# EDUCATION:
# A BEGINNING

# EDUCATION:

Second Edition

Houghton Mifflin Company · Boston

# A BEGINNING

William Van Til

*Coffman Distinguished Professor in Education*
*Indiana State University*

Atlanta · Dallas · Geneva, Ill. · Hopewell, N.J. · Palo Alto · London

Part opening photographs courtesy of:
Lesley College, Cambridge, Mass. (p. 1)
Paul S. Conklin (p. 127)
Ivan Massar, Black Star (p. 277)
Marc St. Gill, Black Star (p. 479)

Printed in the U.S.A.

Library of Congress Catalog Card Number: 73-9405
ISBN: 0-395-17576-3

For the Van Til family—
from Florence Alberta Van Til, 1880–1973,
to Linda Alison Nichols, born 1970,
and Justin Travis Van Til, born 1973,
and, somewhere in between,
Bee,
Jon and Sally, Barbara and Bob, Roy and Linda

# Contents

# Preface

*Education: A Beginning* is for you if you intend to teach or are thinking about the possibility of teaching. It is for you if you are a prospective teacher at any level of instruction from preschool through adult education. It is for you if you are a new teacher of any subject in any school or system. *Education: A Beginning* is especially for you if you are a student in a first course in education. Such a course is often titled Introduction to Education or Social Foundations of Education, among many possible names.

I revised *Education: A Beginning* throughout a year, from summer 1972 into fall 1973. The revision is a summing up of what I think is relevant to the new teacher for the mid-1970s. The book represents what I have learned from teaching in schools and in universities and from working in educational organizations which I have served as president: the Association for Supervision and Curriculum Development, the John Dewey Society for the Study of Education and Culture, the National Society of College Teachers of Education. It represents too what I have learned from intensive study while writing the book. My hope is that *Education: A Beginning* may help you to make a difference through teaching.

Each chapter of *Education: A Beginning* deals with a question which is important to the new teacher:

Chapter 1 initiates thinking on decisions about teaching with the question, "Do you want to teach?"

Chapter 2 asks "Which level will you choose?" and describes the more common divisions or levels in the American educational system. Included are infancy and babyhood years, nursery school, kindergarten, elementary school, junior high school, senior high school, college and university, and adult education.

The purpose of Chapter 3, "Who teaches in American schools?", is to help you to arrive at a realistic picture of who actually teaches in American schools and to consider the implications.

Chapter 4, "What are teachers paid?" describes the salaries of American teachers and gives comparable figures for other professions.

The purpose of chapter 5, "What organizations do teachers join?", is to describe the two major organizations to which teachers currently belong (the National Education Association and the American Federation of Teachers), to acquaint you with the existence of other specialized organizations, and to enable you to consider the degree to which education is a profession.

Chapter 6, "How did the public schools begin?", summarizes some developments in the history of American education from its beginning in colonial times to 1920. The attempt is to sketch some of the highlights in the development of American education.

Chapter 7, "What is the work of the public school today?", concentrates on the past fifty years in American education. It introduces you to some of the controversies which characterize education in our times.

Chapter 8, "What are the roles of independent and parochial schools?", introduces you to the nature and functions of private independent and parochial schools. Descriptions of new "alternative" and "free" schools are included here and in Chapter 18.

Chapter 9, "Who's in charge here?", deals with some of the surrounding conditions and forces which influence the teacher in a public school.

Chapter 10, "What is expected of American teachers?", takes up the expectations of teachers by communities, parents, administrators, students, fellow teachers, and by the teacher himself or herself.

Chapter 11, "What about money to support schools?", deals with the financing of public education.

Chapter 12, "What are the social class and ethnic backgrounds of students?", deals with both social class groupings and with ethnic groups, including immigrants from Western Europe, Indians, blacks, and Spanish-speaking immigrants from Mexico and Puerto Rico.

Chapter 13, "What are the community backgrounds of students?", describes the lives of students from rural communities, small and large cities, and suburbs.

Chapter 14, "How do learners differ?", emphasizes psychological considerations, especially focusing upon the reality of individuality. Delinquency, dropping out, and drug abuse are also considered here.

Chapter 15, "How do social problems affect education?", begins with the fable of The Saber-Tooth Curriculum and then focuses on conflicts in the international setting, interrelated problems of population, pollution and energy, and problems related to racism.

Chapter 16, "What's a school for, anyway?", deals with the purposes of education through summarizing what many thinkers throughout the ages have had to say concerning education and through reporting on studies of the purposes of American education made during the past half century.

Chapter 17, "What should the schools teach?", is an introduction to the curriculum of the schools, including the views of those who advocate basing the curriculum on the needs of the learner, those who stress meeting social demands and learning about social realities, those who emphasize developing humane values, and those who advocate the study of the structure of the disciplines.

Chapter 18, "How do curriculum content and organization change?", describes the processes and ways through which changes in curriculum content and organization come about. Included are programs of non-grading, team teaching, core, modular scheduling, independent study, open schools, and alternatives in public schools.

Chapter 19, "What does the new teacher worry about?", deals with discipline, students with problems, providing for individual differences and developing varied methodologies, and dealing with confrontation.

Chapter 20, "What is the work of the new teacher?", presents a down-to-earth picture of the work of the new teacher, including his teaching responsibilities, the tools of his trade, and parent and community relations.

Chapter 21, "What about evaluation and guidance?", provides an introduction to two specialized fields which are important to teachers: evaluation and guidance.

Chapter 22, "What will the schools of the year 2000 be like?", considers alternative futures. Specifically, education and society and the year 2000 are the subjects of the chapter.

Chapter 23, "Is teaching for you?", returns to many of the same questions with which we opened the book. You are helped to build a list of factors to take into account in deciding whether or not to teach. Common sense approaches to career planning for those who have decided that they will teach, are described.

So the early chapters of this book, Part One, deal with decisions about teaching. The chapters in Part Two consider the nature of American schools. The chapters grouped as Part Three deal with foundations of education. The concluding group of chapters, Part Four, deal with the experiences and the work of the new teacher.

You and your instructor may want to know the major ways in which this revised edition of *Education: A Beginning* differs from the first edition. Obviously, a great many facts and figures and charts are updated. But, in addition, the revised edition considers:

the difficult employment situation faced by many teachers in the mid-1970s and the reasons why teaching positions are hard to come by possible future developments at each of the levels of teaching

participation by teachers in organizations and politics

the contemporary criticisms of schools which the new teacher is reading today

recent developments as to teachers' salaries and as to the way teachers are regarded by parents and community members

changes in the structure of the National Education Association and the development of proposals for merger between the National Education Association and the American Federation of Teachers

the controversy concerning the role of schools in achieving equality of educational opportunity, including the Coleman report, the views of the Nixon administration, and the report by Christopher Jencks, *Inequality*

the outcomes of experimentation with the voucher plan and performance contracting

the programs of free and alternative schools and the criticisms of some of these schools by Jonathan Kozol

the continuing decline in enrollment in Catholic schools

recent court decisions on separation of church and state and the viewpoints on aid to Catholic education of political leaders and of newspapers

the controversy over decentralization of schools

changes in what is expected of teachers in American schools

data on how schools are financed, including conflicts over the property tax stimulated by the Serrano decision in California and by U.S. Supreme Court rulings on equality of educational opportunity

new findings by scholars concerning social class

the extent of the gap between the living conditions of whites and blacks in contemporary America

Indian demands upon the Federal government

the anger of the "new ethnics" of Western European ancestry

the extent of black and white population changes in the big cities

the changing suburbs which contradict the usual stereotype of suburbia

the controversy over Jensen's views on the intelligence of blacks

recent court decisions expanding education for retarded, handicapped and emotionally disturbed children and youth

the views of those who believe that keeping potential dropouts in school is harmful to individuals and society the views of those who believe that staying in school is important to success in life

the extent of the problem of drug abuse

Abraham Maslow's hierarchy of needs

international problems facing the United States after the Vietnam peace agreement and the termination of the bombing of Cambodia in 1973

the relationship of two vs. three children in a family to population growth

the conflict between environmentalists and technologists, between spokesmen for ecology and for growth of energy

the conflict over neighborhood schools and busing for desegregation; related rulings of the courts

new developments in affective education espoused by today's compassionate critics of the schools

the work of free schools

limitations of the structure of the disciplines approach reported by original supporters; *The Process of Education* as revisited by Jerome S. Bruner

open schools as to space, organization, and curriculum; conflict in open education between the new freedom and the new fundamentalism

descriptions of a variety of alternatives in public education

causes of the decline in student protest in the schools of the early 1970s

growth in the use of paraprofessionals, aides, and teaching teams

new instances of community pressures on teachers

the pro and con on the new demand for accountability

Regents and college entrance examinations under fire; alternatives to grading proposed in *Wad-Ja-Get?*

the current extent and need for counseling

developments in the study of alternative futures

recent information on supply and demand in specific teaching fields and at specific levels

Those familiar with the first edition of *Education: A Beginning* will recognize that revised suggestions for *Discussion* and *Involvement* are included in this edition too. They should be useful to the instructor in fostering both discussion and involvement. They should be useful to students who, on their own, wish to think through issues raised in the chapters or who wish to personally involve themselves in schools and communities.

Users of the first edition of *Education: A Beginning* may note that bibliographies and audio-visual suggestions again appear at the close of chapters; please note that these are *in addition* to the important sources which are mentioned in the footnotes. An even greater number of footnotes appear in this revised edition of *Education: A Beginning* for enterprising students who want to grow more acquainted with the sources and authorities mentioned throughout the book. Please use *both* the footnotes and the additional end-of-chapter materials for expansion of knowledge and understanding.

As I wrote at the close of the final chapter, "Through these pages, an attempt has been made to introduce you to education. But an introduction is only a beginning. For you as an educator, there is much more to know, many more experiences to be had, much more living to do. May you learn much, experience widely, and live well in your years as an educator! For yours is a career field where the action is and where human beings can make a difference."

William Van Til
Lake Lure
Terre Haute, Indiana

# Acknowledgments

I am grateful to many people to whom I owe much. Above all, I am grateful to thousands of my predecessors and contemporaries upon whom I have drawn in the first edition and in this revised edition of *Education: A Beginning* for their insights on school and society. Only some of them are individually named in footnotes and bibliographies.

Thanks also to leaders in American education who read, reacted to, and suggested improvements in this author's drafts of content related to their fields of specialization. They contributed markedly to whatever strengths this book may have and their ideas were of the highest importance to this writer. Yet the author alone is responsible for this book and certainly for any inadequacies; until the book was published readers named below saw neither any completed chapter or chapters which evolved from first drafts of the original book and this revision nor the book as a whole. For the first edition the chapter readers included Glen Robinson, Philip Rothman, Edgar L. Morphet, Stanley Elam, W. Richard Stephens, C. Taylor Whittier, Ronald C. Doll, William P. McLure, Helen Storen, Virgil A. Clift, Frank W. Jerse, Jack Allen, Arthur G. Wirth, Fred T. Wilhelms, Gordon F. Vars, Prudence Bostwick, Jean Marani Graetz, Merle M. Ohlsen, and David L. Jesser.

For this revised edition, the chapter readers included:

William S. Graybeal, Assistant Director, National Education Association Research Division, Washington, D.C. (Chapters 1 and 23);

Stanley Elam, Editor, *Phi Delta Kappan,* Bloomington, Indiana (Chapter 5);

W. Richard Stephens, Vice President, Greenville College, Greenville, Illinois (Chapters 6 and 7);

Robert L. Pabst, School of Education, Indiana State University, Terre Haute, Indiana (Chapter 8);

William P. McLure, School of Education, University of Illinois, Urbana, Illinois (Chapter 11);

Jon Van Til, Chairman, Department of Urban Studies, Rutgers University, at Camden, New Jersey (Chapters 12 and 13);

Alvin D. Loving Sr., Assistant Dean, School of Education, University of Michigan, Ann Arbor, Michigan (Chapter 15).

My thanks to the following scholars who read the entire manuscript of this revised edition and made helpful suggestions to me:

Mack A. Ralston, Professor, College of Education, Arizona State University, Tempe, Arizona;

Ronald C. Doll, Professor of Education, Richmond College, The City University of New York, New York;

Virgil A. Clift, Professor of Education, New York University, New York;

John H. Lounsbury, Chairman, Education Department, Georgia College, Milledgeville, Georgia.

Thanks again to the research assistants, secretaries and typists, editors, and specialists in teaching aids who contributed to the first edition including: Marvin Kelly, Ronald M. Leathers, Gail Rudd, Judy Braden, Ola Kelly, Mitzi Williams, R. Joseph Dixon, Jane Angell, William Mac-Donald and Russell McDougal.

For help on the revised edition my thanks to:

C. Wesley Lambert, Director, Audio-Visual Center, Indiana State University, for preparation of the audio-visual sections;

R. Joseph Dixon, formerly with the Des Moines public schools, and Ronald M. Leathers, now Assistant Professor of Education, Eastern Illinois University, for research assistance;

Sandy Sievers and Donna Fisher, for secretarial assistance;

Larry D. Vandeventer and O. Pierre Lee, who checked and verified the footnotes and the quotations, an unglamorous yet essential service, and who also supplied research assistance;

The staff at Houghton Mifflin;

Thousands of my former students and hundreds of my past and present colleagues.

Thanks especially to my wife Bee, my first mate and my best editor since our cruise down the Danube River.

William Van Til
Lake Lure
Terre Haute, Indiana

## QUOTATION ACKNOWLEDGMENTS

Boxed quotations in Chapters 1 and 16 reprinted from *Quotable Quotes on Education* by August Kerber, with permission of the Wayne State University Press. Copyright 1968 by the Wayne State University Press.

Quotations by Ralph D. Winn in Chapter 17 reprinted with the permission of Philosophical Library, Inc. From *John Dewey: Dictionary of Education* by Ralph D. Winn. Copyright 1959 by Philosophical Library, Inc.

Quotation of page 69 reprinted from *Good Morning, Miss Dove* by Frances Gray Patton by permission of Dodd, Mead & Company.

Quotation on page 155 from *The Transformation of the School* by Lawrence A. by permission of Macmillan Publishing Co., Inc. Copyright 1968 by The Macmillan Company.

Quotation of page 155 from *The Transformation of the School* by Lawrence A. Cremin reprinted by permission of Alfred A. Knopf, Inc. Copyright 1961 by Alfred A. Knopf, Inc.

Material on pages 158–159 from *The Story of the Eight-Year Study,* volume 1 of *Adventure in American Education* by Wilford M. Aiken, pp. 111–112, reprinted by permission of McGraw-Hill Company. Copyright, 1942, by McGraw-Hill, Inc.

Quotation on page 238 from "What Makes a Good High School Curriculum" by William Van Til reprinted by permission of *Woman's Day* Magazine. Copyright © 1964 by Fawcett Publications.

Table on page 271, "The Federal Government and Education, 1780–1957," reprinted by permission of Kappa Delta Pi, An Honor Society in Education, from "The Tenth Amendment and Uncle Sam" by John M. Nagle from *The Educational Forum,* November 1969, pp. 21–30. Copyright 1969 by Kappa Delta Pi.

Quotations on pages 379–381 from *The Saber-Tooth Curriculum* by J. Abner Peddiwell, copyright © 1939 by McGraw-Hill Book Company.

Quotation on page 468 from *Individualized Learning through Modular-Flexible Programming* by Gaynor Petrequin, copyright © 1968 by McGraw-Hill Book Company. Used with permission of McGraw-Hill Company.

Material from Encyclopedia of Educational Research, 4th ed., Robert L. Ebel, ed., reprinted with permission of Macmillan Publishing Co., Inc. Copyright © 1969 by American Educational Research Association.

Quotation on page 518 from "The Road Not Taken" from *The Poetry of Robert Frost,* edited by Edward Connery Lathem. Copyright 1916, © 1969 by Holt, Rinehart and Winston, Inc. Copyright 1944 by Robert Frost. Reprinted by permission of Holt, Rinehart and Winston, Inc.

Quotations on pages 535, 545–546, from *Guidance Services in the Modern School* by Merle M. Ohlsen, copyright, 1955, © 1964 by Harcourt Brace Jovanovich, Inc. and reprinted with their permission.

# EDUCATION:
# A  BEGINNING

PART ONE

# DECISIONS ABOUT TEACHING

# ONE

# Do you want to teach?

You have had considerable experience with schools and teachers that will help you decide whether you want to teach. After all, you've been going to school for a long time now, and have had contact with a number of teachers of all sorts.

Some of your teachers you remember well; others you would just as soon forget. Your experience with teaching is based on a considerable number of persons who taught you well, badly, or indifferently during the fifteen years, more or less, that you have been a student.

But even though you are a veteran student, you have been on only one side of the desk; there is much to be learned from the other side—the teacher's side.

This book is intended to give you a look at the many aspects of education that must concern you as you make up your mind whether to teach and as you plan your future in the specialty and level you choose. In doing your own independent thinking you should take into account that the author's viewpoint will not be disguised. The author's view on "Why teach?" permeates this book.

## WHY TEACH?

We must in all honesty admit that some of the tired old answers to the question "Why teach?" persist. We are all familiar with them: "Because I don't know what else to do." "I'll teach until I get the degree I am really after—MRS." "After all, there are long vacations"—a dreary and unexciting list of mindless and expedient reasons for teaching.

5

Teaching offers opportunities for personal satisfaction and for helping others.

But there are far better reasons than these for teaching. One of the best is the possibility of doing something socially useful with one's life in a period that is dangerous, difficult, and explosive, yet simultaneously rewarding, exciting, and meaningful. Many human lives will be needlessly destroyed in the years ahead, yet our times hold for more people than ever the promise of achieving their potential. The British novelist H. G. Wells was at his prophetic best when he wrote, "Human history becomes more and more a race between education and catastrophe."

**MORTIMER ADLER**  *The best teachers are those who make the fewest pretensions.*

**BRONSON ALCOTT**  *The true teacher defends his pupils against his own personal influence. He inspires self-distrust. He guides their eyes from himself to the spirit that quickens him. He will have no disciple.*

**ARISTOTLE**  *Those who educate children well, are more to be honoured than those who produce them; for these only gave them life, those the art of living well.*

**JACQUES BARZUN**  *Teaching is something that can be provided for, changed or stopped. It is good or bad, brilliant or stupid, plentiful or scarce.*

American education must provide for and apply to varying life-styles.

Charles Dickens was describing a different revolutionary period from our own when he wrote *A Tale of Two Cities*. But he might have been writing of our era in the opening sentences of his book when he wrote of the period before the French Revolution, "It was the best of times, it was the worst of times, it was the age of wisdom, it was the age of foolishness, it was the epoch of belief, it was the epoch of incredulity, it was the season of Light, it was the season of Darkness, it was the

**JAMES CASE** *The original, the basic, the indispensable audio-visual device for every classroom is the teacher. No one has yet developed an aid to learning that is nearly as flexible, as dependable, as versatile — and probably no one ever will.*

**JOHN CIARDI** *There are no dull teachers. There are only dull people in classrooms impersonating teachers.*

**ARTHUR COMBS** *The good teacher is the one who has learned to use himself in an effective way. . . . Learning to teach is not learning to do but learning to be.*

**JOHN DEWEY** *His (the teacher's) problem is to protect the spirit of inquiry, to keep it from becoming blasé from overexcitement, wooden from routine, fossilized through dogmatic instruction, or dissipated by random exercise upon trivial things.*

The affluent trends of the late 1960s and early 1970s have not been felt by everyone.

spring of hope, it was the winter of despair, we had everything before us, we had nothing before us, we were all going direct to Heaven, we were all going direct the other way." He was writing about the year 1775.

Two centuries later it is also the best of times, the worst of times. Let us look at the state of the world, and more particularly the United States of America, in the mid 1970s.

There is abundant evidence of both best and worst. The standards of living of the developed nations steadily improve, yet the gap between the standards of living of the developed nations and the underdeveloped nations widens. New and effective techniques for population control have been developed, yet the world population is increasing by leaps and bounds. An explosive element is inherent in any situation in which the rich get richer while the poor get children.

The United Nations continues to try to keep peace through mediation of small conflicts and through the activities of its worldwide agencies. The superpowers increase communication with each other and develop mutual compacts and agreements. For instance, in 1972, for the first time in the history of the United States, an American President journeyed to China and the Soviet Union on behalf of better world understanding. In 1973, Soviet Union leader Brezhnev traveled to Washington to confer further. The target date of 1974 was set for a permanent treaty on offensive-arms controls. Strategic arms limitations were agreed upon through SALT negotiations. But the United Nations lacks adequate financial support and is frequently by-passed by the nations. The superpowers compete for the allegiance of minor powers and new nations. The Middle East Israeli-Arab War broke out again in October, 1973.

The citizens of the United States point proudly to a long period of continued economic growth accompanied by higher standards of living and interrupted only by occasional recessions, such as the economic decline of the early 1970s. After the hungry, depression-scarred decade of the 1930s, Americans experienced the increasingly prosperous forties, fifties, and sixties. Yet it is obvious that this affluence has not been shared by large numbers of Americans, particularly many Negroes, Puerto Ricans, Mexican-Americans, and Indians, white people in Appalachia and some Southern rural areas, the old, those of all ages who are untrained and unequipped vocationally, and residents of the slums and ghettos of American cities. Inflation reduces the buying power of many Americans in the 1970s.

Americans also point proudly to civil rights laws and economic gains by Negroes. But many white Americans, used to a society in which the real power is in white hands, and isolated from the realities of the black experience, are puzzled and frightened by the new sense of black pride, by the drive for power in black communities, and by the apathy and disillusionment of the still larger group whose sense of worth has been destroyed by the ugliness and frustration of ghetto life.

Americans are proud of the development of a universal education system available from elementary school through college and university for those who presumably have the ability, will, and funds to continue their education. But some of the citizenry are appalled by inadequate and outdated education. Some are shocked by violence and physical destruction directed against educational institutions by a revolutionary minority among the many students who seek changes. Others condemn what they term compulsory miseducation and call for the deschooling of society.

Some young men and women build and create, enjoy cultural resources and the expanding sports programs of the nation, live in comfortable homes, and take relatively well-paying jobs on graduation. But some young men and women are blocked by social and economic circumstances from the jobs they want and the lives they hope to live. Young people will long remember that American young men were drafted and killed in a war in Indochina which many of the nation's youth despised.

America builds marvels in the form of bridges, skyscrapers, highway systems, and planes. America also fouls its air, pollutes its waters, and ravages its landscape.

America prizes its democratic dream of a nation in which each man is respected as an individual, where men work together for common con-

---

**TYPICAL RESPONSES GIVEN BY TEACHERS-IN-TRAINING WHEN ASKED,
"WHY DO YOU PLAN TO TEACH?"**

"I want to help people."

"This world's in a hell of a mess. Education seems to be the only answer to our problems."

"My father is a teacher, my mother is a teacher. I suppose I'm part of a tradition."

"I've always been a good student. I think I'll make a good teacher."

"The money."

"It's simple; I like kids."

"As a black, I'm interested in black people. What we need is good education to compete with whitey."

"I had a great teacher in my sophomore year of high school who genuinely inspired me. I'd like to have that same effect on others."

"What I really want to do is go to law school. Teaching will give me some good experience and a few bucks."

"It's a good job for a married woman."

"The long vacations and the short hours are what I'm interested in."

"I like to work with people."

"It's a good life for a person who deals in ideas."

"I don't know what else to do."

"It's a good, respectable profession. My parents want me to amount to more than they did."

"My fiancé and I will be married following graduation. I'll teach to support us while he goes to graduate school."

"An education major is a snap course."

"I'm fed up with irrelevant education. I want to teach to tell it like it is."

"I don't plan to teach. A teaching certificate is a good insurance policy. If I can't find a better job, I can always fall back on teaching and support myself."

"Security. The fringe benefits are good."

"Teaching requires talents and personal attributes which I believe I have."

"I think I can make a difference through teaching."

---

cerns, and where the use of intelligence is the instrument of progress. Yet, Americans doubt themselves as gross and materialistic, careless and despoiling, and lacking in a worthy philosophy. The Watergate scandal and the Agnew case contribute to their disillusionment.

Into this setting comes a new generation of American teachers. Theirs is no easy task. Instead their job is tough and demanding. As to the outcome, the gods give no guarantees.

Unfortunately, every so often many Americans forget what education is supposed to do for human beings. Then cultural crises force a reassessment. This happened in America as the 1960s yielded to the 1970s.

Some of these crises were the Vietnam quagmire, rebellion of world

Larry Keenan, Jr.

Among the central challenges of the 1970s are the development of a sense of international understanding and solutions to problems of pollution and population.

youth against meaningless and obsolete educational practices, alienation and hostility of protesting students on scores of American campuses, decay of the central cities, the rioting and looting as Negro ghettos burned, persistence of poverty in the richest nation the world has ever known, fouling of the air we breathe and the waters that wash our shores, and assassination of such magnificent human resources as Martin Luther King and Robert F. Kennedy. Many Americans were forcibly reminded that education, which is supposed to improve human existence, faces tremendous tasks if it is to make a difference in people's lives.

**JOHANN WOLFGANG VON GOETHE**  *A teacher who can arouse a feeling for one single good action, for one single good poem, accomplishes more than he who fills our memory with rows on rows of natural objects, classified with name and form.*

**LAURENCE D. HASKEW**  *Teachers make teaching. And teachers are persons first of all, getting the results they get chiefly because they are personalities.*

**THOMAS JEFFERSON**  *Enlighten the people generally and tyranny and oppressions of both mind and body will vanish like evil spirits at the dawn of day.*

**SØREN KIERKEGAARD**  *To be a teacher in the right sense is to be a learner. Instruction begins when you, the teacher, learn from the learner, put yourself in his place so that you may understand what he understands and in the way he understands it.*

Even so, some Americans of the 1970s did not become aware of the major tasks before education. Some, even some teachers, still blindly skirt the central challenges—the challenge to help young people cope with the social realities of our times; the challenge to relate learning to the motivation and concerns of the learner; the challenge to develop commitment to humane and decent values based on mankind's winnowed and reconstructed experiences. Such challenges as these are the proper foci for our best reflection, creativity, and action in education in the mid 1970s.

In the schools of the 1970s we must deal with the real and urgent problems of our times, including the most difficult problems of all, those of international understanding, pollution and population, and democratic human relations at home. We must see young people as individuals, each unique, with his own drives, tensions, and concerns. We must recognize that the anger and intensity of some of the social activists and the indifference and apathy of some of the hippie escapists point to the crucial importance of educators helping young people develop valid values by which to live.

Fortunately, many educators of the mid 1970s are aware that education is inextricably related to people's lives. They recognize the challenges and seek ways to consider social realities, to relate to the individual's needs, and to encourage his search for values by which to live. They do not have all the answers, but they know what the crucial questions are. To ask the right questions is a step toward wisdom and intelligent action.

The new generation of teachers has a genuine potential to effect social changes. They may or may not be able to make education work for

**WILLIAM PENN**   *Good instruction is better than riches.*

**POPE PIUS XII**   *The teacher must make his teaching live, make his students think, and uncover for each of his students the talents he has at his disposal.*

**DAGOBERT D. RUNES**   *We have had teachers for the crown's sake, teachers for God's sake, teachers for Science's sake, teachers for business' sake, but none yet for man's sake.*

**BERTRAND RUSSELL**   *The thing, above all, that a teacher should endeavor to produce in his pupils, if democracy is to survive, is the kind of tolerance that springs from an endeavor to understand those who are different from ourselves.*

**TALMUD**   *Teach thy tongue to say, "I do not know."*

**HORACE MANN**   *A teacher who is attempting to teach without inspiring the pupil with a desire to learn is hammering on cold iron.*

**ALEXANDER MEIKELJOHN**   *No one can be a genuine teacher unless he is himself actively sharing in the human attempt to understand men and their world.*

**H. L. MENCKEN**   *Next to the clerk in holy orders, the fellow with the foulest job in the world is the school master. Both are underpaid, both fall steadily in authority and dignity, and both wear out their hearts trying to perform the impossible. How much the world asks of them, and how little they can actually deliver!*

**THOMAS PAINE**   *One good school master is of more use than a hundred priests.*

**GEORGE HERBERT PALMER**   *Kindling of interest is the great function of the teacher. People sometimes say, "I should like to teach if only pupils cared to learn." But then, there would be little need of teaching. . . . Teaching may be defined as the awakening of another's mind, and, the training of its faculties to a normal self-activity.*

the goals and values they hold and are developing. But the potential is there.

Why teach? Because teaching offers a fighting chance to make a difference. There are other good reasons too, such as liking to work with people and liking the teacher's life-styles. But the main reason for teaching, as the author sees it, is that teaching is where the action is—the action against ignorance and the stifling of human potential, the action of facing today's social realities, meeting the needs of learners, and developing humane values. Through teaching, one can make his life count.

WILL DURANT  *Woe to him who teaches men faster than they can learn.*

FELIX FRANKFURTER  *Teachers must fulfill their function by precept and practice, by the very atmosphere which they generate; they must be examplars of . . . openmindedness and free inquiry. They cannot carry out their noble task if the conditions for the practice of a responsible and critical mind are denied to them.*

JAMES ABRAM GARFIELD  *I am not willing that this discussion should close without mention of the value of a true teacher. Give me a log hut, with only a simple bench, Mark Hopkins on one end and I on the other, and you may have all the buildings, apparatus and libraries without him.*

KAHLIL GIBRAN  *If (the teacher) is indeed wise, he does not bid you enter the house of wisdom, but rather leads you to the threshold of your mind.*

OLIVER WENDELL HOLMES  *I never saw the man that couldn't teach me something.*

HENRY ADAMS  *A teacher affects eternity, he can never tell where his influence stops.*

RALPH WALDO EMERSON  *The secret of education lies in respecting the pupil.*

## HOW MANY OPENINGS ARE THERE FOR TEACHERS?

If you become an American teacher you will join a sizable occupational group. According to the U.S. Office of Education there were almost three million Americans who listed their occupation as elementary, secondary, or higher education teaching at the opening of the 1971–72 school year.[1] Over two million of them were public elementary and secondary school teachers (whom we will often refer to collectively as "public school teachers").

Not only is the occupation of teaching sizable—it has steadily grown. In the early years of the twentieth century, the number of teachers in American public elementary and secondary schools alone was approximately half a million. (For instance, in 1900 there were 423,062 teachers in American public schools.) By the time of the Great Depression, there were some 800,000 to 900,000 public school teachers. (In 1930 there were 854,263 teachers in American public schools.) About the time today's recent college graduates were born, there were approximately a

[1] U.S. Office of Education, *Digest of Educational Statistics,* 1971 ed. (Washington, D.C.: U.S. Government Printing Office, 1972), p. 6.

NUMBER OF TEACHERS
(THOUSANDS)

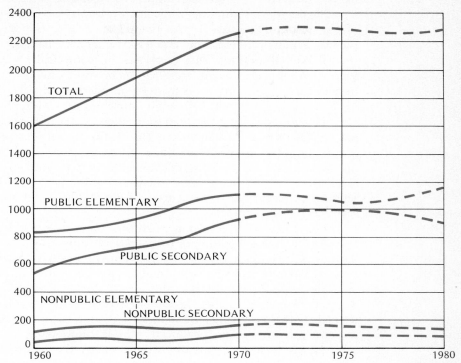

**FIGURE 1-1** Classroom Teachers in Regular Elementary and Secondary Schools, by Institutional Control and Organizational Level: United States, Fall 1960 to 1980

U.S. Office of Education, *Projections of Educational Statistics to 1980–1981* (Washington, D.C.: U.S. Government Printing Office, 1972), p. 6.

million American public school teachers. (In 1950 there were 913,671 teachers in American public schools.)[2]

Then the number of teachers really accelerated in public elementary and secondary schools. By 1969, the number of teachers in American public schools amounted to 2,014,000. When nonpublic school teachers were added, the total of American teachers reached 2,241,000.[3] (See Figure 1-1.)

What happened? One factor was a general population increase. If

[2] U.S. Bureau of the Census, *Historical Statistics of the United States, Colonial Times to 1957* (Washington, D.C.: U.S. Government Printing Office, 1960), p. 208.

[3] U.S. Office of Education, *Projections of Educational Statistics to 1979–80* (Washington, D.C.: U.S. Government Printing Office, 1971), p. 57.

you were born in 1950, you were one of approximately 150 million Americans. By 1970 the American population passed the 203 million mark.

The increased number of teachers is explained not just by the general population increase in the twentieth century but more particularly by the expansion in school attendance which characterized the post-World War II period. This increase is dramatically demonstrated in school enrollment figures. In 1950, there were only 20,716,000 children between the ages of five and thirteen enrolled in schools. But by October 1971 there were 35,641,000 such children. In 1950 there were only 8,143,000 young people fourteen to nineteen years old enrolled in schools. But by October 1971 there were 18,701,000 school enrollees in this age group. Population has boomed and school attendance has grown in the age groups of greatest relevance to you if you are a prospective teacher of the five- to nineteen-year-old span, as the enrollment in this school-age group increased from 28,859,000 in 1950 to 54,342,000 in late 1971.[4] (See Figure 1-2.)

Why then were teaching positions hard to come by in the early 1970s? Why were beginning teachers confronted by unemployment in their chosen field on a scale unprecedented since the depression years of the 1930s? Several factors combined to create a supply of potential teachers substantially higher than the actual demand for teachers. For one thing, the early 1970s was a period of economic recession, a time characterized both by rising unemployment and growing inflation. Consequently, communities reduced school budgets as far as possible; funding for education was often defeated by the voters at the polls. In recession years, Americans tighten their economic belts. Though business and industry again prospered in 1973, a sharp increase in inflation penalized people on fixed incomes and offset wage gains of many workers.

Meanwhile, the rate of growth of the school-age population decreased in the 1970s. While the trend toward enrolling a larger proportion of the school-age population continued, especially at the secondary school level, this trend could not offset the decreases resulting from fewer persons entering the school-age group. Yet the students who were represented in the large increases in school enrollment that occurred in the 1950s had reached the age of college graduation and had enlarged the numbers of potential teachers available for entry into classrooms each year. So two interrelated factors—decreasing rates of enrollment growth in public schools accompanied by significant increases in the annual number of college graduates completing preparation to enter teaching—

---

[4] U.S. Bureau of the Census, *Historical Statistics of the United States,* p. 214; and "School Enrollment in the United States: 1971" ("Population Characteristics") *Current Population Reports,* Series P-20, No. 234 (Washington, D.C.: U.S. Government Printing Office, 1972), p. 2.

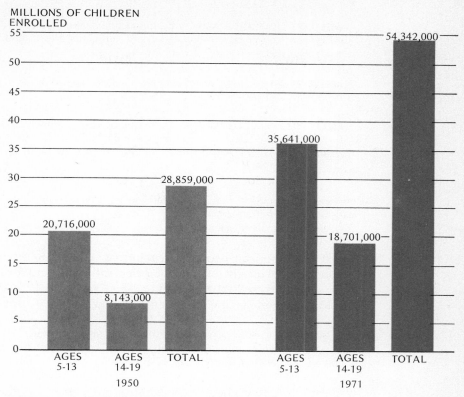

MILLIONS OF CHILDREN
ENROLLED

FIGURE 1-2   Children Enrolled in American Schools, 1950 and 1971

combined to sharply reduce employment opportunities in teaching in
the 1970s.

The abundant supply of college graduates prepared to teach is also
typical of many other occupations for which a college degree has been
required. The number of job offers to college graduates is not growing as
rapidly as the numbers expected to graduate. This means that the United
States faces a critical national problem not only of under-utilization of
teachers but also under-utilization of other college trained personnel.[5]

As a teacher education newsletter put it:

Explanations for the teacher surplus are easy to find: many of today's teachers
were part of the *World War II baby boom;* the 1960s *saw a sharp drop in the birth
rate,* and now the number of children entering kindergarten and first grade is leveling

[5] Task Force on Under-Utilization of Professional Personnel, National Education Association, *A Critical National Problem: Under-Utilization of Teachers and Other College Trained Personnel* (February 1972).

> **WILLIAM O. DOUGLAS** *The constitution guarantees freedom of thought and expression to everyone in our society. All are entitled to it; and none needs it more than the teacher.*
>
> **ALBERT EINSTEIN** *It is the supreme art of the teacher to awaken joy in creative expression and knowledge.*
>
> **ANATOLE FRANCE** *Let our teaching be full of ideas. Hitherto it has been stuffed only with facts. . . . The whole art of teaching is only the art of awakening the natural curiosity of young minds for the purpose of satisfying it afterwards.*

off; and *recent budget cuts,* particularly in big-city schools, have reduced teaching staffs or limited normal expansion.

Answers are another matter. . . .[6]

If the American people had required immediate attainment of minimum levels of quality staffing of schools, the demand for teachers would have sharply increased. (See Figure 1-3.) As early as 1970, *Changing Times,* the Kiplinger magazine, commented upon teacher supply and demand:

. . . according to some experts, there actually are not enough teachers on the job right now to meet the true needs of the schools. The problem, they say, is not an oversupply of teachers but an undersupply of money.

School systems, faced by taxpayer resistance, are starved for the funds they need to lighten teacher loads, replace underqualified instructors and expand course offerings. . . .

Allan W. Ostar, executive director of the American Association of State Colleges and Universities, . . . makes this comment: "How can we talk of a teacher surplus when perhaps half of our communities are without kindergartens; . . . when according to a recent study at Harvard, almost half of the adult population 25 years old and over is functionally illiterate; when a new right-to-read program has been launched by the U.S. Office of Education as a top national priority; when in our high schools we have less than one counselor for every 500 students; when our rural and urban schools are woefully inadequate in meeting the special educational needs of our underprivileged children? There is no teacher surplus. There is an educational deficit which, for the first time since World War II, we now have an opportunity to correct.[7]

In 1972 Herold G. Regier, in *Too Many Teachers: Fact or Fiction?,* reached the same conclusion:

. . . there really is not an oversupply of teachers; there is simply an undersupply of money. For a country that spends about 7 percent of the gross national product on

---

[6] "Reshuffling the Teacher Market," *Concern: AACTE Newsletter for Teacher Education* (November 1971), p. 5.
[7] "Too Many Teachers?" *Changing Times* (October 1970), p. 44.

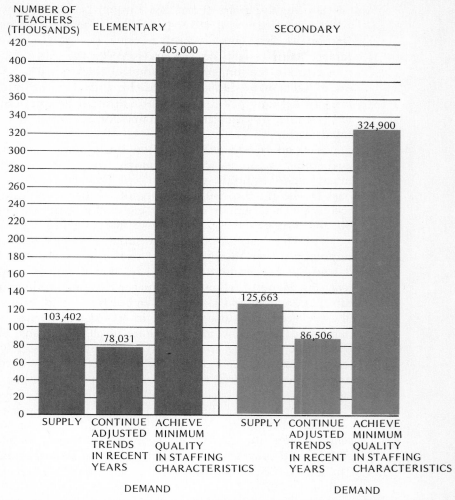

**FIGURE 1-3 Estimates of Supply of Teacher Education Graduates and Demand for Beginning Teachers, 1971–1972**

NEA, Research Division, *Teacher Supply and Demand in Public Schools, 1971,* Research Report 1972-R4 (Washington, D.C.: The Association, 1972), p. 38. Copyright © 1972 by the National Education Association. All rights reserved. (Adjusted trends based on percent of staff who were new teachers previous year.)

education, one can conclude that spending enough for education may be the real problem. Court decisions about providing equal educational opportunity may force the people of the United States to take a new look at how to fund education and how to fund it adequately. Given enough dollars, the conclusion may be that "too many teachers" is fiction; but until the dollar problem is solved, it is a fact.[8]

[8] Herold G. Regier, *Too Many Teachers: Fact or Fiction?* (Bloomington, Indiana: Phi Delta Kappa Educational Foundation, 1972), p. 37.

During the years from 1966 through 1970, the actual demand for additional certificated teachers in public schools reached 1,094,000 (to improve staffing and programs to teach the growing enrollment, and to replace teachers who die, resign, etc.) But the U.S. Office of Education, projecting education statistics, foresaw only 852,000 additional certificated teachers in demand for teaching during the comparable period from 1971 through 1975. For the 1976 through 1980 period, the U.S. Office of Education has projected a demand for only 880,000 additional certificated teachers.[9]

Such predictions were based on the assumptions that: (1) despite the availability of an increasingly ample supply of teachers, the rate of improvement in public education offerings and staffings will continue at past levels; (2) the usual number of teachers will continue to die or resign; (3) there will be a slightly increasing birth rate in the early 1970s. But the birth rate in 1972 was lower than in 1971.

The National Education Association is critical of the current rate of improvement in offerings and of staffing. For instance, Mrs. Catharine Barrett, NEA President in 1972, said that the large supply of qualified teachers, many of whom now must mark time while education deteriorates, can and should be utilized in bolstering and improving education. She deplored the waste of talent in a field tied to the well-being of the nation's children and to the welfare of all Americans. She pointed out that "many teaching and support positions have been eliminated. Subjects like art, music, and physical education, frequently the keys to academic or occupational success, have been casualties of 'economy measures.' In some schools the sizes of reading, math, English, and other classes, including elementary school classes, are unmanageable." She concluded by pointing out that there would be no teacher surplus if all schools were brought up to even minimum acceptable standards of staffing and programs—in fact, there would be a shortage of teachers.[10] The U.S. Office of Education (USOE) estimated a teaching staff of 2.32 million for 1972–73, an increase of only 20,000 over 1971–72 in elementary and secondary schools.[11]

The employment outlook for staff members in the colleges and universities that make up higher education in the United States is for continued growth in faculty jobs during the seventies followed by some reductions in the early 1980s. A ten-year projection of staff positions in higher education made in 1972 anticipated a growth from somewhat under 600,000 staff members in 1970 to more than 800,000 staff members

[9] U.S. Office of Education, *Projections of Educational Statistics to 1980–81* (Washington, D.C.: U.S. Government Printing Office, 1972), p. 62.
[10] "Nation Should Use Record Teacher Supply to Upgrade Education, NEA Leader Counsels Federal Officials," *NEA News* (October 4, 1972), p. 1.
[11] "The New School Year: Calm Before the Storm," *Education U.S.A.* (Washington, D.C.: National School Public Relations Association, September 4, 1972), p. 1.

NUMBER OF INSTRUCTORS
(THOUSANDS)

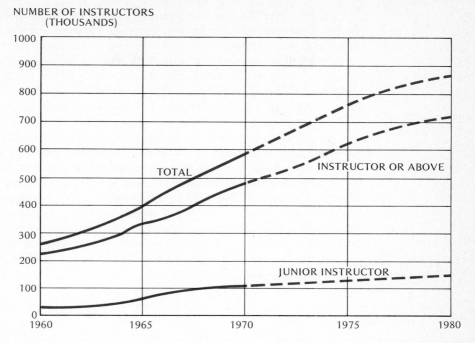

**FIGURE 1-4** **Instructional Staff for Resident Courses in Institutions of Higher Education, by Professional Rank: United States, Fall 1960 to 1980**

U.S. Office of Education, *Projections of Educational Statistics to 1980–1981* (Washington, D.C.: U.S. Government Printing Office, 1972), p. 6.

by 1980.[12] However, comparatively few of the members of the American teaching profession begin their careers as teachers at the college and university level. (See Figure 1-4.) Too, some experts believe the prediction to be overly optimistic.

The experts also point out that the growth in higher education faculties in the future will probably not be as great as the growth during the 1960s. This is a result of the leveling off in the rate of growth in the college-age population. In addition, the percent of the college-age population enrolled in higher education is no longer growing.

So you will have to be a highly competent teacher in the mid 1970s. The days of employing incompetents to meet teacher shortages are over. For each open position, most school systems will be able to choose from a variety of applicants who will have at least minimum qualifications for the position.

[12] U.S. Office of Education: *Projections of Educational Statistics to 1980–81* (Washington, D.C.: U.S. Government Printing Office, 1972), p. 6.

Yet despite the difficult situation faced by the teacher at the varied levels described in this chapter, growing opportunities may lie ahead in the field of education broadly conceived. Consider, for instance, the opportunities for working with very young children through day-care centers. Consider, for another instance, the need for special education to help retarded and handicapped children of all ages, in and out of school, in a nation in which courts and legislatures expand requirements for special education programs for all who need them.

In a growing American economy, consider the need for continuous training and retraining of people in business and industry. Note the recent upsurge of interest in prison conditions in America and the accompanying demand for expansion of educational opportunities in the interest of genuine rehabilitation of the large prison population. Recognize the great opportunity in the neglected field of geriatric education for senior citizens. Take into account the educational aspects of constantly expanding problems of human welfare. There may be major opportunities in the burgeoning field of education that lies outside the classic conception of educational programs.

## DISCUSSION

1. Consider your own teachers. Whom do you remember favorably and why? Whom do you reject and why? Can you generalize from these reactions on the qualities that you consider important in a "good" teacher?

2. In appraising yourself, do you find that you like to work with people, with things? In groups or alone?

3. What are some of the reasons some of your friends have gone into teaching? How would their responses compare with the answers quoted in the chapter in response to the question "Why do you plan to teach?"

4. Which of the reasons given by prospective teachers do you consider worthwhile? Which are selfishly motivated? Which reflect indifference? Which show some dedication to an idea or an ideal? Which are most similar to yours?

5. What has happened to you and the world in your lifetime that indicates to you that you are living in the best of times? The worst of times?

6. What do you conceive to be the major tasks before American educators?

7. What is your answer to the question "Why teach?" Why are you thinking seriously of entering the teaching field? What does teaching really mean to you?

8. Consider the growth in the number of teachers and the decline in teaching opportunities. What is the situation with respect to teacher supply and demand today in your state? Your community? What is the situation as it affects you?

9. Why were teaching positions hard to come by in the early 1970s?

10. What is the meaning of "minimum levels of quality staffing of schools"? How would achievement of quality staffing affect the demand for teachers?

11. In what way is the current problem not an oversupply of teachers but an undersupply of money?

## INVOLVEMENT

1. Make arrangements to visit a classroom (wherever convenient and of most interest to you) to see first hand a teacher and class situation. When you report back to your class, consider what you saw, how the teacher and class interacted, what your reactions were. (Caution: Always go first to the office of the principal of the school visited to request permission to visit.)

2. If the schools from which you graduated are nearby, go back to one of your schools and talk about teaching with a teacher whom you remember favorably.

3. In everyday conversations introduce the possibility that you will become a teacher and consider the ideas and reactions of your friends and relatives. Try out with them the idea that teaching can make a difference in people's lives.

4. Develop a simple questionnaire dealing with possible reasons why people wish to teach. Administer the questionnaire to some who are considering teaching, tabulate the results, and report to the group. (Best results are likely to occur when those answering remain anonymous.)

5. Try to bring to your class a first-year teacher to present his or her reasons for entering the field of education and to answer questions. Perhaps one speaker might be selected from the elementary and another from the secondary school level.

6. Interview the individuals in charge of employment in nearby local school systems as to the actual current situation concerning supply and demand of teachers.

## FURTHER READING

Allen, Dwight W. and Eli Seifman, eds. *The Teacher's Handbook*. Glenview, Illinois: Scott, Foresman, 1971. A massive reference source for the beginner and the experienced teacher made up of contributions on the teacher, human growth and development, the instructional process, the curriculum and methods areas, the school system, the foundations of education and contemporary issues.

Burrup, Percy E. *The Teacher and the Public School System*. New York: Harper & Row, 1972. The major problems that teachers and administrators face today. The major parts of the book deal with "preparing teachers to meet the problems of education; government in education; certification: key to employment; striving for success; the teacher: a law-abiding citizen; increasing our investment in education; and education struggles for professional maturity."

Chandler, B. J., Daniel Powell and William R. Hazard. *Education and the New Teacher*. New York: Dodd, Mead, 1971. An introduction to education which explores major issues, provides an overview of the processes and performance of teaching, and examines the work of elementary and secondary schools.

Crary, Ryland W. and Louis A. Petrone. *Foundations of Modern Education*. New York: Alfred A. Knopf, 1971. A book foundational to inquiry about education and designed for use in the first course in a teacher education program.

Heath, G. Louis. *The New Teacher: Changing Patterns of Authority and Responsibility in the American Schools*. New York: Harper & Row, 1973. An examination of current trends and recent innovations in American education which ranges widely over contemporary developments in education.

Hughes, James Monroe. *Education in America*. New York: Harper & Row, 1970. An introduction to American education stressing the teacher, influential ideas, American schools, and aims and methods in American education.

Muse, Milton. *Selected Readings for the Introduction to the Teaching Profession.* Berkeley, California: McCutchan, 1970. Readings to help beginning teachers become aware of current curriculum theory and practice. Selections from leading contemporary educators to assist teachers to interpret classroom situations and recognize the theoretical concepts upon which understanding is based.

Ohles, John F. *Principles and Practice of Teaching: Selected Readings.* New York: Random House, 1970. An anthology on teachers and teaching; learners and learning; the school; the classroom process; and facilitation of instruction.

Ryan, Kevin and James M. Cooper. *Kaleidoscope: Readings in Education.* Boston: Houghton Mifflin, 1972. Readings in education which include materials from novels, commentaries from educational leaders, cartoons, songs and poems, as well as materials from professional journals and books. Sections deal with "teachers, students, schools, instruction, etc."

Ryan, Kevin and James M. Cooper. *Those Who Can, Teach.* Boston: Houghton Mifflin, 1972. A highly informal introduction to education organized about a series of questions concerning schools, teachers, and the real world.

## SELECTED AUDIO-VISUAL MATERIALS

*Career for You — Teaching* (16 mm film, 28 min., b. & w., WUNC-TV: University of North Carolina, 1965). Illustrates the possibilities in a career in teaching.

*Education — Antidote to Poverty* (16 mm film, 30 min., b. & w., University of Michigan TV Center, 1967). Takes a look at movements in education designed to eradicate some of society's inequalities.

*I Want to Be a Teacher* (35 mm filmstrip, 30 frs/record, color, Educational Enrichment Materials, Inc., 1969). Reveals the workday world of a teacher and stimulates questions and role playing.

*Teacher* (35 mm filmstrips, 44 frs /captions, color, National Film Board of Canada, 196-). Describes educational and personal requirements for teachers, training in specialized fields, opportunities and advantages. Stresses the importance of the teacher in society.

*The Teacher — A Community Helper* (16 mm film, 10 min., color, Sigma Educational Films, 1967). Describes a typical day in the life of a primary school teacher. Shows her as she plans the lesson, teaches, confers with a parent, attends the university, and performs other duties as a mother, homemaker, and responsible member of the community.

*What Right Has a Child?* (16 mm film, 15 min., color, McGraw-Hill, 1969). Children from all over the world speak about what the Declaration of Rights of the Child (passed by the United Nations, November 20, 1959) means to them.

# TWO

# What level of teaching?

At what level of the American educational system do you propose to teach? This chapter will discuss the characteristics of each of the common divisions of the educational system.

## INFANCY AND BABYHOOD YEARS

In America, no organized education now exists for the period from birth to the third birthday. Yet the importance of the first three years of life cannot be overestimated. Freudian psychology particularly emphasizes the importance of these early years, but one does not have to be a Freudian to recognize their significance in the shaping of the human being. The child is first molded by his family and the surrounding home environment during these three years. But in current American culture such education is informal and home-based rather than formal and institution-located. Rarely do American two-year-olds go to nursery schools.

Education at home during infancy and babyhood is not a universal practice, however. Limited opportunities presently exist for educators to work with children during this phase of development; welfare agencies, children's hospitals, and orphanages often require the service of trained educators to help raise babies who have no families. Other societies of the world have developed alternative programs to the informal, home-based education of children during babyhood. For instance, Bruno Bettelheim in *The Children of the Dream* has written a fascinating account of the kibbutz method of rearing Israeli children, many of whom leave home shortly after birth for institutional upbringing. Bettelheim reports:

A meal on a kibbutz.

Courtesy of State of Israel, Government Press Office

The kibbutz experience clearly demonstrated to me that children raised by educators in group homes can and do fare considerably better than many children raised by their mothers in poverty-stricken homes, and better than quite a few raised at home by their middle-class parents.[1]

My conclusion must be that, despite published reports to the contrary, the kibbutz system seems quite successful in raising children in groups by other than their mothers, and this from infancy on. But up to now this success has only been demonstrated for relatively small societies, where an unusually high degree of consensus exists, where there is very little differentiation in style of life or in property rights, and where the entire society functions like an extended family.[2]

Knowing nothing of apartness, they are content with satisfactions not destroyed for them by having to fight for a sense of belonging. Neither must they strive for an individuation that might compensate, through a rich inner life, for what is absent from their group life. They feel no need to push ahead, but neither do they have the impulse to push anyone down. While such people do not create science or art, are neither leaders nor great philosophers nor innovators, maybe it is they who are the salt of the earth without whom no society can endure.[3]

[1] Bruno Bettelheim, *The Children of the Dream* (New York: Macmillan, 1969), p. 43.
[2] *Ibid.*, p. 52.
[3] *Ibid.*, pp. 319–320.

Lunchtime at a federally funded day-care center.

In the U.S., researchers are studying child development in the earliest years of life and particularly focusing on the differences between children of the poor and of the affluent. Maya Pines reports:

If their research confirms that the first three years of life largely determine a human being's future competence, these years can no longer be left to chance, they believe. Thus, armies of tutors could conceivably be sent into the homes of disadvantaged infants, and thousands of expectant parents enrolled in crash programs to teach them modern child rearing. We may be witnessing the end of society's traditional laissez-faire about the earliest years of a human being's life.[4]

Though most students of human development now hope to produce improvements in the way parents, especially mothers, raise their children, some are considering as a possible strategy "starting kibbutz-like day-care centers in which trained teachers would give children an excellent education from earliest infancy."[5] As Pines points out, "As these ideas spread, the nation's educational efforts are likely to include ever

[4] Maya Pines, "Why Some 3-year-olds Get A's and Some Get C's," *New York Times Magazine* (July 6, 1969), p. 10.
[5] *Ibid.*, p. 17.

younger children, and soon the years from birth to three may become a target of first priority."[6]

The federal government is becoming increasingly concerned about fostering the development of day-care centers for preschool children under five years old. Such day-care centers would obviously include the children whom Pines describes who are in the first three years of their lives. So the day-care center for the first three years of the child's life may become the first rung on the evolving educational ladder in the United States. If so, there will be exciting new employment possibilities for many educators in a scarcely explored field of work.

## NURSERY SCHOOL

Presently, the first level in American education is nursery school mostly for children three or four years old. These schools are relatively new to Americans, the value of such education having been underestimated in the past. By October 1971, enrollment of public and private nursery schools had reached approximately 1,100,000.[7] But even when one takes into account both public and private schools, only one out of five children three and four years old was enrolled in nursery schools in the U.S. in 1971.[8] However, nursery school enrollment is growing fast. The U.S. Bureau of the Census reported that enrollment of public and private nursery schools reached approximately 1,283,000 by October 1972.

Also encouraging is the fact that two out of five children who were three through five years old (including kindergarteners with nursery school children) were enrolled in 1971 in an educational program of some kind. In 1970, the pre-primary school enrollment of children three through five years old totalled 37.5 percent of the population for that age range.[9] The 39 percent level was reached in 1971, according to the U.S. Office of Education.

Nursery school education was encouraged by the federal government during the economic depression of the thirties and the manpower shortages of the forties as World War II raged. School services for young children were expanded through the Economic Opportunity Act and the Elementary and Secondary Education Act during the sixties as part of the war on poverty. Proposals for the revision of the welfare system during the early seventies were accompanied by emphasis on opportunities for

[6] *loc cit.*
[7] U.S. Bureau of the Census, "School Enrollment in the United States: 1971" ("Population Characteristics"), *Current Population Reports*, Series P-20, No. 234 (Washington, D.C.: U.S. Government Printing Office, 1972), p. 1.
[8] *Ibid.*, pp. 1–2.
[9] U.S. Bureau of the Census, *Statistical Abstract of the United States, 1971* (Washington, D.C.: U.S. Government Printing Office, 1971), p. 106.

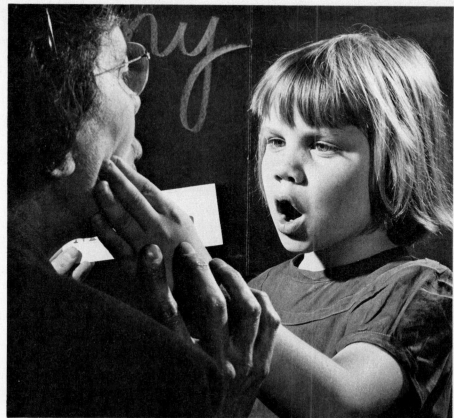

H. Spivak, D.P.I.

In a nursery school for exceptional children a deaf child receives special attention.

welfare mothers to be gainfully employed. Thus, social forces both in recent decades and today have resulted in federal government programs, actual or proposed, which support the expansion of school services for young children.

But nursery school education has a considerable distance to go before the widespread achievement of the goal of enriching a child's first five years of life. Though 38 states provided financial support for kindergartens in 1972, only 6 supported pre-kindergarten programs. Recently a task force of the Education Commission of the States recommended, "The state should provide support for developmental programs for children younger than 6."[10]

In the United States today there are varied types of nursery schools

[10] "Never Too Young To Learn," *Newsweek* (May 26, 1972), p. 99.

for children. Some of them are public, some private; some are sponsored by colleges and universities, others are organized by groups of parents, still others by church groups. A nursery school may be a laboratory nursery school associated with a university, a cooperative nursery school supported by a group of parents, a church-sponsored nursery school. Some nursery schools are conducted as private enterprises or by community agencies and organizations. Some are designed for the exceptional child—blind, deaf, crippled, mentally handicapped, speech impaired. Some are designed for the educationally disadvantaged child and attempt to reduce possible environmental handicaps.

Some nursery schools are part of the regular public school system, serving as the educational enterprise for the year or years preceding kindergarten, organized and maintained as part of the sequential program of the public elementary school under the direction of a qualified teacher.

As to the programs of the public nursery schools, a report from 141 school systems indicated that "about one-half, 51.1 percent, of the total systems had a daily program structure in which activities were provided in a regular sequence. Pupils moved from one activity to another with no regular sequence or definite time allotment in 24.8 percent of the systems. Of the total systems, 23.4 percent had a definite time allotment and sequence for each activity in the daily program. The daily program should be flexible and coincide with the pupil's needs and interests and the goals of the school; hence no one preferred structure exists."[11] The response of nursery school educators about their goals is reported in Figure 2-1.

Katherine H. Read summarized the fundamental goal of nursery school education in *The Nursery School: A Human Relationships Laboratory:*

The nursery school is a place where young children learn as they play and as they share experiences with other children. It is a place where teachers provide the child with a variety of materials and experiences suited to his individual needs, and where they offer guidance and encouragement to him as he learns. The nursery school is also a place where adults learn about child development and human relationships as they observe and participate in the program of the school. . . .

The nursery school as we will define it is a school serving the needs of two-, three-, and four-year-old children in today's world by offering them experiences adapted to what is now known about growth needs at these age levels. It shares with parents the responsibility for promoting sound growth and learning in a period when growth is rapid and significant. Respect for the individual child and his needs is the basis for a good nursery school program.[12]

---

[11] NEA, Research Division, *Nursery School Education, 1966–67,* Research Report 1968-R6 (Washington, D.C.: The Association, 1968), p. 18.

[12] Katherine H. Read, *The Nursery School: A Human Relationships Laboratory* (Philadelphia: W. B. Saunders Company, 1971), pp. 3, 27.

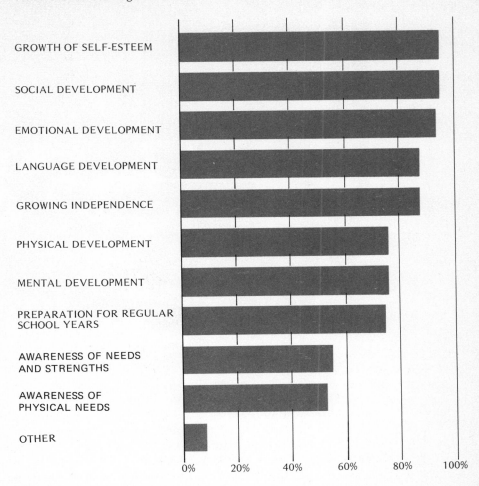

**FIGURE 2-1 Primary Goals of Nursery School Education in 141 School Systems**
NEA, Research Division, *Nursery School Education, 1966–1967*, Research Report 1968-R6 (Washington, D.C.: The Association, 1968), p. 18. Copyright © 1968 by the National Education Association. All rights reserved.

## KINDERGARTEN

The second established educational level is that of kindergarten. A kindergarten year usually takes place for a child (when it does occur) when he is five years old.

The first kindergarten was designed by Friedrich Froebel in 1837 in Germany, in order to provide an educational situation in which children's creative play might be organized constructively. Advocates of the early kindergarten believed that through kindergarten experiences such

A kindergarten class, 1876.

as the use of songs, stories, games, group activities, and simple materials, children could be helped to develop well and to mature.

The first private kindergarten in the United States was founded in 1856 and the first public kindergartens were established in St. Louis, Missouri, in 1873.[13] By 1888 the number of kindergarteners enrolled in public schools almost equaled those enrolled in private schools—15,145 in public schools and 16,082 in private schools.[14] During the depression decade of the 1930s enrollment in kindergarten declined, but aside from this decade, enrollment in kindergartens steadily grew. By October 1972 a total of approximately 3,135,000 children were enrolled in kindergartens. The large majority were in public kindergartens.[15]

But provision of kindergarten as part of the public educational system varies greatly from state to state. In some states practically all local

[13] Josephine Foster and Neith Headley, *Education in the Kindergarten* (New York: American Book Company, 1966), p. 26.

[14] *Early Childhood Education,* 46th Yearbook, Part II, National Society for the Study of Education (Chicago: University of Chicago Press, 1957), p. 46.

[15] U.S. Bureau of the Census, "School Enrollment in the United States: 1972" ("Population Characteristics"), *Current Population Reports,* Series P-20, No. 247 (Washington, D.C.: U.S. Government Printing Office, 1973), p. 4.

A contemporary kindergarten

school districts provide public kindergartens. On the other hand, in a few states there are no public kindergartens. Equality of educational opportunity throughout the United States has not been established for kindergarten-age children.

    A contemporary writer describes the role of a good kindergarten program:

1. The kindergarten program helps to promote and maintain the child's health and physical development. . . .
2. The kindergarten program gives a child the opportunity to further his contact with other children and adults. . . .
3. The kindergarten program provides a rich environment for living, thinking, and learning. . . .
4. The foundation for the three R's, or reading, writing, and arithmetic, is cultivated in the kindergarten. . . .
5. The kindergarten program provides opportunities for the child to expand language as a means of communication and expression. . . .
6. The child's understanding of the social world is broadened. . . .
7. The child's understanding of the scientific world is broadened. . . .
8. The kindergarten program makes provision for satisfying aesthetic experiences for the child. . . .

Schoolroom around the time of the American Revolution. The schoolmaster was responsible for all age groups, usually in a crowded one-room schoolhouse.

9. The kindergarten program provides opportunities for the child to develop his sense of responsibility. . . .[16]

As to the future, the kindergarten is increasingly being conceived as an integral part of early childhood education, a time span which includes the school experiences of young children in nursery school, kindergarten, and the primary grades. The kindergarten of the future will not be regarded as an isolated one-year experience during the early childhood years. Nor will the kindergarten be conceived as the level where learning begins. Today, students of child development are aware of the many learning experiences even so-called deprived children have before reaching the age of five. Children are entering kindergarten with more maturity in social and intellectual development than ever before. As the latest edition of the *Encyclopedia of Educational Research* says:

Much of the literature on kindergartens seems strangely out of touch with the child of today. To speak of his "beginning learning" in kindergarten ignores the tremendous influences on children which exist outside of the school. Unless the child has been isolated from the world completely, he has shared a wealth of experiences with his

[16] Emmy Louise Widmer, *The Critical Years: Early Childhood Education at the Crossroads* (Scranton, Pennsylvania: International Textbook, 1970), pp. 106–114.

concern for the program as a whole rather than separate subjects or fields. Teachers were encouraged to seek outside evaluation in understanding and assessing their own emotional needs. Counselors, psychologists, self-assessment classes, and encounter groups became more widely available and were more often used both by teachers and by students in teacher education programs.

The elementary school in America has been changing. Even your own experience a decade or more ago is no longer a reliable guide to today's elementary schooling. Looking to the future, Alfred Ellison of New York University describes an elementary school "for the day after tomorrow" which develops what he terms "tools for living."

1. Insight into the ideals, historical perspectives, and functioning of a democratic society to the extent of valuing it as a way of life, with consequent acceptance of full personal responsibility for participation in and defense of its instruments and institutions.
2. Respect for and understanding of one's self, leading to respect for others and skills in relating to them, maintaining the integrity of the individual personality as a primary value.
3. A rigorous intellectual development that provides an ability to evaluate facts, put them into proper perspective, and use them with purpose. Mere repetition and memory of a set of facts are inadequate; vitally important is the ability to think clearly and reason effectively.
4. Broad and deep insights into man's accomplishments and trials in his efforts to live together with others at personal, local, national, and international levels; and in his efforts to control, modify, and understand his physical and social worlds.
5. Aesthetic sensitivity — an ability to sense and participate in making the beautiful in a variety of art forms, with enough mastery of at least one art so as to provide a comfortable medium of personal expression.
6. An individual quirk of originality, inventiveness, creativeness, with corresponding strength to be nonconformist when important, so that the unique problems of an unknowable world ahead may find their necessarily unique solutions.
7. A high moral and ethical value structure as a basis for decision-making and personal living, one which serves to enhance the business of everyday living.
8. Knowledge of the many-faceted vocational propensities of a real world of work, including the new occupations now developing, together with techniques for realistic appraisal of one's personal abilities and aspirations.
9. Recognition of the excitement of discovery, the acceptance of intellectual challenge, the intensity of unfilled curiosity, with a fervor for the honest pursuit of ideas.
10. Skill in the communication of ideas, facts, and feelings in many forms and media.
11. Recognition of leisure time as an opportunity for the pursuit of private or public goals, with ability to use it wisely, creatively, and purposefully.
12. The achievement of optimum health through the interaction of the individual's physical well-being, his mental stability, and his personality fulfillment.[23]

[23] Alfred Ellison, "A School for the Day After Tomorrow," in Joe L. Frost and G. Thomas Rowland (eds.), *The Elementary School: Principles and Problems* (Boston: Houghton Mifflin, 1969), pp. 517–518.

## JUNIOR HIGH SCHOOL \ MIDDLE SCHOOL

Junior high school, customarily grades 7, 8, and 9, constitutes one educational level authentically invented in the United States. Americans inherited the organization and structures of the other educational levels, but the junior high school was first established in the United States in Columbus, Ohio, in 1909. Some claim the birthplace to be Berkeley, California, which established its intermediate schools in January 1910, with a program specifically intended to meet the needs of young adolescents. However, Berkeley titled its schools "introductory high schools," a name which never caught on. The Ohio capital was the first city to use the name "junior high school."

Some students never attend an institution labeled "junior high school" because they go from elementary school into senior high in accordance with the popular nineteenth century organization, the so-called 8–4 system. Others spend their junior high school years in an institution which also encompasses the senior high school, the so-called 6–6 division. Yet about one-third of all public secondary schools are two- or three-year junior high schools.[24] Most schools are organized on the 6–3–3 or 6–6 basis.

The newest competitor to the junior high school is titled the "middle school," a way of grouping grades which results in a three- or four-year middle school made up of the fifth through eighth or the fourth through eighth grades, followed by a four-year high school. Translated numerically, this form of organization involves 5–3–4 or 4–4–4 school groupings.

Regardless of how organized or where housed, the junior high school years are intended to: (1) continue the education needed by all citizens in a democracy (general education), and (2) provide experience especially suited to the diverse abilities, needs, and interests of widely varied adolescents (education for diversity). Fulfillment of these purposes imposes on the modern junior high school responsibility for the following functions:

1. Continuing and extending the general education program of the elementary school, including development of the basic skills.
2. Providing for a transition between the organization and approach of the elementary school and that of the senior high school.
3. Introducing new subject areas and additional specialization within basic areas.
4. Providing opportunities for students to discover and pursue their special interests and aptitudes.
5. Providing appropriate experiences to assist and guide the rapid physical development that is characteristic of early adolescence.

[24] U.S. Office of Education, *Digest of Educational Statistics*, 1971 ed. (Washington, D.C.: U.S. Government Printing Office, 1972), p. 46.

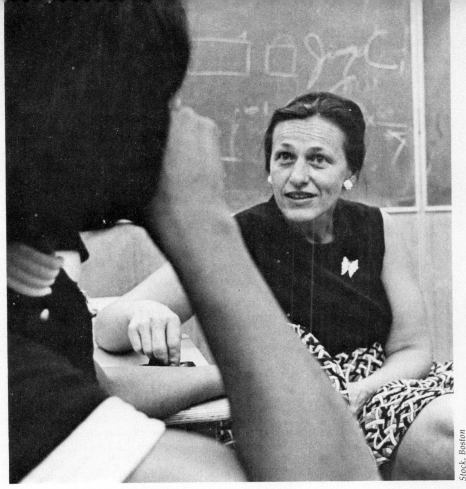

One of the services and responsibilities of the school is providing counseling and guidance to all students.

2. *The junior high school of the future should rely upon a basic policy of experimental development of the instructional program.* So far as we now know or can predict, we never will have permanent answers regarding what constitutes the best education. . . .

3. *The junior high school of the future should seek continually to improve time arrangements for effective learning and teaching.* The quality of learning in almost all areas of the curriculum could be improved if the time allotments could be made more flexible. . . .

4. *The instructional process should be planned explicitly for the junior high school years.* If young people are to examine, study, and develop commitment to articulate democratic values in the junior high school, and if these are to be years of exploration and discovery in terms of self, vocational and life goals, then the kind of instructional process utilized must be geared to these purposes. The read-recite-quiz approach simply will not do. The emphasis in junior high school classes increasingly must be upon discovery, upon finding out what constitutes a fact,

Modern technology has provided varied teaching and learning aids for the schools.

what is an opinion, upon discrimination of sources of information and their relative reliability, and upon the process of problem solving. . . .

5. *The junior high school of the future should be an ungraded institution.* Today, the junior high school recognizes that many students cannot be easily classified by grade levels. In the future, students will be assigned to classes and courses on the basis of individual interests, achievement, and need. . . .

6. *The junior high school of the future should incorporate routines and patterns that encourage civility in living.* . . .

7. *Varying instructional procedures will be used to accomplish the purposes of junior high school education in the future.* It is widely agreed that during the years of early adolescence the student needs special attention and help for exploration and discovery. . . .

8. *The junior high school of the future should provide many means for the student to see himself as a significant individual in a larger world setting.* Many opportunities will be available to young people for experiences designed to help them develop personal values and commitments. One such opportunity can be provided by a school through establishing close ties with a school overseas. . . .

9. *The school year should be extended to provide a richer and more effective education program.* In many metropolitan and suburban areas, the junior high school youngster has few opportunities for constructive and satisfying activities after school. . . .

10. *Aesthetic and creative opportunities and experiences should be abundant in the junior high school of the future.* In today's world, individual maturity and serenity are hard to achieve. Yet, through aesthetic awareness and creative experiences, individuals can find ways in which life becomes more meaningful and manageable. . . .

11. *The junior high school of tomorrow should provide extended guidance for all students.* Adolescence is a crucial period in which many fateful decisions are made—to go to college, to leave school, to prepare for a vocation. Youngsters at this age need all the help that trained personnel can give them. . . .
12. *The staff in the junior high school of the future should be given differentiated assignments.* Just as we know that young people have different talents and strengths, so we must recognize that teachers vary in their skills. . . .
13. *New developments in technology and in materials of instruction should be utilized in the junior high school of tomorrow.* . . .
14. *Administrative responsibilities will be more clearly defined in the junior high school of the future.* . . .
15. *Gaining knowledge, skill and understanding are basic goals for junior high school pupils.* Knowledge must be meaningful; skills must relate to use; and understanding needs a foundation in reasoned and disciplined thought. . . .[27]

## SENIOR HIGH SCHOOL

The high school today is either a three- or four-year institution, depending largely on whether the system uses the junior high school form of organization. The ancestry of the American high school includes the Latin grammar school, designed to teach academic knowledge, particularly the classics, to boys preparing for college; it also includes the academy, which was designed by Benjamin Franklin to foster useful knowledge rather than simply that knowledge which was ornamental.

From 1893 to 1918, five committees of distinguished educators reported to the nation on the functions of high school education. The first four of these committees stressed the responsibility of secondary school for preparing students for college; these committees were called the Committee of Ten on Secondary School Studies, the Committee on College Entrance Requirements, the Committee on Economy of Time in Education, and the Committee of Nine on the Articulation of High School and College.[28]

But in 1918 came the historic report of the Commission on the Reorganization of Secondary Education. Unlike the earlier committees, this commission suggested that schools should base their instruction on the present and prospective lives of the students who attended. The report set forth as the principal objectives of all education and especially of secondary education these seven cardinal principles: health, command of the fundamental processes, worthy home membership, vocation, citizenship, worthy use of leisure, and an ethical character. Stress on the seven cardinal principles strengthened the curriculum claims of such high school subjects as industrial arts, home economics, music, fine arts,

[27] Jean D. Grambs *et al., The Junior High School We Need* (Washington, D.C.: Association for Supervision and Curriculum Development, 1961), pp. 19–29.
[28] William Marshall French, *American Secondary Education* (New York: Odyssey, 1967), p. 147.

Nineteenth century public high school building, Hartford, Conn.

physical education, and business education. Emphasis on the new objectives encouraged the development of a more unitary social studies program for citizenship rather than completely separate history, geography, economics, etc.

There have since been many campaigns in the struggle to make high school education less traditional. Nevertheless, most high schools continued to stress college preparatory programs, supplemented by vocational offerings for the non-college bound through vocational "tracks" within the comprehensive high school. Some large city systems separate academic and vocational education still further through developing a double system of academic high schools and vocational high schools.

With the Soviet Union's successful launching of Sputnik in 1957, American education placed new emphasis on the need for trained manpower to achieve national purposes. The high school curriculum was reconstructed subject by subject, particularly with the aid of the original National Defense Education Act of 1958, which fostered the reconstruction of programs in science, mathematics, and world languages. With the development of concern for the culturally disadvantaged during the 1960s, the forces which urged a high school curriculum to meet the needs of all young people gained ground.

By October 1972, American public high schools (grades 9–12)

44

Modern high schools give the impression of space, light, and expansion—room to learn.

enrolled about 14,015,000 students. Nonpublic high schools enrolled about 1,155,000 students.[29] But the question of the high school's purpose was still unresolved. Some believe the high school exists simply to prepare young people for college; others see it as an extension of general and specialized education intended to serve the needs of all young people whether college-bound or not.

An important proposal for the future of the high school was made by Kimball Wiles of the University of Florida. Taking 1985 as a target date, Wiles envisioned a high school of the future in which "each pupil will develop a set of values to guide his behavior; acquire the skills necessary to participate effectively in the culture; gain an understanding of his social, economic, political, and scientific heritage; and become able to make a specialized contribution to society.[30] Wiles envisioned four educational phases: analysis of experience and values, acquisition of fundamental skills, exploration of the cultural heritage, and specialization and creativity.

[29] U.S. Bureau of the Census, "School Enrollment in the United States: 1972" ("Population Characteristics"), *Current Population Reports,* Series P-20, No. 247 (Washington, D.C.: U.S. Government Printing Office, 1973), p. 4.
[30] Kimball Wiles, *The Changing Curriculum of the American High School* (Englewood Cliffs, N.J.: Prentice-Hall, 1963), p. 301.

Vivienne, D.P.I.

Personal observation and involvement have become integral components of American education today.

In order to achieve analysis of experiences and values, Wiles proposed the pupil spend six hours a week in an "analysis group" with ten other pupils and a teacher-counselor discussing a variety of relevant problems. To acquire fundamental skills he proposed dependence upon teaching machines, especially for learning mathematics, foreign languages, and many scientific processes and formulas. To explore the cultural heritage he proposed exposure to basic knowledge from such fields as the humanities, social sciences, and the physical and biological sciences, through media which would be easily understood and dramatically and forcefully presented. He saw the analysis groups, the fundamental skills work, and cultural heritage courses as the program to be required of all. But in addition he called for each student to develop a specialization through work in shops, studios, work laboratories, work experience, seminars, etc. All students would also be encouraged to engage in creative activity through the varied arts and writing laboratories.

In 1969, nineteen writers contributed their reactions to Wiles' ideas in *The High School of the Future*. While the ideas of the authors naturally varied, there was fundamental agreement with Wiles' projection. For instance, this writer, after reviewing alternative futures of the high school, made the following predictions:

The most likely future high school, 1985–2000, will include as a component "analysis of experience and values," through small groups made up of students of varied social and racial backgrounds who will not only discuss but will also use various media in analyzing the value implications of their individual experiences and of society's social problems. . . .

The most likely future high school will include as a component "acquisition of individual skills" through core-like analysis groups, broad fields, and the specialized and creative approaches. Additionally, acquisition of individual skills will take place through individual study via computers, listening laboratories, and allied technology geared to individual levels and rates of learning.

The most likely future high school will include as its single heaviest component carefully selected "knowledge of the humanities, the social sciences, and the physical and biological sciences." In addition, this component will include world languages because of the world power setting, and that important universal language used in the knowledge explosion—mathematics. Some of the work in these broad fields will be presented through large group instruction via multi-media. But much of it will take place through moderately sized groups characterized by questioning, discussion, and both individual and small group work. . . .

Specialization for the leadership group in a society of expanded higher education will be regarded as an indication of incipient potentiality which must be heavily supplemented on the collegiate and graduate level. Similarly, in a society with expanded on-the-job training for the ordinary worker, specialization in high school through work experience and vocational education will be regarded as little more than orientation. Specialization for those who are unemployable in a highly advanced society will be a problem possibly resolved by rotation in undemanding jobs or by new careers in the human services field which may exist or be created. On the other hand, the creativity dimensions, through a variety of laboratory and field inductions into mental and physical leisure pursuits, will be heavily emphasized for the health of the social order and the fulfillment of the individual person in a society providing multiple options for the use of the abundant time on one's hands. Even the leadership group will be urged to develop creative pursuits, if for no other reason than enhanced productivity and more effective cogitation.[31]

## COLLEGE AND UNIVERSITY

A college may be autonomous or it may be part of a university. The *university* is far more comprehensive than the *college;* they usually differ in

[31] William Van Til, "Alternative Futures of the High School," in W. Alexander (ed.), *The High School of the Future: A Memorial to Kimball Wiles* (Columbus, Ohio: Charles E. Merrill, 1969), pp. 113–115.

FOR EVERY 10 PUPILS IN THE 5thGRADE IN FALL 1961

9.6 ENTERED THE 9th GRADE IN FALL 1965

8.6 ENTERED THE 11th GRADE IN FALL 1967

7.6 GRADUATED FROM HIGH SCHOOL IN 1969

4.5 ENTERED COLLEGE IN FALL 1969

2.2 ARE LIKELY TO EARN 4-YEAR DEGREES IN 1973

FIGURE 2-2    School Retention Rates

U.S. Office of Education, *Digest of Educational Statistics*, 1971 ed., (Washington, D.C.: U.S. Government Printing Office, 1972), p. 8.

size and scope of curriculum, and in the fact that a university grants graduate degrees.

The first colleges were established in the twelfth century in Paris, Oxford, and Cambridge. The college became the principal center for learning within the university. The role of the university was to examine candidates for degrees and grant the degrees. From these seeds grew higher education. In the United States, college education has reached substantial dimensions. In October 1972, American colleges enrolled 8,313,000 students.[32]

A new computation of school retention rates by the Office of Education shows that young people are staying in school longer than ever before. As the accompanying chart indicates (see Figure 2-2), about 96 percent of the fifth graders in the fall of 1961 reached the ninth grade, 86 percent got as far as the 11th grade, and 76 percent received a high school diploma in 1969. The proportion of young people who graduate from high school has risen during the past decade from less than two-thirds to more than three-fourths.

The increase in college attendance in recent years is even more striking. In 1969 about 45 percent of our young adults (or close to 60 percent of the recent high school graduates) entered a degree-credit program in a college or university. A decade ago only about one-third of the appropriate age group entered college. Approximately 22 percent of the persons in their late teens in 1969 can be expected to graduate from college with a 4-year degree. Ten years ago only about one young person in six went on to earn a bachelor's degree.[33]

Though the American colonies inherited the idea of colleges from the Old World, Americans gave it a new twist. They developed the college as an institution separate from the university. A primary purpose was to educate young men for the ministry. The first American college was Harvard in 1636. There followed such colleges as William and Mary in 1693, Yale in 1701, Princeton in 1746, Columbia in 1754, Brown in 1765, and Rutgers in 1766. As the nation moved west, the settlers brought the college idea with them, and now the map of the nation is dotted with colleges, some of which have grown into universities.

In the latter half of the nineteenth century, tax-supported state colleges were formed. Through the Morrill Act of 1862, public lands were granted to the states for state agricultural and mechanical colleges. Out of such beginnings have grown such giants as the Big Ten[34] universities. Throughout the late nineteenth century and into the twentieth, the land grant colleges steadily moved to the status of universities by expanding to include professional schools and graduate instruction.

---

[32] U.S. Bureau of the Census, "School Enrollment in the United States: 1972," ("Population Characteristics") *Current Population Reports,* Series P-20 No. 247 (Washington, D.C.: U.S. Government Printing Office, 1973), p. 4. These census statistics on colleges include only people to the age of 34; therefore, the many older graduate students in universities were not included and total higher education enrollment was somewhat larger in 1972 than the cited figure indicated.

[33] U.S. Office of Education, *Digest of Educational Statistics,* 1971 ed. (Washington, D.C.: U.S. Government Printing Office, 1972), p. 8.

[34] Indiana University, Michigan State University, Northwestern University, Ohio State University, Purdue University, University of Illinois, University of Iowa, University of Michigan, University of Minnesota, University of Wisconsin.

## Colleges for Women

Another American collegiate innovation was the establishment of colleges for women. The first women's colleges included Mount Holyoke, 1837; Elmira, 1853; Vassar, 1861; Wellesley, 1871; Smith, 1871; and Bryn Mawr, 1881. Woman's colleges persist in the closing third of the twentieth century, but today the trend is to coeducation. Today many women's colleges—the prestigious Seven Sisters,[35] for example—have developed further collaborative relationships with their male neighbors—for instance, Barnard and Columbia, Radcliffe and Harvard, Smith and Amherst, and Wellesley and M.I.T. Today the male sanctuaries, having earlier admitted women at the graduate level, are increasingly enrolling women undergraduates. Dartmouth College was the last (1972) of the Ivy League[36] colleges to adopt some form of coeducation. Even the five men's colleges at Oxford University, England, decided to admit their first women undergraduates experimentally in 1974.[37] However, as approximately half of the 298 women's colleges in America closed or became coeducational between 1960 and 1972, some American women's colleges stiffened their resistance to coeducation. As of 1973, women's colleges Mount Holyoke, Smith, Wellesley, and Bryn Mawr did not grant degrees to men. In mid-1973 the president of Wellesley indicated her belief that coeducation had failed and that the trend to coeducation had increased, rather than lessened, male domination of American higher education.

## Colleges for Blacks

The development of Negro colleges also reflects the American social setting. After the Civil War, colleges for black Americans came into existence partially through the philanthropy of such rich men as George Peabody and partially through the activities of Negro leaders like Booker T. Washington, who opened Tuskegee Normal and Industrial Institute in 1881.

In an era first of post-Civil War reconstruction and then of state-enforced segregation, Negro colleges struggled with the handicap that they were separate in status and unequal to white institutions in quality. Legally, the tide turned to desegregation in the late 1930s and the 1940s, when Supreme Court decisions opened the door to the enrollment of Negroes in formerly all-white institutions. In a precedent-setting case, the Maryland Court of Appeals upheld a decision in which Donald Gaines Murray, a Negro graduate of Amherst was ordered admitted to the University of Maryland School of Law in 1935.[38] In a similar case filed by Lloyd Lionel Gaines, the Supreme Court of the United States handed

---

[35] Barnard, Mount Holyoke, Smith, Radcliffe, Wellesley, Vassar, and Bryn Mawr.
[36] Brown University, Columbia University, Cornell University, Dartmouth College, Harvard University, University of Pennsylvania, Princeton University, Yale University.

Black college biology class.

down a decision in 1938 which supported the earlier Murray decision and relied heavily on findings in that case.[39] Other suits followed in other states, so that by 1950 resort to legal action in school segregation questions was not an unusual practice.[40] Although twelve southern and border states and the District of Columbia had initiated desegregation in some of their institutions of higher learning to a limited degree prior to the 1954 Supreme Court ruling, court cases such as the Brown case provided the most influential prod to university desegregation.

Universities, sparked by the demands of black militants, initiated black studies programs in the late 1960s and into the 1970s; Negro colleges, largely in the South, were raided by northern colleges and universities suddenly eager to bring black men to their staff for development of black studies programs. In addition, Negro colleges encountered economic problems brought about by inflation. They were also confronted by demands of black separatists and legal requirements that

[37] "5 Oxford Men's Colleges to Admit Women in 1974," *New York Times*, April 29, 1972, p. 9.
[38] W. A. Low, "The Education of Negroes Viewed Historically," in V. A. Clift, A. W. Anderson, and H. G. Hullfish (eds.), *Negro Education in America: Its Adequacy, Problems, and Needs* (New York: Harper, 1962), p. 54.
[39] *Ibid.*, p. 55.
[40] *Ibid.*, pp. 55–56.

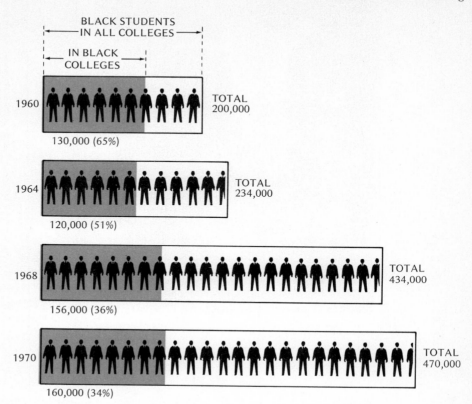

**FIGURE 2-3**   **Black Students in Colleges**

*New York Times,* October 17, 1971, section 4, p. 7.

public education be desegregated. As a result of such social forces, Negro colleges are today struggling for survival.

As the 1970s opened, there were 51 private and 34 public four-year black colleges, and 11 private and 4 public two-year colleges, with a total enrollment of 160,000 black students. Some 310,000 more black students were involved in predominantly white public and private institutions of higher learning. Half of these latter students attended two-year community colleges.[41] (See Figure 2-3.) In the early 1970s, black college enrollment continued to rise. In 1972 black enrollment in all colleges had grown to 727,000. Today black colleges also enroll whites.

Sidney P. Marland, Jr., while he was the U.S. Commissioner of Education, commented: "It is not anachronistic to have literally hundreds of sectarian institutions, a Brandeis or a Notre Dame. So no defense of black institutions is required as they play their special role in focusing

---

[41] "Negro Higher Education: Between Two Worlds," *New York Times,* October 11, 1971, p. 26.

on the needs of their people." [42] Marland urged black colleges to take the lead in developing urban and black studies programs and in filling the pressing need for more black professionals.

### The Junior College

The established four-year undergraduate college has been joined in the twentieth century by a college with a new time span, the junior college. Essentially, the junior college covers the first two years of the customary four-year span. Some junior colleges are private and independently supported; some are affiliated with churches. But the most phenomenal growth is that of the kind of junior college called the public community college. In the late 1950s, approximately one out of five students in the nation began his undergraduate studies in a community college. But in the late 1960s, the number had grown to more than one out of three beginning college students. It is reasonable to predict that the number will reach one out of two sometime during the 1970s.

Edmund J. Gleazer, Jr., executive director of the American Association of Junior Colleges, points out in a 1971 book, *American Junior Colleges:*

> The increasing number of high school graduates, the increasing percentage of college-age persons seeking education beyond high school, the technological advances that require more workers to receive in-service training or embark on new careers, the increasing popularity of adult continuing education, the expansion of community service programs, and the continuing efforts of public junior colleges to recruit and educate the disadvantaged all indicate that both the number of community colleges and the number of students they enroll will continue to grow. More students are beginning their college work in two-year institutions; in California 88 percent of freshmen attending public colleges are enrolled in community colleges; in Florida the reported figure is 65 percent. To achieve the goal of providing a community college within commuting distance of all potential students, the Carnegie Commission estimates 230 to 280 new community colleges will be needed by 1980. It further estimates that 37 percent to 46 percent of *all* undergraduates will be enrolled in community colleges by the year 2000. By 1975, 3,873,000 to 5,055,000 students are expected to enroll. [43]

### Graduate School

Increasingly, the master's degree is being taken for granted as a necessity for teachers—if not immediately after embarking on teaching, then quite soon after. One form of master's degree is the MAT, designed especially for liberal arts graduates who decide to teach. Five years of education for teachers following high school graduation will almost certainly become

---

[42] "Black Colleges Get New Pledge of U.S. Support," *The Chronicle of Higher Education,* April 10, 1972, p. 1.
[43] Edmund J. Gleazer, Jr., ed., *American Junior Colleges* (Washington, D.C.: American Council on Education, 1971), p. 7.

one of the facts of teaching life which you should take into account.

Beyond the master's degree lies a one-year degree which still lacks a dignified title. It is sometimes referred to as the sixth-year degree or the advanced degree in education. This degree is for the practitioners who want to go beyond the master's degree but do not require specialization in research for their career development.

The ultimate degree in the American educational system is the doctorate. A doctor of philosophy (Ph.D.) or doctor of education (Ed.D.) degree has become a must for the graduate staff member and a near must for four-year college teachers and school leadership posts.

Graduate education began in the United States in 1876 with the founding of the Johns Hopkins University. Many of the patterns now being disputed by some of the nation's youth were established at that time. The first president of the Johns Hopkins University, Daniel Coit Gilman, had in view:

. . . the appointment of professors who had shown their ability as investigators, whose duties as teachers would not be so burdensome as to interfere with the prosecution of their research, whose students should be so advanced as to stimulate them to their best work, and the fruit of whose labors in the advancement of science and learning should be continually manifested in the shape of published results.[44]

Sound familiar? This conception of the role of the graduate professor is often under attack from student dissenters who urge more activism and involvement by professors.

### The Future of Colleges and Universities

As to the future of higher education, there is fierce debate and wide disagreement. The controversy goes far beyond the continuing and significant academic questions of how many courses should be required and how many should be elective, how much general or liberal education to include in the curriculum, or how much specialization in a single field. The questions now discussed with earnestness and passion involve the very role of these institutions. In the late 1960s and early 1970s demonstrations, strikes, arson, and closedowns swept through the colleges and universities because of student dissatisfaction on issues related in part to the role of the university in society.

Nineteenth century scholars such as John Henry Newman, a cardinal of the Roman Catholic Church, saw the university as an assembly of scholars who tested and shared ideas and created an atmosphere in which students could develop sound and creative habits of mind. As the twentieth century developed, classical ideals of liberal education such as Newman's were supplemented by demands that higher education prepare Americans for a variety of new professions and careers. Since World

[44] Fabian Franklin *et al., The Life of Daniel Coit Gilman* (New York: Dodd, Mead, 1910), p. 196.

*Charles Harbutt, Magnum Photos, Inc.*

Education of America's adults has also received new emphasis in recent years.

designed to help eliminate such inability and raise the level of education of such individuals with a view to making them less likely to become dependent on others, to improving their ability to benefit from occupational training and otherwise increasing their opportunities for more productive and profitable employment, and to making them better able to meet their adult responsibilities."[48]

Though there are relatively few professional teachers in adult education, there are many volunteers. No one has calculated the number of volunteer adult education workers. For instance, think of the number of program chairpersons in American voluntary organizations. A second

[48] Margaret Samet (ed.), *The Public Continuing and Adult Educational Almanac* (Washington, D.C.: National Association for Public Continuing and Adult Education, 1972), pp. 15–16.

**TABLE 2-1  Participants in Adult Education by Source of Instruction: United States 1969**

| Source of instruction | Total |
|---|---|
| Total (in thousands) | 13,150 |
| | Percent of column totals |
| Public or private school | 27.7 |
| College or university, part-time | 25.2 |
| Job training | 27.5 |
| Correspondence courses | 8.0 |
| Community organizations | 13.4 |
| Tutor or private instructor | 5.8 |
| Other | 10.3 |

Since some adults received instruction from more than
one source, percentage totals more than 100.
U.S. Office of Education, *Digest of Educational Statistics*,
1971 ed. (Washington, D.C.: U.S. Government Printing
Office, 1972), p. 5.

group of adult educators are the part-timers. These are the people who
are regularly employed, often as teachers in universities and school
systems; they take on additional work with classes of adults as moonlighting employment. They are seldom trained especially to work with
adults and tend to find their way through the use of trial and error. Finally, there are the professionals in adult education, such as staff members of university extension programs, the agricultural extension experts,
the adult education specialists in public schools, etc. Increasingly, such
professionals work for graduate degrees. (See Table 2-1 for job clues.)

## CHOOSING AMONG LEVELS

If you are going to be a teacher, you will teach at one of the levels
described. A small minority of new teachers may teach on two levels—for
example, at both junior high and senior high schools levels, or at both
kindergarten and early elementary school levels. Or as his career inten-
tions change, a teacher may move from junior high to a different level,
perhaps to senior high school teaching. Sometimes an outstanding elementary or secondary school teacher, having achieved the doctoral degree, moves into college and university teaching. But most teachers stay
at the level they originally chose.

How do you choose the teaching level that is right for you? Presumably you want to work with people to make a difference. But people at
what stage of development? Perhaps the single most important factor to
take into account is the age level of students with which you feel most
comfortable and to which you are most attracted as a teacher. Do the

Some adults have organized into groups to discuss common interests, such as community participation and child-rearing.

unique experiences which you have had in your family, schooling, work, or recreation lead you to prefer to work with one particular age group?

To decide the teaching level which you prefer, you might also take a realistic look at your own personality characteristics. If you are turned on by watching and helping individuals grow, you might seriously consider some of the lower levels of the educational system; if teaching, to be rewarding to you, requires a lively interchange of ideas on a near peer basis, you might consider the highest levels of the educational system.

As part of your self-examination, you might also ask yourself what essentially you are trying to do through teaching.

If your primary interest is in the communication of a body of content which has awakened and aroused you, you might find yourself most at home on one of the higher educational levels—unless you have concluded that the earliest stages of learning your specialized content offer the most exciting challenge to you.

Or perhaps your motivation is to help human beings develop their values and approach to life. Such a commitment might lead you to work either with the very young, since presumably the young are still forming their values, or with older learners during those periods of their lives when they are reconsidering their life styles.

Perhaps your main interest is in research. Then you probably should plan to get your doctoral degree and teach at a four-year college or, preferably, a graduate school.

For the teacher who wishes to teach on the college level but does not propose to become a research specialist, the American junior college movement, and especially the community college, offers great opportunities. A recent study of community colleges points out:

> The master's degree is the highest one held by most members of the staff. Of those in the national sample, 77.7 percent held an M.A. or M.S. degree. Only 8.6 percent held a doctorate. Slightly more than 10 percent had earned only a bachelor's, and only 3.5 percent were working on less than a bachelor's. . . .
> Community college faculty are recruited from a wide variety of sources. In the study of the 57 institutions, staff members were asked to indicate their principal occupation immediately before their current college position. By far the largest number—almost one-third of the total—came from the public school system, usually as teachers, counselors, or administrators from high schools. The next largest group, approximately 22 percent, were directly from graduate school. Next in line was the group, accounting for 11 percent of the total, who were recruited from four-year institutions. Approximately 10 percent come from business or industry, and the remainder from a variety of other sources.[49]

You cannot be sure that your early decision will be the best for you. But you must think it through carefully now. It is romantic folly to hope that you will become a professor of English in a university through preparing to become a teacher of English in a high school. The road to being a professor of English does not lead through the high school or a college of education program, but requires graduate work in English at a major university.

Yet career changes can and do take place. For instance, it is quite possible that you may find yourself more interested in a career in college teaching as you grow older, rather than immediately after college. Currently the community college staff is made up primarily of those in the 31- to 50-year age bracket. A recent study found that fewer than 18 percent of community college staff members were under 30, and only 23 percent were over 50.[50]

If your career decision is both early and thoughtful, you will avoid such obvious errors as taking adolescent psychology instead of child psychology if you really intend to teach on the elementary school level; and also more sophisticated errors such as insufficient courses in the various social sciences when you intend to teach social studies in junior or senior high school.

Each state has its own patterns of certification; your advisers are familiar with these. Should you find your adviser inadequate, most

[49] Leland L. Medsker, Dale Tillery, and Joseph P. Cosand, *Breaking the Access Barriers* (New York: McGraw-Hill, 1971), pp. 88–89.
[50] *Ibid.*, p. 87.

colleges or schools of education maintain an office of certification intended to help you meet certification requirements. There is additional advice on career planning in the final chapter of this book.

When you have decided about the best level, you can then concentrate on becoming the best possible teacher at the level you have chosen.

## DISCUSSION

1. Which educational level presently most appeals to you? Why?
2. How much do you know about the kibbutz method of rearing children? What do you think about it?
3. What seem to be the advantages and disadvantages of the development of day-care centers for children from disadvantaged homes in America?
4. Why is there presently little or no formal education for the years from birth to age three?
5. What do you know of nursery education in the community or communities in which you have lived? Who sponsors the nursery schools with which you are acquainted?
6. What do you think is the purpose of a nursery school?
7. What do you think of the purposes of kindergartens that are proposed? Do you believe that kindergarten should stress reading? Why or why not? What research data is available?
8. What have been some trends in the development of elementary education in America? Can you cite any evidence to support the idea that elementary school education in America has been rapidly changing?
9. How would you revise Ellison's proposal for an elementary school "for the day after tomorrow"?
10. Can you see any reasons to prefer junior high schools, middle schools, or some other form of educational organization for the middle years?
11. Do the proposed purposes of the junior high school and those of the middle school seem fundamentally different to you in any ways? Do they seem alike?
12. What would be your own proposal for "the junior high school we need"?
13. What are some major developments in the history of the senior high school in America?
14. Why is the senior high school level particularly resistant to program changes? When the program does change, what forces particularly account for such changes?
15. As you see it, what is the relative importance of the four educational phases proposed by Wiles? In what ways do these phases correspond with the seven cardinal principles of education? In what ways do they go beyond them? Can you see any influence of Wiles' thinking in your own high school experience?
16. If you had your way, how would you change the current high school program? What is your picture of a desirable high school for the future?
17. Attendance at colleges and universities is steadily increasing. How is this desirable or undesirable? Is society forcing young people into college?
18. What is to be said for and against coeducation as contrasted to separate colleges for men and women? Do your reasons apply to all educational levels?
19. Speculate on the future of black colleges. Will they survive? If so, how will they be different from Negro colleges of earlier decades?

20. Why has the junior college movement boomed? What are the advantages and disadvantages of this form of educational organization? Why have community colleges grown markedly?

21. What is the status of the junior college movement in your state? Are the junior colleges there a part of the state educational program? Does the junior college play a major or minor role in your state's higher education?

22. Do you see any relationship between the doctoral degree and the teaching ability of instructors and professors who have taught you?

23. What do you think of the emphasis on publications by professors which is characteristic of graduate school education? Is it valid to condemn higher education for so-called "publish or perish" policies? What is your conception of a desirable undergraduate or graduate school professor?

24. Fundamentally, what is a university or college for? Development of the mind? Vocational training? Social action?

25. What is the role of students in your university? What should it be? Should students have voice and vote? Should they have a degree of representation in policy-making groups? Should they have full equality with faculty in number of representatives?

26. Should students determine university and college matters related to tenure, promotion, salary increases of professors? Would academic freedom be threatened by student power?

27. What essentially *is* adult education? Why is adult education less systematically organized than higher education in America?

28. What is your own appraisal of your personality characteristics in relationship to teaching? How important to you is the exchange of ideas with students? How important is helping individuals grow?

29. In deciding to teach, how important is the subject matter in which you specialize? Do you propose to teach subjects or young people—or do you regard that as a false dualism?

30. Do your present ambitions tie into your long-range aspirations? Can you make a case for going in one occupational direction after college and moving in a sharply different direction some years later?

## INVOLVEMENT

1. Get in touch with and interview a member of one of the community agencies which deals with preschool children. Talk with this person about the differences between the behavior and problems of children of the poor and children of the affluent. Consider any differences which emerge and the implications they might have for education. Report to the class on your findings.

2. Visit a day-care center. Observe the teacher and the children and report things which seem significant to you. In what ways are these young children receiving good care? Speculate on whether or not some children are receiving better care than they might receive at home.

3. Visit a nursery school. After observing, ask the teacher why these particular children are in attendance. Do you find any relationship to social forces and developments?

4. Visit a kindergarten. Look for the purposes behind the various activities you observe. Try to find an opportunity to talk with the teacher about why the activities

you observed are taking place. How would you handle (ideally) the program you observed?

5. Visit the oldest and the newest elementary schools in the community in which you live or study. Do you see any differences in the program related to the age of the buildings? Or are the differences due to other factors?

6. Draw up your own proposal for an elementary school geared to today's needs and tomorrow's demands. Consider the physical plant as well as the educational program.

7. Visit a school for the middle years. How is the program which you observe similar to or different from that recommended?

8. Interview a successful teacher who teaches at the level you presently prefer. Find out his or her reasons for teaching and why he or she chose that particular level.

9. Visit a senior high school. Make a point of going to other classes than simply those which represent your own field or fields. As you see it, what are the teachers trying to do in their classes? In general, do the classes seem to be taught in a modern or traditional manner?

10. Create an opportunity to talk with a high school teacher about Wiles' ideas concerning the high school of the future. How does this individual see the future of the high school?

11. Visit the campus of a junior college, preferably a community college, in your area. Go to the administration building and find the individual responsible for visitors. Talk with him about the role and future of the junior college and the nature of its staff.

12. Sum up the degree of engagement of your college or university in current campus dissent. What matters are in debate? What problems are latent, awaiting arousal?

13. Develop a few interview questions to raise with fellow students on the goals, program, problems, etc., of your college or university. Look for common denominators in answers.

14. Examine the process of student involvement in government and university life in general at your institution. Determine whether centers of power exist in the student body. Reexamine your own role and participation in student government and campus life.

## FURTHER READING

Alexander, William M., J. Galen Saylor, and Emmett L. Williams. *The High School, Today and Tomorrow.* New York: Holt, Rinehart, and Winston, 1971. A comprehensive volume on the American high school which takes up the high school in American life, the curriculum of the high school, teaching in the high school, and the high school of tomorrow.

Anderson, Robert H. and Harold G. Shane, eds. *As the Twig Is Bent.* Boston: Houghton Mifflin, 1971. A book of readings on early childhood education which grew out of a special issue of *Kappan,* an important and readable educational journal. Selections deal with early childhood education in perspective, growth and development of the young child, and education of the young child.

Bronfenbrenner, Urie. *Two Worlds of Childhood, U.S. and U.S.S.R.* New York: Simon and Schuster, 1970. A cross-cultural study in child-rearing which describes the making of the new Soviet man through child-rearing and which describes the past, present, and future of child-rearing in America.

Crossland, Fred E. *Minority Access to College.* New York: Schocken, 1971. A Ford Foundation report on the underrepresentation of minorities in colleges and the nature of barriers to college admission.

Funk, Hal D. and Robert T. Olberg, eds. *Learning to Teach in the Elementary School.* New York: Dodd, Mead, 1971. A book of readings primarily designed for elementary student teachers, yet useful prior to student teaching. Chapters take up motivation, individualizing instruction, developing pupil control and discipline, and evaluating and reporting pupil progress.

Goodlad, John I. and Harold G. Shane, eds. *The Elementary School in the United States.* Chicago: National Society for the Study of Education, 1973. The 1973 Yearbook of the National Society for the Study of Education which reports on and looks ahead in elementary education.

Gorman, Burton W. *Secondary Education.* New York: Random House, 1971. Changes that must take place in the high school to bring it abreast of current challenges and to prepare youth for responsible participation in a democratic society.

Hertling, James E. and Howard G. Getz, eds. *Education for the Middle School Years: Readings.* Glenview, Illinois: Scott, Foresman, 1971. A lively and informative anthology on the middle school. Includes purposes, the nature of the early adolescent, curriculum, model programs, physical facilities, and the controversy surrounding the middle school concept.

Hess, Robert D. and Doreen J. Croft. *Teachers of Young Children.* Boston: Houghton Mifflin, 1972. A book which integrates psychological research and theory on child development with early education theory and practice. Especially emphasized are ways of working with the disadvantaged child.

Landreth, Catherine. *Preschool Learning and Teaching.* New York: Harper & Row, 1972. A book on preschool learning and teaching emphasizing how to make these activities absorbing and rewarding.

Mills, Belen Collantes and Ralph Ainslee Mills. *Designing Instructional Strategies for Young Children.* Dubuque, Iowa: William C. Brown, 1972. A book on early childhood education interpreted broadly as encompassing the developmental range from infancy to pre-adolescence. The contributors deal with the teaching-learning process, strategies for teaching, individualized instructional programs, and process of evaluation.

Overly, Donald E., Jon Rye Kinghorn, and Richard L. Preston. *The Middle School: Humanizing Education for Youth.* Worthington, Ohio: C. A. Jones, 1972. Emphasis on individualizing and humanizing instruction through the middle schools. Includes the rationale for the middle school, the learning environment, staff allocations, student outcomes, and facilities.

Parker, Ronald K. *The Preschool in Action.* Boston: Allyn and Bacon, 1972. An anthology of readings concerning early childhood programs by specialists who presented papers at a conference on curricula for young children.

Spodek, Bernard. *Teaching in the Early Years.* Englewood Cliffs, New Jersey: Prentice-Hall, 1972. A special emphasis on the curriculum for the nursery, kindergarten and primary grades which make up early childhood education.

Weber, Evelyn. *The Kindergarten: Its Encounter with Educational Thought in America.* New York: Teachers College Press, Columbia University, 1969. The development of ideas concerning the kindergarten.

Yamamoto, Kaoru, ed. *The College Student and His Culture: An Analysis*. Boston: Houghton Mifflin Company, 1968. What college students are like, as perceived by writers during the 1960s, just prior to the period of student revolt. The diversity of educational institutions of higher learning in the nation—some of the problems faced by them and some possible solutions.

## SELECTED AUDIO-VISUAL MATERIALS

*College* (16 mm film, 19 min. color, Pyramid Films, 1963). Explains the nature and function of an ideal college through the eyes of the scientist, poet and explorer. Ignores the exterior aspects of a college and concentrates on what occurs in students' minds. Filmed at San Fernando Valley State College, Northridge, California.

*From Cradle to Classroom,* Parts I and II (16 mm film, 51 min., color, CBS: McGraw-Hill, 1968). Children from 3 months to 5 years in age are shown in many special types of teaching programs. Programs use professional teachers, nonprofessional instructors, teaching machines, educational toys, and association drills.

*Higher Education* (16 mm film, 30 min., b. & w., Holt, Rinehart, and Winston, 1969). Probes the question whether there is a different education for black students than for other students in higher education, and whether black colleges are valid institutions for higher learning.

*Infant School* (16 mm film, 29 min., b. & w., Educational Development Center, 1963). Explores a typical day in the Gordonbrook Infant School in London in an old building that has been adapted for new teaching methods. Examines the nongraded approach to instruction as practiced in England with children ranging in age from 5 to 7 years and grouped "family-fashion" for a wide variety of learning experiences.

*The Junior College Story* (16 mm film, 23 min., color, Bailey Film Associates, 1964). Explains how a student can acquire professional and technical skills or prepare for advanced college work by attending a junior college. Outlines the types of vocational and academic subjects which are taught and discusses the counseling services which are available.

*Junior High—A Time of Change* (16 mm film, 11 min., color, McGraw-Hill, 1964). Defines some of the problems which arise for the student upon entering junior high school. Suggests techniques to help in adjustment to the new type of school.

*Kindergarten: Twigs From a City Tree* (16 mm film, 22 min., color, Coronet, 1971). Observes a day with black children and a white male teacher in a ghetto kindergarten. A sensitive treatment of school, community, and social problems.

*Learning for Life* (16 mm film, 29 min., color, National Education Association, 196-). Reasons for adult education programs.

*The Precious Years* (16 mm film, 25 min., color, ABC Media Concepts, 1970). How do children learn and when? Evidence that what happens to a child between the ages of 0–6 determines his future.

*Skippy and the 3 R's* (16 mm film, 29 min., color, National Education Association, 1953). Shows how a first-grade child is taught reading and arithmetic by a teacher who utilizes the boy's interest to help him to realize his own need for learning.

*Teaching the 3's, 4's, and 5's,* Part 1: Guiding Behavior (16 mm film, 21 min., b. & w.,

Churchill Films, 1966). Shows several nursery school children in situations where adult help is needed to guide group and individual behavior: a tantrum, a runaway, and other situations. Mistakes as well as examples of skillful handling of situations are shown.

*Teaching the 3's, 4's, and 5's,* Part II: Setting the Stage for Learning (16 mm film, 22 min., b. & w., Churchill Films, 1966). Shows young children at play in a series of nursery school activities. Many simple "props" and play equipment are arranged to allow construction with wood, tests of physical powers, and use of imagination in family life play situations.

*Your First Year in High School,* Part I & II (35 mm filmstrips, Pt. 1–71 frs/record, Pt. II-74 frs/record, color, Guidance Associates, 1965). Defines the purpose of a high school education. Explores the student's relationship to teachers, parents, and classmates. Discusses the academic program.

How did any of Miss Dove's pupils, past or present see her? Off hand, that would seem an easy question. There was nothing elusive about Miss Dove's appearance and it had, moreover, remained much the same for more than thirty-five years. When she had begun to teach geography her figure had been spare and angular and it was still so. Her hair was more shadowy than it had once been but, twisted into a meagre little old-maid's knot, it had never had a chance to show much color. Her thin, unpainted mouth bore no sign of those universal emotions—humor, for instance, and love, and uncertainty—that mark most mouths in the course of time. Her pale, bleached out complexion never flushed with emotion—a slight pinkness at the tip of her pointed nose was the only visible indication that ordinary human blood ran through her veins. . . . All in all, in bearing and clothing and bony structure, Miss Dove suggested that classic portrait of the eternal teacher that small fry, generation after generation, draw upon fences and sidewalks with nubbins of purloined chalk; a grown-up stranger, catching his first glimpse of her, might be inclined to laugh with a kind of relief, as if he'd seen some old, haunting ogress of his childhood turned into a harmless joke. . . . Even the elevated position of her desk—a position deplored by modern educators who seek to introduce equality into the teacher-student relation—was right and proper. The dais of aloof authority suited her as a little hill near Ratisbon suited Napoleon Bonaparte. . . .[2]

Miss Dove had no moods. Miss Dove was a certainty. She would be today what she had been yesterday and would be tomorrow. And so, within limits, would they. Single file they would enter her room. Each child would pause on the threshold as its mother and father had paused, more than likely, and would say—just as the policeman had said—in distinct, formal accents: "Good morning, Miss Dove." And Miss Dove would look directly at each of them, fixing her eyes directly upon theirs and reply: "Good morning, Jessamine," or "Margaret," or "Samuel." (Never "Sam," never "Peggy," never "Jess." She eschewed familarity as she wished others to eschew it.) They would go to their appointed desks. Miss Dove would ascend to hers. The lesson would begin.[3]

Contemporary stereotypes have been created by books, films, and television programs of recent decades. For instance, James Hilton's Mr. Chips of the novel, film, and musical *Goodbye, Mr. Chips* was a warmhearted and generous dodderer who seemed to have been born an old man. Francis Prescott, "probably the greatest name in New England secondary education," was variously perceived as a tyrant, hypocrite, and hero by the characters of Louis Auchincloss's novel *The Rector of Justin.* Television's *Our Miss Brooks,* played by Eve Arden, was a loud-mouthed, amiable, scatterbrained high school teacher, and *Mr. Peepers,* played by Wally Cox, was a shy, confused, and lovable junior high science teacher. In recent television history, only handsome white James Franciosa, playing Mr. Novak, and handsome black Lloyd Haynes in *Room 222* supplied what psychologists term a desirable role model of the teacher. In movies based on novels, teachers have been favorably portrayed by

[2] Frances Gray Patton, *Good Morning, Miss Dove* (New York: Dodd, Mead, 1954), pp. 19–21.
[3] *Ibid.,* p. 8.

Sidney Poitier in *To Sir with Love* and Sandy Dennis in *Up the Down Staircase*. Bill Cosby has played an active and humorous "gym" teacher.

Yet if a composite stereotype exists, it is of the teacher as a patient, tired spinster (though most female teachers are married), or as an ineffectual man. But look around you. Your future colleagues are individual human beings characterized by wide diversity in age, education, motivation, experience, and life-style.

## GENERALIZATIONS ABOUT THE AMERICAN SCHOOL TEACHER

It is, of course, possible to generalize about teachers. But these generalizations must be approached warily, for statistical figures often prove to be descriptions of the "mean" or "median" person. Yet the many people who are not average (mean), or who are not the one in the middle (median), are just as real. With this warning, let us proceed to generalize on elementary and secondary school teachers.

### Sex

As to which sexes teach on what levels, generalizations are easy. Teaching on the preschool or nursery level is a near monopoly of the female sex. So is kindergarten teaching. On the elementary school level, teachers are primarily women, a whopping 84.5 percent in 1971–72. There has been some increase in the number of male elementary teachers, from 127,177 in 1961–62 to 176,913 in 1971–72. But the percentage of men elementary teachers increased only one percent in the decade 1961–62 (14.5%) to 1971–72 (15.5%). However, on the secondary school level, men teachers are now the majority. By 1971–72 the estimated percentage of male secondary school teachers was 54.2 percent.[4] In American public schools as a whole in 1972 approximately one out of every three teachers was male.

Men dominate as teachers on the college and graduate school levels. In 1972, 24.5 percent of faculty men in higher education held the highest rank of full professor, while only 9.4 percent of faculty women had attained that rank. Conversely, 16.3 percent of faculty men held the lowest rank of instructor, while 34.8 percent of faculty women were classified at the instructor level.[5] The women's liberation movement of the 1970s campaigns for much greater representation of women teaching on university faculties than the approximately 16.5 percent of 1972–73, and also for an end to discrimination in promotion and pay.

The generalizations are clear: the younger the learner, the greater the proportion of women teachers; the older the learner, the greater the

---

[4] NEA, Research Division, *Estimates of School Statistics, 1971–72,* Research Report 1971–R13 (Washington, D.C.: The Association, 1971), p. 14.
[5] "The Fight For a Fair Shake On Campus," *New York Times,* October 8, 1972, p. 11.

proportion of men teachers. So discrimination based on sex still persists in education.

Yet your personal decision today about the level at which you propose to teach should not be restricted by your sex. As a matter of fact, men are in high demand in elementary schools where their contribution as a male role model for children is valued. Though discrimination against women persists in higher education (despite supposed enlightenment of professors), and though raising of eyebrows has occurred when male teachers choose the preschool or kindergarten levels (despite the cry for "father images"), sex barriers in teaching are diminishing.

### Age

The age of the American teacher ranges from late teens to the seventies. Both entry into and exit from teaching are becoming increasingly delayed. In a society which prizes degrees and requires certification, practically no one graduates directly from high school into teaching or leaves college before graduation for a teaching post, though many did this in the nineteenth and early twentieth century. In a society of increasing longevity and increasing flexibility in retirement age, some universities and school systems defer teacher retirement or even make a point of employing retired people.

The average age of the American elementary and secondary school teacher is close to that age immortalized by the comedian Jack Benny—going on 39. To be precise, the average age was 41.5 in 1961 and was 38 in 1971. The median teacher was 40.9 in 1961 and 35 in 1971.[6] So the profession is growing younger.

Though the fair sex may not be pleased to hear it, the average female teacher is older than the average male teacher. If you recall your elementary school teachers as older than your high school teachers, you are quite correct. The fact is that elementary school teachers—as you will recall, most are women—*are* older. A 1971 survey by the NEA Research Division showed that the average age of elementary school teachers was 39 and of secondary school teachers 36. Interestingly, the survey also reported that in 1971 the average age of *all* female teachers was 39 and the average age of *all* male teachers (in public schools) was 36.[7]

So, should you ever meet our "average teacher," bear in mind that he or she, while younger than your parents, is nearer to their age than to your own. There may be some generation gap between you and our "average teacher."

[6] NEA, Research Division, *Status of The American Public-School Teacher, 1970–71*, Research Report 1972-R3 (Washington, D.C.: The Association, 1972), p. 59.
[7] *Ibid.* p. 59.

### Education

Do not underestimate the extent of schooling of your colleague-to-be, the average teacher. More than 97 percent of them have bachelor's or graduate degrees. Specifically, more than two-thirds have a bachelor's degree (69.6 percent) and more than a quarter have a master's or higher degree (27.5 percent). Only 2.9 percent of all teachers now teaching have no degree whatsoever.[8]

### Motivation

The motivations which have led experienced teachers into the field are mixed, even as are the motivations of today's new teachers. They include wanting to work with children or youth; salary and community considerations; admiration or rejection of some of their own teachers; parental influence; a desire to make a difference in individual lives and American society; a drive to challenge students, motivate them to learn, and contribute to the solution of social problems.

College juniors and seniors in a teacher education program at a mid-American university were asked why they wanted to teach in the 1970s.[9] Sydney stressed wanting to work with young people and improving democracy:

I am going into teaching because one of the things I enjoy most is working with young people of all ages. I find it very rewarding to help set up situations in which people may discover, and learn to enjoy discovering, ideas and facts about themselves and others. I find it challenging to help others to realize their own resources, to learn to think, to create, and to express themselves. I also have strong feelings about education in a democracy and its role in informing and motivating students to inform themselves as they come into a position of influencing the governing of the country.

Mary stressed belonging to a community:

I am from a small community in which the school is the main industry. The school is the center of activity and the hub of the community. As a student, I was a part of this hub, and I want to continue being an active, involved part. I enjoyed school from the first day through graduation, and I cannot picture myself any place except in a school. Wanting to be a part of a school organization is the first reason that I chose teaching for my career.

Other reasons reinforced my decision. I like working with young people. . . . By teaching, I feel that I can satisfy a need in myself to help others. I can gain a sense of accomplishment by helping others achieve and by being a part of their learning and growing.

[8] *Ibid.*, p. 12
[9] Papers by students in education who plan to teach English gathered by Ronald Leathers (Charleston, Ill.: Eastern Illinois University, February 1970).

this same pleasure whenever I enter the field of teaching and if I ever feel that I am not doing so, I shall no longer be a member of the teaching profession.

## Joyce stressed dealing with social problems:

I have made my decision to become a teacher because it seems that it is a profession which could allow me to make a positive contribution to the development of my students' capabilities. . . . The teaching profession would give me the opportunity to contribute to the prevention of some of society's problems and to the cure of some social problems presently existing.

### Participation in Organizations

Do the extent of the American teacher's educational background and the aspirations characterizing his motivation reveal themselves in his participation in community and civic organizations? The Research Division of the National Education Association, after studying participation by classroom teachers in 1971, reported:

. . . a decrease in teacher participation in organizations since the beginning of the 1960s and especially since 1966. As in 1966, the only two types of organizations in which a majority of teachers hold membership are a church or similar religious group and the Parent-Teacher Association; but percentages of teachers who are members of such organizations have decreased during the last five years, in the former case from 86 to 78 percent and in the latter from 78 to 66 percent. Membership in political parties has decreased throughout the decade to a very considerable extent, dropping from 31 to 22 percent between 1961 and 1966 and then again to 13 percent in 1971. Fraternal organizations also show a large decrease, from 33 to 19 percent in teacher membership during the first half of the decade and a smaller decrease to 15 percent in the ensuing five years. Small decreases have occurred in the percentage of teachers who are members of youth-serving groups and women's groups and in the percentage of men who are members of men's service clubs.[10]

Did you expect something more of the American teacher? What changes do you think there have been since this 1971 study? (See Table 3-1.)

### Political Views

The same NEA status study reports:

. . . in political philosophy, teachers incline to the conservative side but most are middle-of-the-road. Those who classify their political philosophy as either tend to be conservative or tend to be liberal comprise 7 teachers in 10, but those who say they either are conservative or tend to be outnumber those who are or tend to be liberals by 6 to 4. The proportion that label themselves conservative without qualification, 1 in 6,

---

[10] NEA, Research Division, *Status of the American Public-School Teacher, 1970–71*, Research Report 1972-R3 (Washington, D.C.: The Association, 1972), pp. 82, 84.

**TABLE 3-1   Teacher Membership in Organizations**

| | Total | | | Sex | | | | | |
| --- | --- | --- | --- | --- | --- | --- | --- | --- | --- |
| | | | | Men | | | Women | | |
| | 1961 | 1966 | 1971 | 1961 | 1966 | 1971 | 1961 | 1966 | 1971 |
| Church, synagogue, or other religious group | 87.2 | 85.5 | 78.3 | 83.9 | 80.0 | 73.8 | 88.7 | 88.0 | 80.7 |
| Youth-serving group | 21.2 | 19.7 | 15.9 | 30.7 | 23.7 | 19.8 | 16.9 | 17.8 | 13.8 |
| Women's business, professional, civic-social group | 21.7 | 22.1 | 18.9 | ... | 2.5 | 1.9 | 31.6 | 31.0 | 27.8 |
| Men's service club | 6.2 | 5.2 | 5.1 | 19.6 | 15.9 | 14.8 | ... | 0.4 | ... |
| Fraternal or auxiliary group | 32.6 | 19.3 | 15.0 | 40.3 | 24.0 | 22.6 | 29.0 | 17.2 | 11.0 |
| Civil liberties group | ... | 5.5 | 4.4 | ... | 6.2 | 4.0 | ... | 5.1 | 4.7 |
| Veterans group | ... | 4.5 | 4.5 | ... | 11.2 | 11.6 | ... | 1.5 | 0.8 |
| Political party organization | 30.8 | 22.0 | 12.6 | 35.7 | 31.0 | 13.1 | 28.5 | 17.9 | 12.3 |
| Parent-teacher association | ... | 78.4 | 66.3 | ... | 70.0 | 55.5 | ... | 82.2 | 72.0 |
| Hobby club | ... | 17.5 | 16.2 | ... | 16.8 | 17.5 | ... | 17.8 | 15.5 |
| Number reporting | 1,881 | 2,344 | 1,533 | 590 | 730 | 526 | 1,291 | 1,614 | 1,007 |

| | Age | | | | | | | |
| --- | --- | --- | --- | --- | --- | --- | --- | --- |
| | Less than 30 | | 30-39 | | 40-49 | | 50 or more | |
| | 1966 | 1971 | 1966 | 1971 | 1966 | 1971 | 1966 | 1971 |
| Church, synagogue, or other religious group | 82.6 | 74.0 | 85.9 | 74.8 | 86.8 | 83.7 | 88.9 | 85.3 |
| Youth-serving group | 15.2 | 10.5 | 25.4 | 21.2 | 27.3 | 24.1 | 15.7 | 12.7 |
| Women's business, professional, civic-social group | 14.6 | 10.5 | 17.4 | 15.4 | 30.3 | 24.1 | 30.2 | 31.3 |
| Men's service club | 5.1 | 3.4 | 8.4 | 7.0 | 6.2 | 7.0 | 2.4 | 4.7 |
| Fraternal or auxiliary group | 13.2 | 9.6 | 21.6 | 15.1 | 21.3 | 18.9 | 24.5 | 20.9 |
| Civil liberties group | 4.0 | 2.3 | 8.8 | 7.2 | 7.9 | 5.9 | 2.7 | 3.2 |
| Veterans group | 0.8 | 1.2 | 7.3 | 3.2 | 10.9 | 10.4 | 3.0 | 6.8 |
| Political party organization | 23.6 | 12.3 | 26.5 | 11.9 | 22.1 | 11.9 | 16.0 | 14.2 |
| Parent-teacher association | 74.5 | 58.9 | 81.3 | 67.8 | 81.9 | 75.6 | 79.3 | 70.2 |
| Hobby club | 18.2 | 16.7 | 18.5 | 17.4 | 19.1 | 15.9 | 15.3 | 14.5 |
| Number reporting | 781 | 562 | 524 | 345 | 403 | 270 | 593 | 339 |

NEA, Research Division, *Status of the American Public-School Teacher, 1970–71*, Research Report 1972-R3 (Washington, D.C.: The Association, 1972), p. 83.

exceeds the 1 in 8 who are unqualified liberals, while those who tend to be conservative, 44 percent, far exceed the 28 percent who tend to be liberal. In party affiliation, however, a greater percentage classify themselves as Democrats, 43 percent, than as Republicans, 34 percent, but more than 1 teacher in 5 reports that he is not affiliated with any party.

Men and women, and elementary and secondary teachers, show generally similar distribution in regard to both political philosophy and political affiliation. Analysis of responses by age also shows that a majority of teachers in all age groups are on the conservative side of the political spectrum, while Democrats exceed Republicans in every age group except the oldest. However, as would be expected, older teachers are more likely to be conservative than younger teachers; 7 teachers in 10 among those age 50 or older either are or tend to be conservative, compared with about 6 in 10 in each of the two middle age groups, and only slightly more than one-half the youngest teachers. Young teachers, on the other hand, are less likely than older teachers to be Republicans and more likely not to be affiliated with any political party. More than one-third of all teachers under age 30 report that they are not affiliated with any party—about twice as great a proportion as can be found in any of the older age groups.[11]

### Experience

In 1971 the average teacher had taught for eleven years. *She* had been teaching twelve years; *he* had been teaching ten years.[12] Once again the facts for elementary and secondary teachers paralleled the sex differences; the average elementary school teacher had been teaching twelve years and the average secondary school teacher ten years.

### Mobility

Usually, every year about one out of twelve teachers leaves the teaching profession. As the NEA Research Division points out in a 1972 report, "Earlier studies in this series have used an estimate that the number of positions vacated by teachers who leave the profession each year equals about 8 percent of the total number of teachers."[13] Most who leave teaching resign from their posts; a large minority are separated for other reasons, including retirement, death, dismissal, and promotion to non-teaching jobs. Small systems have greater teacher holding power.

Meanwhile, approximately 1 in every 33 teachers returns to teaching annually (3 percent to secondary schools and 3.2 percent to elementary schools), often because their children are grown, other jobs have been disappointing, or a second income in the family appears tempting. The difference between about 8 percent leaving and about 3 percent returning results in a 5 percent gap. These teaching posts are filled by beginning teachers.[14] In addition, beginning teachers are employed to fill new posts created by population expansion and the increased holding power of the high schools.

The majority of male teachers perceive themselves as willing to move out of the state to a better paying job, but not the majority of female teachers. More than 57 percent of the men teachers queried gave a migratory-minded "yes" to the question, "Would you move to a school system in another state that is comparable to the one in which you are

[11] *Ibid.,* pp. 87–88.
[12] *Ibid.,* p. 15.
[13] NEA, Research Division, *Teacher Supply and Demand in Public Schools, 1972,* Research Report 1972-R8 (Washington, D.C.: The Association, 1972), p. 25.
[14] *Ibid.,* p. 31.

presently teaching if the superintendent of the school system offered you a sufficient salary increase and moving costs?" But 79.4 percent of women teachers answered "no" to the same question.[15] In general, the male teacher appears to be more mobile and the female teacher more bound to home and community ties.

Teachers are more likely to have moved within the same state than across state lines. Almost twice as many report that they have taught in another system in the same state (39 percent) as report that they have taught in other states (20 percent). Seven percent of all teachers have taught both in another state and in another system in the same state where they are now teaching.[16]

So teaching no longer means committing yourself to stay forever in your home community or region or even your state. Today's teacher is much more footloose than his predecessor.

## IS THERE A NEW TEACHER IN THE SEVENTIES?

One of the significant conditions of modern life is change—radical change affecting all aspects of life. In the forefront of today's change are many college students and recent graduates.

To predict the outcome of a period of change is extremely difficult, though it is possible to examine the prevalent experiences, values, attitudes, ideas, and actions and thus get some indication of likely outcomes. Yet in so doing there is some danger of developing a new stereotype, one which depicts the college student as an extremist. Let us eliminate this danger of substituting one stereotype for another by recognizing that no single description can encompass all college students or all new teachers. It is clear that present college students and new teachers represent a wide spectrum of types. However, this does not negate the presence of certain strong formative influences which may make *some* new teachers very different from their predecessors. The possibility of a generation gap among teachers is real.

Many new teachers will represent, in varying degrees, the results of a triple revolution—social, political, and educational—which is making itself felt in our society. So far visible effects include increased pressure on schools to change, the development of those schools often called "free" or "alternative" schools, and conflicts in schools between teacher factions and between teachers and administrators.

### The Social Revolution

Many young people have been evolving a new life-style. They have made radical changes in such things as dress, language, music, sexual mores,

[15] "Teacher Opinion Poll," *NEA Journal* (April 1968), p. 60.
[16] NEA, Research Division, *Status of the American Public-School Teacher, 1970–71,* Research Report 1972-R3 (Washington, D.C.: The Association, 1972), p. 18.

Some people question whether new white teachers can contribute to the education of American Indian children.

ceremonies, and values. The problem of whether a school can control the length of its students' hair has been a major controversy in some schools, and has in many cases been brought to court. Schools have also been having trouble with dress codes. Some lower court decisions have supported student choices of hair style and clothing; others have opposed.

The use of drugs by students has become a national dilemma. Student newspapers, both underground and above, have challenged existing standards of obscenity and definitions of free speech. Increasingly, the traditional purposes of education have been challenged as irrelevant to contemporary human needs.

In colleges, many of these changes have been accepted, in varying degrees, by some students as appropriate—even necessary—behavior. The conflict may not remain a simple conflict of the school with its students, because some young teachers will bring with them their own experience with various forms of dissent. The act of graduation or achievement of certification will not bring about a rejection of a style of life which has been chosen as appropriate. There will be young teachers in the schools of the seventies who will find it increasingly difficult or distasteful to make compromises that the schools will seem to demand. Certain of these conflicts are already apparent, as in standards of dress and hair length for teachers. A considerable number of schools, sometimes reluctantly, are learning to live with young, bearded, long-haired or Afro-styled teachers who wear dashikis, or no tie, or jeans as teacher apparel. Rock and soul music are heard in some classrooms. Some teachers have been in trouble with their administrators because they have not objected to taboo words in their students' writing, and have even used such words themselves in their own writing.

### The Political Revolution

Through the sixties and early seventies some young people were increasingly involved in a wide variety of political activity. Many students have been involved with liberal reformist activity—for example, the campaign for Eugene McCarthy in the 1968 primary, the support of peace candidates in the congressional elections of 1970, and the presidential campaign of George McGovern in 1972. Fewer were involved in radical politics, including membership in such organizations as SDS (Students for a Democratic Society) or other new-left groups. Some were engaged in conservative political action through such organizations as YAF (Young Americans for Freedom). A substantial number campaigned for the re-election of President Richard M. Nixon in 1972. Other specific movements now attracting student interest and support are women's liberation, anti-poverty programs, environmental reform, and the various ethnic power groups—blacks, Chicanos, and Indians, for example.

When these students become teachers, many will continue to involve themselves in the political activity of the community and nation. It is also likely that they will approve of and participate in political activities as part of their relationship to the schools. Political activity by teachers' groups, affiliates of both the National Education Association and the American Federation of Teachers, has been accelerating. Teachers' strikes and other vigorous organizational responses to the actions of school boards and administrations have been increasing in recent years. Many young teachers will add to the militancy of such groups and will consider political activism by teachers as appropriate and necessary.

### The Educational Revolution

Many young teachers believe that today's schools are not very good places for the young. Schools in the ghettos and other poverty areas are seen as failures in their mission of providing basic skills and information to those who need such basics in order to find a place in a technical society, and the schools in the suburbs are seen as failures in their role of providing meaning and understanding in the lives of children of an affluent society. New teachers often find the schools failing to deal with problems of institutional racism, pollution and destruction of environmental resources, war and international tensions, and poverty in the midst of affluence.

Students in colleges often express dissatisfaction with their own schooling. Some have had no teacher whom they remember with appreciation and commendation. Some believe that schools are going to have to change radically. One of their major objections concerns the bureaucratic nature of school systems. They see the schools as one of the worst examples of depersonalization in modern society. They feel that students and teachers are treated as objects and recognized as numbers rather than as persons. They believe that school administrators are concerned with budgets, buses, and buildings rather than with students and learning.

Such students wish to bring to the schools and to their pupils more direct personal relationships, more trust, more intimacy, and more love. They have been influenced in their feelings by such activities as T-groups and encounter sessions. They are often advocates of affective education, which emphasizes emotions and feelings. They have been impressed by views of education such as *Education and Ecstasy* by George B. Leonard,[17] *The Lives of Children* by George Dennison,[18] and *How Children Fail* by John Holt.[19]

Many young teachers question the purposes which our schools seem to serve. While recognizing the need for developing basic skills, they challenge the curriculum which seems to be more concerned with preparing students to fit into a society which to them is rapidly becoming obsolete, than with the development of individual self-realization and social improvement. They find confirmation for their misgivings in such books as *Summerhill* by A. S. Neill,[20] and *Compulsory Mis-education* by Paul Goodman.[21] They often read and admire the books of contemporary compassionate critics such as *Death at an Early Age* by Jonathan Kozol,[22] *36 Children* by Herbert Kohl,[23] and *The Naked Children* by Daniel Fader.[24] They find help in books which suggest methods and approaches for becoming a compassionate teacher, such as *What Do I Do Monday?* by John Holt,[25] *How to Survive in Your Native Land* by James Herndon,[26] *The Open Classroom* by Herbert Kohl.[27]

Some of these young educators believe that the only possible approach to take toward the contemporary school system is to abolish it. Their beliefs are supported by such books as *Deschooling Society*[28] by

[17] George B. Leonard, *Education and Ecstasy* (New York: Dell, 1968).
[18] George Dennison, *The Lives of Children: The Story of the First Street School* (New York: Random House, 1969).
[19] John Holt, *How Children Fail* (New York: Pitman, 1964).
[20] A. S. Neill, *Summerhill: A Radical Approach to Child Rearing* (New York: Hart, 1960).
[21] Paul Goodman, *Compulsory Mis-education* (New York: Horizon Press, 1964).
[22] Jonathan Kozol, *Death at an Early Age* (Boston: Houghton Mifflin, 1967).
[23] Herbert Kohl, *36 Children* (New York: New American Library, 1967).
[24] Daniel Fader, *The Naked Children* (New York: Macmillan, 1971).
[25] John Holt, *What Do I Do Monday?* (New York: E. P. Dutton, 1970).
[26] James Herndon, *How to Survive in Your Native Land* (New York: Simon and Schuster, 1971).
[27] Herbert Kohl, *The Open Classroom* (New York: Random House, 1970).
[28] Ivan Illich, *Deschooling Society* (New York: Harper and Row, 1971).

Education in the middle of a city—students on a field trip to the museum.

Ivan Illich and *School is Dead: Alternatives in Education*[29] by Everett Reimer. They find that two of the compassionate critics have now transformed their pleas of the sixties for change "from within" to advocacy in the seventies of establishing alternative forms of education: *Freedom and Beyond*[30] by John Holt, and *Free Schools*[31] by Jonathan Kozol.

Some questioning young teachers enthusiastically accept the challenge of teaching the children of the poor in public schools in disadvantaged areas. They see an opportunity to make changes in the education of children and youth who have been neglected by society. But still others despair of the potential of public schools and turn elsewhere. Philip Rothman of Antioch College, for instance, reports as follows:

Despite working in innovative programs such as the Philadelphia Schools Parkway Project, and despite a usually comfortable and successful student teaching placement in Yellow Springs' mildly experimental public schools, the students are left

[29] Everett Reimer, *School Is Dead: Alternatives in Education* (New York: Doubleday, 1971).
[30] John Holt, *Freedom and Beyond* (New York: E. P. Dutton, 1972).
[31] Jonathan Kozol, *Free Schools* (Boston: Houghton Mifflin, 1972).

with a feeling of frustration when faced with teaching in the public schools. By contrast, while not always in complete agreement with what goes on, the students feel a lot more comfortable with their experiences in the Antioch School, the Pinel School, and other small, private, experimental or "free" schools. Many seniors speak of next year by saying, "*IF* I teach next year . . ." and, "I would like to find a small, private school . . ." It is true that this is not completely new, but the trend seems to have grown. The anti-institutional utopian bias seems to be challenging the public service ethos which had been predominant in the past.

. . . In recent years with the emergence of black identity as a major educational factor and with a growing emphasis on black control and leadership of black affairs,

*Bruce Davidson, Magnum Photos, Inc.*

Some students learn electronics in a special workshop.

few white Antiochians continue to feel that they can serve useful purposes in predominantly inner-city black schools.[32]

A significant difference between new teachers and previous generations is their relationship to technology. Television has been an indigenous part of the new teachers' culture since infancy, computers have increasingly been available for serving their needs, transportation and communication have provided direct access to ideas and places on a global basis, and they have accepted man's steps on the moon as a natural, if difficult, achievement. The writings of Marshall McLuhan on the uses of media have influenced their thinking. Consequently, they look to technology as a normal part of the school environment. They hope that computer-assisted instruction, film-making, video taping and playback, rapid duplication facilities, and inexpensive paperbacks will be at hand so that they can individualize instruction, serve the interests of the students, meet different levels of ability and background, and provide students with a richness and diversity of materials and sources of information.

### A Transitional Period

The above description is not meant to be a portrayal of *all* young teachers as they are today or will be in the near future. A generalization does not describe a population, even if it is an up-to-date generalization. However, these characteristics do represent clear and strong trends which are shaping some young people who will be the new teachers of the seventies. Will the schools be able to accept these teachers, to accommodate their demands, and to help them use their abilities and energies? The most honest answer is that the evidence is mixed and conflicting. Schools are changing, but in many ways the change is reluctant and slow. Many school board members, school administrators, experienced teachers, taxpayers, and parents recognize the changing characteristics of our times and, to different degrees, are in agreement with the younger teachers; others are strongly resistant. Their resistance may be strengthened by the shift in teacher supply and demand. To put it bluntly, those resistant to these changes may be able to screen out some of the new teachers most inclined to dissidence. And, some rebels, eager for jobs, may reluctantly decide to conform.

So the middle seventies are likely to be a period of transition—a time of significant and sometimes disrupting change. The challenge to young teachers who recognize themselves in the description of the past few pages is to face the turmoil, tension, and trials of such a challenge with high competence.

---

[32] Philip Rothman, "Education Majors Found Turned Off By Public School Teaching Prospects," *Antiochian* (July 1970), p. 5.

## THE TEACHER IS AN INDIVIDUAL

Perhaps the most honest answer to our question, "Who Teaches in American Schools?" is simply that many more than two million individuals teach in American elementary and secondary schools. They defy stereotyping. They are as varied as the American people.

What you perceive as you view teachers, whether experienced or new, depends largely upon your own background and perception. There is a story that Carl Sandburg once told of the two visitors about to move to a town. Each called upon an old resident and asked the same question, "What kind of people live in this town?" The old resident responded to the first visitor, "And what kind of people are there in the town you came from?" The visitor said, "Mean people and rude people." The old resident commented, "I guess that's the way you'll find people in this town too." To the second inquirer he also responded, "And what kind of people were there in the town you came from?" The second visitor said, "Fine people, honest and likable." The old resident said, "I guess that's the way you'll find people in this town too."

Teachers have in common that, for multiple reasons, they have chosen to work with learners, whose lives they can influence. They have in common the possibility of making a difference through being teachers.

When you join American teachers in their work, you make an important choice. When you join them, you open up the potential of your own self-realization and of human betterment for others.

## DISCUSSION

1. What has been your stereotype of a school teacher? Why?
2. Is there any validity in the common stereotype of the teacher?
3. What is the current situation as to men teachers in the early school years? How do you think more men can be attracted to the field? Should they be?
4. Are women discriminated against in higher education teaching opportunities? To what extent has the women's liberation movement opened up further opportunities for women in higher education?
5. Why are increasing numbers of men entering teaching?
6. Teachers now customarily teach after receiving a bachelor's degree. Is this sufficient? Should a five-year higher education period of preparation be required?
7. What are the characteristic motivations of teachers, young and old? Which of the motivations described in this chapter seem to you most admirable?
8. Does the information reported on teacher participation and political views agree with your own observations of teachers? In what ways do the teachers you know best differ from the reported generalizations?
9. What advantages and disadvantages do you see of teaching in one's home town? Home region?
10. Is mobility among teachers likely to grow? What factors might influence mobility in a particular direction?

11. What changes in your peers do you see that would support the statement, "The new young public school teacher will be a 'new breed of cat'?" What do you see to disprove such a statement? What forces might bring about a "new" teacher for the 1970s and help create a generation gap among teachers?

12. Essentially what do you find your friends and fellow students saying about education in general? Their own education? Administrators? Purposes of schools?

13. If your friends and fellow students in education had their way, in what types of schools would they teach? Public? Private? "Free"? Parochial?

14. What do you think of the likelihood of the dissenting new teacher finding a teaching post? If you think it would be difficult, do you think it should be?

15. Can you generalize on the American teacher in an intellectually reputable way?

## INVOLVEMENT

1. Test the persistence of the traditional stereotype of the school teacher by asking a variety of people what they envision when you say "school teacher."

2. Develop a letter of support or criticism to a producer of a TV or radio program in connection with some portrayal of American teachers and share the response you receive with others.

3. Develop a simple questionnaire concerning motivations and try it out with a class of teacher education students and a class not planning to enter the field of teaching.

4. Develop a questionnaire parallel to the study cited of the participation and political views of classroom teachers and administer it to your class. Compare the results with the NEA results.

5. Develop a series of character sketches of new teachers. Invite an administrator to class and ask him to react to the employment prospects of these new teachers sketched by you and other class members. When there is disagreement as to employability, explore the reasons for different perceptions.

6. Attempt to reach a consensus among class members as to the characteristics of the school in which they would like to teach. If consensus is not forthcoming, at least clarify different ways of looking at the ideal school.

## FURTHER READING

Ashton-Warner, Sylvia. *Teacher*. New York: Simon and Schuster, 1963.   An unorthodox, readable account of a talented teacher's way of working with children of a culture foreign to her.

Benjamin, Harold R. W. *The Sage of Petaluma*. New York: McGraw-Hill, 1965.   A purported biography of teacher J. Abner Peddiwell which allows author Benjamin to be partially autobiographical yet also, as he himself said, "to lie a little."

Brenton, Myron. *What's Happened to Teacher?* New York: Coward-McCann, 1970.   An examination of why teachers have changed, why they teach, why they strike, what they fear, and how they really view children.

Daniels, Steven. *How 2 Gerbils 20 Goldfish 200 Games 2,000 Books and I Taught Them How To Read*. Philadelphia: The Westminster Press, 1971.   A delightful book by a young teacher who taught children to read through unorthodox, yet effective, techniques.

Frazier, Nancy, and Myra Sadker. *Sexism in School and Society*. New York: Harper & Row, 1973.   The extent of sex bias and discrimination in professional academic life as well as in the educational system from kindergarten through graduate school.

Goodlad, John I., M. Frances Klein and associates. *Behind the Classroom Door*. Worthington, Ohio: Charles A. Jones, 1970. An account of visits to public school classrooms by the staff of a laboratory school. Reports essentially the continuance of ordinary conventional teaching at a mediocre level.

Gross, Ronald and Beatrice Gross, eds. *Radical School Reform*. New York: Simon and Schuster, 1969. Selected readings reflecting the range of radical thought and practice in public education, emphasizing significantly different schools.

Postman, Neil, and Charles Weingartner. *Teaching as a Subversive Activity*. New York: Delacorte, 1969. A lively, refreshing book which calls for teaching to challenge and to generate excitement.

Rousculp, Charles G. *Chalk Dust on My Shoulder*. Columbus, Ohio: Charles E. Merrill, 1969. Presenting by essay and anecdote in a plain-spoken document, the ordeals, the errors, and the triumphs that make a teacher's day and the contribution teachers make to American society.

Stinnett, T. M., ed. *The Teacher Dropout*. Itasca, Ill.: F. E. Peacock, 1970. A symposium report by the Commission on Strengthening the Teaching Profession of Phi Delta Kappa. An exploration of the teacher dropout problem. Insight into possibilities of strengthening the teaching profession.

Van Til, William. *The Making of a Modern Educator*. Indianapolis: Bobbs-Merrill, 1961. A collection of essays and short writings which describe the author's experiences as a teacher in situations ranging from a reform school to a university.

Yamamoto, Kaoru, ed. *Teaching: Essays and Readings*. Boston: Houghton Mifflin, 1969. Varied views on teachers and teaching from a wide range of sources.

## SELECTED AUDIO-VISUAL MATERIALS

*For All My Students* (16 mm film, 36 min., b. & w., University of California, Berkeley, 1967). Presents problems and rewards of teaching high school students effectively. Demonstrates both poor and effective teaching in classroom situations. Suggests ways of providing special help for disadvantaged students. Emphasizes education for blacks.

*Teach Me* (16 mm film, 20 min., color, Teaching Film Custodians, 1968). A beginning teacher in a large inner city high school discovers that the rewards of motivating disadvantaged students outweigh environmental handicaps.

*The Teacher and Technology* (16 mm film, 49 min., color, Ohio State University, 1967). Illustrates the role of the educational media specialist in applying technology to the problems of teaching large numbers of students, and for individual instruction.

*The Teacher Is Between* (16 mm film, 15 min., b. & w., National Education Association, 1970). Discusses the emerging role of the teacher as a mediator of learning experiences and the relationship of teachers to students, parents, the school, and society.

*What Is a Teacher?* (16 mm film, 59 min., b. & w., University of Texas, 1965). Twelve student teachers working with elementary school children in math, social studies, art, and science. Indicates the role of the teacher in helping children to acquire knowledge and self-confidence.

*Who Teaches Them?* (16 mm film, 30 min., b. & w., NET: Indiana University). Com-

pares schools with various orientations and reveals some things about their techniques.

*Youth — The Search for Identity* (35 mm filmstrip, 46 frs/captions, b. & w., Current Affairs, 1968).   The motivations of young people in their search for identity. Points
out that the majority of young people are concerned with today's challenges.

*Youth Forum* (audio tape, 30 min., National Center for Audio Tape, 1968).   Selected
Titles: Changing Values; Is There a Sexual Revolution?; Tensions in Teenagers;
What Is a Relevant Education for Today?

# FOUR

## What are teachers paid?

How important is the teacher's pay in your tentative decision to become a teacher? At one extreme are those new teachers who can honestly say that they are not concerned about salaries. They see their major goal as service to others. As dedicated agents of change, they are not especially interested in present or prospective financial compensation. At the other extreme are those who say, with equal honesty yet with a different social orientation, that the salary must be pretty good or they can be counted out. They are apt to point out that teachers and their families cannot live on dedication. Between these two groups are prospective teachers who realize that the financial compensation of educators is moderate and that one usually does not teach for the money in it; they know that the rewards are primarily in the teacher's recognition that he has made a difference in the lives of others.

Most people want to be well informed as to the economic probabilities of their work. They recognize that they must take financial factors into account as they attempt to determine and establish their life-styles. This chapter is intended for everyone who is at all concerned about financial compensation. It is intended neither to recruit you into nor to repel you from teaching; it is an objective account of some of the material aspects of teaching.

### THE SALARY OF THE AMERICAN TEACHER

The average 1971–72 salary of classroom teachers in public schools was $9,705. Most secondary school teachers were paid more than elementary school teachers by about $600 a year, largely because their average length of preparation was greater than that of elementary teachers. The average salary of secondary school teachers in public schools in 1971–72 was $10,031. The average salary of elementary school teachers in public schools was $9,424.[1]

These averages do not reveal the differences between the beginner's salary and that of the experienced teacher who often holds graduate degrees. The average salary for the beginner holding a bachelor's degree in 1971–72 was $7,061; the classroom teacher holding a doctor's degree and having sufficient years of experience to reach the maximum level in a school system was paid an average salary of $13,805—almost twice as much. But these were also averages for the nation as a whole. The actual range in beginning salaries with the bachelor's degree was from a little less than $5,500 in some school systems to about $9,000 in others; maximum salaries with the doctor's degree ranged from about $9,000 in less wealthy areas to more than $20,000 in a few very wealthy districts (1.3 percent of systems).

Between the extremes there are stages in compensation that depend upon both educational degrees and experience. In 1971–72, the average beginner holding a bachelor's degree was paid $7,061; the maximum for the average experienced teacher with a bachelor's degree was $10,299.

[1] NEA, Research Division, *Estimates of School Statistics, 1972–73,* Research Report 1972-R12 (Washington, D.C.: The Association, 1973), p. 14.

TABLE 4-1 **Mean Scheduled Salaries of Teachers by Preparation Level, 1962–1963 to 1971–1972[1]**

| Preparation level | 1962–1963 | 1965–1966 | 1968–1969 | 1971–1972 |
|---|---|---|---|---|
| Number of reporting systems[2] | 557 | 1,071 | 1,199 | 1,179 |
| Mean scheduled salary for: | | | | |
| Minimum | | | | |
| Bachelor's degree | $4,331 | $4,925 | $ 5,941 | $ 7,061 |
| Master's degree | 4,880 | 5,350 | 6,546 | 7,837 |
| Six years (M.A. +30) | 5,310 | 5,900 | 7,154 | 8,501 |
| Doctor's degree | 5,417 | 6,057 | 7,471 | 8,943 |
| Maximum | | | | |
| Bachelor's degree | 6,428 | 7,262 | 8,690 | 10,299 |
| Master's degree | 7,054 | 8,167 | 9,981 | 11,973 |
| Six years (M.A. +30) | 8,236 | 9,385 | 11,273 | 13,308 |
| Doctor's degree | 8,199 | 9,452 | 11,602 | 13,805 |

[1] Reporting school systems with enrollments of 6,000 or more.
[2] Not all systems report all preparation salary classes.
NEA, Research Division, *Economic Status of the Teaching Profession, 1971–72,* Research Report 1972-R2 (Washington, D.C.: The Association, 1972), p. 41.

The average beginner with a master's degree started at $7,837; the maximum for the average experienced teacher with a master's degree was $11,973. The beginner with a sixth year degree, or the master's plus 30 hours of graduate work, started at $8,501; the maximum for an average experienced teacher with that degree was $13,308. The rare beginner who first taught after receiving a doctor's degree averaged $8,943; the maximum average for the experienced teacher with a doctor's degree was $13,805. (See Table 4-1 for "mean scheduled salaries.")

In the U.S. public education system there are significant geographical differences in compensation. Take, for instance, regional differences in average annual salaries of the total instructional staff in public schools in 1971–72. If a beginning teacher made his decision of where to teach on the basis of salary alone (which doesn't happen to be the case), he would surely follow Horace Greeley's historic advice to his generation, "Go West, young man, go West!" In the Far West the estimated average annual salary paid members of the total instructional staff was $11,653. The next most attractive regions with respect to salaries were the Mideast states, where the average was $11,393; the Great Lakes states, where the average was $10,747; and the New England states, where the average was $10,306. Less attractive economically was the rest of the nation, with an average annual salary in the Plains states of $9,468, in the Rocky Mountain states of $9,122, in the Southwest of $8,657, and in the Southeast of $8,424.[2] Though contiguous, the states in the Far West paid instructional staff an average of three thousand dollars more than states in the Southwest. So, if salary were the sole consideration, many teachers might join a late twentieth century Gold Rush to California, or trek north to Alaska.

How do today's salaries compare with salaries of teachers during the past years? The general answer, of course, is that they have gone up, as have salaries in other fields of work. (See Table 4-2.) Should we regard this increase "optimistically" or "pessimistically"? It depends. Consider, for instance, a partially consumed glass of your favorite beverage resting beside you on a table. If you are an optimist, you may pronounce the glass half full; if you are a pessimist, you may pronounce the glass half empty. Yet it is the same glass with the same amount of liquid in it—it all depends on your own perspective. So it is with respect to the significance of the rise in teachers' salaries and comparisons that might be made with other occupations.

If you look at the world through rose colored glasses, you can truthfully point out that during the period 1960–61 to 1971–72 the salary of the typical instructional staff member of the public schools increased by about seven-eighths (86.2 percent). But if you look at the world through dark glasses, you can equally point out that because of the inflation that

**TABLE 4-2** **Percent Distribution of Estimated Annual Salaries Paid Teachers, 1960–1961 Through 1971–1972.**

| School year | Below $3,500 | $3,500–4,499 | $4,500–5,499 | $5,500–6,499 | $6,500–7,499 | $7,500–8,499 | $8,500–9,499 | $9,500–10,499 | $10,500–11,499 | $11,500 or more |
|---|---|---|---|---|---|---|---|---|---|---|
| 1960–1961 | 9.2 | 26.0 | 27.2 | 19.3 | 10.9 | 7.4%[1] | ... | ... | ... | ... |
| 1961–1962 | 5.7 | 20.9 | 28.9 | 22.6 | 12.9 | 9.0[1] | ... | ... | ... | ... |
| 1962–1963 | 4.3 | 17.7 | 28.0 | 23.4 | 14.5 | 8.1 | 4.0%[2] | ... | ... | ... |
| 1963–1964 | 2.7 | 14.2 | 28.6 | 24.2 | 15.1 | 9.0 | 6.3[2] | ... | ... | ... |
| 1964–1965 | 1.6 | 11.9 | 27.0 | 24.7 | 16.6 | 10.1 | 5.5 | 2.6%[4] | ... | ... |
| 1965–1966 | 0.8 | 8.0 | 22.7 | 26.8 | 19.1 | 11.5 | 6.6 | 4.5[4] | ... | ... |
| 1966–1967 | 0.3 | 4.1 | 19.7 | 26.7 | 19.8 | 13.2 | 8.6 | 4.5 | 3.1%[4] | ... |
| 1967–1968 | (——2.1[3]——) | | 11.5 | 25.5 | 22.0 | 15.3 | 10.5 | 6.6 | 6.5[4] | ... |
| 1968–1969 | (———— 6.9[5] ————) | | | 18.1 | 24.5 | 18.1 | 13.4 | 8.6 | 6.0 | 4.3% |
| 1969–1970 | (———— 2.9[5] ————) | | | 13.2 | 20.5 | 19.7 | 14.4 | 11.4 | 7.7 | 10.3 |
| 1970–1971 | (———— 1.5[5] ————) | | | 7.2 | 15.6 | 18.4 | 16.7 | 14.9 | 11.3 | 14.5 |
| 1971–1972 | (———————— 19.9[6] ————————) | | | | | 17.7 | 15.9 | 13.4 | 10.4 | 22.7 |

[1] $7,500 or more; detailed breakdown not available.
[2] $8,500 or more; detailed breakdown not available.
[3] Breakdown below $4,500 not computed.
[4] Detailed breakdown not available beyond this salary range.
[5] Breakdown below $5,500 not computed.
[6] Breakdown below $7,500 not computed.
NEA, Research Division, *Economic Status of the Teaching Profession, 1971–72*, Research Report 1972-R2 (Washington, D.C.: The Association, 1972), p. 34.

changed the purchasing power of the dollar, the increase was less than it appears. To which the optimist might retort that a near doubling of salary in a twelve-year period is nothing to view darkly.

If you view the world through rose tinted glasses, you might accurately point out that at the beginning of the period, 62.4 percent of the teachers were below $5,500 in salary annually. You can apparently clinch your case by pointing out that almost no teachers received a salary of less than $5,500 in public schools in 1971–72. Further, as one impressed by progress, you can correctly point out that, at the close of the period, about four-fifths (80.1 percent) of teachers had salaries ranging from $7,500 to $11,500 or more, whereas, you might conclude, only 7.4 percent of teachers at the beginning of the period had a salary of over $7,499.

But while you are polishing those rose colored glasses, your colleague who sees the world pessimistically can justifiably remind you that the average salary of the beginning teacher with a bachelor's degree in 1971–72 was $7,061 (for approximately 9 months of service) and he will ask you to set this beside the beginning annual (full year) salaries of male college graduates with a bachelor's degree in engineering, $10,500, or women college graduates in mathematics and statistics earning $9,312. To clinch his point of the comparatively low income of beginners in teaching as contrasted with beginners in other fields of work, he might point out that college graduates in a variety of fields are paid more than teachers. He, too, has statistics to which he can refer you. (See Table 4-3.)

Both the optimist and the pessimist can then turn to the NEA *estimated* average salary figures for classroom teachers in the public schools for 1972–73. (These 1972–73 *estimates,* which are less firm than the 1971–72 figures cited throughout this chapter, became available to the author while *Education: A Beginning* was in press.) The optimist can point out triumphantly that the estimated average salary for teachers passed the $10,000 mark for the first time in the history of American education in 1972–73. The NEA 1972–73 estimates are $10,114 for the average teacher; $10,460 for the average secondary school teacher; $9,823 for the average elementary school teacher. To which the pessimist can retort coolly, "and what about the 1972–73 inflation which gobbled up this

**TABLE 4-3  Average Starting Salaries of Classroom Teachers Compared with those in Private Industry, 1964–1965 to 1971–1972**

| Position or subject field | Average starting salaries | |
|---|---|---|
| | 1964–1965 | 1971–1972 |
| Beginning teachers with bachelor's degree[1] | $4,707 | $ 7,061 |
| Male college graduates with bachelor's degree | | |
|   Engineering | 7,356 | 10,500 |
|   Accounting | 6,444 | 10,260 |
|   Sales-Marketing | 6,072 | 8,736 |
|   Business Administration | 5,880 | 8,424 |
|   Liberal Arts | 5,712 | 8,292 |
|   Production Management | 6,564 | 9,792 |
|   Chemistry | 6,972 | 9,720 |
|   Physics | 7,200 | 9,636 |
|   Mathematics-Statistics | 6,636 | 9,192 |
|   Economics-Finance | 6,276 | 9,216 |
|   Other Fields | 6,360 | 8,580 |
|     Total — all fields (weighted average) | 6,535 | 9,534 |
| Women college graduates with bachelor's degree | | |
|   Mathematics-Statistics | 6,108 | 9,312 |
|   General Business | 4,848 | 8,076 |
|   Chemistry | 6,468 | 9,744 |
|   Accounting | 5,664 | 9,516 |
|   Home Economics | 5,112 | 7,932 |
|   Engineering-Technical Research | 7,224 | 10,608 |

[1] In school systems enrolling 6,000 or more pupils.
NEA, Research Division, *Economic Status of the Teaching Profession,* 1971–72, Research Report 1972–R2 (Washington, D.C.: The Association, 1972), p. 88.

supposed salary increase of approximately 4 percent?" The optimist might comment that the average beginner with a bachelor's degree was paid $296 more in 1972–73, as $7,061 in 1971–72 rose to $7,357 in 1972–73, according to new *firm* NEA figures. But the pessimist might respond with reminders both of inflation and of the degree of unemployment among beginning teachers in 1972–73.

## HOW SALARIES AND INCREASES ARE DETERMINED

When the new teacher with the bachelor's degree is employed, he or she moves into the first niche on the salary scale of the employing public school system (or sometimes private or parochial school). Since this first step is of the most immediate importance to you, you should be aware that beginners' salaries vary among public school systems. For the 1971–72 school year some beginners (10.3 percent of systems) earned salaries of $8,000 or more while other beginners (10.7 percent of systems) earned less than $6,249. However, the most frequent grouping was $7,000–$7,249 for 17.7 percent of the systems reporting. (See Table 4-4.)

With experience, continued study, and higher degrees, the teacher moves along the salary scale. Eventually he reaches the maximum which he can earn in that particular system. Teachers within a school system have usually been paid on the basis of their experience and the extent of

TABLE 4-4  **Range in Salaries for Beginning Teachers in 1971–1972**[1]

| Bachelor's degree, minimum salary | Percentage |
|---|---|
| Less than $5,500 | .1 |
| $5,500–5,749 | 1.0 |
| 5,750–5,999 | 1.3 |
| 6,000–6,249 | 8.3 |
| 6,250–6,499 | 11.2 |
| 6,500–6,749 | 11.0 |
| 6,750–6,999 | 12.4 |
| 7,000–7,249 | 17.7 |
| 7,250–7,499 | 12.2 |
| 7,500–7,799 | 10.7 |
| 7,750–7,999 | 3.7 |
| 8,000–8,999 | 10.0 |
| 9,000 or more | .3 |

[1] 1,179 reporting systems.
NEA, Research Division, *Salary Schedules for Teachers, 1971–72,* Research Report 1971–R12 (Washington, D.C.: The Association, 1971), p. 8.

their higher education. There are currently several controversial questions about the way teachers are paid. Should there be a single salary scale, regardless of sex? Should elementary and high school teachers be paid on the same scale based on training and experience (which has been the policy during recent years), or should high school teachers receive higher salaries? The third question is the most heretical: Should teachers be paid on the basis of single salary schedule, or should they be paid at least partly on the basis of demonstrated merit? These questions have often been considered in discussions of American education. Though the direction in which decisions have gone during the past few decades in respect to each of these questions seem clear, the questions can still engender considerable warmth.

As to the question of the compensation of men versus women, the counterarguments are clear. Those who favor higher compensation for men argue that men usually support families, while women usually do not, and that higher salary scales will attract needed males into teaching. The arguments for a single salary scale for both men and women stress sex equality and declare that a woman often is the single breadwinner in her family.

In the debate, sex equality has won out over sex discrimination in salaries. Legislation such as the Equal Pay Act of 1963, Title VII of the 1964 Civil Rights Act, and counterpart state legislation have ended this issue in most school systems. Women public school teachers are now almost always paid the same as men. The women's liberation movement of the 1970s supports equal pay for equal work in all occupational fields.

The question of whether high school teachers should be paid more than elementary school teachers also has a long history. The arguments for higher compensation for high school teachers have stressed the greater difficulty of teaching on the higher level, the need for more preparatory study and higher qualifications, and the greater importance of high school education as compared with elementary education. The opposite opinion denies these assumptions. Some elementary education protagonists even say that elementary school teaching, since it reaches young people at a stage when they are more malleable, is socially and educationally more important than high school teaching.

In practice, the single salary schedule without differentiation between levels has prevailed during recent years. The professionalization of teaching, and increased understanding of the importance of early education (among other things) are factors that have almost eliminated the dual salary schedule.

The most lively of the questions concerning compensation is the most fundamental—should teachers be compensated solely in terms of years of experience and advanced educational study undertaken, or should they be compensated at least partly on the basis of merit as demonstrated by their teaching performance? This controversy has raged in many communities, often with substantial segments of community leadership advocating merit pay and substantial groups of teachers (with some community support) advocating compensation through fixed scales. The controversy centers around the desirability of using merit rating to determine promotion, increases in pay, and advancement within a school system. Merit rating is an attempt to determine the degree of effectiveness with which teachers perform their duties.

The argument for merit pay and attendant merit rating is clear. Essentially, the argument is that the superior teacher should be rewarded with higher pay. Proponents point out that in many fields—business for example—employees presumably are rated according to the effectiveness of their work and promoted and paid accordingly. But even in business and industry there are many deviations from this policy.

The viewpoint of those who reject merit rating and merit pay is that selecting superior teachers is very difficult, if not impossible. Generations of researchers have not been able to provide a workable and operational definition of superior teaching; as a result, no satisfactory system has yet been developed for selecting these supposedly superior teachers. It is argued that since teaching is a profession marked by cooperation and mutual support between colleagues, one should not be made to compete with other teachers for salary increases. Nor should administrators, supervisors, and others spend their energies attempting to subjectively determine how an individual ranks in relation to a fellow teacher. Those who reject merit pay proposals insist that time and funds would be better invested in helping all teachers continue to improve.

Some state legislatures have initiated studies of merit rating plans. Sometimes such plans have been put into effect and then abandoned as they proved unacceptable or unworkable. The number of systems having a quality-of-service provision in their plans of salary compensation has declined over the past twenty-five years.

According to a 1972–73 NEA study of salary schedules for teachers, of 1,235 school systems reporting (enrollment ranged from 6,000 through 100,000 or more) 94.5 percent had no merit pay provisions while 5.5 percent reported some form of payment for meritorious service. The smaller systems seemed more likely to have adopted or continued merit pay plans. None of the systems exceeding 100,000 enrollment reported merit pay provisions.[3]

Taking some of the edge off the merit pay controversy is a related idea which sometimes has been mistaken for merit rating. This is the approach of differentiated staffing and pay, making salary adjustments relate to increased responsibilities or differentiation of functions among staff members. Differentiated pay is increasingly used in American school systems. For instance, in school systems using team teaching, higher payment is sometimes provided for team leaders or head teachers.

[3] NEA, Research Division, *Salary Schedules for Teachers, 1971–72,* Research Report 1971-R2 (Washington, D.C.: The Association, 1971), p. 26.

Staff members who take on semiadministrative or supervisory roles as staff assistants, heads of departments, etc., are usually compensated accordingly. Moreover, especially competent teachers in many school systems are sometimes selected and provided additional compensation for summer work on the curriculum and other related projects. Paraprofessionals (teacher helpers) with more limited preparation are also employed at somewhat lower pay scales in many school systems.

Yet the advocates of merit pay and merit rating still point out the existence of the system of evaluation and rating which you will probably encounter as a beginning teacher before you achieve tenure. Tenure assures an employee permanence in his position or employment as long as his work is satisfactory. With tenure, a teacher can theoretically only be dismissed after a hearing which determines that clearly defined unprofessional conduct has been demonstrated or that a teacher's service has been below acceptable standards. The beginning teacher who lacks tenure is appraised and evaluated by principals and others for usually three years before he is accepted as a permanent member of the staff. In some states, tenure is granted after two years and in a very few states after four or five years.[4]

Today, administrators are often critical of the idea of tenure for teachers; teacher organizations usually strongly defend the necessity for teacher tenure. The American Association of School Administrators in a 1973 report, *Teacher Tenure Ain't the Problem,* argued that teacher tenure should be replaced with more flexible, but specific, personnel policies, while the American Federation of Teachers escalated its defense of teachers whose tenure rights have been violated. In 1973, tenure for professors came under fire in several states. Some citizens oppose tenure for teachers in both the universities and public schools.

During the non-tenure period, the novice teacher can be dismissed from the system provided he is notified of his dismissal within a reasonable and designated time. If the beginning teacher is rated and judged, argue the advocates of merit pay, why cannot the experienced teacher be so rated? Their opponents admit that the rating of beginning teachers is necessary, but deny its applicability or desirability for experienced professionals.

## LENGTH OF THE SCHOOL YEAR AND VACATION PERIODS

Another economic characteristic of teaching is that traditionally teachers have worked far fewer days a year than people in most other occupations. For most teachers, the school year ends in May or more usually June and begins in September. Christmas vacation begins before

[4] NEA, Research Division, *Teacher Tenure and Contracts,* Research Report 1971-R3 (Washington, D.C.: The Association, 1971) p. 6.

Christmas and ends after New Year's Day. There is usually a week of vacation in the spring, often coinciding with Easter week. Legal holidays are observed. All in all, teachers are employed for a school term of nine or at the most ten months.

But before you reach the conclusion that the teacher's life is a leisured one, consider some additional factors. During the approximately 185 (average) working days, the teacher's work is intensive. It often carries over into the evenings and weekends. Christmas and spring vacations are often used in part to catch up on work that simply cannot be handled during the regular teaching months. Bear in mind, too, the ongoing educational preparation of the teacher. The typical teacher begins as a bachelor's degree holder. For a number of reasons, which usually include both economic and professional improvement, the teacher works for higher degrees. When? Through late afternoon, evening, Saturday, and summer term courses. No other profession makes such systematic provision for continuing education of its practitioners while they are employed.

For beginners in education, the fact of frequent and substantial vacations is an advantage and an inducement into the career of teaching. However, as the teacher grows more mature and the need for increased income becomes more important, many teachers (and most especially male teachers) come to view summer vacations in particular as an economic handicap. They would rather work and earn a better salary than be supposedly free. Such teachers welcome the growing trend in school systems to an extended term or twelve-month contract that allows them Christmas and spring vacations and two to four weeks of summer vacation, but which occupies the rest of the summer season with teaching summer school classes, curriculum work, and committee activities aimed at improving education throughout the school system. In most school systems which use the extended term or twelve-month plan, a teacher has the option of working for the school system at additional compensation during summers or having the summer to devote to other activities.

In recent years extra income from extra work was earned by teachers primarily during the summer months, sometimes from teaching or tutoring in the teacher's own school system but more often from outside jobs. The most usual outside summer jobs for teachers were in the areas of recreation, sales and retail, clerical-secretarial, teaching or tutoring outside of one's own school system, and the building trades.

During the regular school year some teachers also earned extra income. Some took on extra duties for extra pay in their own school system, largely by coaching athletic teams or directing recreational programs, occasionally through drama and music activities, and less often through administration and supervision, work with student teachers, special school duty, club sponsorship, or work with publications. Some teachers supplement their regular salaries from a school system through additional work in a different occupation. The term "moonlighting" has recently entered the American vocabulary. *Webster's New Collegiate Dictionary* did not carry the word at the beginning of the decade of the 1960s, but by the close of the decade the *Random House Dictionary of the English Language* defined moonlighting as "working at an additional job, usually at night, after one's regular, full-time employment." Teachers helped make the invention of such a word necessary.

In 1971, 8.5 percent of all teachers held jobs outside their school system while teaching during the regular school year. Men are especially inclined to moonlight because they are more often the family breadwinners. In 1971, 18.6 percent of all male teachers held some kind of employment, not within the school system, during the school year.[5]

To moonlight or not to moonlight? This is a decision which the teacher, particularly the male teacher, must often make. While it does increase income, moonlighting eliminates many opportunities for community action, further study, additional time devoted to instructional responsibilities, and opportunities for leisure and travel. One should become a moonlighter only after a careful assessment of priorities.

Presumably, if salaries increase for teachers, moonlighting will become less necessary. Yet as the general standard of living of Americans rises, so do the expectations of Americans for their own standards of living. Consequently, moonlighting is likely to persist, especially for those not involved in extended term programs. Extra jobs, particularly in the summer, are attractive to many people psychologically as well as economically. For some, extra work is a solution to a twentieth century problem our ancestors could not have anticipated: "What do I do with the time on my hands?"

## FRINGE BENEFITS

The phrase *fringe benefits* is another twentieth century addition to the English language. Fringe benefits refer to various kinds of protection or benefits that make an occupation more attractive and more economically secure. Fringe benefits in teaching usually include group health insurance, income protection during disability, group life insurance, sick leave, retirement pay, and reasonable time off with compensation for self-improvement and for personal reasons other than illness.

But most young teachers in good health give little thought to the possibility of accident, illness, or aging. Like Eugene Gant, the Thomas Wolfe character in *Look Homeward, Angel* and *Of Time and the River*, they can't really believe that they will ever grow old, become ill, or die. They may recognize that time will prove them wrong, but it is natural that they do not choose to worry much about the distant future.

Consequently, the typical beginning teacher is seldom seriously con-

[5] NEA, Research Division, *Status of the American Public-School Teacher, 1970–71*, Research Report 1972-R3 (Washington D.C.: The Association, 1972), p. 77.

cerned about fringe benefits when he accepts his first position; however, long-term planners are likely to appraise them more carefully. Fringe benefits become of greater concern to teachers as they grow older. They are taken into account in their decisions about whether to move to another post, and most particularly to another state with its different retirement system. If a teacher has accrued sufficient retirement benefits, it may not be in his interest to move. Thus retirement systems, as well as the supposed conservatism of age, inhibit mobility on the part of many teachers.

## FROM YOUR VIEWPOINT

These then are some of the important facts that should be considered in your appraisal of economic prospects. They indicate that through teaching you will become neither a plutocrat nor a pauper. You may neither cruise the Mediterranean on your own yacht, nor starve romantically in a garret. You will be in a field of work in which salaries are rising—but you may ask whether they are rising fast enough. You will be in a field in which your salary increments are reasonably secure—but you may ask whether they are large enough. You will be in a field of work in which the rewards are not primarily financial—but you may wonder whether they are adequate. You can make a difference in lives of other people—but you may ask yourself whether your fellow citizens recognize the value of your contributions. As to your latter speculation, you may find useful some information about how your fellow Americans view your chosen field.

## THE STATUS OF TEACHERS

Where does the American public place teaching in its ranking of the comparative status of occupations? Is the social status of teachers important to you? Should it be? The data which follow will answer the first question, but only you can answer the last two questions.

One early study of the prestige of occupations was conducted in 1947 by sociologists in cooperation with the National Opinion Research Center.[6] The study asked Americans to rank ninety occupations. When the scores were tabulated, the public school teacher was found to be thirty-sixth among the ninety occupations. Slightly above public school teachers were the artists who exhibit in galleries, factory owners who employ about a hundred people, sociologists, accountants for large businesses, biologists, musicians in symphony orchestras, authors of novels, captains in the regular army, building contractors, and economists. Clustered just below the public school teacher were the county

[6] National Opinion Research Center, *National Opinion on Occupations: Final Report of a Special Opinion Survey Among Americans 14 and Over* (Denver: University of Denver, 1947).

agricultural agent, railroad engineer, farm owner and/or operator, official of an international labor union, radio announcer, newspaper columnist, and owner-operator of a printing shop.

The top places on the scale went to the U.S. Supreme Court Justices, physicians, state governors, cabinet members in the federal government, diplomats in the U.S. foreign service, mayors of large cities, college professors, scientists, United States representatives in Congress, bankers, and government scientists. Two-thirds of the way down the list were ranked mail carriers, carpenters, automobile repairmen, plumbers, garage mechanics, local officials of labor unions, owner-operators of lunch stands, corporals in the regular army, and machine operators in factories. Lowest on the list, in descending order, were dock workers, night watchmen, laundry clothes-pressers, soda fountain clerks, bartenders, janitors, sharecroppers (who own no livestock or equipment and do not manage a farm), garbage collectors, streetsweepers, and finally shoeshiners.

So the public school teacher was not at the top of the reported ranking of occupations and social status as reported by the NORC study in 1947. But he was also a long distance from the bottom. His closest occupational kin, the college professor, shared seventh place with scientists and congressmen. Incidentally, Albert J. Reiss, Jr., in a book which reported, analyzed, and criticized the NORC study, commented that younger people tended to rank teachers lower than did older people.[7] You might wish to speculate on why this was the case.

Some scholars who were interested in occupational prestige in America used a sample of 651 persons in June 1963 to replicate the 1947 NORC scales. They found that the public school teacher shared twenty-ninth place. The sociologist was still slightly ahead of him, but the public school teacher had passed the factory owner, contractor, artist, musician, novelist, and economist. Moreover, the public school teacher had not been passed by anyone below him in the prestige order.[8] So the teacher in the public school had gained respect in the eyes of Americans.

Changes in the social status of teaching appear to be continuing. A Gallup Poll in 1972 reported:

The public's high regard for teachers and for the teaching profession has been evidenced in many ways in these annual surveys. In the present study, two out of every three citizens interviewed said they would like to have a child of theirs take up teaching as a career. The vote:

| | |
|---|---|
| Yes | 67% |
| No | 22% |
| No opinion | 11% |

[7] Albert J. Reiss, Jr., *Occupations and Social Status* (New York: Free Press, 1961), p. 187.
[8] Robert W. Hodge, Paul M. Siegel, and Peter H. Rossi, "Occupational Prestige in the United States: 1925–1963," in S. M. Lipset and R. Bendix, *Class, Status and Power,* 2nd ed. (New York: Free Press, 1966), p. 324.

While this percentage is very high, it is worth noting that it was higher in earlier surveys. Comments by those interviewed shed light on the drop. Many are aware that teaching jobs are scarce and that supply in many areas exceeds demand. Another reason, frequently voiced, is that teaching has become "dangerous," with children permitted to run "wild" in many schools.[9]

As with salaries, some potential teachers are not seriously concerned about status considerations. Other potential teachers may regard the social status of an occupation as of major importance. But most potential teachers will probably be pleased to know that regard for teaching has risen, yet may conclude that there are more important considerations in career decisions. Among the most important considerations for any teacher are his self-respect and the way he views his work. Of greatest importance is whether the individual can achieve his own personal and social goals and whether through teaching he can make a difference in others' lives.

## DISCUSSION

1. What position do you take on the importance of teacher salary in deciding to enter teaching? What are the arguments about the importance of the teacher's salary? What assumptions lie beneath different positions?
2. How different is the salary paid in the community you know best from the salaries reported in this chapter? What are the factors which determine the salaries of teachers?
3. In broad terms, how should salaries in differing fields of work be determined? How are they determined now? Ideally, how would you advocate they be determined?
4. What is your viewpoint on equality of pay for men and women? For those who are elementary or high school teachers and for professors?
5. What is the case for and against merit pay? What is your own conclusion? How about teacher tenure? What factors must be taken into account in reaching a decision on tenure and its desirability or undesirability?
6. Is the long summer vacation of teachers an actual advantage or disadvantage to teachers? To society? To children and youth?
7. What do you think of "moonlighting"? Is it good? bad? necessary? detrimental?
8. What specific areas of education are often compensated for with extra pay when additional assignments are undertaken or responsibilities accepted? Should such differential compensation be paid? What criteria determines decision in this respect? Are these valid?
9. How important are fringe benefits to you? What fringe benefits do you regard as important? Are there additional fringe benefits you would suggest?
10. How important is the status of teachers to you? To the class? To teachers as a whole? Does the ranking seem too high or too low? Is teacher status rising, leveling off, or declining?

[9] George H. Gallup, "Fourth Annual Gallup Poll of Public Attitudes Toward Education," *Phi Delta Kappan* (September 1972), pp. 39–40.

11. How important are these economic and status factors in your tentative decision to enter the teaching field?

## INVOLVEMENT

1. Get in touch with the office of your local teachers' association or union, or the office of a school district and obtain a copy of the current salary schedule of teachers in your community. Note the increments for each year of teaching experience and for each additional step in preparation.
2. Attempt to determine the salary you would receive if you were employed in the school or school system in which you currently think you might like to be employed.
3. Obtain salary schedules for several school systems in which you would like to teach. Compile your collection with those of other class members and create a master file for reference.
4. Get in touch with the office of your state teachers' association for the average salary figures for the current year. From the schedule, find the salary for the beginning teacher in your state, for the teacher with the master's degree and ten years of teaching experience, and for the teacher with an advanced degree in education and twenty years of teaching experience. Contrast these figures with the figures presented in the chapter in order to see the direction of the trend.
5. Obtain information on differentiated pay (in contrast to merit pay) in school systems to which you are contemplating applying for a position. Inquire about the extent of moonlighting and summer jobs in local school systems from local educational association or teachers' union officials.
6. Determine the fringe benefits in school systems to which you contemplate applying for a position.
7. Develop an adaptation of the status questionnaire and administer it to your class, to a sample of "people in the street," and to students on campus. Note any differing views expressed by the varying groups.

## FURTHER READING

National Education Association, Research Division. *Economic Status of the Teaching Profession*. Washington, D.C.: The Association. (Refer to most recent report.) One of an annual series of reports on salaries and related economic factors in American public schools.

National Education Association, Research Division. *Estimates of School Statistics*. Washington, D.C.: The Association. (Refer to most recent report.) Another of the continuing NEA publications which supply schoolmen with statistical data helpful in planning.

National Education Association, Research Division. *Rankings of the States*. Washington, D.C.: The Association. (Refer to most recent report.) Financial data on how the states of the American union compare with each other in their educational practices as to spending.

National Education Association, Research Division. *Salary Schedules and Fringe Benefits for Teachers*. Washington, D.C.: The Association. (Refer to most recent report.) One of the regular publications of the National Education Association. Sets forth current salary schedules for teachers.

National Education Association, Research Division. *Status of the American Public-*

*School Teacher*. Washington, D.C.: The Association. (Refer to most recent report.) Interesting and varied data concerning teachers, such as outside jobs held.

National Education Association, Research Division. *Teacher Tenure and Contracts*. Washington, D.C.: The Association. (Refer to most recent report.) What the teacher needs to know about security of tenure and the nature of contracts.

FIVE

# What organizations do teachers join—and why?

When a teacher joins an organization of fellow educators, what kinds of services are provided the teacher in exchange for the dues paid? A general benefit is joining with other like-minded persons to advance shared interests and common ideas.

Your selected organization (or several organizations) is your spokesman in the field of education. Presumably the organization wants to communicate many of the same ideas about your interests that you want to communicate individually. The organization can usually communicate these ideas and advance your interests, often including economic interests, more effectively than you can alone, unless you are unusually influential or eloquent.

Support for organizations can contribute to the advancement of education. Vigorous organizations can be heard at the local, state, and national levels; they can play a role in the decision-making that goes on in boards of education, in community governing bodies, in state legislatures, and in the Congress. Vigorous organizations can protect and extend academic freedom, the freedom to teach that every teacher requires for self-respect and for effective performance in the profession. They can oppose the kinds of loyalty oaths which single out teachers for special statements of their allegiance not required of other citizens. They can help in the production of such statements as the Code of Ethics developed by the National Education Association (NEA) and adopted by a number of other organizations, and the Bill of Rights of the American

Federation of Teachers (AFT), documents which are reproduced at the close of this chapter.

For instance, the National Education Association supplies a wide variety of special services for its members, in addition to helping them toward higher salaries. The organizational divisions that perform these services are at the heart of NEA's activities; the substance of what NEA does for the educational profession is typically conceived, implemented, and coordinated by a wide variety of professional interest organizations, commissions, councils, and committees of educators working with full-time staffs maintained at the Washington, D.C. headquarters.

For example, the Legislative Commission represents the teaching profession before Congress and generally promotes legislation favorable to the interests of public education and teachers. The Human Relations Council fosters good human relationships through education among Americans who are of varied races, ethnic backgrounds, and religions. The Dushane Emergency Fund Division supplies funds to ensure fair treatment of educators when their rights are threatened. The Research Division produces a constant flow of research reports on salaries, court decisions, teacher supply and demand, school statistics, etc., as well as publishes the quarterly *NEA Research Bulletin*. NEA services include such benefits as a program of educational travel for educators; insurance, annuity, and mutual fund programs; and an auto leasing program.

A new NEA Constitution was drafted in 1972 to become effective September 1973. The proposed changes would have eliminated the Executive Committee, an important group, and the state by state director system and set up, as a governing body, a 30-member board chosen regionally and at large, with a classroom teacher majority and with specification of inclusion of racial and ethnic minority members.[1] The document was approved at the 1972 NEA convention in Atlantic City, N.J., by a vote of 4,154 to 2,175 despite a charge by NEA Executive Secretary Sam Lambert that it represented "one more step in NEA's gradual drift toward unionism." He predicted that "the first president you elect under this system will be in for life" and warned that "our 17 national affiliates and 11 associated organizations will depart the scene for good."[2]

In 1973, in a mail ballot, almost 60 percent of NEA members who voted opposed the proposed constitutional changes. Only 17 of the required 27 states approved, so the proposed changes were defeated. Meanwhile, administrative groups, such as the American Association of School Administrators and the National Association of Secondary School Principals, voted to cut the last ties of their organizations with the NEA. The controversy over the NEA's role and governance continued and at the 1973 convention the delegates accepted a compromise version of the

---

[1] "Con Con Draft Okayed, Union Ties Debated," *NEA Reporter* (September 1972), p. 1.
[2] "News Front," *Education U.S.A.* (July 5, 1972), p. 224.

previously defeated document to alter NEA's structure. The major changes accepted were the creation of seven classes of membership, two-year presidential terms, and guarantees for minority group participation in governance.[3]

The American Federation of Teachers also performs a variety of special functions for its members, as well as helping them in collective bargaining and in improving working conditions. Such organizational divisions as the Legal Counsel and Teacher Defense Commission, the Legislative Department, and the Department of Research are similar in function to parallel NEA groupings. In addition to such generalized services, the AFT provides members with insurance coverage of the professional liability, accident and life varieties, and protection against unfair disciplinary or dismissal action through the activities of the federation and the resources of the AFT Defense Fund.

Early in the new teacher's career he will make a decision, either conscious or by default, whether or not to play an active part in whatever organizations he joins. The democratic tradition of active citizenship supports a decision to be an active participant. Both self-interest and advancement of one's social concerns also support active participation by the individual in organizations in which he holds membership. If one refrains from participation, he can scarcely complain in good conscience about the operation of the organization.

Another membership benefit is that you are entitled to participate in the national, regional, state, or local meetings your organization may have. You are entitled to play a role in the development of the organization's program through your elected representatives and sometimes through your own role as a representative.

If you are active in the organization, you can experience personal and professional relations with people who have many of your interests and concerns. If you choose to be a relatively passive participant, you can still receive the publications which almost all such organizations issue.

Many organizations include among their publications a journal or magazine which may either be distributed every school month, quarterly, or sometimes on a six-issue schedule. Such a magazine usually contains articles, columns, and news information related to the teacher's specialty. Many organizations have, in addition, a more informal "house organ" type of publication containing news about the work of the organization and mention of the activities of members. All such publications help the teacher stay up to date. For instance, the National Education Association publishes *Today's Education,* and the American Federation of Teachers publishes *American Teacher.*

For some specialized organizations which deal with particular sub-

---

[3] "News Front," *Education U.S.A.* (February 12, 1973), pp. 128–129. "NEA, AFT to Begin National Merger Talk," *Education U.S.A.* (July 9, 1973), p. 222.

ject matter fields or other interests, publications include a yearbook which, as the name implies, is an annual publication on some topic of special concern to the group. The yearbook is usually made up of chapters contributed by intellectual leaders and prominent practitioners in a specialized field, and it often deals with a topic of current controversy or of concern in the field. In addition, many organizations distribute pamphlets, usually prepared by selected members, on topics of interest to the membership.

## THE STRUGGLE BETWEEN NEA AND AFT

In legend and in literature there have been historic feuds. A famous example is the nineteenth century feud of the Hatfields and McCoys in the mountains of West Virginia and Kentucky. A feud between the Montague and the Capulet families in Verona resulted in the death of a pair of "star-cross'd lovers," Romeo and Juliet.

As a teacher you may be a participant in the final act of another famous feud, the struggle between the American Federation of Teachers and the National Education Association. The years ahead may see the termination of the battle between these major organizations; the struggle for power may be resolved through some degree of conciliation or accommodation or through a merger.

### The Backgrounds of NEA And AFT And Their Differences

The National Education Association was created in 1857 when forty-three people met in Philadelphia to organize the "National Teachers' Association." After World War I the organization began to grow toward its present impressive size. By mid 1973 the estimated membership of the NEA was about 1,400,000.

The American Federation of Teachers was organized and granted affiliation with the American Federation of Labor in 1916. By mid 1973 membership in the AFT was estimated as 375,000. (Some mergers at the lower levels had expanded the membership of both AFT and NEA.)

The National Education Association and the American Federation of Teachers are rival organizations. Historically, they have had differing perceptions of their educational roles, and of each other.

The National Education Association historically has seen itself as the major professional association for American educators. Though teachers have always been a majority, departments of the NEA have enrolled such groups as administrators, supervisors and curriculum directors, high school principals, elementary school principals, and others in administrative and supervisory posts. The NEA has long been devoted to enhancing the professional stature of teachers as well as promoting their economic welfare. Consequently, the organization has stressed a broad spectrum of publications, conventions to improve the competence of teachers and add to their sense of belonging to a profession, and representation of the cause of education in Congress.

The American Federation of Teachers has seen itself as an integral part of the American labor union movement and is affiliated with the AFL-CIO. The organization is made up almost exclusively of teachers; administrators have been barred from membership since 1966 (though they were not retroactively excluded). The AFT stresses its devotion to the improvement of the economic welfare of teachers; it suspects that too much talk about "professional" status serves as a smoke screen obscuring the real economic issues. Nevertheless, in recent years the AFT has expanded its interest into such professional matters as the support of research, promotion of international education in the curriculum, and the encouragement of such educational reforms as New York City's "More Effective Schools." The AFT now has a Council on Effective Schools.

The fundamental differences between the two organizations have been that the National Education Association serves an umbrella function for varied educational groups, including administrative groups, while the AFT is affiliated with the labor union movement. Myron Lieberman pointed out these differences more than a decade ago.

> Essentially there are two basic issues which divide the two organizations. One is the fact that the NEA has no restrictions upon administrator membership. The other is AFT's affiliation with the AFL-CIO.[4]

Thirteen years later, the AFT retained its affiliation with the AFL-CIO. But the new constitution of the NEA, which proposed to give NEA state and local affiliates the option of excluding school administrators as members and which specified that the new 30-member governing board would have a classroom-teacher majority,[5] speeded the departure of administrators from the NEA, even though the proposed constitutional changes were rejected by the membership in the mail ballot of 1973.

Relationships between the NEA and the AFT were not always bad. In fact, some of the earlier leaders of the AFT were also leaders in the NEA. When the AFT was founded in 1916, some thought that it would represent teachers on welfare issues such as wages and tenure, while the NEA would work mostly with research and curriculum and methodology.[6] But as the American Federation of Teachers began to grow following World War I, competition developed. In the period from 1918 to 1921, efforts were made by teachers who had sought affiliation with the labor

[4] Myron Lieberman, *The Future of Public Education* (Chicago: The University of Chicago Press, 1960), p. 231.
[5] "Con Con Draft Okayed, Union Ties Debated," *NEA Reporter* (September 1972), p. 1.
[6] Edward B. Shils and C. Taylor Whittier, *Teachers, Administrators, and Collective Bargaining* (New York: Crowell, 1968), pp. 539–540.

movement to take over the NEA or to bring its policies in line with the AFT view. At the 1918–1921 conventions of the National Education Association, for instance, the Chicago Federation of Teachers urged emphasis upon welfare matters such as salaries, tenure, and pensions. The NEA responded with its usual insistence on professional development and the inclusion of all educators in a concerted effort at educational improvement.[7]

In 1918 the memberships of the NEA and the AFT were approximately equal—each had fewer than 10,000 members. By 1960 the NEA had 713,000 and the AFT 60,000 members. By the beginning of the 1960s some of the leaders of organized labor had become deeply interested in enrolling teachers in teacher unions. They reasoned that if teachers could be persuaded to join unions, other white-collar workers and professional people would follow, which seemed appealing to labor since union rolls were suffering from the decrease in the percentage of blue-collar workers in the nation's work force.

The focus of AFT activity in the early sixties was New York City. After a successful breakthrough in New York City in December 1960—the United Federation of Teachers, an AFT local, won exclusive right to bargain for teachers—the AFT began to grow. The growth occurred primarily in large cities like New York, Chicago, Detroit, Los Angeles, St. Louis, Boston, New Orleans, Washington, and Cleveland.

The battlegrounds of the two organizations were the big cities. The campaigns took the form of competition between the two organizations to serve as the representative of teachers in bargaining and negotiations. Each side had its victories and defeats, but in general the National Education Association maintained a firm hold in rural, small town and small city America while the AFT gained in the larger cities, particularly in the northeast quarter of the U.S. Teachers in metropolitan areas sometimes went on strike; for instance, early in 1973 the teachers of Chicago, Philadelphia, and St. Louis were simultaneously on strike.

With respect to size the NEA remained Goliath and the AFT remained David. But the AFT gains were disturbing to NEA supporters. Since the 1890s the U.S. had been steadily developing as an urban and industrial nation and had grown away from its earlier rural and agricultural orientation. So although the NEA still heavily outnumbered the AFT in memberships throughout the 1960s, the speed of growth of the teachers' unions in big cities and in some suburbs threatened the NEA's controlling position.

### Collective Bargaining vs. Professional Negotiation

For a while, a clear distinction could be made between the major groups of educators as to the instruments of power they used in gaining conces-

[7] T. M. Stinnett, *Turmoil in Teaching* (New York: Macmillan, 1968), p. 19.

sions from boards of education. The AFT used the historical labor union tactics of collective bargaining and strikes; the NEA used the processes of professional negotiations and sanctions.

T. M. Stinnett, a student of the dispute, points out that "collective bargaining" was defined by the Taft-Hartley Act as "the performance of the mutual obligation of the employer and the representatives of the employees to meet at reasonable times and confer in good faith with respect to wages, hours, and other terms and conditions of employment or the negotiation of any agreement or any question arising thereunder, and the execution of a written contract incorporating any agreement reached if requested by either party, but such obligation does not compel either party to agree to a proposal or require the making of a concession." "Professional negotiation" was defined by the National Education Association as "a set of procedures to provide an orderly method for teacher associations and school boards, through professional channels, to negotiate on matters of common concern, to reach mutually satisfactory agreement on these matters, and to establish educational channels for mediation and appeal in the event of impasse."[8]

Certainly there is a similarity. Is there a difference? Stinnett, a long-time worker in the National Education Association and an admitted advocate of the NEA point of view, believes there is and states his position as follows:

The differences are that collective bargaining:
1. Is designed for private employees, and its use is mandatory under law.
2. Uses procedures that are subject to Federal and state laws and interpretations of the courts. Administration of collective bargaining is under jurisdiction of Federal and state labor departments or agencies.
3. Employs, in cases of impasse, the strike, which is recognized under the laws as the weapon of the employee.
In contrast, professional negotiation:
1. Is designed for public employees (teachers).
2. Requires that all processes are to be through professional channels; that is through education personnel and agencies.
3. Must use educational channels for appeals or mediation of impasse.
4. Does not advocate or consider legal the use of the strike as a weapon.
In short, professional negotiation seeks to keep public employees (teachers) out of labor techniques as defined in labor laws. The rationale is that schools and factories are not analogous; schools are not profit-making enterprises, and management and employees are not natural enemies fighting over divisions of profits.[9]

## Strikes and Sanctions

To others, the distinctions between collective bargaining and professional negotiation appear less obvious. To them, the difference dimin-

[8] Cited by Stinnett, p. 90.
[9] Stinnett, p. 90.

ished further as the NEA advocated not strikes but sanctions. A sanction involves curtailment or withdrawal of services of teachers to a given district or state school system. A first step involved is publicizing the dispute; the association involved then requests its members who are employed elsewhere not to seek or accept positions in the unsatisfactory school district. All instruction personnel are then requested to boycott the school district. Finally, the Association declares it professionally unethical for either newcomers or present staff to accept employment in the school district.

Again is there a difference between the strike and the sanction? Stinnett thinks there is:

> There are several differences. Sanctions do not violate a contract. Services to children are not interrupted. Teachers serve out their contracts for the current school year. Under sanctions, there are no picket lines. Under sanctions, school districts are given several months' notice and told that existing conditions make possible only inferior programs for children, that professional people cannot, under the existing conditions, provide first-rate services. As a general rule, sanctions are made effective in the succeeding school year except in the case of withdrawing extracurricular services.[10]

AFT proponents are quick to counter, however, that sanctions do, in fact, negatively affect services to children, particularly in the later stages of a sanction effort. They also argue that strikes do less long-term damage to a district and are usually briefer and "cleaner." In other words, a strike may end and the entire original staff resume teaching, whereas sanctions may result in the departure of teachers over a long period of time.

### The Decline of Differences Between NEA and AFT

Increasingly, NEA local associations used work stoppages which resembled strikes. However titled, work stoppages, strikes, mass resignations, withdrawals, and sanctions were used by both the NEA and the AFT to withhold teacher services. In his final chapter, Stinnett comments sadly,

> Like the teachers' unions up to 1962 with respect to collective bargaining, the NEA and its affiliated associations began advocating professional negotiation in muted tones and with promises of responsible and reasonable action by teachers. Gaining a foothold in some places now, teachers' associations and unions are exhibiting increasing truculency and growing demands. Turmoil and strife have grown alarmingly in frequency.[11]

Edward B. Shils and C. Taylor Whittier summed up the disappearance of differences between the NEA and the AFT in *Teachers, Administrators, and Collective Bargaining,* as follows:

---

[10] *Ibid.,* p. 127.
[11] *Ibid.,* pp. 356–357.

The earlier differentiation between the NEA as a professional organization and the AFT as a labor union is gradually disappearing in the cold light of local organizing actions and tactical planning at national headquarters. Both organizations train organizers, employ strikes and threats of strikes, aim at contracts that are highly complex, and whittle away at traditional staff and board prerogatives, and advocate firm grievance procedures ending with final and binding arbitration. Little by little, the NEA at the local level, like the AFT, is driving principals, supervisors, and administrators out of the bargaining unit. Both organizations press hard for exclusive representation and the NEA is getting as tough in the fighting as the AFT. The two organizations are busy lobbying the legislatures for laws to their own liking that will mandate elections and recognition in each district. While each organization specializes in a particular approach—the educational channels versus the labor channels—their respective lobbyists, in due time, will press for amendments not far apart.[12]

Symptomatic of the point of view of the above authors as to the gradual disappearance of operational differences between the AFT and the NEA is the increasing frequency of the use of the phrase "collective negotiations," a hybrid of collective bargaining and professional negotiations. Shils and Whittier say, "In view of the militancy engaged in by both the NEA and the AFT the difference between NEA's professional negotiations and AFT's collective bargaining is a matter of nomenclature."[13]

By 1973, in response to the collective negotiations movement among teachers and the rapid growth of other public employee groups, more than half the states had passed laws governing the collective negotiations relationship. The NEA was lobbying for a national law which would legalize teacher strikes under certain circumstances.

### The Possibility of Merger

In the early 1970s the two organizations increasingly resembled each other in their daily operations at the community level as to teacher welfare. So talk about and action toward merger began. Discussion of merging was proposed by the AFT in 1968 but was rejected by the NEA. Community action resulting in merger started in Flint, Michigan, in 1969. In Los Angeles in 1970 the Association of Classroom Teachers (ACTLA) and AFT Local 1021 combined; they formed the United Teachers of Los Angeles with more than 14,000 members.[14]

In June 1972, the New York State Teachers Association (NEA) voted in referendum to approve a merger with the United Teachers of New York (AFT). In conjunction with the merger in New York State, a mail ballot of the two organizations was conducted; members of the United Teachers of New York (AFT) approved the measure by 34,171 to 1,706

[12] Shils and Whittier, p. 540.
[13] *Ibid.*, p. 549.
[14] Myron Lieberman, "The Union Merger Movement: Will 3,500,000 Teachers Put It All Together?" *Saturday Review of Education* (June 24, 1972), pp. 51–52.

Conventions offer teachers opportunities to exchange ideas with others of their profession, as well as learn about new publications and innovations.

and members of the New York State Teachers Association (NEA) approved by 45,635 to 19,477.[15] Prior to the vote, the presidents of two organizations, Thomas Y. Hobart, a guidance counselor from Buffalo who headed the State Teachers Association, and Albert Shanker, president of the United Federation of Teachers, traveled 4,000 miles through the state to advocate support for the merger among their organization members.

Consequently, the question of a possible merger of the National Education Association and the American Federation of Teachers was the dominant issue at the 1972 annual convention of the NEA. The President of the NEA, Donald E. Morrison, spoke on behalf of merger, reminding the delegates that they had an obligation to achieve teacher unity and indicating that he supported an independent organization of teachers. The Executive Secretary of the NEA, Sam M. Lambert, cautioned against entering into any more teacher mergers such as the one which had taken place in New York State.[16] (In the fall of 1972, Lambert resigned his post.)

After long and heated debate, the convention voted to bar further mergers such as the New York State development. Though the action was a setback for merger advocates in both groups, a clause in the resolution exempted the recent merger in New York State and others that were already underway or completed. The delegates, by a vote of 3,723 to 2,051, instructed local and state units of the NEA as well as the national organization that they "not enter into a merger requiring affiliation with

[15] "Teachers Vote for a State-Wide Union," *New York Times,* June 15, 1972, p. 17.
[16] "N. E. A. Aide Attacks Mergers by Teachers," *New York Times,* June 29, 1972, p. 43; and "Merger Issue Roils N. E. A. Meeting," *New York Times,* June 27, 1972, p. 23.

A.F.L.-C.I.O.," the labor organization with which the American Federation of Teachers is affiliated. The convention authorized exploration of relationships with organizations. Thus the NEA could discuss merger with the AFT but could accept no agreement that would call for association members to join organized labor.[17] Meanwhile, the AFT, under the presidency of David Selden, who for years has advocated merger, and influenced by AFL-CIO oriented Albert Shanker of the United Federation of Teachers, continued to urge one powerful organization to support the interests of teachers and to improve education through unified action. Two months after the 1972 NEA convention, the AFT voted to make membership in the AFL-CIO mandatory in any merger arrangements. In 1973, Terry Herndon became the new executive secretary of NEA; the press reported that when he was head of the Michigan Education Association he had favored having all teachers united in one strong organization.

During the annual convention of the National Education Association in July 1973, the NEA voted to open discussions on merger with the rival American Federation of Teachers. But the delegates endorsed the position of outgoing President Catharine Barrett that the NEA was not prepared to compromise on the AFT requirement of affiliation with AFL-CIO. So in late 1973 the probability of an NEA-AFT merger still hinged on the difficult question of American teachers affiliating with the organized labor union movement.

At the present writing, the NEA and AFT exist as separate organizations. Membership in such educational organizations is voluntary and so a matter of individual teacher choice. Thus, one can choose to be a member of the National Education Association, or of the American Federation of Teachers, or neither. (A few teachers hold membership in both.) One can choose to belong to a local union of the AFT or the state or local affiliates of the NEA, or belong to none. (However, one cannot join a local of the AFT without paying national dues, a percentage of which goes to the AFL-CIO.) In the early 1970s not all of the members of the NEA affiliates paid dues in the NEA nationally. The NEA is attempting to remedy lack of unification through Uni-Serv, a unified program of services to teachers.

As teachers in local communities increasingly decide that, for purposes of "collective negotiations," they will be represented either by the union or the professional association, a surrounding climate of opinion develops among fellow teachers which strongly encourages the new teacher to join the dominant group. It is quite possible that the 1970s will see such labor techniques as the closed shop with compulsory checkoff of dues mandated by agreements and supported by law. Many contracts

[17] "NEA Votes Ban on New Mergers," *New York Times,* July 1, 1972, p. 1.

negotiated by AFT locals call for dues deductions to be made from salary checks; the money withheld is paid directly to the union by the board of education.

## SPECIALIZED ORGANIZATIONS

One can choose whether or not to belong to a specialized organization within the broad field of education. Here we refer not to the variety of locals of the American Federation of Teachers from the large United Federation of Teachers of New York City down to a handful of union-oriented teachers working toward recognition in a small community, nor to the influential state associations of the National Education Association and the local associations at the community level. Instead, we refer to the many specialized organizations which bring together teachers with common interests in a particular subject matter or other specialty. A U. S. Office of Education directory lists education associations and agencies in the United States. Some of these are affiliated or associated with the National Education Association in an increasingly loose relationship; many others are independent. (See below.) Some of the organizations which historically have been affiliated or associated with the National Education Association are moving away from their former close relationships. For instance, leaders of groups of administrators conceive the concerns of their members as not always in accordance with and sometimes antagonistic to strong current NEA concerns for salaries, welfare, bargaining, and a powerful voice for teachers in decision-making. Some organizations are literally moving out of the NEA building in Washington and occupying new locations as their headquarters.

---

### SPECIALIZED ORGANIZATIONS FOR TEACHERS

**Some Departments, National Affiliates, and Associated Organizations Related to NEA as Reported in 1971--72 NEA Handbook**

#### Departments

Driver and Traffic Safety Education
School Nurses
Classroom Teachers
Rural Education

#### National Affiliates

Supervision & Curriculum Development
Teacher Educators
Public Continuing & Adult Education
Music Educators
Mathematics Teachers
Social Studies

Elementary-Kindergarten-Nursery
Educational Communications & Technology
Industrial Arts
Art Education
Educational Secretaries
Administrative Women
Health, Physical Education, & Recreation
Home Economics
Journalism Education
Retired Teachers Association

**Associated Organizations**

Business Education
Exceptional Children
Educational Data Systems
NTL Inst. for Applied Behavioral Science
Women Deans & Counselors
School Librarians
School Public Relations
Speech Teachers

**A Few Independent Organizations, 1973**

American Educational Research Association
Association for Childhood Education International
Delta Kappa Gamma
Kappa Delta Pi
National Association of Biology Teachers
National Congress of Parents and Teachers
National Council of Teachers of English
Phi Delta Kappa
American Association of School Administrators (left the NEA in 1972)
National Association of Secondary School Principals (left the NEA in 1972)
National Association of Elementary School Principals (left the NEA in 1973)

You are a social studies teacher? For you there is the National Council for the Social Studies. You are research-oriented? For you there is the American Educational Research Association. You are a teacher of the language arts? For you there is the National Council of Teachers of English. You are concerned about the curriculum? For you there is the Association for Supervision and Curriculum Development. Those educators who believe that education should increasingly become a profession rather than an occupation often become members of such specialized groups to share ideas and interests with fellow professionals.

## IS EDUCATION A PROFESSION?

A persisting problem for educators has been whether education is a profession in the fullest sense of that honorable word.

Myron Lieberman has suggested eight characteristics of a profession:

1. A unique, definite, and essential social service.
2. An emphasis upon intellectual techniques in performing its service.
3. A long period of specialized training.
4. A broad range of autonomy for both the individual practitioners and for the occupational group as a whole.
5. An acceptance by the practitioners of broad personal responsibility for judgments made and acts performed within the scope of professional autonomy.
6. An emphasis upon the service to be rendered, rather than the economic gain to the practitioners, as the basis for the organization and performance of the social service delegated to the occupational group.
7. A comprehensive self-governing organization of practitioners.
8. A code of ethics which has been clarified and interpreted at ambiguous and doubtful points by concrete cases.[18]

Should education be a profession marked by this complex of characteristics? *Is* education currently a profession marked by these characteristics? If one is to answer these questions, some specific elements in the definition must be taken into account.

1. A unique, definite, and essential social service. Is education unique, to be carried on only by educators? Or can an untrained person teach well? Is there agreement on the function of education? Or is there substantial disagreement and uncertainty over what education is intended to do? Is education essential to the welfare of children in our society? Or is education a social luxury which should be available only to those who can pay for it?
2. An emphasis upon intellectual techniques in performing its service. Does education require of the teacher complex intellectual operations which are characteristic of professions? Or is education simply a matter of using physical techniques in carrying on the work?
3. A long period of specialized training. Are the four years of college work toward the baccalaureate, including some education courses, equivalent to a "long period of specialized training"? Would the requirement of a master's degree for teaching constitute a sufficiently "long period of specialized training" necessary for a profession? Is the professional training received by teachers-to-be primarily intellectual? Or is it primarily nonintellectual?
4. A broad range of autonomy for both the individual practitioners and for the occupational group as a whole. Does teaching involve freedom to exercise independent skill and judgment? Or must teaching be closely supervised by authorities who make the basic decisions and solve the major problems? Do teachers have a great deal of say in reg-

---

[18] Myron Lieberman, *Education as a Profession* (Englewood Cliffs, N.J.: Prentice-Hall, 1956), pp. 2–6.

ulation of their profession? Or do teachers lack freedom to decide such things as admission to the profession, suspension from work, and the characteristics of ethical conduct?

5. An acceptance by the practitioners of broad personal responsibility for judgments made and acts performed within the scope of professional autonomy. Do teachers accept responsibility for their work and its outcomes? Or do they regard responsibility for outcomes as residing with others outside of their field of work?

6. An emphasis upon the service to be rendered, rather than the economic gain to the practitioners, as the basis for the organization and performance of the social service delegated to the occupational group. Do teachers take pride in the service they render? Or do teachers work simply because of the pay involved?

7. A comprehensive self-governing organization of practitioners. For instance, do teachers have an organization or organizations to foster the profession by setting standards of certification, disseminating new ideas, raising the general and social economic status of the professional group? Or do teachers not have an organization or organizations concerned for the standards and advancement of the profession?

8. A code of ethics which has been clarified and interpreted at ambiguous and doubtful points by concrete cases. Is there a code of ethics for the teaching profession which has been interpreted in practice? Or is there no such code?

As you check over the questions raised in connection with each of the ingredients of the definition of a profession, it is quite possible that you will answer affirmatively to some questions which describe professional status, affirmatively to some questions which describe education simply as an occupation but not a profession, and ambiguously to others. If so, your conclusion will probably be that education is partially but not totally a true profession at the present time.

This latter conclusion is that of several authors who summarize proposed sets of criteria which must be met in order to consider an occupational group a profession. Chandler and his co-authors say:

First, the profession must provide a unique and essential social service. . . .
The second qualification is that a professional must have had a prolonged education. . . .
The final qualification is that of professional autonomy, the achievement of which is especially important to those involved in education. . . .
Although teaching appears to be a profession in several aspects, there are many obstacles preventing full professionalization. Teachers seem to take a narrow view of their potential as contributors to the educational enterprise. Too often the teacher defines himself and his co-workers as classroom operators only. This limited definition does not recognize the valid contribution the teacher can and should make in such related areas as curriculum, instructional organization, evaluation, and methodology.

If teachers fail to take initiative in these areas their role will be a limited one and their function defined by other sources.

Other obstacles preventing full professionalization include the lack of a sufficient number of men in teaching, a source of instability to the profession. Although no significant personality or intelligence differences exist between the sexes, women tend to enter teaching on a temporary basis. Men, in general, consider it as a permanent career. There is some evidence, however, that the number of men entering the field is increasing. Finally, the status and salary of teachers are not always consistent with the service rendered.[19]

We will refer hereafter to education as a "profession" throughout this book. But we hope you will keep in mind that we too recognize that the professional status of education has not been fully achieved. Codes and bills of rights such as those which follow contribute to the achievement of professional standing for teaching.

## NATIONAL EDUCATION ASSOCIATION
## CODE OF ETHICS OF THE EDUCATION PROFESSION

### Preamble

The educator believes in the worth and dignity of man. He recognizes the supreme importance of the pursuit of truth, devotion to excellence, and the nurture of democratic citizenship. He regards as essential to these goals the protection of freedom to learn and to teach and the guarantee of equal educational opportunity for all. The educator accepts his responsibility to practice his profession according to the highest ethical standards.

The educator recognizes the magnitude of the responsibility he has accepted in choosing a career in education, and engages himself, individually and collectively with other educators, to judge his colleagues, and to be judged by them, in accordance with the provisions of this code.

### Principle I
### Commitment to the Student

The educator measures his success by the progress of each student toward realization of his potential as a worthy and effective citizen. The educator therefore works to stimulate the spirit of inquiry, the acquisition of knowledge and understanding, and the thoughtful formulation of worthy goals.

In fulfilling his obligation to the student the educator—

1. Shall not without just cause restrain the student from independent action in his pursuit of learning, and shall not without just cause deny the student access to varying points of view.
2. Shall not deliberately suppress or distort subject matter for which he bears responsibility.
3. Shall make reasonable effort to protect the student from conditions harmful to learning or to health and safety.

[19] B. J. Chandler, Daniel Powell, William R. Hazard, *Education and the New Teacher* (New York: Dodd, Mead 1971), pp. 218–220.

4. Shall conduct professional business in such a way that he does not expose the student to unnecessary embarrassment or disparagement.
5. Shall not on the ground of race, color, creed, or national origin exclude any student from participation in or deny him benefits under any program, nor grant any discriminatory consideration or advantage.
6. Shall not use professional relationships with students for private advantage.
7. Shall keep in confidence information that has been obtained in the course of professional service, unless disclosure serves professional purposes or is required by law.
8. Shall not tutor for remuneration students assigned to his classes, unless no other qualified teacher is reasonably available.

## Principle II
### Commitment to the Public

The educator believes that patriotism in its highest form requires dedication to the principles of our democratic heritage. He shares with all other citizens the responsibility for the development of sound public policy and assumes full political and citizenship responsibilities.

The educator bears particular responsibility for the development of policy relating to the extension of educational opportunities for all and for interpreting educational programs and policies to the public.

In fulfilling his obligation to the public the educator—

1. Shall not misrepresent an institution or organization with which he is affiliated, and shall take adequate precautions to distinguish between his personal and institutional or organizational views.
2. Shall not knowingly distort or misrepresent the facts concerning educational matters in direct and indirect public expressions.
3. Shall not interfere with a colleague's exercise of political and citizenship rights and responsibilities.
4. Shall not use institutional privileges for private gain or to promote political candidates or partisan political activities.
5. Shall accept no gratuities, gifts, or favors that might impair or appear to impair professional judgment, nor offer any favor, service, or thing of value to obtain special advantage.

## Principle III
### Commitment to the Profession

The educator believes that the quality of the services of the education profession directly influences the nation and its citizens. He therefore exerts every effort to raise professional standards, to improve his service, to promote a climate in which the exercise of professional judgment is encouraged, and to achieve conditions which attract persons worthy of the trust to careers in education. Aware of the value of united effort, he contributes actively to the support, planning and programs of professional organizations.

In fulfilling his obligation to the profession, the educator—

1. Shall not discriminate on grounds of race, color, creed, or national origin for membership in professional organizations, nor interfere with the free participation of colleagues in the affairs of their association.

2. Shall accord just and equitable treatment to all members of the profession in the exercise of their professional rights and responsibilities.
3. Shall not use coercive means or promise special treatment in order to influence professional decisions of colleagues.
4. Shall withhold and safeguard information acquired about colleagues in the course of employment, unless disclosure serves professional purposes.
5. Shall not refuse to participate in a professional inquiry when requested by an appropriate professional association.
6. Shall provide upon the request of the aggrieved party a written statement of specific reason for recommendations that lead to the denial of increments, significant changes in employment, or termination of employment.
7. Shall not misrepresent his professional qualifications.
8. Shall not knowingly distort evaluations of colleagues.

**Principle IV**
**Commitment to Professional**
**Employment Practices**

The educator regards the employment agreement as a pledge to be executed both in spirit and in fact in a manner consistent with the highest ideals of professional service. He believes that sound professional personnel relationships with governing boards are built upon personal integrity, dignity, and mutual respect. The educator discourages the practice of his profession by unqualified persons.

In fulfilling his obligation to professional employment practices, the educator—
1. Shall apply for, accept, offer, or assign a position or responsibility on the basis of professional preparation and legal qualifications.
2. Shall apply for a specific position only when it is known to be vacant, and shall refrain from underbidding or commenting adversely about other candidates.
3. Shall not knowingly withhold information regarding a position from an applicant, or misrepresent an assignment or conditions of employment.
4. Shall give prompt notice to the employing agency of any change in availability of service, and the employing agent shall give prompt notice of change in availability or nature of a position.
5. Shall adhere to the terms of a contract or appointment, unless these terms have been legally terminated, falsely represented, or substantially altered by unilateral action of the employing agency.
6. Shall conduct professional business through channels, when available, that have been jointly approved by the professional organization and the employing agency.
7. Shall not delegate assigned tasks to unqualified personnel.
8. Shall permit no commercial exploitation of his professional position.
9. Shall use time granted for the purpose for which it is intended.[20]

**AMERICAN FEDERATION OF TEACHERS**
**BILL OF RIGHTS**

The teacher is entitled to a life of dignity equal to the high standard of service that

[20] *National Education Association Handbook, 1971–72* (Washington, D.C.: The Association, 1971), p. 18.

is justly demanded of that profession. Therefore, we hold these truths to be self-evident:

### I

Teachers have the right to think freely and to express themselves openly and without fear. This includes the right to hold views contrary to the majority.

### II

They shall be entitled to the free exercise of their religion. No restraint shall be put upon them in the manner, time, or place of their worship.

### III

They shall have the right to take part in social, civil, and political affairs. They shall have the right, outside the classroom, to participate in political campaigns and to hold office. They may assemble peaceably and may petition any government agency, including their employers, for a redress of grievances. They shall have the same freedom in all things as other citizens.

### IV

The right of teachers to live in places of their own choosing, to be free of restraints in their mode of living, and the use of their leisure time shall not be abridged.

### V

Teaching is a profession, the right to practice which is not subject to the surrender of other human rights. No one shall be deprived of professional status, or the right to practice it, or the practice thereof in any particular position, without due process of law.

### VI

The right of teachers to be secure in their jobs, free from political influence or public clamor, shall be established by law. The right to teach after qualification in the manner prescribed by law, is a property right, based upon the inalienable rights to life, liberty, and the pursuit of happiness.

### VII

In all cases affecting the teacher's employment or professional status a full hearing by an impartial tribunal shall be afforded with the right of full judicial review. No teacher shall be deprived of employment or professional status but for specific causes established by law having a clear relation to the competence or qualification to teach, proved by the weight of the evidence. In all such cases the teacher shall enjoy the right to a speedy and public trial, to be informed of the nature and cause of the accusation; to be confronted with the accusing witnesses, to subpoena witnesses and papers, and the assistance of counsel. No teacher shall be called upon to answer any charge affecting his employment or professional status but upon probable cause, supported by oath or affirmation.

### VIII

It shall be the duty of the employer to provide culturally adequate salaries, security in illness and adequate retirement income. The teacher has the right to such a salary as will: (a) Afford a family standard of living comparable to that enjoyed by other professional people in the community; (b) Make possible freely chosen professional study; (c) Afford the opportunity for leisure and recreation common to our heritage.

### IX

No teacher shall be required under penalty of reduction of salary to pursue studies beyond those required to obtain professional status. After serving a reasonable probationary period a teacher shall be entitled to permanent tenure terminable only for just cause. They shall be free as in other professions in the use of their own time. They shall not be required to perform extracurricular work against their will or without added compensation.

### X

To equip people for modern life requires the most advanced educational methods. Therefore, the teacher is entitled to good classrooms, adequate teaching materials, teachable class size and administrative protection and assistance in maintaining discipline.

### XI

These rights are based upon the proposition that the culture of a people can rise only as its teachers improve. A teaching force accorded the highest possible professional dignity is the surest guarantee that blessings of liberty will be preserved. Therefore, the possession of these rights imposes the challenge to be worthy of their enjoyment.

### XII

Since teachers must be free in order to teach freedom, the right to be members of organizations of their own choosing must be guaranteed. In all matters pertaining to their salaries and working conditions they shall be entitled to bargain collectively through representatives of their own choosing. They are entitled to have the schools administered by superintendents, boards or committees which function in a democratic manner.[21]

## DISCUSSION

1. For what reasons should a teacher join an educational organization? Should he or she take an active part? Why? Do you think membership should be compulsory?
2. Essentially what is the difference between the two major organizations of teachers and the specialized organizations of teachers?
3. What are the fundamental and historical differences between the National Education Association and the American Federation of Teachers?
4. What current perceptions do the members of the two major organizations have of each other? Is the past hostility decreasing?
5. What are the past differences and present similarities between the two major organizations as to "strikes"; "negotiations"?
6. If you were forced to choose between the two major organizations, which would you choose to join? Why?
7. What forces tend toward merger of the National Education Association and the American Federation of Teachers? Which forces discourage merger?
8. Discuss the advantages and disadvantages of a possible merger of the National Education Association and the American Federation of Teachers.

[21] American Federation of Teachers, *A Bill of Rights for Teachers*, leaflet, no date.

PART TWO

# THE NATURE OF AMERICAN
# SCHOOLS

SIX

# How did the public schools begin?

One function of this book is to provide you with information so that you can responsibly make some important decisions. In the next two chapters we will consider the public education system, its origin, development, and present challenges. A third chapter will deal with private independent schools, and schools sponsored by religious groups, especially the largest such school system, that of the Roman Catholic Church. In what kind of system will you teach—with the large majority of educators in public schools or with those who teach in either private independent or religiously sponsored schools?

## AMERICAN PUBLIC SCHOOLS

There are many things we take for granted. We press a switch and assume the electric lights will come on; we open a book and know there will be print before our eyes; we desire an education and expect the American public school system to provide it. We take so much for granted that we almost forget that there had to be an Edison to discover the uses of electricity, a Gutenberg to invent movable type, a Horace Mann to "invent" the public school system.

Even American historians take American public education so much for granted that they sometimes pay it the dubious compliment of *not* sufficiently including it in their histories. One is apt to find mention of many minor military and industrial figures yet find little recognition of one of the most creative of all American social developments—universal public education.

The idea of universal public education—the opportunity for every child to have a good education sponsored and financed by everyone—is a central idea in American education. The phrase is so familiar you probably consider it an ancient concept; in reality it is uniquely American, and therefore relatively new in the history of educational thought. Education for the elite has far more worldwide historical precedent.

American education has not always been guided by this ideal of universal public education. In fact, the public support part of the idea was not applied to all the major educational levels until the final quarter of the nineteenth century, and educational opportunity for all did not become a reality until the twentieth century. The history of this unique, complex, and something less than perfect institution is important for you as a potential American teacher. To know what education is requires knowing something about the people, processes, and forces which have created it. David B. Tyack in his *Turning Points in American Educational History* argues in favor of the study of educational history:

> As general education for teachers, educational history can rarely be useful or functional in a narrow sense. Instead it should be a kind of knowledge which is interesting and valuable in its own right, though it also can give educators lasting insights and habits of analysis which will benefit them professionally. Inquiry into educational history can assist teachers to interpret and generalize their experience and to free themselves from unexamined routine.[1]

As you prepare for and later practice your chosen specialty, you should continue inquiry into the history of education in more depth than is provided here.

### Before Universal Public Education

Our ancestors from Europe, Asia, and Africa did not bring public education with them when they came to the New World. They couldn't, as it had not yet been invented. The most advanced of the world areas as to education—Europe—regarded education as a privilege of the wealthy and assumed lack of education as inevitable for the masses. So England established tutorial systems and preparatory schools and universities for the children of the prosperous classes. Originally, education was for the children of the landed aristocrats; but increasingly the children of the rising new middle class industrialists were included. Education was still not conceived as education for all, however; instead it was for the sons (and less frequently for the daughters) of the upper class that they might become the elite leaders of society. It was not until the twentieth century that Europe achieved a school system for children and youth of all social classes.

[1] David B. Tyack, *Turning Points in American Educational History* (Waltham, Mass.: Blaisdell, 1967), p. xii.

Page from *The New England Primer*. Puritan education was closely associated with Puritan religious beliefs.

Some European nations did initiate laws requiring local communities to feed, clothe, and shelter paupers; tied to such legislation were provisions for the schooling of charity cases. In 1601, for example, the English Poor Law was passed, and as a result England developed "charity schools," providing a degree of literacy to some impoverished children.[2] But these charity schools were a far cry from the free public elementary schools that were to develop first in the United States and then in Europe.

## EDUCATION IN COLONIAL AMERICA (1620–1776)

To a large extent, colonial life in America was an extension of European, and particularly English, social, political, and commercial systems. As a result, the educational patterns that emerged in the seventeenth century followed European, especially English, models. The Old World dual system of education, which provided formal instruction for the upper classes and charity schools and some apprentice training for the lower classes, was widely practiced throughout the colonial and early national periods. But there were religious, political, and social forces operative in the American colonies that caused the American educational system, as it

[2] Robert Holmes Beck, *A Social History of Education*, Foundations of Education Series (Englewood Cliffs, N.J.: Prentice-Hall, 1965), p. 75.

The Connecticut Historical Society

Early hornbook—now in the Bulkeley Collection of the Connecticut Historical Society.

developed, to differ significantly from the European tradition.

Most influential of these forces was the religious motive of the Quaker, Catholic, Anglican, and Puritan colonists who early established church sponsored and controlled schools. As the educational historians Butts and Cremin point out, this religious-educational diversity inhibited the development of a strong colonial educational system under English civil control and thereby provided the climate for distinctively American ideas to develop.[3]

### Puritan Influence in New England

Among no religious group was education more integral to the social and

[3] R. Freeman Butts and Lawrence A. Cremin, *A History of Education in American Culture* (New York: Henry Holt, 1953), p. 98.

theological order than among the Puritans of New England. In 1629 these English businessmen and craftsmen founded Massachusetts Bay Colony under royal charter to establish a "New Jerusalem" where their rigid Calvinism could be both the religious and civil code. Puritan theology defined both child and adult as sinners, totally depraved and worthy of nothing except God's punishment. Since salvation was always uncertain, it was only natural that the "perfecting of the saints" should be the primary and oftentimes harsh business of the schools.

As early as 1635 the citizens of Boston started the first "public" Latin grammar school for the education of boys between the ages of eight and fifteen. The following year Harvard College was funded from public and private sources and by 1638 was operating in Cambridge, Massachusetts, with one professor and one building. These early schools—models for New England education—placed great emphasis upon the practical Puritan ideal of education for the perpetuation of a "hellfire and damnation" morality, using, paradoxically, the pagan Greek and Roman classics prominently in the curriculum. The Puritans respected education as instrumental in developing reason, in making man a more willing instrument in the hands of God, in counteracting the wiles of Satan, in providing a learned clergy and literate congregation, and in allowing the Bible to be read in the English language and Latin. Consider, for instance, this excerpt from *The New England Primer,* which illustrates the Puritan viewpoint on the proper purpose of reading.

Praise to God for Learning to Read

The Praises of my Tongue
    I offer to the Lord
That I was taught and learnt so young
    To read his Holy Word.

That I was brought to know
    The Danger I was in,
By Nature and by Practice too
    A wretched slave to Sin.

That I was led to see
    I can do nothing well;
And whither shall a Sinner flee
    To save himself from Hell.

Dear Lord this Book of thine,
    Informs me where to go
For Grace to pardon all my sin,
    And make me holy too.

> Here I can read and learn
>   How Christ the Son of GOD
> Has undertook our great concern,
>   Our Ransom cost his Blood.
>
> And now he reigns above,
>   He sends his Spirit down
> To show the wonders of his Love,
>   And make his Gospel known.
>
> O may that Spirit teach,
>   And make my heart receive
> Those Truths which all thy Servants preach,
>   And all thy Saints believe!
>
> Then shall I praise the Lord
>   in a more cheerful Strain,
> That I was taught to read his Word,
>   And have not learnt in vain.[4]

In addition to the Latin grammar schools, so-called "dame schools" operated in housewives' homes. These schools provided reading, ciphering, and religious instruction for a town's young children. For the older child, tax and tuition supported grammar schools appeared as a response to the growing need for education.

As the Bay Colony grew and prospered, the Massachusetts General Court sought to exercise some regulatory influence over education in the various towns with the passage of a 1642 law requiring parents to see to the education of their children or be fined for noncompliance. When many parents failed to comply, the state in 1647 passed an important piece of legislation, commonly called "The Old Deluder Satan Act," which required that every village of fifty families provide a school for instruction in reading and writing. Towns of one hundred or more families were required to employ schoolmasters to prepare young boys for college. Considering that by 1647 Massachusetts "had nearly 20,000 people, some 30 towns, 30 to 40 churches, 7 grammar schools, and a college,"[5] the impact of this law is quite impressive.

In the early years of the New England colonies the church and the state were so closely united that they were essentially one. The church, however, was dominant when any differences arose. So colonial Massachusetts was able to impose the Puritan creed on all citizens by state legislation. The phraseology used in the 1647 law stressed the struggle against the Devil, "it being one chief project of that old deluder, Satan, to

---

[4] From the *New England Primer* (Boston: Ginn, Twentieth Century reprint; Boston: Draper, 1785–90).

[5] Edward A. Krug, *Salient Dates in American Education* (New York: Harper and Row, 1966), p. 9.

keep men from the knowledge of the Scriptures as in former times by keeping them in an unknown tongue. . . ." Though the religious motive was dominant, there were other concerns in the 1642 and 1647 Acts. The 1642 Act specified that parents and masters were required to teach children not only "the principles of religion" but also "the capital laws of the country." The 1647 Act was intended to protect the colonist from "the old deluder," but it also emphasized "that learning might not be buried in the grave of our fathers in the Church and Commonwealth." The responsibility for enforcement of such acts was placed with the community's "chosen men appointed for managing the prudential affairs" rather than with any state organization.

Although the New England schools were predecessors of the modern public school insofar as they were under community control, were in theory open to all a town's children, and were partially supported by public funds, they were not free schools in the contemporary sense. Parents were usually obligated to provide additional support in the form of fees and tuition. Also, of course, these schools were not dedicated to free inquiry but to the maintenance of Puritan moral and religious beliefs.

Butts and Cremin have summarized the control of New England schools in the following way:

1. The state could require children to be educated.
2. The state could require towns to establish schools.
3. The civil government could supervise and control schools by direct management in the hands of public officials.
4. Public funds could be used for the support of public schools.[6]

Some change in this pattern developed in the eighteenth century, however, as the colonial legislatures of New England increasingly transferred the control of schools to local districts. This decentralization rapidly took hold and became the dominant system throughout most of America as school districts multiplied with westward expansion.

### Education in the Middle and Southern Colonies

Not all the colonies were as homogeneous in religious allegiance as Massachusetts under the domination of the Puritans. In the Middle colonies, though religion was still a motivating concern in the establishment of schools, diversity of religious beliefs prevailed. Consequently, the state could hardly force one religion upon a diverse people through education. Instead, the responsibility for education was left to a variety of individuals and institutions, including families, churches, religious and philanthropic organizations.

While Puritan education was spreading through the New England

[6] Butts and Cremin, p. 103.

colonies, the Dutch Reformed Church in New York and the Quakers in Pennsylvania were among those establishing educational systems in the Middle colonies. Prior to the English takeover of New Amsterdam (New York) in 1664, the Dutch had instituted a civil-controlled educational system under the agency of the Dutch Reformed Church. Following the collapse of Dutch control, these town schools became solely church operated, and other religious sects moved to establish their own schools. William Penn, founding Pennsylvania in 1681, likewise sought to develop state responsibility for education. But state influence later faltered, leaving education under the control of church and private interests during most of Pennsylvania's colonial history.

The Dutch schools were similar in curriculum and method to the Puritan schools, but the Quaker approach to education was much more humane. William Penn, in his *Some Fruits of Solitude in Reflections and Maxims,* said children should "be making of Tools and Instruments of Play; Shaping, Drawing, Framing, and Building, &c. than getting some rules of propriety of Speech by Heart. And those also would follow with more Judgment, and less trouble and Time."[7]

The Southern colonies were slowest to mandate a system of public supported education. The system of slavery required an elitist education for the sons of the white gentry who would themselves soon become slave masters; a tutorial system of classical education became the dominant practice. The education of the slave was antithetical to Southern society, and was prohibited by law in many states, as indicated by the following excerpt from a 1740 South Carolina Act prohibiting teaching slaves to write:

XLIV. And whereas, the having of slaves taught to write, or suffering them to be employed in writing, may be attended with great inconveniences: BE IT ENACTED BY ETC. that all and every person and persons whatsoever, who shall hereafter teach, or cause any slave or slaves to be taught to write, or shall use or employ any slave to be taught to write, or shall use or employ any slave as a scribe in any matter of writing whatsoever, hereafter taught to write; every such person and persons, shall, for every such offence, forfeit the sum of $100 current money.[8]

Meanwhile, among the poorer white settlers, there sometimes existed a rudimentary education in the home. Consequently, formal education in the South lagged behind that of the Middle and New England colonies.

[7] Cited in Rena L. Vassar, *Social History of American Education,* vol. 1 (Chicago: Rand McNally, 1965), p. 34.
[8] *An act for Better Ordering and Governing of Negroes and Other Slaves in this Province. In South Carolina, Statutes, The Public Laws of the State of South Carolina from its Establishment as a British Province down to the Year 1790, inclusive* (Philadelphia: R. Aitkin & Son, 1790), p. 174.

The University of Pennsylvania had its beginnings in Franklin's idea of an academy to teach the young ". . . Things that are likely to be most useful and most ornamental. . . ."

## The Enlightenment

The eighteenth century saw ideas imported from Europe that challenged the older religious orthodoxies. The resulting shift in thinking has been described by Butts and Cremin:

. . . proposals for change in the older ways of thinking and acting carried appeals to *human* reason rather than divine law, to *natural* rights rather than supernatural rights, to *scientific* method rather than to established truths, to *social* agreements and *individual* freedom rather than authoritarian control, and to *humanitarian* and *democratic* faith rather than aristocratic privilege. The results of this shift in emphasis in intellectual sanctions were felt in theology and religion, in philosophy, and in political, economic, and social theory. They were likewise seen in the emergence of new forms of educational theory and proposals for educational change that eventually led to changes in educational practice.[9]

Prominent among Americans who exemplified the new emphasis on human reason was Benjamin Franklin. Though he lent his insights and talents to a variety of endeavors, his educational proposals are of particular importance as indicative of directions American education would take.

In 1749 he wrote his *Proposals Relating to the Education of Youth in*

[9] Butts and Cremin, pp. 43–44.

*Pennsylvania,* followed in 1751 by the *Idea of the English School, Sketch'd Out for the Consideration of the Trustees of the Philadelphia Academy.* He proposed that an academy for the education of youth be chartered in Philadelphia, suggesting that: "It would be well if they could be taught *every Thing* that is useful, and *every Thing* that is ornamental; But Art is long and their Time is short. It is, therefore, propos'd that they learn those Things that are likely to be *most useful* and *most ornamental,* Regard being had to the several Professions for which they are intended."[10]

The academy was opened in Philadelphia in 1751 with a curriculum patterned after the one outlined by Franklin. Although the school did not long maintain the practical directions Franklin had mapped for it, it presaged the secondary school.

## EDUCATION IN THE NATIONAL PERIOD (1776–1865)

Two of the most significant educational events immediately following the Revolutionary War were the passage of the Land Ordinance Act of 1785 and the Northwest Ordinance of 1787. First stated in the 1785 act and reinforced by the 1787 legislation was a provision to reserve section 16 of each township of public land for educational purposes. The Northwest Ordinance, which provided specifically for the territorial organization of that area roughly bounded by the Ohio and Mississippi Rivers and the Great Lakes, contained an often quoted indication of the new government's concern for education. "Religion, morality, and knowledge being necessary to good government and the happiness of mankind, schools and the means of education shall forever be encouraged." Thus, the colonial emphasis upon education was an early tradition of the new nation. The new government regarded education as among its proper spheres of action.

The government instituted by the Articles of Confederation in 1781 was superseded in 1789 by a more centralized government under the United States Constitution. The new Constitution had nothing specific to say about education; but its silence on this issue is highly significant, for it left education completely under the control of the states rather than laying the foundation for a national system of education.

However, this silence should not be interpreted to mean that the founding fathers abhorred federal intervention in education. George Washington left a part of his estate to help establish a national university, and Thomas Jefferson as President signed a bill into law which allocated funds to Catholic nuns to "Christianize" and "educate" the Indians. This question of state versus national control has been an important one throughout American educational history; today such debates are evident in conflicts over busing, private segregated schools, school financing, and religion in the schools.

[10] Cited by Tyack, p. 74.

There was a relentless trend in the development of American society toward education for all the people. Thomas Jefferson, an advocate of a nation composed of sovereign individual states, probably best expressed the necessity of education in a republic. In a proposal to the Virginia Assembly in 1779, a Bill for the More General Diffusion of Knowledge, Jefferson said:

. . . it becomes expedient for promoting the publick happiness that those persons, whom nature hath endowed with genius and virtue, should be rendered by liberal education worthy to receive, and able to guard the sacred deposit of the rights and liberties of their fellow citizens, and that they should be called to that charge without regard to wealth, birth or accidental condition or circumstance; . . . it is better that such should be sought for and educated at the common expense of all. . . .[11]

He went on to call for a common school system organized and governed on a county basis. All free white children were to be provided the first three years tuition free; the superior students were then to be selected and sent to regional grammar schools; yearly, the best students in each grammar school were to be selected and sent to the College of William and Mary for a full college education, all of which would be paid for by the public. This plan, calling for only three years of common education, was highly selective in nature. Nevertheless, it was a milestone in the slow move toward universal public education. Regrettably, the Virginia Assembly, imbued with the popular notion that education was a private matter, rejected Jefferson's bill. But the basic ideas were incorporated in legislation passed in 1796 for a comprehensive system of elementary schools and in 1810 for a system of aid from the State of Virginia to counties in order to support public education.

Essentially what Jefferson wanted was the three R's for all free children plus the opportunity for bright boys to obtain still more schooling at state expense. That opportunity, thought Jefferson, must be extended to include university education. So persuaded was Jefferson of the importance of the university that he instructed that his tombstone carry the fact that he was not only the drafter of the Declaration of Independence but also a founder of the University of Virginia.[12]

Jefferson knew that education of the people was essential to freedom. In a letter to Du Pont de Nemours, April 24, 1816, he said, "Enlighten the people generally, and tyranny and depression of body and mind will vanish like evil spirits at the dawn of day."[13] And in a letter to William Charles Jarvis, September 28, 1820, he said, "I know of no safe depository of the ultimate powers of the society but the people

[11] Cited by Vassar, pp. 109–110.
[12] John Dewey, ed., *The Living Thoughts of Thomas Jefferson* (New York: Fawcett World Library, 1963), p. 9.
[13] John Bartlett, *Familiar Quotations*, Fourteenth Edition (Boston: Little, Brown, 1968), p. 473.

themselves; and if we think them not enlightened enough to exercise their control with a wholesome discretion, the remedy is not to take it from them, but to inform their discretion."[14]

Nor was Jefferson alone. As Thayer and Levit point out, "In 1786 Benjamin Rush in Philadelphia produced a plan for the education on a national scale of all American youth, including both sexes, a plan specifically designed to emphasize the principles of democracy and to insure an understanding of the machinery of government with which to maintain the institutions of democracy."[15] Rush also outlined a plan for public schools in Pennsylvania that was comparable to Jefferson's. He called for a four-level system with a free school in each township, an academy in each county, four state colleges, and one state university. He, too, failed to get his plan adopted.

### The Common School Movement

Despite these early failures, the first three decades of the nineteenth century were marked by a rising clamor for public schools. This was the "era of the common man," personified by Andrew Jackson, who was elected president in 1828 largely as a result of support from the "common people." It was these people, the small farmers, the immigrants, the urban laborers, who most vigorously voiced their demand for schools for their children. Encouraged by the democratic promise, they feared that existing private selective educational systems would promote the development of an aristocratic society that would lock their children in the bonds of ignorance and poverty.

It was not that there were no schools. Tyack points out that except in the South and a few rural areas there were schools, but they were a hodgepodge of public, semiprivate, private, and religious institutions with little common direction. They certainly did not adequately meet the demands of the new social conditions—"urbanization, industrialism, immigration, and the democratization of politics."[16]

The movement did not proceed unresisted, however. Religious and private interests, which controlled the largely private system of education, actively opposed the creation of schools that would lessen their control (in the case of the churches) and profits (in the case of school owners). But public education was gaining more support. Labor spokesmen demanded schools for the children of workers that were not charity schools for paupers or schools dependent upon the whims of rich industrialists. Simultaneously, some of the more perceptive of the middle-class leaders and the imaginative business leaders supported public education for its potential contribution to a prosperous society. As a result,

[14] *Ibid.*
[15] V. T. Thayer and Martin Levit, *The Role of the School in American Society* (New York: Dodd, Mead, 1966), p. 59.
[16] Tyack, pp. 120–121.

the states increasingly began to set up funds to help communities fulfill their educational responsibilities. Massachusetts became the first state to establish a free, public, tax-supported, common school system.

The first American high school, enrolling 176 boys, opened in Boston in May 1821. By 1823 a school committee was alarmed that seventy-six pupils had dropped out and that some of the teachers had already deviated from the plan in the disposition of the studies. Said the committee, some teachers had even introduced some studies not originally included. The committee urged that the high school maintain its original purpose and that the most useful and practical studies be taught the first year. Confirming its displeasure with the swing toward a strictly academic curriculum, the committee recommended that the high school's name be changed from "The English Classical School" to "The English High School."

## Horace Mann and Public Education

Historians regard Horace Mann as the outstanding nineteenth century proponent of public schools. He was educated in law at Brown University, entered the legal profession in 1823, and was elected to the Massachusetts legislature in 1827. While a member of that body, he led the fight against the state's increasing abdication of responsibility for education and aided in the successful drive for the creation of a State Board of Education. In 1837 he accepted the position of secretary of the board, thus becoming the chief, though somewhat powerless, administrative officer of Massachusetts' public schools.

The energy and vision which he brought to the office, however, soon made it an influential forum for his views. In his twelve annual reports to the state on the condition of education, Mann combined several arguments to persuade the citizens to support public schools. He played heavily on the self-interests of businessmen and industrialists in pointing out the economic value of education. Simultaneously, he stressed the potential of education for the elimination of both social problems and individual defects. Mann could combine practical economic arguments with appeals to utopian beliefs:

. . . education has a market value; that it is so far an article of merchandise, that it may be turned to pecuniary account; it may be minted, and will yield a larger amount of statuable coin than common bullion. . . . The aim of industry is served, and the wealth of the country is augmented, in proportion to the diffusion of knowledge.[17]

Mann could also make the following sweeping idealistic claim:

. . . there is by nature little or perhaps no distinction among men with respect to their original power of intellect. The seeds of knowledge, of refinement, and of literary ex-

[17] Cited by Thayer and Levit, p. 6.

cellence are implanted with a liberality, nearly or completely equal, in the mind of the ignorant peasant, and in the mind of the most profound philosopher.[18]

Cremin has summarized the common school idea that Mann so vigorously promoted:

The commanding figure of the early public-school movement, he had poured into his vision of universal education a boundless faith in the perfectibility of human life and institutions. Once public schools were established, no evil could resist their salutary influence. Universal education could be the "great equalizer" of human conditions, the "balance wheel of the social machinery," and the "creator of wealth undreamed of." Poverty would most assuredly disappear, and with it the rancorous discord between the "haves" and the "have-nots", that had marked all of human history. Crime would diminish; sickness would abate; and life for the common man would be longer, better, and happier. Here was a total faith in the power of education to shape the destiny of the young Republic. . . . Little wonder that it fired the optimism of the American public.[19]

## Common Schools Realized

Of course Horace Mann was not the only influential supporter of public schools. He was joined by men such as Henry Barnard, John Pierce, and Samuel Lewis. "The reformers emulated each others' articles in the journals, regarding work in other states as social laboratories for reform ideas. Though ranging from Massachusetts to California, the crusaders came to similar conclusions about the purpose and institutional character of the common school. Out of the diversity of American education in the early nineteenth century had come, by mid century, a remarkable degree of consensus."[20]

The struggle for educational reform spanned twenty-five years, but by the beginning of the Civil War public supported education at the elementary level was fairly widespread. Cremin sums up the advances made by the common school movement as follows:

A majority of the states had established public school systems, and a good half of the nation's children were already getting some formal education. Elementary schools were becoming widely available; in some states, like Massachusetts, New York, and Pennsylvania, the notion of free public education was slowly expanding to include secondary schools; and in a few like Michigan and Wisconsin, the public school system was already capped by a state university. There were, of course, significant variations from state to state and from region to region. New England, long a pioneer in public education, also had an established tradition of private education, and private schools continued to flourish there. The Midwest, on the other hand, sent a far greater proportion of its school children to public institutions. The southern states, with the ex-

[18] *Ibid.*, p. 5.
[19] Lawrence A. Cremin, *The Transformation of the School* (New York: Knopf, Vintage, 1961), pp. 8–9.
[20] Tyack, p. 125.

ception of North Carolina, tended to lag behind, and did not generally establish popular schooling until after the Civil War.[21]

Accompanying the rapid growth of common schools was the need for teachers to "keep" them. Young women fourteen to eighteen years of age were the most readily available supply source in the quantity needed. Besides, teaching for a man was considered popularly to be a demeaning job; the image of Ichabod Crane was a deeply embedded image of the male teacher. Young women, by contrast, were thought to be morally pure, politically safe in terms of ideas, and well suited by God and nature to continue the mother's role in the common schools. They also could be hired for a mere pittance. Therefore, young women soon became the backbone of the emerging teaching profession, which was sometimes called the "petticoat profession." There soon appeared in American higher education normal schools and departments of education in colleges and universities to advance pedagogical theory and practice. Public education came about when democratic ideals, labor support, increasing acceptance by the middle classes, and the needs of an increasingly industrial age resulted in a demand for education for more than the few.

## EDUCATION IN EXPANDING AMERICA (1865–1920)

The half century following the Civil War was a period of intense educational activity. The common school gains of the first half of the nineteenth century were consolidated and extended in a variety of important ways. Specifically, the federal government created a Department of Education; Negro education increased; the common school idea was extended to secondary education; public education included the education of the immigrant; and vocational education became an accepted function of the schools.

In 1867 a Department of Education was created by Congress for the purpose of "collecting such statistics and facts as shall show the condition and progress of education in the several States and Territories, and of diffusing such information, respecting the organization and management of schools and school systems, and methods of teaching, as shall aid the people of the United States in the establishment and maintenance of efficient school systems, and otherwise promote the cause of education throughout the country." The name was later changed to the Office of Education in 1868, then to the Bureau of Education in 1870 for 59 years, and back to the United States Office of Education in 1929.

The first Commissioner of Education was Henry Barnard, an educator of Horace Mann's era who had made considerable contributions to

---

[21] Cremin, p. 13.

education as the chief educational officer in Connecticut and Rhode Island. As Cremin notes, however, it was William Torrey Harris, the "commanding figure of his pedagogical era" who towered above post-Civil War commissioners.[22] Prior to his appointment as commissioner, he had distinguished himself as the superintendent of schools in St. Louis from 1868 to 1880. During his superintendency and his tenure as commissioner (1889–1906), he worked to entrench the common school in American tradition.

### Negro Education

For the education of the Negro, the post–Civil War period was not a time for consolidation but for beginning. There had been some scattered interest in educating the Negro during the colonial and early national periods, but for the most part the slave of the "cotton" South had been systematically deprived and denied the benefits of education, often by law, since a slave was seen as mere property to be used as necessary for personal gain. It was widely believed that educating the Negro would threaten the entire social and economic system of the South—a system which through enslavement violated the personal rights and dignity of human beings.

Although the door to education did open somewhat for the Negro before the Emancipation Proclamation, various forces worked to discourage mass education of the black population. The reorganization of education forced by reconstruction policies was for most Southern states the beginning of free public schools for whites and blacks.

The early progress that was made can be credited primarily to the deep, long held desires of black Americans for education and to the educational programs of the Freedmen's Bureau and various church groups, the support of northern philanthropists, and the concern of civic leaders in the North. These forces combined to start the development of Negro education. Yet the hostile attitudes of many whites toward the Negro resulted in more legislation than schools.

The founder of Tuskegee Institute (1881), Booker T. Washington, a self-educated ex-slave, became a spokesman for Negro education. He propagated the doctrine of social regeneration by means of industrial training. In a speech at an Atlanta exposition in 1885, he advanced what has come to be called the "Atlanta Compromise." He said, "In all things that are purely social we can be as separate as the five fingers, yet one as the hand in all things essential to mutual progress."

It was due principally to white leadership that a racially segregated school system grew up in the South after the Civil War. The Negro portion of the dual system that developed was separate but not equal. In 1896, the Supreme Court ruled in *Plessy v. Ferguson* that it was legal for a

[22] Cremin, p. 14.

state to operate separate but equal facilities for the white and black races. De jure segregation developed.

Although this decision was invalidated by the Supreme Court in 1954 (*Brown v. the Board of Education of Topeka*), de facto segregation has continued throughout many parts of the country. One of the many challenges to education in the 1970s is to provide high quality education without racial and ethnic discrimination.

### Education for the Immigrants

Immigration to the U.S. began in substantial volume in the 1830s and 1840s. Many emigrated from Ireland with the failure of potato crops in 1845–1846. After the Civil War large numbers of Englishmen, Germans, Irishmen, and Scandinavians came looking for a better life than Europe

*The Bettmann Archive, Inc.*

Americanization became one of the functions of education during the immigration movement of the 19th century.

had offered them. In the 1880s and 1890s nineteenth century immigration reached its peak with southern and eastern Europe contributing an increasing share of the almost 9,000,000 newcomers. In the next two decades (1901–1920) more than 14,500,000 people arrived.

From the early part of the nineteenth century, the schools had played an important part in Americanizing the newcomers. As the incoming numbers increased in the 1880s and 1890s, however, education was forced by public opinion to respond in a more systematic and deliberate way. The immigrants who came at this time tended to congregate in urban centers and to retain their languages and cultures. Poverty, anti-immigrant attitudes of the white middle class, and political corruption combined to handicap the immigrants. Many Americans who considered themselves the "true" Americans because their families had been here earlier wanted the schools to absorb these newcomers and to eliminate their "foreign" language and cultural patterns. Education for conformity became for some an ideal. In the late nineteenth century a movement to reform the public schools developed. Though humanitarian motivations were held by some school reformers, such as journalists and social workers, many Americans were largely concerned to assimilate the "new immigrant" into the capitalist economic system and endow him with the "virtues" of the Protestant ethic.

To men such as Professor Ellwood P. Cubberley of Stanford University the new immigration represented a threat to American society. They called for the schools to adopt an explicit policy of Americanization in which Anglo-Saxon values would supplant what they considered the inferior ethnic patterns of immigrants from countries like Italy, Austria-Hungary, and Russia. As a result, more attention was paid to English instruction, civics, American history, and the inculcation of values that white Anglo-Saxon Protestant America prized.

Cubberley wrote:

These Southern and Eastern Europeans were of a very different type from the North and West European who preceded them. Largely illiterate, docile, often lacking in initiative, and almost wholly without the Anglo-Saxon conceptions of righteousness, liberty, law, order, public decency, and government, their coming has served to dilute tremendously our national stock and to weaken and corrupt our political life. . . . Our national life, for the past quarter of a century, has been afflicted with a serious case of racial indigestion.[23]

To assimilate these people into our national life and citizenship is our problem. We must do this and we must, if possible, give them the impress of our peculiar institutions and ideals. National safety and welfare alike demand that we not only teach these peoples to use the English language as our common tongue, but that they be educated also in principles and ideals of our form of government. Even under the best

[23] Ellwood P. Cubberley, *Public Education in the United States* (Boston: Houghton Mifflin, 1934), pp. 485–486; also see Ellwood P. Cubberley, *Changing Conceptions of Education* (Boston: Houghton Mifflin, 1909), p. 15.

of conditions this will require time, and it calls for a constructive national program if effective work is to be done. Social and political institutions of value are the product of long evolution, and they are safe only so long as they are in the keeping of those who have created them or have come to appreciate them. Our religious, political, and social ideals must be preserved from replacement by less noble ideals if our national character is not to be weakened.[24]

Needless to say, the school did not go unchanged. While the motives many times were based on prejudice, the result was that children of many backgrounds were educated together. And eventually what was learned by educators contributed to the educational move away from a subject matter orientation, characteristic of American education from colonial times, toward a greater concern for the individual and the society in which he lived.

### Public Secondary Education Develops

It would be a mistake to assume that public elementary and secondary education developed concurrently. The public elementary school was consolidated after the Civil War, but it remained for the educators of the second half of the nineteenth century to extend the common concept up through the secondary level.

The early Latin grammar schools were not strictly secondary schools in the contemporary sense, for their students were not adolescents until the last two or three years. It was the academy, however, which was the prototype of the secondary school to come. Benjamin Franklin's idea had caught on as the nation moved into the nineteenth century, and by 1850 it is estimated that there were 6,000 academies in existence. These schools varied in curriculum from the Latin grammar school classicalism to the more comprehensive English-influenced school of Franklin's type, to the patently vocational school. They were generally not under public control and were not free. They were the best available, but their selectivity was not in the spirit of the democratic ideal which education was increasingly called on to serve.

Consequently, laymen and professional educators alike began to think in terms of a publicly supported educational system spanning the elementary and secondary years. But as the movement started in this direction in the third quarter of the nineteenth century, it met heavy resistance, as had the elementary common school fifty years earlier. Butts and Cremin point out, however, that the earlier fight had been to get education laws on the books while the secondary education issue was centered on whether or not these laws furnished the legal basis for upward extension.[25]

---

[24] Ellwood P. Cubberley, *An Introduction to Education* (Boston: Houghton Mifflin, 1925), pp. 26–67.
[25] Butts and Cremin, p. 418.

This question was first answered conclusively in the Kalamazoo case of 1874. The Michigan State Supreme Court upheld the Kalamazoo school district's right to collect taxes for the support of a high school. The decision, written by Justice Thomas M. Cooley, pointed out that Michigan had already provided for a tax supported elementary system and a state university and that it was inconsistent to exclude secondary education. This decision clarified the legal status of public secondary education in Michigan and set the stage for the national expansion of public high schools.

Development to 1890 was slow, however. Raubinger *et al.* in *The Development of Secondary Education* point out that by 1890 only 203,000 students were enrolled in public high schools. For the approximately 6,000 public high schools in existence by this date, the average enrollment was less than forty.[26] Clearly, much had to be accomplished if universal public secondary education was to become a reality.

### Vocational Education

As the American economy became increasingly commercial and industrial in makeup, there was a parallel increase in vocational education interest and activity. In the early 1900s industry and organized labor collaborated with the National Society for the Promotion of Industrial Education in supporting the passage of federal legislation to underwrite substantial financial assistance for vocational education. The result was the Smith-Hughes Act of 1917.

Specifically, this legislation allowed the federal government to cooperate "in paying the salaries of teachers, supervisors, and directors of agricultural subjects, and of teachers of industrial subjects, and in the preparation of teachers of agricultural trade and industrial and home economics subjects." The continuing interest in vocational education in the nation's high schools is largely due to this piece of legislation and other laws which followed it.

By 1920 the public schools were somewhat more socially relevant. The decline of classical courses was accompanied by the introduction of vocational agriculture, home economics, business and secretarial training, vocational guidance, and industrial arts.

## DISCUSSION

1. What does "universal public education" mean to you? Do you support literally education for everybody? Do you believe that public support should apply to all rungs of the educational ladder? What is the case for the alternatives to "universal public education?"

2. React to the statement "The opportunity for a good education for every child and

---

[26] Frederick M. Raubinger, *et al.* (eds.), *The Development of Secondary Education* (London: Collier-Macmillan, 1969), pp. 2–5.

young person paid for by everybody is a central idea in American education." Is this the way it is? Is this the way it ought to be?

3. What accounts for differences between New England education and Middle region education in the American colonies? What accounts for differences between colonial New England education and Southern education?
4. What are the shifts in thinking brought about by ideas from the Enlightenment?
5. Why does Franklin hold a significant place in American education?
6. What was Jefferson's point of view on education? What was the political basis of his educational convictions?
7. How did Jacksonian democracy encourage the development of public schools?
8. What were the views of Horace Mann? How did he use his position to foster public education?
9. What combination of factors fostered public education in nineteenth century America? What stages did education for blacks go through?
10. What were the circumstances which explain why Booker T. Washington took the position on separation of the races that he did? Do you think his position was necessary or not?
11. What problems did immigration pose for American schools? What support from society did historian Cubberley have for his position on "Americanization" of the immigrant? What criticisms can be directed against his position?
12. How did academies differ from public schools? How did they differ from today's independent schools?
13. What is the significance of the oft-cited Kalamazoo case?
14. What influence did the need for vocational training have on the American public school program?

## INVOLVEMENT

1. To learn more of the tenor of Puritan education, turn to histories of education or collections of early documents to read more about the first learning materials used in American schools.
2. Expand your knowledge of Franklin's ideas through his autobiography and collections of his writings.
3. Expand your knowledge of Jefferson's views through biographies and excerpts from his writings. Study the interrelationship of his educational ideas and his political philosophy.
4. Find out when your college or university was founded. Was it originally a land grant college, a denominational college, state school or other? Report to the class on its background and the place it takes in the history of education.
5. Become more familiar with Horace Mann's contribution through biographies of Mann and books on his educational contributions. Try your hand at using historical sources by finding and reading one of his famous reports to the state on the condition of education.
6. Grow familiar with the lives and accomplishments of nineteenth century Negro leaders. Attempt to understand the total social situation which influenced their convictions and approaches.
7. Trace the development into the twentieth century of ideas such as Cubberley's which attribute inferiority to certain "stocks." What are some of the social consequences in our own times of the continuance of such views?
8. Interview your grandparents concerning their educational backgrounds. What

changes or innovations in education do they remember as significant in their
lives? How do they view education differently from you and your contemporaries?

9. Without indicating the source, try out with friends and family members some of
the educational theories characteristic of an historical figure described in this
chapter. After obtaining reactions, tell the individual with whom you have been
talking the name of the historical figure. Does learning the name affect his
agreement or disagreement with the ideas?

## FURTHER READING

Calhoun, Daniel, ed. *The Educating of Americans.* Boston: Houghton Mifflin, 1969.
A documentary history which includes both major statements of philosophy and
policy and fragmentary records revealing the conditions with which philosophy
and policy try to deal. Highly comprehensive and useful source book in the history of education.

Callahan, Raymond. *Education and the Cult of Efficiency.* Chicago: The University of
Chicago Press, 1962. A classic study of the social forces that have shaped the ad-
ministration of the public schools. Documents the strength of business ideology in
American culture and the weakness and vulnerability of schoolmen.

Good, Harry G. and James D. Teller. *A History of Western Education.* New York: Macmillan, 1969. A comprehensive history of education which includes education in
antiquity, education in the church, adapting education to children, and adapting
education to national aims.

Greer, Colin. *The Great School Legend: A Revisionist Interpretation of American Public
Education.* New York: Basic Books, 1972. Greer attacks as a myth the thesis that
American schools were instrumental in the assimilation of America's immigrants
and in their eventual economic success.

Katz, Michael B. *Class, Bureaucracy, and Schools.* New York: Praeger, 1971. Inadequacies of American urban education and the ineffectiveness of reform as
reported by an author who sees the American educational system as essentially
unchanged since about 1885 despite the prevalent illusion of educational change
in America.

Kneller, George F., ed. *Foundations of Education.* New York: John Wiley & Sons, 1971.
An introduction to ideas and findings in education as perceived by scholars in
several foundations areas—historical, social, philosophical, scientific, structural.

Lawrence, Elizabeth. *The Origins and Growth of Modern Education.* Baltimore, Maryland: Penguin Books, 1970. A comprehensive though brief book on the history of
education from the Greeks into the twentieth century. Stress is placed on the ideas
of outstanding individuals, as viewed by a British educator.

Stephens, W. Richard and William Van Til, eds. *Education in American Life.* Boston:
Houghton Mifflin, 1972. A book of readings on the history of American education intended for high school seniors but also used at the college and university
level. Deals with "European Transplants in Colonial America: 1620–1776; The
Search for the New America: 1776–1900; and Urbanization of American Education: 1900–present."

Wirth, Arthur G. *Education in the Technological Society.* Scranton, Pennsylvania: Intext Educational Publishers, 1972. An account of the development of vocational
education in the early twentieth century and of the controversies which accompanied the movement as reported by a competent historian of education.

## SELECTED AUDIO-VISUAL MATERIALS

*Education for a Free Society* (16 mm film, 29 min., b. & w., NET: Indiana University, 1961).   R. Freeman Butts discusses freedom from constraint; freedom of thought, religion, speech and press; and freedom to make choices and to act on those choices.

*Education in America: The Seventeenth and Eighteenth Centuries* (16 mm film, 16 min., color, Coronet, 1958).   The beginnings of American education are reenacted from the early New England school laws to the Northwest Ordinance. Includes scenes of dame schools, Latin grammar schools, church schools, and pauper schools.

*Education in America: The Nineteenth Century* (16 mm film, 16 min., color, Coronet, 1958).   Discusses development of schools from the Northwest Ordinance to 1900, including westward movement, change to secular education, rise and decline of district schools, struggle for tax support, and contributions of educational pioneers.

*Education in America: Twentieth-Century Developments* (16 mm film, 16 min., color, Coronet, 1958).   Effects of industrial revolution; the influence of Binet, Dewey, Thorndike, and others; junior high school movement; growth of the graduate school; consolidated schools and effects of new court decisions.

*Horace Mann—The Fight for Education* (35 mm filmstrip, 43 frs/record, color, McGraw-Hill, 1968).   Explains how Horace Mann instituted reforms in the educational system that influenced the improvement of education throughout the United States.

*How Technological America Transformed the World* (35 mm filmstrip, 18 filmstrips/records, color, Current Affairs, 1972).   The first American revolution was political; the second was technological and has changed the world. Subtitles are: Colonial Times to Civil War; Civil War to First World War; World War I to Tomorrow.

*Our Schools Have Kept Us Free* (16 mm film, 30 min., color, National Education Association, 1964).   Based on an article of the same title by Henry Steele Commager. Discusses the role of education in helping to shape and preserve democracy in the United States.

*School—Time and Space— A Series* (35 mm filmstrips, 8 filmstrips, color, McGraw-Hill Films, 1970).   Presents the similarities and differences of schools around the world and of schools of yesterday and today.

*Then and Now* (audio tape, 15 min., Indiana University: National Center for Audio Tapes, 1961).   A series of 53 programs illustrating that history is the result of what people have said, done, and thought in the past. Selected Title: Americans Plan for Education—Beginning of Public Education.

# SEVEN

# What is the work of the public schools today?

The past half-century has been a period of quest for more significant and appropriate education. The public schools had been created and their powers extended in earlier periods. The question then became "what now should be the work of public schools in a rapidly changing twentieth century?" Concern shifted to the nature of programs of the public schools.

Urban schools in the early years of the twentieth century were essentially agrarian schools which had grown large. Nineteenth century schools had originally been intended for a relatively homogeneous population. Such schools largely ignored the growth of pluralism in American society as waves of immigrants settled in the large cities. The typical course of study in American high schools in the early twentieth century was oriented toward college preparation. Most colleges stressed the classics, especially the literature of Rome and Greece, so they usually required a mastery of Latin and sometimes Greek. In the twentieth century, high school programs of this type caused thousands of the sons and daughters of the common man and of the "new immigrant" to quit school.

Many people became disenchanted with schools that were insufficiently related to the needs of children and youth. They were also troubled about the lack of attention in schools to the problems of industrial America.

teacher-pupil planning through which young people participated in determining content, methods, and program. Teachers were proud of student activity in self-initiated projects; the focus of instruction moved increasingly from formal subject matter to the self-initiated and self-directed activities of children. Critics, of course, claimed that children were allowed to "run wild."

With worldwide economic depression and the rise of fascism in the 1930s, progressive education became increasingly oriented to social needs and interests. Rather than stressing the importance of child needs alone, progressive schools attempted to include content to help Americans meet urgent and pressing social problems. Consequently, progressive schools of the 1930s included in their programs studies of international relations and alternatives for the American economy.

The issues of secondary education which seemed important to educators in the middle thirties were stated by the Department of Secondary School Principals (later retitled the National Association of Secondary School Principals) of the National Education Association as follows:

1. Shall secondary education be provided at public expense for all normal individuals or for only a limited number?
2. Shall secondary education seek to retain all pupils in school as long as they wish to remain, or shall it transfer them to other agencies under educational supervision when, in the judgment of the school authorities, these agencies promise to serve better the pupils' immediate and probable future needs?
3. Shall secondary education be concerned only with the welfare and progress of the individual, or with these only as they promise to contribute to the welfare and progress of society?
4. Shall secondary education provide a common curriculum for all, or differentiated offerings?
5. Shall secondary education include vocational training or shall it be restricted to general education?
6. Shall secondary education be primarily directed toward preparation for advanced studies or shall it be primarily concerned with the value of its own courses, regardless of a student's future academic career?
7. Shall secondary education accept conventional school subjects as fundamental categories under which school experiences shall be classified and presented to students, or shall it arrange and present experiences in fundamental categories directly related to the performance of such functions of secondary schools in a democracy as increasing the ability and the desire better to meet socio-civic, economic, health, leisure-time, vocational, and pre-professional problems and situations?
8. Shall secondary education present merely organized knowledge, or shall it also assume responsibility for attitudes and ideals?
9. Shall secondary education seek merely the adjustment of students to prevailing social ideals, or shall it seek the reconstruction of society?
10. Granting that education is a "gradual, continuous, unitary process," shall secondary education be presented merely as a phase of such a process, or shall it be

organized as a distinct but closely articulating part of the entire educational
program, with peculiarly emphasized functions of its own?[3]

## The impact of the progressive movement on education was obvious.

### Evaluation of Progressive Education

As progressive education developed, interest in evaluating its outcomes
grew. Consequently, the Progressive Education Association, formed in
1919, appointed a Commission on the Relation of School and College. In
the 1930s, 300 colleges and universities agreed to cooperate in an eight-
year experiment and to release a selected group of secondary schools
from the usual pattern of requirements for college admission. Students
from the progressive high schools would be admitted to college and a
careful evaluation would be made of the success of these students in
college. The resulting study, sometimes called the Eight-Year Study or
the Thirty Schools Study, involved 1,475 matched pairs of students. Each
graduate from the thirty schools was matched with another student in
the same college who had taken the prescribed courses, who had graduated from some school not participating in the study, who had met the
usual entrance requirements, who was of the same age, sex, race, scholastic aptitude scores, home and community background, interests, and
even probable future. The college follow-up found that the graduates of
the thirty schools:

1. Earned a slightly higher total grade average.
2. Earned higher grade averages in all subject fields except foreign language.
3. Specialized in the same academic fields as did the comparison students.
4. Did not differ from the comparison group in the number of times they were placed
   on probation.
5. Received slightly more academic honors in each year.
6. Were more often judged to possess a high degree of intellectual curiosity and
   drive.
7. Were more often judged to be precise, systematic, and objective in their thinking.
8. Were more often judged to have developed clear or well-formulated ideas concerning the meaning of education. . . .
9. More often demonstrated a high degree of resourcefulness in meeting new situations.
10. Did not differ from the comparison group in ability to plan their time effectively.
11. Had about the same problems of adjustment as the comparison group, but
    approached their solutions with greater effectiveness.
12. Participated somewhat more frequently, and more often enjoyed appreciative
    experiences, in the arts.

[3] Department of Secondary Principals of the National Education Association, "The Issues of
Secondary Education," Bulletin No. 19 (Washington, D.C.: The Association, January, 1936).
In later years, the publication of the secondary principals was retitled in accordance with
the new name of the organization, National Association of Secondary School Principals.

13. Participated more in all organized student groups except religious and "service" activities.
14. Earned in each college year a higher percentage of nonacademic honors. . . .
15. Did not differ from the comparison group in the quality of adjustment to their contemporaries.
16. Differed only slightly from the comparison group in the kinds of judgments about their schooling.
17. Had a somewhat better orientation toward the choice of a vocation.
18. Demonstrated a more active concern for what was going on in the world.[4]

## The College Follow-Up Staff said:

Some of the differences were not large, but wherever reported, they were consistent for each class. It is apparent that when one finds even small margins of difference for a number of large groups, the probability greatly increases that the differences cannot be due to chance alone.

It is quite obvious from these data that the Thirty Schools graduates, as a group, have done a somewhat better job than the comparison group whether success is judged by college standards, by the students' contemporaries, or by the individual students.[5]

If the proof of the pudding lies in these groups and a good part of it does, then it follows that the colleges got from these most experimental schools a higher proportion of sound, effective college material than they did from the more conventional schools in similar environments. If colleges want students of sound scholarship with vital interests, students who have developed effective and objective habits of thinking, and who yet maintain a healthy orientation toward their fellows, then they will encourage the already obvious trend away from restrictions which tend to inhibit departures or deviations from the conventional curriculum patterns.[6]

In the 1940s, the Educational Policies Commission of the National Education Association and the American Association of School Administrators proposed better programs for two illustrative communities, which the commission called Farmville and American City. They called for a common learnings course, interdisciplinary in nature, as an important component of secondary education to deal with the major personal and social problems of young people of high school age. The Commission set forth ten imperative needs of youth:

1. All youth need to develop salable skills and those undertakings and attitudes that

[4] Wilford M. Aikin, *The Story of the Eight-Year Study,* vol. 1 in Commission on the Relation of School and College of the Progressive Education Association (ed.), Adventure in American Education Series (New York: Harper and Bros., 1942); Reprinted by permission from *The Story of the Eight-Year Study,* volume 1 of *Adventure in American Education* by Wilford M. Aikin, Copyright, 1942, by McGraw-Hill, Inc., pp. 111–12.
[5] Dean Chamberlin *et al., Did They Succeed in College?* vol. 4, Commission on the Relation of School and College of the Progressive Education Association (ed.), Adventure in American Education Series (New York: Harper and Bros., 1942), p. 112.
[6] *Ibid.,* p. 113.

make the worker an intelligent and productive participant in economic life. To this end, most youth need supervised work experience as well as education in the skills and knowledge of their occupations.

2. All youth need to develop and maintain good health and physical fitness.

3. All youth need to understand the rights and duties of the citizen of a democratic society, and to be diligent and competent in the performance of their obligations as members of the community and citizens of the state and nation.

4. All youth need to understand the significance of the family for the individual and society, and the conditions conducive to successful family life.

5. All youth need to know how to purchase and use goods and services intelligently, understanding both the values received by the consumer and the economic consequences of their acts.

6. All youth need to understand the methods of science, the influence of science on human life, and the main scientific facts concerning the nature of the world and of man.

7. All youth need opportunities to develop their capacities to appreciate beauty in literature, art, music, and nature.

8. All youth need to be able to use their leisure time well and to budget it wisely, balancing activities that yield satisfactions to the individual with those that are socially useful.

9. All youth need to develop respect for other persons, to grow in their insight into ethical values and principles, and to be able to live and work cooperatively with others.

10. All youth need to grow in their ability to think rationally, to express their thoughts clearly, and to read and listen with understanding.[7]

But many high schools disregarded the needs oriented recommendations of *Education for All American Youth* or the proposals of the Progressive Education Association. When the typical high school experimented with the "ten imperative needs," such as the need to be an intelligent consumer, it more often offered an elective course or placed an emphasis on the problem in an established course, rather than creating the interdisciplinary "common learnings" course. Most high schools continued to stress college preparatory programs, supplemented by vocational offerings for the non-college bound.

During World War II, the energies of the nation and school men turned increasingly to the international struggle. Reconstruction of the program of the schools assumed a subordinate position and when it did occur it was often in the interest of meeting wartime demands for manpower and homefront support. The report of the Eight-Year Study was given less attention that it would have been given had it not been published during World War II.

[7] Educational Policies Commission, *Education for All American Youth* (Washington, D.C.: NEA, 1944), pp. 225–226.

## REACTIONS AGAINST PROGRESSIVE EDUCATION

### Right Wing Criticism

Reactionary rightist criticism of the public schools flourished in the early 1950s. Public school education was condemned by some as communistic and socialistic, as godless and atheistic, and as disloyal and unpatriotic. This wave of criticism, coinciding with the late Senator Joseph McCarthy era, represented an educational counterpart to the McCarthyism which accused government employees of being disloyal, liberals of having Communist sympathies, and the United States Army of harboring traitors. The National Education Association was portrayed by some rightists as a part of a Communist conspiracy to take over the country.

A cause célèbre of the period was that of Willard Goslin, an outstanding American educator. Goslin, as superintendent of schools in Pasadena, California, was assailed because of his support for UNESCO, his inclusion of sex education in the curriculum, his concern for Negroes, his advocacy of racial integration, and his support of progressive education. A vigorous reactionary minority forced his resignation.[8]

In attempted responses to criticisms of the public schools, educators faced a familiar dilemma. On the one hand, the public schools belong to the people and should never be exempt from critical examination and appraisal by the people; nor should schoolmen be unduly defensive or smug about claimed achievement for schools. On the other hand, the attacks on the schools were incited and supported by a minority and were manifestly unfair and distorted. Schoolmen had to resist or good school systems would be picked off one by one.

### Academic Criticism

A second major wave of criticism of education came from a quite different source, the academic critics of progressive education. Because this criticism immediately succeeded that of the reactionary right wing, and because the academic critics also singled out progressive education as a foe, some educators mistakenly lumped the two criticisms. Actually, the academic criticism was an expression of an educational counterphilosophy to the progressive education philosophy which had contributed to what historian Cremin called "the transformation of the school."

The academic critics were led by Arthur E. Bestor, a liberal arts professor at the University of Illinois, and by Hyman G. Rickover, an admiral in the United States Navy and the developer of the nuclear-powered submarine. They urged an alternative conception of education. Steadily maintaining that they were supporters and not enemies of public education, the academic critics called for an end to "life adjust-

[8] David Hulburd, *This Happened in Pasadena* (New York: Macmillan, 1951).

ment education" and "life problems in schools." Instead they called for increased emphasis upon the separate disciplines of knowledge. Bestor, a historian, described the social studies as "social stew." He urged the teaching of history, geography, and political science as separate disciplines rather than as taught in interrelationship with each other:

> The "social studies" purported to throw light on contemporary problems, but the course signally failed, for it offered no perspective on the issues it raised, no basis for careful analysis, no encouragement to ordered thinking. There was plenty of discussion, but it was hardly responsible discussion. Quick and superficial opinions, not balanced and critical judgments, were at a premium. Freedom to think was elbowed aside by freedom not to think, and undisguised indoctrination loomed ahead. I am surprised at how accurately we as students appraised the course. I cannot now improve on the nickname we gave it at the time: "social stew."[9]

Bestor generalized his arguments in another statement and referred to all the disciplines:

> What is falsely called "integration" in most secondary schools and many colleges is actually a fallacious but disguised attempt to bypass the stage of analysis entirely . . . the programs themselves, when examined with care, turn out to be schemes for finding a shortcut to intellectual discipline. They propose, contrary to all reason and experience, to train men to perform the culminating acts of thought while skipping all the antecedent steps . . . we must remember . . . that the various disciplines can only be coordinated; they cannot be fused. If a real synthesis of knowledge is to take place, it must take place in the mind of the student. Our responsibility as teachers is to aid him in acquiring a range of intellectual powers—each clear-cut, precise, and controlled—which he can employ in various combinations to solve problems that may never arise in our lifetimes.[10]

Rickover, alarmed at what he saw as the Soviet threat to American military strength, charged that neglect of science and mathematics by the schools had weakened the American capacity to survive in a physically dangerous world:

> . . . the Russians are increasing their engineering and scientific talent faster than we are. Mr. Allen Dulles, director of our Central Intelligence Agency, estimated that between 1950 and 1960 Soviet Russia will have graduated 1,200,000 scientists and engineers, compared with 900,000 in the United States. And by 1960 it is estimated she will have more scientists and engineers than we. Thereafter, the situation will steadily worsen unless we take steps to upgrade mathematics and science teaching in the high schools and increase enrollment in our engineering colleges.[11]

> The greatest mistake a nation can make is to underestimate a potential enemy.

---

[9] Arthur E. Bestor, *The Restoration of Learning* (New York: Alfred A. Knopf, 1955), pp. 142–143.
[10] *Ibid.*, pp. 61–65.
[11] Hyman G. Rickover, *Education and Freedom* (New York: E. P. Dutton, 1959), p. 45.

Special early education programs have attempted to expose the disadvantaged child to more varied experiences.

porting Head Start was that poor children, including many blacks and minority group members, were socially disadvantaged as compared to middle class children because of the lack of opportunities for good audio-lingual development, limited neighborhood and community trips with family members, and few stimulating experiences or materials, such as books and educational toys. A preschool experience, it was urged, would provide disadvantaged children the head start needed so that they might enter the first grade at the same level as middle class children.

The same concept of compensation for social deprivation character-ized such junior and senior high school programs as New York City's Higher Horizons. The idea was to open up greater opportunities for youth in slum areas through increased guidance, remedial programs, parental education, and—the most highly publicized aspect of the pro-grams—trips to historical locations and cultural institutions. For instance, New York City's Higher Horizons students visited Franklin D. Roose-velt's home in Hyde Park, college campuses, Philharmonic concerts, and the Modern Art and Metropolitan museums.

Similarly, at the precollege level, Upward Bound programs were developed as compensatory education for disadvantaged students who required some degree of additional help beyond their high school programs in order to qualify for college entrance. During the summers, such young people attended special high school or college classes, received help from tutors and remedial education specialists, and had such group experiences as trips, living in college dormitories, and so forth.

In addition to many such programs as the above, schools adapted content to the special needs of the culturally deprived students. New textbooks were developed especially at the primary levels to recognize the variety of skin colors of Americans. Some early efforts were rightly dismissed as "color me brown" books—the same textbooks except for darker faces. Increasingly, books adapted to the realities of urban life and the actualities of the black experience were published. Historians rewrote textbooks to include the black experience and to weed out prejudicial statements. By 1972 an AFT publication reported considerable progress in eliminating racism from history textbooks.[18] Progressive education techniques such as planning with students, recognition of learner needs, and attempts to identify and use relevant content came back into vogue as their necessity became apparent, though the term "progressive education" stayed out of style.

### The Controversy over Equal Educational Opportunity

Since the publication of *Equality of Educational Opportunity*[19] in 1966, a study directed by James S. Coleman, the effectiveness of compensatory education has been widely discussed. This massive survey, which came to be known as the Coleman Report, raised substantial questions as to the extent of the contribution of schools to a child's educational performance. The Coleman Report indicated that the most important attribute of the child's performance in school had to do with his own family background. Characteristics of other students in a school also strongly influenced the child's achievement, though not as heavily as the effects of his own family background. For instance, children from working class families gained by going to school with children whose parents had educational backgrounds that were stronger, in the sense that such parents had more schooling, read more, and conversed more. A follow-up study in 1972, *On Equality of Educational Opportunity*, edited by Frederick Mosteller and Daniel Patrick Moynihan, criticized some of the research and analysis in the Coleman Report but found that its conclusions were substantially correct.[20]

[18] Irving Sloan, *The Negro in American History Textbooks,* fourth ed. (Washington, D.C.: American Federation of Teachers, 1972).
[19] James S. Coleman *et al., Equality of Educational Opportunity* (Washington, D.C.: U.S. Office of Education, 1966).
[20] Frederick Mosteller and Daniel Patrick Moynihan (eds.), *On Equality of Educational Opportunity* (New York: Random House, 1972).

In an interview, James S. Coleman was asked, "Then, is it fair to say that peer-group influence and the education of the parents are more important than per-pupil expenditure, teachers, and curriculum?" Coleman responded:

All factors considered, the most important variable—in or out of school—in a child's performance remains his family's educational background. The second most important factor is the educational background, the social-class background, of the families of the children in the school. These two elements are much more important than any physical attributes of the school. . . . a child's learning is a function more of the characteristics of his classmates than of those of the teacher.[21]

In a message to Congress concerning the Equal Educational Opportunities Act of 1972, President Richard M. Nixon said:

For some years now, there has been a running debate about the effectiveness of added spending for programs of compensatory or remedial education. Some have maintained there is virtually no correlation between dollar input and learning output; others have maintained there is a direct correlation; experience has been mixed. . . . While there is a great deal yet to be learned about the design of successful compensatory programs, the experience so far does point in one crucial direction: to the importance of providing sufficiently concentrated funding to establish the educational equivalent of a "critical mass," or threshold level. Where funds have been spread too thinly, they have been wasted or dissipated with little to show for their expenditure. Where they have been concentrated, the results have been frequently encouraging and sometimes dramatic.[22]

A report of the Department of Health, Education, and Welfare, *The Effectiveness of Compensatory Education,* affirmed that compensatory education could be made to work and that the application of concentrated compensatory resources invested in basic learning programs could make successful compensatory education more probable. After reviewing evidence of successful programs in California, Colorado, Connecticut, Rhode Island, and Wisconsin, the report described a national Follow Through evaluation:

The Follow Through evaluation is the most rigorous in design of all evaluations of compensatory education; but it has not been completed. The following are the preliminary conclusions which can be drawn from the data at this time: children receiving compensatory help show very small but consistent improvement in learning compared with matched children without compensatory help; and, the more disadvantaged the children are, the more effective this compensatory help has been in improving their academic performance compared with similar children not receiving any help.[23]

[21] James S. Coleman, "Class Integration—A Fundamental Break With the Past," *Saturday Review of Education* (May 27, 1972), pp. 58–59.
[22] Department of Health, Education, and Welfare, *The Effectiveness of Compensatory Education* (Washington, D.C.: U.S. Government Printing Office, 1972), p. 4.
[23] *Ibid.,* p. 8.

However, the report included "some honest and prudent qualifications which should be attached to these 'yes' answers."[24] The report on the effectiveness of compensatory education then cited evidence against the effectiveness of compensatory education:

The most pessimistic view of compensatory education is that it has not worked and probably cannot be successful with disadvantaged children. The evidence we have just discussed contradicts this totally negative conclusion. Yet there is considerable evidence indicating that many compensatory education programs can be assessed as unsuccessful either because too few children improved their academic performance or the rates of improvement did not exceed that typical for poor children. Both large scale and situational evaluations contain evidence of this kind. . . .

Yet another body of evidence against the effectiveness of compensatory education is the national evaluation of the Head Start program which concluded that full year Head Start programs produced cognitive gains for a small proportion of participants but not for most; and that the gains dissipated rapidly when the children entered normal school programs. This study was a well designed and well implemented one, and its findings should be accepted. We would note, nevertheless, that Head Start is concerned with preschool, rather than school programs and that little is known concerning the extent to which Head Start programs attempted to concentrate on cognitive improvements for the participating children. In addition, the children showing most gains were minority children in cities. The schools which the children entered after Head Start were not necessarily able to provide them with the enriched learning environment needed to preserve the achievement gains; we consider that effective compensatory education will require more than a single year's effort for most disadvantaged children.

The situational evidence against compensatory education is more impressionistic—there are relatively few validated failures of compensatory programs but there are many, many instances where close investigations of claimed success showed that the evidence was lacking or unreliable. Undoubtedly, many specific efforts labeled as compensatory education at all levels of cost and intensity have failed.

The evidence indicating that compensatory education has not worked is, we judge, sobering but not overwhelming, a counsel of caution but not of despair.[25]

The controversy over the effectiveness or ineffectiveness of compensatory education was heightened by the publication in 1972 of *Inequality: A Reassessment of the Effect of Family and Schooling in America* by Christopher Jencks and his associates.[26]

Jencks contended that "None of the evidence we have reviewed suggests that school reform can be expected to bring about significant social changes outside the schools. More specifically, the evidence suggests that equalizing educational opportunity would do very little to

[24] *Ibid.*, p. 5.
[25] *Ibid.*, pp. 8–9.
[26] Christopher Jencks *et al.*, *Inequality: A Reassessment of the Effect of Family and Schooling in America* (New York: Basic Books, 1972).

make adults more equal. . . . Furthermore, the experience of the past 25 years suggests that even fairly substantial reductions in the range of educational attainments do not appreciably reduce economic inequality among adults. . . . The evidence suggests . . . that educational compensation is usually of marginal value to the recipients."[27]

Jencks believed that children were more influenced by what happened at home than by what happened in the schools; that curriculum revision and pupil reassignment were less important than the relationships between teachers and pupils; that even when schools did influence children the results were not likely to continue into the adult years. To Jencks, "Our research suggests . . . that the character of a school's output depends largely on a single input, namely the characteristics of the entering children. Everything else—the school budget, its policies, the characteristics of the teachers—is either secondary or completely irrelevant."[28] In an article on *Inequality*, Bane and Jencks said:

> The main policy implication of these findings is that although school reform is important for improving the lives of children, schools cannot contribute significantly to adult equality. If we want economic equality in our society, we will have to get it by changing our economic institutions, not by changing the schools.[29]

Specifically, *Inequality* concluded:

> In America, as elsewhere, the general trend over the past 200 years has been toward equality. In the economic realm, however, the contribution of public policy to this drift has been slight. As long as egalitarians assume that public policy cannot contribute to economic equality directly but must proceed by ingenious manipulations of marginal institutions like the schools, progress will remain glacial. If we want to move beyond the tradition, we will have to establish political control over the economic institutions that shape our society. This is what other countries usually call socialism. Anything less will end in the same disappointment as the reforms of the 1960s.[30]

Jencks' conclusions stirred furious debate among social scientists, research scholars, and educators. In 1973, the annual meeting of the American Educational Research Association vigorously discussed Jencks' findings. The American Association of School Administrators released a pamphlet called "Christopher Jencks in Perspective." Most of the *Harvard Educational Review* for February, 1973 was devoted to attacks (and rebuttals) on Jencks' thesis. Conservative forces cited his findings as a support in their campaigns to reduce school appropriations.

[27] *Ibid.*, p. 255.
[28] *Ibid.*, p. 256.
[29] Mary Jo Bane and Christopher Jencks, "The Schools and Equal Opportunity," *Saturday Review of Education* (Sept. 16, 1972), p. 38.
[30] Jencks *et al.*, p. 265.

## SOME PROBLEMS OF AMERICAN PUBLIC EDUCATION

A fair analysis requires the recognition that in recent years some Americans have concluded that universal public education has failed in several areas.[31] It has not yet provided a relevant education for blacks, who experienced centuries of slavery followed by decades of enforced segregation. It has failed the children of many poor Americans, whatever their skin color. It has not produced the social understandings which Jefferson said were requisite for an educated citizenry. It has not solved the social and personal problems which Horace Mann confidently anticipated that it would soon conquer. In the 1970s public education, because of such failures, is under attack by many who judge it inadequate.

Criticisms of big city schools are particularly vigorous. Some blacks, despairing of help from the entrenched bureaucracies of large public school systems, call for decentralized education in large cities. They favor greater community control of schools in black ghettos. They believe that black schools manned by black teachers would be superior to the present centralized city systems largely controlled and staffed by whites. Those both black and white who disagree see this course as the road back to segregation; they point out that some whites use decentralization to maintain segregated white schools.

The viewpoint of militant blacks is still within the tradition of support for public education. Indeed, it may be argued that the contemporary black demands for black community control are simply an extension of Jefferson's decentralization concept. But whether decentralization is the best way to achieve good education in a nation characterized by increasing centralization in government is difficult to determine.

### Vouchers

Some critics of public education express the belief that rather than universal tax-supported education, individuals should be given a sum for education to spend as they see fit, in public, private, or parochial schools. Competition among such schools, accompanied by accountability through rigorous appraisal of results, would be an improvement in education, it is argued. To those who oppose this, the danger of throwing out the baby with the bath seems imminent.

Two years before his study, *Inequality,* described above, Christopher Jencks of Harvard University proposed giving parents money for schooling by way of educational vouchers, and the U.S. Office of Economic Opportunity agreed to support experimentation with "tickets to schools." According to Jencks' proposal, parents ought to choose between competing schools; the schools must be open to all applicants and must accept the voucher as full payment for the cost of a young

[31] See Henry J. Perkinson, *The Imperfect Panacea: American Faith in Education, 1865–1965* (New York: Random, 1968).

person's education. Private and religious schools would be included as well as public schools. Schools would inform parents of alternative programs so that parents might decide wisely. The value of the vouchers would be supplemented for the poor so that schools could develop special programs for the disadvantaged. An independent Education Voucher Agency would enforce the regulations and administer the program.

Opponents of the Jencks plan quarreled with such aspects as parents, not educators, choosing educational programs for children. They opposed government funds going to private and parochial schools as well as public schools, and the replacement of school boards by the new Education Voucher Agency. The voucher plan was especially criticized by those who called for greater investment in public school education in the slums and the ghettos of the inner cities. The president of the American Federation of Teachers warned that the voucher plan would bring more problems than it would solve, including "hucksterism" as competing schools attempted to sell parents on their peculiar merits. The chairman of a commission on law and social action of the American Jewish Congress saw the plan as a disaster for the country because of the possible proliferation of hundreds of school systems segregated on the basis of religion.[32]

In the fall of 1972 a feasibility study of the use of vouchers began in the Alum Rock School District of San Jose, California, a district in which half the families speak Spanish. However, only public school programs, not nonpublic, were involved, and the local board of education retained control, though it was advised by a committee composed of parents. Parents chose between competing school programs rather than competing schools. However, as in the original Jencks plan, the programs were open to all who applied, parents were informed of possible choices, and a supplement was added to the vouchers of poor children.

Both conventional schools and innovative schools were available to parents at Alum Rock. A larger number of parents than expected, approximately 60 percent, chose nontraditional programs with such titles as Open-Activity Center, Individualized Learning, Continuous Progress Nongraded, Daily Living School, School 2000, and school programs stressing one particular subject area such as Fine Arts—Creative Expression, Fine Arts and Creative Arts, Math—Science, Cultural Arts, and Multicultural.[33]

### Performance Contracting

Another approach to meeting the current problems of American public education is performance contracting. In performance contracting,

---

[32] *Education, U.S.A.* (July 1, 1970), p. 25.
[33] James A. Mecklenburger, "Vouchers at Alum Rock," *Phi Delta Kappan* (September 1972), pp. 23–26.

a company enters into an agreement with a school system to improve the performance of students in such basic skills as reading or mathematics. The company as contractor specifies set amounts of improvement that are to be achieved. The company entering into the contract is paid according to the degree of its success. If the contractor brings the students' performance up to the level the contractor has specified in advance, the company makes a profit. If the contractor does not bring the students' performance up to the proposed level, the company does not get paid. General guidelines are established by the school board involved. Within these guidelines, the company uses whatever approaches it believes to be most effective. The companies involved usually use particular instructional techniques in which they have faith, develop incentive systems for motivation and reward, and employ a variety of audio-visual and technological teaching aids. In using such approaches, the company usually has a high degree of flexibility.

In the late 1960s and early 1970s performance contracting boomed. The target of the projects was often better education for disadvantaged young people. The hope of many performance contractors was to bring poor children to the level of achievement, especially in basic skills, of children from homes with greater economic advantages. Along with its advocates, performance contracting had its critics, who did not approve of public school programs being turned over to business groups, who criticized reliance in performance contracting on the reinforcement theory of the behaviorists, and who were dubious of the desirability of competitive incentives and rewards for students such as trading stamps and free recreational time.

The Office of Economic Opportunity of the federal government, which had seen promise in performance contracting, sponsored an evaluation of many performance contracts. In 1972, the Office of Economic Opportunity reported on the outcome in *An Experiment in Performance Contracting: Summary of Preliminary Results*. The OEO reported:

> In half of the 10 cases, there was no difference at all between the gains of the experimental and control groups. In four of the cases, there was a difference of only one-tenth of a grade level and in only one case was there a difference of as much as two-tenths of a grade level. These overall differences are so slight that we can conclude that performance contracting was no more effective in either reading or math than the traditional classroom methods of instruction.[34]

The Office of Economic Opportunity added:

> Not only did both groups do equally poorly in terms of overall averages, but also these averages were very nearly the same in each grade, in each subject, for the best

[34] Office of Economic Opportunity, *An Experiment in Performance Contracting: Summary of Preliminary Results,* OEO pamphlet 3400-5 (Washington, D.C.: Office of Economic Opportunity, February 1972), p. 17.

education for all is essential to democracy. Thus, to many prospective educators, American public education, with all its difficulties and complexities, is the place where the action truly is. It is the opportunity to contribute to the American dream through the education of all, regardless of race, creed, or class; it is the opportunity to help make a better world.

Doubters point out that, given our social structures, education in public schools is often racially segregated, and sometimes exclusive and socially classified. As evidence they point to both ghetto and homogenized suburban schools. Others are appalled by the extent of the challenge of educating the disadvantaged and underprivileged. To them, the American dream of a strong public school system for all is an unattainable dream. Others think that schools cannot contribute much to equal educational opportunity; to them, the school is a marginal and ineffective institution in the struggle for equality.

Thus the question of whether or not to teach in the public school system eventually comes down to the matter of one's basic philosophy and aspirations and beliefs.

## DISCUSSION

1. How did the progressive movement in education come about? Did John Dewey "invent" progressive education?
2. What is the essential meaning of a "child-centered school"? What weaknesses or strengths do you see in such a school program?
3. Why did an increasing social orientation come into the progressive education movement? Do you see any possible strengths or weaknesses in a socially oriented school program?
4. What were the fundamental findings of the Thirty Schools Study? What are the implications of such findings for college entrance? For school programs? For controversies on education? Why was so little attention paid to the Thirty Schools Study after it was completed?
5. How did the report of the Educational Policies Commission on ten imperative needs of youth reflect the emphases of the progressive education movement?
6. Why do most high schools continue to stress separate subject college preparatory programs rather than create the interdisciplinary "common learnings" course?
7. What was the nature of right wing criticism of public schools in the 1950s? What dilemmas did educators face in attempting to respond to such criticism?
8. How did the academic criticism of education in the 1950s differ from right wing criticism? What did the two have in common?
9. What was Arthur E. Bestor's fundamental criticism of progressive education? How is this similar to or different from Admiral Hyman G. Rickover's?
10. What social events in America and the world contributed to the reconstruction of certain disciplines in American schools during the 1950s?
11. How did the scholars perceive their task of reconstructing the disciplines? How did they proceed? What were some of their triumphs and perplexities?

12. What accounts for the development of educational concern for the culturally disadvantaged? What legislative enactments supported programs for the disadvantaged?

13. So far, how successful has the campaign against culturally disadvantaged backgrounds been? Which programs are currently receiving support? Which programs seem to be minimized today?

14. What is the nature of the debate over the effectiveness of compensatory education and the achievement of equal educational opportunity? What position did James S. Coleman take? The Nixon Administration? Christopher Jencks and his associates in *Inequality*? What do you think of the view that if we want economic equality in our society we will have to get it by changing our economic institutions, not by changing our schools?

15. Some critics say that American education is failing. In what respect? Do you agree?

16. What proposals are currently being made for the improvement of education in large cities?

17. What are the pros and cons of the voucher plan? How would it affect American public education and financial support for public education? How would it affect parochial schools? Segregated schools? Independent schools? Is the Alum Rock project a true test of the feasibility of the voucher plan?

18. What are the arguments for and against performance contracting? What does the evidence currently indicate as to the success of performance contracting?

19. What have been the latest Supreme Court rulings involving education? What has been the latest legislation enacted that affects education?

20. What advantages and disadvantages can you see in teaching in the American public school system? How might a decision to teach or not to teach in the public schools be related to one's philosophy of life? Philosophy of education? View of the potentiality and effectiveness of public schools?

## INVOLVEMENT

1. Learn which school available to you for a visit is popularly regarded as the "best" school in the community or region. Visit the school to observe whether it has characteristics of what has been termed progressive education. In what ways does it differ from what you understand progressive education to be? Do you see evidence of child-centering? Do you see evidence of social orientation?

2. Seek out the reports of the Thirty Schools Study. Through the indexes to the volumes, locate the names of schools nearest to your own geographical situation. Read about these schools and compare or contrast their present programs with their programs in the past.

3. Interview three persons who were young adults during the depression years (1929–1935). Do they see the depression as related to educational failures? As a force for change in the pattern of public education?

4. From news weeklies, and reports by educational journals, determine what are the current criticisms of schools by right wing forces in America; left wing forces. To what extent are the criticisms similar to those of the 1950s?

5. Review your own educational experience to determine whether the projects that followed the launching of Sputnik influenced your own high school experiences

and education. In retrospect how do you see the importance and significance of these projects? Do you have any criticisms of them?

6. Visit some outstanding contemporary compensatory programs for the disadvantaged. After asking questions of teachers and sponsors, reach some tentative conclusions on their influence and success. (*Caution:* quick conclusions may be inaccurate.)

7. Visit an Upward Bound program for high school students and a Head Start program for young children. What do they have in common and how do they differ?

8. Obtain recent figures for unemployment and for persons on welfare rolls in the United States. Look carefully at percentages, at trends. Do these comparisons lead you to form any theories about the needs of people today?

9. Interview the director of the local unemployment services to obtain his view on the success or failure of the Manpower Development and Training Act and its programs to train unemployed youth and functional illiterates.

10. Find out whether any schools in your area are experimenting with the voucher plan, performance contracting, etc. If so, plan an individual or group visit.

11. Draw up your own bill of particulars in support of American public education and in criticism of American public education. Venture possible improvements.

12. Foster a debate on whether or not to teach in American public schools.

## FURTHER READING

Fantini, Mario D. *The Reform of Urban Schools.* Washington, D.C.: National Education Association, 1970.   An analysis of the urban crisis accompanied by concrete suggestions for renewing urban education through what Fantini calls public-schools-of-choice to open up a range of educational opportunity and choices.

Katz, Michael B. *School Reform: Past and Present.* Boston: Little, Brown, 1971. Readings on recurring issues in education from a point of view highly critical of schools written in the hope of providing a liberating perspective. Deals with the public school and the city, the uses of pedagogy, black education in the urban North, and the triumph of bureaucracy in urban education.

La Noue, George R., ed. *Educational Vouchers: Concepts and Controversies.* New York: Teachers College Press, Teachers College, Columbia University, 1972. Anthology on the pro and con of vouchers including varied proposals, court decisions, and Congressional responses.

Leight, Robert L., ed. *Philosophers Speak on Accountability in Education.* Danville, Illinois: Interstate Printers & Publishers, 1973.   Essays by Maxine Greene, John Stoops, Martin Levit, Alice Rinehart, Beatrice Sarlos, and Donald Gertenback to clarify the dimensions of educational accountability.

McClure, Robert M., ed. *The Curriculum: Retrospect and Prospect.* Chicago: National Society for the Study of Education, 1971.   An important yearbook by able scholars who survey twentieth century developments in the curriculum, including the progressive movement, and who look ahead to possible developments in the curriculum of American schools.

Mecklenburger, James A. and Richard W. Hostrop, eds. *Education Vouchers: From Theory to Alum Rock.* Homewood, Ill.: ETC Publications, 1972.   A collection of articles and policy statements on the voucher plan, including the experiment at Alum Rock.

Ozmon, Howard. *Contemporary Critics of Education*. Danville, Illinois: Interstate Printers & Publishers, 1970. A variety of contemporary writers who criticize education from their varying perspectives. Included are Arthur E. Bestor, Jerome S. Bruner, Paul Goodman, A. S. Neill, H. G. Rickover, and others.

Spring, Joel H. *Education and the Rise of the Corporate State*. Boston: Beacon Press, 1972. Spring's thesis is that the public schools were used by the economic elite to support economic efficiency and social control. He suggests that the schools have done little to meet the real human needs of the majority.

Squire, James R., ed. *A New Look At Progressive Education*. Washington, D.C.: Association for Supervision and Curriculum Development, 1972. A yearbook of the Association for Supervision and Curriculum Development which reviews major ideas and efforts associated with progressive education and relates these to today's efforts to reform American education. The implications of progressive education for today's schools are emphasized by the curriculum-oriented chapter authors. The major parts of the yearbook stress the child, the classroom, the curriculum, and school in society.

## SELECTED AUDIO-VISUAL MATERIALS

*All in a Lifetime* (16 mm film, 29 min., b. & w., National Education Association, 1962). Shows the changes in the public schools during the last 60 years. Discusses why the one-room school cannot meet the educational needs of contemporary children.

*Children Without* (16 mm film, 29 min., b. & w., National Education Association, 1964). Shows how a school in an economically substandard urban area attempts to solve the educational problems of culturally deprived children.

*Education as Intellectual Discipline* (16 mm film, 29 min., b. & w., NET: Indiana University, 1961). Arthur E. Bestor comments on the importance of a disciplined mind and outlines the methods of obtaining intellectual discipline in a democratic society.

*Education: The Public Schools* (16 mm film, 29 min., b. & w., NET: Indiana University, 1961). Indicates the forces which have influenced the form of our public schools. Includes population mobility, increased number of students in the past two decades, new educational theories, and increased government participation.

*The Negro and the American Promise* (16 mm film, 60 min., b. & w., NET: Indiana University, 196-). Presents Kenneth Clark interviewing James Baldwin, Martin Luther King, Jr., and Malcolm X.

*Operation Head Start* (16 mm film, 16 min., b. & w., Bailey Film Associates, 1966). Tells the story of the home and classroom experiences of an underprivileged American child who is participating in the Head Start program.

*Operation Head Start* (16 mm film, 29 min., b. & w., USOEO: U.S. National Audiovisual Center, 1966). Shows the need for the Head Start project, various facets of the program, and its policies as observed in a variety of localities. Includes scenes of the poverty existing in urban and rural ghettos.

*Should You Go to College?* (35 mm filmstrip, 80 frs/record, color, Guidance Associates, 196-). Compares college with its alternatives—trade schools, technical institutes, and nonspecialized occupations.

*Teaching the Disadvantaged* (35 mm filmstrip, 52 frs/record, color, National Education Association, 1967). Describes the characteristics of disadvantaged children and discusses their learning handicaps. Contrasts the teaching methods by which they may be reached with those which are ineffective, and points out some of the problems of each age group.

*Thurgood Marshall — Mr. Civil Rights* (35 mm filmstrip, 45 frs/captions, color, Bailey Film Associates, 1967). Portrays Thurgood Marshall's leadership in the civil rights movement. Shows how he challenged the "separate but equal" doctrine. Deals with the Supreme Court decision to integrate all public schools.

*Worlds Apart* (16 mm film, 16 min., b. & w., Anti-Defamation League of B'nai B'rith, 196–). Demonstrates techniques for developing a sense of self-esteem, for teaching concept formation and language efficiency. Techniques bridge the gap between the ghetto and the "all-white world" to which the child cannot relate.

# EIGHT

# What are the roles of independent and parochial schools?

Though the large majority of American teachers teach in public schools, still other forms of organization are the private schools (or, to use the phrase which private school educators think more appropriate, "independent schools"), and church systems of education, such as maintained by the Roman Catholic church, commonly called parochial schools. Both of these are nonpublic.

Both independent and parochial schools which meet the legal requirements of a state, when such requirements exist, have been adjudged legal alternatives to public schools. In other words, approved independent and parochial schools are deemed able to achieve the same goals that public schools achieve while accomplishing their own characteristic objectives. This principle was confirmed by the United States Supreme Court in the 1925 Oregon Decision. An Oregon law passed in 1922 required all normal children between eight and sixteen years of age who had not completed the eighth grade to attend the public schools. Both a church school and a nonsectarian military academy challenged the law. The court ruled:

We think it entirely plain that the Act of 1922 unreasonably interferes with the liberty of parents and guardians to direct the upbringing and education of children under their control. . . . The fundamental theory of liberty upon which all governments in this Union repose excludes any general power of the State to standardize its children by forcing them to accept instruction from public teachers only. The child is not the mere creature of the State; those who nurture him and direct his destiny have the right, coupled with the high duty, to recognize and prepare him for additional obligations.[1]

## INDEPENDENT SCHOOLS

The private or independent school is a school open to selected students, rather than a school committed to a public responsibility for educating children in a particular neighborhood or community. Independent schools are supported primarily by tuition and by philanthropic funds. Yet such private schools are not completely independent of government control or supervision; they are subject to whatever state controls exist. They are also subject to whatever community controls are established; for instance, a headmaster and a board of trustees cannot conduct a school in a firetrap. A useful definition is supplied by an official of the National Association of Independent Schools:

> What is an independent school? In contrast to the public school, it is supported chiefly by nonpublic funds, and it is controlled by a nonpublic body, usually a board of trustees. It is relatively independent of state control; conditions and regulations vary from state to state, but as a general rule it has considerable freedom to set its own standards and curriculum, admit and dismiss students, and hire and dismiss teachers, without state supervision or control. It is free, legally, to incorporate religious teaching in its curriculum, and free, practically, to encourage discussion of controversial topics. Of course, it must meet health, fire, and safety standards, and the state has ultimate control in the equivalency laws.[2]

The independent school is usually nonsectarian, but a degree of church affiliation occasionally exists. Whenever the independent school's board is essentially the controlling force and control by the church is actually or relatively nonexistent, as in the case of many Friends and Episcopal schools, the school is usually regarded as an independent school. When a school is essentially under the control of a central church authority, as have been Roman Catholic parochial schools, it is not usually regarded as in the independent category. With the growth of lay boards at the parish level, some educators regard Roman Catholic parochial schools today as independent schools: i.e., open to selected students and supported by tuition and philanthropy. This issue will be resolved in time; meanwhile, because of their size and scope, private "independent" schools and Roman Catholic parochial schools will be considered separately in this chapter.

---

[1] Pierce, Governor of Oregon *et al.* v. Society of Sisters; and Pierce, Governor of Oregon *et al.* v. Hill Military Academy, Appeals from the District Court of the United States for the District of Oregon, Nos. 583, 584. Argued March 16, 17, 1925; decided June 1, 1925.
[2] Francis Parkman, "Independent Schools," in American Educational Research Association, *Encyclopedia of Educational Research,* 4th ed. (New York: Macmillan, 1969), p. 633. Copyright © 1969 by American Educational Research Association.

Some states make no real provision for regulation, some have regulations ranging from moderate to demanding, and some states regulate only some phase of the operation of independent schools, such as curriculum, teaching methods, and ratio of pupils to teachers. Wide variation also exists in accreditation; some independent schools comply with all provisions for accreditation and others refuse to do so in the interest of freedom in the employment of teachers regardless of their professional training.

### The Original Private Independent Schools

Private independent schools have a long lineage. Private education antedates public education; the first schools established in centers of civilizations such as ancient Egypt or classical Greece were private schools. The Egyptians had schools for royal children in early times, and later such schools trained young men to conduct government. The Greeks did not have free schools, but the son of an Athenian citizen began attending a private school at the age of seven. He was taught reading, writing, literature, and arithmetic; then he went to another school for physical training. At sixteen, he entered the "gymnasium," a state school, and learned the duties of citizenship. The famed philosophers had no classrooms; they gathered students around them on tree-shaded athletic grounds. Plato met his pupils in the field called the Academy, and Aristotle held sessions with his students in the Lyceum. Later, the Romans founded schools on the Greek pattern.[3]

When European universities arose, Latin was the language of the scholars. So Latin schools were established to prepare young scholars for the universities. By the fourteenth century, some cities established schools for the teaching of arithmetic, reading, and writing of the common speech rather than of Latin, and for teaching other subjects of practical value to merchants and traders.

As Europe moved from medievalism, when education was a church function, into the modern world, private education became a part of the home; aristocratic families employed tutors or teachers to instruct young family members. In time education moved from a room within a family home to a building or cluster of buildings termed a school. Great Britain developed its famous private schools in which generations of British leaders were educated. Eton College, largest and most famous of the English private schools, was founded by King Henry VI in 1440; Harrow was established in 1571. Such schools were called by the British "public schools," a phrase baffling to the American ear and requiring reverse translation, since in our terms these schools are private.

[3] For a broader, more detailed discussion, see Frederick A. G. Beck, *Greek Education: 450–350 B.C.* (New York: Barnes and Noble, 1964).

Phillips Exeter Academy, First Academy Building, restored.

### Private Independent Schools in America

The American colonies followed the pattern of private education. "Dame schools" were first taught by housewives in their own homes in exchange for payment by their students' families. Later, early American schoolmasters conducted private schools in school buildings.

Some independent schools, still existent, date from the seventeenth century. They include the Roxbury Latin School in Massachusetts (1645), the Collegiate School in New York City (1638), the Hopkins Grammar School in New Haven, Connecticut (1660), and the William Penn Charter School in Philadelphia (1689).[4]

So America, too, developed outstanding private schools, which specialized in preparing young men for entry into such colleges as Harvard, Yale, and Princeton as part of the education of a young elite who were to become American leaders. The Phillips Academy in Andover, Massachusetts, for example, was opened in 1778 and chartered in 1780 by Samuel Phillips, a state senator from Massachusetts. The school, often called Andover or Phillips Andover, is the oldest incorporated academy in America. The Phillips Exeter Academy was chartered in 1781 and

[4] Parkman, p. 634.

opened in 1783 by John Phillips, an uncle of Samuel Phillips and a provider of financial backing to both schools. Academies flourished in the mid nineteenth century when more than 250,000 pupils were enrolled in 6,000 academies.[5]

Today private independent education is a minority segment of the total American educational enterprise. After pointing out that the large majority of nonpublic schools in the mid sixties were Roman Catholic parochial schools, Parkman said in 1969, "The remainder comprises some 1,000 non-church related and 2,900 church related elementary schools with about 400,000 students and in the secondary area about 1,500 schools (800 nonsectarian, 700 church related) with nearly 200,000 students. According to our definition, not all of these schools can be counted as truly independent schools but certainly a large part of them can be. Over 90 percent are nonprofit schools."[6]

By contrast, in 1970 enrollment in Catholic elementary schools was 3,359,000 and in Catholic secondary schools 1,008,000, a total of 4,367,000. Enrollment in public elementary schools was 30,001,000 and in public secondary schools 13,545,000, a total of 43,546,000.[7]

In 1972 *Newsweek* reported that in the previous two years, enrollments declined by about 11 percent in military schools, 10 percent in girls' boarding schools, and 4 percent in boys' boarding schools.[8] As a result, some long-established independent schools have closed and others are becoming coeducational. In the 1972–73 school year, after three years of decline, there was an upturn in enrollment.

There is also a decline in that type of private school which recently was created in some states to maintain segregation. These so-called "instant academies" often played on the fears and prejudices of white parents who enrolled their children. In situations in which desegregation of public schools was successful, the influence of the quickly-created segregated private schools for whites waned. In 1973 the U.S. Supreme Court, in an unanimous decision, prohibited state distribution of textbooks to private segregated schools in Mississippi.

In the 1973 meeting of the National Association of Independent Schools, stress was placed on the need to increase minority group enrollment which is only approximately 5% in independent schools, on the desirability of financial relief for middle income families, and on the expansion of the open classroom concept. In his inaugural address in 1972 at Phillips Academy in Andover, Massachusetts, headmaster Theodore R. Sizer called on schools such as his to collaborate closely with the public schools so that many students might have a residential experience, whether for months or years, in private boarding schools.

[5] *Ibid.*
[6] *Ibid.*
[7] U.S. Bureau of the Census, *Statistical Abstract of the United States, 1972*, 93rd Edition (Washington, D.C.: U.S. Government Printing Office, 1972), pp. 106, 121.
[8] "Can Prep Schools Survive?" *Newsweek* (January 31, 1972), p. 45.

## Alternative or Free Schools

A new development in the private sector of American education is the "alternative" or "free" or "innovative" school, developed to provide alternatives to the restrictiveness of some public schools. In March 1970, Donald W. Robinson reported that over 700 alternative schools had been founded during the past three years, about half of them in the inner cities.[9] Many alternative schools are child-centered and youth-centered. Harvey Haber, founder of the New Schools Exchange, estimated the average life of a new school at eighteen months, after which it may die completely, merge with another school, or alter its course so severely as to cease to be a radically innovative institution.[10]

In the late 1960s and early 1970s a variety of alternative schools proliferated. Some were inner city schools for black children; others were situated in suburbs and rural areas and were attended largely by white children and youth. Some alternative schools were designed to bring young people together in integrated, multicultural experiences. Alternative schools grew up in abandoned city stores, in barns or former churches in the open country, in the homes of teachers or parental enthusiasts, among other settings.

Varied interpretations of educational freedom and of humanizing education developed. Some alternative schools stressed highly individualized tutorial work in the classrooms. Others put heavy emphasis upon social travel or on learning at the side of adults in community enterprises. Some emphasized projects such as rebuilding the school or constructing a geodesic dome for faculty and student living quarters or to house classes. Some stressed the concerns of particular minority groups or sponsoring communes. As Jonathan Kozol put it,

Free schools at the present moment cover the whole range of beliefs from the Third World Institute of all black kids and all black teachers, operated by a group of revolutionary leaders wearing military jackets, boots, and black berets, to a segregated Summerhill out in the woods of western Massachusetts offering "freedom" of a rather different kind and charging something like $2,000 or $3,000 yearly for it. But free schools that I care most about stand somewhere in between, though surely closer to the first than to the second.[11]

[9] Donald W. Robinson, "'Alternative Schools': Challenge to Traditional Education," *Phi Delta Kappan* (March 1970), p. 374.
[10] *Ibid.*, p. 375. New Schools Exchange at 301 East Canyon Perdido, Santa Barbara, California, lists jobs in alternative schools. Teacher Drop-Out Center, Box 521, Amherst, Massachusetts, publishes a directory of private and public alternative schools as well as a monthly newsletter. Educational Alternatives Project, School of Education, Indiana University, Bloomington, Indiana 47401, publishes a newsletter that focuses on the development of options (alternative schools) in *public* education.
[11] Jonathan Kozol, "Free Schools: A Time for Candor," *Saturday Review of Education* (March 4, 1972), p. 51.

The kinds of free schools Kozol supports are:

(1) outside the public education apparatus, (2) outside the white man's counter-culture, (3) inside the cities, (4) in direct contact with the needs and urgencies of those among the poor, the black, the dispossessed, who have been the most clearly victimized by public education, (5) as small, "decentralized" and "localized" as we can manage, (6) as little publicized as possible.[12]

Just as John Dewey in 1938 thought it necessary to write *Experience and Education* to criticize and caution against some undesirable trends in progressive education, Jonathan Kozol in 1972 wrote *Free Schools*, which questions trends and tendencies in some of the alternative or free schools.[13]

Kozol is particularly concerned about "the paralyzing inhibition about the functions of the teacher." He believes the teachers must provide adult direction and not make the mistake of reducing themselves to "ethical and pedagogical neuters." He believes that "hard skills" must be taught and that power can be gained by the poor and the minorities only through acquiring complex and intricate knowledge.

"Wow!" I hear some of these Free School people say. "We made an Iroquois canoe out of an oak log!" Nobody, however, needs an Iroquois canoe. Even Iroquois do not. The Iroquois can buy aluminum canoes if they should really need them. They don't, however. What they need are doctors, lawyers, teachers, organizers, labor leaders.[14]

### Whether or Not to Teach in Private Independent Schools

A new teacher contemplating whether or not to teach in the private schools should take into account some of the advantages and disadvantages. The arguments below apply to most long-established private independent schools; some, but not all, apply to alternative schools too.

A strong argument for teaching in a private independent school is the freedom to experiment, released from some of the imputed restrictions characteristic of public school education. Classes are frequently small; there is a low pupil-teacher ratio. Independent schools, it is sometimes said, are free from the petty hobbles placed on teachers by the public school bureaucracy, from the restrictions of conformity-centered public educators, from the system-wide homogeneity of public schools. Under creative leadership, the private school teacher is free to innovate and as Ralph Waldo Emerson put it, "to do his thing." In such circumstances, the only test is whether the teacher achieves educational results. For instance, approximately half of the schools in the Progressive Education Association's Eight-Year Study were independent. Independent schools fostered the advanced placement programs of the 1950s and 1960s.

[12] Jonathan Kozol, *Free Schools* (Boston: Houghton Mifflin, 1972), p. 16.
[13] *Ibid.*
[14] *Ibid.*, p. 59.

But the skeptic with a counter argument quickly points out that the independent school teacher may have merely traded one master for another. Upper and upper middle class parents are notoriously concerned about their children's entrance into the best colleges. They are apt to throw their weight in conservative rather than experimental directions. Most long-established independent schools are educationally conservative and oriented to close conformity to college entrance requirements, rather than progressive or experimental in approaches. Headmasters and principals, it is said, have been known to sacrifice their principles to the practical goal of parental support manifested by the continuing payment of tuition. So the supposed freedom from restrictions and for experimentation may be illusory. The skeptic adds that independent school teachers are seldom tightly organized in a teachers' union or educational association and must pay for their supposed individualism by acceptance of lower salaries and even more administrative controls than public school teachers.

Controversy also exists as to the social class biases of independent schools. Parkman of the National Association of Independent Schools, after citing the volume of scholarships granted by private schools, defends independent schools against "misconceptions held by the public":

Many people cherish one or another (and some people all) of the following illusions: that independent schools are run for somebody's private gain, that they are all richly endowed, that they are "exclusive," that they are only for the rich and/or for disciplinary cases, that children from poor families cannot gain admission, that attendance at an independent school guarantees admission to highly selective colleges, that the New England boarding school is typical of all independent schools.[15]

An opposing view frequently advanced against teaching in independent schools is that independent schools (but usually not alternative or free schools) are essentially "class" institutions in which education has been and remains, despite scholarships, essentially for the upper and upper middle classes. In the independent school the new teacher essentially works with an American elite, which is sometimes conscious of being an elite and in which social snobbery often exists. Critics say that the independent private schools evade the social challenge of public education to educate the children of the common people that they may improve the quality of their lives.

Some new teachers teach in private independent schools precisely because they want to teach upper income children who accept upper or middle class values, who may not present as many discipline problems, and who are culturally advantaged. Such a teaching situation is precisely what some new teachers prefer, even though their more socially mo-

---

[15] Parkman, p. 637.

tivated colleagues may regard them as "copping out" on the tougher responsibilities.

An interesting footnote to the matter is provided by the junior and senior high school dissent of the late 1960s, which was led by upper middle class youth. In the 1970s will the new teacher who prefers the private independent school, or his public school counterpart who prefers the upper class suburbs, be able to escape student anger and hostility through his choice of a "privileged" setting?

## PAROCHIAL EDUCATION

Several religious groups have developed their own schools in America, among them the Lutherans and the Jews. But by far the largest of the private religion related school systems is that of the Roman Catholic Church. Consequently, only the Catholic educational system is treated here. Roman Catholic schools represent the second major type of school system in the United States in size.

Catholic schools were established to provide for the religious formation of the young. As early as 1606, Franciscan missionaries established a short-lived school in St. Augustine, Florida. In the nineteenth century, Catholic schools were created in response to both the secular theory of the public schools and the religious practices of Protestant Christianity—such as reading the King James Bible and holding prayers— which were a daily part of nineteenth century public schools. Catholics initially sought to free the public schools of such religious practices but without success. After several court decisions favoring Protestant religious practices in public schools and after several "religious riots" in cities such as Philadelphia, Catholics began their own school system in order to ward off the Protestantizing of their children.[16]

As early as 1840 there were 200 Catholic schools in the United States.[17] They were created largely because Catholic citizens of the New World wanted to keep alive their religion in the minds and hearts of their children. The development of Catholic schools was encouraged by nineteenth century immigration, including the major migration of the Irish in the decade of the 1840s.[18] In 1820 there were only 195,000 Catholics in the United States but by 1850 there were 1,606,000.[19] Catholic schools often reduced the immigrants' shock of transition. Support for

---

[16] Among references see John F. Wilson, *Church and State in American History* (Boston: D. C. Heath, 1965); Robert Michaelsen. *Piety in the Public Schools* (New York: Macmillan, 1970), pp. 85–98; J. A. Burns and Bernard J. Kohlbrenner, *A History of Catholic Education in the United States* (New York: Benziger Brothers, 1937), p. 24.

[17] George N. Shuster, *Catholic Education in a Changing World* (New York: Holt, Rinehart & Winston, 1967), p. 26.

[18] *Ibid.,* p. 27.

[19] Neil G. McCluskey, S.J. *Catholic Viewpoint in Education* (New York: Doubleday, 1962), p. 189.

A contemporary Catholic classroom

Don Getsug, Rapho Guillumette Pictures

the establishment of a parochial school system came from American Catholic bishops gathered at the Third Plenary Council of Baltimore in 1884. The Council decreed:

> That near every church a parish school, where one does not yet exist, is to be built and maintained in perpetuum, within two years of the promulgation of this council, unless the Bishop should decide that because of serious difficulties a delay may be granted.
>
> That all Catholic parents are bound to send their children to the parish school, unless it is evident that a sufficient training in religion is given either in their own homes, or in other Catholic schools; or when, because of a sufficient reason, approved by the Bishop, with all due precautions and safeguards, it is licit to send them to other schools. What constitutes a Catholic school is left to the decision of the Bishop.[20]

In practice, prior to the twentieth century, the usual pattern of Catholic education in the United States placed great emphasis on the ele-

[20] Reginald A. Neuwien (ed.), *Catholic Schools in Action: A Report, the Notre Dame Study of Catholic Elementary Schools and Secondary Schools in the United States* (Notre Dame, Ind.: University of Notre Dame Press, 1966), p. 9.

mentary and college levels. "The first provided most of the schooling the average youngster received, and the second was relied upon to provide, among other benefits, the supply of teachers needed. In the Catholic system the elementary school was a place in which children were taught discipline—at an earlier stage, rigorously, and later on, persuasively—as well as the rudiments of their religion, while learning secular subjects appropriate to their time of life. The sexually segregated college, which was often an adaptation of the European Gymnasium or lycée to the American environment, was normally conducted by a religious community."[21] Catholic secondary education grew markedly in the twentieth century until the 1960s when a decline began.

At the 1972 meeting of the National Catholic Educational Association, Reverend George Elford, Research Director for the association, said that on the basis of preliminary figures from an association survey about 4.1 million children were then attending parochial elementary and high schools. He reported that this was a 6 percent decline from the 4.4 million children enrolled in parochial schools during the school year ending in June, 1971. The peak of parochial school attendance was about 5.5 million during the 1960s.[22]

Table 8-1 reports a decline in total private school enrollments (including Catholic schools) when these enrollments are compared with total school enrollment in the United States, including public schools.

For years, Catholic leaders supported the idea of the bishops of 1884 of educating every Catholic child in a Catholic school. However, in the present age of ferment in the world and in Catholicism, and especially following the Second Vatican Council, Catholics have reopened the discussion of the desirability and practicality of this. A Notre Dame study reports that as of 1962–1963, a high point in enrollment in Catholic

[21] Shuster, p. 7.
[22] "Catholic Schools Continue Decline," *New York Times,* April 6, 1972, p. 23.

TABLE 8-1 **Private School Enrollments (including Catholic Schools) as Percent of Total Public and Private Enrollments**

| Year | K–8 | 9–12 | K–12 |
|------|------|------|------|
| 1951 | 11.7 | 9.0 | 11.0 |
| 1955 | 13.4 | 9.8 | 12.6 |
| 1961 | 14.7 | 10.4 | 13.7 |
| 1965 | 15.3 | 11.2 | 14.2 |
| 1971 | 11.6 | 7.4 | 10.4 |

National Education Association, Committee on Educational Finance, *Financial Status of the Public Schools* (Washington, D.C.: National Education Association, 1972), p. 11.

schools, only 52.21 percent of Catholic children in the United States were enrolled in Catholic elementary schools — in other words, somewhat more than four million of a potential enrollment of more than eight million.[23] Only 32.22 percent of eligible Catholic children were enrolled in Catholic secondary schools — slightly more than a million of a potential enrollment of more than three million.[24]

With the dwindling of immigration, the characteristic enrollment in the Catholic school has changed. George N. Shuster says, "The comment is often made that Catholic education serves 'nice' middle class boys and girls. To a certain extent, due allowance having been made for the pejorative quality of the adjective, this is true. The average Catholic school youngster, apart from a few exceptional diocesan elementary and high schools, has a better family background, a higher I.Q., and more learning motivation than does the average public school child . . . the situation arises because not all who would like to attend Catholic schools can do so."[25] Shuster concludes, "By reason of the structure of its schools, particularly from the admissions point of view, the Church in the United States may be in some peril of becoming an intellectualized Church and of losing what for a lack of a better term we may call the working class."[26]

A great debate now rages in Catholic educational circles as to which aspects of the total educational structure are most vital for Catholic education. The problem is complicated by financial considerations because Catholic schools have depended heavily upon instruction by the members of religious orders and by the relatively low-paid lay teachers. Writing in 1972, Louis R. Gary, former chairman of Cardinal Spellman's Committee on Educational Research and consultant to President Nixon's Commission on School Finance, and K. C. Cole, editor of New York State's Fleischmann Commission Report on education, said:

> Along with falling enrollments, the decline in numbers of teaching brothers and nuns is the most serious economic problem for Catholic schools. In dollar terms, the presence of the religious-order teacher represents a great subsidy to the school. On a national average, religious-order teachers receive cash stipends and room and board worth $2,550 for teaching in Catholic schools, compared with the average salary of $5,597 paid to laymen [in the Catholic schools]. The problem is that this kind of sacrifice is coming to an end. Fewer young people are entering religious orders.[27]

Some Catholic educators believe the best course would be reduction of elementary education and particularly the early years of elementary school programs. Shuster points out,

[23] Shuster, pp. 55–56.
[24] *Ibid.*, p. 56.
[25] *Ibid.*, pp. 78–79.
[26] *Ibid.*, p. 80.
[27] Louis R. Gary and K. C. Cole, "The Politics of Aid — and a Proposal for Reform," *Saturday Review of Education* (July 22, 1972), p. 32.

Notable is a trend, first seriously inaugurated by the Archdiocese of Cincinnati, to lop off the earlier grades of the elementary school. Also, we read reports that schools are being closed in a number of smaller towns and cities, presumably because keeping them going is too difficult. Do these things portend a serious effort to curtail, if not indeed to abandon, the elementary school? . . . We have now come to the point where not only laymen but priests, religious, and even bishops are asking whether it may not be wise and necessary to think of a drastic curtailment of the parochial school effort.[28]

. . . Whether it is desirable to concentrate on the high school, in order to provide a measure of Catholic education for all children whose parents wish them to have it, is a query which must be submitted to those in charge of Catholic education as a whole. As has been said, its adoption would not automatically mean the demise of the parochial school, but that school would henceforth be in some measure peripheral.[29]

Another aspect of the debate about the future of Catholic education centers on the matter of maintaining neighborhood schools. Parish members who send their children to parochial elementary schools often identify strongly with the elementary schools established in their parish. Sometimes they tend to support these neighborhood elementary schools in preference to giving support to programs of Catholic secondary schools, which are relatively costlier.

### Issues in Catholic Education

Like the public schools and the private independent schools, Catholic schools face fundamental problems today. Two sociologists, Andrew M. Greeley, who is a Catholic priest, and Peter H. Rossi, who is a non-Catholic, have explored these issues in *The Education of Catholic Americans,* a study conducted by the National Opinion Research Center. In the preface to the book several issues are set forth:

The first of these concerns is the major manifest reason for the establishment and maintenance of the Catholic school system—the preservation of religious faith. Since the *raison d'etre* of religious schools is that they assist in the teaching of religion, it is crucial that any research project on Catholic schools address itself to the question: "Are the people who attend Catholic schools better Catholics?" . . .

A second issue of major concern in discussions of Catholic education has been the question of the potentially divisive nature of a separate, value oriented educational system. Does the Catholic school system set its students apart from other Americans and create barriers to their cooperation with Protestants and Jews? . . .

A third issue which underlies the research project is the evaluation of the part which Catholic education plays in preparing individuals for economic success. The significant question here concerns the competency of Catholic schooling to prepare one for life in a secular world, where occupation success not only contributes to his

[28] Shuster, pp. 171–172.
[29] *Ibid.*, pp. 176–177.

general level of economic well-being but also has a significant impact on his general social status.[30]

## The authors conclude that:

> The first theoretical question was whether the values of a religious group can be effectively taught in a religiously oriented educational system. Our answer to this question is that, to some extent, they can. The students who attend such schools can be expected in adult life to do even better those things which most members of their religious group do reasonably well. Value oriented education can affect behavior in adult life in precisely those areas in which adults can be expected to adhere to the norms of their religious group even without education. Those who have the education will simply be even more likely to exhibit the desired behavior.
>
> The second theoretical question was whether such separate systems of education were "divisive." We could find no evidence that the products of such a system were less involved in community activities, less likely to have friends from other religious groups, more intolerant in their attitudes, or less likely to achieve occupationally or academically. On the contrary, we found that they were slightly more successful in the world of study and work and — after the breaking point of college — much more tolerant. The achievement, and perhaps even the tolerance, seems to be related to the degree to which a young person was integrated into his religious subculture during adolescence.[31]

### Who Teaches in Catholic Schools?

A Notre Dame study shows that, although members of religious orders once substantially outnumbered lay teachers in Catholic schools, the lay staff was growing rapidly during the 1950s. Between 1950 and 1961 "the number of lay teachers had grown approximately four times as fast as the number of religious at the secondary school level, and nearly twenty-three times as fast at the elementary school level."[32] From 2,768 lay teachers in 1946, the number grew to 44,000 in Catholic elementary schools in 1965–66.[33]

In 1972 Gary and Cole summarized the situation as to the proportion of members of religious orders as contrasted to lay teachers in Catholic schools: "In 1950, 93 percent of the teachers in Catholic schools across the country were brothers or nuns; today (1972) fewer than half are brothers or nuns."[34]

Among the problems encountered by lay teachers in Catholic schools have been the lack of career opportunities to become administrators.

---

[30] Andrew M. Greeley and Peter H. Rossi, *The Education of Catholic Americans* (Chicago: Aldine, 1966), pp. vi–viii.
[31] Greeley and Rossi, pp. 228–229.
[32] Shuster, pp. 56–57.
[33] C. Albert Koob, "Parochial Schools—Roman Catholic," in American Educational Research Association, *Encyclopedia of Educational Research*, 4th ed. (New York: Macmillan, 1969), p. 927. Copyright © 1969 by American Educational Research Association.
[34] Gary and Cole, p. 32.

FIGURE 8-1    Teachers in Roman Catholic Parochial Schools

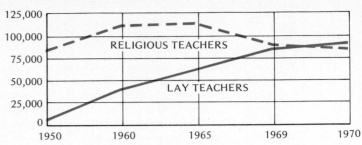

"Teachers in Roman Catholic Parochial Schools," *New York Times*, December 25, 1971. p. 15. © 1971 by The New York Times Company. Reprinted by permission.

These posts were usually reserved for the sisters and brothers in religious orders. However, Neil G. McCluskey, in *Catholic Education Faces Its Future*, points out that in recent years "the ranks of administrators have opened significantly, again indicating the pattern of the future."[35]

### Whether or Not to Teach in Catholic Schools

As teachers contemplate service in Catholic schools, many factors will have to be taken into account. How deep is the individual's commitment to a distinctive Catholic education? If the commitment is deep, to what extent does it reflect traditional approaches to Catholicism or to what extent does it reflect the new self-examination that followed Pope John and the Second Vatican Council? Will the individual be content with a presumably lower salary than is paid in the public schools and will he or she accept somewhat fewer opportunities to move ahead to administrative posts? Can the teacher adapt to larger class size than is usually characteristic of public schools? Will parochial elementary schools be curtailed?

An official of the National Catholic Education Association concludes his contribution to the *Encyclopedia of Educational Research* with several questions concerning Catholic parochial education:

Should an all-out effort be made to expand the system in order to meet the rising demands of the immediate future, or should the system be held at its present level of size or even cut back, while efforts are concentrated instead on new educational and religious formation programs? If the decision is for expansion, where will the money to build the schools and pay the teachers come from? Will the American public, legislatures, and courts accept the arguments of parochial school proponents that their institutions and/or students are constitutionally entitled to aid from tax funds, or will decisions of public policy or constitutional interpretation instead go against the interests of parochial education? Can parochial schools continue to meet the mounting demands for educational excellence?[36]

[35] Neil G. McCluskey, S.J., *Catholic Education Faces Its Future* (Garden City, N.Y.: Doubleday, 1969), p. 112.
[36] Koob, p. 929.

Ernest Bartell, C.S.C., who administered the national economic study of Catholic elementary and secondary schools for the President's Commission on School Finance, reports on the national study in the Catholic magazine, *America:*

Certainly the results of the national study are not cheery. If not checked, the declines in enrollment of Catholic elementary and secondary schools that have been evident since the peak year of 1962 can be expected to increase at an expanding rate. Elementary schools are hardest hit with 1970 enrollments of 3.4 million expected to drop to 2.15 million by 1975 and 1.4 million by 1980 unless checked. While this represents a 60 percent decline in a decade, the rate of decline in secondary school enrollments is somewhat less dramatic, predicted to fall from slightly over one million in 1970 to 822,000 in 1975 and to just less than 700,000 by 1980, for a rate of decline of about 30 percent through the decade. The percentage of Catholic elementary school age children actually enrolled in Catholic elementary schools will have fallen from a peak of almost 54 percent in 1958 to 31 percent in 1970, and down to 22 percent by 1975 and less than 20 percent by 1980.[37]

Gary and Cole, who have worked with national and state commissions on school finance, conclude their article with the controversial recommendation:

. . . the time has come to rapidly reorder public thinking on the future of Catholic schools. If the courts do rule that substantial public aid to nonpublic schools is unconstitutional—and they probably will—then the country must prepare for not only a 50 percent drop in Catholic school enrollment but a substantial phasing out of the system that now holds several million Catholic pupils. The public schools could absorb such an influx over the decade with adequate planning and preparation. But the myths and rhetoric that now dominate the Catholic school debate will lead only to collapse, dislocation, and severe overcrowding in the public schools.

To prevent this collapse, the Catholic leadership must begin immediate, massive consolidation of Catholic schools. At the same time political leaders must tell Catholics how much public aid they can expect over the decade. The remaining aid alternatives should be tested in the courts. Only then can church leaders be freed from their current state of uncertainty. Only then can Catholics confront the present-day value of their schools and decide how much they would be prepared to sacrifice to preserve them if large amounts of public funds are not forthcoming.[38]

You might take all of these views and still more into consideration as you decide about teaching in Catholic schools.

## CONTROVERSIES OVER RELIGION AND SCHOOLS

Since a large majority of America's nonpublic schools are Catholic and a substantial proportion of the independent schools are church-related to some degree, religion is an important factor in nonpublic edu-

---

[37] Ernest Bartell, "Good News and Bad for Catholic Schools," *America* (April 1, 1972), p. 343.
[38] Gary and Cole, p. 33.

cation. The right of a nonpublic school to instruct in the tenets of the sponsoring religious group is not in dispute in the United States today. But does the government have any responsibility for the financial support of religiously controlled nonpublic schools? And does the public school, an institution maintained by public funds for the benefit of a highly diverse population as to religion, have any responsibility for religious instruction in the public schools?

The principle of separation of church and state is embodied in the first amendment to the United States Constitution, "Congress shall make no law respecting an establishment of religion, or prohibiting the free exercise thereof; . . . " The new nation chose freedom of religion rather than the earlier colonial concept of an established church supported with public funds.

To the Founding Fathers, the religion clause of the first amendment meant that a "wall of separation" was erected between church and state. For instance, Thomas Jefferson wrote in 1802, "I contemplate with sovereign reverence that act of the whole American people which declared that their legislature should 'make no law respecting an establishment of religion, or prohibiting the free exercise thereof,' thus building a wall of separation between church and state." James Madison, who wrote the first amendment, said, "We maintain, therefore, that in matters of religion no man's right is abridged by the institution of civil society; and that religion is wholly exempt from its cognizance."

Supporters of the "wall of separation" interpretation of the first amendment believe that it has saved America from the religious conflicts that troubled the Old World, has permitted a great religious diversity in which approximately 300 sects and denominations exist peaceably, has guaranteed religious freedom for all, and has given religions the opportunity to be free, independent, and strong.

But some interpret the first amendment as simply intended to keep the Congress from establishing a national church. Some Catholic spokesmen, for instance, have argued for a limited and literal interpretation of the amendment. James M. O'Neill, in *Religion and Education Under the Constitution,* said that "the question of 'an establishment of religion' for the whole United States . . . was a subject which Congress should not touch. It neither approved nor disapproved of the established religions existing in the States. It made explicit the fact that Congress was powerless to act in favor of an establishment of religion for the nation."[39]

Another interpretation of the first amendment calls for friendly cooperation between church and state and increasing flexibility. For instance, an official of a council of the United Church of Christ said:

Between the poles of "nonestablishment" and "free exercise" lies a vast realm of

[39] James M. O'Neill, *Religion and Education Under the Constitution* (New York: Harper and Bros., 1949), pp. 9–10.

functional interaction which cannot—and should not—be proscribed by legal and judicial acts. Instead of a "wall" we ought to have a "wavy line" between church and state. They are in dynamic relation to each other and the boundaries of their respective spheres cannot be determined once and for all.[40]

The Supreme Court of the United States has frequently been called on to rule on cases involving separation of church and state. In the *Everson* decision in 1947, the Court said:

Neither a state nor the Federal Government can set up a church. Neither can pass laws which aid one religion, aid all religions or prefer one religion over another. Neither can force nor influence a person to go to or remain away from church against his will or force him to profess a belief or disbelief in any religion. No person can be punished for entertaining or professing religious beliefs or disbeliefs, for church attendance or nonattendance. No tax in any amount large or small can be levied to support any religious activities or institutions, whatever they may be called, or whatever form they may adopt to teach or practice religion. Neither a state nor the Federal Government can, openly or secretly, participate in the affairs of any religious organization or groups and vice versa. In the words of Jefferson, the clause against establishment of religion by law was intended to erect a "wall of separation between church and state."[41]

But in the *Everson* decision, the Court held that the state could provide free bus transportation to children attending private schools, including church-related schools. In 1968, in the *Allen* case, the United States Supreme Court upheld the constitutionality of a New York State statute requiring local boards of education to lend secular textbooks that were approved by public school authorities to children in nonpublic schools, including parochial schools, without charge. Operating on a "child benefit" theory, which conceived the loan of textbooks as aid to children rather than aid to religious schools, the Court said:

Private education has played and is playing a significant and valuable role in raising national levels of knowledge, competence and experience. Americans care about the quality of the secular education available to their children. They have considered high quality education to be an indispensable ingredient for achieving the kind of nation and the kind of citizenry that they have desired to create. Considering this attitude, the continued willingness to rely on private school systems, including parochial systems, strongly suggests that a wide segment of informed opinion, legislative and otherwise, has found that those schools do an acceptable job of providing secular education to their students. This judgment is further evidence that parochial schools are performing, in addition to their sectarian function, the task of secular education.[42]

[40] Ray Gibbons, "Protestantism and Public Action," *Social Action* (February 15, 1949).
[41] U.S. Supreme Court, *United States Reports,* October Term, 1947, *Everson* v. *Board of Education,* 330 U.S., pp. 59–60.
[42] U.S. Supreme Court, *United States Reports,* October Term, 1967, *Board of Education* v. *Allen,* 392 U.S., p. 236.

Several basic Supreme Court rulings have affirmed that the public school must be a secular institution—the Court's rulings in the *Everson* case, the *McCollum* decision against "released-time programs" for religious instruction on public school premises, the *Engel* v. *Vitale* case declaring unconstitutional the recitation in the public schools of a prayer composed by the New York Board of Regents, and the *Schempp* case holding that devotional reading of the Bible and school sponsored prayers are violations of the first amendment. But with the *Allen* case it became obvious that the question of how far the state may go in aiding parochial schools or their students had not yet been fully determined.

Under the "child benefit" theory, public aid is frequently shared by public and nonpublic schools. The Elementary and Secondary Education Act (ESEA) of 1965 was a compromise providing funds for educationally deprived students in both public and nonpublic schools. Grants to public school children were shared by nonpublic school students through educational radio and television programs, mobile educational services, library resources, textbooks and other instructional materials, and "dual enrollment" programs through which the school time of children was shared between state-supported schools providing general education and church-supported schools providing the religious emphasis of a denomination.

Based on the child benefit theory that the student and not the school must receive the aid, several states passed laws in the 1960s providing for some type of indirect aid to financially-pinched private schools. A 1968 Pennsylvania law provided state aid for the "purchase of secular educational services." These services were defined as made up of courses in mathematics, modern foreign languages, physical science, and physical education. The reimbursement was for teachers' salaries, textbooks, and instructional materials used in the teaching of these courses in nonpublic schools.[43] Simultaneously, the Supreme Court heard the Rhode Island case of *DiCenso* v. *Robinson* concerning the constitutionality of appropriating state funds for a 15 percent salary supplement for eligible teachers in nonpublic elementary schools. The *Lemon* and *DiCenso* cases were consolidated and in 1971 the Supreme Court decided that the Pennsylvania and Rhode Island statutes had the effect of advancing religion and of fostering excessive government entanglement with religion.

How then did the situation with respect to public aid to parochial schools stand during 1971? The forms of state aid to public schools which were judged permissible were summarized in the *Lemon* case by the Supreme Court as follows:

Our decisions from *Everson* to *Allen* have permitted the states to provide church-related schools with secular, neutral, or nonideological services, facilities, or materials.

[43] Patrick S. Duffy, "The First Amendment Is Not for Sale," *Phi Delta Kappan* (September 1971), p. 55.

Bus transportation, school lunches, public health services, and secular textbooks supplied in common to all students were not thought to offend the Establishment Clause.[44]

What is unconstitutional was summarized by the Supreme Court as follows:

The Pennsylvania statute . . . has the . . . defect of providing state financial aid directly to the church-related school. This factor distinguishes both *Everson* and *Allen*, for in both those cases the Court was careful to point out that state aid was provided to the student and his parents—not to the church-related school.[45]

Thus the Supreme Court specified that any state benefits to nonpublic education must be secular and must be provided to the student and to his parents, not to the school itself.

During April of 1972 a Panel on Nonpublic Education proposed to President Nixon that the government grant income tax credits to parents of middle class children and provide direct tuition grants to parents of poor children. The chairman of the panel, Clarence C. Walton, President of the Catholic University of America, said in a covering letter to President Nixon: "The panel has given serious attention to the constitutional issue. It is persuaded that, although direct aid to nonpublic schools is prohibited, aid to parents and to children will pass judicial muster."

After noting that the Supreme Court had declared the Pennsylvania and Rhode Island statutes unconstitutional, the panel said: "The law is still being molded and shaped by both judicial philosophies and political events so that the final phase in the Federal drama over nonpublic school education is still to be enacted.[46]

President Richard M. Nixon, addressing the annual convention of the National Catholic Education Association in 1972, said:

I am irrevocably committed to these propositions: America needs her nonpublic schools; that those nonpublic schools need help; that therefore we must and will find ways to provide that help. . . . I feel that the only responsible way to proceed is to take the extra time required to guarantee that the legislative recommendations which we finally submit will be equitable, will be workable, and will be constitutional and so held by the Supreme Court.[47]

The *New York Times* commented editorially on the address:

President Nixon appears to ignore two key issues—the fact that the public schools

[44] *Ibid.,* p. 57.
[45] *Ibid.,* p. 57.
[46] "Panel Urges U.S. Act Quickly to Rescue Nonpublic Education," *New York Times,* April 21, 1972, p. 45.
[47] "Nixon Vows To Aid Catholic Schools But Asks Caution," *New York Times,* April 7, 1972, p. 1.

are themselves in desperate financial straits and the danger implicit in any erosion of the separation of church and state. There is a lack of realism in Mr. Nixon's theorizing about the hypothetical consequences to the public schools in the event of the collapse of the nonpublic ones, when the actual consequences of underfinanced public education should be his immediate concern. As for the constitutional question, the President's first duty is to protect—not try to circumvent—a principle that safeguards essential freedoms of both the state and religion.[48]

During the Presidential Campaign of 1972, the Democratic Party candidate, George McGovern, endorsed "a system of tax credits to aid the parents of children attending parochial and other bona fide nonpublic schools."[49]

Again the *New York Times* editorialized:

The proposal by Senator George McGovern to grant tax credits to parents who pay private school tuition is virtually identical with a plan previously submitted by President Nixon's advisory panel on aid to parochial schools. Although this form of aid has not yet been tested in the courts, it appears to us a threat to the principle of the separation of church and state, no less real for being an indirect subsidy. Since tax credits would apply to all nonpublic school tuition, this form of Federal support moreover could easily become a windfall for those private academies that have been established to perpetuate segregation.

The additional and intolerable risk in any major move toward the financing of nonpublic schools with tax funds is the probability of simultaneous reduction in the support of public education. This would come at a time when public schools in many communities are actually being forced by budgetary difficulties to reduce their teaching staff and face curtailed academic terms.[50]

In October of 1972 the Supreme Court struck down, by an 8 to 1 vote, an Ohio plan providing direct tuition grants to parents of children in private and parochial schools. The plan had been regarded as a testing ground for new methods of public aid to church-related schools. The Court affirmed a Federal Court ruling that the 1971 Ohio law violated the principle of separation of church and state.[51]

In June of 1973 in major decisions, the Supreme Court ruled against New York and Pennsylvania statutes that offered tax credits and tuition reimbursements to parents of students attending nonpublic schools. The Supreme Court ruled that even the indirect method of supporting parochial schools by providing tax credits to parents instead of money for the schools had "the impermissible effect of advancing the sectarian activities of religious schools." The Court also ruled against state maintenance payments to parochial schools and state financing of record keeping and

[48] "Church and State," *New York Times*, April 10, 1972, p. 34.
[49] "McGovern for Tax Credit to Aid Parochial Schools," *New York Times*, September 20, 1972, pp. 1, 34.
[50] "The School Aid Issue," *New York Times*, September 22, 1972, p. 40.
[51] "Court, 8 to 1, Bars Ohio Tuition Plan," *New York Times*, October 11, 1972, pp. 1, 20.

testing in parochial schools. Through such decisions, the U.S. Supreme Court emphatically reaffirmed the principle of church-state separation in 1973.[52]

It seems likely that future Supreme Court decisions may relate to proposals providing support to the student and his parents through, for instance, voucher plans. In such future cases the courts may be called on to rule whether the proposed aid is secular rather than sectarian and whether it involves excessive government entanglement with religion. So the arguments on the constitutionality of forms of state aid for parochial schools are not over. The courts will be heard from again on church-state issues.

The argument over public aid to parochial schools grows increasingly tense as predictions are made that the Catholic system of education will collapse without further support and, therefore, will load the already overburdened public schools with the students who now attend Catholic schools. But opponents of public aid doubt that Catholic schools will collapse without government support and advise instead investment of federal funds in inner city public schools, which are sadly in need of money.

## DISCUSSION

1. On what basis has the United States Supreme Court ruled that independent and parochial schools are legal alternatives to public schools?
2. What are the characteristics of an independent private school?
3. To what extent is an independent school subject to state regulation? How might the existence of state regulations relate to you and your career and training if you chose to work in an independent school?
4. What are the major developments in the evolution of the private independent schools in America?
5. How do the "alternative" or "free" or "innovative" schools differ from the long-established private independent schools? Do you agree with Kozol's criticisms?
6. What are the advantages of teaching in an established private independent school, according to its proponents? What are the disadvantages, according to its critics? What is your own point of view on advantages and disadvantages? Apply the questions to alternative or free schools.
7. What accounts for the development of parochial schools in America in the nineteenth century?
8. What reactions do you have to the 1884 decree that "all Catholic parents are bound to send their children to the parish school"? Have there been changes in the interpretation or implementation of this decree in recent years?
9. Why did parochial education place great emphasis on the elementary and college

[52] "Church, State and School," *Newsweek* (July 9, 1973), p. 64; "The Court Reverses a Trend," *New York Times*, July 1, 1973, p. 7.

levels? Does this seem to you to have been a wise decision from the point of view of its sponsors or the public at large?

10. Who enrolls in Catholic schools? Are social class factors involved?

11. What have been some recent trends in Catholic education as to levels of instruction to be stressed and maintained? What do you think of the advisability of these tendencies?

12. According to *The Education of Catholic Americans,* what are the fundamental issues being faced by Catholic schools today? What conclusions do the authors of the cited study reach? Do you agree with their conclusions?

13. Who teaches in Catholic schools? What are the trends as to employment of lay and religious teachers? What seem to be likely future developments as to Catholic teachers? As to career opportunities in administration for lay teachers?

14. What are the factors to take into account in deciding whether or not to teach in Catholic schools? What seem to you to be the advantages and disadvantages advanced by proponents and critics and perceived by yourself? What would be your own tentative decision as to whether you, if a Catholic, or a friend of yours, if a Catholic, should teach in parochial schools?

15. What are the central controversies over religion and schools? What are some subordinate issues?

16. What interpretations have been advanced on the meaning of the first amendment pertaining to schools? What position do you take on the matter? Why?

17. What position has the United States Supreme Court historically taken on separation of church and state? What position is the Court currently taking on the public schools as secular institutions?

18. Do you see any possible shift in the United States Supreme Court position through the "child benefit" theory? In what ways do parochial schools now share with public schools resources provided by public funds?

19. What are the arguments about public funds for the support of religiously sponsored education?

20. What are the newest developments as to tuition grants? What are the latest decisions of the Supreme Court in connection with such support to students and parents? What are the latest decisions as to tax credits?

## INVOLVEMENT

1. Have a panel of students describe the program and problems of independent private schools, if your class includes students who have attended such schools.

2. Make arrangements to visit a class in an independent school. From personal observation, what do you see as differences between this class and those you have observed in public schools?

3. Through panels, debates, extended discussions, etc., explore the pros and cons of teaching in private independent schools. Include fundamental issues such as student characteristics and the values of teachers.

4. If a 'free' or 'alternative' school exists in your region, visit it to learn of its program and problems. How stable or impermanent is this school? What is your appraisal of its program?

5. Determine the dates of the founding of private independent schools in the region in which you live or attend school.

6. Invite an administrator or teacher or sponsor of a private independent school or an alternative school to class to describe the program and problems of his school.

7. Sponsor an exchange visit or a shared class session with a teacher education class in a Catholic college if you attend a non-Catholic college, or plan to visit a public college if you are attending a Catholic institution. Explore similarities and differences in programs. Look for agreement and clarify different ways of seeing education.

8. Talk to selected Catholic leaders, both members of the clergy and laymen, concerning probable directions of Catholic education. Invite nuns to class to talk with you on the matter.

9. Write your own summary of the major issues in Catholic education.

10. Make arrangements to visit a class in a parochial school. From personal observation, what do you see as differences between this class and those you have observed in public schools?

11. During a visit to a parochial school attempt to talk to both lay and religious teachers. Are there apparent differences in their points of view? Similarities?

12. Draw up a check list of factors to be taken into account in deciding about teaching in Catholic schools. Include in your list the possible advantages and disadvantages.

13. Research the various positions people take with respect to religion and the schools. Organize panel presentations of the varying viewpoints with documentary support.

14. Visit programs in your community in which parochial schools share a degree of public support. Do the programs you observe seem to be "secular" or "sectarian"?

## FURTHER READING

Brown, William and Andrew M. Greeley. *Can Catholic Schools Survive?* New York: Sheed and Ward, 1970.   The future of Catholic education.

Buetow, Harold A. *Of Singular Benefit: The Story of Catholic Education in the U.S.* New York: Macmillan, 1971.   A history of the development of Catholic schooling in America.

Butts, Freeman. *The American Tradition in Religion and Education*. Boston: Beacon Press, 1950.   The history of separation of church and state by an able educational historian.

Clayton, S. Stafford. *Religion and Schooling*. Waltham, Massachusetts: Blaisdell, 1969. The place of religion in the American public school system, including examination of patterns of European countries.

Erickson, Donald A., ed. *Public Controls for Nonpublic Schools*. Chicago: University of Chicago Press, 1969.   A collection of essays reflecting ideas which grew out of a national conference on government regulation and private schools.

Fraser, W. R. *Residential Education*. New York: Pergamon Publishing, 1968.   Explores the nature of the residential school, conceptual frameworks for its existence, and its struggle to function successfully.

Jacobson, Philip. *Religion in Public Education*. New York: American Jewish Committee, 1969.   A compact and objective guide to discussion of the major issues, upon which a section of this chapter draws.

Koob, C. Albert and Russell Shaw. *S.O.S. for Catholic Schools: A Strategy for Future Service to Church and Nation*. New York: Holt, Rinehart and Winston, 1970. An analysis of approaches to be used for the continuation of Catholic education.

Seidl, Anthony and Sidney G. Tickton, eds. *Long-Range Planning for Catholic Schools: A Guide for Action*. New York: Joseph F. Wagner, Inc., 1969.   A workbook on

institutional planning, including essays by such educators as Rev. C. Albert Koob,
Rev. Edmund W. Olley, Rev. Louis F. Generes, and E. Bruce Heilman.

## SELECTED AUDIO-VISUAL MATERIALS

*Bible Reading in the Public Schools* (audio tape, 56 min., CBS: National Center for
Audio Tapes, 1963).  A report on the Supreme Court decision. One aspect of the
problem of religion and the schools.

*Keystone for Education* (16 mm film, 27 min., color, CCM Films, 1969).  Shows many
ways in which to approach the teaching of religion, using both interviews and examples. Includes ideas expressed by religious educators from varied faiths.

*Roman Catholic View of Education* (16 mm film, 29 min., b. & w., NET: Indiana University, 1961).  Father Robert J. Henle discusses a Roman Catholic view of education.

# NINE

# Who's in charge here?

The teacher works in a particular school, usually in a particular public school system in a particular community. What are the surrounding conditions and forces influencing the teacher in such a public school? In other words, who's in charge here?

## INFLUENCES ON THE PUBLIC SCHOOL IN THE COMMUNITY

### The Power Structure

Michael Y. Nunnery and Ralph B. Kimbrough have defined power structure as follows: "the power structure of the community is the systematic, relative distribution of social power among the citizens in determining the kind of community they want and the kind of institutional arrangements that will best serve them. The exercise of power by citizens is not equal; there is an unequal distribution of influence in the system."[1]

Within the specific community in which the new teacher will work, a power structure exists. The term *power structure* was popularized by the Southern sociologist Floyd Hunter in a study of the early 1950s.[2] He recognized that one could not simply explain decision-making in communities through reference to the legal channels alone. Many factors, including social class, also influence the decision-making process. So Hunter studied a city of over 500,000 population and found that decision-

---

[1] Michael Y. Nunnery and Ralph B. Kimbrough, *Politics, Power, Polls, and School Elections* (Berkeley, Calif.: McCutchan, 1971), p. 8.
[2] Floyd Hunter, *Community Power Structure* (Chapel Hill, N.C.: University of North Carolina Press, 1953).

making was largely the province of a few men who dominated the economic system of the city. The influential men in this informal power structure usually did not hold public offices; instead they were the key industrialists, financiers, and commercial leaders of Regional City, as Hunter called his community. The public officials followed the decisions of the men in the informal power structure; few citizens actually participated in community decisions.

Not all of the studies which followed Hunter's found the degree of monopolization of power that Hunter did in Regional City. Yet most studies agreed that only a small percentage of the people were involved in basic community decisions. For instance, Robert Presthus concluded from his studies, "In sum, our findings in Edgewood generally support earlier research of sociologists who found a tendency toward elitism in community power structures which were usually dominated by economic elites. In Riverview, the decision structure remains highly concentrated, but political leaders play the major role. Regarding the restriction of active participation to the few, the more recent findings of political scientists are quite similar."[3]

Recognizing the importance of the question of who makes the basic decisions in communities concerning public education, students of power such as Ralph B. Kimbrough have explored the process of educational decision-making.[4] Stephen K. Bailey and others examined particularly the relationship of school decisions and politics.[5] While the students of decision-making in school systems recognized that the community power structures differed from one school district to the other, they were able to generalize on some common characteristics. Based on their conclusions, the new public school teacher might well assume that, despite the equalitarian ideals of democracy, power in a school district is not equally distributed among all the people. At the top of the structure are usually the influentials, for instance a powerful industrialist or a vigorous mayor. Below them are the leaders who perform a variety of roles, such as a superintendent in a school system or an official appointed by the administration at the city hall.

In power systems there are ground rules, or procedural norms, which vary in accordance with the type of power structure, the people involved, their interests and goals. People who do not observe these rules usually lose their power to influence the system. Latent centers of power composed of people who potentially have strength but who do not usually choose to exercise their power must also be considered. Given a community crisis, those who are silent yet powerful may be heard from.

[3] Robert Presthus, *Men at the Top* (New York: Oxford University Press, 1964), p. 430, quote found in Ralph B. Kimbrough, *Administering Elementary Schools: Concepts and Practices* (New York: Macmillan, 1968), pp. 73–74.
[4] Ralph B. Kimbrough, *Political Power and Educational Decision-Making* (Chicago: Rand McNally, 1964).
[5] Stephen K. Bailey, Richard L. Frost, Paul E. Marsh, and Robert C. Wood, *Schoolmen and Politics* (Syracuse, N.Y.: Syracuse University Press, 1962).

Students of power structures have pointed out that informal as well as formal power structures exist and exert substantial influence.

### The Types of Power Structure

Students of community power structures in relationship to schools have identified four main types of community power structures. Kimbrough, for instance, recognizes the *monopolistic power structure*, in which the influentials, through consulting together, dominate the decisions, though often with some opposition. *Multi-group noncompetitive structures* are often found in rural areas where each village has its own power structure and where political change comes about through temporary unions of the influentials from the different villages. *Competitive elite structures* exist when power struggles occur between coalitions of influentials. *Pluralistic power structures* occur in which power groups specialize in particular fields; for instance, those providing leadership in the field of education may not be heavily involved in other areas of community activity.[6]

Kimbrough also points out that the resultant power systems may be open or closed. He cites his research in Florida in two counties he refers to as Beach County, a closed social system, and River County, an open social system. In Beach County, the few dominant influentials, largely from the business groups, were hostile to outside influences, opposed to economic and social changes which might threaten the status quo, and were, in general, conservative. In such a closed system, educational innovation would be difficult to carry on, particularly if it required funds from outside sources such as the federal government. However, in River County, with a more varied group of influentials including some active educational administrators, there was much more openness to and interest in change. River County was closer to the democratic ideal than Beach County; yet even within River County, characterized as it was by an open competitive elite, there was far from maximum effective democracy. However, the climate for innovation was favorable in open River County, partly due to the fact that many new residents had recently come into the county because of a new economic development in the area.

## INFLUENCES ON THE TEACHER IN THE SCHOOL SYSTEM

### The Board of Education

High in the legal framework in public schools is the local school board, which holds the general policy-making authority in communities. Though most frequently called the school board or the board of education, the local governing body for public education is sometimes called a committee; the members of the board are sometimes described as the school directors, trustees, commissioners, or inspectors.

Though the board is the local controlling agency and though there

[6] Ralph B. Kimbrough, *Administering Elementary Schools*, pp. 73–74; Nunnery and Kimbrough, pp. 14–18.

can be no school district without a school board, it is important to bear in mind that this local agency's powers and operation are influenced by the state legislature as the controlling state authority. The school board is a civil subdivision of the state; it looks to state statutes for its administrative powers. Yet school board members have substantial autonomy to make decisions.

With increased consolidation, the number of school boards has declined from 22,010 local education agencies in 1968. In 1972 there were 16,771 school districts in the United States and, assuming that a typical board had slightly more than five members, approximately 85,464 school board members. Since consolidation of school districts produces a board somewhat larger than the two boards which preceded it, the actual number of board members might be two or three thousand more than the 85,464 estimate.[7]

The American school board grew out of the early New England town government. Committees of selectmen carried through the decisions of the New England town meeting. In 1721 the heavily burdened selectmen of Boston appointed a committee on school visitation. At first such school committees were the agents of the selectmen, but an 1826 Massachusetts law established school committees as a separate entity. So school boards governed separately from other community governing bodies date from the early nineteenth century in America.

School boards are usually elected directly by the people: a commonly accepted estimate is 85 percent; the remaining 15 percent are appointed by public officials such as mayors or occasionally the governor. The usual number of members is five-plus, though the size of local school boards sometimes ranges from one to fifteen members; a school board member usually serves from three to six years, though again the length of a term may range from one to seven years.

The large majority of school board members receive no pay but perform their office as a public service. The large majority are men who, relatively speaking, represent the higher social levels in their community. They are generally better educated than the population of the community which elects them; most of them are college graduates. Historically, school board members come from backgrounds more representative of the haves than the have-nots. Among school board members, there are usually a disproportionate number of lawyers, businessmen, and doctors.[8] Men outnumber women.

Currently, the number of black, Puerto Rican, and Mexican-American members of boards of education is increasing. In 1972 the two candidates for the presidency of the New York City Board of Education

---

[7] Letter from James A. Mecklenburger, Research Director, National School Boards Association, September 15, 1972.

[8] This was noted as early as 1927 by George Counts in his study, *The Social Composition of Boards of Education: A Study in the Social Control of Public Education.*

were a black and a Puerto Rican. In 1972 there were 684 black school board members in the nation; four years earlier there were only 125 black school board members.[9]

Today, despite increasing minority group representation, a general disproportionate distribution of power still exists. Consequently, many school board members are consciously or unconsciously predisposed to the interests of the more prosperous and propertied members of the community. They often interact with such associates in their daily work and they often encounter them in school affairs, since the propertied and prosperous carry the largest burden of taxation and are sensitive to getting their money's worth.

The responsibilities of a local school board are summarized by Knezevich as follows:

1. To satisfy the spirit as well as the word of state laws dealing with education and of the regulations of the state education authority.
2. To ascertain goals or objectives of public education and to prepare general policies in tune with them.
3. To select a superintendent of schools, designate him as the chief executive officer, and work harmoniously with him.
4. To strive continuously to develop further and improve the scope and quality of educational opportunities for all children and youth in the district.
5. To create policies which will attract and retain professional and other personnel needed to realize educational objectives.
6. To provide educationally efficient and safe school plant facilities.
7. To plan for and obtain financial resources necessary to achieve educational goals.
8. To keep the people of the district informed and aware of status, progress, and problems of their schools.
9. To appraise activities of the school district in the light of its objectives.
10. To discharge its responsibilities as a state agency by participating in statewide efforts to promote and improve public education.[10]

The single most important responsibility of a school board is to determine policy for the school system. A policy statement is a guideline which describes an objective to be achieved. Increasingly school board policies are written; written policies save time, money, and effort, reduce inconsistencies in school board action, and prove especially useful when community controversies develop. They are particularly helpful to the staff; all should be familiar with them. However, too often the teacher is unaware of these statements.

School board policies usually deal with such matters as the work of the board and the superintendent, personnel relations, the instructional program, school food services, business matters, student transportation,

[9] Ronnie Moore and Marvin Rich, "When Blacks Take Office" (Scholarship, Education and Defense Fund for Racial Equality, Inc., undated unpaged release, 1972?); also Ronnie Moore and Marvin Rich, "When Blacks Take Office," *The Progressive* (May 1972), p. 31.
[10] Stephen J. Knezevich, *Administration of Public Education* (New York: Harper and Row, 1969), pp. 216–217.

selection and retention of personnel, procedures as to pupils, public relations, and salary schedules.

School boards are constantly exhorted by experts on school organization to make a clear distinction between policy-making and administration; nevertheless, a gray area persists. A major function of a school superintendent and his team is to supply leadership and thus constantly advise and consult with the board on the development of policy. On the other hand, a board member wants to see his policies embodied in rules and regulations and thus is likely to take a substantial interest in the precise courses of action which are developed to carry out the broad framework of policy.

Meetings of school boards are usually open to the public. But sometimes a school board finds it desirable to hold an executive session in such cases as disciplinary action directed against particular pupils, accusations brought against teachers, and decisions on the purchase of school sites. But when boards use executive sessions too frequently and use open sessions primarily for voting with a minimum of discussion, they are naturally subject to suspicion by the public and the mass media.

The school board member has a difficult job. He not only has the responsibility for formulating policy but also for evaluating results. He is expected to play down his own self-interests and play up board unity. He is expected to support the superintendent who, after all, was selected by the board. He should be a leader and be effective in personal human relations; he must also be able to relate to teachers and to the administrative staff. Above all, he should have the courage of his convictions in situations beset by pressures.

School boards operate in difficult circumstances. Today there is a demand for high quality education; teachers are militant, and decisions about salaries and working conditions are difficult. The federal government enters the picture through special programs of aid and support. Today court decisions as to desegregation and students' rights play an important role in school affairs. The school is increasingly regarded as an institution to deal with problems traditionally viewed as noninstructional and to correct social injustice. Pressure groups flourish and grow more vigorous. Innovation is expected from schools. Criticisms proliferate. Many community forces and varied expectations must be taken into account. Yet few citizens are enthusiastic about helping board members obtain the kind of financial support the schools need to meet such demands.

One problem today is how the residents of a local district will exercise influence over their schools. In some cases minority groups claim they must have authority to hire and fire neighborhood principals and teachers, thus carrying decentralization of decision-making to a point where it is difficult to see the relationship of these functions to the total school district. This is defended as a way of involving minorities in the vital process of education. But it raises the question of whether local residents not organized as a board of education have the competence, authority, and final accountability to carry out their wishes. Consequently, proposals for community control within large cities should be accompanied by plans for community boards of education with defined legal powers and a carefully spelled out relationship to any centralizing board and administration.

In New York City, control of community elementary schools and intermediate schools was assumed by nine-member elected local boards in July, 1970. Eighteen of 31 district school superintendents either resigned or were let go from their posts during the two years that followed the start of school decentralization.[11]

Opinions as to the success of the school decentralization vary. Kenneth B. Clark, a black leader and a member of the New York State Board of Regents, said in May 1972:

My assessment of the consequences of decentralization as of now is quite different from my anticipation two, three years ago when we were fighting for it. I personally do not see evidence that decentralization has resulted in an increased quality of education for the children in the school. . . .

The purpose was not a struggle for power or control. The purpose was to try to find some way in which the quality of education provided children in a particular school could be increased by more direct monitoring, supervision, more effective teaching accountability.

I do not see that we have kept—or the local boards have concentrated on—quality and methods for raising quality as much as they have concentrated on power, actions, control of finances. . . .

I am not suggesting that we scrap decentralization. I suggest we try to make it a more effective means toward the goal and that we give it every opportunity.[12]

However, in response, Mayor John Lindsay of New York City declared that the city's decentralized school boards had brought "a new vigor to the whole process of achieving quality public education," and indicated that it was much too early to make a final judgment on decentralization.[13] Superintendent Scribner of New York City said, "We sometimes lose sight of the fact that there are 31 local school districts in the city—not just the handful that make the headlines because of their troubles—and the majority of the community school boards went through the year with hardly a major problem. . . . Considering that decentralization is a new experience for us—that this city is pioneering this concept—I think things went very well."[14]

In November 1972, Kenneth B. Clark termed New York's decentrali-

[11] "Eighteen of 31 District School Superintendents Have Left Jobs Since Decentralization Began," *New York Times,* May 21, 1972, p. 64.
[12] "Decentralization of Schools Fails, Kenneth Clark Says," *New York Times,* May 8, 1972, p. 1.
[13] "Local School Units Defended by Mayor," *New York Times,* May 9, 1972, p. 53.
[14] "School Ends, but Problems Don't," *New York Times,* July 1, 1972, p. 25.

zation experiment a "disastrous" experience and declared himself "a vehement foe" of school decentralization. Supporters of decentralization were dismayed that Clark, an influential black scholar upon whose research the U.S. Supreme Court leaned in its 1954 school desegregation decision, now opposed decentralization.

Citizens of a community often know very little about how a centralized (or even a decentralized) board operates; teachers are frequently suspicious of boards. Meanwhile the power structure continues to operate, regardless of whether board members are high in the power structure or not. So the typical board of education in America presides over a situation marked by considerable conflict. The board member often relies heavily upon his executive officer, particularly the superintendent.

### The School Superintendent

The general executive agent for a school system is the superintendent, sometimes known as the general superintendent, the supervising principal, or the district school superintendent. The superintendent is the implementer and the executive for the board.

In the early years of American education the executive and implementing body was the school committee itself, operating through a standing committee of the board of education. But the demands on such standing committees grew heavier as school systems grew more complex. By 1837, Buffalo and Louisville established the post of school superintendent. Some of the early city school superintendents were elected by popular vote, and though this approach was soon terminated, election of county and state superintendents still exists in many states.

The early superintendent was "the board's man" and was responsible for a variety of chores rather than for leadership. His work was primarily superintending instruction; it was not until the twentieth century that he took over financial and building functions. In 1972 there were 14,010 school superintendents in the United States. This included the state superintendents, superintendents of intermediate units, and local superintendents of public schools.[15] Even today some superintendents are bogged down with "administrivia." However, more superintendents are assuming leadership responsibilities.

The job of the superintendent today is a complex one. Knezevich describes it as follows:

1. The superintendent is the chief executive officer of the board.
2. He is responsible for carrying out all policies, rules, and regulations established by the board. In matters not specifically covered by board policy, he is to take appropriate action and report the same to the board not later than the next regular meeting.

[15] Letter from Paul D. Salmon, Executive Secretary, American Association of School Administrators, August 17, 1972.

3. All individuals employed by the board are responsible directly or indirectly to the superintendent of schools.
4. The superintendent has the authority to prepare regulations and to give such instruction to school employees as may be necessary to make the policies of the board effective. He may delegate responsibilities and assign duties. Such delegation and assignment do not relieve the superintendent of responsibility for actions of subordinates.
5. Except when matters pertaining to his reemployment are being considered, the superintendent is to be present at all meetings of the board and its special committees.
6. He is responsible for preparing and submitting the budget to cover school operations.
7. The superintendent has the authority, within limits of major appropriations approved by the board, to authorize and direct all purchases and expenditures.
8. He recommends all candidates for employment. The board has the authority to reject specific candidates recommended, but personnel finally accepted should be employed only upon the recommendation of the superintendent.
9. The superintendent formulates and recommends personnel policies necessary to the functioning of the school.
10. The superintendent provides professional leadership for the educational program of the schools and is responsible for developing a system of regular reporting to the board on all aspects of that program.
11. The superintendent is responsible for keeping the school board informed on all vital matters pertaining to the school system.
12. He is responsible for the development of a program of maintenance and improvement or expansion of the buildings and the site. This includes recommendation for employment and supervision of all building custodians.
13. He is responsible for formulating and administering a program for supervision for all schools.
14. The superintendent is responsible for submitting an annual report on the operation of the school system.[16]

Yet, in a sense, the superintendent is still "the board's man" for the board still retains the right to dismiss him. But a school board should not too lightly dismiss a superintendent. If a superintendent is to be more than a puppet, he may well be involved in disagreements with board members or indeed the board as a whole. The relationship of the school board members and the superintendent should be one of mutual responsibility in which each supplies his ideas, listens to the others and all work for the best interests of children and youth.

Today's superintendents have usually had a broad background of experience and interests, and have been especially concerned with the social aspects of education. The stereotype that most superintendents are former successful athletic coaches is false. "The fields of major study most frequently listed by superintendents were the behavioral sciences (sociology, economics, psychology, anthropology, and human relations),

---

[16] Knezevich, p. 239.

17.6 percent; education, 16.8 percent; physical and biological sciences, 14.8 percent; history and political science, 14.7 percent; mathematics, 11.4 percent; and English, 8.6 percent."[17] Almost all superintendents have a master's degree. By 1968 more than a fourth of the school superintendents of the country had a doctorate and others were working toward this degree. Educator Barbara Sizemore, black and a woman, became Washington, D.C., superintendent of schools in 1973.

Yet today as the post of superintendent involves increasing competence in politics and human relations, some school systems are turning from the educator-superintendent to the nationally prominent civic figure in the search for capable superintendents. A few years ago, New York City, seeking a superintendent, sounded out such national figures as Ralph Bunche, a black United Nations official, and Arthur Goldberg, a leader in government and labor relationships, and other well-known Americans before choosing an educator for the post. In 1972 a lawyer sought appointment as a district superintendent in New York City. Because of rising costs and the need for managerial skills in conducting large enterprises, some boards have considered selecting a superintendent from the top ranks of industrial leadership.

### The Central Office Administrative and Supervisory Staff

If the superintendent is to serve as the executive for the policy-making school board, he needs help from a team or staff. This is particularly true as the school system grows larger and as school programs grow more complicated. The early American superintendents sometimes found themselves responsible not only for administering the schools but for some of the teaching. Boards of education soon found it necessary to relieve superintendents of such assignments and to supply them with secretaries and similar clerical assistance in order to get the job done. But even secretaries and clerks were not enough; professional assistance in staff positions had to be provided. This was the beginning of the professional team, usually headquartered and working with the superintendent in the central office of the school system.

The size and organization of the supporting staff depends on the size and nature of the school system. For instance, it is still possible in small systems for the superintendent to have no more help than a school secretary. But the larger the school operation, the more special functions emerge—such as the general supervisor whose task is to help teachers, system-wide, to improve the quality of their teaching, or the curriculum director whose function it is to update and improve the curriculum through teacher participation in curriculum building. In the larger school systems, the general supervisor who attempts to better instruction in all fields and at all school levels yields to specialized supervisors, who know

[17] *Ibid.*, pp. 243–244.

intimately particular specialized fields, such as music or science, or are especially informed about a particular level, such as elementary or junior high school or senior high school.

A logical first addition to the superintendent's staff was the assistant superintendent, first appointed in the large cities in America in the middle of the nineteenth century. In small systems, the general superintendent and his assistant superintendent still handle matters of personnel, instruction, business management, and public relations.

Assistant superintendents are often placed in charge of major responsibilities within the school system. For instance, an assistant superintendent may be in charge of instruction, or business affairs, or personnel service, or pupil services, or school-community relations, or human relations.[18] In other words, an assistant superintendent may work with an instructional area or a service function of the school.

As cities grew and the number of assistant superintendents in big city systems increased, the post of deputy or associate superintendent was created to coordinate the work of various assistant superintendents. The geographical sprawl of big cities also necessitated the appointment of area or district superintendents who are in charge of geographic areas within a large city though ultimately responsible to the superintendent. As the current drive for greater decentralization of the school bureaucracies of big cities grows, the district or area superintendent will probably increase his responsibilities and influence along with his worries.

If a system contains a considerable number of supervisors, they may be responsible to a director of supervision who in turn reports to an assistant superintendent. In addition to supervisors, school systems often develop directors or coordinators of special functions. The audio-visual function is an illustration. The audio-visual director or coordinator may be responsible to the assistant superintendent who is in charge of curriculum or instruction.

Supervisors were first conceived to be inspectors, and it was first thought that laymen could do this job. After the Civil War, however, professional inspectors or evaluators became necessary.

In time, American educators learned that there were more effective ways of helping teachers than to place inspectors or evaluators over them. In the twentieth century supervision became increasingly concerned with helping teachers improve their instruction through classroom observation by supervisors, rather than inspection or rating. With the growth of emphasis upon human relations techniques both in industry and in education, supervision became an earnest attempt to help teachers develop as professionals and to encourage curriculum

[18] American Association of School Administrators, *Profiles of the Administrative Team* (Washington, D.C.: American Association of School Administrators, 1971), pp. 29, 49, 61, 76, 103, 123, 136.

changes through teachers. But, the old image of the supervisor as an inspector or evaluator who reports to '' the boss'' persists.

In an attempt to eliminate, or at least reduce, the inspector-evaluator image, school systems have developed a distinction between ''line'' and ''staff'' officers. The line officer is the individual who is directly subordinate to the superintendent, yet has the authority to act as a chief almost as if he were himself the superintendent. People in line positions can and do exert their authority with respect to those who are subordinate to them in the educational structure. On the other hand, a person in a staff position, though still subordinate to the superintendent, sees himself primarily as a person acting as a service agent. Such a person can exert no direct authority; he or she attempts to be perceived as a helper or consultant. Supervisors today usually prefer the role of staff worker rather than line authority.

In professional baseball, when the manager of a ball club is fired, the coaches he has brought to the club are usually dismissed too. When a new manager takes over a ball club it is usually assumed that he will bring his own coaches with him. To a lesser degree this is the same situation when a superintendent is employed or dismissed; his top level staff may go with him. Lower level line officers and almost all staff officers still stay on, for they are regarded as ''career'' people within the school system, even as, despite changes in a national administration, the ''career diplomats'' of the State Department stay on. One result is that the key men around the superintendent are sometimes more personally loyal to him than those somewhat removed from the superintendent's ''cabinet.''

In today's complicated operation the superintendent needs staff members who have specialized skills he lacks. In the effective large system, the operation becomes a team effort in which the superintendent coordinates the efforts of several specialists. Yet because a common training pattern for all members of the superintendent's staff often persists, the superintendent may find himself working with staff members with skills like his own rather than with the specialists who are really needed.

In the day-to-day decisions that carry out the board policies and the superintendent's rules and procedures many different interpretations may develop. The problem of communication, both written and oral, can result in countermanding an ''order'' from the superintendent. Getting through to principals and teachers is difficult and almost impossible if those in the line want to block or modify the message. The reverse is also true. The teacher who wishes to communicate with the superintendent has a long and difficult road, especially in a large system. Similarly, communication by students and community members to the superintendent and his central office staff is often difficult. As a veteran spokesman for democracy in administration, Ernest O. Melby, points out, decisions are

The principal's responsibilities include conferring with teachers.

made at a considerable distance from the persons affected by the decisions.

The principle of separation of planning and performance, borrowed from industry and the military, is basic to educational administration. This means that planning is done by the central administration and performance by subordinates. In decision-making the more important a decision is, the further it is made from the person affected by the decision—the child—the teacher—the parent—the citizen. This also means that in a very large degree decisions are the same for all even though each child, each person, is unique and the decision will have different effects on each person. A certain amount of . . . misfit is initially guaranteed.[19]

Though the headquarters of the varied members of the superintendent's team is frequently the central office (or, with decentralization, the office of the district or area superintendent) members of the superin-

[19] Ernest O. Melby, "New Dimensions to the Roles of Educational Personnel when the Community Education Approach to Learning is Implemented," *The Community School and Its Administration* (August 1972), p. 1.

tendent's team are frequently found at work in individual schools. This is particularly true of the staff officers. Thus, members of the superintendent's staff form an important ingredient in the answer to the question, "Who's in charge here?" Sometimes their relationships with the man who is supposedly in charge in the individual school—the principal—grow complex indeed.

### The School Principal

The school principal is the chief executive officer or administrator of the basic unit of the school system—the individual school. In the 1969–1970 school year there were 60,275 principals or assistant principals in public elementary schools.[20] In 1972 there were approximately 30,250 public secondary school principals in the United States; in addition, there were approximately 35,000 assistant principals, vice principals, deans, etc.[21] The smaller the school the more likely it is to have only a principal; the bigger the school the more likely it is to have one or more assistant principals or deans.

The evolution of the principalship resembles the evolution of the superintendency and the superintendent's team. The early American schools were staffed only by teachers. Then certain teachers were charged with some responsibilities for the school's administration. A later step was the hybrid of principal-teacher with administration responsibilities primary and teaching secondary. Latest was the creation of the full-time principal. Yet even today one finds, particularly in rural or in small communities, situations where the principal also teaches.

In the evolution of the principalship, the principal started out as a glorified clerk. In the twentieth century, the principal's major responsibility is seen as leadership for his students, teachers, and building or buildings. A good principal today skillfully uses the special services and supporting staff from the central office and encourages the development of improved instruction through resource people within the school itself, such as "helping teachers." But even the good principal is sometimes perplexed as to what services he should supply and which should come from central staff people or delegated individuals within the school.

Concerning the work of the principal, Knezevich says,

The principal in a public school, whether at the elementary or secondary school level, is a counselor of students, the school disciplinarian, the organizer of the schedule, the supervisor of the instructional program, the pupil-relations representative for the attendance area, the liaison between teachers and the superintendent, the director and evaluator of teaching efforts, the manager of the school facilities, the supervisor of custodial and food-service employees within the building, and a professional leader.

[20] Letter from National Association of Elementary School Principals, Washington, D.C., August 16, 1972.
[21] Letter from Douglas W. Hunt, Associate Secretary for Professional Programs, National Association of Secondary School Principals, Washington, D.C., September 1, 1972.

Little wonder that this is a demanding position as well as one of considerable significance determining the direction of public education.[22]

The high school principal occupies a higher status position than other principals, partly because there are fewer high school principals than elementary or junior high school principals. Since the high school is usually the largest of the community's schools, the high school principalship is viewed as a senior position. But the reasons are also largely historical. One of the most prestigious posts of the nineteenth century was headmaster of an academy, the predecessor of the American high school. The high school principalship preceded the development of the superintendency. Thus in the nineteenth century there was sometimes conflict as to authority between the high school principal and the superintendent.

### The Teacher

Teachers within a school constitute still another force affecting decision-making in the individual school. The "good old days" in which the American teacher was a humble and subservient follower of orders seems to be gone — and few forward-looking people mourn this passing. With the new teacher militancy, teacher concerns have gone beyond salary and immediate welfare conditions and have included participation in shaping the curriculum. No precise design for teacher participation in the conduct of the school has yet emerged, but greater participation by teachers is a reality.

Two tendencies appear to support this development. Enlightened supervisors and other central office staff members have long been saying that teachers should be a genuine force in the shaping of the school's program. So supervisors have long secured participation by teachers in shaping and forming the curriculum, rather than simply implementing what others have mandated. A second tendency is for many teachers to recognize that, if they are to be maximally effective, their concerns must go beyond salaries and working conditions and into the realm of curriculum. True, some demands by teachers' unions or associations may have been misguided; they may have been too concerned about the time which teachers devote to committee work and too anxious to avoid the authority of principals and central staff members. But there is great promise and potentiality in teacher union and teacher association participation in creating a more relevant curriculum.

### The Student

Nor can the teacher of the 1970s afford to overlook the student as a participant in decision-making. Again, granted that student participation has

---

[22] Knezevich, p. 283.

often been clumsy, conflict oriented, and even violent, the potential of student participation is clear. New York City accepted a forward looking code concerning students' rights:

1. In each high school there should be established an elective and representative student government with offices open to all students. The student government will establish reasonable standards for candidates for office. All students should be allowed to vote in annual elections designed to promote careful consideration of the issues and candidates.
   a. The student government shall have the power to allocate student activity funds, subject to established audit controls and the by-laws of the Board of Education. Extracurricular activities shall be conducted under guidelines established by the student government. The student government shall be involved in the process of developing curriculum and of establishing disciplinary policies.
   b. Representatives selected by the student government shall meet at least monthly with the principal to exchange views, to share in the formulation of school student policies and to discuss school-student relations and any other matters of student concern.
2. A parent-student-faculty consultative council, as established by previous Board of Education resolutions, shall meet at least monthly to discuss any matter relating to

Teachers in an in-service training session.

*Paul S. Conklin*

the high school. The Consultative Council shall organize a subcommittee to consider matters of school-wide concern submitted by individual students. The subcommittee shall place such problems on the agenda of the consultative council when appropriate.

The consultative council shall establish a continuing relationship with the principal to secure information regarding the administration of the school, to make recommendations for the improvement of all school services and to promote implementation of agreed upon innovations. Its structure and operating procedures shall be placed on file with the Chancellor.

3. Official school publications shall reflect the policy and judgment of the student editors. This entails the obligation to be governed by the standards of responsible journalism, such as avoidance of libel, obscenity and defamation. Student publications shall provide as much opportunity as possible for the sincere expression of all shades of student opinion.

4. Students may exercise their constitutionally protected rights of free speech and assembly so long as they do not interfere with the operations of the regular school program.

   a. Students have a right to wear political buttons, armbands, and other badges of symbolic expression, as long as these do not violate the limits set in 4c, below.

   b. Students may distribute political leaflets, newspapers and other literature at locations adjacent to the school.

   c. Students shall be allowed to distribute literature on school property at specified locations and times designated. The principal and the student government shall establish guidelines governing the time and place of distribution at a site that will not interfere with normal school activities. They will also provide for sanctions against those who do not adhere to prescribed procedures.

      No commercial or obscene material, nothing of a libelous nature or involving the defamation of character nor anything advocating racial or religious prejudice will be permitted to be distributed within the school. In noting these exceptions it is clearly the intention of the Board of Education to promote the dissemination of diverse viewpoints and to foster discussion of all political and social issues.

   d. Students may form political and social organizations, including those that champion unpopular causes. These organizations, however, must be open to all students and must abide by Board of Education policies as developed in guidelines established by the student government acting in concert with the principal. These organizations shall have reasonable access to school facilities.

5. Faculty advisers shall be appointed by the principal after consultation with the student group.

6. Students have the right to determine their own dress, except where such dress is clearly dangerous, or is so distractive as to clearly interfere with the learning and teaching process. This right may not be restricted even by a dress code arrived at by a majority vote of students, as Dr. Ewald Nyquist, Acting State Commissioner of Education, held this year in Decisions No. 8022 and 8023.

7. Students shall receive annually upon the opening of school a publication setting forth rules and regulations to which students are subject. This publication shall also include a statement of the rights and responsibilities of students. It shall be distributed to parents as well.

8. A hearing must be held within five school days of any suspension as prescribed by law and the circulars of the Chancellor (Superintendent of Schools).

9. The extent and definition of student rights and responsibilities are subject to discussion by the consultative councils. Appeals from the decisions of the head of the school, relating to rights and responsibilities herein enumerated, must first be lodged with the assistant superintendent in charge of the high schools, then the Chancellor and finally the central Board of Education. All such appeals shall be decided as quickly as possible.

10. Rights also entail responsibilities. One of the major goals of this document is to establish a new trust, one based on the humane values of self-respect and respect for others. No student has the right to interfere with the education of his fellow students. If dialogue is interrupted or destroyed, then the bonds that hold us together are broken. It is thus the responsibility of each student to respect the rights of all who are involved in the educational process.

*Explanation.* This resolution is an attempt to state systematically some of the rights and responsibilities of senior high school students. In no way does it diminish the legal authority of the school officials and of the Board of Education to deal with disruptive students. The resolution recognizes the student's responsibility for his conduct and at the same time extends the range of his responsibility. It is meant to foster greater understanding so that students, parents, teachers and administrators can more effectively participate in an active educational partnership.[23]

Let us grant that students cannot possibly know completely what is best for them. Yet the fact remains that they are the ultimate consumers of the curriculum. They too deserve a voice in the making of decisions. The quality of their education is involved. After a period of struggle which may be particularly sharp in schools that previously have been indifferent to viewpoints of students, we may move into a period in which the student relationship to decision-making proves productive. This is a frontier on which the new teacher, who is nearest to the contemporary student generation, might be active.

### The Curriculum

The curriculum is also a force in decision-making in the individual school. Some educators believe it to be a more important force than the individuals who supposedly make the decisions as they set policies, administer, and teach.

The curriculum is made up of all of the learning experiences under the control of the school. Therefore, such subjects as arithmetic in the third grade or French in high school are part of the school curriculum. So is the school trip or the interscholastic football game. Whatever learning experiences a school affords are part of the curriculum. (The curriculum will be defined further in Chapters 17 and 18.)

The curriculum of the specific school in which you will teach is

[23] Board of Education's amended resolution on "Rights and Responsibilities of Senior High School Students," *New York Times,* July 8, 1970, p. 16.

influenced by historic backgrounds and social forces. The curriculum is influenced by whether the school is public, parochial, or independent. It is influenced by individuals, by the broad educational policies, and by the various forces which exist in the system and school in which you work.

If we look for the central defining agency of the curriculum of your school, we must again turn to the individual state. For the broad framework of subjects and requirements are set forth by the state legislature and are more specifically defined by the state department of public instruction or education. The law of a state often defines in a general way the minimum curriculum offerings. Sometimes laws go further to specify particular areas or emphases, such as American history or driver education, which must be taught in all the schools.

The total educational program of a state is administered and supervised by a State Department of Education. The chief administrator is appointed or elected to a position called State Superintendent, Commissioner of Education, Superintendent of Public Instruction, or a similar title. The chief administrative officer is responsible to a state board of education, which functions much like boards of education at the local level. In accordance with policies established by the state board of education, the administrative officer and his staff often function in a regulatory manner with respect to such matters as finances, teacher certification, and pupil attendance. Legislatures often assign to state departments of education responsibility for fostering within the schools programs of instruction in citizenship, adult education, vocational education, etc. State department personnel often participate in workshops, in-service programs, and conferences at local and regional levels. The state staff often develops bulletins and guides for use in schools throughout the state.

Despite this apparent restriction, local school systems have substantial latitude in arriving at curriculum decisions. After all, it is the local board of education that is responsible for broad curriculum policies and it is the superintendent and supporting staff who must execute these policies and realize the goals set by the board. So curriculum making is an activity which utilizes the energies of many educators at the local level. In the United States there is considerable variation in the degree to which local school systems depend on standardized resources supplied by the state and by textbook publishers and the degree to which they depend on local initiative and teacher-influenced curricular approaches.

For instance, some school systems depend heavily upon whatever courses of study or curriculum guides are provided by the state. Such courses of study are often prepared by a single individual or a few "experts." In some schools, the "curriculum" is almost synonymous with textbooks adopted for use throughout the state. What some teachers teach is exactly what a textbook prescribes.

Fortunately, educators are becoming increasingly more active in making curricular programs. Today, when curriculum guides are used they are sometimes the products of high level curriculum projects carried on jointly by scholars in the disciplines and by educators, including teachers. Projects such as PSSC (physics) or BSCS (biology) or SMSG (mathematics) are the products of scholars organized in a physical science study committee, a biological science curriculum study, and a school mathematics study group respectively.

Today even more enterprising educators stress curriculum development to meet the needs of students in the individual school situation. Such curriculum development even refuses to be bound by the names of established subject matter. Out of such experimentation has grown concern for interdisciplinary problems such as race relations and international relations. Out of such experimentation has grown the combination or fusion of subjects, such as the combining of English and social studies into a unified studies or core program. Out of such experimentation has grown open education and more informal approaches to learning.

## WHO IS IN CHARGE HERE?

This chapter has emphasized forces contributing to decisions in a particular school within a particular school system. The question is, "Who *is* in charge here anyway?" Nominally within the individual school it is the principal—who, it is important to remember, works within a larger setting. He is in constant and sometimes complex interaction with members of the superintendent's team. Because he represents only one school, he sometimes conflicts with administrators who must make decisions that affect all schools in the district. He is very much subject to decisions made at the level of the superintendent of schools and to the policy-making responsibility of the board of education. The surrounding power structure, whether completely understood by him or not, plays its part in the complex process of decision-making. The individual principal also has to take into account the students and teachers in his school and those who live in the immediate area of the school and the views of all these individuals.

Perhaps the best answer to our question is to recognize that no single person is "in charge here," as there would be within an authoritarian system. Instead, the affairs of the individual school are subject to the interaction of a variety of forces, some far beyond the community at the national level. These forces interrelate and shape and reshape each other and out of the interplay come the decisions reached within the individual school.

The new teacher may look with some degree of anxiety at a situation marked by dynamic forces and constant flux. He may prefer the security of clear-cut decisions made by clearly identifiable persons. As Erich

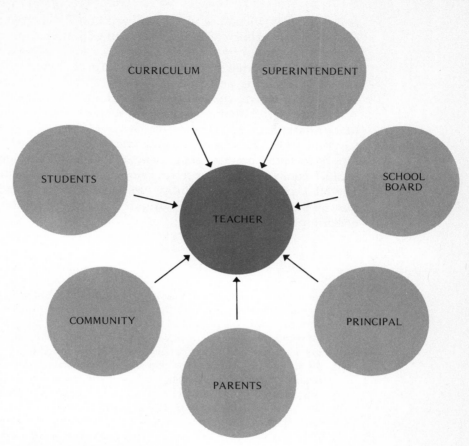

**FIGURE 9-1    Influences on the American Teacher**

Fromm pointed out, many people fear freedom; perhaps such individuals will be unhappy in a situation marked by a balance of forces rather than by a dominating decision maker (whether it takes the form of a human being such as a principal or a medium of instruction such as the textbook for the course).

On the other hand, the new teacher may have the type of personality that welcomes the challenge of flexibility and flux. The very existence of a variety of influences gives him the opportunity to make decisions for himself, particularly with respect to his classrooms and students. Rather than imposing a high degree of restriction on his teaching, the variety of forces influencing the program of individual schools often results in less restrictiveness than the new teacher expects.

The wide variety of individuals responsible for decision-making makes it important for teachers and administrators to identify the goals and objectives which are to be achieved and the degree to which each educator responsible contributes to good education. "Accountability" is strongly advocated by some citizens and educators today. Variation in responsibilities often causes parents to urge common standards and ways of measuring achievement. Teachers are being asked to develop evidence which will show whether or not they are successful in teaching. Administrators are being asked to be accountable for their performance. Many individuals and groups which have different perceptions are attempting to hold educators accountable for results. The National Education Association opposes state mandated accountability programs which compel, constrain, and coerce educators and students, as the NEA sees it. The NEA prefers "responsibility" to "accountability" and recommends that teachers have sufficient authority and decision-making power to perform professional work.

## DISCUSSION

1. What is the meaning of power structure as applied to American communities? To American education? What are the variations in power structures in America, according to students of power?
2. What seems to you to be the power structure in the community in which you live or in which you study? Find out how valid your reported impressions are.
3. In the schools you attended did you see any evidence of pressure groups at work in establishing or changing school policy or emphases in the curriculum?
4. In what ways might a large number of new people moving into a community create a change in the community's educational system?
5. What is the usual role of board of education members in the power structure? What are possible roles in the power structure which board of education members could play?
6. Why did boards of education come into being in the United States?
7. What is the usual social composition of boards of education? What is the situation in your own community? Is any change in the social composition becoming obvious? Any minority group members? Discuss and revise the list of responsibilities of a local school board summarized by Knezevich.
8. What is the function of written policy statements for a school system? Do they exist in your community?
9. What are some illustrations of distinctions between policy making and administration in education? Have there been any controversies in this connection in your community?
10. How has the work of the school board member grown increasingly complicated in recent years?
11. How did the superintendent's responsibility change over the years?
12. What are the academic backgrounds of the superintendents in school systems which have been attended by members of your class?
13. Revise the cited list of responsibilities of the superintendent in accordance with your perception of his proper responsibilities.
14. To what extent is the American superintendent "the board's man"?

15. How did the central office staff evolve? What were some first additions to the staff? What is the nature of the staff in the community you know best?

16. What are some issues in the question of centralization or decentralization of the administration of school systems? What are the latest developments in decentralization?

17. How does a supervisor perceive his responsibility?

18. What are the usual channels of communication between members of the public or teachers and the superintendent of schools and the board of education? How can these channels of communication be improved? What is the situation in your own community?

19. Basically, what is the role of the school principal? How did this post evolve?

20. To what extent are teachers participants in decision-making in schools? Should they be? What gains or losses come from greater teacher participation?

21. Should students play a role in the determination of educational matters? In determining the curriculum? In presenting and handling grievances? In teacher rating? In promotion and tenure and salaries?

22. How is the curriculum a force in decision-making in an individual school?

23. Who has been in charge in the schools you have attended? Do you agree that this individual or combination of individuals should have been in charge? Who do you think should be in charge in an individual school? Should educators be held "accountable" for results?

## INVOLVEMENT

1. With the help of a sociologist, work out approaches to determine the power structure in a community. Interviews and questionnaires might be employed. Conclusions should be drawn with care, and throughout the investigation the possible negative repercussions should be recognized.

2. Attempt to generalize on the nature of the power structure in the community you know best.

3. Find the names, educational backgrounds, and areas of work of the members of your local board of education. Does your board membership represent the more affluent and socially prominent elements of your community? Does it represent pressure groups? Are minority groups represented? In what ways does it reflect the model outlined in the chapter? In what ways does it differ?

4. Attend some meetings of the board of education of your home community or the community in which you are a student. Inquire about how people attain their posts on school boards, their positions on issues before the board, etc. If an opportunity occurs, speak up for any viewpoint which you think the board should take into account.

5. Locate a copy of the Policy Handbook of your local school corporation. What areas does it cover generally? What are some of the exact rules and regulations it spells out? What kinds of implications do you see in these?

6. Draw up some distinctions between policy making and administration for consideration by the class.

7. Invite the superintendent or one of his representatives to describe the program and problems of a local school system to your class. Ask the superintendent or his representative about recent changes in his work, including negotiations regarding salary, etc.

8. Invite a school supervisor to class to describe his relationship to the new teacher and the help he attempts to provide.

9. Invite a school principal to class to discover the kind of teacher he would like to employ. Discuss the desirable characteristics of such a teacher.

10. Visit the central office of your local school district. Obtain or make a chart of the organization of the administrative staff including both line and staff officers.

11. Invite several teachers to class to discuss their role in decision-making in schools. Attempt to clarify differences and similarities among them.

12. Interview a teacher you admire and ask him or her to frankly report to you his or her views of the functions and responsibilities of the school principal and the supervisor.

13. Invite the president of the school government organization and a student critic of his school to your class to comment on the proper role of the students in decision-making.

14. Ask teachers about the role of the curriculum in decision-making within a particular school. If specific materials are cited as influential in decision-making, attempt to obtain copies of them.

15. Sum up what you have learned about who is in charge in a particular school system. Advance your own theory on who should be in charge. In so doing, take into account the variety of influencing forces.

## FURTHER READING

Bowers, C. A. (Ed.). *Education and Social Policy: Local Control of Education.* New York: Random House, 1970.  Original readings dealing with the complex relationship between politics and public education.

Cronin, Joseph M. *The Control of Urban Schools.* New York: Macmillan, 1973.  A history of school district organization over the past one hundred years.

Fantini, Mario, Marilyn Gittell, and Richard Magat. *Community Control and the Urban School.* New York: Praeger, 1970.  An account of developments in urban education from a point of view favoring community control.

Haubrich, Vernon F. (Ed.). *Freedom, Bureaucracy and Schooling.* Washington, D.C.: Association for Supervision and Curriculum Development, 1971.  A yearbook on bureaucracy which analyzes the problem, examines specific organizational structures in education, and examines the future of the common schools in America.

Heald, James E., Louis G. Romano, and Nicholas P. Georgiady (Eds.). *Selected Readings on General Supervision.* New York: Macmillan, 1970.  A variety of articles on current trends and practices in effective supervision.

Hencley, Stephen P., Lloyd E. McCleary, and J. H. McGrath. *The Elementary School Principalship.* New York: Dodd, Mead, 1973.  A theory-based presentation on the elementary school principalship.

Hostrop, R. W., J. A. Mecklenburger, and J. A. Wilson (Eds.). *Accountability for Educational Results.* Hamden, Conn.: Linnet Books, 1973. An anthology in which accountability is examined by thinkers and practitioners in education, business, government, and the media.

Kraft, Leonard E. *The Secondary School Principal in Action.* Dubuque, Iowa: Wm. C. Brown, 1971.  An anthology on the role of the principal at a time when there have been profound changes in philosophy and practices of secondary school administration.

Leeper, Robert R. (Ed.). *Supervision: Emerging Profession.* Washington, D.C.: Association for Supervision and Curriculum Development, NEA, 1969. An anthology on supervision made up of selections from *Educational Leadership,* the readable magazine of ASCD.

Netzer, Lanore A., Glen G. Eye, Marshall E. Dimock, Matthew P. Dumont, Lloyd Homme, Fremont E. Kast, Stephen J. Knezevich. *Education, Administration, and Change.* New York: Harper & Row, 1970. A comprehensive book that acquaints the reader with administrative programs and problems.

Sexton, Patricia Cayo. *Readings on the School in Society.* Englewood Cliffs, N.J.: Prentice-Hall, 1967. An anthology that contributes a sociological perspective to educational analysis through the study of power, the economy, social stratification, values, organizations, structures within the school, and research and development.

Townsend, Robert. *Up the Organization.* New York: Alfred A. Knopf, 1971. An amusing and irreverent compendium of suggestions on improving administration within American corporations. Many suggestions of the author, a highly successful businessman, apply also to school administration and the work of board members and chief executives.

Wasserman, Miriam. *The School Fix, NYC, USA.* New York: Simon & Schuster, 1971. The community-control movement and the conflicts between it and various groups in the school system. The author's vivid report on power and status struggles in the New York City public schools.

## SELECTED AUDIO-VISUAL MATERIALS

*The Administration Series* (35 mm filmstrip, 4 filmstrips/record, color, Scott Education, 1970). Delineates the functional relationship of school personnel. Titles are: Superintendent of Schools, the School Principal, the Board of Education, and the Instructional Supervisor.

*An Approach to School Site Development* (16 mm film, 22 min., color, International Film Bureau, Inc. 1966). A case study in Ann Arbor, Michigan, shows the planning committee, various classes and teachers, local citizens, and youth groups helping with the environment and utilizing the natural features of the land for an enriched educational program.

*Helpers At Our School* (16 mm film, 11 min., color, Coronet, 1966). A school custodian, lunchroom cook, principal, teacher, and other members of the school community describe the operation of the school.

*The Principal* (35 mm filmstrip, 34 frs/captions, color, McGraw-Hill, 1969). The work of the principal.

*School Buildings, 1967* (35 mm filmstrip, 164 frs., color, American Association of School Administrators, 1967). Examines school building programs—views of interiors, exteriors, sites, and plans of schools ranging from elementary through junior college level.

*School Workers* (35 mm filmstrip, 8 filmstrips, color, McGraw-Hill Films, 1969). Presents important aspects of school life including the interdependence of people, division of labor, and specialization.

*You and Your School* (16 mm film, 9 min., color, ABC Media Concepts, 1970). Encourages students to get to know their school better—how it works and who works for it.

TEN

# What is expected of American teachers?

The word *role* once meant simply a part or a character to be played by an actor or actress. In more recent years, however, it has been borrowed from the theatre for sociological and educational purposes, and an adaptation has been made of its secondary definition, "the proper or customary function of a person or thing." Grace Graham, for instance, writes,

> Adolescents, like adults, have many statuses and roles. Status refers to one's position in a group, and *role* to the behavior associated with a particular status. A teenager may be a son, a brother, a steady boy friend, a buddy, a part-time employee, a student, a football player, a class president, and a leading character in a school play. In each of these statuses, he plays a different role. How he plays the role is determined to a considerable extent by the manner in which others expect him to play it.[1]

Harold L. Hodgkinson specifically compares the theatrical role with the individual's role in society: "Just as an actor learns a given role which he will perform, so each individual acquires a role for each reference group to which he refers. This role represents the desired norms and performances of the reference group."[2] Educators apply this concept to the varied people related to the educational process.

## THE ROLES OF THE TEACHER

Today the individual teacher is expected to assume a variety of activities and behaviors. If you are to be an effective teacher, you must be familiar

[1] Grace Graham, *The Public School in the New Society* (New York: Harper & Row, 1969), p. 336.
[2] Harold L. Hodgkinson, *Education in Social and Cultural Perspectives* (Englewood Cliffs, N.J.: Prentice-Hall, 1962), p. 3.

with your self-expectations and with the expectations others hold for you. With an understanding of these differing expectations, you can better recognize and react to praise and criticism you will necessarily encounter. If you become skillful in managing your responses to criticism, you may be better equipped to encounter potential conflicts. With knowledge of expectations, you may more intelligently appraise and respond to current emphasis on "accountability."

If your knowledge of roles is supplemented by an understanding of social realities, of your students' personal-social needs, and of an educational philosophy in which you are confident, you will be well-equipped for the conflicts and criticisms that may arise.

But not all citizens are critics of teachers. In general, American community members regard teachers with a degree of respect; the status studies described in Chapter Four indicate that Americans consider teachers as within the upper third of occupational groups. The perceptions of community members vary according to community locales, parental and social class backgrounds, and inevitably, according to individual idiosyncrasies.

### Community Expectations in Differing Locales

Rural community members are often well acquainted with the community's teachers. The rural teacher customarily lives in or near the village or town in which he teaches. He is one of the neighbors and is known not only as a teacher but as a resident, a householder, a citizen, and a participant in community life. As a result, he is frequently appraised in these roles rather than just as a teacher. If the morality of the community tends toward provincialism, he is usually expected to conform to what the community regards as reasonable limits on ideas and behavior. This does not mean that he is denied some degree of individuality, or indeed, eccentricity; it does mean that he is usually denied conspicuous violations of the community's accepted codes.

In the city the situation is somewhat different. In the first place, the teacher often lives outside the neighborhood in which he teaches. Though he is far from wealthy, he is by background or has become by occupation a middle class person. As such, he may be somewhat removed in ideas as well as in income from the poorer or wealthier section of the city in which he may teach.

Since the middle classes steadily leave the city, the middle class teacher usually either joins the flight to the suburbs or lives in one of the remaining middle class neighborhoods. He is therefore less often encountered by the community as a householder or community participant than his rural counterpart. Indeed, this is one of the criticisms urban low income community residents have of their middle class teachers. In the urban community the teacher is often viewed somewhat impersonally and is met only on those occasions when community organizations or individual necessities bring the community member to the school. The result is twofold: more freedom or opportunity for variation in the teacher's personal life-style, and more parent and student interest in his teaching role and performance than in his total personality. This does not mean that the teacher's personal life can outrage the urban community's sensibility; it does mean that his personal life is less visible to community members in the city setting.

Almost the same relationship of the teacher to the community is present in the suburb as in the city, though to a different degree. Few teachers can afford to live in conspicuously upper income suburban communities. Indeed, some prefer not to live in such communities because perceptions of them as community service persons might interfere with their social patterns of living. Similarly, teachers are usually paid at a higher level than most residents of working class suburbs and often prefer to live elsewhere. Many middle class suburbs do exist in which teachers both live and work, and where teachers become known as householders and participants. A suburban teacher may also live in a middle class community near the community in which he teaches. Since suburban newspapers often cover a county-wide area, or at least a larger area than one community, teachers may become known to citizens in the community in which they teach through accounts of community and social activities, community participation, etc. Occasionally a teacher may teach in a neighboring school system and serve concurrently as a member of the school board in his home community; thus, both communities become familiar with his views as he records his votes on school board issues.

### Parental Expectations Influenced by Class and Minority Group Backgrounds

A teacher encounters expectations and perceptions by community members which are closely related to the social class backgrounds of the particular neighborhood. For instance, an upper class parent's expectations of the teacher may be to impart to the child the technical skill and knowledge he or she will need to enter the college of his choice. Support for educational innovation also exists in such communities, particularly on the part of parents alert to psychological insights and convinced of the importance of motivation; these parents, as a rule, take pride in having their schools do the "in" thing. But even supporters of innovation seldom support change at the expense of student admission into the best colleges.

Socioeconomic factors account for some contrasting parental conceptions concerning the community's teachers which may be surprising, or even alarming to the young teacher. Some rich persons equate teachers directly with the servant class. The comment of a matron in a wealthy suburb of Westchester County, New York, represents the view of a few very wealthy persons: "I don't see why that nice young school teacher hasn't married one of our chauffeurs." On the other hand, some first

*Ford Foundation, (Arthur Liepzig)*

Counselor visits a home to discuss a student's problems and his school program with family.

generation Americans from middle or working class neighborhoods highly respect teachers and want their children to teach.

Until recently, the characteristic experience of a teacher in a working class district was to encounter few parents. The typical working class community member seemed to assume that the school as an institution knew what it was doing and that teachers knew far more than community members about education. Only when school authorities required their presence because of their children's misbehavior did parents appear at the school. The prevalent attitude was not so much indifference as a feeling that education was not the parent's business.

In contemporary life this attitude has been replaced in some communities by militant concern by the poor, especially minority groups, regarding the quality of education their children are receiving. Rather than passive acceptance, a tone of disappointment, anger, and hostility often characterizes the new relationships of some local community residents to the schools. Militant community members have not only picketed and demonstrated; they have sometimes entered the schools in sit-ins or have withdrawn their children from schools in boycotts or strikes. In some major cities there have been confrontations between striking teachers and militant community members bent on keeping the schools open. Charges of racism by blacks against predominantly white

235

teaching staff members, and by teachers against black militants have become commonplace.

The spokesmen for militant community groups charge that the schools have failed to teach many children to read, write, spell, and handle arithmetic adequately. Repeatedly, some minority group children have failed tests devised by educators to appraise the success of outcomes of teaching. Curriculum content relevant to blacks and other minority groups in America has been ignored or dealt with lightly, say the critics. Demands have mounted for school studies which take into account the black experience, including black history. The qualifications of whites to teach blacks have been sharply questioned by vigorous propo-

Sex education in the schools is one area in which community influence is felt.

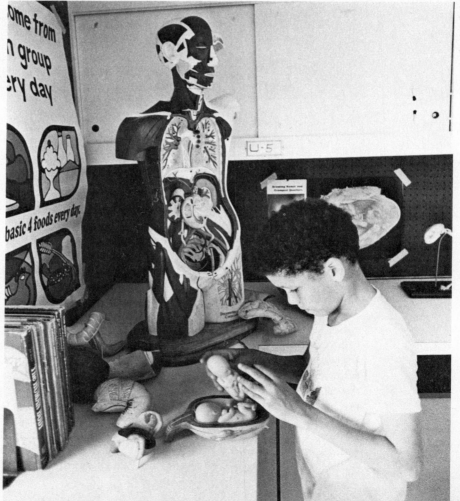

Stock, Boston

Busing to achieve desegregation continues to be a controversial issue in many communities.

nents of relevant education. Some black communities have demanded the replacement of white teachers and administrators by members of their own race. In many communities, the former passivity of parents has been replaced by involvement and often turmoil. Community groups increasingly believe that teachers and administrators must be held accountable for the educational product of the schools.

Simultaneously, some residents of white working or middle class districts have grown suspicious of schools and teachers because of what some white residents regard as favoritism and partiality to minority group members. Parents in such communities have sometimes resisted programs of intercultural or intergroup education and have demonstrated against minority group students being bused into "their neighborhood," or majority group students being bused out into minority group neighborhoods. The anger and hostility of such white groups are growing and their influence on school and political programs is evident. Busing children to achieve desegregation became a hot issue in the Presidential campaign of 1972.

In community conflict situations, the parents of students play an important part. They see themselves as being most intimately concerned, for it is their children's welfare and lives which are at stake.

### Individual Expectations by Citizens

Teachers at any level of a public school system can testify to the completely individualized set of perceptions and problems brought to school by the parents of individual children. Even some of the most helpfully motivated parent-teacher association members often have difficulty in dealing with the real issues concerning the needs of a school in general because they are so concerned for the welfare of their own children. Differing individual expectations concerning the purposes of education are characteristic of parents in communities which appear homogeneous but which actually are not.

Let us illustrate impressionistically the variety of individual expectations by describing the views of some citizens of a community:

A neighbor who works for Bell Telephone Laboratories says, "There has been a tremendous explosion of knowledge in the past few years. Do you realize that 87 percent of all the scientists who ever lived are alive at this very moment? Knowledge is multiplying fantastically. I want my son to master concepts and relationships and to have the skills to acquire and use the new knowledge, especially in the sciences and modern mathematics."

Another neighbor, who is a member of the local League of Women Voters, says, "I listen to my daughter's friends when they're sitting around our house. They want to make a difference in this world but they have no idea of how to go about it. High schools ought to teach them how to participate in community life as young citizens and how to deal with social forces and problems."

Another of my neighbors has a deserved reputation as a good mother. She says, "I want my children to be good human beings. For instance, I hope they will hear and play music, read widely and love knowledge, be creative in the arts, take part eagerly in sports, and enjoy their leisure. The need is for well-balanced people who hold to humane values. I hope the high schools help the young to solve their problems and to live with themselves."

Another neighbor owns a garage. He says, "Not everybody goes to college for further education and for preparation for a professional career. High schools ought to teach practical skills too so that a youngster can move into a job after he gets his high school diploma. Girls ought to know more than they do about making a good home; they get married young these days and homemaking and child raising soon become their jobs. Now the courses my son and daughter are taking. . . ."

My neighbors and your neighbors have a variety of ideas on what their children should be taught in high schools. And no wonder. A variety of young people from a wide diversity of family and economic backgrounds go to high schools today.[3]

### Administrative Expectations

The administrators with whom the teacher usually has the closest working relationship, whether good or bad, are the school principal and/or assistant principal. The principal is usually a former teacher who has been

---

[3] William Van Til, "What Makes a Good High School Curriculum?" *Woman's Day* (October 1964), pp. 42, 104.

recognized for his ability in organization and his skill in human relations. The assistant principal, who carries on those functions delegated to him by the principal, has usually had even more recent experience in teaching than the principal. Since both types of leaders usually have come to their posts via teaching responsibilities, they may be expected to view education in somewhat the same way as the teacher.

In addition to practical classroom experience, today's building administrator holds a master's degree and has taken a number of graduate courses in administration; the more ambitious are working towards a doctoral degree in education. Thus they are acquainted with current ideas on organization, curriculum innovation, supervision, human relations, and administrative procedures in general. This background inclines them to look with approval on teachers who are experimental and innovative. But, at the same time, the responsibility they feel for the efficient administration of their schools inclines them to lack sympathy with those who unduly cause problems. Administrators do not often enjoy conflict or particularly appreciate teachers who are controversial; teachers who are able to manage their own affairs within the classroom without excessive calls upon the principal's office are valued. Administrators are inclined to view with distinct reservations those teachers who bring them long lists of grievances or a variety of complaints.

Thus, the principal is pulled in two directions. In general, his graduate work and his own perceptions of himself as a former teacher and present administrative leader conflict with his desire to "run a tight ship" and to minimize conflicts. Consequently, principals have been known to talk one way about desirable innovations and experimentation and to behave in another way by rewarding conformity.

But it is extremely difficult to generalize on the expectations of principals since principals are as varied as teachers. Whenever possible, the new teacher might attempt to include an interview with the principal prior to teaching in a school. The quality of the principal and his administrative staff can make a great difference in the experience of the new teacher.

The superintendent, though a vital factor in the development of the school system, is often a somewhat remote figure to the classroom teacher. In some school systems, the superintendent is seen as he presides over the opening of school in-service education sessions before or after each Labor Day; then he becomes invisible to the teacher for the balance of the year as he presides over mysterious operations developed through the central office. Obviously, this is not the case with the better superintendents, who participate ex-officio in many committees and who are familiar figures in individual schools. Yet even the most active superintendent must depend heavily on his supporting staff for supervision and the improvement of curriculum and instruction.

Consequently, in the usual school system the teacher encounters the superintendent's supporting staff more often than the superintendent himself. The superintendent's supporting staff members may include assistant superintendents, curriculum directors, personnel directors, and business managers with whom the new teacher often comes into contact during interviews, contract negotiations, certification procedures, curriculum planning, and supply requisition.

The role of the supporting staff is to improve the quality of the school system in the particular area of specialization represented by the supporting staff member. He gains his professional recognition and salary increments through success in his specialization. Consequently, many supporting staff members are genuinely eager to help teachers perform better—especially in the area of the staff member's specialization! If the teacher's perception of his work coincides with that of the specialist, a harmonious relationship is predictable. If the teacher's perception varies to a noticeable degree, it is likely that the supporting staff member will attempt, preferably (but not invariably) through democratic procedures and human relations techniques, to modify the teacher's approach. Whether the supporting staff member will be regarded by the teacher as a helpful person or as a menacing "snoopervisor" depends heavily upon the personalities and the professional skills of the interacting individuals. Fortunately, during the past decade supervision has moved steadily away from a scientific management approach toward a human relations oriented approach and from authoritarian procedures toward democratic processes.

### Board of Education Expectations

Members of boards of education occupy a strategic place in the total pattern of perceptions and expectations in a school system. The board member sees himself as responsible to his community. Yet at the same time, he is not bound to simply reflect the community majority; in many cases he is a vigorous spokesman for education in community debates concerning financing schools or in criticisms directed against the school. Ideally, he is a spokesman for good education and a mediating force between the school and the community.

The typical school board member is more often called upon to deal with financial factors, such as the ever-pressing questions of budget and financial support for the schools, rather than with matters of content and instruction. Unless curriculum matters become controversial in the community, the board member tends to leave content and instruction to the professionals. The school board member thus often finds that his role is political in nature rather than a role of educational leadership.

As teachers bargain collectively, the board of education member may find himself cast in the role of antagonist to the teacher. Increasingly, teachers discriminate between those board members who are "for" them and those who are "against" them. Thus, the school board member has an ungrateful task. Though he supplies unsalaried service to the community, he is sometimes unpopular with large or small segments of the community and the professional staff. Seldom is this more evident than in matters which are financially controversial such as determining salaries, or in situations which are programmatically controversial such as sex education, teaching about communism, etc. If one wishes to be universally loved, one does not become a school board member.

The school board member's expectation of the teacher is that the teacher "do a good job." But definitions of what is a good job vary from board member to board member, even as performance of a good job varies from teacher to teacher.

### Student Perceptions and Expectations

Relatively innocent of such community and administrative expectations are the students. While other forces may react to teachers as a collective group, the student is usually much more concerned with the specific teachers who teach him than with intangible abstractions concerning the "teacher." Studies have been made as to what students value in teachers. A common thread running through such studies is the preference of students for teachers who are fair though firm, who have a sense of humor, who see and help students as individuals, who know their subjects, and who try to make their teaching relevant to students' lives and experiences.

For example, Hulda Grobman asked members of her New York University undergraduate education class who had no previous teaching experience to list "things they hoped as teachers they would never do in the classroom." The top seven items on their list were the following: "be ill-mannered; lose temper, scream; lack love of all individual students; pick a favorite or scapegoat; use sarcasm; be unfair (closeminded); do the same routine each year."[4] Alton Harrison, Jr., and E. G. Scriven asked students at Northern Illinois University to "describe the best teacher you ever had and state why you selected that particular teacher." These students indicated that the most important teacher characteristics are "respects students, empathetic, understanding, provides student participation, encourages self-direction, excellent presentations, knowledgeable."[5] The twenty self-rating questions on p. 242 should help you in understanding student perceptions and expectations.[6] How do you rate?

### Fellow Teacher Perceptions and Expectations

Colleagues also have their perceptions and expectations of the new teacher. Since teaching is essentially not a competitive business, as is, for example, advertising, the new teacher is usually welcomed by his col-

---

[4] Hulda Grobman, "To See Ourselves as Others See Us," *Childhood Education* (March 1969), p. 396.

[5] Alton Harrison, Jr. and E. G. Scriven, "Is There a Relevancy Gap in Education?" *Peabody Journal of Education* (March 1969), pp. 303–307.

[6] Gordon A. Sabine, *How Students Rate Their Schools and Teachers* (Washington, D.C.: National Association of Secondary School Principals, 1971), pp. 2, 75, 76.

## TWENTY SELF-RATING QUESTIONS FOR TEACHERS

### Answer "yes" or "no":

_____ Do I really care and let my students know?

_____ Do I really listen to my students and hear what they say?

_____ Am I there when my students need me—after class, after school, at home by the telephone?

_____ Do students bring their personal problems to me?

_____ Do I know all my students' names?

_____ Am I there to make each student feel important, rather than just to make myself feel powerful?

_____ Can I tell when a student is "uptight" and respond to his feelings?

_____ Do I know my subject matter well enough to welcome all questions in class?

_____ Do I get my students to think instead of merely parroting back what I say?

_____ Is there an orderly climate for learning in my classroom?

_____ Do I emphasize learning more than discipline?

_____ Do I spend time with the slow learners who really need it, rather than "copping out" by concentrating on just the bright ones?

_____ Do I keep my students from getting bored or going to sleep in my class?

_____ Do all my students participate?

_____ Do I work my students and myself hard enough so we both end the year with a sense of accomplishment rather than merely a feeling of relief?

_____ Do I grade on learning, rather than on a like-dislike basis?

_____ Can I admit my own mistakes openly?

_____ Can we still be friends if one of my students disagrees with me and proves me wrong?

_____ Do students learn from my tests, instead of merely memorizing and then forgetting?

_____ Would my students have characterized me on YOUTHPOLL as their best teacher?

(These are among the characteristics of teachers the YOUTHPOLL* students said they most needed and admired. Give yourself 5 points for every "yes" answer. Score above 75 and you're pretty good.)

*YOUTHPOLL was conducted through the American College Testing Program in the fall of 1970. The students were selected from the million high school juniors and seniors who had taken the ACT battery of tests during 1969–70. The YOUTHPOLL was based on responses of 1,603 students who were college bound.

leagues. The typical teacher, who you will recall is "going on thirty-nine years in age," in contrast to the new teacher, who is about twenty-two, often adopts a semiparental as well as professional attitude toward the newcomer. So the experienced colleague is likely to adopt the role of an insider advising an outsider as to the practical facts of life in respect to students, program, administration, and even other teachers. Some experienced teachers make a point of putting an arm around the shoulder of the new teacher, figuratively if not always literally, and advising him or her to forget the nonsense learned in teacher education programs and to proceed in accordance with the experienced colleague's advice—which will then immediately be tendered the newcomer. Such advice should be carefully listened to and appraised, yet taken with several grains of salt by the new teacher. The natural insecurity of the newcomer should not lead him to abandon in panic all he has learned and planned. Above all, advice from the veterans should not lead him to reject his own teaching style arrived at through his own experience in living and his thoughtful consideration of education. Sensible modifications, yes; total rejection, no. Respectful listening without express commitment, accompanied by attempts to develop good human relationships with the colleague, seem to be the best approach for the new teacher.

As the months go by, the new teacher will probably build intellectual identifications and sometimes friendships with particular teachers who are closest to his own life-style and goals, accompanied by increasing respect for the perceptions and expectations of such selected colleagues. Simultaneously, the teacher may experience a degree of widening gap between himself and other colleagues who do not see things his way. But life will be better for all involved if the new teacher does not dramatize the gap through publicly or privately expressed contempt for the ideas, techniques, or performance of colleagues. Professional ethics supports mutual toleration, as does enlightened self-interest, since experienced colleagues may have developed their own ways of manifesting disapproval of their untenured young colleagues.

As America learned in the 1960s, wars should be chosen with great caution and care. Choosing one's "wars" applies not only to countries but also to the individual. A new teacher should be quite sure of the harmfulness of a colleague to whatever the new teacher holds vital before he engages in any warlike activities. The new teacher should carry his torch as a person of conviction, but should avoid burning people with it.

## The Teacher's Self-expectations

The most crucial and complex of the variety of expectations and perceptions of the teacher's role are those held by the teacher himself. To suggest a fixed pattern of desirable expectations which you should hold would be presumptuous and unrealistic. Instead, we suggest some factors to take into account in arriving at your own expectations. Above all, you might ask yourself why you have chosen teaching as your career. What do you hope to achieve through teaching? What is your guiding philosophy? What contribution to society do you hope to make through teaching? What kind of teacher do you want to be?

The young teacher's self-expectations are often unrealistically high; conversely, his self-image is often unrealistically low. He tends to overestimate the influence that he is expected to have on his students and he is often alarmed at the exhaustion which he experiences as he encounters the myriad of responsibilities and long hours of work related to teaching. He is often fearful during his first weeks of teaching that the expectations of his supervisors, students, community, and fellow teachers are too high for his background and ability.

There is no substitute for thinking through your self-expectations, for recognizing the existence of expectations by others, and for using your own intelligence in reconciling conflicting expectations. Recognize that being a teacher will be a learning experience for you, yet that you have much to contribute. Rely on yourself yet be able to respect the varying outlooks of others and to evaluate their suggestions. By all means, use the help when needed of counselors, psychologists, or self-assessment classes in examining your self-expectations.

## WHO OWNS THE SCHOOLS?

Even though you understand the differing self-expectations of the teacher and the varying perceptions of teachers by individuals and groups, you still face a perplexity. In such a context, who should set the broad policies to guide the schools? What forces should determine the general direction in which education should go? Whose schools are these anyway?

Part of the answer is found in the modifiers of the word "school." If a school is private, it essentially belongs to the private board in which responsibility for policy-making is vested. If a school is parochial, it is usually thought of as belonging to the church which administers it. If it is a public school, it belongs to the people. In the case of the American public school system, it belongs to the people of the United States, the basic source of political authority.

### The People Own the Public Schools

But, you may ask, how about the teachers? Do the public school teachers own the public schools? They own the public schools no more than Richard M. Nixon owned the American presidency. In the American political system, whoever happens to be President occupies the Presidency but does not own the Presidency. Presidents can be removed and have been removed by the electoral process or can even, at congressional discretion, be removed by the impeachment process. Similarly, teachers occupy their positions by virtue of the people and at the discretion of the people.

Certainly the people should give substantial autonomy to those they have empowered to teach. But when the chips are down, public school teachers are the representatives of the people and not the owners of the schools. The ultimate power and ownership of the schools is vested in the American people. You may have possibly met teachers and administrators of whom it was said, "They act as if they own the school." But they don't own the school—the people do.

But "the people" is a large and amorphous abstraction. How have the people exercised their responsibility for setting the broad policies concerning the public schools?

### The Democratic Consensus

As we have seen, colonial governments such as the one in Massachusetts required communities to establish schools. With the formation of the nation and through the mechanism of the U.S. Constitution, education was delegated to the states as one of their "implied powers." Article X of the additions and amendments to the United States Constitution states, "The powers not delegated to the United States by the Constitution, nor prohibited by it to the States, are reserved to the States respectively, or to the people." Education was not specified as a power of the Congress; indeed, education is not mentioned in the U.S. Constitution. Through the states, the people established free public education in the nineteenth century and wrote provisions for free schools into the constitutions of nearly all of the states.

Obviously, with education the province of a number of expanding states, no mandate by a centralized federal government as to the proper work of the schools was ever handed down from Washington, D.C. Yet nations have a way of developing a general consensus without specific mandates. To the extent that a consensus as to the responsibilities of education exists in the United States, it is a reflection of the democratic values of Americans.

Americans vary in their ways of phrasing their constellation of values. Yet important in American value patterns, however variously phrased, is respect for the worth and dignity of the individual. Important too is concern for the general welfare to be achieved by working together for common purposes. Important is freedom to use one's own intelligence rather than accept authoritarian dictates. The history of ideas in America testifies to the American dedication to such central ideas in the democratic creed even though the pages of our history are blotted with violation of democratic values.

### Societal Spokesmen for the Democratic Consensus

Abraham Lincoln, for instance, was an outstanding spokesman for the American consensus on the importance of the democratic way of life. He once said, "As I would not be a slave, so I would not be a *master*. This expresses my idea of democracy. Whatever differs from this, to the extent of the difference, is no democracy."[7]

---

[7] Fragment (August 1, 1858?). From Roy P. Basler, *The Collected Works of Abraham Lincoln,* vol. 2 (New Brunswick, N.J.: Rutgers University Press, 1953), p. 532.

In the Lincoln-Douglas debate, Lincoln spoke of

. . . the eternal struggle between these two principles—right and wrong—throughout the world. They are the two principles that have stood face to face from the beginning of time; and will ever continue to struggle. The one is the common right of humanity, and the other the divine right of kings. It is the same principle in whatever shape it develops itself. It is the same spirit that says, 'You toil, work and earn bread, and I'll eat it.' No matter in what shape it comes, whether from the mouth of a king who seeks to bestride the people of his own nation and live by the fruit of their labor, or from one race of men as an apology for enslaving another race, it is the same tyrannical principle.[8]

He also said,

When . . . you have succeeded in dehumanizing the Negro; when you have put him down and made it impossible for him to be but as the beasts of the field; when you have extinguished his soul in this world and placed him where the ray of hope is blown out as in the darkness of the damned, are you quite sure that the demon you have roused will not turn and rend you? What constitutes the bulwark of our own liberty and independence? It is not our frowning battlements, our bristling sea coasts, our army and our navy. These are not our reliance against tyranny. All of those may be turned against us without making us weaker for the struggle. Our reliance is in the love of liberty which God has planted in us. Our defense is in the spirit which prized liberty as the heritage of all men, in all lands everywhere. Destroy this spirit and you have planted the seeds of despotism at your own doors. Familiarize yourselves with the chains of bondage and you prepare your own limbs to wear them. Accustomed to trample on the rights of others, you have lost the genius of your own independence and become the fit subjects of the first cunning tyrant who rises among you.[9]

In the twentieth century, Franklin D. Roosevelt phrased the American aspiration in terms of four freedoms. In a message to Congress some months before the United States entered World War II he said,

In the future day, which we seek to make secure, we look forward to a world founded upon four essential human freedoms. The first is freedom of speech and expression—everywhere in the world. The second is freedom of every person to worship God in his own way—everywhere in the world. The third is freedom from want . . . everywhere in the world. The fourth is freedom from fear . . . anywhere in the world.[10]

In the last year of his life, John F. Kennedy said,

So let us not be blind to our differences—but let us also direct attention to our common interests and the means by which those differences can be resolved. And if

[8] *Ibid.*, vol. 3, p. 315. Reply, seventh and last joint debate, Alton, Illinois (October 15, 1858).
[9] Speech, Edwardsville, Illinois (September 13, 1858).
[10] The State of the Union Message (January 6, 1941).

we cannot end now our differences, at least we can help make the world safe for diversity.[11]

In his inaugural address in 1969 Richard M. Nixon said,

Our greatest need now is to reach beyond government, to enlist the legions of the concerned and the committed. What has to be done has to be done by government and people together or it will not be done at all. The lesson of past agony is that without the people we can do nothing; with the people we can do everything.[12]

Martin Luther King, Jr. spoke for the American dream. He said,

I have a dream that one day this nation will rise up and live out the true meaning of its creed: "We hold these truths to be self-evident; that all men are created equal."

I have a dream that one day on the red hills of Georgia the sons of former slaves and the sons of former slaveowners will be able to sit down together at the table of brotherhood. . . .

I have a dream that my four little children will one day live in a nation where they will not be judged by the color of their skin but by the content of their character.

I have a dream today.[13]

John W. Gardner, formerly Secretary of the Department of Health, Education, and Welfare and more recently Chairman of Common Cause, has written of

. . . the great basic goals of our educational system: to foster individual fulfillment and to nurture the free, rational, and responsible men and women without whom our kind of society cannot endure. Our schools must prepare *all* young people, whatever their talents, for the serious business of being free men and women.[14]

## BROAD INFLUENCES ON EXPECTATIONS

Despite the consensus on a constellation of values defining the democratic way of life, expectations of public school teachers are influenced by many factors. Even though there may be agreement at a verbal level on respect for the individual, fostering the common welfare through working together for common purposes, and the use of intelligence in human affairs, there exist variant perceptions of what these mean in practice.

---

[11] Allan Nevins, ed., *The Burden and the Glory* (New York: Harper & Row, 1964), p. 57.
[12] Inaugural Address (January 20, 1969).
[13] Speech delivered to March on Washington participants, Washington, D.C. (August 28, 1963).
[14] John W. Gardner, "National Goals in Education," *Goals for Americans* (Englewood Cliffs, N.J.: Prentice-Hall, 1960), p. 100.

### Special Interest Group Influences

For instance, special interest groups have varying expectations of teachers. But special interest groups do not own the school—though they too sometimes act as though they do, particularly when their members are high in the community power structure. The schools do not belong to any special group, however praiseworthy or deplorable. For instance, the schools do not belong to the League of Women Voters, or to the American Legion, or to a parent-teacher association, or to a chamber of commerce, or to the National Education Association, or to the Black Panthers, or to the Episcopal Church, or to the John Birch Society, or to the Southern Christian Leadership Conference, or to the Young Americans for Freedom, or to Americans for Democratic Action, or to Planned Parenthood—and so on, ad infinitum. The schools neither belong to those who are prominent in the community power structure nor to those who challenge the existing power structure. All such groups are heard and should be heard in the continuing debate on the work of the schools. Many individual members of such groups will also be heard. But the schools belong to the people as a whole, not to any special group or its spokesmen, not to any power structure or its challengers.

Though the schools do not belong to the special interest groups, such groups bring their influence to bear on the shaping of education. Often they see themselves as representatives of American values; infrequently they are frankly antidemocratic. But their interpretations of the values they support are often influenced by their special interests. Often they do not see eye-to-eye with other protagonists. They bring their influence to bear on behalf of their interpretations of their values and often, in the process, attempt to influence the work of schools. So the programs of the schools are influenced through the policies of voluntary organizations, whether they be labor or management groups, peace or war groups, religious or agnostic groups, minority or majority groups, and so on.

### Higher Education Influences

Simultaneously, influences on educational policies and on expectations of teachers are also being exerted by groups within the field of education, even though they too do not own the public schools. The colleges, as a component of American higher education, influence the policies pursued by the schools through college entrance requirements. Since college is the next educational level beyond high school and since college education is highly valued both as a means of making a better person and as a means of upward mobility occupationally, colleges can exert substantial influence on schools and on expectations of teachers through their prescriptions as to what content and even what personality characteristics are necessary for college entrance.

Meanwhile, formidable social pressures have been applied to colleges to revise their college entrance requirements to admit a larger proportion of relatively disadvantaged youth, especially disadvantaged blacks. Consequently, such a university system as that of the City of New York has markedly relaxed college entrance requirements to achieve open admissions. Some hail open admissions as a major step toward sound educational opportunity. But some scholars and political leaders foresee the decline and decay of higher education if student and community pressures result in wider admissions. Thus, conventional college entrance requirements, as one operating force in higher education, meet counterforces in the form of pressures for open admissions.

Another influence on the policies of schools comes from the various faculties of the institutions of higher learning. Differing perceptions as to desirable educational programs have long existed between liberal arts faculties and teacher education faculties within colleges and universities; individual proponents often sound as though they own the public schools. This cold war between faculty members centers on such questions as the most appropriate content, materials, and methodologies for use in schools. Liberal arts faculty members incline to established academic approaches to education; teacher education faculties incline to learner-adapted approaches. Consequently the college student is apt to hear from the liberal arts faculty member the claim that if one knows his subject, he can teach it without taking education courses, and from teacher education faculty members the contention that much knowledge concerning the learner and society exists and much adaptation of subject matter to the learner and to society is necessary for effective education. While the debate is less heated than it used to be and while reconciliation of the conflict has been achieved on some campuses, the debate on many campuses between the variant perceptions among professors still goes on.

### Financial Support Influences

Still another influence on school policies and expectations of teachers derives from sources which can supply financial aid to school systems which must chronically cope with a shortage of financial support. One such source of support is the philanthropic foundation, typified by the largest of all such foundations, the Ford Foundation. Such foundations frequently make supplementary funds available to schools for the development of new media such as television, or for use with special groups of learners such as the disadvantaged, or to support certain content areas such as citizenship education and science, or to foster open education programs. No school system is forced to accept foundation funds. But school systems, notoriously needy, often do. The acceptance of funds often leads to an acceptance of the emphasis supported by the philanthropic foundation.

Today the federal government, and to a lesser extent state governments, play similar roles with respect to the provision of funds. Federal aid to schools is for special purposes presumably related to the national interest. The federal government supplies help for special concerns, such as vocational education early in the twentieth century, or support for programs for the culturally disadvantaged in our own times. Again, school systems are under no compulsion to accept such aid. Yet their needs are great and, consequently, certain aspects of the school programs are strengthened through selected "categorical" programs of federal aid to education.

Such programs are administered through a wide variety of federal agencies. Prominent among them is the United States Office of Education. Throughout much of the twentieth century the U.S. Office of Education collected statistics and provided informational reports on American education. In the United States, the Office of Education has not been given by the American people the total power and authority in education which has been given to ministries of education abroad. The American tradition in education rejects a high degree of centralization through an all-powerful national ministry.

In recent years the Office has administered extensive programs of federal aid. Recently, under the leadership of Sidney P. Marland, the United States Office of Education has fostered the development of career education, a concept broader than vocational education and emphasizing career orientation and career training in academic as well as vocational fields. Of career education, Marland said,

. . . it implies a structured orientation and preparation program for every student as an integral part of his academic course work throughout the school and college years. Whatever terminology we use, inherent in the concept is the principle that our schools and colleges are accountable to students not only for developing their problem-solving skills, self-awareness, and social consciousness, but for equipping them as well to earn a living in a personally satisfying career field.

The idea that American education has such an obligation did not begin with me or my stewardship of the U.S. Office of Education. It is a proposition that has been around a long time.[15]

After pointing out that the federal thrust now runs to considerably more than $100 million a year, Marland concluded, "I think it is fair to say that the country regards career education as one answer, among many answers, to some of our more serious social and economic problems, including high unemployment and the attendant problems of disaffection and drug excess among the young. I think it is equally clear that our schools are already moving to put career education into action."

Broad policies which supply American education its mandate are

[15] Sidney P. Marland, Jr., "The School's Role in Career Development," *Educational Leadership* (December 1972), p. 203.

also influenced by the action of state legislators. Though there is common agreement among educators that state legislatures should not prescribe the content of specific courses, but should rather depend upon their state education department to establish standards for instruction and to provide leadership, some legislatures do prescribe specific content. Perhaps the most famous illustration of prescription by a legislature is the evolution law once passed by the Tennessee Legislature mandating a Biblical interpretation of the origin of man rather than the evolutionary thesis.

### Relationships of Teachers and Groups

The realistic new teacher knows that such influences exist and that they affect the expectations of individuals and groups as to his role. He must acknowledge their influence yet attempt to maintain his own integrity and his responsibility to the American people. For despite the pressure of a variety of interests, in a democracy the schools belong to the people.

## DISCUSSION

1. What is the meaning of "role" as used in sociology and education? How does it differ from "status"?
2. What are the various roles you as an individual play as you go about your daily life? As you assume the role of teacher what changes in your life-style do you see yourself making?
3. How do community expectations generally differ in rural, urban, and suburban areas? What about expectations of the teacher in the community you know best?
4. How do parental expectations differ? To what extent does social class appear to be a factor? To what extent do individual differences within the groups appear?
5. How have the expectations of teachers by lower income Americans—especially members of minority or disadvantaged groups—changed in recent years?
6. What are characteristic administrative expectations of the teacher? The school board members? The superintendents? The central staffs? The principals?
7. What are characteristic student perceptions and expectations of the teacher? What were your own expectations of the teacher at varying stages in your school life? How did you score on the twenty self-rating questions?
8. How important are the perceptions and expectations of fellow teachers? On what basis is the new teacher likely to be judged by his colleagues?
9. What are some of the self-expectations which members of your class hold? Which do you hold?
10. What can be done to help the young teacher identify realistic self-expectations?
11. What are the possible viewpoints on who "owns" the public schools? What is the relationship of teachers to the people, in broad terms and in specific instances with which you are acquainted?
12. Does a democratic consensus on the work of the schools exist? If so, how might it be phrased? Who has contributed to it? What other public figures have expressed themselves on the goals of American society and the proper goals of American schools?

13. What special interest groups affect education nationally? What special interest groups have influenced the schools with which you are most familiar?
14. How does higher education influence school programs? In the college or university you know best, is there some degree of disagreement among liberal arts professors and education professors?
15. How might financial factors influence the program of schools? How do philanthropic foundations relate to school systems? Federal government?

## INVOLVEMENT

1. Talk with friends or family members about their expectations of schools. Attempt to relate their expectations to class backgrounds, community backgrounds, individual preferences, etc.
2. Visit a meeting of a PTA reputed to have more than routine meetings. Attempt to determine the characteristic expectations of teachers held by parents and, conversely, the expectations of parents held by teachers.
3. Try a "man in the street" interview as to the expectations of schools by varying individuals. Look for similarities and differences.
4. Attempt to interview a board of education member. Try to understand his perceptions and how they are similar to or different from your own and those of your friends. Consider the reasons behind these similarities or differences.
5. Visit an administrator or invite a representative of administration to class in order to learn of his expectations of a teacher. Clarify similarities and differences of his point of view with those of students engaged in the interview or acting as an audience.
6. Invite several teachers to class to discuss their expectations of their colleagues, both new and experienced.
7. Recall your own expectations of teachers at various points in your experience as a student. Talk with contemporary elementary and high school students to see what differences in perception might exist.

8. Extend further your study of the democratic consensus. Read the ideas of others who have contributed to viewpoints on the proper role and responsibility of schools.
9. Talk informally with both liberal arts and education professors to determine their ideas about what constitutes a good teacher and what they expect of American education.

## FURTHER READING

Breasted, Mary. *Oh! Sex Education*. New York: Praeger, 1970.   A lively account of the controversies which surround sex education in the public schools.

Brubaker, Dale L. *The Teacher as a Decision-Maker*. Dubuque, Iowa: Wm. C. Brown, 1970.   A variety of cases are set forth, each requiring decisions by teachers.

Hass, Glen, Kimball Wiles, and Arthur Roberts (Eds.). *Readings in Secondary Education*. Rockleigh, N.J.: Allyn and Bacon, 1970.   A collection of articles which combine discussion of educational theory and attention to practical problems of teaching. One section devotes particular attention to the high school teacher's role in school and community.

Hurwitz, Emanuel, Jr. and Charles A. Tesconi, Jr. (Eds.). *Challenges to Education*. New York: Dodd, Mead, 1972.   Readings helpful in analysis of such major issues as school and society, the courts, school control, teacher power, rebellious students, ethnic groups, urban school finance, and alternatives.

Morphet, Edgar L., David L. Jesser, and Arthur P. Ludka. *Planning and Providing for Excellence in Education*. Denver, Colorado: Improving State Leadership in Education, 1971.   A publication of a project on improving state leadership in education which stresses state leadership in planning improvements in education in a dynamic society and in effecting needed changes in education. For citizens, educators, and legislators active at the state level.

Nielsen, Waldemar A. *The Big Foundations*. New York: Columbia University Press,

1972. A survey and analysis of 33 large foundations which is critical of their passivity in operation and which suggests approaches to revitalization.

Reutter, E. E., Jr. *Schools and the Law*. Dobbs Ferry, New York: Oceana Publications, 1970. A brief book describing the legal framework for the public schools, including local school boards, state government, federal government, laws regarding teaching and both church-state relations and race relations.

Sarason, Seymour B. *The Culture of the School and the Problems of Change*. Boston: Allyn and Bacon, 1971. A book on the culture of schools which deals with the nature of change and stresses the roles of principals and teachers with their attendant problems.

## SELECTED AUDIO-VISUAL MATERIALS

*How Good Is Your Child's School?* (35 mm filmstrip, 80 frs/record, color, National Education Association, 1967). Appraisal of elementary and secondary schools by lay individuals and groups, and criteria for evaluation.

*I Wish I'd Known That Before I Went to College* (35 mm filmstrip, 2 filmstrips/records, color, Guidance Associates, 1965). Presents a conversation between Eugene S. Wilson, Dean of Admissions at Amherst College, and Abraham N. Lass, principal of a New York high school, in which they discuss the academic side of college life, such as faculty and the ways of teaching.

*Is Anybody Home?* (audio tape, 15 min., University of Texas, National Center for Audio Tapes, 1968). A series of 37 tapes on home and family life education. Selected Titles: What a Teacher Expects of Her Student, What a Teacher Expects of Parents, Are Teachers Necessary?

*"Keith"—A Second Grader* (16 mm film, 23 min., b. & w., Indiana University, 1966). Records a typical school day. The purpose is to provide behavioral data for observation and analysis.

*Teachers Contributing to Educational Advance* (35 mm filmstrip, 51 frs, color, Ohio State University, 1960). Presents a review of curriculum activities. Describes the role of the teacher as a creative personality responsible for developing creativity in pupils and contributing to their educational advancement. Discusses the special responsibility of the laboratory school.

# ELEVEN

# What about money to support schools?

Today education is a major enterprise in the United States. More than 60,000,000 people in the population of the United States 3 to 34 years old were enrolled in American educational institutions in 1972.[1] In other words, almost 29 percent of our population were enrolled in American schools and colleges. If we include teachers and administrators, the field of education engages roughly a third of the total population of the United States. Among the major functions of government, public education is second only to national defense in amount of tax revenues spent. Obviously, so large and crucial a service must be financed in some way.

## SOURCES OF FINANCIAL SUPPORT

### Support from Local, State, and Federal Governments

The American public educational enterprise is a decentralized activity. School districts are the primary units of local government charged with responsibility for education, a responsibility delegated by the state legislatures. Other local governments such as township, municipal, and county units provide services including tax collection, fire and police protection, water and sanitation, etc. In addition, about half the states have regional agencies such as county school offices to provide educational services to the local districts. State governments affect education through the legislature, the state department of education, and agencies such as the revenue department and the state judiciary. The federal gov-

[1] U.S. Bureau of the Census, "School Enrollment in the United States, 1972," ("Population Characteristics") *Current Population Reports,* Series P-20, No. 237 (Washington, D.C.: U.S. Government Printing Office, 1973), p. 3.

ernment exercises its educational activities through major departments as well as the United States Office of Education.

Local control is still a key concept in financing public education and local authorities still receive most of the funds for schools through local tax revenues. But, since an individual school district is limited in its ability to raise funds, local funds are supplemented by grants from federal and state governments. Though the federal government plays a greater role in the funding of education than it formerly did, state and local governments are still the major participants in the financing of education.

About half the direct outlay for elementary and secondary public schools comes from funds of local governments. State governments supply approximately two-fifths of school revenue. The third partner is the federal government, which supplies the remainder, constituting 7.2 to 8.8 percent during the 1965–66 through the 1972–73 period. Federal participation has almost doubled since the period 1962–63 through 1964–65 when the percentage of school revenues derived from federal sources averaged about 4 percent annually. (Table 11-1 shows the percentages of revenues from these sources from 1962–63 through 1972–73.) Meanwhile in the eleven school years from 1962–63 through 1972–73, the percentage of school revenue derived from local sources dropped from 57.1 percent to 51.2 percent. Over the same time the percentage of all school revenue derived from state sources increased from 39.3 percent to 41.0 percent. The absolute amount increased from each source during this decade.

### Spending for Schooling

What is the revenue, whether from local, state, or federal funds, spent for? Primarily for salaries. The salaries of the instructional staff of public elementary and secondary schools account for approximately 61 percent of the combined local, state, and federal current expenditures for education.[2] ("Current expenditures" do not include capital outlay such as building schools or repayment of debt or payment of interest on debt.) The salaries of the nonteaching academic staff such as administrators, librarians, and counselors are included in the above figure of 61 percent. The remaining 39 percent goes for transportation, maintenance, etc.[3] When auxiliary staff such as bus drivers, custodians, and other noninstructional personnel are included, when the cost of retirement programs are included, and if the school system is not spending large amounts for school building, "it is common to find that salaries and fringe benefits account for roughly 80 percent of the annual budget."[4]

School revenues, then, are derived from local, state, and federal

[2] U.S. Office of Education, *Projections of Educational Statistics to 1980–81* (Washington, D.C.: U.S. Government Printing Office, 1972), p. 70.
[3] *Ibid.*
[4] Charles S. Benson, *The Economics of Public Education* (Boston: Houghton Mifflin, 1968), p. 30.

TABLE 11-1 **Distribution of Total Revenue Receipts for Public Elementary and Secondary Schools, 1962–1963 through 1972–1973**

| School year | Percent of school revenue derived from: | | |
| --- | --- | --- | --- |
| | Federal sources | State sources | Local and other sources |
| 1962–63 | 3.6 | 39.3 | 57.1 |
| 1963–64 | 4.4 | 39.2 | 56.4 |
| 1964–65 | 3.8 | 39.7 | 56.5 |
| 1965–66 | 7.9 | 39.1 | 53.0 |
| 1966–67 | 7.9 | 39.1 | 53.0 |
| 1967–68 | 8.8 | 38.5 | 52.7 |
| 1968–69 | 7.4 | 40.0 | 52.6 |
| 1969–70 | 8.0 | 39.9 | 52.1 |
| 1970–71 | 7.2 | 40.0 | 52.8 |
| 1971–72 | 8.0 | 40.2 | 51.8 |
| 1972–73 | 7.8 | 41.0 | 51.2 |

NEA, Research Division, *Estimates of School Statistics, 1972–73*, Research Report 1972–R12 (Washington, D.C.: The Association, 1973), p. 16.

sources. Salaries are the largest category in the current spending of those revenues. Salaries of the instructional staff (teaching and other academic personnel) constitute almost two-thirds of the operating expenditures for public schools. Quite soon the instructional staff may include you, and your salary may depend on revenues which are derived from taxation. Yet, can you think of anything more unpopular with people than taxes?

Nevertheless, all signs point to an increase in the cost of education. America's large governmental activity—public elementary and secondary education—grows larger and costlier annually. (See Table 11-2 for total expenditures for schools.) Notice how much larger public expenditures are in contrast to private spending. Notice the growing expenditure for higher education, which may affect the nation's allocation to public elementary and secondary schools.[5]

### Why Tax-supported Education?

If you become a public school teacher, you may often be called on to defend the support of education through taxation. You should therefore be familiar with the arguments for tax-supported education.

You may propose as a possible defense for public education that individuals will be benefited. Any comparison of what a person earns after various stages of graduation—from elementary school, from high school, from college, from graduate school—demonstrates the economic benefits of education to the individual. But this is essentially a *private* argument; it may not persuade many citizens that they have any financial responsibility for education. A more persuasive argument with the

[5] NEA, Committee on Educational Finance, *Financial Status of the Public Schools* (Washington, D.C.: National Education Association, 1972), p. 21.

**TABLE 11-2 Total Expenditures for Schools, 1970–1971 and 1971–1972, and Percent of Increase (Expenditures in Billions)**

|                                  | 1970–71 | 1971–72 | % INCREASE |
|----------------------------------|---------|---------|------------|
| Elementary & Secondary Education |         |         |            |
| Public                           | $43.7   | 46.8    | 7.1        |
| Private                          | 5.0     | 5.3     | 6.0        |
| Total                            | 48.7    | 52.1    | 7.0        |
| Higher Education                 |         |         |            |
| Public                           | 18.1    | 20.1    | 11.1       |
| Private                          | 9.9     | 10.9    | 10.1       |
| Total                            | 28.0    | 31.0    | 10.7       |
| Total, All Levels                |         |         |            |
| Public                           | 61.8    | 66.9    | 8.3        |
| Private                          | 14.9    | 16.2    | 8.7        |
| Total                            | 76.7    | 83.1    | 8.3        |

NEA, Committee on Educational Finance, *Financial Status of the Public Schools* (Washington, D.C.: National Education Association, 1972), p. 21.

tax-paying citizen is that education provides a substantial amount of social benefits as well as private benefit.

A first defense for public support of education is the contention that education of the common man is necessary in a democracy. In a nation which proposes to be a free society, the people must participate in the democratic process. They can do so only if they are an educated citizenry.

There are strong economic arguments for public education as a social benefit. There is a relationship between expenditures for education and the extent of the national economic growth. Theodore W. Schultz, former president of the American Economic Association and a professor of the University of Chicago, once said that there are long-standing puzzles about economic growth, changes in the structure of wages and salary, and changes in the personal distribution of income that can be substantially resolved by taking account of investment in human capital.[6]

Increasingly, economists point out that the most productive investment in human capital that can be made is education. As Professor William G. Bowen has put it, "The results obtained for the U.S. economy do offer rather consistent (some might say surprisingly consistent) support for the notion that education on the average, has paid significant financial as well as nonfinancial rewards."[7]

[6] Theodore W. Schultz, *Economic Value of Education* (New York: Columbia University Press, 1963), p. 65.
[7] William G. Bowen, *Economic Aspects of Education: Three Essays* (Princeton, N.J.: Princeton Industrial Relations Section, Princeton University, 1964), p. 32.

Yet some contend that these economic benefits could come from a private education system just as well if not better. Therefore, some propose that school services be provided more by private sources than they are now. But the arguments against this point of view stress that, along with economic benefits, public education provides desirable non-economic outcomes. Public schools help develop the common values of the democratic way of life; public education contains the potential to reduce class distinction and to provide equal educational opportunities to every individual for fullest development. Thus, public education is needed to achieve the democratic way of life, to reduce class distinctions, and to combat segregation.

### Sources of Tax Revenue

Taxes are collected at the three major levels of government: federal, state, and local. Each level of government mentioned has a relationship to the levying of taxes.

Several sources of tax money for state and local governments exist. Property taxes are the largest single revenue producer, though their proportion in the local and state tax structure is steadily declining. Following property taxes in importance are sales and gross receipt taxes, including general and selective (earmarked) taxes which are levies on retail sales of particular articles and services, such as gasoline, cigarettes, or liquor. The third large source, increasing in importance during recent years, includes individual and corporate income taxes. A fourth source is the federal government. (See Table 11-3.)

Where does the federal government turn for revenue? Over 82 percent of tax revenues for the federal government in 1971 came from individual income taxes, corporate income taxes, and employment taxes. The rest came to the federal government through excise taxes, insurance trust funds, estate and gift taxes, customs duties, and miscellaneous receipts. (See Table 11-4.) No wage earner in the United States can be unfamiliar with the income tax, which withholds income for tax purposes from one's weekly or monthly pay.

As a concerned citizen and as a new school teacher you should consider which types of taxes should be depended on for future revenue. A commonly accepted tax standard is equal treatment of equals. In other words, people who have equal amounts of income or goods should contribute equally; none of the equals should be arbitrarily favored by the tax structure. But obviously not all people are equal in their ability to pay; some have a much higher income than others. Therefore, another proposed tax standard is that the tax burden should be shared according to the amount of income of the individual or corporation. Such a tax is called a "progressive" tax, one under which the high income household pays a higher ratio of tax than a low income family.

**TABLE 11-3  State and Local Government Revenues and Expenditures 1970–1971**

| General revenue by source | Amount (in millions) |
|---|---|
| Property Taxes | $ 37,852 |
| Sales and Gross Receipts Taxes | 33,233 |
| Individual Income Taxes | 11,900 |
| Corporation Income Taxes | 3,424 |
| From Federal Government | 26,146 |
| All Other | 53,535 |
| Total | 166,090 |

| General expenditures by function | Amount (in millions) |
|---|---|
| Education (all public) | 59,413 |
| Highways | 18,095 |
| Public Welfare | 18,226 |
| All Other | 75,032 |
| Total | 170,766 |

U.S. Department of Commerce, *Governmental Finance in 1970–71* Governmental Finances/G.F. 71 No. 5 Bureau of the Census (Washington, D.C.: U.S. Government Printing Office, 1972), p. 18.

**TABLE 11-4   Federal Budget Receipts by Source, 1968 to Estimated 1973 (in Millions)**

| Source | Actual | | | | Estimate | |
|---|---|---|---|---|---|---|
| | 1968 | 1969 | 1970 | 1971 | 1972 | 1973 |
| Budget receipts | 153,671 | 187,784 | 193,743 | 188,392 | 197,827 | 220,785 |
| Individual income taxes | 68,726 | 87,249 | 90,412 | 86,230 | 86,500 | 93,900 |
| Corporation income taxes | 28,665 | 36,678 | 32,829 | 26,785 | 30,100 | 35,700 |
| Employment taxes and contributions | 29,224 | 34,236 | 39,133 | 41,699 | 46,367 | 55,113 |
| Unemployment insurance | 3,346 | 3,328 | 3,464 | 3,674 | 4,364 | 5,016 |
| Contributions for other insurance and retirement | 2,052 | 2,353 | 2,701 | 3,205 | 3,361 | 3,554 |
| Excise taxes | 14,079 | 15,222 | 15,705 | 16,614 | 15,200 | 16,300 |
| Estate and gift taxes | 3,051 | 3,491 | 3,644 | 3,735 | 5,200 | 4,300 |
| Customs duties | 2,038 | 2,319 | 2,430 | 2,591 | 3,210 | 2,850 |
| Miscellaneous receipts[1] | 2,491 | 2,908 | 3,424 | 3,858 | 3,525 | 4,052 |

[1] Includes both federal funds and trust funds.
Economic Report of the President, "Report to the President on the Activities of the Council of Economic Advisers During 1971 " (Washington, D.C.: U.S. Government Printing Office, 1972), p. 271.

### Progressive and Regressive Taxes

It is frequently said that the only things which are certain are death and taxes. We might add that, as to how to distribute taxes, it is equally certain that people will quarrel about what is fairest or best. If there is a consensus among economists on this controversial issue, it is quite possibly the one expressed by Benson:

> In general, economists express a preference for a progressive rate structure and on two grounds: (1) Taxation should not take dollars that are necessary for a minimum standard of living. As long as demand for government services are high and as long as there are several million very poor households in the country, it follows that taxation will have to be levied at proportionately higher rates on the rich than on the poor; (2) Taxation should do something to reduce extreme inequality in disposable income.[8]

Standards as to fairness might be kept in mind as we examine the four major types of taxes used for support of education in the 1970s. The four types are property taxes, sales taxes, state income taxes, and federal income taxes.

The property tax, it will be recalled, is the primary source of revenue for local governments. A property tax is collected from owners of property and is presumably based on the value of the taxable property of the owner. The property tax taxes real property, a phrase for land and the improvements upon the land including houses, garages, etc. In addition, in most states certain kinds of tangible personal property are taxed. Tangible personal property includes automobiles, furniture, clothes, jewelry, business and farm equipment, farm animals, etc. Of these two, the more important source of revenue is locally assessed real estate. Though the assessment is supposed to represent the market value of the real estate, the county or district assessor usually assesses property at less than its actual present buying and selling (market) value.

Property taxes are usually regressive rather than progressive taxes. "A 'regressive tax' is one under which the ratio of tax paid to income is greater in poor families than in rich."[9] Since property taxes are regressive, they are unpopular with many people, particularly those who are not rich. If a tax is unpopular, the person advocating taxes for a social service, such as education, is often ineffective in making his case, despite his possible eloquence as to the social benefits of the service.

Yet the property tax persists because of its long tradition and a certain convenience. It is a stable tax producing a stable yield. Property tax rates can be raised or lowered without much difficulty. A bill is received in a household once or twice a year and a check or money order made out—not a very complex process. The property owner knows how much he is paying and thus the tax is visible; the payer of a visible tax may be

[8] Benson, p. 94.
[9] *Ibid.*, p. 94.

more inclined to keep his eye on how the government spends his money.

A second type of tax is the sales tax, usually levied by the state. The tax on sales (or gross receipts) may be, for instance, as low as 2 percent, regarded as fairly low, or as high as 7 percent, regarded as fairly high. Sales taxes are also regressive taxes. The poor spend a higher proportion of their income in sales taxes than do the rich, while the poor are able to save a lower proportion of their income than rich families do. Rich families usually spend proportionately more of their money than poor families on travel, education, and personal services, on which there is usually no sales tax.

The state has another recourse in collecting taxes to be used in large part for education. This is the state income tax, now used in many states. The state income tax is similar to the federal income tax except that exemptions are usually higher and rates usually much lower. Thus most state income taxes are only slightly progressive. Sometimes uniform tax rates are applied to variable incomes. In contrast, the income tax of the federal government is a markedly progressive tax because the ratio of tax paid to income is substantially larger for the high income family than for the low income family.

The tax of which one most often hears is the federal individual income tax. This tax is not simply the major source of revenue for an increasingly large federal government; it has genuine consequences in the economy, and has become an instrument of social policy. For instance, sometimes the government raises income taxes to fight inflation by reducing the amount of money individuals and corporations have for the purchase of goods and services.

The federal individual income tax asks the taxpayer to total his taxable sources of income; it then allows him certain deductions and exemptions for himself and the members of his family, and it specifies a tax rate to be paid on the difference between his income and his deductions and exemptions.

The income tax has proven a highly productive source of funds for government. It is, of course, a progressive tax and the result is that rich people pay far more than poor families. All taxes are unpopular. But the federal income tax tends to be particularly unpopular with the wealthier segment of the community.

In summary, then, four types of major taxes supply revenue for the support of education. Two of them are primarily regressive taxes—the property tax levied by local government and the sales tax levied by states. Two of them are primarily progressive taxes—the state income tax and the federal income tax. Overwhelmingly, local government uses the property tax as its instrument and the federal government uses the income tax.

State governments, however, have a choice of whether to use the income tax or sales tax. Those states which use both have the choice as to which one to use more heavily. Those legislators who favor regressive taxes tend to favor the sales tax; those who favor progressive taxes tend to favor the income tax. In broad terms, labor usually supports the income tax while business supports the sales tax. The educator is frequently recruited on either side of the battleground. Clearly, there is no tax on which all harmoniously agree.

Each tax base—property, sales, and income—should be evaluated. Complete evaluation of any one tax base cannot be made solely by examining the base without reference to the combined effect of all taxes. For example, some authorities on taxation believe that after making special allowances for extremely low income families, retired persons, and other adjustments, the regressivity of property and sales taxes may not be unfair, particularly when viewed in relation to the progressivity of income taxes. The end result of all taxes is the best basis on which to make final judgment on the reasonableness of any one tax base.

An illustration of variations in percentage of income spent in each of these tax forms by home-owning families with three family members is shown in Table 11-5. These percentages do not provide all the information necessary to judge either a particular tax base or the total of all three. However, they do represent the context for making a fair and rational evaluation.

Sweeping reforms of school financing have been proposed by a few individuals and groups from time to time during the past quarter of a century. One proposed reform is to have the state pay the full cost of local schools. The concept of shifting the full cost of local schools to the state is not a new one; this idea has been around for a long time, though it has not received wide acclaim in this country by school finance scholars and educational leaders. In recent years this approach has been proposed as an alternative to the traditional one of using state and local revenues. This concept was advocated in a report by the Advisory Commission on Intergovernmental Relations, a commission of twenty-six members established by an act of Congress for continuing relationships

TABLE 11-5 **Percentages of Income Spent on Taxes by Homeowners, 1968**[1]

| Income (family of three) | $3,000 | $5,000 | $7,000 | $9,000 | $13,000 | $20,000 |
|---|---|---|---|---|---|---|
| Property tax | 7.2 | 4.0 | 3.1 | 2.9 | 2.8 | 2.2 |
| Sales tax | 2.9 | 2.4 | 2.1 | 1.9 | 1.6 | 1.4 |
| Federal income tax | 3.2 | 8.0 | 10.7 | 12.1 | 14.0 | 18.0 |
| Total | 13.3 | 14.4 | 15.9 | 16.9 | 18.4 | 21.6 |

[1] Data from a survey of homeowners in Illinois in 1968.
William P. McLure, "Major Issues in School Finance," *Educational Administration Quarterly* (Fall 1969), p. 6.

among local, state, and federal levels of government.[10] Some states are currently considering assuming the full cost of local schools, a practice already followed in Hawaii.

## EQUALIZING SUPPORT FOR PUBLIC SCHOOLS

### Inequalities in State and Local Support

The question of support for education is more than a question of what are the most appropriate taxes to levy and administer. Anyone who thinks seriously of the importance of the educational enterprise must take into account the entire program needed by a nation in order to avoid shortages or surpluses in the national life. As the economists remind us, economic goods are by definition scarce and must be used wisely and in relationship to the basic purposes and goals of the people of a nation.

The fact of life is that in the United States there is inequality in income distribution. Consequently, school districts that are among the less wealthy have some of the greatest social needs and yet the least available economic support and educational opportunities. Not only are some districts prosperous and others poor in this land which contains both rich suburbs and miserable slums; this is also a nation of prosperous states such as California and New York and poorer states such as Mississippi and Arkansas.

The decisions concerning the extent of financial support for schools are not made by educators. Basically such decisions are made by the people or their representatives. Thus, the matter of financing of schools is essentially a political decision. At all levels of government, some political administrators are most concerned for what they term the interests of the taxpayer; others are more concerned about fostering what they describe as the broad welfare of the nation by spending for education. Consequently the tug-of-war for funds goes on between taxpayer oriented and education oriented members of state legislatures on the state level, and members of school boards on the local level. On the state level, various pressure groups vie for their share of the state budget. On the local level, the board of education is one group among many competing for a share in the local tax dollar. However, only a very few boards operate under special laws requiring them to argue their case before county trustees, council members, mayors, etc.; with few exceptions, school boards make decisions on amount of local tax levies for schools which they can determine within limitations set by state laws. Federal funding decisions channel through the Congress of the United States,

---

[10] Advisory Commission on Intergovernmental Relations, *State Aid to Local Government,* ACIR Report A-34 (Washington, D.C.: The Commission, April 1969).

**TABLE 11-6** Current (1972–1973) Expenditure per Pupil
in Average Daily Attendance for Elementary
and Secondary Day Schools

| Amount | Number of states (and D.C.) |
|---|---|
| $   550–599 | 1 |
| 600–649 | 0 |
| 650–699 | 3 |
| 700–749 | 5 |
| 750–799 | 3 |
| 800–849 | 4 |
| 850–899 | 4 |
| 900–949 | 8 |
| 950–999 | 2 |
| 1,000–1049 | 4 |
| 1,050–1099 | 1 |
| 1,100–1149 | 6 |
| 1,150 and over | 10 |

NEA, Research Division, *Estimates of School Statistics, 1972–73,* Research Report 1972-R12 (Washington, D.C.: The Association, 1973), p. 18.

which, in turn, is subject to a variety of pressures from the people and
their representatives as to priorities.

That there are inequalities in educational opportunity is apparent.
For instance, in 1972–73 the estimated current expenditure per pupil in
average daily attendance was $590 in Alabama, while the state of New
York was spending $1,584 and Alaska, $1,473.[11] Table 11-6 shows a distribution of average current expenditure per pupil by states in 1972–73.
One state spent $550–599 per pupil in average daily attendance. But ten
states spent $1,150 or more per pupil in average daily attendance. The
ratio of the highest state average ($1,584) to the lowest state average
($590) is nearly three to one; the variations of school district averages
within some states are even greater.

Inequality among states is not a matter of malice or penury on the
part of a particular state. There are great variations among the states in
financial ability to provide support. For example, in 1970 New York had
much more than twice the personal income for each pupil in average
daily attendance than did Mississippi.[12] At the same time there are major

[11] NEA, Research Division, *Estimates of School Statistics 1972–73,* Research Report 1972-R12
(Washington, D.C.: The Association, 1973), p. 35.
[12] NEA, Research Division, *Rankings of the States, 1972,* Research Report 1972-R1 (Washington, D.C.: The Association, 1972), p. 36.

differences as to spending within each state. In some states, some districts support education at twice the level of other districts.

So the social question which arises is whether or not a nation has an obligation to provide equal educational opportunities for its citizens. Does a nation at least have an obligation to move toward greater equalization of opportunity? All states apply the principle of equalization in their state finance plans, but there is a wide variation in the extent to which the actual distribution of state aid accomplishes this purpose.

Most states use a "foundation" plan to equalize a minimum level of support. Each school district is expected to make a local contribution at some prescribed level, applied uniformly to estimated property tax valuations. The state provides the difference between the funds raised locally and the cost of the foundation. In other words, a basic foundation as to scope and cost of education is guaranteed for all districts.

There are reasons, however, why this plan falls short of equalization of educational opportunity among school districts, even in the states judged by the most competent analysts to have the best finance plans. School districts have leeway to raise local taxes beyond the amount required to participate in the foundation; those with high taxing ability can raise more beyond the foundation than those with low taxing ability. There are numerous special aids, state and federal, that are distributed without reference to funds otherwise available. Equal amounts of funds per pupil alone cannot accomplish equal educational opportunity; some pupils require twice, perhaps three or four times, as much to be spent to meet their needs. Since some districts have a higher proportion of pupils with special needs than do other districts, an average amount per pupil will not provide comparable support for such pupils among districts. While some states use procedures for "weighting" pupils with high cost needs, these methods do not fully compensate for the real differences. Finally, most states distribute flat grants to those districts that do not qualify for equalization aid, thus creating a degree of disequalization.

The courts of the nation are now playing an increasingly significant role in the movement toward equalization of educational opportunity. In 1971 the Supreme Court of the State of California reached a decision in the Serrano case.

We are called upon to determine whether the California public school financing system, with its substantial dependence on local property taxes and resultant wide disparities in school revenue, violates the equal protection clause of the Fourteenth Amendment. We have determined that this funding scheme invidiously discriminates against the poor because it makes the quality of a child's education a function of the wealth of his parents and neighbors. Recognizing as we must that the right to an education in our public schools is a fundamental interest which cannot be conditioned on wealth, we can discern no compelling state purpose necessitating the present method of financing. We have concluded, therefore, that such a system cannot withstand constitutional challenge and must fall before the equal protection clause.[13]

The court recognized that poor school districts, even if they had high property tax rates, could not produce enough funding to match wealthier districts. Yet the wealthier districts could raise money for schools with less effort.

As a specialist in school finance has put it:

. . . For example, as the Serrano decision has made clear, school taxes amount to $2.83 per each $100 of assessed property value in Beverly Hills, California, which translates into a $1,232 expenditure per pupil in elementary schools. At the same time, the nearby Baldwin Park rate of $5.48 for each $100 assessed value (two and one-third times greater than in Beverly Hills) generates only $577 expenditure per pupil (less than one-half the expenditure per pupil in Beverly Hills).[14]

As the court put it, "Thus, affluent districts can have their cake and eat it too; they can provide a high quality education for their children while paying lower taxes. Poor districts, by contrast, have no cake at all."[15] In effect, the court said that equality of a child's education in the public schools of a state must be based on the wealth of the state as a whole.

So the property tax, already under political fire in local communities struggling to finance their schools, came under fire from the courts. Suits were instituted in other states. In 1973, in the Texas case of San Antonio Independent School District *v.* Rodriguez, the U.S. Supreme Court held that the states could finance their public school systems in part with property taxes that provided more funds and better facilities for pupils who resided in wealthier districts. The 5-4 decision demonstrated a split in the Supreme Court; four justices appointed by President Nixon joined in the majority decision whereas Justice Thurgood Marshall, among the minority members, in his dissent called the decision "a retreat from our historic commitment to equality of educational opportunity."[16]

The U.S. Supreme Court decision to reverse a lower court in the San Antonio *v.* Rodriguez case slowed but did not stop financial reform efforts which shifted toward financial equalization on a state-by-state basis. Shortly after the Rodriguez case, the New Jersey Supreme Court ruled the state's system of financing schools in violation of the state constitution which requires "a thorough and efficient system of free public

---

[13] "Serrano *v.* Priest: Implications for Educational Equality," *Harvard Educational Review* (November 1971), pp. 503–504.

[14] John E. Peck, "Future Developments in School Finance," *School Management* (August 1972), p. 13.

[15] "Serrano *v.* Priest: Implications for Educational Equality," *Harvard Educational Review* (November 1971), p. 514.

[16] "Court, 5-4, Backs Schools on Property Tax," *New York Times*, March 22, 1973, p. 1.

schools." The state court did not strike down the property tax as unconstitutional, but it did comment that any system of financing which depends largely on the property tax would fail to provide a "thorough and efficient" education.[17]

Decisions on financing schools were to have widespread consequences in a nation in which about 52 percent of the money for schools was supplied by local property taxes with about 41 percent provided by the states and the remaining 7 percent from the federal government. Greater involvement in the financial support of local schools by state governments seemed likely in the future. Increased financial contributions by the federal government to the state appeared to be in the offing. In future years the financial responsibility of local governments might be eased. Because of the possibility of such developments and because of the political unpopularity of the property tax, many states worked on plans for changing their approaches to school financing.

But the prospect of greater educational financing by the state in partnership with the federal government rather than by local sources raised many controversial questions. For instance, what would happen to the American tradition of local control of education with respect to policymaking, if funding shifted from the locality to the state and nation? If equality of educational opportunity among districts was socially desirable, was there not also a case for equality among poor and rich states?

Should more money be spent on children and youth with special needs, such as those with handicaps or from underprivileged backgrounds? (The costs of such programs are usually higher than costs of normal programs, and some districts might have a high proportion of students with special needs.) Would a trend away from local financing of schools increase housing opportunities for minority groups? (If financing shifted to the state, opponents of low-cost housing could no longer claim that such housing would increase local taxes because of increased school enrollment and cost.)

### Federal Aid to Education

The federal government also enters into greater equalization of educational opportunity through *categorical aid.* Categorical aid is support for special aspects of the educational program considered important to the development of the nation. Typically, categorical aid relates to such national concerns as full employment or elimination of educational deficiencies associated with poverty. Table 11-7 shows the extent of the federal program for education and manpower.

Many educators urge that categorical aid should be eliminated or restricted to support only a few selected aspects of school programs and that most federal support be *general aid* that provides revenue from na-

"News Front," *Education, U.S.A.,* (April 9, 1973), p. 175.

**TABLE 11-7  The Budget for Fiscal Year 1973 Education and Manpower (in Millions)**

| Program or agency | Outlays | | | Recommended budget authority for 1973 |
|---|---|---|---|---|
| | 1971 actual | 1972 estimate | 1973 estimate | |
| Education revenue sharing (additional amount under proposed legislation) | ... | ... | 110 | 224 |
| Elementary and secondary education: | | | | |
| Child development | 367 | 376 | 386 | 409 |
| Emergency school assistance (proposed legislation) | ... | 81 | 381 | 1,000 |
| Aid to school districts | 2,533 | 2,607 | 2,507 | 2,349 |
| Other | 264 | 319 | 345 | 344 |
| Vocational education | 415 | 531 | 568 | 554 |
| Higher education: | | | | |
| Student assistance | 745 | 913 | 918 | 951 |
| Institutional aid and personnel development | 684 | 529 | 424 | 356 |
| National Foundation for Higher Education (proposed legislation) | ... | 1 | 30 | 100 |
| Other education aids: | | | | |
| National Institute of Education (proposed legislation) | ... | 2 | 50 | 125 |
| Education renewal | 378 | 398 | 416 | 573 |
| Cultural activities | 156 | 231 | 279 | 331 |
| Subtotal, education | 5,541 | 5,987 | 6,412 | 7,316 |
| General science (National Science Foundation) | 522 | 538 | 596 | 653 |
| Manpower training and employment services: | | | | |
| Emergency employment activities | ... | 660 | 1,100 | 1,250 |
| Manpower training services | 1,448 | 1,587 | 1,614 | 1,695 |
| Work incentives | 129 | 195 | 270 | 205 |
| Federal-State employment service | 374 | 408 | 442 | 442 |
| Unemployment Insurance Service | 428 | 468 | 492 | 492 |
| Other manpower aids | 223 | 326 | 387 | 397 |
| Subtotal, manpower | 2,602 | 3,643 | 4,305 | 4,481 |
| Deductions for offsetting receipts: | | | | |
| Proprietary receipts from the public | −12 | −29 | −32 | −32 |
| Total | 8,654 | 10,140 | 11,281 | 12,416 |
| Expenditure account | 8,520 | 10,055 | 11,215 | 12,383 |
| Loan account | 134 | 85 | 65 | 34 |

*The Budget of the United States Government, 1973* (Washington, D.C.: U.S. Government Printing Office, 1972), p. 131.

tional taxation for the use of schools throughout the nation. In effect, what they urge is a type of foundation program not simply at the state level but at the federal level. Yet the counter argument made is that with increasing federal (or state) support comes increasing control by the fund suppliers. Still others argue that laws can be developed which could safeguard against encroachments and unreasonable federal or state controls.

The present probability seems to be that categorical aid will be continued while general federal aid to education increasingly gains favor. Some believe that the supposed threat of federal control can be reduced by allocating federal monies to the states for control and administration. Yet this raises the question of whether the states, through their agencies, have made the best and most effective use of funds in the past, or whether adequate procedures exist for judging effectiveness. Some educators prefer federal standards. In 1973, President Richard M. Nixon proposed a federal budget for the next fiscal year that would share revenue for education with state and local governments. President Nixon defended his proposal as restoring a greater sense of responsibility at the local and state levels by giving the people and their locally elected representatives a greater voice through revenue sharing. Congressional critics attacked the proposal as a dismantling of federal aid programs of the Lyndon B. Johnson administration and charged that the victims of revenue sharing would be educationally deprived children. The Nixon proposal of education revenue-sharing with the states, which was faced with hostility from Congress and the education community, was dropped for the time being in mid-1973.

Supporters of federal aid to education point to a long history of federal support which is sometimes overlooked by critics. Federal legislation supporting schooling in America began far earlier than is sometimes assumed. (See Table 11-8.) A considerable body of legislation existed previous to the mid-century federal legislation which provided schooling for veterans of World War II through the G.I. Bill of Rights and prior to the National Defense Education Act which grew out of American fears that the schools were not sufficiently geared to a Space Age.

Despite the long history of federal aid to education and the substantial sums now being spent for federal support of education in the nation, the debate over federal aid to education is still heated. Here are the more frequent arguments used on both sides of this issue, as adapted from Howard R. Jones' expanded treatment in *Financing Public Elementary Education and Secondary Education.*[18]

The proponents of federal aid to education say:

1. Every American child, regardless of whether he happens to grow up in a rich state or a poor state, should have at least a minimum level of opportunity to receive an education and, at most, the quality of educational opportunity provided to most American children and youth.
2. The United States needs all of its citizenry to be well educated, in the interest of both national welfare and national security. Even more broadly, educational opportunity for all is necessary if we are to consider ourselves a democracy.

[18] Howard R. Jones, *Financing Public Elementary and Secondary Education* (New York: The Center for Applied Research in Education, 1966), pp. 103–106.

**TABLE 11-8  The Federal Government and Education, 1780–1957**

| Major pre-Sputnik congressional activity in education | | |
|---|---|---|
| Land Ordinance | 1785 | Provided an orderly format for distribution and settlement of public lands and encouraged use of public monies to establish and maintain public schools in the newly created townships. |
| Northwest Ordinance | 1787 | |
| Ohio Statehood Enabling Act | 1802 | First of the Enabling Acts which provided land grants (a total of 98 million acres) for public schools in newly created states. |
| Morrill Act | 1862 | Provided 30,000 acres of land per congressman for establishment of agricultural, scientific, and industrial colleges; assisted 68 institutions currently enrolling 40 percent of the nation's college population. |
| Hatch Act | 1887 | Provided land grants for agricultural experimental stations at land grant colleges. |
| Second Morrill Act | 1890 | Provided permanent annual endowment for developing instructional programs in agricultural and technical colleges and universities; original $15,000/year/state appropriation eventually increased to $50,000/year/state. |
| Smith-Lever Act | 1914 | Created Agricultural Extension Service to "aid in diffusing . . . useful and practical information on subjects pertaining to agriculture and home economics"; original $5 million/year appropriation eventually increased to $50 million/year. |
| Smith-Hughes Act | 1917 | Provided matching funds to help states develop high school vocational programs; original $1.7 million program expanded four times and incorporated in 1958 NDEA. |
| "New Deal" Activity | 1930s | Encouraged education as part of the Public Works Administration, Civilian Conservation Corps, National Youth Administration, Works Progress Administration, etc. |
| Lanham Act | 1941 | Provided funds to construct and operate schools where war-incurred federal activity created burdens upon local governments; expanded in 1950 by Impact Laws 815 and 874, which provided money for school construction and district operating costs respectively. |
| Serviceman's Readjustment Act (GI Bill) | 1944 | Provided education and training for returning World War II veterans; expanded subsequently to include veterans of wars in Korea and Vietnam. |
| National School Lunch Program | 1946 | Provided funds for school lunch programs in public and non-public school; expanded in 1954 to include a school milk program. |
| National Science Foundation | 1950 | Established a federally supported foundation to provide scholarships and fellowships for study and research in scientific fields. |
| School Construction Act | 1957 | Provided $325 million/year for four years for financing school construction. |

John M. Nagle, "The Tenth Amendment and Uncle Sam," *The Educational Forum* (November 1969), pp. 23, 28.

3. Some states and regions of the nation have been particularly handicapped economically in their efforts to supply sufficient classrooms and employ adequate teachers. Even though great improvements have taken place, some areas of the country still face substantial problems.
4. Since most of our taxes are collected at the federal level, primarily through an income tax which reflects the individual's ability to pay better than do state and local taxes, a substantial amount of federal aid derived from the income of the entire nation and used on behalf of the entire nation is eminently fair.
5. Federal aid is the greatest reservoir of resources for taxation; local and state taxes for education have grown tremendously and the capacity for further use of these resources is more limited than at the federal level.
6. The federal government collects taxes relatively efficiently as compared to state and local sources.
7. People in the United States frequently move and this mobility supports national programs for greater equalization.
8. We are spending millions abroad through foreign aid in behalf of the educational programs of newly developing countries. The educational welfare of our own children is at least equally important.
9. If the federal government is able to build highways, protect the public health and provide housing, it should be able to make a substantial investment in the welfare of children.

The opponents of federal aid to education urge:

1. The responsibility for education in the American system rests with the states. Education is not even mentioned in the United States Constitution.
2. Federal control is a reality; schools adapt their purposes and programs in order to receive federal funds. The agency which controls the purse strings will control the educational product.
3. This is no time to add responsibility for education to the national priorities. The present staggering costs of federal government should be decreased, not increased.
4. The emergency is over with respect to the public schools. The boom in elementary enrollment is past, so why support federal spending now?
5. Wealthy states should not be taxed more heavily than poor states to achieve equalization.
6. When tax money must be funneled into Washington before being distributed to the states, substantial overhead and administrative costs will be incurred.
7. Since private and parochial schools may not constitutionally be granted federal support, many citizens with children in private and parochial school programs may be expected to resist expanded federal taxation for education.

8. Perhaps the federal government should support other state activities such as welfare, road building, etc., through grants to the states and thus leave the states more funds for state support of education so there will be less necessity to call upon the federal government.

As the controversy has continued, federal aid has steadily grown, though it has taken the form of federal support for certain aspects of the educational program. It has been a response to emergencies in the name of national interest and in the form of categorical aid. For instance, when during World War I vocational education seemed to be sadly lagging, the Smith-Hughes Act was inaugurated. During the depression of the 1930s, schools were built through federal funds, in large part to provide employment. When the veterans returned from World War II, more educational opportunities were made available through federal funds. School lunch programs came about in large part because of the desire to use America's agricultural surplus. As we have already seen, the National Defense Education Act came about because of fears that the United States was lagging behind the Soviet Union in a space age and most particularly as to subjects judged necessary for national survival—mathematics, science, and modern languages. The federal stress on programs for the disadvantaged was a recognition of a national problem in the inner cities, involving the poor and the culturally disadvantaged in particular.

So, until the present time, financial help provided by the federal government has taken the form of assistance to parts of the school program which seemed to be falling behind, thus potentially or actually handicapping the national interest. Other support to schools came about as a by-product of attempts to aid aspects of the economy.

The result was not general aid to education but what might better be described as a broken-front approach on the part of the federal government. A crucial problem for the seventies is whether or not the federal government has a responsibility to provide aid so that at least a minimum program for all children and possibly a program of genuine educational equalization might be established throughout the nation.

## THE EXPANSION OF EDUCATIONAL EXPENDITURES

### The Growth of Educational Expenditures

The total expenditures for the public schools have risen sharply during the last decade. From the 1962–63 school year through the 1972–73 school year, the total amount spent has increased 162.3 percent. Table 11-9 shows the total expenditures for public schools each year from 1962–63 through 1972–73. Despite inflation during the period, this is an increase which has far out-distanced inflationary forces. The increase over this same period for current operating expenses only, excluding capital outlay and interest on debt, was 180.0 percent.

The probability is that expenditures for schools will continue to rise.

TABLE 11-9 **Expenditures for Public Elementary and Secondary Schools 1962–1972**

| | | TOTAL EXPENDITURES* | |
| | | Percent increase | |
| School year | Amount (in thousands) | Over 1962–63 | Over previous year |
|---|---|---|---|
| 1962–63 | $19,735,070 | ... | ... |
| 1963–64 | 21,324,993 | 8.1 | 8.1 |
| 1964–65 | 23,029,742 | 16.7 | 8.0 |
| 1965–66 | 26,248,026 | 33.0 | 14.0 |
| 1966–67 | 28,352,330 | 43.7 | 8.0 |
| 1967–68 | 32,977,182 | 67.1 | 16.3 |
| 1968–69 | 35,782,262 | 81.3 | 8.5 |
| 1969–70 | 40,683,276 | 106.1 | 13.7 |
| 1970–71 | 43,716,076 | 121.5 | 7.5 |
| 1971–72 | 48,907,413 | 147.8 | 11.9 |
| 1972–73 | 51,762,628 | 162.3 | 5.8 |

* Current expenditures plus capital expenditures plus interest on debt services.
NEA, Research Division, *Estimates of School Statistics, 1972–73*, Research Report 1972–R12 (Washington, D.C.: The Association, 1973), p. 17.

Take, for example, the future oriented studies of a committee of the National Society for the Study of Educational Administration. As the committee projected a financial structure for administering the public education system of the 1980s, the members generalized:

1. The population to be served by public education will be substantially increased in both number and proportion of the population.
2. Educational programs will be perceived as an investment so educational experiences will be continuous as economic and technological advances are made and labor forces will need to be trained and retrained.
3. Most of the presently constituted educational programs will be broadened and deepened.
4. New programs will be instituted which will require unique personnel and material resources.
5. Educational program emphases will include both individual and social benefits.
6. Education in the 1980s will require a substantially larger expenditure than it did in the 1970s in terms of total dollars, per pupil expenditure, proportion of public sector expenditures, and proportion of the gross national product.[19]

So there is no doubt that the problem raised in this chapter as to "where the money comes from" is a real and continuing one. As a new teacher, you have the social responsibility of knowing not only the

[19] Walter G. Hack and Francis O. Woodard, *Economic Dimensions of Public School Finance: Concepts and Cases* (New York: McGraw-Hill Book Co., 1971), p. 222.

dimensions of the problem but thinking through your viewpoint on the social issues involved. You need to consider whether public education should be supported by tax funds, and, if so, why. You need to consider the types of taxes which should be depended on for revenue in the future. You need to consider the social implications of progressive and regressive taxation. You must determine your position on inequalities in support for the schooling of Americans. You need to think about the desirability or undesirability of federal aid and whether the present program of grants-in-aid for special national needs is preferable to a broader program of general aid from federal sources. You need to think about the possible consequences of the federal government's sharing education revenue with states and localities. If your decisions are to be well based, you will have to continually expand your knowledge of finances to become a reasonably literate person in this field.

Your decisions are important in your role as a citizen and they are crucial in your role as a teacher.

## DISCUSSION

1. In what way is American public education a decentralized activity? How important is local control?
2. Where does the money for public education come from? What are the relative proportions of contributions from the various sources?
3. Should public education be supported by tax funds? If so, why? If not, how?
4. What is to be said for achieving economic and social benefits through a private rather than a public system of education? How do public and private expenditures for education compare with each other?
5. What are the sources of taxation in America? What proportion of taxes go to education?
6. How would you defend the support of education through taxation?
7. Discuss the difference between a progressive and regressive tax.
8. Why does a regressive tax measure aid the wealthier segment of our population? How does a progressive tax aid the poorer segment? What are the taxes in your state that are characterized as being regressive? Progressive?
9. What seem to you to be appropriate standards for tax equity? What is the case for, respectively, property taxes, sales taxes, and income taxes? What are some trends and tendencies with implications for the future?
10. Can you document the existence of inequality in income distribution and consequent inequality of educational opportunity in the United States? How do these inequalities manifest themselves in particular states? In local communities?
11. What essentially is the meaning of a "foundation" plan? Could the idea of a "foundation" be equally used at the federal level?
12. What are the latest developments with respect to the use of property taxes in financing schools? How have court decisions affected the financing of public schools? What controversial questions are raised by financing of schools primarily by the state rather than the local community?
13. How has the federal government contributed to education?

14. What is the case for "general" versus "categorical" aid from the federal government?

15. Were aspects of your own elementary or secondary education at least partially supported with federal aid funds or programs? If so, what? Why were these particular aspects singled out?

16. What are the pros and cons on federal aid to education? Which of the arguments seem particularly impressive to you? What social forces encourage and discourage federal aid to education? Federal revenue sharing with states?

17. To what extent have educational expenditures grown in past years and to what extent do they simply reflect inflationary forces? What seems to be the probable future for expenditures for education?

18. What arguments support large additional sums of money being spent on public education? Which oppose? Give specific examples.

19. Should additional funds be allocated by governing bodies to determine and implement a more effective—preventive and developmental—compensatory education program?

20. Discuss this comment: "Adequate financial support alone does not solve the problems facing the school: it facilitates their solution."

## INVOLVEMENT

1. Attempt to determine attitudes toward community and state support of education through local sources in your community.

2. Obtain from local school sources the budget for the local school system. How do the proportions spent compare with the national figures contained in this chapter?

3. Interview a school administrator. Which funds are earmarked for special activities from the federal government? Which from the state? If additional funds were available to him, what would be his priorities for spending them?

4. Determine where your state stands nationally with respect to educational expenditures. (Relevant data might be obtained from your State Department of Education.)

5. Appoint a member of your class to visit the legislature when educational appropriations are under consideration. Better still, plan a group trip by your class to the legislature which might include visits with your own representatives.

6. Interview local school officials on the extent to which the property tax is currently being used in the financing of local schools. Discuss with them problems of financing the schools through property taxes in light of recent court decisions, and recent actions by your state legislature.

7. Report on the federal budget. Attempt to determine the current proportion of funds invested in support of education and in support of the military establishment of the nation. Consider the views of various class members on desirable national priorities.

8. Write to your senators or congressmen concerning your opinions on educational support and solicit their positions on educational appropriations. Share with them your own point of view on federal aid to education and ask for their viewpoints.

9. Interview the student personnel services administrator in your school district. What groups of children need the largest educational expenditures?

10. Develop panel presentations concerning the arguments about increased expenditure for public education. Include value factors.

11. Bring a local administrator to your class to clarify the present situation in your local community and state as to the financing of public education.

# PART THREE

# FOUNDATIONS OF EDUCATION

# TWELVE

# What are the social class and ethnic backgrounds of students?

To this point in the book we have talked largely of teachers. We have dealt mainly with decisions you as a new teacher must make. Knowledge of the social and historical setting in which education takes place and of the forces to be taken into account is essential in your decision-making. But important though your decisions and surrounding forces are, there is another element in education which is of high importance to you and your work. After all, education is for students, young or old. This chapter will deal with the social class and ethnic backgrounds of these students.

The sheer number of human beings who attend schools is impressive. The simplest statistic to describe the volume is three-tenths of the nation. It's no wonder that education is occasionally referred to as America's major enterprise.

But the people who attend schools in America are not statistics—they are individual human beings. Even within categories, students still remain individuals. An impressionistic description of the high school population, which the writer once wrote for the readers of a popular magazine, may illustrate the point of individuality:

What a range of young people attend our public high schools in America! Here's Susan: brilliant, already accepted by one of the "Seven Sisters" colleges, studying PSSC physics devised by the best brains of M.I.T. and elsewhere, speaking French fluently, reading William Faulkner and Jean Paul Sartre, wrestling with calculus, learning international economics, planning to travel on the Continent with her family next summer.

Here's Mike: indifferent, ready to quit high school, attending remedial reading class, seeing some sense in the industrial arts program he calls "shop" but repelled by geometry and world history, counting the days till he's sixteen and free to make the wrong decision.

Here's Jane: of average ability, reading *Silas Marner* at school and movie fan magazines at home, doing well in the health unit in biology but poorly in civics, finding mathematics only tolerable, coming fully alive only in home economics and band, confiding in her counselor that there's only one degree she wants—the MRS.

Here's Joe: alienated from both school and society, hating every moment spent in every subject, proud of being chosen War Lord by his gang, itching for the next rumble or, better still, for some student or teacher to knock off the invisible chip he wears to school, when he comes to school at all.

Here's Maria: physically deprived of good nutrition, adequate housing and clothing; culturally deprived of books, magazines, newspapers except for gutter journalism, games, travel, dinner table conversation, privacy, and desperately trying to master ways of living and learning she has never known which are taught to her in a strange foreign tongue.

Here's Harry: creative and individualistic, understanding what the poet Edna St. Vincent Millay meant by saying "Euclid alone has looked on beauty bare" now that he has fallen madly in love with mathematical analysis. He pays no attention whatsoever to his other subjects.

Add to Susan, Mike, Jane, Joe, Maria, and Harry . . . other young people who attend all types of secondary schools today. Include those wondrously individual youngsters whom you know best from your own family and immediate neighborhood.[1]

## SOCIAL CLASS IN AMERICA

Groupings do exist to help us categorize, however loosely, highly varied people. One such grouping is social class. A society characterized by divisions of people into relative strata or ranks is a society characterized by social classes. To some, the mention of social class is anathema, for they associate social class only with the theories of Karl Marx who conceived capitalist societies as divided into two hostile, antagonistic classes: the proletariat versus the bourgeoisie. But, increasingly, students of society are looking at social class more dispassionately; they recognize that social class has been a characteristic of past societies and is characteristic of American society today. Twentieth century sociologists such as W. Lloyd Warner, August B. Hollingshead, Herbert Gans, and C. Wright Mills; educators such as Robert J. Havighurst, Allison Davis, and Patricia C. Sexton; novelists such as John O'Hara and John P. Marquand; and even cartoonists such as Al Capp, creator of Li'l Abner and the society of Dogpatch, testify to the existence of a social class structure in America.

To describe American social classes, some sociologists have adopted the conventional divisions of a society into upper, middle, and lower

[1] William Van Til, "What Makes a Good High School Curriculum?" *Woman's Day* (October 1964), pp. 42, 104.

classes. They have then subdivided each of the major divisions. As a result, W. Lloyd Warner and his followers, by dividing each category into upper and lower, describe the lives of upper uppers, lower uppers, upper middles, lower middles, upper lowers, and lower lowers. The subdivisions are based on how people perceive other people as to their relative status and rank in the total society.[2]

Some fellow sociologists have criticized Warner's six-fold structure (reduced for some communities to five) as more applicable to an America of the past, characterized essentially by towns and small cities than by modern, complex metropolitan giants. It is true that Warner carried on his studies primarily in the 1940s, but his categories still provide a useful introduction to major class categories, despite the date of his field research and the difficulty of making sharp demarcations between classes in contemporary America. Some new developments since Warner wrote will be included with his description of social class below.

### Upper Upper and Lower Upper

Warner found that the upper upper group is distinguishable from other social classes in that it is made up of families long established in the community that exercise considerable influence in the making of important community decisions. Upper uppers are prominent in what we earlier described as the power structure. Since this group is prosperous, such families often live in old and well-kept residences in what the community considers the most desirable section. The clubs to which family members belong are the most exclusive in the community; they include clubs based on the length of one's ancestry in America and exclusive organizations that raise money for charities. Such families derive their income from inherited wealth, investments, and property ownership.

Children and youth from upper upper families are carefully trained for their roles in life. They have no worries about food, clothing, and shelter. They too belong to the exclusive groups of the community; for them these groups often provide instruction in social dancing and etiquette. Upper upper youngsters often learn their sports skills, such as tennis, through special tutors and camps; national and international travel is taken for granted. In some communities, public school teachers never encounter such students because they often attend exclusive independent schools. Babies may be enrolled at birth for future attendance at a particular prep school. Some upper upper children are sent to public schools in a conscious attempt at democratization of their experiences.

Below the upper uppers in the social scale, yet sometimes equivalent

[2] W. Lloyd Warner, *Social Class in America: A Manual of Procedure for the Measurement of Social Status* (Chicago: Science Research Associates, 1949). See also W. Lloyd Warner and Leo Srole, *The Social Systems of American Ethnic Groups* (New Haven, Conn.: Yale University Press, 1945) and W. Lloyd Warner and Paul S. Lunt, *The Status Systems of a Modern Community* (New Haven, Conn.: Yale University Press, 1942).

to upper uppers in wealth, are the lower uppers, who are also influential in the power structure. Yet, according to Warner and his school of thought, the lower uppers are not perceived by the community as equivalent in social status to the upper uppers because lower uppers represent families who have more recently acquired their substantial share of the world's goods. Though their dollars may be just as green as upper upper dollars, lower uppers are regarded by communities as *nouveau riche* who are not top level in status because they are not the long-time possessors of wealth.

The homes of such lower upper families are among the best in town; sometimes parents have been known to purchase the mansion (though not the status) of an old family. Their clubs are outstanding but not as exclusive as those of the upper uppers. Membership is usually held in the country club. Entertaining is frequent and may be more lively than gracious. The men of the families work for a living as top level business leaders, doctors, lawyers, etc. Cars are new and numerous. Alliances with the upper uppers as a way of social climbing, particularly through marriages, are frequent.

The child or youth from such a family background is somewhat more likely to attend public schools than the upper upper young person. But since his school is located in the most exclusive section of town, he usually does not have much relationship with social classes other than his own and the upper middle class, along with the upper uppers who happen to be in attendance at public rather than private schools. Like the upper upper young person, the young lower upper family member is often trained for the social struggle through social dancing lessons, ballet, tennis instruction, and sometimes fencing. He or she often is destined by the family for entrance into either the best college of the region or an exclusive college on the East or West coast. Families are deeply concerned for academic success, which will ensure college admittance into the selected college. Today, the usual lower upper youth follows the patterns established by parents. But in our turbulent times, some totally repudiate their training and adopt the ways of hippies and other dissenters; they may adopt a life-style from the counter-culture.

In some communities, particularly old communities in New England or in the South, the distinction between upper upper and lower upper classes is clear. In some Middle Western communities and often in young communities, this distinction blurs. Sociologists consequently report, in such communities, a single upper class. Such was the case in Jonesville, a small city of 6,108 in Abraham County, state of North Prairie, a fictional title for an actual community near Chicago described by W. Lloyd Warner in *Democracy in Jonesville.*[3]

In Jonesville the upper group was represented by the Will Taylor

---

[3] W. Lloyd Warner, *Democracy in Jonesville: A Study in Quality and Inequality* (New York: Harper and Row, 1949).

family, which lived in a fine old mansion built by Will's grandfather. The Taylor home was located in Top Circle, the best section of town. The Taylor family were social leaders, prosperous and secure, people in the society pages. Earlier generations of the family often thought of moving to Chicago and taking part in social life there, but the men of the family wanted to be near their farm lands in order to confer with the farm managers on the crops and to see how the tenants were producing. People like the Taylors in Jonesville belonged to the country club and a social club; other similar upper class people belonged to organizations open only to those whose ancestors lived in America during settlement and colonization. According to Warner, the upper class—approximately three percent of Jonesville—included both the few old and respected families who had lived a long time in the community and a few new families of wealth who were accepted by the old families. As to prestige and influence, the lines between upper uppers and lower uppers in Jonesville blurred.

## Upper Middle and Lower Middle

The upper middle group in an American community consists of families in which the men are prominent in managerial and professional work and active in the community through luncheon clubs, community-support organizations, and community affairs. The women of the upper middle group are frequently active in such organizations as the League of Women Voters, the parent-teacher association, and the American Association of University Women. The homes of upper middle class citizens are comfortable and pleasant, often located in the better suburbs or in urban apartments regarded as desirable though not top level. Adults of such families are usually regarded as solid and substantial citizens. Some are members of professions; others are entrepreneurs engaged in business. Their life-styles and political preferences sometimes differ; some professionals tend toward liberalism; many entrepreneurs are more conservative.

Children and youth from upper middle families are often taught (by example, if not directly) the desirability of being well-liked by contemporaries and of making good impressions; teamwork is stressed. In a sense, such families often emphasize the salability of personalities in American life. Perhaps because of this conformity emphasis, it is from this group and the lower upper class that much of the contemporary youth rebellion stems. From the point of view of many young people the lives that their parents have led are not worthwhile. Some see their parents as too materialistic, insufficiently concerned with the larger issues in society, too conventional and conforming. Studies of youth dissent show that the leadership in protest comes particularly from upper middle group young people in revolt against what they regard as a trivial and superficial heritage.

Warner and his associates dramatized the upper middle group

through the entrepreneur-type George Hill family of Jonesville. The father was a successful businessman who had never questioned the desirability of working hard and "getting somewhere' in life. He was active in the Rotary Club, and his wife was a community leader in town. He lived in one of the better residential districts in town, sometimes called the Country Club district. But the George Hill family was not as well off or as accepted in high society as the Taylors. Instead, Jonesville citizens described people like the George Hills as community leaders, respected citizens, prominent business and professional people. The adults of the Hill family worked with community oriented luncheon clubs and service organizations rather than with exclusive society oriented organizations. Approximately 11 percent of Jonesville residents were upper middle class, according to Warner.

In the American class structure, there is a difference in prestige between the upper middle class and the lower middle class members. Families in the lower middle class often earn their living from white collar jobs such as sales positions, clerical pursuits, and employment in small businesses. Their houses, while perhaps neat and tidy, seldom resemble the advertising displays found in the "home and garden" magazines. The clubs to which they belong are certainly not exclusive; often they are lodges which also sponsor women's auxiliaries. Characteristic lower middle class life is marked by a good deal of work by the family about the house and the yard. Domestics are not employed; the lower middle class does its own work in the house and on the lot.

Since Warner conducted his studies, many highly skilled and well-paid workers seem to have joined the lower middle class group. Many of the building construction workers (termed "hard-hats" by the journalists) who demonstrated in New York City in 1970 against student dissent and who carried signs supporting the "Establishment" were probably lower middle class Americans. (One of the problems of the Warner classification is to account for the spillover of workers into the lower middle class.)

The children and youth of lower middle American families are sometimes regarded as typical young people. They are in school primarily, as they see it, to ready themselves for a place in the world of work. Yet they are not usually great social or financial strivers. Today they are usually somewhat more conventional than the youth above them in the social scale, and often, like their parents, they actively or passively oppose rebels and dissenters.

Warner in *Democracy in Jonesville* personified the lower middle class in the Henry Johnson family. As a clothing store clerk, Henry Johnson drew a regular weekly salary. His family lived in an ordinary bungalow which was in a part of town not regarded by Jonesville as the worst part of town or the best part. Henry was a simple man who enjoyed his vegetable gardening and his lodge meetings; his wife was proud of her ability to keep the house without any paid help. People of Henry Johnson's class often worked as small shopkeepers, skilled workers, or clerks; they received salary checks for their office work or obtained weekly wages in pay envelopes for semiskilled jobs in mills or factories. Warner indicated that approximately 31 percent of Jonesville people might be grouped as lower middle.

### Upper Lower and Lower Lower

The upper lower class is roughly synonymous to the working class. Upper lowers pour steel in Pittsburgh, assemble cars in Detroit, mill flour in Minneapolis, and sew garments in New York City. They are usually labor union members; they strike when necessary but usually without revolutionary enthusiasm and they may or may not follow their union leaders on political endorsements. They work primarily with things rather than people, and they are relatively unskilled and not as well paid as skilled building trades workers. Their homes are usually relatively simple but clean, but they do not live in the best section of town. TV's *All in the Family,* featuring the misadventures of Archie Bunker, always includes camera shots of such working class houses.

Children of the working class are often disadvantaged by their parents' somewhat limited outlooks. Often, from the parental point of view, education is simply a way of entering a vocation; consequently, parents tend to deprecate the academic aspects of education. Family travel takes the form of short vacations or day-long trips to the beach or to the park. Books are scarce, though newspapers are read and reread. TV replaces former family relationships. Conversation seldom deals with social or political issues; when it is judged appropriate at the dinner table it usually deals with family affairs, sports, or local activities. While higher education is often aspired to, there is little knowledge of the ways of obtaining scholarships or other financial support.

If one judges by middle class standards, the upper lower young people are often culturally disadvantaged. Yet there often is a closeness and affection in a working class family which compensates for certain disadvantages. This closeness is not always evident in the upper middle class suburban family where commuting distances are long and father's work often takes him out of town.

Warner portrayed the working class through Joe Bird. Joe, who had a steady job at the mill, was perceived by other residents as a man who had little money and not much of a house. But the town saw him as personally honest and as raising a respectable family. When Jonesville described families like the Bird family they talked of "good substantial working class people," "ordinary folks," "poor but honest," "decent and hard working," "respectable." Joe's work was steady. When economic recession or depression occurred, Joe moved onto relief but moved off as fast as he possibly could. He joined the lower middles in clubs and lodges while his wife attended women's auxiliaries. He liked small informal groups to play poker or gossip with. In Jonesville, upper lower residents amounted to a substantial 41 percent of the citizens.

Essentially, the upper lowers are different from the lower lowers in the way they are regarded by the community: lower lowers are regarded as no-account. The difference between upper lower and lower lower on the social scale is not strictly financial: much of it relates to the way society perceives and ranks people as to their status. On one thing all upper classes seem agreed—the lower lowers are not "good people." The community often thinks they don't particularly care or try; and they are often regarded as "trash."

Not only are they often unemployed, but they make little effort to get off relief, according to their neighbors. Their homes are not particularly well-kept. Fathers occasionally disappear (rather than go through the formalities of a divorce, a custom more popular in upper and upper middle classes). The lower lower seldom belongs to a club or organization. He and his family are often isolated and alone.

As a result, children and youth from lower lower families find themselves extremely handicapped in a materially oriented, upward aspiring society. The scholars searching for identifying group features regard them as culturally disadvantaged. Their neighbors above them on the social scale regard them as young people from undesirable backgrounds. By this, people mean that their families, judged by conventional American standards, are disreputable. Young people themselves scarcely have any way to avoid assuming undesirable family characteristics.

Dropping out of school is particularly attractive to young people of this social group, for everything in the school experience and life experience seems to conspire against them. Without a middle class background, they often find school highly unrealistic and irrelevant. Often these young people experience repeated failure unredeemed by any particular success in the school framework. When their best friends drop out at 16, and find jobs that temporarily sound attractive or do not get jobs but insist they are enjoying life just hanging around, it is very difficult for these young people to stay in school. Since their parents have no great respect for education, they do not provide much encouragement to staying in school either. As a result, most lower lower young people leave school at relatively low educational levels and thus cut themselves off from opportunities to rise in American life. To put it bluntly, the dice are loaded against the lower lower class children and youth. To many observers they represent a self-perpetuating American tragedy.

Yet other observers warn us not to sell some of the values of lower lower life short. They point out that there is a kind of tough realism in many lower lower young people, that there exists a quality of loyalty to those who belong to their immediate groups, that struggles for survival have taught lower lower youth a kind of ingenuity, that buried beneath expression in the form of profanity and obscenity lie genuine creative responses. Others, such as sociologist Edward C. Banfield in *The Unheavenly City*, regard such claims as sentimentalism and arrant nonsense for they see little that is redeeming in lower lower class culture.

Again Warner dramatized the lower lowers through the Tom Dow family. As seen by Jonesville people, Tom was shiftless and lazy. He didn't try because he didn't care. He was definitely poor and certainly not respectable. He had no regular work and made no great effort to stay off the relief rolls. He did as little as he could about the house and the yard and he escaped through drinking when he could. He was not active in clubs and organizations, though he complained loudly about life. He certainly did not bring up his children according to Spock. People like the Dow family constituted approximately 14 percent of Jonesville.

### Interaction and Separation among Jonesville Young People

In *Democracy in Jonesville,* Warner and his associates did not particularly report on the interaction and the separateness among the young people. But from the Jonesville data provided and from August B. Hollingshead's *Elmtown's Youth*[4] (Elmtown and Jonesville are the same community) we can readily visualize the relationships. It is quite apparent that belonging to one group or another affected the young person. It made a difference in whom a teenager had as friends, where he went for recreation and what he did, whom he dated, whether he graduated from high school, and whether he got a job after graduation and the kind of job it was.

Who were the friends of these high school students? Who made up these small informal groups of about five friends who stood around talking before school, who tried to sit together at lunch and at the drug store, who went to classes together, who went somewhere together after school? Ask a Jonesville High student and he would say, "I never particularly thought of *who* they are. I guess they are people like me."

He was right. They were like him. About four out of five members of his group were in the same grade. Also the members of his group resembled each other in that about three out of five of them were from family backgrounds similar to his. The chances in Jonesville High were strongly against belonging to a crowd two levels away from the social group of any one's family. When a Jonesville High School student did happen to belong to such a group, people frequently commented about it.

Whom did Jonesville High students date? Six out of ten of their dates were with people from similar family backgrounds. Almost four out of ten of their dates were with young people in the next family background groups.

---

[4] August B. Hollingshead, *Elmtown's Youth: The Impact of Social Classes on Adolescents* (New York: John Wiley and Sons, 1949).

Did Jonesville youth intend to go around with and date people with family backgrounds like their own? Or did it just happen? A little of both. For instance, two fashionable out-of-school clubs of high school students, the G.W.G., a girls club, and the Cadet Club, a boys club, consisted of members largely from upper and upper middle class families who belonged to the Country Club. The other students called the two groups "the combine" because it was understood that the majority of the Cadets dated G.W.G.'s and the majority of G.W.G.'s dated Cadets.

All of Jonesville's youth of high school age were not found in Jonesville High. Young people in Jonesville could choose one of two alternatives. One—usually taken by the upper, upper middle, and the lower middle youth—was that of attending classes, enjoying himself with school friends, taking part in extracurricular activities, holding part-time jobs, doing homework, and taking examinations. The other path was taken by the upper lower and especially the lower lower youth, who often dropped out of school. He looked for a job, and—if he found one—got used to long, regular hours, made job friends, and frequently came to realize that without more education it was hard to get ahead.

Two major explanations by students for dropping out of school are: the need for money and the feeling of not belonging and of being left out or far behind. But do these explanations go far enough? Why do some children from families with little money drop out of school while others, equally poor, stay in? Why do some children and not others feel that they don't belong and that they are left out of things?

The underlying explanation is closely related to family social class background and the attitude of the family toward education. Some parents with little money are eager for their children to have an education; many believe that education will help their children "do better than their parents." They sacrifice to keep a child in school and they encourage him in his schoolwork. It is quite a blow to them when one of their children drops out.

Frequently, lower lower class families are opposed or indifferent to much education. Sometimes they tell their children: "Your father never had a high school education," or "It's up to you; I don't care." When the family is uninterested or hostile, or they do not provide an appropriate atmosphere in which to study, there is a greater chance that children will drop out.

So the way Jonesville-Elmtown families were regarded or rated or thought about by many people in the community made a great difference in the young person's life. It influenced whom he had as friends, who belonged to his group and whom he dated. The family background was important in whether he stayed in school and had a better chance for a better job or whether he dropped out early and eventually settled in a poorer job.

### Later Studies of Social Class

During the past two decades, sociologists have studied the class patterns of other American communities and have investigated the ways of living of many American subgroups within social classes. For instance, Arthur Vidich and Joseph Bensman, in a study of a small town they called "Springdale," reported five classes: the middle class, a marginal middle class, the old aristocracy (which was a fallen upper upper group), the traditional farmers, and the "shack people."[5] C. Wright Mills explored the traditions and values of the American middle class symbolized by the white collar,[6] and in another study reported on three powerful groups in what he termed the power elite: the corporation executives of big business; the political influentials in Washington; and the military leaders of the Pentagon.[7] Herbert Gans studied the residents of a massive housing development, Levittown, and reported on the patterns and interactions of the several classes represented in the community.[8] Gans described upward mobility from the working class, tension between middle class teachers and working class families, and the intergroup relations among suburbanites of various social class cultures. Gans has also reported on ethnic groups in the city in *The Urban Villagers*.[9] A useful appraisal of contemporary social class relationships is Gerhart Lenski's *Power and Privilege*.[10]

Among contemporary writers on school and society, Patricia C. Sexton has made significant contributions to the understanding of the role of class and status. In *Education and Income* she reported on inequality of opportunity in the public schools through her study of Big City located in the American middle west. She found that the reality of Big City was different from the national dream of equal educational opportunity for all, without regard to race, religion, class, or status.[11] In 1965 in *Spanish Harlem*, she studied poverty among the Puerto Rican, Negro, and Italian residents of the area and described the schools as a broken ladder to success.[12] In *The Feminized Male* she discussed the relationships among middle class values and lower class activities in the shaping of contemporary male roles. Among her conclusions were that "schools alone

---

[5] Arthur Vidich and Joseph Bensman, *Small Town in Mass Society* (Princeton, N.J.: Princeton University Press, 1958).
[6] Charles Wright Mills, *White Collar: The American Middle Classes* (New York: Oxford University Press, 1951).
[7] Charles Wright Mills, *The Power Elite* (New York: Oxford University Press, 1956).
[8] Herbert Gans, *Levittowners: Ways of and Politics in a New Suburban Community* (New York: Pantheon Books, 1967).
[9] Herbert Gans, *The Urban Villagers* (New York: Free Press, 1962).
[10] Gerhart Lenski, *Power and Privilege: A Theory of Social Stratification* (New York: McGraw-Hill, 1966).
[11] Patricia C. Sexton, *Education and Income* (New York: The Viking Press, 1961).
[12] Patricia C. Sexton, *Spanish Harlem* (New York: Harper and Row Publishers, 1965).

cannot free men from the apron strings that bind them." But she asks that society become increasingly aware that "schools have feminized boys mainly because society turned education over to women and feminized males."[13] In 1971, in collaboration with Brendan Sexton of the United Automobile Workers, she reported on the relationships between contemporary politics and the values of working class Americans in *Blue Collars and Hard-Hats*.[14]

Rather than focusing on the social class factor alone, contemporary sociologists are increasingly studying subcultural groups in America, such as blacks, "the new ethnics" from European backgrounds, or the residents of inner cities and suburbs, in respect to a combination of factors including class, status, race, values. Social class backgrounds are important ingredients in such subcultural studies, for social stratification continues to play a role in the lives of Americans.

## ETHNIC BACKGROUNDS OF STUDENTS

Despite the melting pot idea in American life, leading to the disappearance of ancestral backgrounds and the emergence of a standard "American type," ethnic differences do exist and are often sharpened in our own times. No tidy and neat classifications exist for the ancestral backgrounds of Americans. So we will use two broad and admittedly clumsy classifications for want of better groupings. These are the Americans who came early from the British Isles and Western Europe and the Americans who came later from Southern and Eastern Europe; and the Americans often collectively called minorities and typified by the original Americans (the Indians), the Negroes or blacks (who came early but in chains), and such groups as the Spanish-speaking people from Mexico and from Puerto Rico. These classifications are adapted from Max Lerner's several categories described in *America as a Civilization;* they provide us a useful framework for analysis of ethnic backgrounds.

### Americans from Europe

In broad terms, settlement in America from the Colonies to the middle of the nineteenth century was largely a story of people from the British Isles and Western Europe who colonized, settled and conquered the wilderness, and built towns and cities. American history books chronicle the traditions they brought with them and developed, including political democracy, concern for civil liberties, the free enterprise system, the belief in hard work, the creation of a legal system, and an ethic which was primarily Protestant in orientation. Subconsciously, and often con-

---

[13] Patricia C. Sexton, *The Feminized Male* (New York: Random House, 1969), p. 199.
[14] Patricia C. Sexton and Brendan Sexton, *Blue Collars and Hard-Hats* (New York: Random House, 1971).

America's ethnic groups have often retained many aspects of their own cultures while contributing to the culture of the American scene.

sciously and blatantly, the descendants of such people think of themselves as being the "real Americans." They often appoint themselves to the roles of the protectors and guardians and extenders of what they see as an early American heritage. But the Indians were here when the English landed at Plymouth Rock and in Virginia, and the Negroes came early.

The first major wave of what came to be called the "new" immigra-

[15] Nathan Glazer and Daniel P. Moynihan, *Beyond the Melting Pot* (Cambridge, Mass.: MIT Press, 1963). John J. Appel and A. S. Eisenstadt (Eds.), *New Immigration* (New York: Pitman, 1971). Ann Novotny, *Strangers at the Door: Ellis Island, Castle Garden, and the Great Migration to America* (New York: Chatham Press, 1971). Wilton Tifft, *Ellis Island* (New York: Norton, 1972). Thomas C. Wheeler, *The Immigrant Experience* (New York: Dial Press, 1972).

tion to the United States consisted of middle and southern Europeans with a sprinkling of people from border lands in the Near East and North Africa. Such immigrants often brought with them faiths different from the prevailing Protestant faith—notably Catholic and Jewish. These new immigrants, especially in the late nineteenth and early twentieth centuries, saw America as the land of opportunity; they had magnificent and misguided stereotypes of gold in the streets and easy acceptance in American life. Actually, they encountered resistance from those who had come earlier. Because they landed at the large city ports and knew little of the country, they tended to concentrate in areas of the Eastern seaboard and to a lesser extent on the West coast. With time, they fanned out across the country and created new centers, somewhat oriented to their own ethnic backgrounds, in rural areas as well as cities.

Their ethnic identities still exist, typified by the Polish in Chicago, the Italians in New York, or the Irish in Boston. They acculturated and they intermarried; yet they retained some of their distinctiveness with respect to such customs as cookery, child rearing, and religion. Their stories are well chronicled by scholars.[15] They struggled for acceptance and their share of the American dream in an America which was essentially becoming more industrial and capitalistic.

Many members of ethnic groups from Southern and Eastern Europe achieved what Americans have traditionally termed "success." Many others stayed at relatively low levels in the American status system. They were not alone in this; we have only to recognize the persisting economic problems of low income whites from the British Isles and Western Europe to recognize that all do not automatically rise to "the top" in American life. Some of those left behind in the American success race were particularly alarmed by what they conceived as an infringement on their lives by others who also wanted to stake their claims to a share in American life. So in the 1970s an increasing uneasiness and even hostility was apparent among some members of some ethnic groups, particularly toward new immigrants from Mexico, the Orient, and Puerto Rico and toward longer established Americans such as blacks and Indians. But other members of such ethnic groups reject charges of racism and emphasize the need for a major social movement among the millions of people of European descent employed in the industrial cities. For instance, at an urban ethnic conference, Barbara Mikulski, a Baltimore community worker and later a city councilwoman, said:

The ethnic American is sick of being stereotyped as a racist and dullard by phony white liberals, pseudo black militants and patronizing bureaucrats. He pays the bill for every major government program and gets nothing or little in the way of return. . . . Unfortunately, because of old prejudices and new fears, anger is generated against other minority groups rather than those who have power. What is needed is an alliance of white and black, white collar, blue collar, and no collar based on mutual

*Oscar Buitrago, Black Star*

New Year celebration in New York City's Chinatown.

need, interdependence, and respect, an alliance to develop the strategy for a new kind of community organization and political participation.[16]

**American Indians**

To some observers of the American scene, the minority with the greatest concentration of human and social problems are the Indians, who were, paradoxically, the first Americans. Despite originally friendly relations, wars between whites and Indians soon occurred. Whites made their conquests not only with guns and treaties but also through some of the harmful accompaniments of so-called civilization—disease and alcohol. Eventually, the Indians were forced onto reservations.

On the reservations there was always ambivalence as to whether education should absorb the Indian into American majority patterns or respect his civilization and identity. The vacillation between opposing poles of thought was accompanied by the growth of a large governmental

[16] "Angry Ethnic Voices Decry a 'Racist and Dullard' Image," *New York Times,* June 17, 1970, p. 49.

bureaucracy, the Bureau of Indian Affairs. Report after report was prepared and filed by governmental and philanthropic groups, with very little change in the low economic level of the remaining members of the Indian tribes. Today the desperate situation of many Indians is documented in their high suicide and alcoholism rates, and their alienation from white society. However, many Indians have recently reassumed a forceful and militant attitude and have become more determined to receive the benefits of American society. In 1969 some Indians dramatically took over Alcatraz Island in San Francisco Bay; they proposed that the all but deserted island become a center for Indian cultural development in the future. In 1972, while Americans were electing a President, some Indians occupied the offices of the Bureau of Indian Affairs in Washington. In 1973, some Indians confronted federal marshals during the occupation of Wounded Knee, South Dakota.

There were nearly 800,000 American Indians in the United States in 1970, according to the census. Possibly there are even more Indians than the census indicates. The Census Bureau includes in the category "Indian" those persons who indicated their race as American Indian or who reported to the 1970 census takers for this item only the name of an Indian tribe. Almost half of the Indian population live in the West.[17] More Indians live on 263 reservations in the West than live in the cities of America, but the number of urban Indians is growing. The Bureau of the Census reports that in 1970 241,699 Indians lived in urbanized areas. ("An urbanized area generally contains at least one city of 50,000 inhabitants or more and includes that portion of the surrounding territory, whether incorporated or unincorporated, which meets specified criteria relating to population density.") In the urbanized area of Los Angeles and Long Beach, California, there were 27,958 American Indians. In the urbanized area of New York City and northeastern New Jersey, there lived 14,669 Indians. The Indian population of the San Francisco-Oakland area was 11,582.[18]

Today there is a major conflict as to whether reservations should be "terminated" or maintained. The conflict is reflected in education as some Indian groups demand control of education on reservations through the creation of Indian school boards. The conflict is partly related to the broader social conflict as to minority policies between integrationist and separationist tendencies. The new cry in the continuing conflict is "Indian power"; the automobile bumper stickers which

[17] U.S. Bureau of the Census, "Supplementary Report: Race of the Population of the United States, by State: 1970," *1970 Census of Population* (Washington, D.C.: U.S. Government Printing Office, 1972), pp. 1–3.
[18] U.S. Bureau of the Census, "Supplementary Report: Race of the Population for Standard Metropolitan Statistical Areas, Urbanized Areas, and Places of 50,000 or More: 1970," *1970 Census of Population* (Washington, D.C.: U.S. Government Printing Office, 1972), pp. 1-324,1-333.

American Indian children, San Juan Reservation, New Mexico.

increasingly report American viewpoints now include such slogans as "Indians discovered America" and "Custer had it coming." Today the American Indian Movement (AIM) is a vigorous factor in Indian protest. Some Indians, however, oppose militant tactics.

### Black Americans

In Jamestown, Virginia, in August 1619, twenty black people were brought ashore to be farmed out as servants. The American tragedy of slavery was about to begin. American Negro slavery has been called the most awful thing the world has ever known. The brutal facts are that the Negro slave in America had no protection from organized society; his children could be sold; his wife could be both violated and sold. He could be subject to any barbaric action his master deemed appropriate. He was sharply cut off from a past that he could learn little about. Laws specified that he could not be taught to read or write without the specific permission of his master. He could not even practice any religion through meeting with his fellow slaves unless a white was present.

Lerone Bennett, Jr. describes the situation:

No slave could stand up to life as a human being. To live, for a slave, especially a male slave, was to renounce, to renounce anger and love and indignation, to renounce hate and human hurt, to renounce the claims and the rewards of love, the responsibilities of parenthood and the pride of ownership—to renounce these things not voluntarily in the service of a higher ideal, but at the command of another human will arbitrarily imposed by society. . . . Slavery destroyed the Negro's family, emptied his mind, and impoverished his soul. More than that, it made him doubt himself.[19]

The institution of slavery troubled the consciences of some of the makers of the United States Constitution. But it did not trouble them sufficiently to result in the abolition of slavery and, as the American nation began, the quality of life was being destroyed for 600,000 human beings, the slaves who existed in America in 1790.

It is little wonder that earnest men deplored slavery. Possibly the first recorded protest came from a group of German Mennonites in Pennsylvania in 1688. They asked, "Pray, what thing in the world can be done worse towards us, than if men should rob or steal us away and sell us for slaves to strange countries; separating husbands from their wives and children?"[20] It is no wonder that physical struggles for human rights took the form of slave mutinies and insurrections. These occurred during the eighteenth century and reached their culmination shortly before the Civil War. Notable uprisings included the revolt by Cato in 1739 near Stono, South Carolina. Probably best known are the Virginia rebellion of Nat Turner in 1831 and John Brown's famous raid on Harpers Ferry in 1857 immortalized in the song *John Brown's Body.* There were hundreds of less celebrated struggles. Yet by 1860 there were almost four million slaves in America.

The white abolitionists, such as William Lloyd Garrison and Wendell Phillips, crusaded, as did the black abolitionists such as Frederick Douglass. But the final confrontation of the Civil War had to take place before the Emancipation Proclamation by Abraham Lincoln freed the slaves of the South. The war was followed by the thirteenth, fourteenth, and fifteenth amendments to the Constitution that forbade slavery, fostered equal protection laws, and specified that rights of citizens to vote should not be denied.

But as the reconstruction period ebbed, racial segregation was established throughout the South by both law and custom. The North acquiesced and practiced its own version of segregation. The Negro response was first a policy of accommodation, typified by the educational efforts of Booker T. Washington. But more militant leadership emerged, as evidenced in 1905 at Niagara Falls in Canada and a year later at Harpers Ferry. The Negro leaders who convened wrote, "We will not be satisfied to take one jot or tittle less than our full manhood rights." Organization of the National Association for the Advancement of Colored People followed in 1910.

[19] Lerone Bennett, Jr., *Confrontation: Black and White* (Baltimore: Penguin Books, 1965), p. 27.
[20] John W. Caughey, John Hope Franklin, and Ernest R. May, *Land of the Free* (New York: Benziger Brothers, 1966), p. 113.

In the middle twentieth century, after numerous sit-ins, marches, and protests, the struggle moved into the courts and the legislatures. The civil rights drive got support from the Supreme Court school desegregation decision of 1954, the Civil Rights Law of 1964, and the Voting Rights Act of 1965. Many racial strategies combined to achieve these triumphs. They included the vigorous legal pressure under the leadership of the NAACP and such men as Thurgood Marshall and Roy Wilkins. They reflected the direct action strategy of A. Phillip Randolph, who sponsored influential marches. They were inspired by Martin Luther King, who developed a combination of passive resistance and social action

299

through the activities of the Southern Christian Leadership Conference. They were stimulated by the militancy of the rebels of the Student Non-Violent Coordinating Committee (SNCC), the Congress of Racial Equality (CORE), and the anger of the Black Muslims and Malcolm X.

Today the confrontation continues. Clearly, civil rights laws are not enough. There are too many people whose lives remain the same despite such laws. They see themselves as still powerless, subordinated, and lacking full rights. Too many people are not treated as free and equal. So militancy grew, particularly among young blacks. It spilled over into rioting during the "long hot summers" of the late 1960s.

This is part of the heritage of black children who will be attending many of the schools in which you will teach. It is part of the background that accounts for much of the anger, hostility, and militant rebellion which the new teachers of the middle 1970s, black or white, will encounter.

Some wonder why there is rebellion and militancy on the part of the blacks when conditions are seemingly growing better for them. In some areas of employment and in some areas of human endeavor, conditions are better for some blacks. Yet there still remains a wide gap between whites and blacks in America. The Bureau of the Census, in its 1972 report on the social and economic status of the black population, indicated that 7.4 million (32 percent) blacks lived below the official poverty level (recently retitled the "low income level" in government reports), which was $4,137 during 1971. There had been little change since 1970 when 7.5 million (34 percent) blacks lived below the official poverty level, then set at $3,968. Meanwhile in 1971, 17.8 million (10 percent) of the white population was living below the official poverty level.

Thus, 1.5 million black families, or about 29 percent of all black families, lived below the poverty level in 1971. Meanwhile, 3.8 million, or 8 percent, of all white families were below the official poverty line. So, as to poverty, the gap between whites and blacks in America persists.[21]

As to unemployment, the gap between whites and Negroes and other nonwhites (such as Indians) in America still persists. In the relatively prosperous year of 1951 the unemployment rate for Negroes and other nonwhites was 5.3 percent while the unemployment rate for whites was 3.1 percent. Ten years later in a year of relatively high unemployment, the unemployment rate for Negroes and other nonwhites was 12.4 percent while the unemployment rate for whites was 6.0 percent. Another ten years later in the year 1971, which was marked by recession,

[21] U.S. Bureau of the Census, "The Social and Economic Status of the Black Population in the United States, 1971," Current Population Reports, Series P-23, No. 42 (Washington, D.C.: U.S. Government Printing Office, 1972), pp. 38–39. The gap described in this study is apparently widening rather than closing. The New York Times, January 5, 1973, p. 25, reported that the U.S. Bureau of the Census estimated that in 1972, 9 percent of whites and 33 percent of blacks in the United States were living below the poverty level then set at $4,275.

TABLE 12-1  **Unemployment Rates: 1948 to 1971[1] (Annual Averages)**

| Year | Negro and other races | White | Ratio: Negro and other races to white |
|------|-----------------------|-------|----------------------------------------|
| 1948 | 5.9 | 3.5 | 1.7 |
| 1949 | 8.9 | 5.6 | 1.6 |
| 1950 | 9.0 | 4.9 | 1.8 |
| 1951 | 5.3 | 3.1 | 1.7 |
| 1952 | 5.4 | 2.8 | 1.9 |
| 1953 | 4.5 | 2.7 | 1.7 |
| 1954 | 9.9 | 5.0 | 2.0 |
| 1955 | 8.7 | 3.9 | 2.2 |
| 1956 | 8.3 | 3.6 | 2.3 |
| 1957 | 7.9 | 3.8 | 2.1 |
| 1958 | 12.6 | 6.1 | 2.1 |
| 1959 | 10.7 | 4.8 | 2.2 |
| 1960 | 10.2 | 4.9 | 2.1 |
| 1961 | 12.4 | 6.0 | 2.1 |
| 1962 | 10.9 | 4.9 | 2.2 |
| 1963 | 10.8 | 5.0 | 2.2 |
| 1964 | 9.6 | 4.6 | 2.1 |
| 1965 | 8.1 | 4.1 | 2.0 |
| 1966 | 7.3 | 3.3 | 2.2 |
| 1967 | 7.4 | 3.4 | 2.2 |
| 1968 | 6.7 | 3.2 | 2.1 |
| 1969 | 6.4 | 3.1 | 2.1 |
| 1970 | 8.2 | 4.5 | 1.8 |
| 1971 | 9.9 | 5.4 | 1.8 |

[1] The unemployment rate is the percent unemployed in the civilian labor force.
U.S. Bureau of the Census, "The Social and Economic Status of the Black Population in the United States, 1971," *Current Population Reports*, Series P-23, No. 42 (Washington, D.C., U.S. Government Printing Office, 1972), p. 52.

the unemployment rate for Negroes and other nonwhites was 9.9 percent while the unemployment rate for whites was 5.4 percent.[22] (See Table 12-1.)

When employed, blacks and other nonwhites continued to be over-represented in occupations frequently regarded as less desirable, such as service, private household, and laborer occupations and to be under-represented in positions commonly regarded as desirable such as professional, technical, and managerial occupations.[23] Table 12-2 represents the 1971 distribution of employed workers by occupation and sex.

To complicate the problem further, there is also a deepening schism

[22] *Ibid.*, p. 52.
[23] *Ibid.*, p. 67.

TABLE 12-2 **Percent Distribution of Employed Workers, by Occupation and Sex: 1971 (Annual Averages)**

| Occupation | Negro and other races | | White | |
| --- | --- | --- | --- | --- |
| | Male | Female | Male | Female |
| Total, employed   thousands. | 4,746 | 3,658 | 44,499 | 26,217 |
| Percent | 100 | 100 | 100 | 100 |
| Professional, technical, and managerial | 13 | 13 | 30 | 20 |
| Clerical and sales | 9 | 25 | 13 | 43 |
| Craftsmen and kindred workers | 13 | 1 | 21 | 1 |
| Operatives, including transport | 26 | 15 | 17 | 13 |
| Nonfarm laborers | 18 | 1 | 7 | 1 |
| Farmers and farm workers | 5 | 2 | 5 | 2 |
| Service workers, except private household | 15 | 27 | 7 | 16 |
| Private household workers | —[1] | 16 | — | 3 |

[1] represents zero or rounds to zero.
U.S. Bureau of the Census, "The Social and Economic Status of the Black Population in the United States, 1971," *Current Population Reports*, Series P-23, No. 42 (Washington, D.C., U.S. Government Printing Office, 1972), p. 67.

in the black community itself between the middle and lower groups, between the well prepared and those with few skills. So American education faces the formidable task of reducing the gaps and disparities and providing equal educational opportunity for all children and youth.

### Spanish-speaking Americans

Two groups are prominent among contemporary Spanish-speaking minority groups in the United States. Though their cultures are substantially different, Americans from Puerto Rico, and the Hispano-American immigrants from Mexico trace part of their heritage back to Spain. The common problems of the recent migrants from Puerto Rico and Mexico include mastery of English and adaptation to an industrial and technological civilization.

The close relationship of Puerto Rico with the United States dates back to the Spanish-American War of 1898. Puerto Rico is now a Commonwealth of the United States. Understanding the ways of two cultures requires bilinguality. In Puerto Rico social problems are pressing. Young Puerto Ricans must learn to earn their living on an island steadily shifting from rural to urban ways, in a world that permits easy migration to the mainland U.S.

As citizens of their localities and of the Commonwealth, as potential migrants to the mainland of the United States, they are learning to participate in democratic government, despite a social heritage marked by the authoritarianism of colonialism and imperialism. Young Puerto Ricans are also learning to improve human relationships in the kaleidoscope of colors, classes, and cultures which characterizes Puerto Rico. As young people in a space age, young Puerto Ricans must become more versed in the mathematical and scientific underpinnings of scholarship which relate to island industrialization.

Puerto Rican youngsters are facing life problems on their island which bewilder them. They are trying to relate to parents who are struggling with the urban-rural transition and the breakdown of older village traditions of family control. They are trying to find their way in peer groups colored both by island ways and by American ideas imported via mainland television, magazines, and publications, sometimes influenced for better or worse by youth who have returned from the streets of New York City. They must learn the new ways of recreation which are now superimposed on the older patterns. They must come to terms with their roles as men and women in society, with early maturation and early marriage. They are threading their way through the maze of vocational decisions and preparation on an island where unskilled work persists, yet new opportunities for the skilled proliferate as the island attracts investments and industries.

Complex choices are presented individuals through the continuing restless migration from village and *barrio* ways to the urbanization of San Juan, Ponce, Mayaguez, and a dozen other major centers, and from the rural stretches of sugar cane and coffee and tobacco lands and from the cities of large plazas and colorful houses and ever open windows to the canyons of cold New York lined by tenements, marked by strange folkways, and, sadly enough, by less than a warm welcome for "the foreigner." Many young Puerto Rican immigrants have to decide whether to band together in street gangs, whether to use militant techniques of confrontation.

For teachers of very low income Puerto Ricans, Oscar Lewis's *La Vida*[24] is essential reading. This frank and haunting book describes the experiences of a Puerto Rican family first in San Juan and then in New York, always living in poverty. But many Puerto Ricans are better off economically and socially than the family Lewis depicted.

Helping Puerto Rican young people to think for themselves should be an important goal in mainland and island education. Respect for each individual personality must prevail over vestigial class consciousness and invidious racial distinctions inherited from earlier aristocratic traditions. Fortunately, the democratic value of working together for common purposes commonly arrived at had strong roots in the *barrio* and is emphasized today through a determined campaign by the Com-

[24] Oscar Lewis, *La Vida: A Puerto Rican Family in the Culture of Poverty* (New York: Random House, 1966).

monwealth government, using many agencies of social work, education, and information, to help Puerto Ricans work together toward a rising living standard and a good life.

Migration to the mainland ebbs and flows according to job opportunities on the island and mainland. While New York City is usually the first home of the Puerto Rican newcomer, many have now moved into New York's suburbs, into adjoining states, and to metropolises throughout the nation.

A lively political struggle is taking place in Puerto Rico over the desirability of Commonwealth status involving immunity from United States income tax (but also no voting representation in the U.S. Congress) versus complete independence from the U.S. versus complete immersion in the U.S. by way of statehood. A teacher in the mid 1970s who works with Puerto Ricans should at least be aware of the varying stances on this issue.

Courtesy of OEO

Puerto Rico is part of the United States whereas Mexico is an independent nation, our neighbor to the south with which we share a long common boundary. Throughout history, people from Mexico have crossed that border to live permanently or temporarily in the United States.

Indeed, some Spanish-speaking Americans lived in what is now the United States long before the present border with Mexico existed. Some states now in the southwestern and western U.S., including Arizona, New Mexico, Texas, and California, were first settled by Spanish-speaking Americans, many of whom came north from Mexico during Spain's colonization of the New World. So some families of Spanish-speaking ancestry have lived on United States soil for centuries; if their children visit Mexico it is as tourists since their birth place is the United States. To term such families "Mexican" or "Mexican-American" is a questionable use of language. How many generations does one have to live in the United States to be regarded as a native?

The terms Mexican-American or Hispano-American or Spanish-American apply more properly to twentieth century immigrants, including those who cross the border for temporary or permanent residence in the United States. Workers from such families have long labored in the fields and ranches and mines of the Southwest and today often work in the industries of such growing cities as Los Angeles, San Francisco, Oakland, and Denver, as they fan out through California and the Rocky Mountain states. Some migrate to urban centers of the midwest and east. Since Mexico, despite gains for the common people growing out of its early twentieth century revolution and despite the growth of a middle class, is a land in which the living standard is still below that of the U.S., the migrants to the U.S. are usually poor people searching for a better life and a higher standard of living. Some plan to settle permanently in the United States; others plan to return to Mexico. Some intend to find permanent work; others have come as *braceros,* entering as authorized temporary agricultural laborers; a few have crossed the Rio Grande as "wetbacks" in illegal immigration.

The families participating in the contemporary immigration from Mexico face many problems. For many, theirs is the culture of poverty. Economically, they are often exploited. Their homes are frequently rural or urban slum shacks or migrant work camps. Only recently, through such charismatic leaders as Cesar Chavez, who led the grape pickers' strike, are they beginning to organize effective agricultural unions.

The educational problems of their children in U.S. schools are formidable. Their native language is Spanish and in Mexico bilingual instruction has not been as essential as in Puerto Rico. Schooling is interrupted by frequent moves to follow the crops from region to region within the states or to return home to Mexico. Low standards of living, sometimes including hunger, handicap effective education. When the

parents reside in cities, the entire family faces the problems of adjustment that rural people worldwide are forced to make to the strange ways
of cities. To cap the problem of education, their culture is essentially
Mexican and the schools, even when sensitive adaptations such as bi-
lingualism are made, are essentially oriented to U.S. culture.

The median number of school years attained by Mexican-Americans fourteen
years old and over is as follows: Arizona 8.3; California 9.2; Colorado 8.7; New
Mexico 8.8; and Texas 6.7.[25]

An educational attainment of eight years or less is automatically bracketed with
the occupational capability and income level of a manual worker. As automation in-
vades clerical and related occupations, educational preparation for those who are to
hold the new jobs must advance at least through high school and, sooner or later,
beyond. As an ethnic group, therefore, the Mexican-Americans have a present handicap of from four to seven years vis-à-vis the rest of the population. The rapid general
increase in high school and college enrollment of the recent past serves but to
emphasize the gap.[26]

Among the very young, different, though equally pressing, cultural gaps appear.
On one side stand the impoverished households, the alien family style, the ancestral
language, the insecure community. On the other there is the school with its inadequate budgets, its administrative molds, its distance from the families of its pupils.
Between them is the preschooler who speaks only Spanish, who falters in his first and
crucial encounter with Anglo-American because his native speech is still regarded as a
barrier and not a road, and because in addition he brings with him all the handicaps of
poverty.[27]

A self-identification as "Chicanos" has arisen among Mexican-
American activists. The Chicano is frequently impatient with those who
term themselves Spanish-Americans and who seem to the Chicano to be
aristocratically inclined upper class people proud of their Spanish past
and disdainful of Mexican origins. The Chicano prefers to be loyal to *La
Raza* and to the Mexican and Mexican-American people. He sees his people as an exploited group who must assert themselves more aggressively.
As he expresses his anger and demands, the Chicano often finds himself
at odds with the Anglo majority in community and school environments.

For teachers of Hispano-American students from Mexico, books by
Oscar Lewis are helpful, especially if the reader avoids stereotyping all
Mexicans as similar to the families portrayed. They include *The Children
of Sanchez*,[28] the autobiography of a Mexican family, and *Five Families*,[29]
case studies in the Mexican culture of poverty.

[25] Ernesto Galarza, Herman Gallegos and Julian Samora, *Mexican-Americans in the Southwest*
(Santa Barbara, Calif.: McNally & Loftin, 1969), p. 38.
[26] *Ibid.*, p. 39.
[27] *Ibid.*, pp. 46–47.
[28] Oscar Lewis, *The Children of Sanchez: Autobiography of a Mexican Family* (New York:
Random, 1961).
[29] Oscar Lewis, *Five Families: Mexican Case Studies in the Culture of Poverty* (New York: Basic
Books, 1959).

## RELATIONSHIP BETWEEN BACKGROUND AND EDUCATIONAL ACHIEVEMENT

The outcomes of education are related to the social class of students; this relationship holds for majorities and minorities. The educational attainment of an individual student appears to be related both to his social class and to the social class level of his classmates. The *Equality of Educational Opportunity* survey—one of the most extensive studies of student attitudes and performance ever made—found that the achievement differences among students are largely accounted for by the differences in their social class.[30] In a study of Richmond, California, performed for the U.S. Civil Rights Commission by Professor Alan Wilson of the University of California at Berkeley, the relationship between a student's social class and his school achievement was assessed; social class was found to be an important factor closely related to the academic achievement of children in the early grades.[31] Attitudes and aspirations of students also seem directly related to their social class.

In addition to suffering educational damage which stems from poverty, many minority group children develop negative self-images and low self-esteem because of segregation and discrimination. These differences do not suggest, however, that to be of low social class or of minority status in America necessarily implies failure in school. They do suggest that, on the average, the social class and ethnic status of a student have a strong relationship to his academic success and aspirations.

One of the most challenging and compelling educational problems of this decade continues to be that of providing equal and adequate education for all groups in America.

## DISCUSSION

1. To what extent do the classifications of social classes proposed by Warner and his followers seem valid to you? To what extent invalid? Do contemporary sociologists conceive social class in large cities as being somewhat different from the Warner conception based on towns and small cities? Is the concept of social class in America still important today or is it obsolete?
2. Elaborate upon the life experiences and educational backgrounds of upper class families based both on your own reading and your own experiences in living. Do the same thing for each of the other major social class groups.
3. In what ways have the behaviors and life experiences of the various classes described by Warner changed in the past two decades?
4. Of what social class do you consider yourself a member? What are the distinguishing characteristics of this class? Do you belong to the same social class as your parents? Your grandparents? If not, what has made the difference?

[30] James S. Coleman, *Equality of Educational Opportunity* (Washington, D.C.: U.S. Office of Education, 1966), pp. 298–300.
[31] Alan Wilson, *Educational Consequences of Segregation in a California Community*, A Report of the U.S. Commission on Civil Rights, 1967, I, 165–206.

5. What is the meaning of culturally disadvantaged? Who judges? To what extent can both upper lowers and lower lowers be described as culturally disadvantaged in America today?

6. Relate your own experiences in growing up to social class theory. Any influences on friends, dates, college entrance, etc.? Does the Elmtown story reflect your own experiences?

7. Are the immigrant ethnic groups from Europe currently "forgotten"? Do you think another group is the "forgotten" one? Is attention now being given to "new ethnics" of European backgrounds?

8. What are the most recent government proposals for improving the life of the American Indians? What is your own view on the maintenance of Indian reservations or their phasing out through absorption of Indians into the mainstream of current American life?

9. What are some possible influences of slavery and a long period of segregation on the personalities of blacks? Do you think it likely that some characteristics might be passed on to later generations?

10. Define the present gap between opportunities of blacks and whites in America. Is the gap closing? Are upper and middle class blacks gaining economically?

11. How is life for the Puerto Rican young person different on the island than on the mainland?

12. What are the major educational problems of Mexican children and youth?

13. How does an individual's class or ethnic background relate to his probable educational experience?

## INVOLVEMENT

1. Study Warner's system of arriving at social class rankings in *Social Class in America*. Apply his approach to your own background and that of friends and acquaintances.

2. Develop a categorization of social classes for the community with which you are best acquainted.

3. Trace your ancestry to the time your family came to America. To which ethnic groups do your ancestors belong? How has this background affected your life?

4. If your school is not located in an inner-city area, develop as a class project a trip to a major metropolis which will include opportunities to become acquainted with the patterns of living of a variety of ethnic and racial groups.

5. Look for opportunities to develop relationships with people of groups other than your own, whether they represent majorities or minorities. Find, if you can, opportunities through recreational leadership, settlement house work, community action programs, etc.

6. Invite to class representatives of a variety of minority groups. Do not overlook ethnic groups from Europe, if substantial clusters of Americans from such backgrounds exist in your community. Groups which might supply speakers include the National Association for the Advancement of Colored People, the Urban League, Mexican-American groups, etc.

7. Discover and take advantage of opportunities to tutor children and youth of minority group backgrounds or those from disadvantaged homes. Church and community groups are often sources of information.

## FURTHER READING

Bottomore, T. B., *Classes in Modern Society*. New York: Pantheon Books, 1966. An introduction to the study of class as a sociological concept.

Cabrera, Y. Arturo. *Emerging Faces, the Mexican-Americans*. Dubuque, Iowa: William C. Brown, 1970. A discussion of Mexican-Americans which does not limit itself to cultural conflict and social pathologies, but which deals with positive and constructive aspects of Mexican-American life.

Deloria, Vine, Jr. *We Talk, You Listen*. New York: Macmillan, 1970. An Indian leader describes the background and the struggles of American Indians. A vigorous call for recognition of Indian issues and demands.

Grambs, Jean Dresden and John C. Carr (Eds.). *Black Image: Education Copes with Color*. Dubuque, Iowa: Wm. C. Brown, 1972. Essays on the black experience which deal especially with the way black people in the United States have been and are depicted through textbooks and other books read by young people of school age. The book includes an extensive annotated bibliography of integrated books for young people of school age.

Howe, Louise Kapp (Ed.). *The White Majority: Between Poverty and Affluence*. New York: Random House, 1971. A study of the white working class American and his discontents.

Kronus, Sidney. *The Black Middle Class*. Columbus, Ohio: Charles E. Merrill, 1971. Interrelationships of people who are black, middle class, and American.

Lerner, Max. *America as a Civilization*. 2 Vols. New York: Simon and Schuster, 1967. An ambitious and classic overview of American life by one of America's most versatile social scientists upon which this chapter draws for categories.

Lightfoot, Alfred. *Inquiries Into the Social Foundations of Education*. Chicago: Rand, McNally, 1972. Readings in social foundations especially for those preparing to teach in urban schools or already teaching. Includes sections on social change, social class, and problems of equal educational opportunity.

Marshall, Kim. *Law and Order in Grade 6-E; Chaos and Innovation in a Ghetto School*. Boston: Little, Brown, 1972. In a black ghetto school similar to Kozol's in Boston, the author transformed a seemingly hopeless situation into a meaningful learning situation. Using his own striking photos, the author shows what can be done with modified open classroom techniques.

Novak, Michael. *The Rise of the Unmeltable Ethnics*. New York: Macmillan, 1972. A fresh and original description of the lives of lower middle class whites who are often blue collar workers, and whose ethnic backgrounds are Polish, Italian, Greek, Slavic, etc. The author contends that these "invisible men" are the new potent political force of the 1970s.

Rose, Karen. *A Gift of the Spirit*. New York: Holt, Rinehart and Winston, 1971. Readings in black literature for teachers which constitute a history of the black experience and of the ways blacks have dealt with that experience in America.

Shinn, Ronald. *Culture and School*. Scranton, Pa.: International Textbook Co., 1971. Essays on the sociocultural determinants of learning by youngsters in the public school which help teachers to relate to children from diverse subcultures.

Webster, Staten W. *Knowing and Understanding the Socially Disadvantaged Ethnic Minority Groups*. Scranton, Pa.: Intext Educational Publishers, 1972. A collection dealing with those ethnic minority groups which can be classified as being socially disadvantaged in America, including black Americans, Mexican-Americans, Puerto Ricans, Chinese- and Japanese-Americans.

## SELECTED AUDIO-VISUAL MATERIALS

*Mexican-American: A Historic Profile* (16 mm film, 30 min., b. & w., Anti-Defamation League of B'nai B'rith, 196-).   Traces the history of the Mexican-American from the time of the Spanish period to the present. Particular emphasis on the various prejudices against migrants during the last one hundred years.

*Mexican-Americans — The Invisible Minority* (16 mm film, 38 min., color, PBL/NET: Indiana University, 1969).   Describes the struggle of Mexican-Americans for identity. Discusses economic poverty, employment, and education in a system designed for white English-speaking students.

*The Negro American* (16 mm film, 15 min., color, Bailey Film Associates, 1966).   Discusses the contributions of the Negro to American civilization.

*No Hiding Place* (16 mm film, 59 min., b. & w., NET: Indiana University, 1968).   A study of the tensions which divide the Negro and white communities. Ghetto youth, housewives, the local NAACP president, an alderman, and others are interviewed on racial problems of the town.

*Portrait of a Disadvantaged Child: Tommy Knight* (16 mm film, 16 min., b. & w., McGraw-Hill, 1965).   A day in the life of a slum child. Shows many of the factors that affect Tommy's ability to learn.

*The Pride and the Shame* (16 mm film, 30 min., b. & w., BBC-TV: Time-Life Inc., 1968).   Focuses on the Sioux Indians and deals with the plight of the American Indians across the country who live on reservations.

*Prior and Present Experience* (16 mm film, 30 min., b. & w., Indiana University, 1968).   Explains the need for the teacher to consider the differences between teacher background and that of students as shown by language used and assumptions made.

*Sixteen in Webster Groves* (16 mm film, 47 min., b. & w., CBS: Pyramid Films, 1966).   A "slice-of-life" survey of teenage opinions, attitudes, goals in an affluent suburban community.

*Some of My Best Friends Are White* (16 mm film, 30 min., b. & w., BBC-TV: Time-Life Inc., 1968).   A provocative look at middle class Negro attitudes, values, and approaches to racial equality.

*Strangers in Their Own Land: The Puerto Ricans* (16 mm film, 14 min., color, ABC Media Concepts, 1970).   Presents problems of those Puerto Ricans who are unskilled and uneducated. The Puerto Rican Family Institute, run by and for Puerto Ricans, attempts to keep the family together despite unfavorable living conditions which may break down relationships.

*The Way It Is* (16 mm film, 60 min., b. & w., NET: Indiana University, 1967).   Presents the chaos of the ghetto school and reports on a New York University special learning project in Junior High School 57, Brooklyn. Shows visits with parents, teachers' meetings, and project workers in classrooms.

*Where Has the Warrior Gone?* (16 mm film, 13 min., color, Centron Educational Films, 1971).   Explores the life of a Navajo father who leads a life devoid of purpose and meaning — a man living in a society that no longer has a place for him.

# THIRTEEN

# What are the community backgrounds of students?

American communities are classified by the Census Bureau as either urban or rural. The term rural is limited to farm families, to hamlets which contain less than 500 people, and to villages or towns in which 500 to 2500 persons live. Any place with 2500 or more inhabitants or any area with 1500 or more people per square mile is defined as urban. As a result, "urban" becomes an omnibus category which includes not only large and small cities but also many suburban communities.

A somewhat sharper contrast is needed to understand the ways of living that will be encountered by new teachers. Perhaps a more helpful categorization for purposes of sketching American community backgrounds is three-fold: (1) rural communities including farms, hamlets, villages and towns, (2) small and large cities, and (3) suburbs.

## RURAL BACKGROUNDS

If you choose to teach in a rural area, you will be working among a dwindling group. Americans are steadily moving from rural areas to urban centers. The farm population dropped from 15 million in 1960 to 9 and a half million in 1972. In 1960, farmers and their families comprised about 8 percent of the U.S. population. In 1972, the ratio had fallen to 4½ percent.[1]

[1] U.S. Bureau of the Census, "Farm Population of the United States: 1972," *Current Population Reports*, Series P-27, No. 44 (Washington, D.C.: U.S. Government Printing Office, 1973), p. 1.

Rural life has been eulogized by many Americans as the quiet, unharried life, but in recent years rural areas have lost large percentages of their population; now less than 30% of America's population lives in rural areas.

### Rural Communities

What happened? In the 1890s, we crossed the "watershed of American history," as the historian Henry Steele Commager phrased it. On the nineteenth century side of the watershed lay a country that was essentially rural and agricultural. On the twentieth century side emerged a primarily urban and industrial nation. In 1910 approximately 45 percent of the American people lived in the locations classified by the census as urban; but by 1970 approximately 73 percent of the American people lived in such areas.[2]

In the twentieth century, Americans steadily moved from the farms, hamlets, villages, and towns, and took up residence in large and small cities and in the suburbs. In addition, the life-style of those who remained in the rural communities became more urban oriented as rural

[2] U.S. Bureau of the Census, *Statistical Abstract of the United States, 1972* (Washington, D.C.: U.S. Government Printing Office, 1972), p. 17.

people increasingly assumed the characteristics of whose who lived in cities. Mechanization, the mass media, and mobility steadily influenced the traditional rural ways of living celebrated in nineteenth century American literature. True, some isolated pockets of homespun and sturdily independent farmers persisted, particularly in the hill country of Appalachia and the Ozarks. But such American yeomen were becoming rare.

Mechanization changed the farm. Electricity became commonplace and with it came electric ovens, refrigerators, and household appliances. Farming itself became mechanized with increasing use of tractors, combines, potato harvesters, cotton pickers, corn pickers, hay stackers, citrus sprayers, etc. Many farms have become, in Carey McWilliams' classic phrase, "factories in the fields" conducted by businessmen of the soil.

The outside world entered the farm home through mail delivery, the telephone, and the mass media. Newspapers and magazines are read; radios play; television is watched. Mobility characterizes the farmer and his family.

The automobile ended the isolation of the American farm early in the twentieth century. Outside communities are now within an easy cruising range of farm families. Even the village and town cannot hold the mobile rural residents, for the automobile has brought the big city into the farmer's range for buying and selling. Along with the world-changing force which Henry Ford fostered, came superhighways, supermarkets, and supergovernments. Shopping by mail order developed; national advertising campaigns were launched. With the rural resident no longer dependent upon a single trade area, the historic justification for the village or town disappeared. Some villages and towns were able to make the adjustments and continue to attract some rural customers. Some turned to tourism as an income-producing resource. But, in general, the rural community is declining and the young are leaving for the cities.

Though, historically, farming has been the reason for living in rural areas, today only about one-fourth of rural residents are farmers. Many are local business and professional men; others are daily commuters to jobs in the cities. Some residents of rural areas are among the most prosperous of Americans; they are successful in their city occupations but prefer to live in the country.

But no one should leap to the conclusion that farmers and village and town residents who remain in rural areas are universally prosperous. Many farm laborers and tenant farmers who stayed with the rural areas have a miserable standard of living. Some live on subsistence farms; some shuttle between city and farm; some become migrant workers. Rural poverty is a reality in America today, as a trip off the turnpike on the backroads will readily demonstrate to the city resident. As Michael Harrington pointed out in *The Other America*, poverty has a way of

Poverty in rural America—Appalachia.

Paul S. Conklin

hiding up back roads. In his book, which encouraged a federal governmental war on poverty, Harrington wrote of Appalachia:

> Though the steep slopes and the narrow valleys are a charming sight, they are also the basis of a highly unproductive agriculture. The very geography is an anachronism in a technological society. Even if the farmers had the money, machines would not make much difference. As it is, the people literally scratch their half-livings from the difficult soil. . . .
>
> This, for example, is how one reporter saw the independent yeomanry, the family farmers, and the laid off industrial workers in the Appalachians: "Whole counties are precariously held together by a flour-and-dried-milk paste of surplus foods. The school lunch program provides many children with their only decent meals. Relief has become a way of life for a once proud and aggressively independent mountain people. The men who are no longer needed in the mines and the farmers who cannot compete with the mechanized agriculture of the Midwest have themselves become surplus commodities in the mountains. . . ."
>
> One study, for instance, estimated that the Appalachians would need slightly more than one million new jobs if the area were to begin catching up with the rest of America. As of now, the vicious circle is at work making such a development unlikely; the mountains are beautiful and quaint and economically backward; the youth are leaving; and because of this poverty modern industry hesitates to come in and agriculture becomes even more marginal.[3]

As Robert Coles points out, there are many rural people "still hungry

---

[3] Michael Harrington, *The Other America* (New York: Macmillan, 1962), pp. 41–42.

in America" years after the war on poverty began.[4] Researchers are increasingly pointing out causal relationships between poverty and mental retardation. For instance, Rodger L. Hurley, in *Poverty and Mental Retardation,* says:

> The thesis of this book is that the supposed mental retardation of many of the poor is not mental retardation at all but environmental deprivation. . . . It appears that on many occasions we are not measuring mental retardation but our society's callousness toward the poor.[5]

With the loss of population and economic power in the rural areas may come some possible losses to American life. Historically, the small town has been celebrated for the sense of belongingness it cultivated, for neighborliness at the grassroots level, for day-by-day personal relations and for a simple homespun philosophy. Its civic contribution is symbolized by the New England town meeting in which the neighbors get together for full participation in the civic decisions affecting their lives.

However, some observers do not see the decline of the small town and of rural life as catastrophic. Contributors to American literature such as Hamlin Garland and Sherwood Anderson have long decried the small town as dull and lifeless and provincial. They feel that there is no loss in the disappearance of patterns of small town conformity which have been based on narrow and provincial morality. So some commentators on American life welcome the movement to urban areas where the educational level of the residents is higher, the people are more cosmopolitan, and more women are included in the labor force.

### Rural Children and Youth

If new teachers in rural areas are to be realistic in their education of rural children and youth, the steady movement toward erasing distinctions between rural and urban personalities in contemporary America must be taken into account. In the nineteenth century and well into the twentieth century, it could be taken for granted that rural young people, because of their backgrounds, experienced life differently from urban young people, and consequently viewed the world and behaved differently. Living close to the soil, and working closely with their parents, rural children and youth tended to be more conservative and more accepting of traditional American values; they were characterized by close-knit family loyalty and a degree of reserve rather than ready acceptance of strangers. Some personality tests in past decades have indicated that rural young people were more likely than urban young people to be shy, self-deprecating, withdrawn, and submissive. Such tests showed that farm

[4] Robert Coles, *Still Hungry in America* (New York: World Publishing, 1969).
[5] Rodger L. Hurley, *Poverty and Mental Retardation: A Causal Relationship* (New York: Random House, 1969), p. 44.

New England town meeting.

children tended to be less poised, less confident, and less articulate. Rural children depended more upon parents and their authority than did urban children, were less likely to rebel against authority, and were not particularly optimistic about the power of human beings to improve and better the surrounding environment.[6] Such self-perceptions, along with few horizon-widening experiences, particularly in poor farm homes, contributed to rural young people making lower scores than urban young people on tests of school achievement and of mental ability.

To some extent, these differentiations continue to exist in rural areas. But as the outside world increasingly enters the rural home and as mod-

[6] Grace Graham, *The Public School in the New Society* (New York: Harper and Row, 1969), p. 220.

ern transportation brings increasingly easy access to larger towns and urban centers, the differences between rural and urban youth steadily diminish. Today there is much less difference or, some even say, no significant difference between rural and urban youth as to their attitudes and ideas. Youth opinions increasingly tend to be alike, regardless of whether the individual lives in the city or the country. So the new rural teacher cannot count upon rural young people supporting individualism, hard work, or fixed moral standards to the degree that rural parents support these values.

In addition, rural youth, when grown up, continue to leave the farm for the city. The continuing movement in America from an agrarian to an industrial society sweeps them up. The good rural school and teacher therefore have the extremely difficult job of helping those rural young people, now a minority, who plan to stay with the farm and small town while simultaneously helping those others who (whether they currently plan to or not) will migrate toward the larger community.

Because they have been accustomed to educating youth for rural life, country schools do better with the first task than the second. Yet vocational agriculture, a frequent offering in the rural schools, does little to

4-H Club member at county fair. The good rural school must combine the education of young people who will stay with the farm with that of others who will eventually migrate to urbanized areas.

*Stock, Boston*

prepare rural youth for the forthcoming city experience. In the city, much emphasis is placed on verbal abilities and skills; reading, writing, and speaking are more in demand. Specialized occupational skills are required if one is not to remain at the lowest vocational levels or find himself technologically obsolete. Other people constantly impinge upon one's life. The more isolated and culturally disadvantaged the back-ground of the young rural migrant, the greater these problems loom. Yet it is the schools in such areas that have the least relevant curriculum.

Consequently, rural schools must adapt to urban demands rather than rest content with agricultural programs alone. Realistic teachers must stress the acquisition of social skills along with enhanced knowl-edge of industry through studies of occupations accompanied by trips, student exchanges, and outside visitors.

The establishment of vocational and technical schools in rural areas is helpful to adjustment to a broader occupational scene. Yet many rural parents, who provide the financial support for rural schools, resist. As they see it, the establishment of area technical institutes or urban oriented community colleges is a way of financing and supporting com-petition to their rural way of life and thus encouragement to rural youth to leave their homes.

Not the least of rural education difficulties is that teachers too tend to move cityward. Teachers, like young people, tend to reject what they sometimes regard as the more restrictive and limited environment of the village. Yet for those who do choose to stay with rural education, the challenges are many and the opportunities to make a contribution are great. Not all the ghettos and the poverty are found in the cities. One can find many mountain and other relatively isolated areas where a teacher's contribution could make a significant difference in the life of rural chil-dren. Writers like Jesse Stuart, a mountain poet and teacher, testify to the rewards of teaching in the hills.

Seldom if ever did one of my Lonesome Valley pupils stay out of school because he wanted to. He stayed out of school usually for one of three reasons: he was sick; he had to help harvest the crops; he didn't have sufficient clothes, shoes, or books. . . .

My attendance was down considerably in September. There wasn't an attendance officer to see why they didn't come to school. If the pupil went, it was all right. If he didn't, it was all right too. It was a land of freedom and work. But we had made our school so attractive in appearance that the pupils loved the place. They had had a hand in helping to make it beautiful—to make their school their home during school days, their workshop, their beehive. This was their place and my place. It was the liveliest spot in our community. It was the only place they could go, and many would never go beyond this school. . . .

I thought of these things when I taught my pupils all the practical things I could teach them. How to write letters, measure land, be clean with drinking water, about personal sanitation, screens for their windows, and so many things aside from the dry-as-powder, uninteresting textbooks I was forced to teach because they were *standard,* selected by someone in the state department who didn't teach, perhaps never had, and if he had taught once upon a time was far removed from it now.[7]

## CITY BACKGROUNDS

Despite the warnings of the devoted agrarian Thomas Jefferson, cities have grown. In 1790 there were only two U.S. cities of more than 25,000 population. By 1970, the nation contained 33 metropolitan areas with over one million population, ranging in size from 11,529,000 (New York City) to 1,009,000 (Portland, Oregon).[8]

The word "cities" was no longer comprehensive enough to describe the size of the biggest cities; even the word "metropolis" would not suffice. A new description—"megalopolis"—was borrowed from the Greeks to describe emerging intermeshed cities such as Boswash, a complex of interlocking metropolises stretching from Boston through New York and Philadelphia to Washington; Chipitts, a middlewestern complex stretching from Chicago and past the Great Lakes to Pittsburgh; and Sansan, stretching initially from San Diego to Santa Barbara and eventually to San Francisco. Kahn and Wiener predicted in *The Year 2000* that these three developing megalopolitan complexes would hold almost half of the American people by the end of the twentieth century.[9]

A complex of circumstances led the American people into the cities. Changes in science and technology, which influenced developments in production, power, transportation, and communication, resulted in vastly increased urbanization, particularly throughout the twentieth century. Technical developments in industry combined with social developments—stable central government, expanded markets throughout the world, and the specialization of labor—to foster the growth of cities. Steadily Americans migrated to the cities. Once, at the time of the American Revolution, approximately 90 percent of the American people were employed in agriculture. Today the large majority is engaged in work other than the production of food; much of this work necessitates cities.

### Urban Communities

Sociologists have looked for patterns of living or characteristic life-styles within cities. One popular sociological theory in the first half of the twentieth century stressed the loss of relationships to the community which came with the movement from rural to urban areas. The theory emphasized the impersonality of urban life. City people, it was pointed

[7] Jesse Stuart, *The Thread That Runs So True* (New York: Charles Scribner's Sons, 1949), pp. 57–58.
[8] United States Bureau of the Census, *Statistical Abstract of the United States, 1972* (Washington, D.C.: U.S. Government Printing Office, 1972), p. 18.
[9] Herman Kahn and Anthony J. Wiener, *The Year 2000* (New York: Macmillan, 1967), p. 61.

out, meet many people, so many people that they pass them by indifferently with little or no recognition. Searching for more intimate relationships, city people join special groups which reflect their own special interests, whether occupational or avocational. So the city dweller was perceived as a sophisticated cosmopolitan and individualistic person who found his common interests in groups made up of people from across the city.

In recent years, this conception of the urban style has been modified by scholars who believe that insufficient emphasis has been placed on urban neighborhoods, where people resemble each other in life-styles. Frequently their social class and ethnic backgrounds are similar. Such neighborhoods are by no means as closely knit as rural neighborhoods, yet the city neighborhood has not disappeared, as assumed in the earlier theory. Nor have family relationships disappeared in cities. Urban dwellers do visit relatives and friends and neighbors, as traffic tie-ups on weekends testify. Only a few urban residents are loners who are disattached from contacts with their fellow men. Only a few are constantly seeking "action" and are ceaselessly on the go with new people. Indeed, many residents of the city live a life which is not drastically different from life in small towns.

But the urban dweller is often isolated in respect to relationships with people who are not of his familial group or neighborhood. Particularly, he is separated from people across class, racial, and ethnic lines. Yet as equal employment opportunities increase, he meets a greater variety of people through his job. Sometimes romance defies family lines, as in the love affair of Maria and Tony in *West Side Story;* marriages across ethnic, racial, and class lines do occur and are increasing. But in general the city remains a mosaic of social worlds; the ways of living of the jet setter and the solid middle class citizen and the slum dweller differ markedly from each other.

All city dwellers are vulnerable to breakdowns in their environment, whether they be newspaper or garbage collection strikes, power blackouts or brownouts, smog or pollution, riots or crime in the streets. Some residents are more vulnerable than others; usually the poorer the individual the more vulnerable he is to the events which result in social disorganization.

Sometimes urban policies have contributed to greater social disorganization. For instance, urban renewal became, in practice, a program of demolition of old buildings in the center of cities. As a result, new downtown commercial centers were rebuilt, but poor families and homeless isolates had to move into new slums. The increase in automobile travel resulted in massive programs of highway construction. Communities of poor people who blocked the paths of new super highways were cleared away. Planners and political leaders sometimes found it expedient to place new highways in areas in which poor people lived. The result was

Georg Gerster, Rapho Guillumette Pictures

Los Angeles traffic pattern, the "stack" (at least four levels of roadways).

the dislocation of still more people. High-rise public housing projects often became the focus of vandalism and destruction rather than centers for comfortable community living.

Crucial to any prospective teacher's appraisal of city life is a frank recognition of the wide diversity of life patterns in the city. The patterns vary with areas and with degrees of wealth. The variation grows more noticeable as the middle classes flee to the suburbs.

With the migration of the middle classes toward the suburbs, a city increasingly becomes a place of extremes. Left behind are the wealthy and the poor. The wealthy live on their social islands, often huge, self-contained apartments, hotels, and town houses with preempted views of the lake, river, park, or other city scenic attraction. Sometimes the park overlooked by plush housing is not safe for walking after dark. The transportation to work or play or school is by cab or private bus, car or limousine or, when very hurried, by subway. The poor people, conspicuously including the most recently arrived groups such as the Puerto Ricans and Negroes in New York, Negroes in Chicago, Mexicans and Negroes in Los Angeles, live in run-down areas, including once-respectable brownstone houses now crowded with families. They sit on the front steps and occupy the roofs in hot weather. They jam the subways and elevateds and public buses returning from their work at a variety of unskilled and semiskilled jobs.

321

The middle class group, a potential mediator between extremes, steadily dwindles through flight to the suburbs.[10]

Playwrights have long dramatized city contrasts of rich and poor living side by side, but increasingly in the cities the neighborhoods grow more residentially distinct. Both income and life-styles contribute to the succession of social islands which make up a modern city. For example, clerical workers who frequently earn less than blue collar workers live in more prestigious neighborhoods primarily as an expression of life-style and desired social differentiation from working class people.

### City Children and Youth

In so diverse a city pattern, the life and the educational experience of children and youth depends heavily upon the neighborhood in which the individual lives. In turn, the neighborhood situation is heavily influenced by social class and ethnic backgrounds.

There still exist in American cities enclaves (distinctly bounded areas enclosed within the larger area) in which upper class city dwellers and their children live. Sometimes the enclave is a city neighborhood in which large and imposing houses persist; Riverdale in New York City is such a section. More often in contemporary times the enclave takes the form of luxury apartment buildings grouped together, each with its own doorman and security system. Babies and small children from such families are often taken to nearby parks or playgrounds by maids and household employees playing the role formerly occupied in Britain by nannies. School-age children are frequently transported by car to private schools which combine both academic and recreational facilities. The cultural resources of the city are often used by both old and young upper class family members. Vacations are frequently taken at a considerable distance from the city. In general, the patterns of living of children and youth of such families are the urban counterpart of the upper upper and lower upper social class experiences described in Chapter 12.

Similarly, upper middle and lower middle class youth frequently live in city neighborhoods much in the manner described in the section on social class. However, middle class families in cities increasingly move to the suburbs when opportunities occur. Moving to the suburbs is a way of bettering oneself and of living the good life in America, as many middle class Americans see it. Unfortunately, it is also a way of separating middle class citizens from the problems experienced by the lower class who remain of necessity in the city. Many white middle class Americans see themselves as beleaguered by pressures from lower income city dwellers and, more particularly, from blacks and other minor-

---

[10] William Van Til, Gordon F. Vars, and John H. Lounsbury, *Modern Education for the Junior High School Years* (Indianapolis: Bobbs-Merrill, 1967), p. 95.

The city offers few play areas for its young people.

ity groups. As new migrants who are largely of upper lower and lower lower class background press in upon the borders of former middle class neighborhoods, the residents grow uneasy. They perceive any lower class groups as bringing with them the virus of crime and neighborhood blight. Reaching the conclusion that "the old neighborhood is not what it used to be," they move. They explain the move as "being good for the children."

Many middle class young people who remain in cities stem from ethnic group backgrounds related to the earlier immigration waves. Some middle class young people in urban areas, however, stem from the contemporary minorities; their ethnic backgrounds are largely Negro, Puerto Rican, Mexican-American, etc. Their way of looking at the world is heavily influenced by middle class backgrounds.

Some middle class children and youth from minority group backgrounds accept the conventional American system of economic rewards and work within it toward good jobs and material satisfactions. Within the system they hope to achieve better housing, better opportunities for the use of leisure time, and better total social surroundings. Often they are just as eager as majority group members to move out of the city to the conventional grass-surrounded house in the suburbs. Thus, a new teacher would make a grave error by stereotyping young people from upwardly mobile families as having the same attitudes and reactions as socially disadvantaged children.

The errors schools sometimes commit because of insensitivity to changing social class circumstances in neighborhoods verge on the ludicrous. For instance, Estelle Fuchs in *Pickets at the Gates* tells of one minority group rising toward middle class status, which was misinterpreted by the schools. In a dilapidated area which had long been populated by working class Negro people, new housing developments arose, including Skyview Terrace Apartments. Skyview Terrace attracted as tenants 60 percent Negro, 20 percent Puerto Ricans, and 20 percent others. The heads of families were semiskilled and skilled workmen and many were at the factory foreman level. Still others were civil service employees including postal workers, policemen, and teachers. To the Slater School came children from Skyview Terrace (45 percent) and children from the old neighborhood outside the project (55 percent). The more articulate new residents of Skyview Terrace became active in the P.T.A.

The community exploded in anger when the principal of Slater School wrote a well-intentioned but misguided letter to his faculty which over-generalized on the disadvantaged backgrounds of the children. Resentful parents petitioned for his removal from the principalship, on the basis that he had made the following comments about the community, parents, and children:

Compared with middle class homes, they are poorer financially, academically, socially.
Many of our children are on welfare . . . the school lunch is the best meal they get.
The mother is so busy with her brood that the individual child is lonely.
Many of our children have no fathers at home.
Our children are living in a noisy atmosphere.
There is a lack of encouragement at home to achieve.
Families on welfare for the third generation lack academic drive.
Coming from a poor environment, socially, culturally, economically, physically, it is no wonder that our children are not ready for school.
The people of the Appalachian Mountains, the Ozark hill-billies, the Mexican-American migrant workers, have these attributes as well as poor Negroes and poor Puerto Ricans.[11]

[11] Cited by Estelle Fuchs, *Pickets at the Gates* (New York: Free Press, 1966), pp. 10–11.

Larry Cuban, in a book on teaching in the inner city, *To Make a Difference,* comments on the same situation. He says of the principal:

> Where had he erred? First, he misread totally the diversity of social economic class that exists in segregated neighborhoods. Second, his middle-class prejudices (the ones he warned new teachers about) slipped into the discussion and colored his views of youngsters and parents. Third, he combined sense and nonsense in his descriptions of children and parents by borrowing generalizations from sociology and psychology and applying them uncritically to the children and the community his school serves. . . . He discovered that he did not know the range of income and style of living of his students and their parents.[12]

Sociologist E. Franklin Frazier, in *Black Bourgeoisie,* described with a degree of irony the renunciation of their heritage by some upwardly mobile Negroes.[13] Members of the black bourgeoisie are sometimes called "strivers" and a section of Harlem is even referred to as Strivers Hill. Contemporary invective directed against them includes "Oreo," a reference to the product of a biscuit company which is a cookie black on the outside and white on the inside.

But a contemporary E. Franklin Frazier would find that much of today's leadership in minority group struggles to attain status is being taken by adult and youthful ethnic group members from families that have become middle class. Today the middle class status of some minority group youths does not necessarily mean they will accept conventional economic and social American patterns. For instance, leadership in black militancy and Puerto Rican and Chicano dissent often stems from young people who are not themselves poverty-stricken. Their deep loyalty to the cause of underprivileged blacks, Puerto Ricans, and Mexican-Americans leads them into social activism on behalf of the group with which they identify.

Crucial to the urban problem of America in the 1970s are the children and youth of the lower classes, especially the lower lowers. Frequently, they live within what the sociologists have termed the inner city, that section of the city which includes slums and ghettos and which houses those who have the least materially. Many inner-city residents today are black. But it should not be forgotten that 57.5 per cent of the urban poor are white.

The past decades have been periods of substantial migration of the poor, of all racial and ethnic backgrounds, to the cities of both the North and the South. Though the parents of many children and youth have come to the city in search of a better life, they have often encountered

---

[12] Larry Cuban, *To Make a Difference: Teaching in the Inner City* (New York: Free Press, 1970), pp. 18–19.

[13] E. Franklin Frazier, *Black Bourgeoisie* (New York: Free Press, 1957).

deprived living conditions. They have moved into the neighborhoods in which they could find the least expensive housing, which is usually also the oldest and most deteriorated. They have often been exploited by absentee landlords who refused to maintain the buildings and who have charged exorbitant rents. The jobs they found (when they could find them) were low paying and primarily for the untrained and unskilled. The new migrants have swelled the relief rolls.

In 1940, three-fourths of all black people in America lived in the Southern states. Increasingly, blacks moved into the central cities of both North and South; by 1970, 54 percent of all American blacks lived in central cities and another 15 percent were located on the urban fringe. Over 45 percent of the black Americans who are poor live today in central cities rather than in rural, small towns or suburban areas.[14] According to the 1970 census, nearly half of the nation's black population now lives in 50 cities. One third of the total black population lives in 15 cities. Six of these cities now have black majorities (Washington, D.C.; Compton, California; East St. Louis, Illinois; Newark, New Jersey; Gary, Indiana; and Atlanta, Georgia). Eight other cities have 40 percent or more black people in the population (Baltimore, New Orleans, Savannah, Detroit, Birmingham, Richmond, St. Louis, and Jackson).[15] New York City added one million black and Puerto Rican residents during the 1960s. Segregated housing patterns intensified as former residents moved out while the new migrants were moving in.[16] Some areas declined economically.

A sixth grade child in Harlem describes a block in a highly deteriorated neighborhood:

My block is the most terrible block I've ever seen. There are at lease 25 or 30 narcartic people in my block. The cops come around there and tries to act bad but I bet inside of them they are as scared as can be. They even had in the papers that this block is the worst block, not in Manhattan but in New York City. In the summer they don't do nothing except shooting, stabbing, and fighting. They hang all over the stoops and when you say excuse me to them they hear you but they just don't feel like moving. Some times they make me so mad that I feel like slaping them and stuffing and bag of garbage down their throats. There's only one policeman who can handle these people and we call him "Sunny." When he come around in his cop car the people run around the corners, and he won't let anyone sit on the stoops. If you don't believe this story come around some time and you'll find out.[17]

[14] U.S. Bureau of the Census, "Consumer Income," *Current Population Reports*, Series P-60, No. 77 (Washington, D.C.: U.S. Government Printing Office, 1971), p. 1. A central city is a city of 50,000 or more in an urbanized area with surrounding closely settled territory.
[15] "One-Third of Blacks Found in 15 Cities," *New York Times*, May 19, 1971, p. 20.
[16] "Blacks and Puerto Ricans Up Million Here in Decade," *New York Times*, March 6, 1972, p. 1.
[17] Herbert Kohl, *36 Children* (New York: The New American Library, 1967), p. 36.

Increasingly America is having to face up to the fact that the education being received by upper lower and lower lower class children and youth in the inner city as yet cannot compensate for the environmental conditions which these young people experience. Indeed, some of the irrelevant education which lower class children receive even adds to their handicaps. The handicaps brought to school with the child from the slums already include deteriorating housing, the weak family structures in some (but by no means all) families, the prevalence of crime in the neighborhood, the spread of drug addiction, the lack of recreational facilities, the incidence of disease, etc. Take any index of social ills in America and you will find that the lower class bears the brunt of the burden.

The schools of the cities, historically conceived as institutions in which young people of all backgrounds could come together, have become increasingly one-social-class and one-ethnic-group institutions. This is particularly true of elementary schools, which are usually located so as to be within walking distance of the young child; it is less true of the secondary schools, which draw young people from a wider area. Schools, like the neighborhoods, are part of the urban mosaic. But *each* elementary school and *each* neighborhood is not likely to have the characteristics of a mosaic because contemporary urban living results in limited interaction among people who live in differing social worlds. The walls between lower and middle class neighborhoods may be invisible, yet they do exist in psychological terms. So lower class groups feel estranged from other groups.

The children of lower class groups in large cities often share societal alienation. Forces encouraging alienation include the isolation and insecurity of children in the environment of the cities. It is no accident that two outstanding black writers have titled their books *The Invisible Man* (Ralph Ellison) and *Nobody Knows My Name* (James Baldwin). In such a setting, low self-esteem combines with low motivation. One of the hardest things for whites to understand is that riots, such as the summer disturbances of the late 1960s, and social anger such as that of the Black Panthers of the early 1970s are ways troubled people use to establish self-identity and self-esteem. One of the problems facing American society is whether alienation can be replaced by identity only through violence or whether, on the other hand, the schools can play a role in establishing identity and reducing alienation through education.

Teachers in inner-city schools often encounter formidable difficulties. The buildings in which they work are often old; needed equipment is frequently lacking. And, above all, the children who are to be educated are beset by problems. Sometimes they are emotionally disturbed. Sometimes they reject the discipline which the school attempts to maintain. Sometimes they bring into the schools the obscenities of the streets and the anger communicated to them by role models in homes and neighborhoods. As a result, many such children respond with anger and hostility.

On the other hand, some say that school systems and the teachers themselves help create their difficulties. Critics say that educators do so through insistence on irrelevant curriculum, by taking for granted that if one is poor and from a minority group background he will be unable to learn, by expecting little or nothing from disadvantaged students, and by blaming all school failures upon the community and the environment which surround the student. Consequently, scholars like Kenneth B. Clark believe that "the schools are presently damaging the children they exist to help."[18]

But in an effort to help, a torrent of books replete with suggestions has recently poured from the presses. Among the experts on socially disadvantaged children and youth are Robert J. Havighurst, Helen Storen, A. Harry Passow, Staten W. Webster, and Mario D. Fantini.

Since the new teacher is likely to be assigned to schools containing substantial proportions of poor children, he has an obligation to read current literature concerning the disadvantaged and to be willing to train in deprived areas. For much still needs to be done to change both school and community situations which perpetuate the problems of the disadvantaged.

Jules Feiffer, the cartoonist, developed a series of drawings to illustrate the following ironic comments, attributed to a sad-looking, tired man:

I used to think I was poor. Then they told me I wasn't poor, I was needy. Then they told me it was self-defeating to think of myself as needy, that I was culturally deprived. Then they told me deprived was a bad image, that I was underprivileged. Then they told me underprivileged was overused, that I was disadvantaged. I still don't have a dime, but I do have a *great* vocabulary.[19]

## SUBURBAN BACKGROUNDS

Though cities have grown markedly during the twentieth century, the fastest growing community grouping in the United States today is the suburb. In 1790, according to the first census, only one of every twenty Americans lived in a city or its immediate surroundings. By 1910 about one of every three Americans who lived in a metropolitan district was a suburban resident. By 1970, a majority of Americans who lived in what by then was termed Standard Metropolitan Statistical Areas (SMSA) lived in suburbs rather than in the city.

In 1960, the percentages of American people living in the suburbs,

[18] Kenneth B. Clark, *Dark Ghetto* (New York: Harper & Row, 1965), p. 124.
[19] Jules Feiffer, *Reader's Digest* (March 1967), p. 145.

*Charles Gatewood*

One of the complaints against suburbia is that its very physical arrangement encourages and is a reflection of its conformity.

the cities, and the small towns or rural areas were almost exactly equal—33.4, 33.3, and 33.3 respectively! In 1970, 37 percent of the American people lived in the suburbs while only 31 percent lived in the cities and only 31 percent lived in small towns or rural areas. So by 1970 the suburbs had pulled ahead in population.[20]

### Suburban Communities

When Americans think of the suburbs, they often visualize an upper or upper middle class setting. But with the growth of the suburbs, other types of suburbs must be included—lower middle class suburbs and working class suburbs in which some upper lower Americans live. One cannot make the assumption that all suburban teachers work in affluent communities. A growing proportion of low income people live in the suburbs. By 1970, 21 percent of the American poor lived in the suburbs![21]

The suburbs resemble the frontier in American history. Like the frontier, the suburbs refuse to be confined; they move steadily outward. What used to be an inner suburb has often been embraced by the city as city limits expand. Houses that once were surrounded by vacant space are then often surrounded by looming apartments. The outer suburbs grow more populated and new outer suburbs develop far beyond what

[20] U.S. Department of Commerce, Bureau of the Census, *1970 Census of Population*, Vol. 1, Characteristics of the Population, Part A, Section 1, Figure 38, p. 34.
[21] "Poverty Growing Faster in Suburbs," *New York Times*, November 14, 1971, p. 41.

formerly was thought reasonable commuting distance. Eventually the suburbs give way to the exurbs, that strange new blend of suburban and rural.

A common characteristic of suburbanites, whether inner, outer or exurban, is to be acutely aware of travel time. The suburbanite often works in a city, returns home to his bedroom community, and spends a substantial fraction of his life in commuter trains, buses, or automobiles.

The more well-to-do of the upper class or upper middle class communities usually are a considerable distance from the central city. Homes are along quiet tree-shaded streets, lawns are well kept. The men commute regularly; the women play a considerable role in social life and community affairs. In the comfortable homes of the prosperous suburban community there is considerable emphasis upon entertaining, gardening, and college entrance. Critics often blast such communities for conformity, striving to outrank others, and a general complacency. For instance, Fred M. Hechinger says:

> Too many of the suburbs have become compounds which, even though they are not protected by the barbed wire of their military counterparts in occupied territories, nevertheless set their inhabitants apart from the "outside" world. They are pervaded by a sameness—in income levels, in taste, in mutual entertainment and admiration, in outward indicators of material status and attainments, and in aspirations especially for the children's collegiate careers.[22]

If you ask the typical prosperous suburbanite why he has come to the suburbs, he usually responds that this is the best place to raise his children. By this, he (or she) means that near home there is space for the young to play and opportunities for them to attend good schools. Critics of suburbia claim that one of the actual reasons for moving to suburbia, yet one not often mentioned, is to avoid lower class contacts for the family as a whole, especially contacts with blacks, Puerto Ricans, and other minorities.

Lower middle class suburbs are increasing. Frequently they are made up of nearly identical houses in a development which has been bulldozed from farm lands and denuded of trees. The occupational status of the residents is not as high as in the upper or upper middle class suburbs. In both types of suburbs, family relationships continue to be important. Neighboring with the people in nearby houses is frequent.

The working class suburb is also different from the various upper or middle class suburbs. Sometimes such suburbs are actually small cities on the edge of larger ones; sometimes they are genuine residential suburbs from which people travel to the central city. These suburbs differ from the middle class suburbs in that the residents are largely

[22] Fred M. Hechinger, Foreword. In Alice Miel, with Edwin Kiester, Jr., *The Shortchanged Children of Suburbia* (New York: Institute of Human Relations Press, 1967), p. 5.

semiskilled or unskilled workers often classifiable as upper lower class. More minority group members live in working class suburbs than in upper or upper middle class suburbs. Customarily people in working class suburbs have less formal education than those who live in the upper middle class suburbs. Their homes are not used for the large-scale entertaining, such as cocktail parties, characteristic of the upper middle class suburb. Instead, entertaining in the working class suburb often takes the form of having relatives in for dinner. Organization membership is not as high in the working class suburbs as in the upper middle class suburbs.

Business and industry are spreading to all types of suburbs. Even upper or upper middle class suburbs now frequently welcome neat electronics plants or handsome company headquarters or buildings housing light industries. Working class suburbs are often less choosy about the appearance of plants providing jobs for those who live nearby. The suburbs are well on their way to having as many jobs available per resident in the area as the cities have per resident. As metropolitan areas spread out, suburbs are no longer simply places for residence; they are also sources of nearby jobs for suburbanites.

The exurbs are a kind of community smorgasbord. Since they are located at the meeting place of urban and rural, one hardly knows whether to categorize them as suburban or rural. Residents vary from necessarily gregarious residents of trailers and mobile homes to isolates living on extensive estates. Since the area is not restricted by building regulations and is characterized by little community organization, anything goes with respect to residences. Residences may be expensive homes or shacks. They may house people who work in the city or who work on the farm. The life-styles of people are mixed and varied; the exurbs are marked by great heterogeneity.

### Suburban Children and Youth

The social class of the area in which the suburban child lives makes a difference in his life.

In the relatively upper class suburb, the schools are frequently oriented to college entrance. The programs, while academic, frequently reflect the best that a coalition of scholars can develop for instruction in the varied disciplines. Many students in such situations are acceptant of their schools and willing to play by the implicit rules of the game. So they struggle for grades and attempt to qualify themselves for the college of their choice. Yet such programs have also spawned contemporary rebels. Drug addiction worries suburban residents today. Confrontation with the administration of schools by dissidents has grown.

James A. Meyer says of suburbia,

At first glance most of our suburban youth share a common background of comfortable homes, loving parents, "good schools," high intelligence, excellent health,

Standardized tests often encourage learning merely to do well on these exams.

and almost unlimited opportunities for self-development. They have almost all the advantages that many of their mothers and fathers growing up during the Great Depression and World War II were denied. Yet many of today's middle class suburban youngsters exhibit disturbing character qualities—sexual libertarianism, vehement rejection of adult authority, and a widespread disposition to experiment with drugs.[23]

Dan Dodson, director of the Center for Human Relations and Community Studies at New York University, has long pointed out that a problem for upper and upper middle class young people in suburbs is "their essential uselessness." Young people are supported by their parents and often can make little contribution to the family except to strive for good grades, says Dodson. Consequently, the "college rat race" becomes surpassingly important to many such young people, as Frances R. Link points out in an article on pressures on youth.

The youth of suburbia is a young person under pressure, and the pressure for him is "awesome." It "preys" on his mind; it is a continual sense of foreboding and dismay. One suburban teenager said, "It is the feeling, as each academic day breaks,

[23] James A. Meyer, "Suburbia: A Wasteland of Disadvantaged Youth and Negligent Schools?" *Phi Delta Kappan* (June 1969), p. 575.

that there is always something, or rather some million things, to be done, and all count terribly much and hold enormous importance for the future."

When he says future, the suburban youth means college. He must get into a "good" college. It requires getting good grades, taking part in extracurricular activities, and "taking tests until your eyes fall from their sockets." This necessity bombards the suburban high school student from all possible angles, from parents, teachers, and counselors, whose bywords are: "Don't forget that every test counts," and "A college will look at your total record." The pressure sometimes seems impossible, sometimes murderous, but it must be lived with, for in our society there is no other way, no alternate route—to "success."

. . . The child of suburbia is the organization child, and his social and psychological pressures, as well as his solutions to them, are very significantly rooted in the family, in the nature and quality of family interaction.[24]

Upper and upper middle class suburban schools are often made more pleasant for those who attend them by an emphasis on student participation and the use of modern teaching methods, such as committee work, independent study, and problem solving. In addition, suburban schools are noted for the variety and extent of the extracurricular or co-curricular programs. So even when students are not stirred by classroom experiences, they do have opportunities for educational challenges in athletics, school publications, dramatic clubs, and a host of other activities.

Yet the forgotten person in such schools is often the individual who is not oriented toward college and who needs vocational preparation during his secondary school years. Since suburban schools are frequently weak in vocational education because of community emphasis on the academic program, such children and youth are overlooked or pressured to conform to the majority pattern. The upper and upper middle class suburban school, despite a peaceful outer appearance, is often a frustrating place for those who are not academically inclined.

Some feel that upper upper, lower upper, and upper middle class youth in suburbs are cheated of an opportunity to live and work together with young people of varied backgrounds. Alice Miel and Edward Kiester, Jr., in *The Shortchanged Children of Suburbia* point out that in relatively upper income suburbs, the housing situation itself deprives the young of the opportunity to know lower class students, though their future success may often depend heavily on their human relations skills with people of a variety of economic groups. Young people in "lily-white" suburbs are cheated of the opportunity to know young people of minority backgrounds, particularly black, Puerto Rican, and Mexican-American, though the rapidly changing occupational patterns makes it almost inevitable that as adults they will work with these people. Though the world has become a global village populated largely by colored races

[24] Frances R. Link, "Pressures on Youth: Suburbia," *Theory Into Practice* (February 1968), p. 23–24.

in lands less industrialized than the U.S., such suburban children and youth experience only their own homogeneous villages. It is difficult to bring about meetings of such young people with other young people different from themselves.

Miel and Kiester say:

. . . the child of suburbia is likely to be a materialist and somewhat of a hypocrite. In addition, he tends to be a striver in school, a conformist, and above all a believer in being "nice," polite, clean and tidy. Besides dividing humanity into the black and the white, the Jew and the Christian, the rich and the poor, he also is apt to classify people as "smart" or "dumb," "clean" or "dirty," and "nice" or "not nice." What is more, he is often conspicuously self-centered.

In all these respects the suburban child patterns his attitudes and goals chiefly after those of his parents. But he can never be sure that he won't fall short of their hopes for him—that he is measuring up to the standards (especially of academic achievement, behavior, and tidiness) that they have set for him. He is therefore likely to be an anxious child. Our study as well as other inquiries indicate clearly that to grow up in an American suburb today is not a wholly enviable lot.[25]

Such an analysis enrages some suburban parents who regard it as a distorted version of their lives and their children's lives. But some proportion of suburban parents admit a degree of validity in the authors' portrait of "New Village" and support their recommendations that upper and upper middle class suburban schools should (1) develop higher thought processes; (2) foster understanding of the students' own community, its structure and operation; (3) help children attain some insight into their own values and those of others; and (4) develop an empathic understanding of others.[26] Such parents are sometimes active in programs of suburban-urban pupil exchange aimed at breaking down the barriers between cities and suburbs. They work actively through P.T.A.s and school boards so that their children experience the social learning necessary to the achievement of the American dream and so that no social shortchanging takes place.

Because substantial financial support and well-equipped modern school plants are available, and genuine concern for their children is manifested by parents, education in upper and upper middle class suburban communities has high potential. Needed are more adventuresomeness in the teaching of controversial issues; more and better use of resources outside the classroom in the suburban community and in the neighboring city; more opportunities for the young to clarify and achieve democratic values; and above all, the creation of opportunities for surburban children to become acquainted with and to work beside others of a variety of racial, religious, national, and socioeconomic back-

Asked what he is or would like to be, he would most likely say: A good guy. This translates to some degree into someone who is both tough and sentimental, someone who can be pushed just so far, but no one—including himself—appears to know just how far that is.[30]

The authors also say,

With his father he essentially shares an outlook characterized by resignation, but resignation without a basis in experience. He is, in relative terms, active rather than introspective. He is not a moralist. He is prepared to take life as it comes, expecting frighteningly little as long as it comes in predictable ways. It is when it does not come this way, when it becomes unpredictable, and he is required to respond, that he does so as a moralist and a very rigid moralist indeed.[31]

Schools in working class suburbs can make a contribution by helping young people examine themselves, their values and goals, and recognize that education is more than simply vocational training. The development of understanding of people at other economic levels and of those who dissent from established values (which the working class youth often takes for granted) is particularly desirable in the interest of broader American unity.

## THE INFLUENCE OF COMMUNITY BACKGROUNDS

So, community factors such as rural, city, or suburban backgrounds continue to make a difference in the lives of American young people. As we try to illustrate in the next chapter, individuality remains, despite all attempts at grouping. Despite all of the conditioning influences in our backgrounds, the human being is unique and develops in ways which are often unpredictable.

## DISCUSSION

1. How do the census definitions of categories differ from the groupings employed for explanation of community backgrounds in this chapter?
2. Why is the rural American "the disappearing American"?
3. What were formerly the characteristics of rural youth, according to studies? Do these characteristics differ from those of rural youth today? How and why?
4. What is the dual task of many rural schools?
5. What accounts for the steady growth of urbanism in America?
6. What are the varying theories of life-styles within American cities? Specifically

---

[30] William Simon, John H. Gagnon, and Donald Carns, "Working Class Youth: Alienation Without an Image," *The National Association of Secondary School Principals Bulletin* (September 1969), p. 69.
[31] *Ibid.*, p. 68.

how do urban theories of the 1930s differ from contemporary theories concerning neighborhoods, etc.?

7. What are the characteristics of life in the city as experienced by children and youth of different social classes?

8. Why do some young people aspire to and others reject upward economic mobility? Why do some young Americans accept while others reject middle class patterns?

9. What were the major misinterpretations by the principal in the account of Skyview Terrace and Slater School?

10. Why are the problems of the poor so pressing in American life today? Why is the problem more exaggerated than it was in earlier years? How does migration by blacks to cities affect the problems?

11. What are the handicaps which the slum child brings to school with him? What are the actions of schools which sometimes increase those handicaps? What are the actions of schools which decrease such handicaps? What are the difficulties against which the city teacher struggles in teaching children and youth from slum and ghetto areas?

12. How do teachers in the inner city sometimes help create their difficulties?

13. What do you consider the role of a teacher of culturally disadvantaged students? Should he or she adapt his or her approach to meet individual differences or maintain a careful uniformity in relationships with all students?

14. What are some major cues from books on the disadvantaged to help new teachers who will work in the inner cities?

15. Distinguish among various types of suburbs. Discuss the emphasis of Dobriner and others on the existence of suburbs other than upper class communities. How are some suburbs changing as to industries and proportion of low income residents?

16. Why do people move to the suburbs?

17. Can you generalize on children and youth from the upper income suburbs? From the lower income suburbs? How do their school experiences differ? How important is social class in accounting for differences in patterns of behavior?

## INVOLVEMENT

1. Use students in your class who have rural or urban or suburban backgrounds as resources for a panel presentation on the characteristics of such community backgrounds and the influences they believe these backgrounds have had upon them.

2. Make arrangements to visit a classroom in an inner-city school, a suburban school, and a rural school. Note any significant differences you discover—differences in pupils, teachers, settings, facilities, methods, etc.

3. Make a conscious attempt to see the different neighborhoods of the city nearest you. A group may visit a particular neighborhood and generalize on it to the class.

4. Interview a teacher or an administrator who has been in an inner-city school for at least ten years. Get his reactions to the changes in the pupils and their family backgrounds.

5. Volunteer your services to the administration of a school in the inner city. Learn of the challenges to education in such a school by immersing yourself in the environment of that school. Then write an objective account of your experiences.

6. Develop your own reading program of books by authors who have grown up in the inner city, typified by James Baldwin's *Nobody Knows My Name* and Claude Brown's *Manchild in the Promised Land.*
7. Compile a list of suggestions for working with disadvantaged children and youth from class members' reading on the culturally disadvantaged.
8. Develop and carefully plan at least two major trips for the class as a whole. One trip would explore living patterns and experiences in a community background familiar to the students, whether rural, urban, or suburban. The other would explore a community background quite unfamiliar to the students. In each case, emphasize not only the physical experience of being in a neighborhood but also exchange ideas with residents through meetings, discussions, etc.

## FURTHER READING

Bottom, Raymond. *The Education of Disadvantaged Children.* New York: Parker Publishing Company, 1970. An appraisal of the problem of developing an appropriate education for disadvantaged young people.

Coleman, James S. *The Adolescent Society.* New York: The Free Press of Glencoe, 1961. A classic study of the social life of the teenager and its impact on education. An analysis of the social systems of ten high schools, with an emphasis upon value systems.

Coles, Robert. *The South Goes North.* Boston: Atlantic—Little, Brown, 1972. A description of the lives of poor people from the South who migrated North in search of a better life. Deals with the problems of the poor in both geographical settings.

Coles, Robert. *Migrants, Sharecroppers, Mountaineers.* Boston: Atlantic—Little, Brown, 1972. An investigation of the lives of poor people by a sensitive observer with a background in psychology.

Frost, Joe L. and Glenn R. Hawkes (Eds.). *The Disadvantaged Child.* Boston: Houghton Mifflin, 1970. Issues and innovations in education for the poor which range widely over many social, political, and educational forces.

Gentry, Atron, Byrd Jones, Carolyn Peelle, Royce Philips, John Woodbury, and Robert Woodbury. *Urban Education: The Hope Factor.* Philadelphia, Pennsylvania: W. B. Saunders, 1972. The authors see poor and minority students as the victims of a general failure of urban schools, but they believe that teachers can survive and facilitate learning in classrooms through transforming ideas, goals, and atmosphere.

Henderson, George, and Robert F. Bibens. *Teachers Should Care.* New York: Harper & Row, 1970. An overview of factors related to culturally disadvantaged students. The uniqueness of each student is emphasized and the reader is shown how effective teachers respond to culturally different children in crisis situations. Human relations and the struggle against prejudice are emphasized.

Levy, Gerald E. *Ghetto School.* New York: Pegasus, 1970. An account of the struggle between teachers and students in an elementary school in the ghetto. The clash of values is graphically portrayed by a sociologist who accepted a teaching assignment in Midway School.

Miller, Harry L. and Roger R. Woock. *Social Foundations of Urban Education.* New York: Dryden Press, 1970. A comprehensive examination of sources of massive educational retardation of lower class minority groups in the cities.

Passow, A. Harry (Ed.). *Opening Opportunities for Disadvantaged Learners*. Teachers College, Columbia University, New York: Teachers College Press, 1972. Some critiques and analyses of existing programs; reviews of research from preschool through college; descriptions of alternative education programs; and some predictions of what might be ahead in urban education.

Walberg, Herbert J. and Andrew T. Kopan (Eds.). *Rethinking Urban Education*. San Francisco: Jossey-Bass, 1972. An anthology which grew out of a Phi Delta Kappa project that examines urban education from the following perspectives: psychological, evaluation, sociological, systems, historical, and philosophical. The authors are among today's outstanding authorities on urban problems and solutions.

## SELECTED AUDIO-VISUAL MATERIALS

*Critical Moments in Teaching: First and Fundamental R* (16 mm film, 12 min., color, Holt, Rinehart, and Winston, 1968). An elementary class of culturally deprived children is making very little progress in learning to read. The children are inattentive and generally uninterested. The problem of what to do is explored.

*Critical Moments in Teaching: Tense Imperfect* (16 mm film, 11 min., color, Holt, Rinehart, and Winston, 1966). Problems of teaching adolescents from a low socioeconomic background in a secondary school. A stimulus for discussion and analysis of the situation.

*A Desk for Billie* (16 mm film, 57 min., color, National Education Association, 1956). The true story of a child of migrant parents and her struggle to get an education in the public schools.

*Four Families, Part I* (16 mm film, 29 min., b. & w., NFBC: McGraw-Hill, 1960). Family life and child care in India and France. Intrafamily relations, duties and responsibilities, and relationships to child care are discussed by Margaret Mead.

*Four Families, Part II* (16 mm film, 31 min., b. & w., NFBC: McGraw-Hill, 1960). Family customs in Japan and on the Canadian prairies are explored. Margaret Mead discusses infant dress, roles of family members, eating patterns, bathing the baby and the child's place in the home.

*How to Raise a Boy* (16 mm film, 20 min., b. & w., Teaching Film Custodians, Inc., 1967). Concerning the influence of a farm environment, the necessity of assuming responsibility, and how the faith and trust of loving foster parents contribute to the rehabilitation of an orphan boy.

*John Kenneth Galbraith: The Idea of the City: History, Economics, Future* (16 mm film, 29 min., color, University-at-Large, 1968). Galbraith traces the historical transition from the preindustrial to the industrial city and explores the nature and consequences of commitment to "economic efficiency."

*New Kid on the Block* (16 mm film, 11 min., color, King Screen Productions, 1971). Families move, and each time their children enter a new and unfamiliar world. Empathetic insights into the newcomer's world.

*Portrait of the Inner City* (16 mm film, 15 min., b. & w., McGraw-Hill, 1965). Pictures life in the inner-city slum area. Shows both the positive and negative aspects of growing up in poverty-stricken areas.

*Portrait of the Inner-City School — A Place to Learn* (16 mm film, 18 min., b. & w., McGraw-Hill, 1965). Discusses some of the creative ways in which school teachers and administrators can approach the problem of teaching pupils from the disadvantaged inner city. Points out how these pupils view school. Underscores the importance of the classroom climate.

*The Search for Excellence* (16 mm film, 29 min., b. & w., North Carolina Film Board, 1964). Discusses the role of the consolidated school with reference to changing communities, boundary shifts and teaching resources. Photographed in Winston-Salem, Greenville, Charlotte and Waynesville areas.

*Stay On, Stranger—Alice Geddes Lloyd, Teacher* (16 mm film, 22 min., b. & w., Teaching Film Custodians, Inc., 1966). Dramatizes incidents in the life of a teacher who started a school in Appalachia whose graduates were pledged to return to the mountains and work among their own people.

*Teaching Deprived Kindergarten Children* (35 mm filmstrip, 91 frs/record, color, Teachers College Press, Columbia University, 1966). Describes an experimental program for teaching kindergarten children from a disadvantaged neighborhood in New York City. Outlines the major teaching strategies, discusses the formulation of academic needs and concept development, and shows how these needs can be met.

# FOURTEEN

# How do learners differ?

No matter how we try to group people, we eventually have to acknowledge individuality. To get some clues to human behavior we may use such sociological groupings as those described in the last two chapters: social classes, ethnic backgrounds, and community backgrounds. Yet experience repeatedly tells us that the resulting classifications are imperfect. Each person remains an individual. Whatever the measurements we use—whether they be anatomical, biological, physiological, mental, or social—we find that human beings differ, each from the other.

The inevitability of individuality is certainly apparent in education and the schools. No matter how we try to group children and youth we find that each young person is unique; each differs in interests, motives, talents, aptitudes, ideas. Each has different habits and different life-styles; each differs in his needs and in his sensitivities. In education as in life, the norm is a myth.

Yet societies develop schools with supposedly natural groupings. American society provides rough groupings in the form of rural, city, and suburban schools, since students come to the schools from these community backgrounds. American society often provides still more supposedly homogeneous groupings—neighborhood schools attended by students of some particular ethnic background whose families live in that particular neighborhood.

When students appear at the doors of these schools, educators attempt to group them further, presumably on the assumption that greater homogeneity leads to better instruction. One such grouping, until recently taken for granted as desirable, is grouping on the basis of age. The

Both the cynical and the serious have sometimes said that intelligence is what the tests measure! But surely this is not a sufficient definition.

An early interpretation of intelligence was that the test measured not only specific factors but also a general factor, called "g"; it was thought that there existed a measurable unitary trait of general intelligence. Charles E. Spearman stressed this concept, and he proposed that a single test be substituted for the heterogeneous collection of items found in most intelligence tests.

But later researchers concluded that there were multiple factors in intelligence. J. P. Guilford recognized three broad classes which he termed operations, products, and content. Content factors are essentially figural, symbolic, semantic, or behavioral. Product factors involve units, classes, relations, systems, transformations, or implications. Operations factors have to do with memory, cognition, divergent thinking, convergent thinking, and evaluation.[5] Today many psychologists think that intelligence is not a simple unitary trait, but a complex combination of many components.

### New Dimensions Concerning the IQ

Yet as the psychologists have struggled with their definitions of intelligence, the schools have continued using the relatively simple instrument called the IQ test. However, the familiar assumptions concerning IQ tests are being challenged today.

The earlier mental testers thought that the IQ remained constant throughout one's life (assuming that the original basic test and follow-up tests were well conducted). Yet, while it is true in general that the bright remain bright and the dull remain dull, it is not true that an individual IQ always remain constant. Shifts as high as fifty IQ points have occurred; the more usual changes, however, do not go beyond fifteen points during the school years of the child.

How can such large changes as fifty points be accounted for, assuming the tests were competently handled? According to the strict advocates of the importance of heredity, such marked changes should never take place. According to the exponents of the power of the environment, such changes can be accounted for through changes in the setting and situation in which the young person grows up. The English scholar-philosopher, John Locke, recognized the two schools of thought on this question. As early as 1693 Locke wrote, "God has stamped certain characters upon men's minds, which, like their shapes, may perhaps be a little mended but can hardly be totally altered and transformed into the contrary."[6] Yet in his discussions on the choice of a tutor and on the relative influence of the home and school on the child's upbringing, he was

[5] *Ibid.*, p. 657.
[6] F. W. Garforth (ed.), *John Locke: Some Thoughts Concerning Education* (Woodbury, N.Y.: Barron's Educational Series, 1964), p. 92.

well aware of environmental influences on the individual's behavior.[7]

The conflict between proponents of the power of heredity and supporters of the strength of environment has persisted through the centuries and each side has had its say. In the struggle about "nature" (heredity) and "nurture" (environment), contemporary scholars often take a middle position. They hold that both the genes and the social situation are important. This middle position supports the possibility that an IQ can be influenced by the intellectual or educational level of the family or, indeed, by migration to a more stimulating geographical environment.

Research has documented that, *in general*, the higher the individual's social class the higher he will score on the usual IQ tests. Similarly, in the past Negroes have *in general* recorded lower scores on the usual intelligence tests than whites. Some have attributed such differences to racial characteristics but psychologists overwhelmingly reject this theory. The question was reopened by Arthur R. Jensen in the *Harvard Educational Review*, Winter 1969.[8] Vigorous criticism of Jensen's position by fellow psychologists followed in the Spring issue of the *Review*,[9] and the debate continues. In January 1972, in *Phi Delta Kappan*, William Shockley[10] presented views similar to Jensen's in an article which was accompanied by a response from N. L. Gage, "I.Q. Heritability, Race Differences, and Educational Research."[11] In the March issue Shockley[12] and Gage[13] again debated, along with Arthur R. Jensen.[14] During the past few years, Jensen and Shockley have encountered disruption or threats by radical activists on the occasion of some of their lectures and speeches. So civil liberties issues have entered into the continuing discussion and have partially diverted attention from the central issue of the existence or nonexistence of genetic factors in relationship to the IQ of Negroes.

Studies of intelligence of blacks and whites show wide overlap between distributions of scores, rather than support the assumption that "all" whites are superior in intelligence through hereditary factors to "all" Negroes. Differences within the white race are equally as large as

[7] *Ibid.*, pp. 24, 98 ff.

[8] Arthur R. Jensen, "How Much Can We Boost IQ and Scholastic Achievement?" *Harvard Educational Review* (Winter 1969), pp. 1–123.

[9] Jerome S. Kagan, J. McV. Hunt, James F. Crow, Carl Bereiter, David Elkind, Lee J. Cronbach, and William F. Brazziel, "Discussion: How Much Can We Boost IQ and Scholastic Achievement?" *Harvard Educational Review* (Spring 1969), pp. 273–356.

[10] William Shockley, "Dysgenics, Geneticity, Raceology: Challenges to the Intellectual Responsibility of Educators," *Phi Delta Kappan* (January 1972), pp. 297–307.

[11] N. L. Gage, "I.Q. Heritability, Race Differences, and Educational Research," *Phi Delta Kappan* (January 1972), pp. 308–312.

[12] William Shockley, "A Debate Challenge: Geneticity is 80% for White Identical Twins' I.Q.," *Phi Delta Kappan* (March 1972), pp. 415–419.

[13] N. L. Gage, "The Causes of Race Differences in I.Q.: Replies to Shockley, Page, and Jensen," *Phi Delta Kappan* (March 1972), pp. 422–427.

[14] Arthur R. Jensen, "The Causes of Twin Differences in I.Q.: A Reply to Gage," *Phi Delta Kappan* (March 1972), pp. 420–421.

differences within the black race. Studies of intelligence of Negroes also show that regional differences within those Americans who were classified as blacks, particularly Northern-Southern differences, have been as large as the differences between the races. Similarly, studies of American Indians and Mexican-Americans do not support those who believe that innate differences exist and that such minorities are "inferior people as to brains."

The question of whether environment is a powerful factor that makes a significant difference in the IQ scores engages many scholars. That it does is indicated by such studies as that of Benjamin Bloom which testify that impoverishment of the environment may depress the IQ by as much as twenty points.[15] Many scholars have pointed out that IQ tests are not completely culture free or culture fair. Recent reconsiderations of intelligence testing lend support to those who refuse to accept the result of intelligence tests as a necessary predestination for the individual. For instance, in 1972 a young black earned a straight A grade average in the University of Louisville graduate school, although years earlier his IQ had been recorded in a reform school as 69.[16]

Too long have children and youth suffered from teachers learning of an individual's IQ score and then promptly assuming that nothing can be done for the relatively low scoring individual. Scholars now think that there is a range within which the individual can operate. Whether he operates toward the bottom or the top of his range depends on factors susceptible to change, such as family influences, the quality of the environment, and—most important of all to teachers—the quality of the educational experiences he encounters.

So the assumption is invalid that an intelligence quotient provides us with so remorseless a natural grouping that we can ignore the law of diversity. What is learned by each individual differs from what is learned by the rest of a group, despite similarities in IQ.

### Categorizing Intelligence

It can be argued that generations of work with intelligence quotients have been useful in helping educators divide young people into broad descriptive categories—mentally retarded, normal, gifted, etc. The terms used for such categories are not completely standardized, so do not be surprised if your professor of psychology or of psychology of education uses somewhat different cut-off points concerning categories from those described below.

Lowest of the IQ categories is the grouping of the mentally deficient, feeble-minded or mentally defective who range from zero to 50 on IQ

---

[15] Tuddenham, p. 663.
[16] Associated Press, " 'Retarded' Grad Student Doesn't Believe Tests," *Terre Haute Tribune*, September 9, 1972, p. 14.

scales. They include individuals on the nontrainable level, technically defined as between zero and about 20 or 25 on intelligence tests; these people can learn no more than a two-year-old. The trainable level ranges from about 25 to 50 on IQ scales. People at this level are trainable to carry out simple routines or to care for their bodily needs; they are not educable in the usual sense of the word.

People with a tested IQ between approximately 50 and 70 are sometimes called the mentally handicapped or mentally retarded. Today the usual term is the educable retarded. Such people are educable in the sense that they can learn to read, write, and do simple arithmetic. They can develop limited occupational proficiency and can manage in society. Unlike the nontrainable and trainable, they usually attend regular schools and are often enrolled in classes titled "special education" or "education for the mentally retarded." The educable mentally retarded are usually placed in special classes rather than educated with other children and youth.

In 1971 a Philadelphia Federal Court decided, in response to a suit filed by the Pennsylvania Association for Retarded Children, that the state of Pennsylvania must provide public education for all retarded children. Every retarded child denied a public education must be identified by the state. Using the Pennsylvania decision as a precedent, organizations have filed suits across the nation on behalf of retarded children.

The higher up the IQ scale analysis goes, the more difficult it is to describe precisely the categories. This is the case with the borderline or slow learner category made up of people with IQs ranging roughly from 70 to 90. Even the category of "slow learner" is controversial, for some researchers—including Leona E. Tyler, a specialist on individual differences—warn us that slow learning or dull children are often slow developers. Such children may move to higher levels of understanding in time, but achieving understanding will take them longer. It is worth recalling that the British statesman Winston Churchill was thought by some of his teachers to be a slow learner!

Some authorities have estimated that about 20 to 24 percent of the child population falls into the category variously described as borderline or dull, slow learner, or slow developer. Whatever the title given such a child, the fact remains that he is usually found in a regular class where he faces real difficulty in dealing with skills or information that normal or gifted children can readily acquire. School is a constant and frequently losing struggle for him.

Which grouping for the mentally retarded pupil and for the slow learner is best? Some educators attempt to resolve the problems by regarding the separation of the mentally retarded (IQ range of 50 to 70) as desirable, particularly when skillful and trained teachers of special education use appropriate methods and materials with such students. They argue that the gap separating the retarded individual from members of the regular class is too large and that the mentally retarded child is likely to be overwhelmed in the setting of the regular class and to be rejected by classmates. But, on the other hand, categories and labels can stigmatize children unfairly; some learning disabilities may be aggravated by isolation; some children may be mislabeled and misplaced. So other educators support "mainstreaming," some degree of absorption of mentally retarded youngsters in regular classes, particularly when classroom teachers have small classes, abundant support services, and "back-up" specialists as helpful consultants. Today many educators contend that pupils in the range above mentally retarded, the slow learners (IQ range of 70 to 90), are sufficiently like the rest of the regular class in personality and background that they will be socially accepted, may make friends who may challenge them, and may not perceive themselves as failures. However, a minority of educators would also separate slow learners from other students.

The middle category is, of course, the average or normal range made up of children with IQs from approximately 90 to 110. Since about 45 to 50 percent of the population of pupils falls into this middle category, teachers who have difficulty dealing with individual differences often aim their lessons and teaching at this middle group.[17] Whether they hit their target is another matter.

Above average or superior students as to IQ are those whose intelligence quotients fall somewhere in the range between 110 and 130. Pleasant names are applied to them—rapid learners, superior students, able people, apt students, etc. They too are usually found in the regular classes. Consequently, they are often the class leaders academically and socially; teachers point to them with pride.

In the category of an IQ ranging roughly from 130 to 170 are the students who are classified as gifted or very superior. Such students often regard school work as very easy. If the teacher focuses his instruction only on the average student and ignores individual differences, a gifted youngster may soon become bored and may even develop antisocial behavior in the classroom. It is sometimes surprising to a new teacher to learn of the sizable number of gifted people attending his school.

There is a good deal of controversy as to what IQ constitutes the lower level of giftedness. When a school begins a program of grouping certain students as gifted, the controversy is particularly sharp. In some situations, the gifted group is open to only those above 140; in other situations, a student with a measured IQ of 115 may be admitted. Contrary to the prevalent stereotype, gifted children are not usually sickly, weak,

[17] R. Murray Thomas and Shirley M. Thomas, *Individual Differences in the Classroom* (New York: David McKay, 1965), p. 90.

and nonathletic; studies show them to be above average in general in health, strength, and physical agility.[18]

At the top of the groupings by intellect is, of course, the category made up of persons who are exceptionally superior. Arbitrarily, the lower level for this category has sometimes been set at 170. There is no known upper cut-off point. Such people at the very top of the intellectual scale are often well rounded as to various aspects of intelligence, at least well rounded enough to score above 170 on intelligence tests. The need for recognizing individual differences in the case of the exceptionally superior thinker, sometimes called "the genius," is obvious. The word genius, incidentally, might best be reserved for those who have produced works of genius through significant contributions of enduring value, as in the case of the musical genius or the artistic genius or the scientific genius, a person of magnificent virtuosity regardless of his IQ score.

### Homogeneous versus Heterogeneous Grouping

With respect to intellectual differences among children and youth, educators face a familiar dilemma. On one hand, they cannot help but be aware of the existence of individual differences. On the other hand, the school is not organized today as an individual tutorial system but operates through groups, some of them quite large. How can there be provision for individual differences in an institution geared not to individuals but to groups? Possibly the new technology being developed for schools, such as computer-aided instruction, will contribute in the future to the achievement of greater individualization.

Possibly the most popular way of attempting to meet individual differences that relate to learners' intellectual abilities involves the organization of groups. One organizational way of dealing with divergent intellectual abilities which has been used in American education is "homogeneous" grouping on the basis of intelligence. Homogeneous grouping brings together students who are presumably similar in intellectual ability. It is the opposite of "heterogeneous" grouping, which involves grouping together students who represent a wide range of intellectual ability.

In homogeneous grouping, pupils are usually first sorted according to grade levels, which primarily represent divisions according to age. Then the students are divided according to their ability, frequently on the threefold basis of slow, normal, and fast learner. On the elementary school level such groups are frequently named for various members of the bird world or animal kingdom. But a child soon learns what it really means to be classified as a redbird or a bluebird or a robin.

18 *Ibid.,* p. 91.

Proponents of homogeneous ability grouping advance several arguments. They claim that when the materials and methods and specific objectives are adjusted to the particular learning group, students make better academic progress in a class with others in the same ability range than if they were in a heterogeneous class. In this case the teacher does not have the problem of dealing with as wide an ability range. Nor is it fair to the learner to expect him to compete with a person of superior ability or to be held back by slow learners. In general, parents support ability grouping (though they sometimes have inaccurate but firm ideas as to which group their own child should be in!), and in general teachers prefer teaching intellectually similar children to teaching diverse children in heterogeneous groups.

The case for homogeneous ability grouping sounds persuasive; why then does ability grouping not universally prevail? Why does the introduction of ability grouping ebb and flow in American education, rising in one period and falling during a subsequent decade?

Opponents of ability grouping contend that in large part the difficulty is traceable to the undeniable fact of human individuality. While the bright tend in general to be bright in all ways and the dull tend in general to be dull in all ways, significant individual variations persist. As a result, an elementary school student may rate placement in the bright group in verbal abilities but only in the normal group in quantitative abilities. The supposedly dull student may prove to be quite competent in some particular subject. And even in the group which appears homogeneous intellectually, there is actually a considerable range of variation. If the teacher of this group does not individualize through a variety of techniques—just as he presumably individualizes in teaching in a heterogenous group—learning will not go forward very briskly.

As Vernon L. Replogle says,

. . . the idea of a homogeneous group is largely an illusion. Groups designated as homogeneous on the basis of reading test scores are actually quite heterogeneous with regard to specific areas of reading achievement. For example, two children who make the same score on a standardized reading test may have very different profiles of specific sub-skills and instructional needs. . . . This condition prevails in virtually every area used as a base for grouping whether it be I.Q. tests, math tests, or physical tests. Abilities are diverse and stubbornly fluid.[19]

Another argument used against homogeneous grouping is of a social nature. The American democratic ideal envisions the classless and integrated school which teaches children and youth of all backgrounds to live and work together with mutual respect and acceptance. What

[19] Vernon L. Replogle, "Another Look at Heterogeneous-Homogeneous Grouping," *Illinois Principal* (March 1971), p. 3.

happens to the dream in schools which use homogeneously grouped classes in a society in which the supposedly intellectual differences actually reflect differing social and cultural backgrounds? Is the result a degree of snobbery on the part of the "superior" group often made up of socially advantaged young people? Is the result submission or rebellion on the part of the "inferior" group, often composed of the socially disadvantaged?

Another claimed disadvantage of homogeneous grouping has a psychological base; it can best be comprehended by considering the "slow learners." Their perceptions of themselves must be taken into account, too, and their self-identities must not be derogated. Each person has a picture of himself which he learns in large part from the way others see him. He tends to accept this picture of himself as true and behave accordingly. If this be so, say the psychologists, the lesson may be driven home every day to the slow learners that they are the dull and stupid, the "dummies," who will never amount to much. Would they not build more constructive and positive self-identities if placed in heterogeneous classes?

One compromise offered as an alternative to homogeneous grouping is assigning students to special classes or to tutoring for part of the school experience, perhaps through an hour or two during the school day or after school. A slow learner might have remedial reading experiences or a gifted child might work in a science laboratory or an honors class. Special interests and needs are thus maximized.

### Acceleration and Retention

Another approach in the eternal quest by the school to place supposedly similar children and youth together and thereby outwit the law of human variability, takes the form of acceleration and retention (sometimes called "skipping" or "being left back").

Accelerating the child a grade or a half grade on one or more occasions gives him the opportunity to take on advanced work. Since presumably his ability level is closer to the intellectual level of students a grade level beyond him than to the intellectual level of his present classmates and age mates, the child or youth is advanced to the higher grade. Yet the haunting question as to acceleration is whether possible resulting social, physical, and emotional handicaps offset the possible intellectual gain. Consequently, when acceleration takes place, forward-looking educators find it advisable to take into account not only intellectual factors but also the social maturity, emotional stability, the physical prowess, and even quite literally the size of the individual. One well-known study, which has reassured some educators concerning the effects of acceleration, was conducted by the same Lewis E. Terman who developed IQ tests. Terman and his associates, in *Mental and Physical Traits of a Thou-*

*sand Gifted Children*[20] and *The Gifted Child Grows Up*,[21] reached the conclusion that acceleration was not usually harmful, in general, to the gifted child's social, physical, or emotional development. Terman pointed out that in most cases feelings of inferiority were soon overcome. Yet some educators are not persuaded of the desirability of acceleration and the haunting question persists.

As to retention, the idea that a student will benefit from nonpromotion has not been supported by research. Retention or nonpromotion is often defended on the assumption that the student would master on a second try the material he did not understand before and that he would work harder because of a fear of failing. As early as 1954, Henry J. Otto in a book on elementary education made the following statements:

> It is now evident that practically all of the notions previously held about the value of nonpromotion or the motivating value of the threat of failure have been exploded. Out of a group of repeaters, about 20 percent will do better than they did the preceding term, about 40 percent will show no change, and about 40 percent will actually do worse. If doubtful cases are divided into two groups appropriately matched on essential items, and one group is promoted and the other group is held back to repeat the grade, several studies have shown that the achievement of the promoted group, as measured by standardized tests, is equal to or greater than the achievement of the group held back. . . . As far as personality adjustment is concerned, group studies show that the adjustment of pupils of low achievement is not more satisfactory when they are retained in grade groups more nearly representative of their levels of achievement. Numerous cases are on record which show the contribution which nonpromotion, especially repeated nonpromotion, has made to the personality maladjustment of individual cases.[22]

Those educators favoring retention cannot defend their case through the argument that the child benefits; consequently, they fall back on arguments that school standards must be maintained and that the work of the teacher will be simplified by retention. Opponents retort that standards must be flexible and individual-related and that schools are for learners, not for the convenience of teachers.

## DIFFERENCES IN CREATIVITY

Just as children and youth differ in intellectual competencies, they also differ with respect to special abilities. Some are especially creative in the

[20] Lewis M. Terman, *Mental and Physical Traits of a Thousand Gifted Children,* vol. 1, *Genetic Studies of Genius,* Lewis M. Terman (ed.) (Stanford, Calif.: Stanford University Press, 1925).
[21] Lewis M. Terman and Melita H. Oden, *The Gifted Child Grows Up,* vol. 4, *Genetic Studies of Genius,* Lewis M. Terman (ed. (Stanford, Calif.: Stanford University Press, 1947).
[22] Henry J. Otto, *Elementary School Organization and Administration* (New York: Appleton-Century-Crofts, 1954), pp. 268–269.

The preschool offers very young children varied experiences to help their total development.

arts or music or science, etc. Throughout history man has been aware of the existence of especially creative people. Indeed, man's recorded history is largely the account of the activities of such people. But only since approximately 1955 has substantial research begun on a variety of unknown matters relating to creativity.[23] Among the present findings of the scholars of creativity is the conviction that all people are to some degree creative or potentially creative, regardless of their age, their cultural background, or the field in which they specialize. Yet students of creativity also recognize the law of individual variability, for they assure us that individuals differ in their creative potential in various fields and in their varied ways of expression.

[23] Calvin W. Taylor (ed.), *Creativity: Progress and Potential* (New York: McGraw-Hill, 1964), p. 2.

One of the lively arguments concerning creativity deals with the extent to which the creative person is or is not identical with the intellectual person. Few deny some degree of relationship; students of creativity have also pointed out differences. Calvin W. Taylor, a researcher and writer in the field of creativity, says:

> Certain intellectual characteristics, for instance, appear to have some relationship with creative performance; these fall within the categories of memory, cognition, evaluation, convergent production, and divergent production. The divergent-production factors, including fluencies and flexibilities, seem to be most important. The fact that these intellectual aspects of creativity are relatively distinct components indicates the probability of multiple types of creative talent. The generally low correlation of these factors with intelligence test scores suggests that creative talent is not only various, but relatively different from intelligence.[24]

[24] *Ibid.,* p. 179.

Education offers much more than just academic subjects.

*Dan McCoy, Black Star*

No one claims that all frontiers of creativity, including its relationship to intelligence, are yet explored. Among the scarcely known areas of high interest to students of creativity are explanations for the decrease in creativity which seems to occur in the early school years. Too, we know relatively little about the development of creativity during the later school years. Still further specific suggestions, tested materials, and procedures are needed if we are going to develop, rather than block, creative learning at the various school levels.

But some suggestions of ways to develop creativity are ventured, as those summarized by E. Paul Torrance who considers nurturing creativity in elementary schools:

1. Value creative thinking.
2. Help children become more sensitive to environmental stimuli.
3. Encourage manipulation of objects and ideas.
4. Teach how to test each idea systematically.
5. Develop tolerance of new ideas.
6. Beware of forcing a set pattern.
7. Develop a creative classroom atmosphere.
8. Teach the child to value his creative thinking.
9. Teach children skills of avoiding or coping with peer sanctions without sacrificing their creativity.
10. Give information about the creative process.
11. Dispel the sense of awe of masterpieces.
12. Encourage and evaluate self-initiated learning.
13. Create "thorns in the flesh," making children aware of problems and deficiencies.
14. Create necessities for creative thinking.
15. Provide for active and quiet periods.
16. Make available resources for working out ideas.
17. Encourage the habit of working out the full implications of ideas.
18. Develop skills of constructive criticism.
19. Encourage acquisition of knowledge in a variety of fields.
20. Be adventurous-spirited yourself.[25]

In general, it makes good sense for the creativity-fostering teacher to introduce all youth to various media and opportunities in such fields as art and music. It is helpful to open up many possibilities to the student. The teacher should also individualize potential creative experiences by using such techniques as working in small groups, giving individual assignments, sponsoring projects, and generally individualizing classroom procedures so that as many students as possible can realize their creative potentials.

## DIFFERENCES IN PHYSICAL AND EMOTIONAL HANDICAPS

Just as there are intellectual and creative abilities which differ widely, handicaps also unfortunately exist and greatly differ. Physical obstacles

[25] *Ibid.*, pp. 92–93.

of students most often encountered by teachers include those of sight, hearing, speech, and cerebral palsy. Some students are crippled or disfigured. Mental obstacles include emotional disturbances.

In an important decision in 1972, a federal court ruled that all handicapped and emotionally disturbed children have a constitutional right to a public education. The court ruling resembles the 1971 Pennsylvania decision which ruled that all retarded persons are entitled to a public education. In a Washington, D.C. case, a federal district judge gave the District of Columbia schools 30 days to enroll all handicapped children already identified by the school system.[26]

With respect to such handicaps, the first necessity is to recognize them. The teacher certainly recognizes total blindness, deafness, inability to communicate, etc. But the teacher may not be equally aware of visual defects, hearing problems, and speech problems serious enough to require special attention. Many children and young people with such handicaps will be found in the regular classroom.

Too, the teacher sometimes fails to diagnose the problems he encounters with a sufficient degree of accuracy. Many hard-of-hearing students who are not deaf but who are below the normal hearing level are wrongly diagnosed by teachers as slow learners. Some stutterers are thought to suffer from an unremediable physical handicap, though actually it may be some degree of emotional disturbance. However, many teachers are increasingly aware of the nonphysiological origins of speech handicaps and of the availability of speech therapy resources. The referral of handicapped children to such specialized sources, whether within the school or the community, is desirable. But special help, when available, will only be used if the teacher is sensitive to the existence of a problem.

After recognition of handicaps and seeking help from available school and community sources, the teacher might well stress two approaches. For one, the teacher should do all of the common sense things by way of adaptation of the school environment to reduce the degree of the individual's handicap. These include attention to lighting problems, moving hard-of-hearing young people within close range of the center of the classroom action, and special attention to children and youth with speech handicaps. The most useful adaptation of all is individualizing instruction.

There is an additional adaptation which cannot be overlooked—working with the class as a whole for greater understanding and acceptance of the individual with the handicap. How easy it is for a child with a handicap to become the butt of the cruelty, however innocent or unintentional, directed against him by classmates! The scorn or jeering of classmates can contribute further to the difficulties the handicapped child may be experiencing.

---

[26] "News Front," *Education, U.S.A.* (August 7, 1972), p. 230.

## DIFFERENCES IN BEHAVIOR PROBLEMS

Individual differences occur not only with respect to the intelligence, creativity, and physical handicaps of children and youth. Individual differences in the form of behavior variations also occur, and are myriad. From the teacher's point of view, behavior differences are particularly obvious when they take such negative forms as delinquency, dropping out of school, or the use of drugs. These three types of behavior are, of course, only a small sample of possible behavioral manifestations growing out of the pressures of the surrounding society. Would that teachers were always especially sensitive to positive behavior, such as the behavior of children and youth who exercise constructive leadership in the school and community! But behavior problems are more obvious and appear more urgent to new teachers.

### Juvenile Delinquency

In a period in which Americans are deeply troubled by the prevalence of crime, juvenile delinquency poses a major problem for schools. Who is the juvenile delinquent? The juvenile delinquent is a person who is in trouble. He (or she) can be of any race or social class. The delinquent reacts to his problem with outward aggressive behavior. He does so in a society which finds his conduct bothersome and contrary to how it believes life should be. Again, we must recognize that he is an individual and must be treated as such.

Social forces largely account for delinquency. Today few hold to the obsolete theories of the nineteenth century Italian criminologist Cesare Lombroso, who compared anthropological measurements of human beings and reached the conclusion that the criminal was a type marked by distinct physical traits. The related idea that criminality is somehow inherited through the genes has also been abandoned. This is not to deny that criminals may not breed criminals through family environmental influences. But the locus of the making of the criminal and the delinquent, it is commonly agreed, is to be found in his surroundings rather than in the bumps on his head or in his genetic history.

According to research studies of delinquency, summarized by William C. Kvaraceus among others, the delinquent is more likely than the nondelinquent to be characterized by the following environment and experience:

Living in slum areas
Overcrowded, poorly furnished and badly kept homes
Poverty and deprivation
Bad home conditions
No family recreation
Parents less interested in his future

Home characterized by quarreling, rejection, and indifference
Discipline, if not completely lacking, depending heavily on physical punishment
Less mental ability
Ten points lower than nondelinquent on IQ scales
Instability
Resentment of authority
Emotional conflicts
Inclination to look for adventure away from home
Disliking school
Lacking career plans
Doing poorly in school
Receiving low grades
Failing to be promoted
Behaving badly
Escaping through truancy

A word of caution is in order. As you read such characteristics as "living in slum areas," "poverty and deprivation," "bad home conditions," the thought may occur to you that you know of—or you may even know personally—some delinquents who live in relative affluence surrounded by good home conditions in privileged communities. Yes, juvenile delinquency does exist in America's Dariens and Scarsdales and Evanstons, and in exclusive "Main Line" and "North Shore" communities, as well as in the bitter city slums. But the generalization nevertheless holds—the life of the delinquent is *more likely* to be marked by the characteristics cited above than the life of the nondelinquent. Yet your recognition of the reality of delinquency among upper middle and lower upper class young people supplies further evidence that the juvenile delinquent, like other human beings, must ultimately be seen as an individual.

Schooling is no panacea for juvenile delinquency. The roots of delinquency are social, emotional, and deep. Juvenile delinquency is complex; it is multiple-caused.

A good illustration of what is meant by "multiple-caused" and the significance of this conception is furnished by the history of investigations into the causes of delinquency. During the 1920's and 1930's, investigators such as Shaw and McKay (1931, 1942) provided data indicating that there is a relationship between urban delinquency rates and distance from the center of the city. The highest rates were found near the center of the city, with rates decreasing gradually as one moved away from the center. Although there was a significant correlation, it was not high. There were many exceptions. This led Healey and Bronner (1936) to pose the question, why, of two children living in the *same* home and under the *same* environmental conditions, one becomes delinquent and the other does not. Their inquiry involving 105 delinquents paired with 105 sibling controls, indicated that a variety of blocked emotional forces such as feeling rejected, deprived, or thwarted, internal mental conflicts, or a sense of guilt, characterized 96 of the 105 cases. The remaining nine without marked emotional stress

Members of two gangs take part in a work project combatting delinquency.

revealed such factors as various social pressures, lack of supervision, and poor family standards.[27]

Delinquency similarly requires multiples cures, some of which are hard to apply. For instance, we know delinquents often need love; yet of all the persons whom it is hard to love, it is the angry, hostile, suspicious juvenile delinquent! Nevertheless, the need for love is inescapable.

If a school—or even one teacher—can create for the potential or

[27] Ralph H. Ojemann, "Behavior Problems," in American Educational Research Association, *Encyclopedia of Educational Research*, 4th ed. (New York: Macmillan, 1969), p. 101. Copyright © 1969 by American Educational Research Association.

in contact with an increasingly wider world. If his school is one in which students sit passively while teachers tell them exactly what to do and exactly how to do it, there is likely to be classroom warfare between the teacher and the rebellious delinquent.

The potential juvenile delinquent especially needs a curriculum which includes vocational education and work experience. College entrance is seldom a motivating goal for a delinquent. A school which forces youngsters to work toward unattainable and/or irrelevant goals only contributes to delinquency. We should not forget that the typical delinquent is more likely to be a slower learner than others and often needs remedial help.

Certainly one major contribution to the prevention and control of delinquency which can be made by the schools is early identification of the problem. Once identified, the young person should be referred to diagnostic facilities so that the variety of factors operating in his case may be studied and remedial programs developed. Increasingly, remedial programs provide for consultation by mental health workers with teachers and other school personnel working closely with the youth involved. Though still woefully lacking, such diagnostic facilities are fortunately on the increase. They take the form of community child-guidance clinics, which have resulted in part from the work of the National Institute of Mental Health, and of residential receiving centers for juvenile delinquents. Diagnostic approaches are also provided by an increasing number of school psychological and guidance services. The best diagnosis of the difficulty and an appropriate plan of action is more likely to come from a multi-dimensional approach involving a variety of sources such as community clinics, schools, churches, employment facilities, recreational facilities, and health agencies rather than from any single source. Teachers should learn to work with a variety of community agencies if they are serious about combating delinquency.

Important though diagnosis may be, the importance of primary prevention should not be minimized. A delinquent child may benefit from the understanding help of a teacher or a counselor and a delinquent youth may be helped by placement in a job. But if other social circumstances remain the same and the delinquent returns nightly to a slum area or an inadequate family, there may be little real progress. The multiple causation of delinquency includes persisting social problems.

## The Dropout

The dropout is also an individual. A combination of circumstances account for his leaving school before graduation; each combination is different. Yet generalizations on the dropout can be stated, though not every dropout will represent each generalization.

Who is the typical dropout? The dropout is more likely to be a boy than a girl. He is usually just beyond his sixteenth birthday. His intelligence is average or slightly below average, as measured by intelligence tests. But he is usually not reading at his appropriate grade level. It is a good bet that academically he will rank in the lowest quarter of his class. He is probably slightly older than others in his grade for he has usually had the experience of having been held back once during the elementary or junior high school grades. The typical dropout leaves after the junior high school years and does not enter the doors of the senior high school.

The average dropout has encountered discipline problems in his career. But, contrary to an erroneous stereotype, the usual dropout is not a juvenile delinquent; most dropouts have no police record. Yet as compared with the nondropout, the dropout has been in trouble more frequently with the law and more often has a police record.

The dropout feels that the school is not for him. He seldom takes part in extracurricular activities; he feels that the school and its representatives reject him and he in turn rejects the school. For instance, at Modesto (California) High School students who graduated and students who dropped out answered questions about their self-concepts. Sixty-two percent of the dropouts answered affirmatively to the question "Do you feel spiteful toward other pupils?" whereas only 11 percent of the graduates answered affirmatively. Only 39 percent of the dropouts answered yes to the question "Has a teacher ever rewarded or praised you?" whereas 88 percent of the graduates testified that this was the case. Sixty-two percent of the dropouts responded yes to the question "Do you feel you are a slow learner?" whereas only 18 percent of the graduates saw themselves in this role. Forty-one percent of the dropouts answered affirmatively to the question "Do you have any skills that will help you get a job?" whereas 90 percent of the graduates thought they had such skills.[28] Feeling rejected by the school, the dropout in turn rejects the school.

The parents of the dropout often were themselves dropouts; it is more than likely that the dropout's older brothers and sisters also dropped out of school early. His friendships are usually made with people outside of the school and these include older dropouts.

His explanations as to why he dropped out of school are profuse and often antischool. He frequently says that school is uninteresting, that he wants to earn money for himself, that he wants to contribute to his parents' support, etc. It is understandable that he cannot describe, at this stage of his life, the combination of factors which made his dropping out predictable. The dropout often explains that he intends to work for a high school diploma at night or through correspondence. But he usually does not achieve that diploma.

[28] Daniel Schreiber, "Dropout Causes and Consequences," in American Educational Research Association, *Encyclopedia of Educational Research*, 4th ed. (New York: Macmillan, 1969), p. 314.

TABLE 14-1    **Relationship Between Years of Education and Earnings**

| Education of family head | Mean income in 1968 | Total | Less than $3,000 | $3,000 –4,999 | $5,000 –7,499 | $7,500 –9,999 | $10,000 –14,999 | $15,000 or more | Number of cases | Median |
|---|---|---|---|---|---|---|---|---|---|---|
| 0–5 grades | $ 4,000 | 100 | 52 | 22 | 13 | 7 | 4 | 2 | 143 | $ 2,920 |
| 6–8 grades | 6,300 | 100 | 33 | 16 | 19 | 14 | 13 | 5 | 410 | 5,170 |
| 9–11 grades, some high school plus noncollege* | 8,820 | 100 | 17 | 15 | 20 | 17 | 22 | 9 | 402 | 7,260 |
| 12 grades, completed high school | 9,480 | 100 | 6 | 12 | 18 | 24 | 29 | 11 | 415 | 8,940 |
| Completed high school plus other noncollege* | 9,890 | 100 | 5 | 14 | 18 | 20 | 31 | 12 | 264 | 9,060 |
| College, no degree | 10,830 | 100 | 14 | 9 | 12 | 17 | 31 | 17 | 329 | 9,610 |
| College, bachelor's degree | 13,030 | 100 | 6 | 10 | 14 | 13 | 29 | 28 | 239 | 11,240 |
| College, advanced or professional degree | 16,460 | 100 | 3 | 6 | 6 | 15 | 31 | 39 | 109 | 13,120 |

* Author's note: Noncollege refers to the further education of the family head through courses and studies which were not part of a college education.

Stephen B. Withey et al., *A Degree and What Else?* a report prepared for The Carnegie Commission on Higher Education (New York: McGraw-Hill, 1971), pp. 56–57.

After dropping out, he has a hard time finding and keeping a job. Some studies have shown that at least half the dropouts are unemployed for a substantial period immediately after leaving school. The jobs dropouts do get are frequently menial, such as washing cars, mowing lawns, cleaning up, household help, etc. Unemployment is usually markedly higher in the age groups from sixteen to nineteen than in other age groups. If the dropout also happens to be a member of a minority group, his chances of unemployment are usually still higher. The lifetime income of the dropout is substantially lower than that of the individual who graduates from high school. There is a direct relationship between the number of years of education of family heads and the earnings of American families. The longer individuals stay in school the higher their incomes become. A chart from a 1971 publication of The Carnegie Commission on Higher Education reports the average family head who dropped out somewhere between the completion of the sixth and eighth grades as earning $6,300. The average family head who completed high school earned $9,480 and the average family head who obtained a bachelor's degree from college earned $13,030. Table 14-1 reports the relationship between years of education and earnings.[29]

Yet some believe that keeping potential dropouts in school is harmful to individuals and society. For instance, Paul Goodman says:

[29] Stephen B. Withey et al., *A Degree and What Else?* a report prepared for The Carnegie Commission on Higher Education (New York: McGraw-Hill, 1971), pp. 56–57.

The belief that a highly industrialized society requires twelve to twenty years of prior processing of the young is an illusion or a hoax. The evidence is strong that there is no correlation between school performance and life achievement in any of the professions, whether medicine, law, engineering, journalism, or business. Moreover, recent research shows that for more modest clerical, technological, or semiskilled factory jobs there is no advantage in years of schooling or the possession of diplomas. . . .

Forcing the nonacademic to attend school breaks the spirit of most and foments alienation in the best. Kept in tutelage, young people, who are necessarily economically dependent, cannot pursue the sexual, adventurous, and political activities congenial to them. Since lively youngsters insist on these anyway, the effect of what we do is to create a gap between them and the oppressive adult world, with a youth subculture and an arrested development.[30]

## Theodore Roszak advises:

*Let them go.* Help them to escape, those that need to escape. Find them cracks in the system's great walls and guide them through, cover their tracks, provide the alibis, mislead the posse . . . the anxious parents, the truant officers, the supervisors and superintendents and officious superegos of the social order.

At least between ourselves and the young, we might begin talking up the natural rights of truancy and the educative possibilities of hooky—which is after all only matriculating into the school without walls that the world itself has always normally been for the inquisitive young.

And who knows? Once we stop forcing *our* education on the children, perhaps they will invite a lucky few of us to participate in *theirs*.[31]

Some researchers believe that current antidropout campaigns give dropouts a bad name, are based on invalid assumptions about the consequences of dropping out, and distract Americans from more basic educational problems and issues. For instance, the Senior Study Director of the University of Michigan's Institute for Social Research reports that

. . . while unemployment rates may be twice as high among dropouts as among stayins, it is very misleading to claim that the act of dropping out will double a young man's chances of being unemployed. That difference in unemployment rates is linked primarily to family background and ability factors, and these things are not changed because someone drops out of school.

Are dropout's jobs unattractive and poorly paid? When employed dropouts were compared with employed high school graduates, we found their weekly income levels to be nearly identical. . . . We cannot, of course, answer the argument that the long-range earnings of graduates will be higher—at least not until we conduct further follow-up studies of the Youth in Transition respondents. But we can say that in the

[30] Paul Goodman, "Freedom and Learning: The Need for Choice," *Saturday Review* (May 18, 1968), pp. 73–74.
[31] Theodore Roszak, "Educating Contra Naturam," *A Man for Tomorrow's World* (Washington, D.C.: Association for Supervision and Curriculum Development, 1970), p. 27.

short run there is little justification for the assertion that dropouts who get jobs will earn less than their counterparts who finish high school.

There is also little justification for the view that dropouts get less satisfying jobs. Three-quarters of the dropouts rated themselves "quite satisfied" or "very satisfied" with their jobs, while two-thirds of the graduates expressed similar levels of satisfaction.[32]

If you believe that dropping out is undesirable, whether we seem to be doing well or badly in the 1970s on the problem of dropping out depends on how we state the situation. We can, for instance, say that in 1900, of every 100 pupils who once made up the fifth grade only seven graduated from high school. By 1950 of every 100 pupils once in the fifth grade, more than half graduated from high school. By 1970, of every 100 pupils once in the fifth grade about three-fourths graduated from high school. For instance, of 1,000 who entered the fifth grade in 1962, 752 graduated from high school in 1970.[33] Thus the percentage of students who dropped out before high school graduation has declined steadily throughout the twentieth century, with one-sixth anticipated as the probable dropout proportion in the mid 1970s. So some say we are doing well on the secondary school level in reducing dropouts.

But ours is a land in which college education is increasingly regarded as important to successful living. Clark Kerr, chairman of The Carnegie Commission on Higher Education, has said, ". . . going to college—any college—does give to the individual a chance for a more satisfying life and to society the likelihood of a more effective community, even at the cost of intensifying certain inherent problems and cleavages in the postindustrial world."[34] Dr. Kerr reports of the Carnegie study:

Individuals who go to college tend to be:
- More "liberal" and tolerant in their attitudes toward and in their relations with other individuals and groups in society.
- More satisfied with their jobs.
- More highly paid and less subject to unemployment.
- More thoughtful and deliberate in their consumer expenditures.
- More likely to vote and to participate generally in community activities.
- More informed about community, national, and world affairs.

Women who go to college are more likely to work and also to have fewer children on the average. All these characteristics may be viewed as being on the constructive side. But college attendance also gives greater accent to certain problems in society:

[32] Jerald G. Bachman, "Anti-Dropout Campaign and Other Misanthropies," *Society* (February 1972), pp. 6, 60.

[33] U.S. Bureau of the Census, *Statistical Abstracts of the United States,* 92nd Annual Edition (Washington, D.C.: U.S. Government Printing Office, 1971), p. 125.

[34] Clark Kerr, "Foreword," *A Degree and What Else?* a report prepared for The Carnegie Commission on Higher Education (New York: McGraw-Hill, 1971), p. xiii.

*Bob Coombs, Rapho Guillumette Pictures*

Students learning auto mechanics through a work-study program developed to keep young people in school.

- To the prolongation of youth with its inherent tensions.
- To the generational conflict between the more highly educated younger generation and the less educated older generation.
- To the conflict within the younger generation between those who go to college and those who do not.
- To the opposition between those who have more "liberal" and those who have more "conservative" points of view on social issues.[35]

Take four young people today; only one of them graduates from college. Of these four people, one left school without even graduating

[35] *Ibid.*, p. xii.

from high school and three of them graduated from high school. Of these same four people, two entered college but one of these dropped out along the way. Thus, one of the four graduated from college. Consequently, some say we have a considerable distance to go before we can say we are doing well as to reducing the number who drop out before completing a college education.[36]

### Drug Abuse

Though the use of drugs has a long history, the problem of drug abuse by students became a major social concern in America during the late 1960s and early 1970s. Prior to recent years, drug abuse had been regarded as largely a ghetto problem affecting disadvantaged youth. But in recent years drug usage has spread through American society, including urban and suburban communities with primarily white youth populations.

The recent increase in the use of drugs by some children and youth appears to be related to a combination of several factors. Some speculate that increased drug use is related to observation by youth of widespread adult acceptance of social drinking, cigarette smoking, and mood-altering pills. Some attribute increased drug use to boredom of some young people, rebellion by others, and searching for escapes from society by still others. Some think increased drug use by the young stems in part from quests for new experiences and attempts to arrive at new cosmic philosophies. Still others think that the spread of the use of drugs stems largely from youth anxiety to be accepted by friends and to belong to the current youth culture.

Presently, reliable statistics on drug users and abusers among students are hard to come by. Complicating any calculations are the varying patterns of drug use and the wide variety among currently available drugs.

For instance, one classification of possible patterns of drug use by students includes the experimenter, the dabbler, the social smoker, the pan-drug user, and the abuser.[37] The experimenter may try a drug once or a dozen times and then quit. The dabbler may smoke marijuana perhaps once or twice a week. The social smoker may use marijuana frequently on social occasions, but not allow it to interfere with staying in school or working on a job. The pan-drug user indiscriminately and constantly uses a variety of drugs. The abuser chronically and regularly uses marijuana, hashish, amphetamines, and LSD, or turns on with the notorious drug heroin. (But some observers believe *any* use of drugs constitutes abuse and regard all users as abusers.)

The question of the extent of drug abuse is complicated by con-

[36] U.S. Office of Education, *Digest of Educational Statistics,* 1971 Edition (Washington, D.C.: U.S. Government Printing Office, 1972), p. 8.
[37] TIME Education Program, *A TIME Guide to Drugs and the Young,* undated, pp. 3, 4.

Due to increased drug use among seventh to twelfth graders, many states have instituted compulsory drug education programs in their schools.

troversies concerning the relative harmfulness of drugs. There is no doubt in the minds of experts that heroin is addictive and destructive; there is also clear evidence that heroin users repeatedly turn to crime to support their habit. The use of LSD and similar hard drugs is also broadly condemned. But the extent of the harmfulness of marijuana is argued hotly. The legalization of marijuana is opposed by many and defended by some. Its opponents argue that marijuana involves as yet unknown health hazards, that widespread habitual use might develop a passive and fatalistic population, that it is bad enough to have alcohol as an intoxicant in American society without legalizing a second escape mechanism. Those who support the legalization of marijuana usually do not contend that marijuana is harmless. But they do point to its widespread use by millions of Americans and claim that if marijuana were legalized, its appeal to the young as a kind of forbidden fruit would be reduced.

*A TIME Guide to Drugs and the Young* estimates that there are roughly 100,000 heroin addicts in the nation. As to marijuana:

A conservative White House staff estimate recently revealed that at least 5,000,000 Americans have used marijuana alone. Dr. Stanley Yolles, Director of the National Institute of Mental Health, puts the total far higher: at least 12 million, and perhaps even 20 million, have used marijuana at least once. By the time adolescents become college students, some 25% to 40% have at least tried it, Yolles adds.

Yolles estimates that abusers account for less than 10% of all those who use marijuana—a far cry from the level sometimes claimed by alarmists, and many fewer than the nation's estimated 6,000,000 alcoholics, but still a serious number, which may include as many as 2,000,000 people.[38]

How many of these millions are children and youth is currently unknown. A 1972 estimate by a New York State Commission claimed that 45 percent of the students in the tenth through twelfth grades and 20 percent of those in the seventh through ninth grade in New York City were "currently users of some psychoactive drug." By "users," the commission referred to more than "just weekenders" or occasional users. The Commission's estimate for the state's next largest cities—Albany, Buffalo, Rochester, Syracuse, and Yonkers—was 25 percent of youngsters in grades ten through twelve and 10 percent in grades seven through nine. For suburban New York State areas, the estimate was 25 percent of students in the junior and senior grades in high school. For rural areas, 10 percent of twelfth graders were estimated to be drug users.[39] The State Commission recommended drug education in the curriculum of the New York schools. By the end of 1972, twenty-four states had instituted compulsory drug education programs in their schools. But evaluation of results was often lacking.

A variety of federal government agencies and business and civic organizations are producing materials on drug abuse. Some materials are helpful but other materials may do more harm than good. To learn of sources of information, to acquire material, and to obtain descriptions of school programs, an initial step for the beginning teacher might well be a request for general information directed to the National Coordinating Council on Drug Abuse Education and Information, Inc., Suite 212, 1211 Connecticut Avenue, N.W., Washington, D.C. 20036. Teachers might also familiarize themselves with the 1973 report of the National Commission on Marijuana and Drug Abuse which contended that the nation's most serious drug problem was not marijuana but instead remained compulsive use of alcohol. It makes good sense for a teacher to have his facts straight, to be honest and convincing, to understand current terminol-

[38] *Ibid.*, pp. 2, 4.
[39] "Forty-five Percent of High School Pupils Here Said to Take Drugs," *New York Times*, October 13, 1972, p. 22.

ogy, and to recognize the social and psychological factors involved in the current drug problem.[40]

## HOW THE NEEDS OF LEARNERS ARE ALIKE

Throughout this chapter emphasis has been placed on how learners differ because of the inescapable fact of individuality. But individuality does not mean that no likenesses among people exist, including among learners in schools. There do exist basic human needs or urges or drives. Some of these are clearly physical, some are related to ego satisfaction, some arise through the social nature of man, and some occur because of man's insistent desire to know. For instance, Abraham H. Maslow, in *Motivation and Personality,* has described certain basic needs.[41] A student of Maslow's work has charted his hierarchy of needs (Figure 14-1).

Yet even with respect to such recognized human needs, one must recognize variation in intensity of a need among different individuals. The strength of the drives differ from learner to learner. Some categories of needs may be so weak in any one person as to approach the point of disappearance.

One of the verified laws in the behavioral sciences upon which educators can rely is that of individuality.

## DISCUSSION

1. Why do schools group on the basis of age? What is the case for and against the use of age grouping?
2. In what ways have intelligence tests made an important difference in American life? What have been some of the social results of using intelligence quotients?
3. What are some possible meanings of intelligence? What seems a reasonable definition?
4. What is the point of view of the advocates of "nature"? Of "nurture"?
5. What seems to be the relationship of social class and ethnic backgrounds to scores on intelligence tests? What are the theories that attempt to account for the results? Which theories seem to have the greatest scientific support?
6. What are the dangers of abuse of IQ scores by teachers and parents?
7. What are the major categories of human intelligence? How reliable do they appear to be?
8. What is the case for teaching the educable mentally retarded child in a special education class rather than absorbing him in a "regular" class? Is there a case for teaching the "slow learner" of an IQ range of 70 to 90 in a special class rather

---

[40] See also Pharmaceutical Manufacturers Association, "Identification of Drug Users," *Teaching About Drugs, A Curriculum Guide, K-12.* The guide is available through The American School Health Association, P.O. Box 416, Kent, Ohio 44240.

[41] Abraham H. Maslow, *Motivation and Personality* (New York: Harper & Row, 1970), pp. 35–58.

**FIGURE 14-1 Maslow's Hierarchy of Needs**

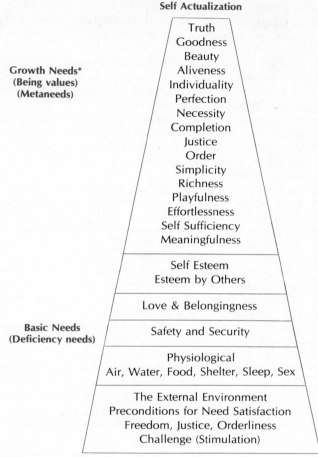

Self Actualization

Growth Needs*
(Being values)
(Metaneeds)

Truth
Goodness
Beauty
Aliveness
Individuality
Perfection
Necessity
Completion
Justice
Order
Simplicity
Richness
Playfulness
Effortlessness
Self Sufficiency
Meaningfulness

Self Esteem
Esteem by Others

Love & Belongingness

Basic Needs
(Deficiency needs)

Safety and Security

Physiological
Air, Water, Food, Shelter, Sleep, Sex

The External Environment
Preconditions for Need Satisfaction
Freedom, Justice, Orderliness
Challenge (Stimulation)

*Growth needs are all of equal importance (not hierarchical).
From *The Third Force: The Psychology of Abraham Maslow* by Frank Goble. Copyright © 1970 by Thomas Jefferson Research Center. All rights reserved. Reprinted by permission of Grossman Publishers.

than a "regular" class? Should the highly gifted be taught in separate classes or in relatively homogeneous classes with their fellow students?

9. Do you know of any recent legislation in the area of special education? What have been the results of earlier legislative decisions for education? What are recent court decisions on educating the retarded and the handicapped?

10. What special services are available to your school district's classroom teachers in serving the needs of children with special problems?

11. What constitutes giftedness? At what measurable level with respect to IQ does giftedness begin? Do you consider this accurate or arbitrary?

12. What are the arguments for and against homogeneous versus heterogeneous grouping in school? Is there a middle position? What types of groupings are most defensible?

13. What are the arguments for and against the use of acceleration by schools? The use of retention? Does supporting evidence for any of the positions in controversy exist?

14. To what extent are intelligence and creativity synonymous? To what extent do they differ?

15. What are some ways of developing creativity in elementary school? In high school? In higher education?

16. What are some common sense things a teacher can do to reduce an individual's physical handicap through adaptation of the school environment?

17. What are some characteristics of "positive" or "healthy" behavior? Why are these sometimes of less concern to the new teacher than negative or unhealthy manifestations of behavior?

18. Essentially, who is the juvenile delinquent? What characterizes him?

19. What do we know of possible ways of working against juvenile delinquency? What can the community contribute? What can education contribute?

20. Essentially, what are the characteristics of the dropout? How does he differ from the young person who stays in school?

21. How serious is the dropout problem? Is the problem of dropping out shifting from the secondary school level to the college level? What is the argument of those like Paul Goodman and Theodore Roszak who reject current concern over dropouts?

22. What is the case for college as an avenue to a more satisfying life as described by The Carnegie Commission on Higher Education?

23. What is your own appraisal as to how well or badly we are doing with respect to dropping out of school and college?

24. What are the current patterns of drug use? What appear to be the facts as to the extent of drug use by the population as a whole and by students in particular? What is the nature of the debate on legalization of marijuana?

25. Is there a legitimate difference between drug "use" and drug "abuse"?

26. To what extent are the needs of learners alike? Different? Do the common needs of learners invalidate the claim that one of the verified laws in the behavioral sciences is the law of individuality?

## INVOLVEMENT

1. The next time you visit a school look particularly for whether or not the school provides "natural" groupings by way of the dimensions of social class, ethnic background, community background, age, homogeneous ability grouping, etc. According to your observations, do the resultant groupings markedly reduce the degree of heterogeneity?

2. Get acquainted with the nature of intelligence tests either from psychology of education books or from examining actual intelligence tests.

3. Report on your own experiences with the influence of intelligence testing on life decisions. Listen to the reports of others attempting the same analysis. What seem to be some of the implications concerning the use of intelligence tests in American life?

4. Carry on some careful investigation of the influences of social class, community background, and ethnic backgrounds — including racial backgrounds — on scores

in intelligence tests. Take into account such problems as the criticism that tests are not "culture free" or "culture fair."

5. Take advantage of possible opportunities to visit classes which reflect the various categories as to intelligence reported in this chapter. Include special education classes. In what way do these differ from "regular" classes?
6. Interview a teacher involved in special education. Why was he attracted to this area and what does he see as its place in the total educational program?
7. Interview an experienced classroom teacher to get his perception of the differences that exist among children who collectively have been labeled "slow learners."
8. Visit a class where the teacher is working with the gifted. Find out what modern concepts are being used. How is the teacher of the gifted meeting the special needs of the learner?
9. Attempt to get at the "feeling level" with respect to homogeneous grouping by discussing candidly your own reactions to a possible proposal by your instructor that the group hereafter be taught by him in section groups according to intellectual ability.
10. Conduct a panel on such controversial issues as homogeneous versus heterogeneous grouping and questions of acceleration and retention. Attempt to clarify the case for approaches and recommendations.
11. Share your own experiences with others as to similarities or differences between creativity and intelligence.
12. Develop a set of suggestions applying particularly to your own subject field and/or level with respect to developing creativity in students.
13. Develop a list of common sense things you would do in a classroom to compensate for the physical handicaps of young people.
14. Visit social agencies in your community and nearby institutions for juvenile delinquents in order to get some exposure to the problem of juvenile delinquency. Visit court sessions. Talk to community workers and police officials, consult experienced teachers. Attempt to build your own program for combating juvenile delinquency.
15. Invite to class for interaction with your group the most knowledgeable people concerning juvenile delinquency available to you.
16. Talk with a guidance counselor about the problem of the dropout in the schools with which you are best acquainted. Consider with him what the schools might do to retain students. Should they? Is there a case for those who advocate dropping out rather than captivity in programs of "compulsory mis-education"? How should school programs be improved to reduce the desire to drop out?
17. Obtain reliable information on drug use. After study of such materials, carry on full and frank discussion of the nature and extent of drug use in the communities with which you are most familiar. Attempt to define approaches to abuse of drugs which should be sponsored by schools and community agencies.
18. Develop your own summary of how individuals are alike and how different. What commonalities and what diversities exist?

## FURTHER READING

Alexander, Theron. *Human Development in an Urban Age.* Englewood Cliffs, N.J.: Prentice-Hall, 1973. Fundamental concepts of human development. Emphasis on the relationship between social structures and the individual in an urban society.

Bachman, Jerald G., Swayzer Green, and Illona Wirtanen. *Dropping Out—Problem or Symptom?* Ann Arbor, Mich.: Institute for Social Research, The University of Michigan, 1972. New insights into the experiences and conditions affecting dropping out of high school as compared to staying in school.

Biehler, Robert. *Psychology Applied to Teaching.* Boston: Houghton Mifflin, 1971. A comprehensive and up-to-date textbook in educational psychology which encourages the reader to think about his development as an educator.

Craig, Eleanor. *P.S. Your Not Listening.* New York: Richard Baron, 1972. Experiences with a transitional class to prepare emotionally disturbed children to return to regular classrooms.

Drug Abuse Survey Project. *Dealing with Drug Abuse.* New York: Praeger, 1972. A report to the Ford Foundation by the Drug Abuse Survey Project which comprehensively reviews the entire drug problem, including the nature of the drugs and an analysis of addiction, rehabilitation, and treatment programs.

Freedman, Jonathan L., J. Merrill Carlsmith, and David O. Sears. *Social Psychology.* Englewood Cliffs, N.J.: Prentice-Hall, 1970. A textbook in social psychology organized around important behaviors such as affiliation, conformity, attitude change, compliance, etc.

Girdano, Daniel A. and Dorothy D. Girdano. *Drug Education: Content and Methods.* Reading, Mass.: Addison-Wesley, 1972. A presentation of knowledge related to the content of a drug education course and a guide to the presentation of information through methods, activities, and discussion topics.

Gowan, John C. and E. Paul Torrance (Eds.). *Educating the Ablest.* Itasca, Ill.: F. E. Peacock, 1971. A book of readings on programs and curricula for gifted children.

Johnson, Lloyd. *Drugs and American Youth.* Ann Arbor, Mich.: Institute for Social Research, The University of Michigan, 1972. Attitudes related to drug use among a nationwide sample of young men during and after the high school years.

Jones, Reginald L. (Ed.). *Problems and Issues in the Education of Exceptional Children.* Boston: Houghton Mifflin, 1971. Emphasis on areas of disagreement and conflicts in the field of the education of exceptional children.

Joseph, Stephen M., (Ed.). *The Me Nobody Knows.* New York: Avon, 1969. Writings by ghetto children which not only achieved publication but became the theme for a theatre production.

Long, N. J., W. C. Morse, and R. G. Newman (Eds.). *Conflict in the Classroom.* Belmont, Calif.: Wadsworth Publishing, 1971. A handbook on helping children with their emotional problems.

McCandless, Boyd R. *Adolescents: Behavior and Development.* New York: Dryden Press, 1970. A treatment of adolescence, including clinical material and case histories.

Raubinger, Frederick M. and Harold G. Rowe (Eds.). *The Individual and Education: Some Contemporary Issues.* New York: Macmillan, 1968. Articles on the individual and his work, how individuality is being threatened, and how teachers can help preserve the integrity of the individual in an increasingly nonpersonal educational system.

Rothman, Esther. *The Angel Inside Went Sour.* New York: David McKay, 1970. An account of ten years of work in a public school devoted to troubled teenage girls who can't be contained in a regular high school. The experiences of a principal in attempting to meet the problems of such girls are reported.

Torrance, E. Paul and R. E. Myers. *Creative Learning and Teaching.* New York: Dodd, Mead, 1970. Aids to elementary school teachers on helping children to think creatively.

## SELECTED AUDIO-VISUAL MATERIALS

*The Child Beyond* (Audio tape, 30 min., University of Texas: National Center for Audio Tapes, 1961). An educational series of 13 programs, semidocumentary in nature, with dramatized interludes and discussions by experts on the exceptional child's area of difficulty and the avenues of adjustment open to him. Selected titles: "The Hurdles too High"; "Hear No Evil, See No Evil, Speak No Evil"; "Neither Devilish nor Divine"; "The Child Out of Step."

*Dialectics of a Dropout* (16 mm film, 9 min., color, Centron Educational Films, 1971). Probes the world of the dropout. A commentary on the quality of contemporary life and personal solutions to the stress and frustration of modern society.

*Dropping Out—The Road to Nowhere,* Pt. I, World Today; Pt. II, World Tomorrow (35 mm filmstrip, Pt. I-85 frs/record, Pt. II-85 frs/record, color, Guidance Associates, 1966). Documents that dropouts can expect lower pay and poorer jobs. Points out the rapid disappearance of unskilled jobs and stresses the necessity of education as a job credential in the automated future.

*Drug Abuse: Everybody's Hang-Up* (16 mm film, 12 min., color, National Education Association, 1970). Dramatically depicts the problem of drug abuse among young people. For stimulating discussion by students, teachers, parents, administrators, and community groups. All films on drugs should be screened by the teacher before being shown.

*Grouping Students for Effective Learning* (35 mm filmstrip, 44 frs/captions, color, Bel-Mort Films, 1960). Considers what happens when students are grouped according to age, ability grouping, or flexible grouping.

*Hey, What About Us?* (16 mm film, 57 min., b. & w., ETS/PS: Indiana University, 1968). Depicts job situations after high school for the majority who don't go to college. Reviews the functions of counselors, industry training, employment agencies, and the military.

*How Do Children Think?* (16 mm film, 30 min., b. & w., BBC-TV: Time-Life, Inc., 1967). Piaget's theory on how children think is discussed. Explanations and examples are given of preconceptual, intuitive, concrete, and formal operations in the process.

*IQ—Questionable Criterion* (16 mm film, 13 min., color, Stuart Finley, Inc., 196-). Shows the utilization of all pertinent information, besides testing, in evaluation. Points out the fallacies and dangers of using one test to identify and categorize the complex human being.

*Jimmy* (16 mm film, 29 min., b. & w., National Education Association, 1966). The story of a high school sophomore dropout. Documents his discussions with his teachers, friends, guidance counselor, and employers.

*High Wall* (16 mm film, 30 min., b. & w., McGraw-Hill, 1952). Uses a case history involving teenage gangs to present analysis of one kind of background that fosters bigotry and antisocial attitudes.

*Mike Makes His Mark* (16 mm film, 29 min., color, National Education Association, 1955). Mike hated school and challenged it by making an ugly mark on the front of the school. The mark remained on his conscience and on the wall until his resentment was changed through the school program.

*More Different Than Alike* (16 mm film, 30 min., color, National Education Association, 1967).  Depicts some unique and creative techniques which provide for individual learning differences. The progress each student is making—a special school for the slow learner—a learning center in which high school students have access to materials and technology for self-instruction—a program of student-planned work schedules and learning projects.

*Understanding the Gifted* (16 mm film, 33 min., color, Churchill Films, 1965).  Uses student participants to point up four primary traits common to the gifted—ability to abstract and generalize; diverse and complex interests; the urge to create; and a well defined sense of ethics and values.

# FIFTEEN

# How do social problems affect education?

Why should teachers be concerned about new developments in the social order? Many students of the social foundations of education (comparative education and the history, philosophy, and sociology of education) have answered the question in sober and pedantic terms. But no one has said it better than Harold R. W. Benjamin in *The Saber-Tooth Curriculum*, a satirical fable about imaginary cavemen who developed the first program of education.

The fable of the Saber-Tooth Curriculum[1] tells of New-Fist, a thoughtful caveman who asked himself what the tribesmen must know in order to live with "full bellies, warm backs, and minds free from fear." He concluded that they had to catch fish with their bare hands, club the little wooly horses, and drive away the saber-tooth tigers with fire. So New-Fist developed a sensible curriculum for the children who lived in the cavemen's country. The curriculum stressed the three fundamentals—fish-grabbing with the bare hands, wooly-horse clubbing, and saber-tooth-tiger-scaring with fire. New-Fist took his children with him as he went about and he gave them an opportunity to practice these three subjects. As the children grew older they had an advantage over other children who had not been educated systematically. So other intelligent members of the tribe imitated New-Fist and the teaching of fish-grabbing, horse-clubbing, and tiger-scaring became recognized as the heart of good education. The tribe prospered and had adequate meat,

[1] Adapted from Harold R. W. Benjamin's (J. Abner Peddiwell) *The Saber-Tooth Curriculum* (New York: McGraw-Hill, 1939).

skins, and security. The curriculum fitted neatly into the demands of the social order in the cave realm.

But a glacier came down from the north and life in the country of the cavemen changed markedly. The life of the caveman which had once been safe and happy became insecure and disturbing. For the glacier melted and dumped dirt and gravel into the creek which became muddy. It was no longer possible to catch fish with the bare hands because the fish could not be seen in the muddy water. Even the tribesmen who had studied advanced fish-grabbing with their bare hands in the secondary schools and even the university graduates who had studied ichthyology could not grab fish with bare hands.

The melting waters from the glacier made the ground marshy so the little wooly horses went east to the dry open plains, far away from the cavemen's country. However, their places were taken by antelopes who were so speedy no one could get near enough to them to club them. The best trained horse-clubbers of the tribe returned home empty-handed though they used all the techniques which the schools had taught them. But they couldn't club horses when there were no horses left to club.

As a final disruption of paleolithic life and education, the dampness gave the saber-tooth tigers pneumonia and most of them died, while the rest crept south to the desert. But with the advancing ice sheet came ferocious glacier bears. These bears were not afraid of fire, could not be driven away even by the best methods taught in the tiger-scaring courses. The tribe was now in deep trouble for there was no fish or meat for food, no hides for clothing, and no security from the hairy death that walked the trails both day and night.

New-Fist had long ago been gathered by the Great Mystery to the Land of Sunset far down the creek. Other intelligent tribesmen devised nets for catching fish, snares for capturing antelopes, and deep pits for trapping bears. They called these new developments "inventions" and the knowledge of these new devices spread throughout the tribe. The tribesmen worked hard at making fish nets, setting antelope snares, and digging bear pits, which were essential to the tribe's prosperity and safety. Meanwhile the schools went on teaching fish-grabbing with the bare hands, wooly-horse clubbing, and saber-tooth-tiger-scaring with fire. So some intelligent tribesmen, whom author Benjamin refers to as "radicals," suggested changes in the school curriculum. Let us listen to the dialogue that ensued, as reported by Harold Benjamin:

"Fishnet-making and using, antelope-snare construction and operation, and bear catching and killing," they pointed out, "require intelligence and skills—things we claim to develop in schools. They are also activities we need to know. Why can't the schools teach them?"

But most of the tribe, and particularly the wise old men who controlled the school, smiled indulgently at this suggestion. "That wouldn't be *education*," they said gently.

"But why wouldn't it be?" asked the radicals.

"Because it would be mere training," explained the old men patiently. "With all the intricate details of fish-grabbing, horse-clubbing, and tiger-scaring—the standard cultural subjects—the school curriculum is too crowded now. We can't add these fads and frills of net-making, antelope-snaring, and—of all things—bear-killing. Why, at the very thought, the body of the great New-Fist, founder of our paleolithic educational system, would turn over in its burial cairn. What we need to do is to give our young people a more thorough grounding in the fundamentals. Even the graduates of the secondary schools don't know the art of fish-grabbing in any complete sense nowadays, they swing their horse clubs awkwardly too, and as for the old science of tiger-scaring—well, even the teachers seem to lack the real flair for the subject which we oldsters got in our teens and never forgot."

"But, damn it," exploded one of the radicals, "how can any person with good sense be interested in such useless activities? What is the point of trying to catch fish with the bare hands when it just can't be done any more? How can a boy learn to club horses when there are no horses left to club? And why in hell should children try to scare tigers with fire when the tigers are dead and gone?"

"Don't be foolish," said the wise old men, smiling most kindly smiles. "We don't teach fish-grabbing to grab fish; we teach it to develop a generalized agility which can never be developed by mere training. We don't teach horse-clubbing to club horses; we teach it to develop a generalized strength in the learner which he can never get from so prosaic and specialized a thing as antelope-snare-setting. We don't teach tiger-scaring to scare tigers; we teach it for the purpose of giving that noble courage which carries over into all the affairs of life and which can never come from so base an activity as bear-killing."

All the radicals were silenced by this statement, all except the one who was most radical of all. He felt abashed, it is true, but he was so radical that he made one last protest.

"But—but anyway," he suggested, "You will have to admit that times have changed. Couldn't you please try these other more up-to-date activities? Maybe they have some educational value after all?"

Even the man's fellow radicals felt this was going a little too far.

The wise old men were indignant. Their kindly smiles faded. "If you had any education yourself," they said severely, "you would know that the essence of true education is timelessness. It is something that endures through changing conditions like a solid rock standing squarely and firmly in the middle of a raging torrent. You must know that there are some eternal verities, and the saber-tooth curriculum is one of them."[2]

In *The Saber-Tooth Curriculum,* Benjamin twitted not only the traditionalists but also the progressives. Though the traditionalists insisted that "the essence of true education is timelessness," the progressives did no better when confronted with the new social demands on the cave realm. The progressives simply transferred fish-grabbing with the bare hands from the heated school pool to the banks of the real creek. They described the new approach as creative fish-grabbing. But it was still no

[2] Harold R. W. Benjamin (J. Abner Peddiwell), pp. 41–44. If you wish to learn more of the perils of the cavemen and of the educational system they developed, you may want to read the rest of *The Saber-Tooth Curriculum,* q. v.

*Los Alamos Scientific Laboratory*

Explosion of the first atomic bomb, July 16, 1945.

longer possible to grab agile and intelligent fish in muddy waters with the bare hands. Despite creative tiger-scaring through waving fire brands before the caged and ancient toothless tigers which were the last of their kind, the giant bears, which were unafraid of fire, still prowled the trails. But no one in caveman education recognized the threat of the giant bears or even acknowledged their existence.

The message of *The Saber-Tooth Curriculum* is clear. Whatever our philosophies and whatever our methodologies, we in education cannot ignore developments in the social order. If we insist on ignoring social developments, we imperil our society and the people who comprise it.[3, 4]

The glacier comes at Americans today not from the North but from developments in the social order. Today the glacier brings with it the problems of modern warfare, the quality of the environment, and race relations. This chapter considers these three developments in the social order. Obviously, there are other significant developments; but problems of the international setting, of pollution and population, and of race relations are among the most critical for our survival.

[3] Robert M. Bruker (ed.), *Wakan: The Spirit of Harold Benjamin* (Minneapolis: Burgess Publishing, 1968). If the wit and wisdom of Benjamin appeal to you, you may wish to read this collection of his writings.

[4] Harold R. W. Benjamin, *The Sage of Petaluma* (New York: McGraw-Hill, 1965). This is a semi-autobiographical book which is purportedly a biography of J. Abner Peddiwell, to whom Benjamin attributes *The Saber-Tooth Curriculum*.

Hiroshima evidenced the atomic bomb's destructive powers.

*U.S. Air Force Photo*

## CONFLICTS IN THE INTERNATIONAL SETTING

### International Problems

To some scholars the paramount problem of modern man is the avoidance of nuclear war through resolving international conflicts. Today one problem that faces the world is the tremendous increase in destructive power which has taken place in the second half of the twentieth century. After years of research and of development of nuclear weapons, the power of the tremendous bomb which destroyed Hiroshima and, in effect, ended World War II in 1945 seems insignificant in comparison to the potential power for destruction possessed by both the Soviet Union and the United States. Nor are nuclear weapons the monopoly of the two superpowers. In 1970 the Stockholm International Peace Research Institute, financed by the Swedish government and chaired by the political economist Gunnar Myrdal, supplied some dramatic facts. The Institute reported that the world's nuclear stockpile amounted to about 50,000 megatons and thus represented about 15 tons of TNT per person on the globe or about 60 tons of TNT per person in the NATO and Warsaw Pact nations taken together. Military expenditures by the world were approximately equivalent to the total income of the lower half of the world's population. A fear haunted mankind that a local or regional war might ignite a total world war and destroy the planet.

So, in the United States in the late 1960s, a counterforce to the acceleration of the Southeast Asian war and the expansion of the military establishment developed. The counterforce had many components ranging from absolutist pacifists to those who regard militarism as too expensive, and ranging from destroyers of draft office files to Congressmen appraising national priorities. Many movements contributed to the counterforce, including widespread youth opposition to the war in Vietnam, spearheaded by a small yet influential segment of the youth population which demonstrated and campaigned against war. One wing of the dissenters took to the streets in the 1967 march on the Pentagon and in the struggle on the lakefront of Chicago during the 1968 Democratic National Convention. Another wing of the activist group crusaded through political involvement that took such forms as support of Senator Eugene McCarthy in his unsuccessful bid for the 1968 Presidential nomination and the development and conduct of the October 1969 Mobilization Day. The counterforce against war has also been supported by many older persons, including those who felt that the quality of American life was deteriorating as funds which might have been spent to reduce urban slums, support schools, improve the natural environment, train and employ more blacks, etc., were appropriated for military purposes.

In 1970 President Nixon announced that American troops had crossed the border of Cambodia. Campuses were rocked by protests. By the end of June 1970, American troops left Cambodia. But the war in southeast Asia continued.

In the early 1970s, activities by the counterforce against war were markedly reduced. Some observers attributed the reduction of protest and dissent to the steady withdrawal of American troops from Vietnam during the early 1970s. Some believed that a powerful factor was changes in draft procedures, which sharply reduced military calls upon youth. A program of acceleration of conflict in Vietnam which marked the Johnson administration was succeeded during the first Nixon administration by a program of gradual withdrawal of troops accompanied by continued bombing and by mining of harbors in North Vietnam and by supplying of military equipment to South Vietnam.

One of the issues in the 1972 Presidential campaign in the United States was termination of American participation in the unpopular Vietnam war. George McGovern, the candidate of the Democratic Party, called for immediate withdrawal. During his first term, President Nixon fostered negotiations to end the war through his envoy Henry Kissinger. In the closing weeks of the Presidential campaign of 1972, Kissinger indicated that a peace agreement was very near. McGovern charged that President Nixon had only pretended to be near a negotiated settlement of the Vietnam war. For months following the election of 1972, political commentators speculated on the influence of negotiations toward a peace in Vietnam upon the landslide victory which returned President Nixon

Stock, Boston

Many young people attempted to help bring about change through the established political system during the campaigns of the early 1970s.

to office. Peace negotiations broke down and the United States resumed bombing of Hanoi in North Vietnam. In 1973, shortly after President Nixon's second term began, a peace agreement was reached and a cease-fire ensued.

However, the bombing of Cambodia continued until August 15, 1973, when congressional action forced its termination. Meanwhile, the American people learned, to their surprise, that they had not been informed that the bombing of Cambodia, presumably a neutral nation, had begun in March, 1969, fourteen months before the American troop invasion of that nation.

But the Vietnam war was not the only fever spot of international tension across the world during the two Nixon administrations. Hostilities frequently flared between Israel and the Arab world as the Israelis continued to hold the land they had taken after the Six-Day War of 1967. Arab guerrillas developed raid tactics, which included hijacking and dynamiting American and European planes and the murder of Israeli athletes at the 1972 Olympic games in Europe. In 1973, war broke out between Arab states and Israel. Secretary of State Kissinger negotiated a cease-fire in November, 1973. The world of the early 1970s avoided the fearful holocaust of total war.

In search of better international relationships, President Nixon journeyed in 1972 to both the People's Republic of China and to the Soviet Union. Treaties to limit armaments grew out of these visits. Negotiations on arms reductions continued and cultural exchanges were increased. Soviet Union leader Brezhnev visited the U.S. in 1973.

Keeping peace in such a world is a difficult business. Notwithstanding the efforts of the United Nations, which stubbornly continued its unspectacular work despite the handicap of lack of sufficient funds, revolution and violence continued to haunt the world. The economic gap between the developed and underdeveloped nations stubbornly increased. The existence of the economic gap coincided with a population explosion characterized by higher birth rates in the underdeveloped nations than in the developed lands. Observers in our society recognized that there was considerable social dynamite lying about any international scene in which the gap between the rich and the poor grew wider while the birth rates of the poorer people rose.

### International Understanding and Survival

That relevant education of American children and youth in the middle 1970s must deal with international relations and associated problems of war and peace seems self-evident. The survival of the world is related to international relationships; it is not mere rhetoric to point out that the physical existence of mankind depends upon the solution of our international problems. International decisions in this area quite literally mean the difference between life and death for many human beings. It is essential that all men learn to view themselves and their nations in the larger context of international understanding. Inclusion of international education in the curriculum of American schools is imperative.

## PROBLEMS OF PEOPLE AND POLLUTION

### Population

There are other perils to survival on this planet than nuclear war alone. Though less dramatic than the mushroom cloud of the atomic bomb, the population explosion and the pollution of the surrounding environment imperil mankind.

The population explosion raises the brutal question as to whether there will be sufficient space for man on the earth unless effective population controls are put into practice. The facts of world population growth are hard to live with but they are real. Paul R. Ehrlich presents the facts dramatically:

It has been estimated that the human population of 6000 B.C. was about five million people, taking perhaps one million years to get there from two and a half million. The population did not reach 500 million until almost 8,000 years later—about 1650 A.D. This means it doubled roughly once every thousand years or

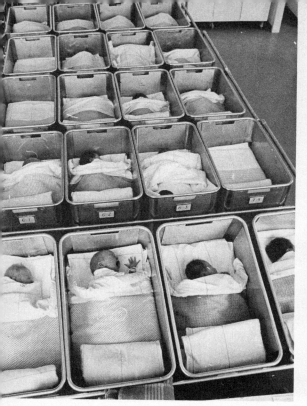

Will there be breathing space for everyone?

so. It reached a billion people around 1850, doubling in some 200 years. It took only 80 years or so for the next doubling, as the population reached two billion around 1930. We have not completed the next doubling to four billion yet, but we now have well over three billion people. The doubling time at present seems to be about 37 years. Quite a reduction in doubling times: 1,000,000 years, 1,000 years, 200 years, 80 years, 37 years. Perhaps the meaning of a doubling time of around 37 years is best brought home by a theoretical exercise. Let's examine what might happen on the absurd assumption that the population continued to double every 37 years into the indefinite future.

If growth continued at that rate for about 900 years, there would be some 60,000,000,000,000,000 people on the face of the earth. Sixty million billion people. This is about 100 persons for each square yard of the Earth's surface, land and sea.[5]

As a 1969 Presidential message to Congress on the U.S. population problem and the world population crisis pointed out:

Today the world population is three and one-half billion persons. If this rate of population growth continues, it is likely that the earth will contain over seven billion human beings by the end of this century. . . .

[5] Paul R. Ehrlich, *The Population Bomb* (New York: Ballantine, 1968), p. 18.

It is in the developing nations of the world that population is growing most rapidly today. In these areas we often find rates of natural increase higher than any which have been experienced in all of human history. At present rates, many will double and some may even triple their present populations before the year 2000.

As a result, many already impoverished nations are struggling under a handicap of intense population increase which the industrialized nations never had to bear. Their standards of living are not rising quickly, and the gap between life in the rich nations and life in the poor nations is not closing.[6]

The steepest rates of population increase occur in the poorer and less developed nations. Yet, even in the United States, population experts are expecting about 251 million to 300 million residents by the end of the twentieth century. In 1966 Philip M. Hauser and Martin Taitel, of the University of Chicago, wrote: "The population of the United States . . . is being projected to exceed three hundred million by the turn of the century."[7] They added that the projections utilized conservative assumptions about the future. However, late in 1972 the Census Bureau issued a new set of projections of future population which were strikingly low.

According to the new calculations, the population in the year 2000 could fall short of previous estimates by at least 20 million and by as much as 71 million. The population in that year is currently projected to be between 251 and 300 million. Prior estimates ranged from 271 to 322 million. The present population is 209.3 million.[8]

Thus, even the ablest demographers have found that predicting population figures is a risky business. The critical factor is the changes in family practices which affect the birth rate. As the Commission on Population Growth and the American Future said in 1972:

Even a one-child difference in average family size makes an enormous difference over the decades. A century from now, with continued immigration, the two-child average would result in a population of 350 million [in the United States], while growth at the three-child level would result in nearly a billion.

Demographic events have the quality of persisting over time—for example, the baby-boom generation born after World War II is still working its way through the age structure, with many repercussions. . . .

It takes a long time to affect population growth rates in a democratically and ethically acceptable manner. Even with a two-child average from now on, it would take sixty years or so to achieve a nongrowing population. . . .[9] (See Figure 15-1.)

[6] Message to Congress, July 18, 1969.
[7] Philip M. Hauser and Martin Taitel, "Population Trends—Prologue to Educational Problems." In Edgar L. Morphet and Charles O. Ryan (Eds), *Prospective Changes in Society by 1980* (Denver: Designing Education for the Future, An Eight-State Project, 1967), p. 24.
[8] "Census Estimate at Century's End Cut by 20 Million", *New York Times*, December 18, 1972, p. 1.
[9] U.S. Commission on Population Growth and the American Future, "A Summary of the Final Report and Recommendations" (New York Times Supplement, *Population: The U.S. Problem, the World Crisis*, Population Crisis Committee 1972), p. 6.

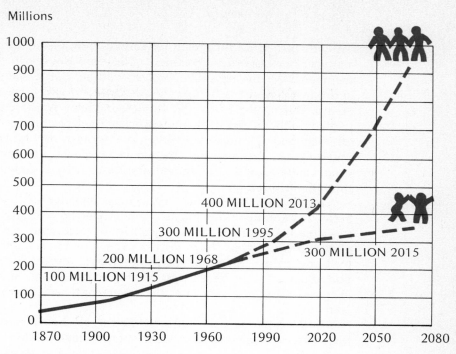

Millions

| | 1870 | 1900 | 1930 | 1960 | 1990 | 2020 | 2050 | 2080 |

400 MILLION 2013

300 MILLION 1995

200 MILLION 1968

300 MILLION 2015

100 MILLION 1915

**FIGURE 15-1 U.S. Population 2- vs. 3-Child Family**

The Report of the Commission on Population Growth and the American Future, *Population and the American Future* (Washington, D.C.: U.S. Government Printing Office, 1972), p. 23.

The population problem in the United States is complicated by the fact that Americans of the year 2000 will live primarily in urban territories. As the Commission said:

In 1970, nearly 70 percent of the United States population was metropolitan—the figure will approach 85 percent by the year 2000. For better or for worse, we are in the process of becoming an almost totally urban society. Most metropolitan growth now results from natural increase, not migration. Thus, the trend toward bigness of metropolitan areas, if undesirable, cannot be substantially checked except as national growth is slowed or stopped.

Migration is from low-income rural areas and abroad to metropolitan areas, from one metropolitan area to another, and from central cities to suburbs. Nearly 40 million or one in five Americans change homes each year. About one in fifteen, a total of 13 million, migrate across county lines.[10]

**Pollution**

At the same time that man is overpopulating the nations of the world, he is increasingly polluting his environment. Recognition of the importance of ecology, the science of the relationships between organisms and their environment, seemed to burst suddenly upon Americans in the 1970s.

[10] *Ibid.*, p. 6.

True, there had been concern for conservation throughout the twentieth century; one American President, Theodore Roosevelt, was largely remembered for his efforts to protect wildlife, halt exhaustion of timber and mineral supplies by private interests, and add lands to public ownership. During the 1930s, the Tennessee Valley Authority (TVA) accompanied public power development with a policy of conservation of natural resources. Popular depression-era writers on economics, such as Stuart Chase, deplored the creation of ravaged lands through the fumes from smelters and condemned the unrestricted gouging of the soil through strip mines.

In the early 1960s, one of the most effective of the pioneers for a better environment was Rachel Carson. Her book, *Silent Spring,* dramatized the threat of the many insecticides which man used to protect his plant life—and which have proven to be lethal poisons to a much wider bird and animal kingdom than bothersome insects. News weeklies reported that she was an alarmist and her message was, at first, deprecated or ignored. But a decade later she was recognized for the wisdom of her warnings.

In the opening pages of *Silent Spring,* Rachel Carson wrote of some future spring season in America when the silence of death would prevail.

Some evil spell had settled on the community: mysterious maladies swept the flocks of chickens; the cattle and sheep sickened and died. Everywhere was a shadow of death. The farmers spoke of much illness among their families. In the town the doctors had become more and more puzzled by new kinds of sickness appearing among their patients. . . .

There was a strange stillness. The birds, for example—where had they gone? Many people spoke of them puzzled and disturbed. The feeding stations in the backyards were deserted. The few birds seen everywhere were moribund; they trembled violently and could not fly. It was a spring without voices.

On the farms the hens brooded, but no chicks hatched. The farmers complained that they were unable to raise any pigs—the litters were small and the young survived only a few days. The apple trees were coming into bloom but no bees droned among the blossoms, so there was no pollination and there would be no fruit.

The roadsides, once so attractive, were now lined with browned and withered vegetation as though swept by fire. These, too, were silent, deserted by all living things. Even the streams were now lifeless. Anglers no longer visited them, for all the fish had died. . . .

No witchcraft, no enemy action had silenced the rebirth of new life in this stricken world. The people had done it themselves.[11]

By the early 1970s, the problem of pollution and attendant deterioration of the quality of the environment had become so widespread that the nation was shocked into action. The combination of difficulties experienced by all Americans with smoke, sewage, noise, garbage, chemical

[11] Rachel Carson, *Silent Spring* (Boston: Houghton Mifflin, 1962), pp. 1–3.

Improvements in mass transportation will help to reduce pollution caused by automobiles.

the sooner they begin working to attain it, the greater will be their chances of success.[14]

The conclusions as to breakdown and worldwide collapse were criticized by some as "doomsday" claims.[15] Meanwhile, the debate goes on as to what degree of slowdown in the birth rate (perhaps approaching Zero Population Growth) and what leveling off of industrial growth in the developed countries (perhaps approaching Zero Economic Growth) is necessary if "spaceship Earth" is to continue to maintain human life and achieve acceptable living standards. Shortages became apparent when a world-wide energy crisis appeared late in 1973.

### Population, Pollution, and the New Factor—Energy Crises

In American schools, study of pollution by children and youth is developing rapidly. Study of population lags behind because of the persistence of objections by some on religious grounds to full consideration of the issues involved. Yet the two problems, pollution and population,

[14] Donella H. and Dennis L. Meadows et al, *The Limits to Growth: A Report for the Club of Rome's Project on the Predicament of Mankind* (New York: Universe Books, 1972), pp. 23, 24.
[15] "The Big Cleanup," *Newsweek* (June 12, 1972), pp. 36–55.

are necessarily interrelated in American life and indeed on the world scene too. In the mid 1970s, mankind also discovered the relationship of both problems to the energy crisis. Belatedly, educational efforts began.

## RACISM

A third cluster of survival problems confronting Americans in the mid 1970s centers on racism. True, the problem is worldwide, as blacks in South Africa and Rhodesia as well as Indians and Pakistanis living in Great Britain can testify. But, for residents of the United States, our own domestic problem of racism, largely centered upon white-black relationships but also manifested in society's discriminatory treatment of American Indians, Hispano-Americans, and others, is particularly obvious and acute. In Chapter 12, the history of minority group experiences in the United States was briefly sketched. In the present chapter, we will look at the present status of racism in the United States and the strategies for dealing with race relations which are currently proposed and which markedly affect education.

### The Nature of Racism

Racism is essentially the notion that one's own ethnic stock is superior. Racism persists; yet the concept of race itself has mythological characteristics. *The Columbia Encyclopedia* (second edition) began its entry on race as follows:

. . . obsolete division of humanity based on criteria of hair texture and color, of skin color, of head shape and other conspicuous physical features. . . . The classification never worked at all but it had great prestige in the 19th and the early 20th century.[16]

Racism takes the form of denying individuals equal opportunities because of their ethnic stock which is often manifested by a skin color different from the majority. Racism becomes institutionalized through policies of discrimination and segregation. For instance, following the Civil War in the United States and despite amendments to the U.S. Constitution, Negroes were segregated by law in many southern states and by custom in many northern states. Through segregation, they were shut away from an equal share in community life. Segregation to reinforce white dominance took the form of separate schools and colleges for blacks, separate sections in railroad cars, buses, and other forms of transportation, denial of admission to recreational facilities or, if admitted, the

---

[16] William Bridgwater and Elizabeth J. Sherwood, *The Columbia Encyclopedia,* 2d ed. (New York: Columbia University Press, 1950), p. 1632.

provision of a separate section for Negroes in attendance, and even segregation with respect to hospitals, churches, and jails.

## The Struggle over Segregation

Since the 1940s the fight against institutionalized segregation and discrimination has been waged on many fronts. In June, 1941, President Franklin D. Roosevelt created the Fair Employment Practices Committee; clauses against discrimination were included in most governmental contracts. In 1948 a directive by President Harry S. Truman called for an end to segregation in the U.S. military forces. In education the historic step away from the institutionalization of segregation and discrimination came in 1954 with the *Brown v. Board of Education of Topeka* decision, which declared that segregation was "inherently unequal" and a denial of the protection of the fourteenth amendment. The Civil Rights Law of 1964 resulted from a combining of many of the desegregation efforts. The battle has been waged state by state and in community after community; yet progress toward the elimination of segregation has been slow and grudging in both school and society.

Following the 1954 *Brown* decision the struggle against segregation in public schools first took place largely in the South. In the later 1950s, conflicts sometimes occurred in the streets. For instance, in 1957 in Clinton, Tennessee, a school was bombed, and in Little Rock, Arkansas, President Dwight D. Eisenhower ordered federal troops to restore order and to protect the right of nine Negro students to enter Central High School.

Increasingly, however, the struggle between segregationists and integrationists shifted to the courts. Southern school districts often proposed freedom-of-choice plans which placed the burden of desegregation on the children and families which sought changes. In 1968 the U.S. Supreme Court held that school districts had a duty to set up a unitary or single system without racial division. Freedom-of-choice methods were regarded by the Supreme Court as inadequate if they did not end school segregation as rapidly as other methods. School boards and administrations were told that they had a duty to set up unitary systems and eliminate segregation "root and branch."

Slowly and steadily, moderate opinion prevailed in the South and school desegregation moved forward during the 1960s in communities and states which had formerly resisted. Among the tools for desegregation which were used was transportation of white and black students by bus to newly desegregated schools.[17] By 1973 there were fewer black pupils remaining in all-minority schools in the South than in the North.

[17] James C. Harvey and Charles H. Holmes, "Busing and School Desegregation," *Phi Delta Kappan* (May 1972), pp. 540–542, and The United States Commission on Civil Rights, *Your Child and Busing* (U.S. Commission on Civil Rights, May 1972), pp. 8–9.

In the 1970s American problems of desegregation and integration increasingly moved North. Some northern communities had segregated their schools through racial gerrymandering by shifting boundaries related to school attendance in order to insure racial separation. In 1972 political and social controversy focused on busing to achieve school desegregation. Northern communities attempting to achieve school desegregation have sometimes used open enrollment, allowing any child to attend any school in his school district with free transportation provided. Some northern communities also redrew neighborhood boundaries so as to achieve racial balance. One-way busing of blacks into largely white schools was also used. But when two-way busing was initiated, including busing white children into largely black schools or black communities, and when proposals included transporting some suburban white middle class children into black areas, active protest arose in some northern communities.[18]

In 1972 President Richard M. Nixon called for a moratorium on new busing and for emphasis on upgrading neighborhood schools. Bills to this effect were introduced in the U.S. Congress but were not passed during 1972. Some political leaders called for a Constitutional amendment against busing for racial balance. The issue of busing—described by opponents as "massive" or "forced" busing and by supporters as a necessary "tool" in the achievement of desegregation—entered into the 1972 Presidential Campaign. Richard M. Nixon, who opposed "forced busing," defeated George McGovern, who accepted busing as a necessary "tool."

In 1971, in a Charlotte, North Carolina case, the U.S. Supreme Court unanimously upheld the constitutionality of busing, though the Nixon Administration and the Justice Department intervened on the side of the defendant to support the neighborhood school concept. However, the Justices also ruled that this decision did not apply to de facto segregation in the North. In 1972 a Federal District Judge in Richmond, Virginia, declared that the public schools of Richmond and those of two suburban counties must be merged into a single metropolitan district.[19] A United States Court of Appeals reversed the District Court. The Richmond case reached the U.S. Supreme Court in 1973 and the highest court divided 4 to 4, thus striking down a school desegregation plan for Richmond that would have merged white suburbs with the heavily black Virginia city in a single school system. Since the vote was a tie, no precedent was set for future cases, such as the one involving Detroit and its suburbs.

The stage was set for an important decision by the U.S. Supreme Court in 1973 in the case of *Keyes v. School District No. 1* of Denver,

[18] Christopher Jencks, "Busing—The Supreme Court Goes North," *New York Times Magazine* (November 19, 1972), pp. 40–41, 118–121, 125–127.
[19] James C. Harvey and Charles H. Holmes, "Busing and School Desegregation," *Phi Delta Kappan* (May 1972), pp. 541–542.

Colorado. The N.A.A.C.P. Legal Defense Fund argued that Denver was essentially using the same kind of de jure segregation used by Southern school boards. A decision favoring *Keyes* could result in large scale desegregation in the North involving busing among other means of achieving racially mixed schools.

By a vote of 7 to 1, the Supreme Court ruled that a school district with a substantial amount of officially imposed segregation can be forced to desegregate its entire system, not just the schools immediately affected by such techniques as gerrymandering in order to restrict minority children to a few schools. The U.S. Supreme Court sent the case back to a district court, which must decide if Denver school authorities intentionally segregated a substantial portion of the school system. If there is proof of de jure segregation—official action segregating the races—Denver or other northern cities will be required to desegregate the whole system through, for instance, redrawing school boundaries and instituting extensive busing. In the decision against Denver, the United States Supreme Court did not deal with the issue of de facto segregation resulting, for instance, from housing patterns. So court cases in northern communities went forward in 1973 primarily on the basis of the existence of de jure, rather than de facto, segregation.

### Strategies for Achieving Rights

By the 1970s two broad lines of strategy for the improvement of the lot of blacks in the United States had emerged. One continuing strategy called for the replacement of segregation by desegregation, and the achievement of integration. Desegregation occurs when minority group members are physically present and are accorded nondiscriminatory treatment along with majority group members in social settings. But integration means more than just physical presence and nondiscriminatory treatment. Integration involves full acceptance of all persons as individual human beings in a variety of social settings such as employment, schools, housing, and the armed forces. Desegregation and integration has been the historic commitment of such groups as the National Association for the Advancement of Colored People and of such Negro leaders as Roy Wilkins, Executive Secretary of the NAACP; Bayard Rustin, a civil rights spokesman who organized effective and orderly marches upon Washington; and Kenneth B. Clark, a psychologist whose assembling of research was used by the United States Supreme Court in arriving at its decision as to the inherent inequality of segregated schools.

But a new and militant approach to the achievement of the rights of blacks emerged in the late 1960s. It was called black power by its proponents and condemned as black separatism by its opponents. The new approach stressed black awareness and black identity; it called for programs of black studies in colleges and school systems; it supported black control of communities in which blacks lived, rather than integration attempts. Spokesmen included such organizers as H. Rap Brown and Stokely Carmichael; Black Panther spokesmen such as Bobby Seale and Huey Newton; CORE spokesmen such as Roy Innis; and prominent writers such as Eldridge Cleaver and LeRoi Jones (Imamu Amiri Baraka); and university staff members such as Angela Davis and Charles V. Hamilton. Though they often differed from each other in ideologies, strategies, and emphasis, all saw promise in new militant approaches stressing blackness.

The views of proponents of each of these strategies is set forth below, as stated by Roy Wilkins, defending the strategy of desegregation and integration, and Stokely Carmichael and Charles V. Hamilton, defending the strategy of black power.

Roy Wilkins wrote:

To the dismay of at least 95 percent of the Negro-American population, many of the Negro college students to whom nearly everyone looked for new ideas on race advancement have come up with a theory of racial self-segregation.

For all the adult lives of every black American, 40 to 60 years old, the primary goal has been the abolition of obviously unjust racial segregation. No textbooks or philosophical theses are needed to drive this point home. The practical operation of the system is plain enough to a fourth grader. If one separates a minority from the majority culture (and the Negro-American is a distinct and relatively powerless minority), it is easy to build it into a deprived population.

Lily-white politics disfranchises blacks. The latter have no say in the election of men to office, in taxes, in legislation that literally affects their very lives. Lily-whiteism seals off the blacks' living quarters, their recreation, travel, employment, and schools. They are (and have been) ripe for exploitation. The white majority also administers the law and can fasten a criminal label on the black population through convictions and imprisonment.

Aided by the many tentacled communications media, the white majority can build an evil conception into racial policy almost overnight. Heavy tomes by "scholars," textbooks for millions of white children, picture books, tabloid and staid newspapers, magazines, opinion polls, and radio and television all can help create and maintain the net of public opinion that will hobble black people. If one adds the sermons and pastoral advice that can be given each week to, say, 50,000 congregations and parishes, he can envision and appreciate the enormous anti-Negro machinery. . . .

The separatism called for by a highly vocal minority of Negro-Americans will harm the multiracial, pluralistic society America is seeking to perfect. It is certain to isolate the black population, to the joy of the white segregationist. With its unconcealed aspects of racial hatred and violence, especially its predilection for paramilitary strutting and boasts, it could foreshadow a tragedy in human relations comparable in concept, if smaller in scope, to the hateful Hitler dictatorship.[20]

The case for black control of black communities was equally well argued by Charles V. Hamilton and Stokely Carmichael in *Black Power:*

---

[20] "Black Leaders Speak Out on Black Education," *Today's Education* (October 1969), p. 32.

Some approaches to race relations stress black consciousness.

The adoption of the concept of Black Power is one of the most legitimate and healthy developments in American politics and race relations in our times. . . . It is a call for black people in this country to unite, to recognize their heritage, to build a sense of community. It is a call for black people to begin to define their own goals, to lead their own organizations and to support those organizations. It is a call to reject the racist institutions and values of this society.

The concept of Black Power rests on a fundamental premise: *Before a group can enter the open society, it must first close ranks.* By this we mean that group solidarity is necessary before a group can operate effectively from a bargaining position of strength in a pluralistic society. Traditionally, each new ethnic group in this society has found the route to social and political viability through the organization of its own institutions with which to represent its needs within the larger society. Studies in voting behavior specifically, and political behavior generally, have made it clear that politically the American pot has not melted. Italians vote for Rubino over O'Brien; Irish for Murphy over Goldberg, etc. This phenomenon may seem distasteful to some, but it has been and remains today a central fact of the American political system. There are other examples of ways in which groups in the society have remembered their roots and used this effectively in the political arena. . . .

The point is obvious: black people must lead and run their own organizations. Only black people can convey the revolutionary idea—and it is a revolutionary idea — that black people are able to do things themselves. Only they can help create in the community an aroused and continuing black consciousness that will provide the basis for political strength. In the past, white allies have often furthered white supremacy without the whites involved realizing it, or even wanting to do so. Black people must come together and do things for themselves. They must achieve self-identity and self-determination in order to have their daily needs met. . . .

Black Power recognizes — and must recognize — the ethnic basis of American politics as well as the power-oriented nature of American politics. Black Power therefore calls for black people to consolidate behind their own, so that they can bargain from a position of strength. . . . The ultimate values and goals are not domination or exploitation of other groups, but rather an effective share in the total power of society.[21]

The same division between the desegregation and integration approach and the black power and separatist approach developed in other minority groups. While the majority of Puerto Ricans held to either Commonwealth status or statehood for Puerto Rico and for integrated acceptance into mainland life, a very small minority of Puerto Ricans called for complete independence of the island and for Puerto Rican control of Puerto Rican communities on the American mainland. American Indians were similarly affected; some called for full acceptance of American Indians in American life and others held to increasing Indian control of Indian reservations. Among the Hispano-Americans, a militant minority called for Mexican-American control of lands which formerly belonged to Mexicans in the American Southwest.

The new militancy had immediate repercussions in the schools. Among those Negroes who supported integration, such as the large body of southern blacks, the struggle in the schools took the form of the attempt to achieve desegregation and integration. In many northern urban areas, the dominant groups were the new black militants who fought for community control, including black teachers and administrators and black boards of education. As black rage mounted, educators found it increasingly difficult to carry on an orderly process of education in ghetto schools.

In the struggle between the two strategies, some observers have attempted to find a middle ground. For instance, some contend that the search for black identity, independence, pride, and power is a necessary phase through which minorities must go. Once power is achieved, they say, the struggle for desegregation and integration can proceed. But others point out that the ends of mankind are shaped by the means used and express skepticism that an integrated America can be reached by following a path resembling the *apartheid* policies of South Africa.

Virgil A. Clift, a student of Negro education in America, writes concerning a middle way in higher education:

[21] Stokely Carmichael and Charles V. Hamilton, *Black Power: The Politics of Liberation in America* (New York: Vintage, 1967), pp. 44–47.

The notions of "black separatism" and "black power" on the college campus shock administrators and professors. Yet every major ethnic or religious group makes use of its separate organizations to formulate goals, determine priorities, and plan strategy. When Catholics, Jews, or Protestants call their special separate meetings for these purposes, it is treated in the press and other media in a salutary fashion. Black students do not understand why they should not be able to separate themselves to determine priorities within the American pluralistic society. "Black power" in terms of developing black leadership within the economic and political system is to employ the same strategy that others do who have power. The term *black* associated with this idea seems to turn off administrators and faculty members. If we lived in a free and open society that did not suppress and oppress black people without power, this would not be the case. It is difficult to admit that schools, universities, churches, and other similar organizations represent institutional power that has frequently been used to dominate and abuse blacks. When they did not dominate and abuse, they condoned it by inaction because they are a part of the system. The black and white higher institutions will have to get their houses in order. . . .

On the other hand, black academic separatism, out of the context of our national history and aspirations in a pluralistic society, can lead to segregated education which does not provide young people with the competencies and skills needed in this highly competitive industrialized society. It is not an either/or proposition. The challenge to students and the university is one of making it possible for the black student to achieve identity and self-esteem while developing essential competencies and skills.[22]

### Racism and Survival

Wise decisions as to the best strategy to overcome racism without creating new forms of racism will be crucial for America in the 1970s. A teacher should study the competing approaches carefully in their historical context before arriving at commitment and action. Many social consequences will stem from decisions as to the best ways to overcome racism, judgments which Americans will be making during the 1970s. The welfare of all Americans is involved in the issue, and the decisions made will vitally affect the organization, conduct, and content of American education.

## HOW THE SOCIAL ORDER AFFECTS TEACHING

In this chapter we have considered three specific survival problems of Americans in our times: conflicts in the international setting, problems of people and pollution, and the problem of racism. Many other problems also confront the American people. A sampling of additional contemporary problems includes energy, housing, drug addiction, violence, hunger, inadequate job preparation, provision for the poor, etc. The mid 1970s undoubtedly will be a period when still other problems are added to this already formidable list. For instance, in 1973 the American people

---

[22] Virgil A. Clift, "Higher Education of Minority Groups in the United States," *The Journal of Negro Education* (Summer 1969), pp. 301–302.

were shocked by revelations of unethical and illegal practices such as the bugging of Watergate during the 1972 Presidential campaign and the Watergate cover-up that followed. So the three selected problems with which we have dealt are only representative of the "glaciers from the north" of which Benjamin wrote in *The Saber-Tooth Curriculum.*

The fundamental reality for the new teacher to remember is that we live in a time of rapid and sweeping social change in which new developments inevitably arise. Some social problems are resolved and new social problems emerge. In a world characterized by rapid and sweeping social change, education must keep up with change or become hopelessly obsolete and irrelevant. If education attempts to ignore social changes, then today's educators, like Benjamin's cavemen, will be teaching the young to grab fish with bare hands, club wooly horses, and scare saber-tooth tigers with fire long after the necessity for such programs has passed and long after it is sensible to carry on such programs. Meanwhile, new developments in the social order will have taken place and new imperatives will be facing Americans.

The schools can ignore developments and imperatives in the social order only at the risk of imperiling society. Teachers can ignore such developments and imperatives only at the risk of their potential contribution—improvement of the lives of human beings—fading into insignificance, irrelevance, and triviality. Schools can be meaningful institutions only if they stay abreast of changes in the social order and teachers can be meaningful human beings only if their teaching recognizes the contemporary social realities.

## DISCUSSION

1. Talk over the fable of *The Saber-Tooth Curriculum.* Behind the humor, what essentially is the author saying? Can you apply the fable to contemporary education?
2. In *The Saber-Tooth Curriculum,* the author talks about "the glacier from the north." What are some modern equivalents of Benjamin's "glacier from the north?" Describe and discuss the international setting of your times as one possible illustration of "the glacier" which changes lives.
3. What is the real purpose of the school in society? Should the school function as a social agent or should it function as a non-committed preserver and expounder of the organized, traditional bodies of knowledge?
4. Should the public school system attempt to accept and *reflect* the tendencies and the forces of society or should it set as its major goal the *improvement* of society?
5. Describe the current state of weaponry in America and the world. What is the present status of the counterforce to militarism? What is the present political situation in relationship to problems of war and peace? How have international problems affected presidential politics in the past and presently in the United States?
6. Is the necessity to deal with international relations and associated problems of war

and peace self-evident? To what extent do schools currently deal with such matters? If there appears to you to be a lag, attempt to account for the reasons.

7. What is the significance of the present rate at which the population doubles? What problem does it pose?

8. What are the latest estimates of the population of the United States by the year 2000? What factors influence such calculations? Have there been marked changes in expectancies in the past few years? What is the relationship of two or three children in a family to estimates of the future population of the United States?

9. What do you remember as pertinent lessons you learned in school on conservation or ecology? Is there a need for change in this area? How would you teach it differently?

10. Why was the earlier American pollution problem less crucial than the present problem? What are some recent illustrations of threats to human life in urban areas through pollution?

11. How has the campaign against pollution fared? Is there greater cause for encouragement or alarm? Do you see evidence of an increasing conflict between supporters of a clean environment and supporters of a growing technology?

12. To what degree are problems of population and pollution being dealt with in today's education? Is one a more popular topic for instruction than the other?

13. What really is the meaning of the word "race"?

14. What has been the history of segregation in the United States? What have been some of the landmarks in the fight against segregation? What is the case for or against busing students in the interest of desegregation and integration? How is the busing issue being resolved?

15. Discuss major strategies for achieving minority rights. Summarize the view of desegregationists and black power advocates.

16. Is there a middle way in racial strategy between emphasis on black power and emphasis on uncompromising desegregation?

17. Meet with a close friend, preferably of a different race, and discuss with him or her the issues and problems of racism touched on by this chapter.

18. In what ways does the problem of integration versus separatism manifest itself in minority groups other than blacks?

19. How does the social order actually affect teachers and schools?

## INVOLVEMENT

1. Using Benjamin's style and approach, attempt to extend the fable of *The Saber-Tooth Curriculum* through some further experiences of the cavemen.

2. Examine your own subject field and/or level to determine how you could best work on emerging problems of the social order.

3. Identify yourself with a group which follows the strategy which you support in connection with problems of war and peace.

4. Explore how your subject matter field contributes to consideration of problems of international relations.

5. Associate yourself with the work of a political candidate who most closely reflects your own views on war and peace and on international relations.

6. Develop a chart which dramatically portrays growth of population in the world in the last 100 years. Post the chart so that others might become acquainted with the facts.

7. What organizations exist which attempt to cope with pollution problems? If you regard pollution as a major problem, identify the problem closest to your own convictions and work on it.

8. Sponsor a serious discussion among your friends and fellow students as to the emerging conflict between those who support a cleaner environment and those who support a growing technology. Avoid the easy answers and take a hard look at this difficult problem of "ecology versus energy".

9. Set down a list of ways in which teachers of a variety of subjects and levels could educate for better human relations and against racism. Specify the ways in which a teacher at the particular subject and level you plan to teach could foster such programs.

10. After carefully thinking through your own beliefs as to strategy for improvement in human relations, associate yourself with a community or campus group which represents your convictions.

11. Sponsor forthright and serious discussion among friends, students, and relatives as to the various positions taken by Americans with respect to the desirability or undesirability of school busing for purposes of greater desegregation.

12. Talk to a friend or relative who was in school 30 years ago. What does he perceive as the changes in society and culture that have affected education during the last 30 years?

## FURTHER READING

Adams, Don. *Schooling and Social Change in Modern America*. New York: David McKay, 1972. The interaction between education and its social and economic setting. Included are problems of the industrial-social order, the social environment, the social structure, the choices in control and planning, and the alternatives as to educational change.

Atchley, Robert C. (Ed.). *Understanding American Society*. Belmont, California: Wadsworth, 1971. An introduction to sociology through examination of institutions and underlying trends which have helped to shape these institutions. Readings by specialists on the economy, politics, the military, education, religion, the family, the arts, recreation and leisure, science, technology, health, welfare, crime, and law enforcement.

Falk, Richard A. *This Endangered Planet: Prospects and Proposals for Human Survival*. New York: Random House, 1971. An analysis of overpopulation, deterioration of the environment, and depletion of natural resources.

FitzGerald, Frances. *Fire in the Lake*. Boston: Atlantic–Little, Brown, 1972. A perceptive study of the backgrounds and relationships of the Vietnamese and the Americans during the recent war in Vietnam.

Halberstam, David. *The Best and the Brightest*. New York: Random House, 1972. A Pulitzer Prize winning author argues that unwillingness to learn from the past propelled America's leaders into the longest war in its history.

Hurwitz, Emanuel Jr. and Robert Maidment (Eds.). *Criticism, Conflict, and Change*. New York: Dodd, Mead, 1970. Readings in American education dealing with several dimensions—critical, social, political, legal, technical, operational, as well as the teacher education dimension.

Mack, Raymond W. (ed.). *Prejudice and Race Relations*. Chicago: Quadrangle, 1970.

Analyses of prejudice and race relations which have appeared in *The New York Times* during the decade of the 1960s.

National Advisory Commission on Civil Disorders. *Report of the National Advisory Commission on Civil Disorders.* Washington, D.C.: Government Printing Office, 1968. The Kerner report on the disturbances in the ghettos during the summer of 1967, when rioting and burning occurred.

Saxton, Lloyd and Walter Kaufmann (Eds.). *The American Scene: Social Problems of the Seventies.* Belmont, Calif.: Wadsworth, 1971. A collection of readings on major social problems which deals with "the accelerating destruction of our natural environment; the increasing unlivability of our cities; inequities based on class and color; the growing concentration of power in the hands of a few; the senselessness but the seeming inevitability of war; the crippling shortcomings of our institutionalized education," and resistance and reform in shaping the future.

Stamp, Dudley L. *Land for Tomorrow: Our Developing World.* Bloomington, Ind.: Indiana University Press, 1969. The pressure of population on land and its physical resources.

Taylor, William L. *Hanging Together: Equality in an Urban Nation.* New York: Simon and Schuster, 1971. A book on racism and the struggle for equality in an urban nation. Deals with problems of race and inequality in the context of education, employment, economic security, and housing. Analyzes "not making it," the federal effort, and emphasizes future strategies for change.

## SELECTED AUDIO-VISUAL MATERIALS

*Bill Cosby on Prejudice* (16 mm film, 25 min., color, Pyramid Films, 1972). Presents Bill Cosby in a monologue which stresses that there is nothing funny about prejudice. Cosby's portrayal of a bigot leads to serious thought and an honest examination of attitudes.

*Eye of the Storm* (16 mm film, 25 min., color, ABC Media Concepts, 1970). Documentary of an innovative attempt to introduce children to the realities of prejudice. The criterion of superiority was the color of eyes.

*The Human Race Is Losing* (16 mm film, 30 min., color, WOOD-TV: Time-Life, Inc., 1970). Points out the reasons why the human race is losing the fight against all forms of pollution. Leading ecologists predict that after 1990 it will be too late.

*No Deposit—No Return* (16 mm film, 10 min., color, Centron Educational Films, 1971). A literate and sensitive indictment of America's pollution, overpopulation, and environmental desecration.

*A Plague on Your Children* (16 mm film, 72 min., b. & w., BBC-TV: Time-Life, Inc., 196-). Investigates chemical and biological warfare and the fact that secret production has continued since 1945. Urges public disclosure and discussion.

*Pollution Is a Matter of Choice* (16 mm film, 53 min., color, NBC: Pyramid Films, 1970). Examines the dilemma of modern man who has it in his power to preserve or ruin his environment.

*Population Explosion* (16 mm film, 15 min., color, NFBC: McGraw-Hill, 1968). Discusses factors which have contributed to the imbalance between population and wealth-producing elements in the mid twentieth century world.

*The Right to Go to School* (35 mm filmstrip, 4 filmstrips/record/cassette, color, Schloat Productions, 1968). Describes the right to attend school by discussing the 1954 Supreme Court decision in the case of student Linda Brown. Describes other cases

in America's long struggle to provide equal educational opportunity for all citizens.

*The Silent Spring of Rachel Carson* (16 mm film, 54 min., b. & w., CBS-TV: McGraw-
Hill, 1963).   Explains how chemicals were used with little investigation of their
effect on soil, water, wildlife, and man in interaction.

*The Time of Man* (16 mm film, 50 min., color, Holt, Rinehart, and Winston, 1970).
Traces animal populations and primitive human cultures that have survived or
perished according to their ability to adapt to their environment. If man is to survive, he must maintain the environment that sustains him.

*Tomorrow's Children* (16 mm film, 17 min., color, Perennial Education, 1971).
Shows the relationship between man and nature as it evolves from give-and-take
to control. Describes the effects of the number of humans and their quantitative
needs. Projects the problem of overpopulation.

*Where Is Prejudice?* (16 mm film, 60 min., b. & w., NET: Indiana University, 1968).
Pictures twelve college students of different races and faiths participating in a
workshop to test their common denial that they are prejudiced. Proves that
prejudice exists even in those who believe themselves to be unprejudiced.

*You've Got to Be Taught to Hate* (audio tape, 30 min., National Center for Audio
Tape, 1970).   Deals with racial prejudice and the perceptions people have of one
another.

# SIXTEEN

# What's a school for, anyway?

What's a school for, anyway? It sounds like a simple question. Each of us individually can answer it—to our own satisfaction at least. But trouble develops when others set forth their interpretations of the purposes of education. Try asking your fellow students, friends, neighbors, or family about the goals of education and notice what varying perceptions they present. Place the whole problem in the wider setting of differing cultures and societies, changing social circumstances, and various epochs and eras, and you will have some idea of the complexity of our seemingly simple question.

Of the many possible ways of approaching the matter of purposes, goals, aims, or objectives—terms that we will here use interchangeably prior to your studying philosophy of education in some course later in your program—we have chosen two: (1) We will summarize what many thinkers throughout the ages have concluded concerning education. (2) We will report on several studies of the purposes of American education which have been made during the past half-century. Then, we will leave up to you your tentative decision on "What's a school for, anyway?" Bear in mind that there are many philosophies and viewpoints other than those which follow.

## THINKERS THROUGH THE AGES

### Socrates (469–399 B.C.)

Socrates the Greek philosopher should strike a responsive chord in many young Americans, for Socrates lived by his principles; there was no

Causing others to doubt their assumptions was one of the ideas Socrates believed essential to education.

hypocrisy in this man. When he became convinced that his responsibility was to discuss ideas with Greek citizens wherever they congregated, he went about Athens applying his dialectic and developing discourses. His dialectical approach was intended to get people to examine their values by clarifying what they meant by them. ("Justice?" "For enemies as well as friends?" "In time of war as in peace?") If his pursuit of knowledge necessitated some degree of neglect of his domestic duties, including those to his reputedly shrewish wife Xanthippe, he would neglect his household in the interest of philosophy.

Socrates not only lived by his principles; he died by them after his trial for allegedly corrupting the youth of Athens. Though the oracle of

**HENRY BROOKS ADAMS** *Nothing in education is so astonishing as the amount of ignorance it accumulates in the form of inert facts.*

**ARISTOTLE** *All who have meditated on the art of governing mankind have been convinced that the fate of empires depends on the education of youth.*

**WYSTAN HUGH AUDEN** *Unless an individual is free to obtain the fullest education with which his society can provide him he is being injured by society.*

**SIR JOHN BUCHAN, BARON TWEEDSMUIR** *Education is the only cure for certain diseases the modern world has engendered, but if you don't find the disease, the remedy is superfluous.*

Delphi acclaimed him the wisest man in Greece, Socrates himself felt only that he differed from others in that they thought they were wise and did not realize their own ignorance, while he was acutely aware of his own ignorance.

Socrates thought that knowledge and virtue were essentially the same. He believed that no man consciously or knowingly did wrong. If virtue was the same as knowledge, then virtue could be taught. Socrates' test therefore became a search for wisdom through his dialectic so that men might achieve right conduct. He was a self-appointed guide to the improvement of his fellow citizens in the intellectual and moral realms. In effect, he was a one-man university. Socrates often preferred to leave people with questions to live with rather than to present them with ready-made answers.

Socrates, through his discussions, demonstrated his faith in the ability of men to think. He was the embodiment of the educational ideal of reason as he constantly inquired into ideas, and remorselessly probed into uncharted areas of thought. He sought for ideas in the social life of his community and he believed that each man had the potentiality to make a genuine contribution to society. Consequently, he is often regarded as a precursor of the democratic tradition.

### Plato (427?–347? B.C.)

The philosopher Plato grew up in a chaotic period when struggles between Athens and Sparta were dividing the loyalties of Greeks. Plato was an enthusiastic, faithful student of the master teacher, Socrates, and the great mentor's influence on his pupil's philosophy was substantial.

But Plato was no democrat. Plato subordinated education, law and order, and human virtue to his ideal conception of a state guided by a timeless Supreme Good. His ideal society (or state) rejected pure democracy. Plato's utopian state—described in *The Republic*—was predicated on

---

**MARK TWAIN (SAMUEL LANGHORN CLEMENS)**  *I have never let my schooling interfere with my education.*

**LOTUS D. COFFMAN**  *The chief support of an autocracy is an uneducated people.*

**JOHANN AMOS COMENIUS**  *Education is the development of the whole man—to be acquainted with all things.*

**JAMES B. CONANT**  *The primary concern of American education today is not the development of the appreciation of the "good life" in young gentlemen born to the purple. Our purpose is to cultivate in the largest number of our future citizens an appreciation both of the responsibilities and the benefits which come to them because they are American and free.*

Pompeian mosaic of Plato with students.

elitism; each man, though possessing equal rights with all others, was to serve the state in the manner for which his individual abilities best suited him. According to Plato the ability to govern, the ability to organize and preserve, and the ability to work and produce are found in all men, but in varying amounts. He categorized the abilities of man into three basic classes: those who were destined to govern, those who were to defend the state, and those who were to perform the menial tasks of labor. The three classes neatly paralleled the three functions of the state

**RALPH WALDO EMERSON** *I believe that our experience instructs us that the secret of education lies in respecting the pupil. It is not for you to choose what he shall know and what he shall do. It is chosen and foreordained, and he only holds the key to his own secret.*

**EDGAR Z. FRIEDENBERG** *Regardless of the uses to which any society may put its schools, education has an obligation that transcends its own social function and society's purposes. That obligation is to clarify for its students the meaning of their experience of life in their society.*

**ROBERT FROST** *Education is turning things over in the mind.*

and these, in turn, paralleled three functions of the individual personality. Thus, class structure was characteristic of Plato's ideal state and regarded by Plato as intrinsic to human nature.

To Plato, education and society were inseparable. It was the purpose of the educational system to preserve the state by training each man to prepare himself for citizenship to the best of his ability and according to his civic class. An educated elite was to identify the abilities and consequent class of each individual; men were to be trained to accept beliefs and values passed on to them by this elite. According to Plato, a man's civic virtue must be his life's pursuit; he must conduct his life according to established standards of good, evil, truth, knowledge, and reason. Since true understanding of virtue requires a man's total commitment, only the elite who have devoted their lives to the attainment of intellectual and moral truth were qualified to rule wisely and supervise the education of the majority.[1]

In *The Republic*, Plato placed strong emphasis on method of study as the road to proper knowledge. The acquisition of knowledge required intellectual exercise and the use of reason. Education began in the nursery with the telling of stories to children, properly censored to ensure a suitable moral tone. In his view of the educational curriculum, Plato included gymnastics for the body and the arts for the soul.

Music and mathematics were essential as far as Plato was concerned in the training of the good Greek citizen; music was taught to develop a

[1] Frederick A. G. Beck, *Greek Education: 450–350* B.C. (New York: Barnes and Noble, 1964), pp. 199–200.

---

**NORMAN COUSINS** *Education fails unless the Three R's at one end of the school spectrum lead ultimately to the Four P's at the other—Preparation for Earning, Preparation for Living, Preparation for Understanding, Preparation for Participation in the problems involved in the making of a better world.*

**JOHN DEWEY** *Education is life, not preparation for life. . . . The aim of education should be to teach the child to think, not what to think. . . . The idea of education as preparation and of adulthood as a fixed limit of growth are two sides of the same obnoxious untruth.*

**ALBERT EINSTEIN** *The aim of education must be the training of independently acting and thinking individuals, who, however, see in the service of the community their highest life problems.*

**DWIGHT D. EISENHOWER** *In this country we emphasize both liberal and practical education. But too often it is liberal education for one, and a practical education for another. What we desperately need is an integrated, liberal practical education for the same person.*

sense of rhythm and harmony, which he viewed as essential in a responsible citizen, and the basic value of mathematics was its training and sharpening of the intellect. Study of music and mathematics helped one become more efficient in thinking and helped one learn other subjects more effectively and rapidly.

Plato developed several ideas still present in our contemporary educational system: compulsory public education, state sponsorship and support of education, the tradition that education as intellectual discipline was correct for the elite and that useful training was appropriate for the masses, and an authoritarian approach to methodology and curriculum selection.

### Aristotle (384–322 B.C.)

Aristotle studied under Plato, became a tutor to Alexander the Great, and opened a school in Athens in which he lectured. He emphasized direct observation of nature and believed that theories must be checked against facts. He constantly looked for the first principles which he regarded as changeless and forming the basis for all knowledge, and he clarified the nature of logical thought and showed how syllogistic reasoning could be an aid to clear thinking. He fostered the pursuit of the life of contempla-

Aristotle with his pupil Alexander.

tion, stood for virtue as the mean between the extremes, and strove for rationality.

Therefore, Aristotle's conception of education emphasized the intellectual and cognitive. To Aristotle, the finest citizen was the man who tried to know and understand through speculating, thinking, and contemplating.

Like Plato, Aristotle believed that education for citizens, for warriors, and for leaders should be differentiated. Democracy was not an essential form of government to Aristotle; in fact, he viewed it with strong reservations. Man as a political being could fulfill his civic function in an elite society as well as in a democratic society, thought Aristotle.

In later years medieval scholastics were influenced by Aristotle's mode of philosophical inquiry; St. Thomas Aquinas was moved to effect an integration between Aristotelian philosophy and Christian theology. Aristotle's studies in rhetoric, logic, ethics, and political theory became major ingredients of the classical tradition in education.

### Johann Amos Comenius (1592–1670)

Comenius was born in 1592 in Moravia in central Europe. He lived and worked amidst the religious and political struggles of the Reformation and the Thirty Years War. In the social struggle, Comenius was Protestant in sympathy and an ordained minister in his sect. During childhood and youth, he attended a typical Latin school; he was disappointed and disillusioned by the traditional authoritarian approach to learning, the rote memory methodology, and the classical curriculum.

Comenius felt a deep personal relationship with God, and he believed that education should have a Christian orientation. He assumed that God was the author of the natural order of things and that a proper education would be one that followed man's natural development. In his major work, *The Great Didactic*, Comenius developed his ideas on education into a system of universal education based on principles of learning suggested by natural law and the ordering of things as he observed them.[2] He used his convictions concerning the rightness of natural law to suggest reforms for school curricula and methodology.

Through his analysis of the principles of natural law, Comenius developed logical timetables for the progression of a young man's education and he argued the case for universal education as a natural human right. He illustrated the importance of effective motivation and methodology through step-by-step graded presentation of one subject at a time and through the realization that "education begins with the universal and ends with the particular."

Comenius developed new textbooks and visual aids for use in the classroom. These were virtually unheard-of innovations in classical and

[2] Harry S. Broudy and John R. Palmer, *Exemplars of Teaching Method* (Chicago: Rand McNally, 1965), p. 96.

A master teaching (sixteenth century).

authoritarian schoolrooms. He was influenced by the new science and scientists of his time; he considered science more useful than the humanities, and stressed the practical, useful subjects in the school.

Comenius anticipated the conclusions of modern educators in several areas: a better life as the central goal of education, education in special buildings and in graded groups, and the need for an affectionate, mutually respecting rapport between children and their teachers. He believed that a teacher should be a most influential force in his students' lives and he stressed patience and guidance in the classroom as opposed to strict authoritarianism.

---

**EDWARD GIBBON** *Every man who rises above the common level has received two educations; the first from his teacher, the second, more personal and important, from himself.*

**SAMUEL GOMPERS** *We can advance and develop democracy but little faster than we can advance and develop the average level of intelligence and knowledge within the democracy. That is the problem that confronts modern educators.*

**JOHANN FRIEDRICH HERBART** *The end of education is to produce a well-balanced many sidedness of interest. Morality is universally acknowledged as the highest aim of humanity, and consequently of education.*

### Jean Jacques Rousseau (1712–1778)

Rousseau was born in Geneva, Switzerland. The conduct of his life reflected his philosophical theses: the glorification of nature, individuals, and man's communion with the elements of nature. He was an avowed romanticist, in keeping with the trend of thought sweeping Europe during his lifetime. He claimed that too much civilization, too much society, corrupted man. Social convention directed man away from his natural life and subjected him to artificiality and external standards of conduct, reason, and evaluation. Rousseau insisted that "civilization represented a constant state of war and that it only produced a parasitical aristocracy which had enslaved the common people."[3] Rousseau did acknowledge the state and society as a necessary organization, however, and held that the question of how to maintain and refine the natural freedom of the individual within the boundaries of society was the basic human dilemma.

Rousseau regarded the purpose of education as fostering the natural inward growth of the individual. The basic objective of the school is to foster the natural development of the individual child; everything else is secondary. The schools of his day, however, were largely entrenched in external processes; they were authoritarian, uncreative, and stereotyped.

Rousseau believed that education must deal with life and must teach the child how to utilize his abilities and recognize his potential. School should give the child experience in living, not merely preparation for life. It must train his senses and give him a knowledge of natural objects and forces. He advocated a one-to-one ratio of student and teacher in order that the teacher might know his student well, establish authentic teacher-student relationships, and plan meaningful learning experiences and actions around the needs and interests of the student.[4]

Rousseau believed that education should be student-centered, that it should be an action-oriented experience which would develop the individual's ability to manifest the power of his senses, to feel and express emotion, to create, and to utilize his knowledge in practical action for his individual well-being.

### Johann Pestalozzi (1746–1827)

Schooled in Zurich, Pestalozzi tried several professions, but was unsuccessful. At Neuhof, he established an orphanage and the remainder of his life was devoted to the care and education of impoverished children.[5] He developed a special interest in the underprivileged children of his communities and became dedicated to the ideal of equal educational opportunity for all children.

---

[3] Frederick Mayer, *A History of Educational Thought* (Columbus, Ohio: Charles E. Merrill Books, 1960), p. 235.
[4] *Ibid.,* pp. 241–243.
[5] *Ibid.,* p. 265.

Pestalozzi's idea of student involvement at the individual ability level has had a great effect on education.

His ideas rest firmly upon his social philosophy[6] and his philosophy was a logical product of the kind of life that he lived. He was a simple, humble man, weak in his abilities to organize, administer, and rule, but powerful in his sensitivity to and awareness of the human condition. The educational ideas of Pestalozzi have much in common with those of Rousseau and Comenius.

Pestalozzi recognized the presence in all men of three basic drives:

[6] *loc. cit.*

> **ADOLF HITLER**  *Universal education is the most corroding and disintegrating poison that liberalism has ever invented for its own destruction.*
>
> **OLIVER WENDELL HOLMES**  *Your education begins when what is called your education is over.*
>
> **ROBERT H. JACKSON**  *Free public education, if faithful to the ideal of secular instruction and political neutrality, will not be partisan or enemy of any class, creed, party, or faction.*

the primitive impulse, the social impulse, and the ethical impulse. Education, according to Pestalozzi, is the process whereby the ethical impulse triumphs over the others. This belief conflicted with the artificial training common in the schools of his time and favored an inward development whereby the human capacities of love, understanding, and creativity were nurtured.[7] Like Comenius, he emphasized the necessity of pleasant rapport between teacher and student, the need for motivation in learning, and the object lessons which nature can teach us. Noticing that children learn much about their lives and their world naturally if left to their own devices, he channeled his observations into laws of learning and methodology.

He taught geography, for example, by taking walks with the children about the countryside and having them draw maps and construct clay models of what they observed and discussed. He believed in the object lessons of nature as one of the most effective teaching methods. He believed that every child must be free to become involved in learning and develop at his individual ability level. Each man's knowledge is his power in life, according to this philosopher, and the instincts of the child are much more effective in helping him satisfy his needs than the logic of the adult.

## Johann Herbart (1776–1841)

Herbart, a German, is an interesting contrast to Rousseau, Pestalozzi, and other progressive or romantic thinkers. He combined the reigning educational theories of the time and advocated a common ground between the authoritarian, classical education prominent in the schools and the student-centered, action-oriented educational ideas of the romantic or progressive thinkers.

Morality and development of character were the fundamental pur-

[7] *Ibid.*, p. 266.

---

**IMMANUEL KANT** *The purpose of education is to train children, not with reference to their success in the present state of society but to a better possible state, in accordance with an ideal conception of humanity.*

**JOHN LOCKE** *The attainment of a sound mind in a sound body is the end of education.*

**GEORGE PEABODY** *Education—a debt due from the present to future generations.*

**JEAN PIAGET** *The principal goal of education is to create men who are capable of doing new things, not simply of repeating what other generations have done—men who are creative, inventive, and discoverers.*

**PLATO**   *By education I mean that training in excellence from youth upward which makes a man passionately desire to be a perfect citizen and teaches him to rule, to obey, with justice. This is the only education which deserves the name. The other sort of training which aims at acquiring wealth or bodily strength is not worthy to be called education at all.*

**WALTER P. REUTHER**   *We need to move to overcome the deficit in our educational system. Millions of American children are being denied their rightful educational opportunity. All of them made in the image of God—are entitled to an educational opportunity so that they can grow intellectually, spiritually, and culturally, limited only by their own individual capacity. We are robbing our nation of the tremendous creative contribution that these young people will make later in life, because we are denying them their educational opportunity.*

poses of education, according to Herbart. He advocated a middle-ground approach between freedom and authority. The idea of individual worth and an atmosphere of emotion and creativity must be fostered in the schools, but these must be balanced by reason and by a sense of responsibility and duty to society. He believed in student motivation and involvement in learning activity; but he also believed that students must learn to accept the organization and structure of the subjects as they are presented by their elders, the authorities in society who know best the proper content and structure of knowledge which children and youth must attain. The freedom advocated by Rousseau and others must be combined with the authority essential in good education, for the "natural exuberance (of youth) must meet enough resistance to avert offense."[8] Children must develop self-control and learn to obey, he wrote, for self-control in the interest of common good is essential to character development.

Herbart's central maxim was that our minds are formed by the ideas that the world and our teachers impress on us. He felt, therefore, that it was centrally important that teachers employ correct means to attain desirable ends. He felt that he had located the scientific laws of learning and formulated from these a correct methodology for classroom practice. It was based on five basic steps: preparation, presentation, association, generalization, and application. These steps were supposed to provide the teacher with the definitive answer to the question of how to teach. But Herbart's system was so tightly structured that it tended to stifle the creativity of both teachers and students.[9]

### Friedrich Froebel (1782–1852)

Froebel's life spanned a period of seventy years in German history. His

---

[8] *Ibid.*, p. 273.
[9] *Ibid.*, pp. 277–278.

A typical Froebel kindergarten.

early years were similar to those of another man of his time, the English romanticist, William Wordsworth. Both of the men spent lonely childhoods; they enjoyed solitary, exhilarating hours in the forests and fields. Each developed a great appreciation for the natural world and formulated theories about the spiritual relationship of God, man, and nature.

Childhood experiences formed the foundation for Froebel's deep religious faith which animated his educational ideas. Froebel joined the

---

**THEODORE ROOSEVELT** *Education must light the path for social change. The social and economic problems confronting us are growing in complexity. The more complex and difficult these problems become, the more essential it is to provide broad and complete education; that kind of education that will equip us as a nation to decide these problems for the best interest of all concerned. Our ultimate security, to a large extent, is based upon the individual's character, information and attitude — and the responsibility rests squarely upon those who direct education in America.*

**BERTRAND RUSSELL** *The sentiments of an adult are compounded of a kernel of instinct surrounded by a vast husk of education. . . . Throughout education, from the first day to the last, there should be a sense of intellectual adventure.*

**WILLIAM F. RUSSELL** *The defense against a bad idea is a better idea; the defense against propaganda is education; and it is in education that democracies must put their trust.*

> **ERIC SEVEREID**  *Ours is not an age of reason, but one of anxiety and feelings of frustration. Educators can help in this crisis by substituting courage for fear and intellect for emotion.*
>
> **GEORGE BERNARD SHAW**  *Civilization is dying of what it calls education.*
>
> **HERBERT SPENCER**  *The great aim of education is not knowledge, but action.*
>
> **HAROLD TAYLOR**  *Education is good only as it helps people to enrich and fulfill their lives, both in leading toward personal joy and in leading toward the extension of one's talents into modes of helping other people.*
>
> **ARNOLD TOYNBEE**  *My own guess is that our age will be remembered chiefly for having been the first age since the dawn of civilization in which people dared to think it practicable to make the benefits of civilization available to the whole human race.*

educators who formulated a theoretical base and practical frame of reference for child-centered education. His beliefs embodied Wordsworth's insight, "The child is father of the man."

He believed that the education of an individual should begin as soon as possible, and he regarded a home united by love as the best educational institution. But according to Froebel, many homes fail in providing love, so the school must take over very early. The early years are the most vital, as Froebel saw it. He believed that education should be based on the needs of children; one learned about the processes of life, the overall unity of all things, by experiencing them through involvement of the whole person.

Froebel established a kindergarten at Blankenburg where directed play activities for children were designed to prepare them for adult activities. The development of the abilities and talents necessary for the social games and the discovery and analysis of nature and objects were parts of Froebel's kindergarten program. He conceived such experiences as essential to successful, happy adult life.

Concerning curriculum and methodology in the school, Froebel believed that the two most important aspects are creativity and freedom. He was especially concerned with problems of creativity; the school's main purpose must be to search for ways of identifying and nuturing creativity. He believed that facts are secondary to experience—memorization should be avoided in the classroom.

### Francis Wayland Parker (1837–1902)

Francis Parker was an American educational pioneer of the latter half of the nineteenth century, a time when new social and scientific forces were emerging in America to make an impact on man and his institutions. He was a democratic educator who believed in the sanctity of the individual and his relationship to his fellow man and to mother nature. He has often been cited for his influence on the teachings of John Dewey, who regarded Parker as the father of modern progressive education.

His educational ideas were clearly influenced by his background of a rural New England childhood, service in the Civil War, and early midwestern teaching experiences. He became a staunch humanist and a lover of nature; he was also an Emersonian in his distrust of "second-hand book-learning."[10]

Parker condemned conventional education as too bookish, too artificial, and too authoritarian. He saw the formal school as suppressive. He recommended direct study in science through observation and field trips in biology, geography, and nature study. The development of affinity for the natural world was to Parker the key step to individual awareness and basic morality.

In one of his basic works, *Talks on Teaching*, Parker condemned the textbook teacher and the academic curricula and courses of study of many school systems because of their emphasis on fixed quantities of skill and knowledge which seemed to take everything into account except the interests and abilities of the individual teachers and students. He allied himself with Comenius, Pestalozzi, and Froebel in the "learning by doing" concept. He advocated an action oriented approach

---

[10] Merle Curti, *The Social Ideas of American Educators* (Paterson, N.J.: Littlefield, Adams and Co., 1965), p. 377.

---

**GEORGE MACAULAY TREVELYAN**   *Education . . . has produced a vast population able to read but unable to distinguish what is worth reading.*

**EARL WARREN**   *Today, education is perhaps the most important function of state and local governments . . . It is the very foundation of good citizenship. Today it is a principal instrument in awakening the child to cultural values, in preparing him for later professional training, and in helping him to adjust normally to his environment.*

**DANIEL WEBSTER**   *On the diffusion of education among the people rest the preservation and perpetuation of our free institutions.*

**ALFRED NORTH WHITEHEAD**   *In the conditions of modern life the rule is absolute, the race which does not value trained intelligence is doomed. Not all your heroism, not all your social charm, not all your wit, not all your victories on land or at sea, can move back the finger of fate. Today we maintain ourselves. Tomorrow science will have moved forward yet one more step, and there will be no appeal from the judgment which will then be pronounced on the uneducated.*

**WOODROW WILSON**  *Without popular education no government which rests on popular action can long endure.*

**PAUL WOODRING**  *A statement of the aim of education need not be a long list or even a short list; it can be in a single sentence. In a society of free men, the proper aim of education is to prepare the individual to make wise decisions. All else is but contributory.*

to teaching and to formulation of courses of study; the scientific method was essential to him. Spontaneity, student discovery, creativity, individual artistry, nondirected, pleasurable work—all of these were important characteristics in the classroom advocated by Parker.

Parker had the opportunity to put his ideas into effect as superintendent of the Quincy, Massachusetts, public schools from 1875 to 1880. The "Quincy Movement" emphasized informal instruction and eliminated rigid discipline; it stressed the teaching of science and emphasized group activities. Parker applied his ideas further as a supervisor in the Boston schools, as principal of the Cook County Normal School in Chicago, and as founder and principal of the Chicago Institute which became part of the school of education of the University of Chicago.

### William Heard Kilpatrick (1871–1965)

William Heard Kilpatrick's career in American education began in the latter decade of the nineteenth century and included more than half of the twentieth century. Kilpatrick has often been described as the leading and most productive disciple of John Dewey. At a time when changing community and family structures were influencing the evolution of the American way of life, Kilpatrick was an educator who stressed the reality of social change and the need for new directions in education.

"Learning by doing," "student-centered," "activity-oriented," "pupil involvement," "problem-centered"—these were Kilpatrick's keys to interpreting education. He believed that their implementation would facilitate the updating of educational practices in keeping with the rapidly changing social conditions in America. He explored democratic ideals and ethics and showed how they are emasculated by traditions and by vested interests, and insisted that creative, integrated personalities can be achieved only through genuine sharing of social activities.[11]

Kilpatrick rejected the organization of subject disciplines apart from each other, and denied that the sole purpose of education was to impart knowledge in the traditional, classical sense. In his words, the school should emphasize the development of "desirable, inclusive character and personality, with especial regard to the dynamic quality of such a character."[12]

[11] *Ibid.,* pp. 561–562.
[12] William Heard Kilpatrick, *Philosophy of Education* (New York: Macmillan, 1963), p. 300.

At Teachers College, Columbia University, Kilpatrick developed the "Project Method" as a theoretical base with practical implications for the classroom teacher. Kilpatrick believed that we learn what we live; he believed that the school must foster experiences through projects, whereby the student can develop his skills and understandings through actual involvement—group problem solving, discussion, evaluation, judgment, analysis, etc.

Kilpatrick saw formal knowledge as being of value in the school only insofar as it contributes to the development of improved character and citizenship.[13] While he emphasized the importance of the individual learner, he did not ignore the power of society in shaping human beings. Yet always he returned to the importance of the learner.

"Don't you think that the teacher should often supply the plan?" asks one of the participants in Kilpatrick's dialogue. "Take a boy planting corn, for example; think of the waste of land and fertilizer and effort. Science has worked out better plans than a boy can make." Kilpatrick answers, "I think it depends on what you seek. If you wish corn, give the boy the plan. But if you wish boy rather than corn; that is, if you wish to educate the boy to think and plan for himself, then let him make his own plan.[14]

### George S. Counts (1889– )

George Sylvester Counts, born on a Kansas farm, became a student of school and society. Heavily influenced by sociology, he saw education as a social function inevitably conditioned by time, place, and the culture. He saw the school as a force which could help determine the direction of societal change; he became a spokesman for social reconstruction.

Counts looked at the social order of the twentieth century and found it inadequate as a means for realizing democratic ideals. Though the social order was characterized by problems of war, an unplanned economy, and racism, Counts found boards of education made up of conservative citizens and dominated by middle class thinking and found schools either traditional or overly child-centered. So he called for more study of social problems in the schools and asked, "Dare the schools build a new social order?"

Counts believed that education should develop individual excellence, strengthen the principles of equality, achieve an economy marked by security and plenty, build a great and enduring civilization, and contribute to the building of a world community. He was critical of progressive education as having failed to elaborate any theory of social welfare, and called upon progressive education to:

. . . face squarely and courageously every social issue, come to grips with life in all of its stark reality, establish an organic relation with the community, develop a realistic

---

[13] Harry S. Broudy and John R. Palmer, *Exemplars of Teaching Method* (Chicago: Rand McNally, 1965), p. 150.
[14] Lawrence A. Cremin, *The Transformation of the School* (New York: Alfred A. Knopf, 1961), p. 218.

and comprehensive theory of welfare, fashion a compelling and challenging vision of human destiny, and become somewhat less frightened than it is today at the bogeys of imposition and indoctrination. In a word, Progressive Education cannot build its program out of the interests of children: it cannot place its trust in a child-centered school.[15]

Counts was criticized for supporting indoctrination of liberal or radical answers to social questions. He steadily responded that a degree of indoctrination was inherent in all education and maintained that he supported free inquiry. But he believed that complete neutrality was impossible.

I believe firmly that a critical factor must play an important role in any adequate educational program, at least in any such program fashioned for the modern world. An education that does not strive to promote the fullest and most thorough understanding of the world is not worthy of the name. Also there must be no deliberate distortion or suppression of facts to support any theory or point of view. On the other hand, I am prepared to defend the thesis that all education contains a large element of imposition, that in the very nature of the case this is inevitable, that the existence and evolution of society depends upon it, that it is consequently eminently desirable, and that the frank acceptance of this fact by the educator is a major professional obligation.[16]

### Boyd H. Bode (1873–1953)

Boyd Henry Bode was another constructive critic of education, but with a different viewpoint from that of George S. Counts. Bode, the son of a midwestern preacher, found that his encounters with Darwin's theory of evolution forced him to reconstruct his religious beliefs. After extensive study of philosophy and initial rejection of the ideas of William James and John Dewey, he decided that the experimental viewpoint of life made the most sense to him.

Bode believed that a fundamental cleavage existed between authoritarian ways of living marked by unchanging absolutist answers to human perplexities in such fields as politics, theology, and economics, and the democratic way of life marked by faith in the intelligence of the common man and a dedication to continuous free inquiry. He held that the essential work of the school was to clarify differences between these ways of living and to examine the consequences of the alternatives.

Bode became a progressive critic of progressive education because, like Counts, he judged the progressive education of his times to be overly child-centered. To Bode, progressive education was at the crossroads. He urged that it take the road toward a free play of intelligence upon man's problems. He rejected imposition and indoctrina-

---

[15] George S. Counts, "Dare Progressive Education Be Progressive?" *Progressive Education* (April 1932), p. 259.

[16] George S. Counts, *Dare the Schools Build a New Social Order?* (New York: The John Day Company, 1932), pp. 11–12 (New York: Arno Press reprint, 1969).

tion of the social reconstruction school of thought as smacking too much of authoritarianism, albeit of the liberal brand. So he called on education to liberate intelligence and to help each student to clarify his personal philosophy of life. He tested human action by asking whether it resulted in the widening of the area of shared interests, and whether it freed men to think for themselves; he fostered the scientific method.

Bode, rejecting both the overly child-centered school and the social reconstruction viewpoints, became a spokesman for the schools as a force in clarifying alternatives and developing a democratic way of life in which the use of intelligence was prized. His critics claimed that he indoctrinated for the democratic way and attendant democratic values. Bode insisted that he did not indoctrinate and that he asked of students only that they use their intelligence. Their conclusions were up to themselves for, in Bode's phrase, "The gods give no guarantees." Using the Socratic method of dialogue, Bode himself fostered independent thought in his classes at Ohio State University and the University of Illinois through humorous and lively exchange of ideas.

Bode wrote of democracy:

> The democratic school, in brief, is an institution which aims to promote the ideal of "free and equal" by taking proper account of individual differences and by reliance on the principle of community living. . . .[17]
>
> The school, therefore, is clearly under the obligation to show that democracy is a way of life which breaks sharply with the past. It must not merely practice democracy but must develop the doctrine so as to make it serviceable as an intellectual basis for the organization of life.[18]

### John Dewey (1859–1952)

Though the American philosopher John Dewey was born before Kilpatrick, Counts, and Bode, he lived into his nineties and was their contemporary. John Dewey, professor at Chicago and Columbia, was an extraordinary man. During his long lifetime, he managed to combine several lives. He lived a full life as an individual and father of five children; he was constantly active in social and civic action; he conducted the most famous laboratory school in history. He left for posterity a legacy of 5,000 pages of articles and 18,000 pages in book form. Dewey was the intellectual inspiration of the progressive movement, though he himself preferred to talk simply of education without any preceding adjectives.

Like other towering figures in American life, John Dewey has had both detractors and disciples. The detractors have frequently condemned him vitriolically, often without bothering to read him. The disciples have sometimes taken one aspect of the broad corpus of his work and iden-

[17] Boyd H. Bode, *Democracy as a Way of Life* (New York: The Macmillan Company, 1937), p. 82.
[18] *Ibid.*, p. 94.

John Dewey.

tified their selected aspect as the totality of his contribution. A student of education owes it to himself to read Dewey rather than exclusively depend on detractors and disciples; a brief and understandable starting point might be Dewey's *Experience and Education*, followed by the longer and more complex *Democracy and Education*.

Stated perhaps too baldly, Kilpatrick was learner oriented, Counts was society oriented, and Bode was values oriented. But the philosopher of education who came closest to reconciliation of these three emphases was John Dewey, who drew freely for his educational theories on psychological, sociological, and philosophical foundations of education. He regarded the individual learner as the starting point in the educational process and thus respected the needs and interests and emotions of children and youth. But he never forgot the necessity of helping people cope with the social problems of their times. He stressed the importance of the development of reflective thought and the use of the scientific method.

Dewey rejected fixed ends and believed that continuous growth was a preferable aim for education. He believed that humans could improve their lives through a continuous reconstruction of experience. For Dewey, the test of an educative experience was whether the learner was led to see himself or some aspect of his world with new meaning. Contrary to the impression of many, John Dewey did believe in the importance of organized subject matter, which to him represented the "ripe fruitage of experience."

## REPORTS ON THE PURPOSES OF AMERICAN EDUCATION

To this point, the thinking of a few individuals who have influenced the course of education has been reported to you. These thinkers often differ from each other in their conceptions of the relative roles of reason and emotion, of freedom and authority, of democracy and elitism, of the individual and society, and of the learner and the teacher. Consequently, their conceptions of the best content and methodology vary. Their basic philosophic assumptions account for their conclusions as to what is good education.

Another approach that might help you is to study outstanding reports on the purposes of education by influential groups of American educators and laymen during the past half century. Below are several such reports which deal with "What's a school for?"

### Cardinal Principles of Secondary Education (1918)

A pioneering report on educational purposes was that of the Commission on the Reorganization of Secondary Education which in 1918 set forth "Seven Cardinal Principles." Unlike earlier reports by other commissions that prescribed amounts of content in the several subject matter fields, the "Cardinal Principles Report" went to the heart of the matter by boldly setting forth purposes for modern schools. Though the Commission specifically refers to secondary education, the recommendations have been found to be applicable to elementary education as well.

1. *Health*. Health needs cannot be neglected during the period of secondary education without serious danger to the individual and the race. The secondary school should therefore provide health instruction, inculcate health habits, organize an effective program of physical activities, regard health needs in planning work and play, and cooperate with home and community in safeguarding and promoting health interests.
2. *Command of fundamental processes*. Much of the energy of the elementary school is properly devoted to teaching certain fundamental processes, such as reading, writing, arithmetical computations, and the elements of oral and written expression. The facility that a child of 12 or 14 may acquire in the use of these tools is not sufficient for the needs of modern life. This is particularly true of the mother tongue. . . .
3. *Worthy home membership*. Worthy home membership as an objective calls for the development of those qualities that make the individual a worthy member of a family, both contributing to and deriving benefit from that membership. . . . The

coeducational school with a faculty of men and women should, in its organization and its activities, exemplify wholesome relations between boys and girls and men and women. . . .

4. *Vocation.* Vocational education should equip the individual to secure a livelihood for himself and those dependent on him, to serve society well through his vocation, to maintain the right relationships toward his fellow workers and society, and, as far as possible, to find in that vocation his own best development. . . .

5. *Civic education.* Civic education should develop in the individual those qualities whereby he will act well his part as a member of neighborhood, town or city, State, and Nation, and give him a basis for understanding international problems. . . .

6. *Worthy use of leisure.* Education should equip the individual to secure from his leisure the re-creation of body, mind, and spirit, and the enrichment and enlargement of his personality. . . .

7. *Ethical character.* In a democratic society ethical character becomes paramount among the objectives of the secondary school. Among the means for developing ethical character may be mentioned the wise selection of content and methods of instruction in all subjects of study, the social contacts of pupils with one another and with their teachers, the opportunities afforded by the organization and administration of the school for the development on the part of pupils of the sense of personal responsibility and initiative, and, above all, the spirit of service and the principles of true democracy which should permeate the entire school—principal, teachers, and pupils.[19]

### White House Conference on Education (1955)

Conferences on education are sometimes called by a President of the United States. In 1955 a White House Conference on Education recommended the following aims in education, especially applicable to elementary education:

1. The fundamental skills of communication—reading, writing, spelling, as well as other elements of effective oral and writing expression; the arithmetical and mathematical skills, including problem solving. . . .
2. Appreciation for our democratic heritage.
3. Civic rights and responsibilities and knowledge of American institutions.
4. Respect and appreciation for human values and for the beliefs of others.
5. Ability to think and evaluate constructively and creatively.
6. Effective work habits and self-discipline.
7. Social competency as a contributing member of his family and community.
8. Ethical behavior based on a sense of moral and spiritual values.
9. Intellectual curiosity and eagerness for life-long learning.
10. Esthetic appreciation and self-expression in the arts.
11. Physical and mental health.
12. Wise use of time, including constructive leisure pursuits.

[19] Commission on the Reorganization of Secondary Education, *The Cardinal Principles of Secondary Education*, Bulletin No. 35 (Washington, D.C.: U.S. Bureau of Education, 1918), pp. 5ff.

13. Understanding of the physical world and man's relation to it as represented through basic knowledge of the sciences.
14. An awareness of our relationships with the world community.[20]

## Educational Policies Commission (1935–1968)

As its name implies, the Educational Policies Commission was set up to help define policies for education and to contribute to the resolution of educational issues. Sponsored by the National Education Association and the American Association of School Administrators, and made up of both educators and laymen, the Commission from 1935 until 1968 prepared a series of reports on the issues facing education.

As to purposes of education, the Educational Policies Commission in 1938 recommended:

The Objectives of Self-Realization:
*The inquiring mind.* The educated person has an appetite for learning.
*Speech.* The educated person can speak the mother tongue clearly.
*Reading.* The educated person reads the mother tongue efficiently.
*Writing.* The educated person writes the mother tongue effectively.
*Number.* The educated person solves his problems of counting and calculating.
*Sight and hearing.* The educated person is skilled in listening and observing.
*Health knowledge.* The educated person understands the basic facts concerning health and disease.
*Health habits.* The educated person protects his own health and that of his dependents.
*Public health.* The educated person works to improve the health of the community.
*Recreation.* The educated person is participant and spectator in many sports and other pastimes.
*Intellectual interests.* The educated person has mental resources for the use of leisure.
*Esthetic interests.* The educated person appreciates beauty.
*Character.* The educated person gives responsible direction to his own life.

The Objectives of Human Relationship:
*Respect for humanity.* The educated person puts human relationships first.
*Friendships.* The educated person enjoys a rich, sincere, and varied social life.
*Cooperation.* The educated person can work and play with others.
*Courtesy.* The educated person observes the amenities of social behavior.
*Appreciation of the home.* The educated person appreciates the family as a social institution.
*Conservation of the home.* The educated person conserves family ideals.
*Homemaking.* The educated person is skilled in homemaking.
*Democracy in the home.* The educated person maintains democratic family relationships.

[20] Committee for the White House Conference on Education, *A Report to the President* (Washington, D.C.: U.S. Government Printing Office, April, 1956), pp. 91–92.

The Objectives of Economic Efficiency:

*Work.* The educated producer knows the satisfaction of good workmanship.

*Occupational information.* The educated producer understands the requirements and opportunities for various jobs.

*Occupational choice.* The educated producer has *selected* his occupation.

*Occupational efficiency.* The educated producer succeeds in his chosen vocation.

*Occupational adjustment.* The educated producer maintains and improves his efficiency.

*Occupational appreciation.* The educated producer appreciates the social value of his work.

*Personal economics.* The educated consumer plans the economics of his own life.

*Consumer judgment.* The educated consumer develops standards for guiding his expenditures.

*Efficiency in buying.* The educated consumer is an informed and skillful buyer.

*Consumer protection.* The educated consumer takes appropriate measures to safeguard his interests.

The Objectives of Civic Responsibility:

*Social justice.* The educated citizen is sensitive to the disparities of human circumstance.

*Social activity.* The educated citizen acts to correct unsatisfactory conditions.

*Social understanding.* The educated citizen seeks to understand social structures and social processes.

*Critical judgment.* The educated citizen has defenses against propaganda.

*Tolerance.* The educated citizen respects honest differences of opinion.

*Conservation.* The educated citizen has a regard for the nation's resources.

*Social application of science.* The educated citizen measures scientific advance by its contribution to the general welfare.

*World citizenship.* The educated citizen is a cooperating member of the world community.

*Law observance.* The educated citizen respects the law.

*Economic literacy.* The educated citizen is economically literate.

*Political citizenship.* The educated citizen accepts his civic duties.

*Devotion to democracy.* The educated citizen acts upon an unswerving loyalty to democratic ideals.[21]

In 1961, the Educational Policies Commission attempted to define the *key* purpose of education in *The Central Purpose of American Education:*

The traditionally accepted obligation of the school to teach the *fundamental processes*—an obligation stressed in the 1918 and 1938 statements of educational purposes—is obviously directed toward the development of the ability to think. Each of the school's other traditional objectives can be better achieved as pupils develop this ability and learn to apply it to all the problems that face them. . . . Development of the ability to reason can lead also to dedication to the values which inhere in rationality: commitment to honesty, accuracy, and personal reliability; respect for the in-

[21] Educational Policies Commission, *The Purposes of Education in American Democracy* (Washington, D.C.: NEA, 1938), pp. 50, 72, 90, 108.

tellect and for the intellectual life; devotion to the expansion of knowledge. A man who thinks can understand the importance of this ability. He is likely to value the rational potentials of mankind as essential to a worthy life.

Thus the rational powers are central to all the other qualities of the human spirit. These powers flourish in a humane and morally responsible context and contribute to the entire personality. The rational powers are to the entire human spirit as the hub is to the wheel. . . .

The purpose which runs through and strengthens all other educational purposes—the common thread of education—is the development of the ability to think. This is the central purpose to which the school must be oriented if it is to accomplish either its traditional tasks or those newly accentuated by recent changes in the world. To say that it is central is not to say that it is the sole purpose or in all circumstances the most important purpose, but that it must be a pervasive concern in the work of the school. Many agencies contribute to achieving educational objectives, but this particular objective will not be generally attained unless the school focuses on it. In this context, therefore, the development of every student's rational powers must be recognized as centrally important.[22]

## Imperatives in Education (1966)

Educational organizations often develop statements which are helpful in thinking about the proper purposes of education. For instance, in 1966 the American Association of School Administrators, an organization primarily made up of the superintendents of schools of the nation, suggested some "imperatives in education":

1. *To make urban life rewarding and satisfying.* Urbanization is one of the most pronounced phenomena of the times. People in great numbers are coming to large cities, seeking better jobs, better education for their children, and a better way of life. They come on the crest of a rising wave of human aspirations. . . .
2. *To prepare people for the world of work.* Appropriate education stands squarely between the individual and the job he expects to get. At a time when the gross national product is at an all-time high and when demands for skilled workmen are increasing in many fields, thousands of young people ready to enter the labor market cannot find jobs because they lack the necessary qualifications. . . .
3. *To discover and nurture creative talent.* Individually and collectively the people of this country are looking to the schools for a great contribution toward developing the reservoir of creative power needed to meet and deal with challenges arising on the forefront of cultural change. . . .
4. *To strengthen the moral fabric of society.* The basic values which undergird the American way of life and which have guided the actions of people for centuries are being put to a severe test in an era of rapid technological change, social readjustment, and population expansion. The results of this test are most visible where they apply to children and youth. . . .
5. *To deal constructively with psychological tensions.* Psychological tensions have been accentuated by, if they are not an actual outgrowth of, cultural change —change that has placed children and youth in new and vastly different situations.

---

[22] Educational Policies Commission, *The Central Purpose of American Education* (Washington, D.C.: NEA, 1961), pp. 5, 8, 12.

In unfortunate circumstances, these tensions have exploded into violent action; in less visible but equally important instances, they have impaired learning and blemished personalities. . . .

6. *To keep democracy working*. The basic purpose of the school is to develop in all people the skills, understandings, beliefs, and commitments necessary for government of and by the people. This is in essence the responsibility for teaching citizenship—but teaching citizenship under a set of circumstances perhaps more trying than in former years. These circumstances are characterized by urbanization, powerful pressure groups, controversies over civil rights, and increasing interdependence between different parts of the country. . . .

7. *To make intelligent use of natural resources*. In keeping with the basic tenets of democracy, the control and use of natural resources have been entrusted to all the people. The question that now confronts everybody, and the schools in particular, is whether control of natural resources can continue to be left with the people or whether, because of dramatic increases in their use and misuse, regulatory measures will have to be imposed. . . .

8. *To make the best use of leisure time*. Leisure time was once a luxury for the few. Now it has become a privilege for the many. With each passing decade the amount of leisure time increases through shorter work weeks, unemployment, a longer life span, labor-saving devices, and customs and legislative action that cause many people to retire while their minds are still active and their bodies still vigorous. . . .

9. *To work with other peoples of the world for human betterment*. Through historical circumstances, a world leadership role has been thrust upon the United States. The hopes of people in other lands are kindled by the ideals and concepts that undergird the American way of life. Because of its strong commitments to maintaining peace; safeguarding the rights of freedom-loving people; and reducing poverty, ignorance, famine, and disease, it becomes increasingly important that the people of this country become familiar with the cultures of other lands and learn how to work in a fruitful manner with people whose customs, values, and traditions differ from their own. . . .[23]

## WHAT IS A SCHOOL FOR?

Certainly, all possible answers to "What's a school for, anyway?" have not been explored in this chapter. For instance, no attempt has been made to report historically the philosophies of education of various denominations or to group and label contemporary philosophic patterns. Nor is any single set of purposes or individual view recommended to the reader. Instead, we have reviewed a range of beliefs from a few thinkers through the ages and from outstanding American commission reports of the past half century. If initial consideration of what a school is for has been encouraged, our purpose in this chapter has been achieved.

[23] *Imperatives in Education* (Washington, D.C.: American Association of School Administrators, 1966), pp. 165–173.

## DISCUSSION

1. Why is the question "What's a school for, anyway?" a complex problem?
2. Which of the thinkers described under the heading "thinkers through the ages" are closest to your own beliefs? In what ways? Which thinkers do you reject?
3. Attempt to devise some groupings or categories into which the thinkers described might best fit—for instance, elitism versus democracy, reason versus emotion, freedom versus authority, individual versus society, learner versus teacher, etc. Which thinkers resemble each other and which markedly differ from others?
4. What are the fundamental similarities and differences in the views of Kilpatrick, Counts, and Bode? Are the differences among them important? If so, why?
5. In what ways were Dewey's fundamental ideas similar to and different from the three figures just mentioned? Why is Dewey usually regarded by educators as the outstanding philosopher of the four men?
6. Why is the Cardinal Principles of Secondary Education report so significant a milestone in American education? Essentially, how did it differ from earlier reports? Do the Cardinal Principles seem valid to you today?
7. Is the proposal of the White House Conference on Education a useful framework for elementary education? Can you reorder the list in terms of priorities?
8. Are the proposed objectives of the Educational Policies Commission, set forth in *The Purposes of Education,* desirable objectives for education today? How would you modify them?
9. What is your own reaction to the idea that a central purpose is appropriate for American education? How important is the rational element in education, in your opinion?
10. Do you find the "imperatives in education" still significant for today's schools? How would you modify or fundamentally change the list?
11. Set forth your own viewpoint on "what's a school for, anyway?" In what ways are your views similar to and different from others in your class who have also attempted to summarize their viewpoints?

## INVOLVEMENT

1. Turn to histories of education or books contrasting philosophies of education to discover the names of other significant thinkers concerning the purposes of schools. Carry on some investigation into their life work and attempt to write sketches about their backgrounds similar to those in this chapter.
2. Choose a particular philosophical school of thought, study it, and attempt to summarize its implications for education.
3. Ambitiously attempt to set forth your own statement of the purposes of American education. Attempt the same thing for your own field or level.
4. Think of the educational experiences you have had. What seems to have been the purposes of your teachers and your schools?
5. Revisit schools to attempt to see in actual teaching practice the pursuit of some of the purposes of education about which you have read. Talk with teachers involved in instruction about what they believe they are fundamentally attempting to do. Compare this with the statement of the purposes of the individual school which may be available from the school administration.

6. Develop a panel for interchange of ideas on the most desirable purposes of American education today.

## FURTHER READING

Boydston, Jo Ann (Ed.). *Guide to the Works of John Dewey*. Carbondale, Ill.: Southern Illinois University Press, 1970. A definitive guide which is a resource for the study of Dewey's writings and a supplement to his collected works through essays by distinguished scholars.

Brameld, Theodore. *Patterns of Educational Philosophy*. New York: Holt, Rinehart and Winston, 1971. An examination of the philosophies of progressivism, essentialism, perennialism and reconstructionism by a leading social reconstructionist.

Broudy, Harry S. *The Real World of the Public Schools*. New York: Harcourt, Brace, Jovanovich, 1972. An educational philosopher takes on the deschoolers and alternative-minded critics. He measures the critics against the school as it must function in the society of which it is part.

Bruker, Robert M. (Ed.). *Wakan: The Spirit of Harold Benjamin*. Minneapolis: Burgess, 1968. A definitive collection of the writings of Harold R. W. Benjamin which are delightful and insightful.

Brumbaugh, Robert S. and Nathaniel Lawrence. *Philosophical Themes in Modern Education*. Boston: Houghton Mifflin, 1972. Deals with theories of learning and knowledge and of human nature and personality from Saint Augustine to Freud, Neill, Skinner, Piaget, Erikson, and others.

Cahn, Steven M. (Ed.). *The Philosophical Foundations of Education*. New York: Harper and Row, 1970. The contributions which philosophers have made to the study of education. An anthology of historical and contemporary works.

Glass, Bentley. *The Timely and the Timeless*. New York: Basic Books, 1970. Reflections on the interrelationships of science, education, and society by an eminent scientist conscious of the critical gap between public understanding and scientific knowledge. A John Dewey Society lecture.

Greene, Maxine. *Existential Encounters for Teachers*. New York: Random House, 1967. An introduction to "the diverse strains of thinking" in existentialism through selections from a variety of existential thinkers, including Sartre, Kierkegaard, Camus, Dostoevsky, Kafka, and others.

Inlow, Gail M. *Values in Transition: A Handbook*. New York: John Wiley & Sons, 1972. On the governing values of the culture, including traditional values, philosophical values, and the values of such groups as the new left and the black community, culminating in a value synthesis.

Simon, Sidney, Leland W. Howe, and Howard Kirschenbaum. *Values Clarification*. New York: Hart, 1972. Practical suggestions for teachers on how to work with students toward the clarification of values.

Strain, John Paul (Ed.). *Modern Philosophies of Education*. New York: Random House, 1971. A collection of essays on progressivism, essentialism, and perennialism by outstanding advocates of these views.

Wirsing, Marie E. *Teaching and Philosophy: A Synthesis*. Boston: Houghton Mifflin, 1972. A book on philosophy and methods demonstrating that they are not two separate operations but part of one process.

## SELECTED AUDIO-VISUAL MATERIALS

*Abraham Kaplan* (16 mm film, 59 min., b. & w., NET: Indiana University, 1968). Abraham Kaplan, professor of philosophy, explains his own immediate background and cultural heritage, his beliefs and attitudes toward teaching and the difference between instruction and education. This film is one of a series of five films from the "Men Who Teach" series showing some of America's inspiring college and university teachers.

*The Classical Realist Approach to Education* (16 mm film, 29 min., b. & w., NET: Indiana University, 1961). Defines classical realism and discusses the theory's basis in the "natural law." Shows the application of the theory in a physics class.

*Education for Cultural Reconstruction* (16 mm film, 29 min., b. & w., NET: Indiana University, 1961). Theodore Brameld defines cultural reconstruction. He elaborates on the reconstructionist viewpoint.

*An Experimentalist Approach to Education* (16 mm film, 29 min., b. & w., NET: Indiana University, 1961). H. Gordon Hullfish elucidates the experimentalist viewpoint, answers objections, and comments on a film sequence of a progressive classroom.

*Glasser on Schools* (16 mm film, 19 min., color, Media Five, 1970). Dr. William Glasser discusses his "no fail" educational philosophy and the principles which he thinks should be applied to teach people how to learn rather than how to fail.

*Learning by Doing* (16 mm film, 30 min., b. & w., BBC-TV: Time-Life, 1967). Asserts that the good elementary school promotes learning by organizing significant discovery for each child and by confirming and extending his experience.

*Oral Essays on Education* (audio tape, 30 min., WKAR: National Center for Audio Tapes, 1961). A series of 17 tapes of talks by prominent personalities discussing some aspects of education. Selected titles: Can Education Change, Margaret Mead; Education in Our American Culture, Margaret Mead; The Here and Now, Hubert Humphrey; Pursuit of Excellence, Arthur S. Flemming; What Price Creativity, Fred Hechinger; The Public Enterprise, Henry Steele Commager; The Red Blackboard, George S. Counts; New Challenge, New Techniques, William Benton.

*Plato's Apology—Life and Teachings of Socrates* (16 mm film, 30 min., color, Encyclopedia Britannica Educational Corp., 1954). A study of Socrates, a man whose influence on the minds of men still endures.

# SEVENTEEN

# What should the schools teach?

## CURRICULUM

The word curriculum has a Latin derivation which stems from *currere*, to run. So curriculum originally meant "a running" or "a racecourse" or "a racing chariot." This origin of curriculum may be a source of wry amusement to students who have been running in the curriculum race since they entered school!

A curriculum should carry out the purposes of the school. Just as the seemingly simple question, "What's a school for, anyway?" is complex, the follow-up question, "What should the schools teach?" proves to be more complex than it first appears.

From the standard dictionary definition—"all the courses of study offered by an educational institution" or "a particular course of study, often in a special field"—one would not think curriculum to be an especially complex matter. According to this, the school curriculum could be described by listing all the courses of study or describing particular courses of study offered by that educational institution. Thus an administrator might present to a visitor the curriculum of his school by handing him a heavy bound volume containing the total courses of study or a slimmer volume containing the course of study for a particular subject.

Nor does the matter of curriculum appear particularly complex to many parents and, indeed, to many administrators, teachers, and students. Many people assume that there exists a fixed body of knowledge and skills which all need to master in order to be educated. They assume that in some way (which they do not specify) this body of knowledge and skills has been defined for educators and the public during the ages, has become clear to all and accepted by all, and, having been finally established, now constitutes the curriculum for all. They assume that the curriculum is now neatly packaged into fixed and established courses of study.

But these conventional assumptions are flatly contradicted by what we have learned from our study of education. The history of American education testifies to constant change in society and education, rather than to school and society remaining static (Chapter 6). The past half century has been a period of controversy over the proper work of the public schools, rather than an era of unanimous agreement (Chapter 7). The existence of such nonpublic schools as independent, alternative, and parochial schools indicates differing conceptions of the functions and programs of schools, rather than monolithic unanimity (Chapter 8). A variety of forces influences schools, rather than a making of decisions for all involved by some single authority (Chapter 9). Expectations of the teacher's role vary from group to group and individual to individual instead of one role expectation prevailing (Chapter 10). Students have different social class and ethnic backgrounds which influence their experiences and their schooling, rather than reflect uniform class, racial, and ancestral backgrounds (Chapter 12). Students come to schools from varied community backgrounds—rural, city, and suburban—and their needs are not identical from community to community (Chapter 13). Learners differ widely from each other. No ways of grouping can repeal the inexorable law of individuality and replace it with uniform education (Chapter 14). Social change is inescapable and rapid and new social problems, including human survival crises, face mankind, rather than society remaining immobile and changeless (Chapter 15). The purposes of education are complex and multiple, rather than simple and singular (Chapter 16).

Consequently, as to curriculum, varied learning experiences are necessary for individuals from a variety of cultural and community backgrounds in a changing world. A fixed body of skills and knowledge to be mastered by every person cannot be taught or learned. Curriculum opportunities and experiences must change with the growth of knowledge concerning the individual, society, values, and the disciplines. Curriculum cannot stay constant over the ages, established and fixed for all learners, in a world in which knowledge explodes.

Contemporary educators recognize that the curriculum is made up of the learning experiences under the control of the school. For instance, Saylor and Alexander say, "Curriculum encompasses all learning opportunities provided by the school. Thus we think of 'the curriculum' and 'the program' of the school as synonymous. In another sense the curriculum of an individual pupil includes the learning opportunities he actu-

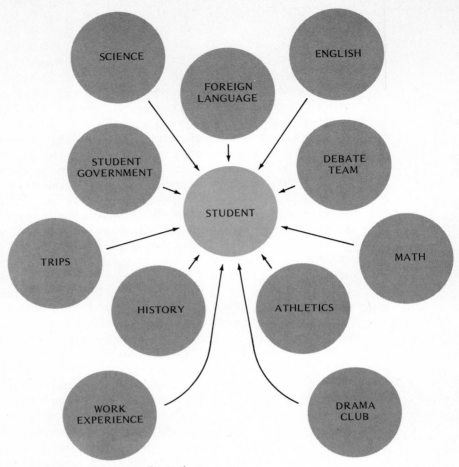

FIGURE 17-1 Curriculum Influences on the Student

ally selects and experiences; this is the 'curriculum had.'"[1] Such a definition places the emphasis where it should be, upon the actual learning opportunities offered by the school and the actual learning experiences had by the students. The wider definition also recognizes that a variety of student activities are part of the program of the school. Formerly such activities were regarded as extracurricular, implying something carried on outside the regular, and presumably much more important, curriculum of the school. The broader definition regards student activities—whether the dramatics club, the debate team, the intramural or varsity athletic events, etc.—as "co-curricular," indicating jointness or mutuality with the regular program.

[1] J. Galen Saylor and William M. Alexander, *Curriculum Planning for Modern Schools* (New York: Holt, Rinehart and Winston, 1966), p. 5.

## FOUNDATIONS OF CURRICULUM

Curriculum leaders today recognize that the programs of schools must bear some relationship to individual learners, the society in which we live, desirable values, and the disciplines of learning. They differ, to a degree, on the proper combination. Few if any educators turn to one of the above referents in isolation. Yet some curriculum proponents stress one referent or source of the curriculum more heavily than the others. They want to be sure that the particular source they emphasize is sufficiently stressed in determining the best learning opportunities and the best learning experiences for Americans in our times. So some curriculum thinkers remind us of the special importance of the individual learners. Others tend to stress the importance of society in shaping persons. Others remind us of the necessity of values to provide us a sense of direction. Still others emphasize ways in which study of the disciplines can contribute to understanding relationships and ways of inquiry. Consequently, we will examine these four logical referents in curriculum making and the reasons why some curriculum workers regard them as important. We will then describe some combinations of sources which contemporary curriculum leaders recommend.

### Needs of the Individual Learner

In developing learning opportunities, say those who emphasize one among these four referents, stress the individual learner. The individual learner has questions, perplexities, concerns, and tensions which he must resolve; he is thus receptive to education which makes sense to him. The curriculum should meet his needs. The individual learner knows best what he most needs; after all, he is the person with the questions, perplexities, concerns, and tensions. Who can know better than the learner what he needs to learn? Furthermore, who can really teach the learner anything that he doesn't really want to know? Consequently, a good school tries to determine what is on the learner's mind and helps to provide him opportunities and experiences to deal with his interests. The only curriculum which can be meaningful to a learner is the curriculum which holds meaning for him personally. So say the advocates of basing the curriculum on the needs of the learner.

Belief in the importance of the individual learner has a long ancestry. Comenius, Pestalozzi, and Froebel, for instance, were concerned about programs for children and youth. Rousseau, about whom we also read in the last chapter, believed that a child at birth was entirely natural and unspoiled. In his book, *Émile*, he afforded his child the opportunity to develop natural gifts in an unhampered way. Émile, shielded from the corrupting influences of civilization, learned from inner realization rather than from books. He followed his own interests, learned from many conversations with his tutor, and grew up to be a wise and humane man.

A wing of the progressive education movement—probably the most influential wing—stressed the importance of the needs of the learner. William Heard Kilpatrick, whose view of education was summarized in Chapter 16, argued for the importance of the learner.

Of the learner, John Dewey said:

The only way to increase the learning of pupils is to augment the quantity and quality of real learning. Since learning is something that the pupil has to do himself and for himself, the initiative lies with the learner. The teacher is a guide and director; he steers the boat, but the energy that propels it must come from those who are learning. The more a teacher is aware of the past experiences of students, of their hopes, desires, chief interests, the better will he understand the forces at work that need to be directed and utilized for the formation of reflective habits.[2]

But he also warned:

The democratic idea of freedom is not the right of each individual to do as he pleases, even if it be qualified by adding "provided he does not interfere with the same freedom on the part of others." While the idea is not always, not often enough, expressed in words, the basic freedom is that of freedom of mind and of whatever degree of freedom of action and experience is necessary to produce freedom of intelligence.[3]

John Holt sums up the views of contemporary educators who call attention to the importance of the learner and who criticize traditional assumptions as to curriculum:

Behind much of what we do in school lie some ideas, that could be expressed roughly as follows: (1) of the vast body of human knowledge, there are certain bits and pieces that can be called essential, that everyone should know; (2) the extent to which a person can be considered educated, qualified to live intelligently in today's world and be a useful member of society, depends on the amount of this essential knowledge that he carries about with him; (3) it is the duty of schools, therefore, to get as much of this essential knowledge as possible into the minds of children. Thus we find ourselves trying to poke certain facts, recipes, and ideas down the gullets of every child in school, whether the morsel interests him or not, even if it frightens him or sickens him, and even if there are other things that he is much more interested in learning.

These ideas are absurd and harmful nonsense. We will not begin to have true education or real learning in our schools until we sweep this nonsense out of the way. Schools should be a place where children learn what they most want to know, instead of what we think they ought to know. The child who wants to know something remembers it and uses it once he has it; the child who learns something to please or appease someone else forgets it when the need for pleasing or the danger of not appeasing is past.[4]

[2] Ralph D. Winn (Ed.), *John Dewey: Dictionary of Education* (New York: Philosophical Library, 1959), pp. 112–113.
[3] *Ibid.*, pp. 40–41.
[4] John Holt, *How Children Fail* (New York: Pitman, 1964), pp. 174, 175.

Today many young people believe that schools fail human beings. For instance, a group of high school students from Montgomery County, Maryland, presented an analysis of their own schooling to their Board of Education. They began with the comment that "It is quite safe to say that the public schools have critically negative and absolutely destructive effects on human beings and their curiosity, natural desire to learn, confidence, individuality, creativity, freedom of thought and self-respect."[5] The students then proposed a series of reforms including a complete rescheduling of the curriculum, voluntary seminars organized by the students, student involvement in choosing teachers, and the elimination of letter grades.

Several angry and earnest books testify to the failure of schools to relate to students as individual persons. Jonathan Kozol titled his book *Death at an Early Age* and amplified the title in his subtitle, *The Destruction of the Hearts and Minds of Negro Children in the Boston Public Schools.*[6]

Herbert Kohl describes, in *36 Children*, his work in creative writing with a class of eleven-year-old Negro children. Yet in following up the children after their meaningful year with him Kohl found, "Robert is not the only one of the 36 children who is now close to being a dropout—John, Margie, Carol, Sam—I stopped searching, don't want to know the full extent of the misery and tragedy of the children's present lives. Recently one of the kids told me: Mr. Kohl, one good year isn't enough . . ."[7]

James Herndon, in *The Way It Spozed to Be*, a record of a year in a metropolitan ghetto school, writes:

> Sitting in a classroom or at home pretending to "study" a badly written text full of false information, adding up twenty sums when they're all the same and one would do, being bottled up for seven hours a day in a place where you decide nothing, having your success or failure depend, a hundred times a day, on the plan, invention, and whim of someone else, being put in a position where most of your real desires are not only ignored but actively penalized, undertaking nothing for its own sake but only for that illusory carrot of the future—maybe you can do it, and maybe you can't, but either way, it's probably done you some harm.[8]

Nat Hentoff, in *Our Children Are Dying*, documents the spirited struggle by Elliott Shapiro, a farsighted and sensitive New York City principal, for a curriculum which makes sense to young people.[9]

As a challenge to the curriculum which fails to recognize the importance of the learner, some educators have founded or conducted their own schools. Currently the most famous is Summerhill, founded in

---

[5] Ronald and Beatrice Gross (Eds.), *Radical School Reform* (New York: Simon and Schuster, 1970), p. 147.
[6] Jonathan Kozol, *Death At An Early Age* (Boston: Houghton Mifflin, 1967).
[7] Herbert Kohl, *36 Children* (New York: The New American Library, 1967), p. 206.
[8] James Herndon, *The Way It Spozed to Be* (New York: Simon and Schuster, 1965), p. 188.
[9] Nat Hentoff, *Our Children Are Dying* (New York: Viking, 1966).

England by A. S. Neill. At Summerhill the children come to school only when they wish to. Yet, paradoxically, when they do attend classes, the curriculum is relatively formal.[10]

George Dennison conducted an "alternative" school in New York City described in *The Lives of Children;* he believes that:

. . . the business of a school is not, or should not be, mere instruction, but the life of the child.

This is especially important under such conditions as we experience today. Life in our country is chaotic and corrosive, and the time of childhood for many millions is difficult and harsh. It will not be an easy matter to bring our berserk technocracy under control, but we can control the environment of the schools, It is a relatively small environment and has always been structured by deliberation. If, as parents, we were to take as our concern not the instruction of our children, but the lives of our children, we would find that our schools could be used in a powerfully regenerative way. Against all that is shoddy and violent and treacherous and emotionally impoverished in American life, we might propose conventions which were rational and straightforward, rich both in feeling and thought, and which treated individuals with a respect we do little more at present than proclaim from our public rostrums. We might cease thinking of school as a place, and learn to believe that it is basically relationships: between children and adults, adults and adults, children and other children.[11]

Educators like George Dennison who are concerned for the lives of individual learners also emphasize the importance of affective (emotion related) education rather than cognitive (intellect related) education alone. For instance, Dennison says:

My purpose is not to castigate the bureaucrats, but to recall parents and teachers to an awareness of one crucial truth, a truth that should be, but is not, the gut-wisdom of everyone: that in humane affairs — and education is par excellence a humane pursuit — there is no such thing as competence without love. . . .

In naming love as the necessary base of competence in humane affairs, I am referring not only to the emotion of love, nor just to the moral actions and feelings that belong to caring, but to loving and caring in the very generalized, primitive sense in which they constitute a background condition of life, as we say of young children that they live "as if in love," and as adults, when they are simplified by disasters and extreme demands, reveal a constructive energy and compassion which are obviously generalized and basic.[12]

Of affective education, Douglas H. Heath says:

The affective education movement is today's most needed catalyst for humanizing our schools. Its principal thrust is to enable students to become more whole and so more healthy human beings. It has not been sharply defined. . . . We need to educate a

---

[10] A. S. Neill, *Summerhill* (New York: Hart, 1960).
[11] George Dennison, *The Lives of Children* (New York: Random, 1969), pp. 6–7.
[12] *Ibid.,* pp. 275–276.

youth, not just his head nor just his heart. The promise of affective education is that it will stimulate us to recover the person lost among our abstractions; its danger is that it may devalue man's most promising adaptive and educable skill: a disciplined intellect." [13]

The affective domain in education is a major concern of today's needs oriented compassionate critics of the schools (for instance, Holt, Kozol, Kohl, Herndon, Hentoff, Neill, and Dennison, described or quoted above). The role of the emotions was also of concern to earlier needs oriented educators (for instance, Comenius, Pestalozzi, Froebel, Rousseau, and Kilpatrick, as described or quoted above). Recently the Philadelphia Public Schools sponsored the Affective Education Research Project to help teachers deal with psychological as well as logical processes. [14]

An issue of *Theory Into Practice*, a journal sponsored by Ohio State University's School of Education, and edited by Jack R. Frymier, past president of the Association for Supervision and Curriculum Development, devoted an issue to the affective dimension in education which stressed the need to teach the young to love. [15] Terry Borton, who served as co-director of Philadelphia's Affective Education Research Project, has

[13] Douglas H. Heath, "Affective Education: Aesthetics and Discipline," *School Review* (May 1972), pp. 353, 371.
[14] Terry Borton, "Reach, Touch and Teach," *Saturday Review* (January 18, 1969), pp. 56–58, 69–70; and *Reach, Touch and Teach: Student Concerns and Process Education* (New York: McGraw-Hill, 1970).
[15] Jack R. Frymier (Ed.), *Theory Into Practice* (April 1969).

Paul S. Conklin

A teaching intern from the Teacher Corps establishes warm relationships with students.

written of another dimension of affective education—fantasy. He re-
minds teachers that it is probable that the amount of time their students
spend in the world of fantasy is greater than the amount of time they
spend in the classroom.[16] A popular anthology on affective education is
titled, *Will The Real Teacher Please Stand Up?*[17] Help for teachers dealing
with emotion related education is increasing.

## Social Demands and Social Realities

Some educators emphasize that learning opportunities and learning
experiences for children, youth, and adults are heavily influenced by the
surrounding society. Exponents of this view stress the importance of the
total environment—the family, the neighborhood, the community, the
nation, and indeed, the world—in determining the educational task.
Though the socially oriented recognize the importance of individual
learners, they point out that individuals must learn in a society.

Historically, many educators have stressed the importance of adaptation or accommodation to the society that surrounds the learner. Such
curriculum workers often use terms such as "acculturation" and "sociali-
zation" in describing the necessity of students adjusting to social demands upon the individual. For instance, immigrant children were asked
to acculturate and become "socialized" (not a radical term) to the demands of the new society which they were experiencing. Sometimes supporters of meeting societal demands emphasize "good citizenship";
however, by this some have meant conformity to societal values and
demands. Thus those who emphasize social demands often tend to stress
keeping things as they are through an educational program emphasizing
the demands that society makes upon the people who live within the nation. Such thinkers provide a conservative emphasis in a time of change.

Though historically the emphasis of those who stress society has been
placed on societal demands, today the views of the socially oriented have
largely shifted to emphasis on changes which must be made in society
by good citizens. Today many socially oriented thinkers stress the need
for human beings to cope with the urgent social realities of the times. If
people's lives are to be improved, they say, social problems must be
studied, understood, and acted upon. Some add that a socially oriented
curriculum is necessary if mankind is even to survive.

Consequently, those who see an important function of the school as
illumination of the social realities of our times advise educators never to
minimize the importance of mankind's dilemmas as the proper content
for study. They want schools to include emphasis on the real and urgent
problems which heavily influence the learner's life. They advocate

---

[16] Terry Borton, "Fantasy in the Classroom," *Learning* (January 1973), pp. 20–25.
[17] Mary Greer and Bonnie Rubinstein, *Will the Real Teacher Please Stand Up?* (Pacific Pali-
sades, Calif.: Goodyear Publishing Company, 1972).

learning about and acting upon international problems such as the threat of nuclear war, ways to achieve a viable peace, relations among nations, problems of imperialism and colonialism, and the gap between developed and underdeveloped nations. They believe that racism is a menacing problem and that black-white relations in America threaten the social order. They call for the study of possible solutions, such as desegregation and integration or black identity and community control; they stress the importance of building democratic human relationships. They point to the need for study and action upon pollution; the population problem must be faced squarely, they say. Making the cities livable is a major challenge; the study of the economic system and of consumer education is needed. They call for more knowledge of government and its operation at all levels from local to federal. They ask for realistic study of communication and the agencies of public information.

Occupational information and training are of high importance to them. Side by side with general education concerning the social realities of our times, they place specialized education by which young people can prepare themselves for socially useful work. In short, this socially conscious school of thought calls the attention of educators to the world outside the classroom windows, to the total surrounding environment which confronts the individual.

John Dewey believed that action was an integral part of education: "Information severed from thoughtful action is dead, a mind-crushing load. Since it stimulates knowledge and thereby develops the poison of conceit, it is a most powerful obstacle to further growth in the grace of intelligence." [18]

The voice of the social realities school of thought is heard particularly during periods of crisis. The 1930s, for example, were a time of economic depression, unprecedented unemployment, and the shattering of customary life patterns of Americans of all social classes. In the same decade, Hitler came to power in Germany, the Nazi conquest in Europe began, and World War II started. In the United States, proponents of a social reconstruction school of thought cried out for an education which came to grips with such problems. It was during this period that George S. Counts, whose view was summarized in Chapter 16, asked eloquently, "Dare the schools build a new social order?"

When the nation threw its energies into World War II with solid support from a citizenry that conceived fascism as a genuine threat to American democracy, less was heard from the supporters of social reconstruction. In the Eisenhower years which followed, *Time* magazine characterized youth as "the silent generation"; the 1950s decade was not a propitious era for those who advocated focusing upon social problems. But in the 1960s, as the revolt of blacks accelerated and as the war

[18] Winn, *John Dewey: Dictionary of Education*, p. 60.

dragged on in Vietnam, concern for dealing with social problems again mounted.

Some educators count upon the schools to contribute to social understanding. For example, in 1970 Theodore Brameld, a veteran social reconstructionist, proposed as a normative model that "a minimum of one-half of the entire time devoted to the curriculum be spent outside the classroom—in the laboratory of direct participation with people and institutions, and always with the close support of teacher-consultants equipped to deal with whatever situations or issues have been selected for analysis and prognosis."[19] He said:

> The structure of the curriculum may be symbolized . . . in the form of a moving "wheel." The "rim" is the unifying theme of mankind—its predicaments and its aspirations. The "hub" is the central question of any given period of learning (perhaps extending over one week, perhaps a semester), while the "spokes" are the supporting areas of concentrated attention that bear most directly upon each respective question. The "spokes" may thus be termed "courses" in art, science, foreign language, or any other pertinent subject or skills. But these are not to be construed as *mere* courses. At all times they are as supportive of the "hub" as it is of them.[20]

But some observers of American life are sweepingly condemnatory of the entire "system" or "establishment." Paul Goodman's view, for instance, is apparent in two of his books on education, *Growing Up Absurd* and *Compulsory Mis-education:*

> Now the organized system is very powerful and in its full tide of success, apparently sweeping everything before it in science, education, community planning, labor, the arts, not to speak of business and politics where it is indigenous. Let me say that we of the previous generation who have been sickened and enraged to see earnest and honest effort and humane culture swamped by this muck, are heartened by the crazy young allies, and we think that perhaps the future may make more sense than we dared hope.[21]

Theodore Roszak, a professor of history, condemned "the educational establishment" and "compulsory schools" in a talk to the Association for Supervision and Curriculum Development Conference in 1970. Roszak views compulsory public schooling as a pedagogical fad destined to become the iron social orthodoxy of all industrial and industrializing societies. He believes the educational establishment, designed to serve the purposes of society, has been successful in the development of scientists and technicians necessary to this industrial way of life. He thinks educators must "let the students go" to bring about the kind of

---

[19] Theodore Brameld, "A Crosscutting Approach to the Curriculum: The Moving Wheel," *Phi Delta Kappan* (March 1970), p. 347.
[20] *Ibid.*, p. 348.
[21] Paul Goodman, *Growing Up Absurd* (New York: Alfred A. Knopf, 1960), p. 241.

Black studies and other socially significant courses are being added to the curriculum in some schools.

man needed for tomorrow's world. Educators should help children and youth escape from the snares of the system. He supports the "voluntary" school where the teacher teaches insofar as the student authorizes. Roszak, like the needs oriented educators, stresses affective relations of adults with young people.[22]

Jonathan Kozol supports the development of free schools which stress confrontations as well as the teaching of reading and the "hard skills." He describes an aspect of a school which he admires in his book which reports on and criticizes the Free School movement:

In Roxbury, Massachusetts, on Leyland Street, a beautiful Free School, nourished and sustained by eloquent young parents and good teachers, discovers that several of its children are in grave medical danger as a consequence of lead poison in the peeling paint and crumbling plaster of the nearby tenement houses. They canvass the neighborhood, enlist physicians, fire broadsides at the press. . . . Forty children in the neighborhood turn out to have been poisoned by the lead paint. . . . The school

[22] Theodore Roszak, "Educating Contra Naturam," in *A Man for Tomorrow's World* (Washington, D.C.: Association for Supervision and Curriculum Development), pp. 12–27.

447

itself becomes the scene of medical examinations for all children, not just those who are the members of its student body. . . . The liberal press does one or two brief stories. . . . The courts do little . . . the city agencies still less . . . In the winter, a child in Roxbury dies of lead-paint poison. . . . The Free School is in the midst of true and human confrontation with the real world of exploitation and oppression that the law, the rental patterns and the medical profession constitute. Teachers at the school do not need to send away to Westinghouse or E.D.C. for "relevant" social studies units "oriented to some of the more serious issues in the urban situation.[23]

Such authors are definitely critical of the system and the establishment. But their concern seems to be more for freeing the young for alternative ways of learning than for changing the curriculum of the public schools to open wider opportunities for dealing with social realities.

The most vigorous spokesmen for dealing with the socially significant in public schools and colleges are some among the young people engaged in dissent. Many contemporary black young people have contributed to setting up programs of black studies; the programs range from conventional historical exploration of the black heritage to radical training for social action on behalf of rebellion in the black ghettos. A substantial number of white students, many of them from middle class suburban schools, have also criticized the current curriculum as out of touch with the great changes in American life. They ask for more study of war, racism, pollution, population. They oppose a curriculum containing much academic material which has little or no connection with the problems of contemporary American life. So they call for curricular change. However, as with adults, some among dissenting young people despair of change through the school and focus on fighting what they conceive to be the repressiveness of both school and society.

### Development of Humane Values

A third emphasis as to the best learning opportunities and experiences for children, youth, and adults stresses the central role of values in human life. On this logic, the basic questions fundamental to education deal with right and wrong, good and bad, desirable and undesirable. The task of education is in large part to help the individual arrive at a pattern of values which gives meaning to his life. One does not indiscriminately gratify all needs; certain needs are selected by educators as appropriate for gratification through the school. The gratification of these needs involves some sense of direction, of orientation, of philosophy. The truly crucial questions as to needs are concerned with the direction toward which the needs lead. Similarly, the crucial question for a society confronted by social problems is to determine guiding values or philosophy. For instance, studying about riots does not help us to determine whether society needs more policemen or more militants, whether soci-

---

[23] Jonathan Kozol, *Free Schools* (Boston: Houghton Mifflin Company, 1972), p. 52.

Students protest pollution, New York City.

ety needs more repression or an improved environment! Only our values help us with such questions, this school of thought argues.

The viewpoint that development of a philosophy of life is the central task of education has a long history. The Greek philosophers, Socrates, Plato, and Aristotle, regarded philosophy as basic to education. Through the ages, religious groups have founded schools to instruct the young in the values of the way of life represented by their churches; this has been an historic justification for Roman Catholic education. In the American colonies, as we have seen, Puritans established schools primarily so that the people would learn to read the Bible, which was regarded by the Puritans as the basic source of morality and philosophy of life.

In twentieth century America, educators also have spoken up for a value oriented and value clarifying education. Accepting that the task of the secular school in America was the development of humane values, Boyd H. Bode (whose work was summarized in Chapter 16), proposed that schools constantly clarify the conflict between authoritarian and democratic ways of living. Bode believed that the value of curriculum content was to be judged by the extent of its contribution to this objective. To Bode, the primary value characteristic of a democratic way of life was the use of the method of intelligence. He called for unremitting application of intelligence to a wide array of human problems. He regarded the work of the school not as the imposition of any single value pattern but the continuous clarification of alternatives.

John Dewey frequently emphasized the importance of freeing intelligence. Yet, he was conscious of its risks:

> Modern life means democracy, democracy means freeing intelligence for independent effectiveness—the emancipation of mind as an individual organ to do its own work. We naturally associate democracy, to be sure, with freedom of action, but freedom of action without freed capacity of thought behind it is only chaos.[24]
>
> Let us admit the case of the conservative: if we once start thinking, no one can guarantee what will be the outcome, except that many objects, ends, and institutions will surely be doomed. Every thinker puts some portion of an apparently stable world in peril, and no one can wholly predict what will emerge in its place.[25]

Lawrence E. Metcalf and Maurice P. Hunt have applied Bode's and Dewey's view to social problems. They believe that the task of the school is to help young people clarify their values with respect to "closed areas" in American discourse, such areas as communism and capitalism, sex and drug addiction, revolution and student dissent, etc. In an article they have proposed "that the schools incorporate in their curriculum a study of an important social movement, rejection by youth, and that this study emphasize examining, testing, and appraising the major beliefs caught up in this movement."[26] They add, "A curriculum that would assist young people in an examination of their basic assumptions about society and its improvement must deal with values and social policies."[27]

This approach is attractive to those who believe improvements must be made within the going system. But some revolutionary students reject any study of values. They disagree with those who believe that democratic ends require the use of democratic means. They prefer intuitive rather than rational thought. One wing of current youth dissent deprecates values and regards goals as illusory. Followers of this view believe that a revolution must come first. The time for talking about goals and the building of a new society is after the overthrow of the establishment, they say.

Some who stress the importance of values believe that the application of values to social problems is only part of the philosophical task of the curriculum. To them, the crisis of our times is a crisis in values which affects all areas of human life. The basic questions deal with the significance and purpose of life itself. They believe there must be

[24] Winn, *John Dewey: Dictionary of Education,* pp. 18–19.
[25] *Ibid,* pp. 13–14.
[26] Lawrence E. Metcalf and Maurice P. Hunt, "Relevance and the Curriculum," *Phi Delta Kappan* (March 1970), p. 359.
[27] *Ibid.,* p. 360.

concern not only for the public sphere but also for the private sphere. They call on schools to deal with the recurring questions of truth, beauty, justice, freedom, etc. Value oriented educators of this persuasion often stress the humanities, including literature, the arts, music, etc. Joseph Wood Krutch said:

> The humanities . . . include every sort of consideration of those human concerns which cannot be treated experimentally and usually cannot be measured — such as right and wrong, the ugly and the beautiful, the nature of happiness, the characteristics of the good life, and so forth — all of which, as soon as they are enumerated, are seen to be the things with which most men are more immediately concerned than with the facts established by science.
>
> Justice Oliver Wendell Holmes once said that science tells us a great deal about things that are not very important; philosophy a little bit about the things which are extremely important . . .
>
> The humanities prove nothing because the things with which they are primarily concerned are not susceptible to scientific proof. But the humanities can and do *carry convictions,* and they are able to do so because they describe human life in terms which we recognize as true to our own inner experience . . .[28]

## Structure of the Disciplines

A fourth referent in considering the opportunities and experiences which should constitute the school curriculum is the study of the disciplines. The historical experience of mankind with respect to knowledge has resulted in a division of knowledge into broad categories which, in turn, can be divided into disciplines. Possible categories of knowledge today are the sciences, mathematics, the social sciences, the humanities, and the arts. In turn, the broad category of sciences can be broken down into the disciplines of psychology, biology, chemistry, physics, astronomy, botany, etc. The broad category of mathematics can be broken down into such disciplines as algebra, geometry, calculus, etc. Similarly, the social sciences can be broken down into history, geography, political science, sociology, economics, anthropology, etc. The humanities embrace literature, philosophy, etc. The arts include music, fine arts, industrial arts, etc. Study of the disciplines comprising the broad categories is required if one is to become educated, say the proponents.

Supporters of study of the structure of the disciplines are critical of the conventional subject matter approach. They believe that current study of subject matter too often takes the form of acquiring miscellaneous and unrelated facts and results in a smattering of knowledge which is inadequate for a true understanding of the disciplines. Instead, they ask for a study of the *structure of the disciplines.* By this they mean understanding the major concepts in a discipline, seeing the rela-

[28] Joseph Wood Krutch, "A Humanist's Approach," *Phi Delta Kappan* (March 1970), pp. 377–378.

tionships of these concepts with each other, and understanding the particular methods of inquiry which are used in that particular discipline. In effect, they advocate that students study geography so that they learn to think like geographers, study mathematics so that they learn to think like mathematicians, study biology so that they learn to think like biologists, etc. According to those who would emphasize structure, such mastery of a variety of disciplines results in the educated person.

Though the study of organized subject matter is old and long established, the idea of studying the structure of the disciplines is relatively new. The major spokesman for the idea in our times is Jerome S. Bruner, formerly of Harvard, a psychologist who described his ideas on curriculum in *The Process of Education.*

. . . the curriculum of a subject should be determined by the most fundamental understanding that can be achieved of the underlying principles that give structure to that subject. Teaching specific topics or skills without making clear their context in the broader fundamental structure of a field of knowledge is uneconomical in several deep senses. In the first place, such teaching makes it exceedingly difficult for the student to generalize from what he has learned to what he will encounter later. In the second place, learning that has fallen short of a grasp of general principles has little reward in terms of intellectual excitement. . . . Third, knowledge one has acquired without sufficient structure to tie it together is knowledge that is likely to be forgotten.[29]

The ways in which scholars conduct inquiry differ from discipline to discipline, proponents say. For instance, a mathematician uses different tools and methods of approaches to inquiry than does a historian. In *Realms of Meaning*, Philip H. Phenix says,

Each discipline has characteristic methods of investigation that distinguish it from other disciplines. By describing the way men of knowledge in a particular field of scholarship go about their professional task, these methods in fact define the discipline.[30]

During the decade which immediately followed the Sputnik anxiety in American education ( a period during which heavy emphasis was placed upon separate subjects and less attention was paid to general education), the structure of the disciplines approach was popular. The scholars developed curricular programs and projects and reconstructed the separate fields. For instance, Zacharias, with his Massachusetts Institute of Technology colleagues, reconstructed instruction in the field of physics and developed the PSSC physics program. Arnold Grobman and his associates at Boulder, Colorado, developed through the BSCS work three versions of biology textbooks. Additional science projects took the form

[29] Jerome S. Bruner, *The Process of Education* (Cambridge, Mass.: Harvard University Press, 1960), p. 31.
[30] Philip H. Phenix, *Realms of Meaning* (New York: McGraw-Hill, 1964), p. 332.

of CHEMS and CBA chemistry, ESCP earth science, and others. New mathematics programs were developed at outstanding universities. After the revision of the National Defense Education Act in 1964, scholars in the social sciences developed projects in such fields as sociology and geography. It is commonly recognized that such developments often eliminated the obsolete from subject fields and resulted in the inclusion of new content. In the better of the projects, principles, relationships, and processes of inquiry were stressed.

With time, some of the limitations of the structure of the disciplines approach were discussed by curriculum leaders. A supporter of the disciplines idea who is, nevertheless, conscious of limitations, Arthur W. Foshay, says:

> What are the limitations of the disciplines idea? . . . First, the disciplines proposal begs the question of the integration of knowledge. We must recognize that the integrity of the fields of inquiry—the disciplines—must be preserved if they are to be learned. But this immediately makes it impossible in theory to combine disciplines into multidisciplines for instruction. . . . But to teach subjects separately leaves the problem of integration of knowledge to the student himself to carry out, more or less unaided.
>
> Second, the disciplines proposal does not deal directly with the relationship between education and life—what we call "relevance." One of the oldest questions in education is how education is to be related to real life. The disciplines proposal deals with the question only in terms of the application of separate fields of knowledge. It does not deal, of itself, with the kinds of life problems . . . which do not come packaged in disciplines. . . . To the degree that we allow the school curriculum to be dominated by the disciplines proposal, we fail to offer students the opportunity to become more than superficially acquainted with great public problems. . . .
>
> The questions of the integration of knowledge and the relevance of knowledge to the real world will not be denied. They demand a response from the school curriculum, one way or another.[31]

In 1971, Jerome S. Bruner, the major exponent of studying the structure of the disciplines, wrote:

> The movement of which *The Process of Education* was a part was based on a formula of faith: that learning was what students wanted to do, that they wanted to achieve an expertise in some particular subject matter. Their motivation was taken for granted. It also accepted the tacit assumption that everybody who came to these curricula in the schools already had been the beneficiary of the middle-class hidden curricula that taught them analytic skills and launched them in the traditionally intellectual use of mind. . . . Failure to question these assumptions has, of course, caused much grief to all of us.[32]

---

[31] Arthur W. Foshay, "How Fare the Disciplines?" *Phi Delta Kappan* (March 1970), pp. 351–352.
[32] Jerome S. Bruner, "The Process of Education Revisited," *Phi Delta Kappan* (September 1971), p. 19.

Bruner then proposed a curriculum which included "immediate and compelling concerns":

> In a recent article . . . I proposed that it is possible to conceive of a Monday-Wednesday-Friday curriculum covering the standard topics, and a Tuesday-Thursday and indeed Saturday way of doing things in which immediate and compelling concerns are given the central place—activism? Let them on Tuesdays and Thursdays prepare "briefs" in behalf of their views, make a case for things they care about. Let them prepare plans of action, whether they be on issues in the school, on the local scene, or whatever.[33]
>
> *I believe I would be quite satisfied to declare, if not a moratorium, then something of a de-emphasis on matters that have to do with the structure of history, the structure of physics, the nature of mathematical consistency, and deal with it rather in the context of the problems that face us.[34]*

By the 1970s, the disciplines proposal, which had ridden high throughout the early sixties, seemed to have passed its zenith. Scholars now are increasingly recognizing the necessity for education related to current social problems. For instance R. Thomas Tanner, of the department of science education at Oregon State University, wrote, "The subject matter developed during the past 13 years may very well constitute a much-improved curriculum in science per se, but it does not go very far beyond science concepts in exploring the societal implications of the scientific enterprise, the interactions of science with society, culture, and human values. Scientists and science educators are beginning to express grave concern over this deficiency in the new status quo of science education"[35] Tanner goes on to propose some urgently needed themes related to the quality of the deteriorating environment; he calls for a multidisciplinary team approach to these problems involving social studies teachers and other educators rather than depending on science or the separate scientific disciplines alone.

## ONE SOURCE FOR CURRICULUM—OR SEVERAL?

In the continuing quest for a relevant curriculum, the question naturally arises as to whether the curriculum should be built on some combination of the sources proposed, the referents just described. Most current curriculum leaders suggest varying combinations of sources. For instance, Arthur W. Foshay, who brought the disciplines proposal to the national convention of the Association for Supervision and Curriculum Development in his 1961 presidential address, has offered what he terms, in a phrase borrowed from Jonathan Swift, "a modest proposal." Foshay

---

[33] *Ibid.*, p. 20.
[34] *Ibid.*, p. 21.
[35] R. Thomas Tanner, "The Science Curriculum: Unfinished Business for an Unfinished Country," *Phi Delta Kappan* (March 1970), p. 353.

depends upon three sources: the child (the needs of the individual learner school of thought), society (the social realities school of thought), and the disciplines proposal (the structure of the disciplines school of thought).

Lawrence E. Metcalf and Maurice P. Hunt support a curriculum based on social realities and examination of values. They say:

A relevant curriculum is sometimes defined as one addressed to the personal problems of youth. This is not good enough. It is more relevant to engage young people in the problems of the larger culture in which many of their personal problems have their origin. The culture of most significance to the young consists of those aspects that are problematic—that is, the large conflicts and confusions which translate into the conflicts and confusions of individuals.[36]

The writer of this book has proposed a general education supplemented by vocational education and study of the special disciplines. He says:

Reassessment of the social setting indicates that there do exist fundamental problems for study by youth which cut across disciplines and which form the heart of problem-centered general education. Such centers of experience are derivative from social realities and grow out of the social foundations of education. They reflect the personal-social needs of learners and grow out of the psychological foundations of education. They offer opportunity for the full development of democratic values, including the key value of use of intelligence, and they stem from the philosophical foundations of education. Reassessment of current social trends and forces reaffirms that such interdisciplinary problems are real, vital, and inescapable for study by the young. A moratorium on dealing with such problems might inhibit long-range individual and societal growth. . . .

Along with the general education of the core curriculum, the specialized education of study of separate subjects for vocational or pre-vocational purposes has long been accepted.

There also exists a "third force" in the curriculum today, mastery at appropriate levels of student maturity of the structure or relationships which characterize the separate disciplines. . . .

Perhaps we can achieve a broader and better curriculum which does not force us to choose among potentially and mutually complementary desirable approaches. To this writer, after reassessment, it seems that what is needed is a general education which focuses on vital problem areas. . . . A specialized education is needed which enables young people to prepare themselves for vocations. Needed is a third force in education, whether regarded as general or special education, which gives those for whom the experience will be meaningful the opportunity to think about separate organized disciplines as specialized scholars think about them.[37]

---

[36] Lawrence E. Metcalf and Maurice P. Hunt, "Relevance and the Curriculum," *Phi Delta Kappan* (March 1970), p. 361.
[37] William Van Til, "What Knowledge Is of Most Worth—A Reassessment," *The High School Journal* (February 1965), pp. 337–338.

Arno A. Bellack proposes a synthesis of structure of the disciplines with a social problems approach. He says:

. . . problems in the world of human affairs do not come neatly labeled "historical," "economic," or "political." They come as decisions to be made and force us to call upon all we know and make us wish we knew more. It was concern for broad cultural and moral questions that go beyond the boundaries of any one discipline that led the progressives to urge that students have the opportunity to deal with them in all their complexity. They proposed a new curriculum, one centered on the problems of youth and broad social issues and drawing upon the academic disciplines as they become relevant to the problems under study. . . .

Giving students an opportunity to grapple with broad social and cultural problems was basically a promising innovation. But at the same time one is forced to recognize that problem solving on such a broad base cannot be pursued successfully without growing understanding of the fields of knowledge on which the problem solver must draw.

Recognizing then the value in systematic study of the fields of knowledge and the importance of developing competence in dealing with problems and issues that are broader than those of any one field, the question arises of why opportunities for both types of activities should not be included in the program of all students. One might envision a general education program that would include basic instruction in the major fields. . . . (the natural sciences, the social sciences, mathematics, and the humanities), together with a coordinating seminar in which students deal with problems "in the round" and in which special effort is made to show the intimate relationships between the fields of study as concepts from those fields are brought to bear on these problems. Such a seminar would also furnish excellent opportunities to help students become aware of the different modes of thought and various types of language usage involved in dealing with problematic situations and the necessity for making clear distinctions among them.[38]

## THE NEW TEACHER'S SEGMENT OF THE TOTAL CURRICULUM

As a new teacher considers what a school should teach, he must take into account such logical referents or sources for a curriculum made up of learning experiences as those described in this chapter. He might well think through the pros and cons of placing emphasis on one or another referent or the desirability of balance among several.

When he has done so, he must face the fact that the level on which he has chosen to teach and/or the broad field of the curriculum he has chosen to emphasize—whether social studies, language arts, sciences, mathematics, world languages, physical education, or the several art fields—are segments of the total curriculum. So the question of foundations of curriculum eventually come home to him at his chosen level and/or broad field. So far as he can influence the learning experiences of children, youth or adults—and teachers can influence those learning

[38] Arno A. Bellack, "What Knowledge Is of Most Worth?" *The High School Journal* (February 1965), pp. 330–331.

experiences more than the new teacher realizes—what sources or referents will he stress? The individual learner? The social realities of the times? Values? The structure of the disciplines? Some balance among several sources? His basic theoretical assumptions will influence the learning experiences which constitute that small part of the curriculum of the totality of American education for which he is responsible. His judgments as to proper stress and balance will make a difference to the human beings whom he is educating—and make a difference to himself as both a person and a teacher.

## DISCUSSION

1. What are the traditional assumptions about the curriculum which are contradicted by the earlier chapters of this book? What are some necessary characteristics of a curriculum in a changing world?

2. What is a useful definition of curriculum, according to contemporary educators? How does this definition differ from the conventional dictionary definition? What are the possible referents or sources upon which educators draw in their curricular theories?

3. What are the arguments for emphasizing the needs of the individual learner in a desirable curriculum? Who supports these arguments? How strong does the case for meeting the needs of the learner seem to be to you?

4. What is the meaning of affective education? Cognitive education?

5. What are the two major different interpretations of social demands? Which one seems more important to you? What types of social problems lead some thinkers to emphasize social realities in contemporary American education?

6. What is the meaning of social reconstructionism? Do contemporary social reconstructionists differ from contemporary critics of "the educational establishment" and "compulsory schools"? In your opinion, would a curriculum based on social realities contribute to revolution or help avoid revolution in America?

7. What is the case for emphasizing values in a curriculum? What is the history of this approach? What form does value emphasis take in secular American education?

8. How are the viewpoints of value emphasis and recognition of social realities sometimes fused? How do values relate to the humanities?

9. How does the structure of the disciplines approach differ from formal education?

10. What is the meaning of study of the structure of the disciplines? What disciplines are involved? Does the number of disciplines complicate the problem of providing for study of the structures of disciplines?

11. What are some of the major projects in subject matter fields in recent American education? What are their strengths and weaknesses?

12. Why is there a possibility that the "disciplines proposal" has passed its zenith? What educational problems appear to be engaging curriculum makers during the 1970s? What is the significance of the proposal of Jerome S. Bruner in 1971 as to two possible types of curriculum?

13. Should a curriculum be based on a single source or referent? Why or why not?

14. What are the proposals of some educators for possible combinations of sources or referents?

15. How does the question of curriculum referents or sources affect classroom teachers? What sources or referents seem most significant to members of your class? To you?

16. What courses in high school that you were required to take have continued to seem irrelevant and unnecessary to you? Why?

## INVOLVEMENT

1. Recheck the preceding chapter on purposes of education and identify the thinkers and the arguments cited which would support one or the other of the referents or sources for curriculum or support some combination of them.

2. Several books by new teachers about their experiences were mentioned in this chapter. Each individual in the class might read one such book and report to the group as a whole.

3. Develop a compilation of significant social problems. Categorize them. If one used an interdisciplinary approach to education, what disciplines would he draw on for the solution of such problems?

4. Assume the existence of a curriculum divided into major subject matter areas. Attempt to allocate contemporary social problems to the most likely areas for purposes of study.

5. Describe some possible approaches to social problems based on Theodore Brameld's model of the moving wheel. Describe possible programs similar to Kozol's.

6. Learn more of the viewpoint of critics of contemporary education such as Goodman, Roszak, Friedenberg, etc., by reading and reporting on their views.

7. Read the views of young people who call for fundamental changes in education as contained in contemporary anthologies. Report to the class on these views and analyze their worth. Invite to your class a young person representative of these views, along with an opponent of these views, for a discussion session.

8. Trace the development of education based on values throughout the history of American education. Determine what forms value education took at varying times.

9. Analyze the possible contributions of the various humanities to value education. Observe the teaching of humanities in schools to determine whether teachers are taking advantage of opportunities for value education inherent in the humanities.

10. Attempt to analyze the discipline you know best as to its structure and especially its methods of inquiry. Attempt to set forth some of the major concepts of the discipline you know best. Compare your results with those of students studying other disciplines to learn more of different tools, methods and approaches in varying fields.

11. In the field with which you are most familiar, what have been the major projects during the past decade? Become familiar with the nature of these projects. Analyze them critically.

12. Attempt to put yourself into the place of any thinker in education described in the previous chapter. What might he say about the referents or sources for the curriculum proposed in the present chapter? Attempt to set down his view. Compare your product with that of others in the class who are attempting the same thing.

## FURTHER READING

Brameld, Theodore. *The Climactic Decades*. New York: Praeger, 1970. Essays from a reconstructionist point of view on the future, the insistent tasks before us, and on religion and education. The author sees education as an an agent of cultural renewal and innovation.

Brown, George Isaac. *Human Teaching for Human Learning: An Introduction to Confluent Education*. New York: Viking Press, 1971. Stresses the flowing together of the affective and cognitive elements in individual and group learning. Draws upon a project at Esalen and upon humanistic psychology.

Crary, Ryland W. *Humanizing the School: Curriculum Development and Theory*. New York: Alfred A. Knopf, 1969. Analysis of school experience from a humanistic point of view. Includes materials on dropouts, the urban crises, black-white relations, etc.

Hart, Harold H. (Ed.). *Summerhill: For and Against*. New York: Hart, 1970. A range of writers evaluating A. S. Neill's book and approach.

Herndon, James. *How To Survive in Your Native Land*. New York: Simon and Schuster, 1971. A book which is both funny and sad concerning a junior high school attended by white students in a middle class suburban setting. Highly outspoken and provocative.

Jones, Richard M. *Fantasy and Feeling in Education*. New York: New York University Press, 1968. A call for the coordination of the cognitive with the affective approach. An emphasis upon the hearts of children as well as their minds.

Patterson, Franklin. *High Schools for a Free Society*. Glencoe, Ill.: Free Press, 1960. Pungent criticism of curriculum practices and a call for a problems centered approach to curriculum.

Rubin, Louis (Ed.). *Facts and Feelings in the Classroom*. New York: Walker and Co., 1973. Contributors contend that cognitive learning must be fused with affective learning in the interest of both the student's emotional well-being and his efficient learning.

Scobey, Mary-Margaret and Grace Graham (Eds.). *To Nurture Humaneness*. Washington, D.C.: Association for Supervision and Curriculum Development, 1970. A yearbook of the ASCD which urges that developing humane capabilities is an educational imperative. The yearbook deals with perceptions of humanness and humaneness, revolutions affecting the nurturing of humaneness, and inhibiting and facilitating forces in the nurturing of humaneness.

Sobel, Harold W. and Arthur E. Salz (Eds.). *The Radical Papers: Readings in Education*. New York: Harper & Row, 1972. A selection of writing by compassionate critics grouped by the editor under "Where It's At; We Must Be Doing Something Wrong; Someone's Doing Something Right; and Where Do We Go From Here?"

Weinstein, Gerald and Mario D. Fantini (Eds.). *Toward Humanistic Education: A Curriculum of Affect*. New York: Praeger, 1970. An exploration of curriculum in the realm of emotion and feeling which represents a start in the direction of a curriculum alternative based on the affective characteristics of children.

Zahorik, John A. and Dale L. Brubaker. *Toward More Humanistic Instruction*. Dubuque, Iowa: Wm. C. Brown, 1972. A presentation of specific behaviors, practices, and strategies which can be used in humanistic education, primarily in the elementary schools.

## SELECTED AUDIO-VISUAL MATERIALS

*As the Twig Is Bent* (16 mm film, 26 min., b. & w., Films, Inc., 1965).  Compares two different approaches to education, "the curriculum centered" approach and the "learning process centered" method.

*Deciding What to Teach* (35 mm filmstrip, 107 frs/record, color, Guidance Associates, 1965).  Discusses four sets of problems related to deciding what to teach: making decisions, establishing priorities, selecting content, and balancing the program.

*How Can the Curriculum for Individualized Education Be Determined?* (16 mm film, 35 min., b. & w., Special Purpose Films, 196–). Presents John Goodlad in a discussion of curriculum for personalized instruction. He considers academic content, teaching skill and school organization.

*How the Historian Decides What Is Fact* (16 mm film, 28 min., b. & w., Holt, Rinehart and Winston, 1966).  Demonstrates the inquiry method of teaching history to students.

*Jerome Bruner: A Time for Learning* (16 mm film, 38 min., color, University-At-Large, 1970).  Presents instructional techniques reflecting Bruner's theory related to the structure of the disciplines and the active learner.

*Summerhill* (16 mm film, 28 min., color, NFBC: McGraw-Hill, 1967).  A visit to a school without fixed rules where no one studies except as he wishes, and where each student is his own master. The founder explains his objectives. The activities of the children illustrate how his methods work.

*Teaching Public Issues: Developing a Position* (16 mm film, 38 min., b. & w., American Education Publications, 196-).  The teacher tries to help students develop justification and reasoning when taking a stand on an issue. Opposing views of the American Revolution were used for this film. The students argue whether or not violent protest is justified and they examine their own positions on the topic in relation to historical and contemporary analogies.

*Teaching Public Issues: Discussion Techniques* (16 mm film, 30 min., b. & w., American Education Publications, 196-).  Illustrates different kinds of teaching and class activities including Socratic debate, small group discussion, deliberate discussion, and role playing.

*To Touch a Child* (16 mm film, 30 min., color, Centron Educational Films, 1969).  Dramatizes the community school concept which utilizes the school buildings as a center for community activities throughout the year.

# EIGHTEEN

# How do curriculum content and organization change?

The curriculum is not static. It may not change rapidly enough to satisfy those who want reform, but it does change. For instance, the curriculum of your college is a far cry from the seven branches of learning which made up the liberal arts curriculum of the Middle Ages: the trivium—grammar, logic, and rhetoric—and the quadrivium—arithmetic, geometry, astronomy, and music.

## CHANGING CURRICULUM CONTENT

### Processes

In American education, one standard approach to changing the curriculum has been to call together a group of experts in a particular subject. The specialists include college professors who convene, confer, and develop a new course of study which usually lists topics to be studied and specific approaches, and provides updated bibliographies of teaching materials. This approach sounds logical, but it has been found that teachers are more likely to use new materials when they have helped develop them; courses of study prepared by outside experts are often filed and forgotten.

Consequently, a major step in curriculum development during the past fifty years has been the increased involvement of teachers in preparing curriculum materials. Teachers have been added to course of study committees as active participating members. They have also played an especially important role in developing resource units for a topic or a problem area. Unlike a course of study which usually prescribes what is to be taught, a resource unit lists many suggestions and allows the teacher considerable freedom of choice among learning experiences. Resource units often include an analysis of the problem or topic, a listing of teaching materials, and a variety of possible learning activities. From the resource unit, teachers select the most appropriate activities and materials for a particular class.

Some school systems try to maintain system-wide curriculum uniformity, but others use a "broken-front" approach, in which the individual school is central in curriculum revision. In the latter approach, within a particular school a committee of teachers might work on the curriculum of a certain grade level. Or a committee might tackle a broad area, such as social studies or science. Committee work in the different schools may be coordinated by a system-wide committee led by members of the central office staff, yet each school usually has a great deal of freedom to develop its own program.

During the 1960s, sponsors of the new curriculum projects, particularly in science and mathematics, developed a more sophisticated approach to curriculum construction. They involved subject matter experts, specialists in the psychology of learning, and public school teachers. Content and methods often were tested with some elementary or secondary school students before more extensive field trials in the schools; programs went through several preliminary versions before formal publication.

The result was often a course package including one or more textbooks, supplementary materials in the form of pamphlets, films, or recordings and comprehensive manuals to guide the teacher. Summer institutes were frequently held to train teachers in the use of such materials. The project approach provided teachers with specific materials and techniques developed by specialists, otherwise inaccessible to teachers. Yet the approach was criticized as converting the teacher into a mechanic who used generalized, expert-prepared materials without sufficient adaptation to local conditions. Despite increasing centralization in American life, many educators continued to value local control of schools to insure that the curriculum would be adapted to community needs and to the needs of particular groups of learners.

Although many educators participate in the process of change of curriculum content, candor and realism compel us to recognize that the motivation for change usually comes from changes in society as a whole. Educators may theorize about the ideal curriculum, but when a significant social change generates a demand for educational change, the schools change, however grudgingly and reluctantly. Educational history records many instances in which particularly threatening social problems were referred to the schools for solution.

In the 1930s the economic and international crisis led to an increase in socially oriented materials in the programs of schools. World War II in the 1940s led to the adaptation of school programs to wartime demands. In the 1950s the schools reacted to the national fear that the United States might be second to the Soviet Union in the space race. This persisted into the early 1960s; emphasis was placed on strengthening programs in science, mathematics, and modern languages, to achieve American national purposes. But the later sixties saw a rediscovery of poverty in America and emphasis shifted to the education of disadvantaged youth, supported by philanthropic and government funds.

In the late 1960s, confronted by angry youth and dissenting blacks and dismay at crime, bombings, and incipient revolution, American society again looked to the schools for help. Such approaches as black studies, free universities, free choice curricula, and problem-centered programs were developed. In the early 1970s, national concern was aroused by sharp increase in the use of drugs by both the college and high school population. Especially in the large cities, then in the suburbs and smaller cities, and finally in rural areas, courses and programs concerning drug abuse have been added to the curriculum.

## CHANGING CURRICULUM ORGANIZATION

Societal demands often bring about change in curriculum content, but how content is organized and taught usually is left to the educational experts.

### Nongraded Schools

A widely approved organizational innovation of the 1960s was the nongraded school. Essentially the nongraded idea is to establish classes on a basis more educationally justifiable than mere age or year in school. The aim is to individualize instruction and eliminate the trappings of grade level school organization, such as annual promotion from grade to grade. Typical primary nongraded programs mix students who might ordinarily be labeled first, second, or third graders.

Exponents of nongraded schools point out that numerous teaching-learning problems have been created by the "lock-step" graded approach to curricular organization. Students have been evaluated and ranked in their achievement by comparison with other children of the same chronological age who were exposed to the same material for the same length of time. Students have lost out in important subject areas because they missed instruction on crucial days and teachers had to move on for the good of the group. Students with cultural deficiencies, but eager to learn, have been inhibited in their work by more aggressive or talented students in their age groups. In short, individuals were expected to adjust to the common standards and goals characterizing a particular grade level. Successful implementation of a nongraded curriculum eliminates most of these problems. But additional responsibility for fostering *learning* falls upon the teacher.

If you teach in a nongraded system, you will probably be less concerned with common standards and uniform performance of the group (and the inevitable inability of certain individuals to meet them) and more concerned with the relevance and value of your teaching to the individual learner. You may provide for the individual needs of slower students without the feeling of futility which often accompanies the realization that the student is so far behind that he will never catch up. In the same manner, slower students may be more readily motivated because they do not experience this feeling of futility in their attempts to catch up.

The threat of failure in the graded system is a coercive device many teachers depend upon. Elimination of failure in the nongraded school will deprive the new teacher of this inducement. He will have to be more original and innovative in his methods and demonstrate more understanding of learning. Initiative and resourcefulness will be called for if the teacher of the nongraded class is to develop logical sequences for instruction, since existing textbooks and curricular aids are primarily organized for the graded program. An English teacher, for example, must have a thorough knowledge of the structure of language and composition in order to permit the student to attain particular understandings and skills sequentially as the student moves through the phases of a nongraded program.

### Team Teaching

Another frequently accepted innovation of the 1960s was team teaching. J. Lloyd Trump, of the National Association of Secondary School Principals, focused national attention on this conception through a study supported by the Ford Foundation and carried through by NASSP's Commission on the Experimental Study of the Utilization of the Staff in the Secondary Schools. Trump, writing in cooperation with Delmas F. Miller, has summarized team teaching as follows:

The term "team teaching" applies to an arrangement in which two or more teachers and their assistants, taking advantage of their respective competencies, plan, instruct, and evaluate in one or more subject areas a group of elementary or secondary students equivalent in size to two or more conventional classes, using a variety of technical aids to teaching and learning through large-group instruction, small-group discussion, and independent study. If one of the foregoing ingredients is missing, the result is *not* team teaching. It may be "cooperative teaching," "rotation of teaching," "utilization of teacher aides," or something else—but it is not team teaching.

The members of a given team may come from one subject department or grade level in the school or from several subject or grade areas. Although present research does not favor one kind of team over the other, we prefer teams that cut across subject lines. Such teams tend to plan instruction that recognizes better the interrelatedness of subject content. (In this regard, teaming has some of the same objectives as the core or common learnings curricular approach.) Teachers still work primarily in their specialties, even with special interests within their subject fields, but they benefit from

Grete Mannheim, D.P.I.                     Charles Gatewood

Team teaching offers an opportunity for free exchange of ideas and can often result in a more creative approach to instruction.

working in group activities with colleagues in other subject fields. Of course we have seen excellent as well as ineffective teams of all types. The organization itself does not produce the goals of team teaching.

A team preferably includes older, more experienced teachers as well as beginners and less experienced ones, each benefiting from contact with the others. The team should select a leader to preside at planning and evaluation sessions. However, formalizing this position too much, or paying extra salary to the leader, may inhibit achievement of team teaching goals. The position of team leader is not analogous to that of a department chairman.[1]

If you teach as a team member, you may find the fishbowl qualities of team teaching difficult to live with at first. Some new teachers prefer the isolation of the self-contained classroom to the demands placed upon them by the sharing of the teaching team; they prefer to carry on their trial-and-error experimentation in private. As a neophyte, however, you may profit considerably from a close, cooperative relationship with experienced teachers. The cooperative approach may offer many opportunities for you to refine your techniques and develop more creative methods sooner than you might in isolation. You may find satisfaction in the greater varieties of small-group instruction offered by team teaching and the resultant opportunities to help individual pupils develop at their own rate.

In a team teaching situation, it is likely that your time and efforts

[1] J. Lloyd Trump and Delmas F. Miller, *Secondary School Curriculum Improvement: Proposals and Procedures* (Boston: Allyn and Bacon, 1968), pp. 318–319.

465

will be used more advantageously. The well-organized team allows the teacher to specialize in areas of particular ability and interest. Teams sometimes include teaching aides or paraprofessionals to assist in the many time-consuming tasks which are necessary in teaching. Assistants may be available to help you grade papers, prepare tests, arrange physical facilities, and maintain student records.

To be effective in team teaching, you must be competent and self-assured, unafraid to expose your knowledge and your ideas to the scrutiny of fellow teachers and laymen. You must believe in the objectives of the team approach and its ability to improve instruction. You must respect the teachers with whom you will work on the team. A spirit of cooperation, mutuality, and willingness to work together is essential to the successful teaching team.

The support of administration is important to effective team teaching. Unfortunately, the development of team teaching has been handicapped by the fact that administrators and school boards may adopt large lecture groups as a means of saving money, while neglecting small discussion groups and independent study.

### Core Curriculum

The core curriculum, like the interdisciplinary team program, emphasizes the interrelatedness of knowledge. It goes even further, however, abandoning arbitrary subject matter divisions to deal directly with human problems in all their complexity. Taught either by one teacher or by a team, a secondary school core class usually lasts two or three periods each day and may be listed on the schedule as "core," "common learnings," or "general education." Similar problem-centered studies are often called "experience units" in elementary schools.

Interdisciplinary courses have long been popular at the junior high or middle school level, and are increasing in the senior high schools. Most core programs take the place of separate classes in social studies and language arts. The two major variations of core are described as follows by Gordon F. Vars:

In *structured core* the students explore broad "problem areas" or "centers of experience" that are specified in advance by the staff. These areas or centers are categories of human experience that embrace both the personal problems, interests, and needs of students and the problems confronting contemporary society. In emphasis they range from those heavily weighted with adolescent concerns, such as "Personality Development" or "Problems of Family Living," to those that emphasize broader social issues, such as "Intercultural Relations," or "Problems of World Peace." Within these areas, students and teachers cooperatively develop learning units focused on specific problems identified by members of that particular class. . . .

To aid in teacher-student planning, many schools provide resource units or guides that explore the ramifications of a problem area, suggest objectives, list possible learning activities and instructional materials. From these a teacher and his students can select or develop learning experiences they deem most appropriate. In preparing resource units, staff members may be joined by parents, students, university consultants, and other knowledgeable people.

In *unstructured core,* students and teachers are free to study any problem that they consider worthwhile. To be sure, classes usually rule out topics that they have studied before, that interest only a minority of the students, or for which the school and community provide insufficient learning resources. In some cases criteria such as these are defined in advance by the staff; at other times they are developed cooperatively by teachers and students.

Units studied in unstructured core may fall within the same problem areas or centers of experience as those of a structured core program. Often as not, however, they may cut across or combine several areas. Consider, for example, the class that started out to study boy-girl relations, became concerned with the problem of juvenile delinquency in the local community, and ended up spearheading a community-wide effort to provide wholesome recreation for young people.[2]

If you teach in a core program, you must be willing to help students work on selected problems. The quest for solutions may involve several subject fields. The fields may not always fall within the areas which you know best. For instance, problems may cut across such broad fields as language arts and social studies. They may interrelate science and mathematics. Reports by students may employ arts media. So core teaching requires versatility on your part; the broader your liberal arts education the better your preparation for core teaching will be. Narrow subject specialists had best not apply!

## Computerized Modular Scheduling

Some schools now use computers for modular scheduling. A module is a unit of time, shorter than the usual class period, that is used as a building block in creating a daily schedule. A pioneer in computerized scheduling was Marshall High School in Portland, Oregon. Its principal described faculty participation in schedule-making:

. . . the staff of each department at Marshall High School was asked the basic question, "How would you like to teach your course next year without the limitations of a conventional schedule?" From the answers given, course structures, teacher team assignments, and room utilization needs were projected. The faculty members were encouraged to think in terms of large- and small-group instruction and various forms of laboratory groups, together with independent study for all students. From the teacher recommendations, the decision was made to divide the school day into 21 twenty-minute modules, or periods of time. Thus, a large-group presentation might be two modules, or forty minutes, less four minutes passing time, and a lab meeting might be

[2] Gordon F. Vars (Ed.), *Common Learnings: Core and Interdisciplinary Team Approaches* (Scranton, Pa.: International Textbook, 1969), p. 9.

as long as five modules, or 100 minutes. Any multiple of these short time blocks could be requested in order to satisfy the needs of the students and of the particular activity taking place in the course.[3]

If you teach in a school which uses modular scheduling, you will participate in decision-making as to the length of your teaching periods. You will have to think through whether your grade level or subject and your characteristic teaching style are best served by sustained periods or shorter periods, by daily instruction or less than five meetings weekly, by large- or small-group work—or by some combination among these. For instance, a physical education teacher may prefer three 100-minute sessions weekly to five 60-minute sessions. A social studies teacher may prefer one long session of 60 minutes for large-group work and the rest of his time in 40-minute blocks for small-group work. A science teacher may prefer two long laboratory sessions and one shorter class meeting.

### Independent Study

Modular scheduling facilitates another valuable innovation, independent study by students. Petrequin says of the Marshall High School experience:

> Proceeding with our working definition that independent study will mean the constructive use of unscheduled time, we can describe the four basic activities in which a student may participate during this time. First, a student often does his regularly assigned classwork; second, the student may become involved in an extensive or intensive extension of his regular class assignment—more likely than not, a student would be given "extra credit" for this type of work; third, a student might be engaged in an independent-study project; finally a student could participate in an enrichment experience. Although the term "enrichment experience" seems a bit unwieldy for a description, it is an appropriate one, for it does suggest the nature of the activity. . . .
>
> Although a student is often engaged in a variety of activities during his unscheduled, independent-study time—he may study in the library or any one of the seven resource centers, confer with teachers or his fellow students, practice on a musical instrument, work on an independent-study project, listen and respond to language tapes—there is a good possibility that he may include an enrichment experience. Enrichment experiences include an array of speciality courses, unique training activities, class auditing on a formal or informal basis, and special programs that are available to the students because of the flexibility of our scheduling system.[4]

If the school in which you teach utilizes independent study, you may find it an effective but a demanding method. In a school using independent study, you may be expected to direct laboratory work or con-

---

[3] Gaynor Petrequin, *Individualized Learning Through Modular Programming* (New York: McGraw-Hill, 1968), p. 3.
[4] *Ibid.*, p. 66.

duct seminars on topics important to students. You may be expected to confer with independent study participants on a regular basis to give direction and check progress. You will undoubtedly spend many hours reading and evaluating project reports which students submit to you. Your work during independent study hours will certainly not be routine.

## Open Schools

''Open'' became a key word in American educational reform in the early 1970s. The drive for openness and informality in education can be traced to several sources. Openness was encouraged by the development of nongradedness, team teaching, the core curriculum, the use of modules, and independent study. It grew out of the emphasis on freedom and the opposition to authoritarianism by the contemporary compassionate critics, such as John Holt and Herbert Kohl. It reflected student demands for relevance. Journalist Joseph Featherstone, writing in *The New Republic,* and educator Lillian Weber of the City College of New York, were among the observers of open informal approaches in British schools who helped popularize open and informal concepts of education. Ideas of earlier progressive educators were reborn and reinterpreted.

The concept of openness was applied to three dimensions in education—space, organization, and curriculum. As to space, the first step in some schools was providing movable walls between adjacent classrooms. A second step was to put three or more classrooms together; corridors were used for study purposes; rooms were grouped in clusters. A third step was to build schools almost completely without internal partitions.

Open space encouraged more open forms of organization. Team teaching was utilized; differentiated roles for teachers developed; time scheduling became more flexible; children were grouped and regrouped. Open schools tried to achieve some balance between individualized and group instruction.

In some schools, openness as to curriculum content was also emphasized. Children worked independently or in small groups; they sat less frequently as total classroom groups listening to a teacher. Children often selected tasks or worked on group-developed projects. They moved about more.

Some of the resultant curriculums stressed a new freedom. Creativity, trips, many resources and options were valued. Others developed what Alexander Frazier has called a new fundamentalism, a formal emphasis upon preplanned programs of individualized instruction. The new fundamentalism stressed mastery, carefully worked out lessons and sequences of learning, and used educational technology and multi-media packages in instruction.[5] (See Table 18-1.)

---

[5] Alexander Frazier, *Open Schools for Children* (Washington, D.C.: Association for Supervision and Curriculum Development, 1972), p. 59.

**TABLE 18-1 Two Major Educational Movements of the Seventies: The New Freedom and the New Fundamentalism**

| The new freedom | Elements | The new fundamentalism |
|---|---|---|
| Walls in the school pushed out<br>Learning areas equal in floor space to several classrooms<br>Expansion out of doors—field trips<br>Use of public facilities as study space<br>Community-centered study projects<br>Some space may be structured as interest or work centers | 1<br>Space | Large study areas—may be several classrooms opened up to form study space<br>Smaller spaces for discussion groups<br>Specialized facilities such as studios, laboratories, workshops<br>Provisions for individual study: carrels, stations, computer terminals |
| Larger units—like 75 to 125<br>May be called learning communities, schools within schools, subschools<br>Grouping may be interage, vertical, family-type<br>Children may remain with same teacher or teachers several years | 2<br>Classification of pupils | Pupils handled as individuals<br>Grouping as such not regarded as too important<br>Grouping for instruction on basis of achievement or need level<br>Regrouping for instruction in basic skills |
| No bells—few fixed time divisions<br>Work going on in many aspects of study at same time<br>Individual pupils planning own use of time within some limits<br>Relatively few occasions for work in large groups—mostly small group and individual or independent study | 3<br>Time schedules | Flexible scheduling related to needs<br>Regular attention, however, to major skills and content areas<br>Individual pacing in progress through study sequences<br>Large amounts of time devoted to individual study |
| Many resources of all kinds—may have media center easily available<br>Live animals—garden—pond<br>Junk or nonstructured stuff<br>Few textbooks in sets—more trade and reference works in or close to wherever study takes place | 4<br>Resources | Boxes, programs, learning packets, multimedia packages: super textbooks<br>Diagnostic devices<br>Assignments highly explicit in terms of study materials to go through<br>Much testing of progress |

**TABLE 18-1    (continued)**

| The new freedom | Elements | The new fundamentalism |
|---|---|---|
| May plan and teach together<br>May be assigned to large group of children as a staff rather than to 25 or 30<br>Paid and volunteer lay workers part of mix | 5<br>Staff | Paraprofessionals to handle routine tasks<br>High level of accountability for getting desired results<br>Teachers coached to ensure greater effectiveness (increased in-service education) |
| More emphasis on learning than on teaching<br>Teacher as guide and helper<br>Planning done by children<br>Emphasis on learning by doing—centered on activities<br>Stress on satisfaction and sense of growth in personal competence | 6<br>Instruction | Mastery the goal<br>Individualized instruction seen as ideal<br>Ends exemplified in behavioral terms—highly explicit<br>Tutoring relationship valued<br>Much small group target teaching<br>Remediation continuous concern<br>Prescriptive teaching |
| Many options and choices for children<br>Use of unexpected incident to lead into group undertakings<br>Much attention to interest, sense of need, current concerns<br>Emphasis on large or global goals<br>Structure for learning exists chiefly in heads of teachers, not on paper | 7<br>Curriculum | Carefully worked out lessons in basic skills and content areas<br>Stress on scientifically determined placement of content<br>Sequences of work very carefully planned<br>Evaluation geared to specific content and its learning |
| Free and easy<br>Children treated as partners<br>Movement from one place to another informal<br>Noise and messiness seen as likely products of meaningful activity<br>Friendly—good humored | 8<br>Environment as a whole | Busy and industrious atmosphere<br>Quiet and orderly<br>Everybody buckling down to work<br>No nonsense<br>Children expected to be where they are supposed to be<br>Formal—firm but concerned with success and good adjustment |

Alexander Frazier, *Open Schools for Children* (Washington, D.C.: Association for Supervision and Curriculum Development, 1972), pp. 60–61.

If you teach in an open school characterized by an emphasis on freedom, you will have to make many decisions on your own. You will not be able to rely upon formal curriculum approaches; instead you will have to relax your demands and try new approaches. You will find yourself in close interaction with other teachers and your ability to be a good team member will be rigorously tested. You will be constantly engaged in experimentation with the outcome never completely assured. Concerning the free type of open classroom, Charles E. Silberman wrote:

> In an informal classroom . . . the teacher is the facilitator rather than the source of learning, the source being the child himself. Learning is something the child makes happen to and for himself, albeit with the teacher's aid, and sometimes at her instigation. The consequence is an atmosphere in which everyone is learning together, and in which teachers therefore feel comfortable saying to children, "I'm awfully sorry, I don't know much about this. Let's go to the library and get a book, and we'll find out together." or "What kind of experiment can we set up together to find the answer?" or "Where might we turn to find out?" Because the classrooms are not self-contained, moreover — because teachers are used to working with one another — they also feel free to direct a child to the head or to another teacher who may be better informed on the subject in question. And since the whole school is their orbit, children feel free to go to one teacher for help with science, another for help with art, still another for music, and so on, without losing respect for anyone. It is manifestly impossible, after all, for any one person to be an authority on everything that comes up in an open classroom.[6]

Should your open school tend more to the new fundamentalism, you will provide prescribed individualized instruction through carefully planned sequences of work. You will need to know your technology and your variety of materials and to be comfortably familiar with the testing of individual progress. Your classroom will be "open" but not "informal." You will probably be held accountable for obtaining good results.[7]

### Alternatives Through Public Schools

The idea of providing alternative schools was first tried out in nonpublic schools, which described themselves as "alternative schools" or "free schools." (See Chapter 8.) However, in recent years experimentation with alternative forms of schooling has taken place in some public school systems. Best known is "the school without walls," the Parkway Program in Philadelphia. John Bremer, the director of the program says, "There is no schoolhouse, there is no separate building; school is not a place but an activity, a process. We are indeed a school without walls. Where do the students learn? In the city. Where in the city? Anywhere and every-

[6] Charles E. Silberman, *Crisis in the Classroom* (New York: Random House, 1970), p. 268.
[7] Frazier, pp. 60–61.

where."[8] For instance, as two observers of the program point out, . . . "students went to art classes and museums, economic seminars and banks, auto mechanics 'classes' and service stations, and leather-making classes and little leather shops."[9]

Instead of being taught in formal classes, students are divided into tutorial groups of fifteen with one full-time faculty member and one university intern assigned to each tutorial group. The students work in the community in "institutional offerings" such as those described above. They also take courses in basic skills, such as language arts and mathematics, and they select electives. Other cities have taken up "the school without walls" idea; for instance, the Chicago Public Schools sponsor the Chicago Metropolitan Studies High School, less formally known as Metro. New York City has an intern plan provided through cooperation of the Human Resources Administration and the Board of Education; in 1973 seven hundred high school juniors and seniors gained a full term of school credit outside classrooms through observing and assisting executives.

An alternative school of a different sort within New York City is John Dewey High School. Within an eight-hour school day for teachers and students alike, students spend approximately one quarter of their time in independent study utilizing independent study kits. Twenty-minute modules characterize the flexible modular schedule. The year is divided into five seven-week cycles and students are regularly reprogrammed. A wide assortment of courses are offered and are supplemented by an extensive guidance program. For some students, there is a degree of community involvement. Throughout the program there is a strong emphasis on learning for mastery.[10]

The Portland, Oregon, Public Schools provides John Adams High School as an alternative. The school emphasizes a general education program based on a study of contemporary or historical issues, problems, and topics. Investigations of problems are frequently accompanied by action within the community. The program utilizes team teaching and resembles the core curriculum for it stresses a problem-centered program. However, unlike most core programs, Adams attempts to use the disciplines as the vehicles for study of the problems.[11]

The Berkeley, California, Public Schools developed a wide variety of alternative schools. Berkeley's public school student body is 45% black, 44% white, and 11% Chicano and Asian. A freelance writer reports:

[8] John Bremer, *The Parkway Program* (Philadelphia: The Philadelphia Public Schools, 1970), p. 4.
[9] James D. Greenberg and Robert E. Roush, "A Visit to the 'School Without Walls': Two Impressions," *Phi Delta Kappan* (May 1970), p. 482.
[10] Sol Levine, "The John Dewey High School Adventure," *Phi Delta Kappan* (October 1971), pp. 108–110.
[11] Alan L. Dobbins, "Instruction at Adams," *Phi Delta Kappan* (May 1971), pp. 516–519.

The experiment in Berkeley centers on twenty-four alternative public schools. All told, they enroll approximately 4,000 elementary and secondary school students—more than one-fourth of the city's entire school population. Some of the new alternative schools are on the grounds of the regular public schools; others are in former factories, homes, churches, and storefronts. Some are deliberately intimate, with a limit of fifty students; others are larger than the traditional schools from which they've drawn their students. Some emphasize multicultural studies; others are racially exclusive. In some, parents are required to participate; in others, they aren't even courted. All twenty-four experimental schools, however, say that they share two priorities: the elimination of institutional racism and the delivery of basic academic skills.[12]

Among the Berkeley alternative schools are Lincoln, housing an "Environmental Studies Program"; Kilimajaro, where "the school is run by parents"; Model A, "which emphasizes basic skills"; On Target, "geared to job awareness experiences"; the School of the Arts, "heavy on drama, music, and dance"; Agora, "designed to teach an appreciation of racial differences"; College Prep, which "is designed to motivate, counsel, and drill them on to higher education"; West Campus Work Study; Casa De La Raza, "a warm child-oriented Chicano-flavored open school"; Black House, emphasizing "a racial consciousness-raising, an independent assertion of identity"; and New Ark, "an all-Asian school." Casa and Black House were "in constant negotiations with the U.S. Office of Education about possible violations of the Civil Rights Act."[13] In 1973, the latter two schools were closed after the Office for Civil Rights of the Department of Health, Education, and Welfare had warned that the schools were violating federal law through being limited to Chicanos and blacks.

Some large high schools have experimented with the development of alternatives through mini-schools within massive buildings. For instance, Haaren High School in New York City, faced by characteristic difficult inner-city school problems, initiated fourteen mini-schools each made up of 150 students and about six or seven teachers. Through a core curriculum combining English, social studies, and mathematics, the mini-schools stressed such themes as ". . . aerospace studies, automotive mechanics, aviation, business, preparation for college, wood-metal-electrical shop, creative arts, English as a second language, cooperative education, preparation for high school equivalency tests, electronics, education of the retarded, work-study, and urban affairs."[14] During the 1971–72 school year, a mini-school focusing on the reading skills of the functionally illiterate was added to the program.

[12] Diane Divoky, "Berkeley's Experimental Schools," *Saturday Review* (September 16, 1972), p. 46.
[13] *Ibid.*, pp. 45–50.
[14] "Mini-School Test Ends First Year," *New York Times*, June 25, 1972, p. 50.

### Relation of Organization to Content

In the case of core programs or open education or alternative schools, changes in organization often affect the curriculum content taught. Nongradedness, team teaching, modular scheduling, and independent study were often initiated to lead to better utilization of manpower, greater efficiency in operation, and more effective management of the time of students and teachers. However, these latter forms of organization may or may not affect the curriculum content taught.

Those educational innovations which are primarily related to management usually are adopted with less community controversy than changes in curriculum content. For instance, the teaching of sex education in a core curriculum or the establishment of an alternative school to teach black studies is likely to arouse more community controversy than the introduction of team teaching or modular scheduling in the curriculum of a more traditional school.

## DISCUSSION

1. What are the processes customarily used in changing the curriculum? What has been learned from such processes and, consequently, what changes in curriculum development have taken place relatively recently?
2. Where does the motivation for curriculum change as to content usually originate? Can you illustrate?
3. What essentially is a nongraded school? What are its advantages and disadvantages?
4. Imagine yourself in a school situation in which nongrading is prevalent. How would your work be different from your anticipated work in a more conventional school?
5. What essentially is the nature of team teaching? What are its advantages and disadvantages? Imagine yourself teaching in a team teaching situation. How would this be different from teaching in a more usual situation?
6. How does team teaching threaten the traditional teacher?
7. What is the meaning of the core curriculum? Of the sources or referents described in the last chapter, which are most likely to be used in core curriculum approaches? Which less likely?
8. What is the difference between structured and unstructured core?
9. If you taught in a core program, how might this experience be different from teaching in a more conventional school program? What kind of educational background and experiences would be maximally useful to you in teaching in a core program?
10. What is the meaning of modular scheduling? In modular scheduling, what is the role of the human being in supplying ideas and the computer in supplying programs?
11. What do you see as the value of having modular scheduling at the high school level? Do you see any problems or possible losses?

12. How might your work as a teacher be different if you taught in a school characterized by modular scheduling?
13. Were there any features of a core approach, ungradedness, modular scheduling, etc., in your school experience?
14. How would your work be different if it included substantial relationships to independent study?
15. What are three dimensions in education to which the concept of openness applies?
16. What is the difference between open education characterized by "the new freedom" and characterized by "the new fundamentalism"? How would your work as a teacher be different if you taught in one or the other of these two forms of open education? How would either of these differ from teaching in a traditional situation?
17. What is the essence of a "school without walls"? What are some illustrations of alternative schooling within the public school system? How do types of alternative schooling differ from traditional forms of education?
18. What type of personality and approach is required if one teaches in an alternative public school?
19. Why are matters of content change often more controversial than matters of organizational change?

## INVOLVEMENT

1. Investigate a curriculum project related to your subject field or level and report upon it to the class as a whole.
2. Learn of the location of a nongraded school and visit classes on several levels. Talk with the teachers about advantages and disadvantages of this approach.
3. After visiting a school in which team teaching takes place, interview several members of a particular team for their perceptions of their responsibilities.
4. A core or block of time program may be found on the junior high school level in your own or a neighboring community. If so, visit such a program. Compare the approaches you observe with those described in this chapter.
5. Draw up a chart for a proposed core curriculum from the seventh through the twelfth grades characterized by learning units which seem most important to you at this time in American life and at varied stages of the learners' development.
6. If a nearby school uses computerized modular scheduling, visit to learn both about the machinery involved and the resultant program. Note the differences in utilization of modules by teachers in subject fields.
7. Observe independent study as it takes place in a school situation. What types of students seem to use this opportunity well? Why do some do badly?
8. Locate an open school situation in your community and arrange a visit. Take abundant time to talk to administrators, teachers, and students. Attempt to define similarities to and differences from the more usual type of schools. Can you identify any students who particularly seem to profit or lose in the open situation?
9. Locate alternative schools in your area. Arrange for a visit. Take substantial time to understand and absorb differences in setting, practice, and procedure. Include discussions with those related to the alternative school visited.
10. Observe any situations of curriculum change in local schools to test the validity of the generalization that content changes are more controversial than organization changes.

## FURTHER READING

Adler, Richard R. *Humanities Programs Today.* New York: Citation Press, 1970. Descriptions of contemporary humanities programs in elementary, middle, but especially in high schools, through 35 case studies.

Alberty, Harold B. and Elsie J. Alberty. *Reorganizing the High-School Curriculum,* 3rd ed. New York: Macmillan, 1962. A classic in curriculum which sets forth the case for an approach centered upon the needs of the learner and democratic values. Advocates and describes the uses of the core curriculum.

Bremer, John and Michael von Moschzisker. *The School Without Walls.* New York: Holt, Rinehart, and Winston, 1971. An account of the Parkway Program of the Philadelphia schools by the creator and director of the program and accounts of the experience by people who were members of this program and by a professional reporter.

Brown, B. Frank. *New Directions for the Comprehensive High School.* West Nyack, N.Y.: Parker Publishing Co., 1972. A critical look at innovations such as team teaching, modular scheduling and performance contracting by the former principal of Melbourne High School in Florida. Purposes of the high school are stressed.

Buffie, Edward G. and John M. Jenkins (Eds.). *Curriculum Development in Nongraded Schools.* Bloomington, Indiana: Indiana University Press, 1971. One of the Bold New Venture series at Indiana University. Deals with nongradedness, its applications and implementations. The book includes reports of outstanding programs at several school levels.

Channon, Gloria. *Homework!* New York: Outerbridge & Dienstfrey, 1970. A New York City public school teacher tells the story of her experiment with an open and freer classroom in which children largely determined for themselves how and what they would study. This is not a treatise on homework; the title stems from conviction that reading about such experiences should be "required" for teachers and parents.

Doll, Ronald C. *Leadership to Improve Schools.* Worthington, Ohio: Charles A. Jones, 1972. A highly readable book for potential educational leaders that emphasizes practical approaches to the performance of five major leadership tasks.

Frymier, Jack R. and Horace C. Hawn. *Curriculum Improvement for Better Schools.* Worthington, Ohio: Charles A. Jones, 1970. The process and the meaning of curriculum change today.

Grobman, Hulda. *Developmental Curriculum Projects: Decision Points and Processes.* Itasca, Ill.: F. E. Peacock, 1970. A study of similarities and differences in methods of producing developmental curricula that provides a critical overview of the curriculum projects of the 1950s and 1960s.

Marsh, Leonard. *Alongside the Child.* New York: Harper & Row, 1970. Experiences in the English primary school as reported by an observer of young children at work.

Rathbone, Charles H. (Ed.). *Open Education: The Informal Classroom.* New York: Citation Press, 1971. A selection of readings that examines the practices and the principles of the British infant schools and their American counterparts, edited by one who has traveled to many open schools in the United States and England.

Repo, Satu (Ed.). *This Book Is About Schools.* New York: Pantheon, 1971. Ideas on education from the activist journal called *This Magazine Is About Schools.* Stresses potentiality of alternatives in education.

Skeel, Dorothy J. and Owen A. Hagen. *The Process of Curriculum Change.* Pacific Pal-
isades, Calif.: Goodyear, 1971. A fictionalized account of the curriculum change
process as it might take place in a typical community. Provides the reader with
open-ended situations from which he can draw his own conclusions.

Weber, Lillian. *The English Infant School and Informal Education.* Englewood Cliffs,
N.J.: Prentice-Hall, 1971. The English approach to informal and open education.
Emphasis on applications in American schools.

## SELECTED AUDIO-VISUAL MATERIALS

*And No Bells Ring* (16 mm film, 56 min., color, National Association of Secondary
School Principals, 1960). Dramatizes new directions planned to improve the
quality of education. Discusses how high schools have handled space and schedule changes.

*Characteristics of a Core Program* (16 mm film, 20 min., b. & w., Columbia University
Teachers College, 1958). Describes the characteristics of the core program at the
junior and senior high school levels.

*Critical Moments in Teaching: Walls* (16 mm film, 11 min., color, Holt, Rinehart and
Winston, 1969). A young high school teacher has tried to expose his high school
class to independent study. All have failed to do assignments on their own. How
can he encourage them to respond?

*High School Team Teaching: The Ferris Story* (16 mm film, 26 min., color, Bailey Film
Associates, 1966). A springboard for further investigation and study by groups
interested in team teaching and flexible scheduling. Compares the modular flexible scheduling system with the traditional class schedule.

*The Improbable Form of Master Sturm* (16 mm film, 14 min., color, Institute for Development of Educational Activities, 1967). Deals with the nongraded school and
concern for individual differences in students. The school shown has practiced
nongradedness for years.

*Individualizing in Duluth* (16 mm film, 12 min., color, Audio Productions, Inc., 1969).
Demonstrates how a Duluth, Minnesota, school teacher used student contracts in
individualized instruction to promote achievement of behavioral objectives and
student decision-making.

*Inquiry: A Teaching Method* (35 mm filmstrip, 2 filmstrips/records/cassettes, color,
Schloat Productions, 1972). Techniques to lead educators to an in-depth understanding of the theory and practice of the inquiry method of teaching.

*Learning Through Inquiry* (16 mm film, 22 min., color, Institute for Development of
Educational Activities, 1970). Illustrates how the inquiry technique changes the
teacher's function and stimulates student interest, interaction, and learning.

*Make a Mighty Reach* (16 mm film, 28 min., color, Institute for Development of Educational Activities, 1967). Shows innovations that have been made in exemplary
schools across the country. Urges educators and parents to support and encourage
innovation in their schools.

*Non-Graded Education for the Modern Elementary School — A Series* (35 mm filmstrips, records, color, Eye Gate House, Inc., 1967). Introduces and explores concepts inherent in nongraded education. Discusses objectives, groupings, and orientation. Titles include: Non-Graded Education — An Overview (111 frs.); Ques-

tion of Grouping for Non-Graded Education (43 frs.); Within the Non-Graded School (43 frs.); Effecting the Change to a Non-Graded Program (43 frs.).

*Why Are Team Teaching and Non-Grading Important?* (16 mm film, 49 min., color, Special Purpose Films, 1965). Presents John Goodlad as he explains how team teaching and nongrading help to bridge the gap between the problems of school organization and individual learning differences.

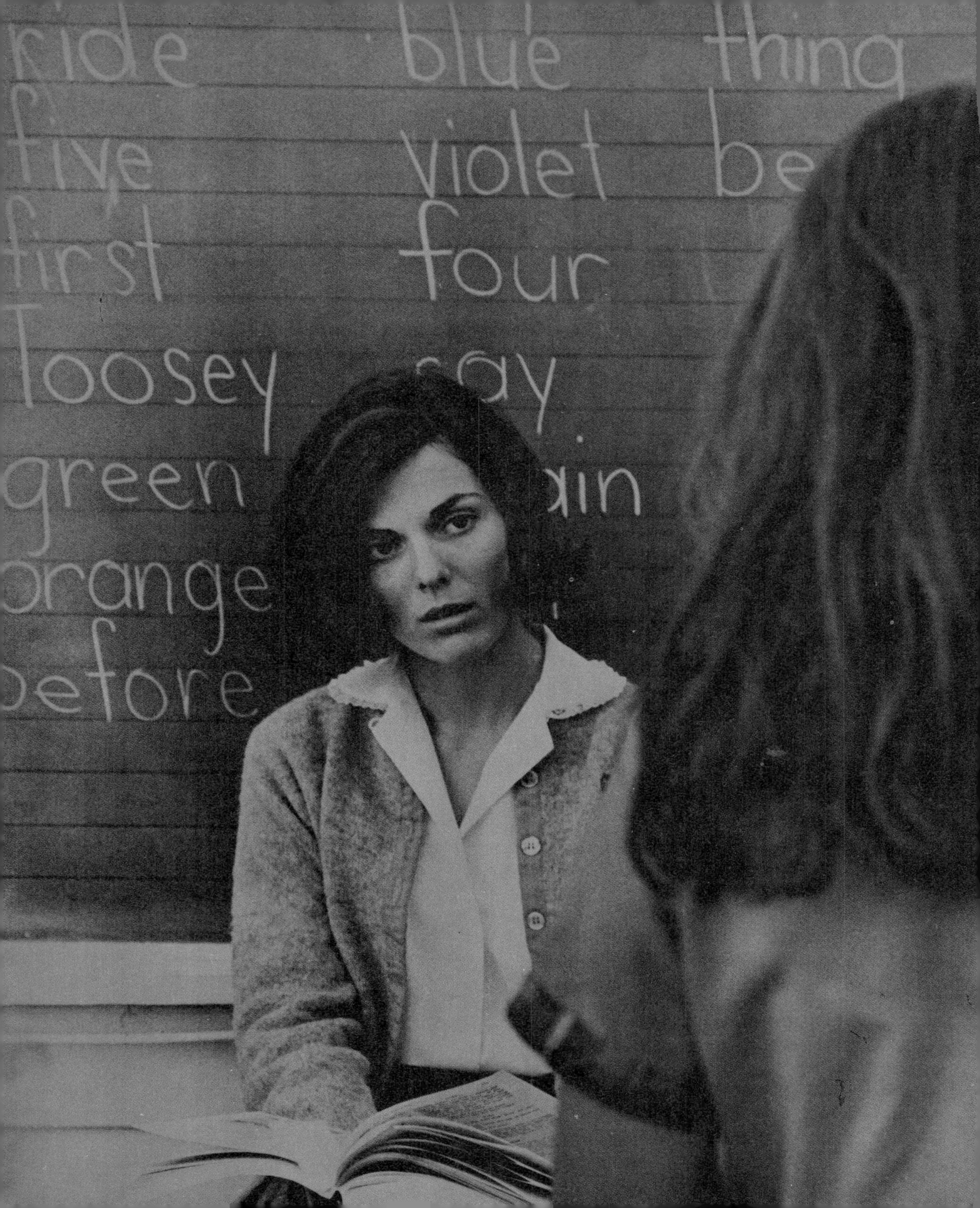
ride
blue
thing
five
violet
first
four
loosey
green
orange

PART FOUR

THE NEW TEACHER

# NINETEEN

# What does the new teacher worry about?

A teacher, like every other human being, is bound to have understandable and natural insecurities, especially when he is just beginning to test his ideas about teaching. He must learn to relate positively and effectively to a variety of individual personalities who are new to him: the children or youth who are assigned to his care, their parents or guardians, and his professional associates who may have a profound influence on his career.

Even if one is a successful teacher with many years of experience, he can never rest secure in predictable patterns of behavior; the good teacher is forever searching for better ways of planning and organizing his work and of developing relationships with others. So most worries of the new teacher are not unique to him (though he may feel that they are); they emerge whenever and wherever human beings come together in purposeful groups. They usually have to do with identifying, clarifying, and achieving group goals, and with maintaining a psychological climate of warmth and mutual respect that encourages participation and responsible behavior by group members.[1]

[1] Findings from inquiry into group processes and group dynamics, a relatively young twentieth century field, are of considerable value to educators. See: Dorwin Cartwright and Alvin Zander (Eds.), *Group Dynamics* (New York: Harper & Bros. 1960); Herbert A. Thelen, *Classroom Grouping for Teachability* (New York: John Wiley & Sons, 1967); David Johnson, *Reaching Out* (Englewood Cliffs, N.J.: Prentice-Hall, 1972); Gerard Eager, *Encounter: Group Processes for Interpersonal Growth* (Belmont, Calif.: Belmont Publishing, 1970); Mark Chesler and Robert Fox, *Role-Playing Methods in the Classroom* (Chicago: Science Research Associates, 1966); Robert Fox, *et al., Diagnosing Classroom Learning Environments* (Chicago: Science Research Associates, 1966); Richard Schmuck, *et al., Problem Solving to Improve Classroom Learning* (Chicago: Science Research Associates, Inc., 1966).

High on the list of a new teacher's concerns are worries about discipline; students with problems; how to provide a variety of methods and materials so that individual differences can be met; confrontations of all kinds. We will attempt in this chapter to deal with these particular worries which grow out of his relationships with children and youth, whether the school is public or nonpublic; elementary, secondary, or college; urban or rural; set in a wealthy suburb, a middle class neighborhood, or an impoverished slum.

## DISCIPLINE

Clearly, discipline is one of the major worries of the new teacher. And little wonder. On the success of his efforts to build relationships of warmth, respect, and trust will depend the quality of his control, the excellence of his teaching, and the opportunity for students to grow.

Too often the new teacher sees discipline and control as processes separate from teaching; instead they are at its very heart. Control is the by-product of the teacher's relations with each student as an individual and with the group as a whole. The new teacher often asks himself whether his relations with students should be permissive or authoritarian. Neither a laissez-faire nor an authoritarian approach to classroom control can create the climate that is necessary for the development of the kind of human relationships necessary for growth. As early as 1939 Kurt Lewin, Ronald Lippitt, and Ralph White conducted an experiment on the reaction of a boys' club to different kinds of leadership: laissez-faire (permissive), authoritarian, and democratic. The results were impressively in favor of the democratic, which is characterized by respect for individuals, careful exploration of goals and methods, and cooperative planning for work.[2]

### Effects of Teacher Personality Patterns

The personality of the teacher will have much to do with the kind of relationships he develops with students and the nature of his control. A new teacher may well ask himself whether his special life-style will permit him to develop an effective classroom control. Can the new teacher be himself? Or must he basically change his life-style and play an unfamiliar role while teaching?

Some educators counsel the new teacher to be completely himself and to follow the style with which he is most comfortable, whether it is open or restrictive, relaxed or taut, permissive or authoritarian. Others counsel the new teacher to begin with tight patterns of control, then gradually loosen certain ones, a practice satirically described as "never

---

[2] See R. Lippitt and R. White, "The Social Climate of Children's Groups," in Barker, Kounin, and Wright (Eds.), *Child Behavior and Development* (New York: McGraw-Hill, 1943), pp. 485–506. The study has since been rewritten and published in *Autocracy and Democracy* edited by Barker and Wright (New York: Harper & Bros., 1960).

smile until Thanksgiving." But there is a middle way in which a new teacher may maintain his basic life-style and be himself, yet watch with a critical eye to see the consequences of his behavior and change his ways of working with others when those ways are ineffective.

For example, though he may be inclined to be open, permissive, and informal, the new teacher might well consider whether to allow students to call him by his first name in classroom situations. He might ask himself whether any gains from first-naming are negated by losses such as overly casual student attitudes toward him as a teacher and resentment or amusement among the young that an older person should consider himself a peer. Similarly, however closed, restricted, and formal his life-style may be, the new teacher must consider the saving contribution which humor makes to a classroom situation. He might ask himself whether some lighthearted words might result in occasional avoidance of trouble.

No one except possibly a gifted actor can successfully maintain a role that is not his, save at the price of great strain; a danger always exists that he will drop the role under tension and revert to his own way. So as to discipline, the best bet is to be oneself, rather than attempt to be an actor, yet modify one's ways of relating to students through self-criticism and recognition of effective approaches to control. The result should be greater respect for the new teacher as an individual. Young people and

Teacher and class enjoy a good laugh together.

Discipline can be maintained with compassion and care.

children value honesty and sincerity and willingness to be realistic; they readily detect phoniness.

There is no single teaching pattern which guarantees success with all students. Some students particularly appreciate and respect the teacher who closely identifies with the problems and concerns of class members. Others appreciate and respect the teacher who is apparently more interested in the content he is teaching than in the individual personalities in the class. And some students equally respect both types.

However, followers of the perceptual school of psychology fostered by Carl Rogers, Earl Kelley, Abraham Maslow, and Arthur Combs, believe that some personality patterns are preferable to others. They call for fully functioning and self-actualizing persons. By way of definition they say that the fully functioning, self-actualizing personality thinks well of himself and of others, and therefore sees his stake in others. He sees himself as part of a world in movement—in process of becoming. Seeing the importance of people, he develops and holds human values. He knows no other way to live except in keeping with his values.[3]

Carl Rogers sees the fully functioning person as a human being in flow, in process, rather than as having achieved some final state. To him

[3] Earl C. Kelley, "The Fully Functioning Self," pp. 18–20 in *Perceiving, Behaving, Becoming* (Washington, D.C.: Association for Supervision and Curriculum Development, 1962).

such a person is sensitively open to all of his experience. He experiences in the present, with immediacy. He permits his total organism to function freely in all its complexity in selecting from many possibilities the behavior which will be most genuinely and generally satisfying.[4]

Arthur Combs says that the truly adequate self-actualizing person is one who has "a positive view of self-identification with others, openness to experience and acceptance, and a rich and available perceptual field."[5] Elaborating upon these characteristics Combs says:

1. Extremely adequate, self-actualizing persons seem to be characterized by an essentially positive view of self. They see themselves as persons who are liked, wanted, acceptable, able; as persons of dignity and integrity, of worth and importance. This is not to suggest that adequate people never have negative ways of regarding themselves. They very well may. The total economy of such persons, however, is fundamentally positive. They see themselves as adequate to deal with life.[6]

2. The feeling of oneness with one's fellows produces in the truly adequate person a high degree of responsible, trustworthy behavior. There is reason for this response. When identification is strong, one cannot behave in ways likely to be harmful or injurious to others, for to do that would be to injure one's self. As a consequence, adequate persons are likely to manifest a deep respect for the dignity and integrity of other people and a strong sense of justice and moral probity.[7]

3. Truly adequate persons possess perceptual fields maximally open to experience. That is to say, their perceptual fields are capable of change and adjustment in such fashion as to make fullest possible use of their experience. Truly healthy persons seem capable of accepting into awareness any and all aspects of reality. They do not find it necessary to defend themselves against events or to distort their perceptions to fit existing patterns. Their perceptual fields are maximally open and receptive to their experiences.[8]

4. The truly adequate person must also be well informed. . . . One need not know everything to be adequate, but one must certainly have a field of perceptions rich and extensive enough to provide understanding of the events in which he is enmeshed and available when he needs them. Adequate people have such perceptual fields. This does not mean that their perceptions are necessarily of an abstract, intellectual character or gained solely from formal schooling. Rich perceptual fields may be derived from quite informal sources through firsthand involvement in human relations in business, in recreation, or in performing a trade or occupation.[9]

What are the implications of the self-actualizing personality for the problem of discipline? The self-actualizing teacher encourages good dis-

[4] Carl Rogers, "Toward Becoming a Fully Functioning Person," pp. 31–32 in *Perceiving, Behaving, Becoming* (Washington, D.C.: ASCD, 1962).
[5] Arthur W. Combs, "A Perceptual View of the Adequate Personality," p. 51 in *Perceiving, Behaving, Becoming* (Washington, D.C.: ASCD, 1962).
[6] *Ibid.*, p. 51.
[7] *Ibid.*, pp. 54–55.
[8] *Ibid.*, p. 56.
[9] *Ibid.*, pp. 59–60.

cipline by showing that he is interested in the individual young person and his welfare. Such a teacher is willing to listen to a young person while reserving or at least not indicating judgment. Such a teacher gives the young person direct evidence that he is liked. He builds mutual trust; he looks hard for ways in which a young person can succeed. He behaves in ways which young people regard as fair. When he makes a mistake, he does not hesitate to say, "I made a mistake; I'm sorry." He has inner security and does not constantly feel personally threatened by misbehavior. He is often able to rally leaders to his side in emergency situations and to avail himself of the group pressure which students themselves can bring to bear. Yet he does not allow group pressure to get out of hand and become punitive. Because of feeling secure, he can maintain a sense of humor. In time, such a teacher may master the delicate combination of being objective enough to look clinically at a class and its members and at the same time maintain human concern for and involvement in the welfare of both individuals and the total class.

The self-actualizing teacher will avoid temptations to maintain discipline through techniques which in actuality often lead to open resentment and rebellion. A self-actualizing teacher will not ridicule either the individual or his family. He will avoid sarcasm. He will not try to command the situation through hollering; he won't filibuster through talking incessantly. Such a teacher will not depend upon idle threats or inflict degrading punishments, nor will he hold grudges or bar students from making fresh starts with a new day or new term. The sensible teacher will avoid punishing indiscriminately a whole class through, for example, keeping everyone after school. He will avoid talking down to the pupils just as he will try to avoid talking over their heads. He will avoid "taking everything personally," that is, seeing all misbehavior as a personal affront to him and his dignity.

Perceptual psychologists believe that a positive attitude toward oneself and toward others does help with respect to discipline. For self-acceptance is a prerequisite to accepting others. Self-understanding is a prerequisite to understanding others. As Rolf Muuss has pointed out," 'Thou shalt love thy neighbor as thyself' seems to contain a deep psychological insight in this respect. . . ."[10]

Whether good relationships and desirable conditions for learning are achieved depends largely on the teacher's faith in himself, the richness of his feeling life, his intellectual power, his fairness and honesty, his awareness of what is happening in the class (a new teacher is often concentrating so much on himself that he can't see the class or the individuals in it), his refusal to vent any frustration by cutting and sarcastic language, his refusal to gain personal satisfaction in exercising power over

[10] Rolf E. Muuss, "First-Aid for Discipline Problems," *Discipline in the Classroom* (Washington, D.C.: National Education Association, 1969), p. 16.

others, and his willingness to alter his carefully prepared plans in the light of new and pressing needs for change. If this seems a high order, it is! Teaching is a field that tests your capacities as a human being.

### Effects of the Curriculum

Behavior problems that challenge the relationships between teacher and child often grow out of a curriculum which does not make sense to the learner. When the academic content bears no relationship to the needs or experience or the world of the learner, the classroom can become a breeding place for rebellion. It is not simply that the content is too hard or too easy, though this may sometimes be the case. The problem is often that the curriculum experiences are trivial and academic. They are unrelated to the learner's needs, irrelevant to the social realities which surround the learner, lacking in relationship to values, and inadequate in developing concepts and stimulating inquiry. In other words, sometimes the real villain with respect to discipline is a curriculum which does not take into account the background of the learner nor provide a wide variety of activities in which each child may satisfy his special needs or interests.

If young people are deeply absorbed in their work and enjoying the activities which the school provides, they are less likely to create discipline problems. To achieve high absorption, careful and systematic planning of classroom experiences is necessary. Such planning can only be successful if the teacher knows the general background and experiences of the young people who make up the class and if he comes to know the backgrounds and experiences of as many individuals as he possibly can. Useful experiences for a college oriented and sometimes intellectually self-motivated group of upper middle class students may not be helpful when they are provided for an occupation oriented and sometimes intellectually less motivated group of the upper lower class young. So-called "bad" language, including profane or obscene four-letter words, may represent genuine defiance in an upper middle class suburb but may represent the only known way of expressing a particular idea in a lower lower class area.

The ingenious teacher usually finds ways of relating content to the needs and interests of young people. Sustained classroom activities may work with some individuals whereas varied activities and methods may be better for pupils who have a short attention span, difficulty in learning through symbols, and who need stimulation through experiences enriched by seeing, hearing, and touching. The teacher keeps an eye on the level of communication and tries to combine adequate understanding with sufficient challenges; he uses a variety of methods and materials.

The successful teacher also arranges the immediate setting to get the best results. He checks the classroom environment for temperature, ventilation, and light; he tries to create a surrounding environment appro-

*Elaine Keenan*

"Better discipline will prevail when learning experiences relate closely to the present interests and needs of children. . . ."

priate to his particular subject or grade level. He may have materials about the room such as an aquarium; separate corners for science, art, or reading; books on hobbies; charts and bright posters to tempt children to explore and think. The teacher may strategically space work centers throughout the classroom to make the room a workroom and to prevent children from clustering in overly large groups and to reduce the time that the teacher stands in front of the room. Time is provided for getting out materials and restoring them. A room left in a disorderly state is an invitation for the new occupants to engage in disorderly behavior.

Some teachers hesitate to plan with students because of fear of disorderly behavior. Actually, the reverse is more frequently the case — undesirable behavior often grows out of lack of sharing in planning with the result that the student sometimes does not understand the work that is going on and cannot find his place in the process. In today's schools, there is less likelihood of the emergence of discipline problems if students have a say in the development of ground rules. There is less chance of disorderly conduct if the content itself is developed cooperatively with young people through the process of teacher-pupil planning. Today's young people often rebel against rules they have not been allowed to participate in developing.

There is reluctance among even experienced teachers to plan cooperatively with students. Some of this comes from a misunderstanding of the kind of opportunities which the curriculum presents for choices. There are many, many situations in which students at any age can be involved in making decisions which affect them. Students can plan together for the details of a field trip including deciding on the standards of conduct that are to be observed; identifying the purposes of the excursion; suggesting what to see, hear, or do; building the criteria for judging the effectiveness of their experience; and evaluating the trip. In preparing to hear a speaker, watch a film or filmstrip or hear a recording, the class may list and present the questions to be asked, then see and judge how adequately they were answered. Students can set up standards for classroom behavior and check from time to time to see whether they are still effective guides to conduct. Students may compose a list of activities which may be pursued when required work is finished and be responsible for carrying through such activities. Such participation is essential for learning. In *The Authentic Teacher,* Moustakas points out three conditions for growth in the individual: freedom to be, choice and the capacity to choose, and responsibility and self-confirmation.[11]

The introductory article of a pamphlet published by the National Education Association notes the close relationship between student behavior and significant learning experiences:

> Better discipline will prevail when learning experiences relate closely to the present interests and needs of children who see the use of what they are learning. Better discipline will prevail when learning is related to the social realities which surround the child. Better discipline will prevail when we practice what we preach as to respect of personality. Better discipline will prevail as we develop active student participation, creative contributions, social travel, and all else that fosters significant experience. Better discipline will grow out of a better curriculum in a better setting.
>
> You may know a little Jimmy who is a discipline problem despite an apparently meaningful curriculum. So do I. But in our concern for nonconforming little Jimmy, let us not neglect improving the environment of millions of Jimmys through gearing our curriculum to the lives of the young and avoiding needless disciplinary struggles.[12]

## STUDENTS WITH PROBLEMS

Let us now look more closely at ways of dealing with nonconforming Jimmy, the individual "problem" student. As the poet Robert Burns has pointed out, "The best laid plans o' mice and men gang aft a-gley." Even the best of teachers encounter discipline problems with particular individuals, however self-actualizing the teacher's personality may be or however relevant the curriculum to the learner's life experiences.

How should a teacher work with a troublemaker who is acting alone

[11] Clark Moustakas, *The Authentic Teacher* (Cambridge, Mass.: Howard A. Doyle, 1966), pp. 9–12.
[12] William Van Til, "Better Curriculum—Better Discipline," pp. 1–2 in *Discipline in the Classroom* (Washington, D.C.: National Education Association, 1969).

or in concert with fellow troublemakers? The first necessity is to deal with the immediate problem so that the class may continue its work and not disintegrate into disorder. Only rules of thumb can be used here; sometimes the best approach is to ignore the problem for the moment, sometimes it may be necessary to check it then and there, or even to remove the disturber from the classroom situation, though this often proves to be a defeating experience.[13]

But as soon as possible, any action should be followed by a talk with the individual and a realistic analysis of the problem confronting the new teacher. The immediate incident may be the focus. However, the perceptive teacher soon tries to determine causation and patterns. To learn still more about the individual student, the teacher may turn to cumulative records or the experiences of other teachers with the individual. Some authorities recommend going to such sources prior to disturbances in order to spot potential troublemakers in advance. But there is a danger that such a procedure may result in a judgment of guilty prior to any offense being committed. One needs also to be sure that he responds only to those recorded comments that are objective descriptions of behavior.

A combination of discussing the situation with the student and reviewing the student's past history through reading records and consulting former teachers should help the new teacher to diagnose what is basically wrong. In some situations a few words may be all that is needed to result in renewed efforts to build trust and respect on the part of both teacher and student. In other situations, the problem may be much more complicated. Sometimes it is a reflection of accepted social class patterns, such as foul language or toughness on the part of a youth influenced by lower lower class life patterns. Sometimes the behavior incident grows out of deep unmet personality needs of the student; for example, hunger for group attention or for approval. Sometimes the negative classroom behavior has to do with racial antagonism. Sometimes the disturbance may grow out of economic factors, such as lack of money to join the group at the drugstore after school or envy of someone's new clothes.

No single prescription can apply to all cases. In each situation, the teacher must use his own judgment and, always conscious that troublesome pupils are really troubled pupils, attempt to do whatever good sense would suggest in the particular setting. Nor is the teacher completely alone in meeting such situations. Principals are sensitive to behavior problems in classrooms and can often aid the new teacher. A good supporting staff can be helpful. The number of guidance counselors in schools is growing. Increasingly schools have relationships with out-

13 Katherine La Mancusa, "Now Enter Billy Bully," *We Do Not Throw Rocks at the Teacher* (Scranton, Pa.: International Textbook, 1966), pp. 51–57.

side agencies, such as mental health centers and guidance clinics. The perceptive new teacher will take advantage of such facilities when they exist. Professional therapy is not the province of the teacher, but in most cases teachers can provide an environment which is nonthreatening and to which insecure or lost individuals may respond.

In schools in which mutual trust among faculty members is characteristic, conferences with other teachers should help. Staff discussion meetings may deal with individual students who baffle their teachers. In most situations teachers, nurses, administrators, and counselors are essentially on the side of new teachers and willing to try to help. Nor should conference with parents be minimized as one technique in working out solutions to behavior problems. For every parent who proves impossible (as perceived by the teacher) in a conference, there are many others who, greeted with tact and without a patronizing attitude, will be enormously helpful to the teacher.

Unfortunately, corporal punishment, which is marked by the use of physical force such as spanking or paddling, still exists in some schools. However, three states, New Jersey, Massachusetts, and Maryland, have outlawed corporal punishment. Law suits in the federal courts of several other states challenged corporal punishment as a violation of civil rights. But in 1972, the U.S. Supreme Court refused to hear an appeal by parents of two Dallas high school students who contended that corporal punishment is "cruel and unusual punishment" that is prohibited by the U.S. Constitution. So the Supreme Court let stand a lower court decision that spanking or paddling by school authorities did not interfere with constitutional rights. Decisions on physical punishment were left up to school boards and lower courts in the states.[14]

The problem is complicated by the belief of some teachers that they need to be allowed the "judicious use" of corporal punishment in difficult situations. Some see the use of bodily force as necessary for protection and even survival. In 1973 the NEA indicated that nearly 18 percent of teachers surveyed had reported that a teacher in their school had been attacked by a student during the 1971–72 school year. Twenty-five percent of teachers surveyed reported personal property of teachers maliciously damaged in their school. Faced with both teacher fears of violence directed against them, and with crime in the schools, some school systems are shifting responsibilities for security and safety to security directors who are in charge of school guards. In those inner-city schools which are characterized by violence and crime, the guards and policemen face problems of the sale of drugs, assaults on teachers, vandalism, and shakedowns of students for their money or belongings. Intruders from outside the school are often the offenders.

---

[14] "News Front," *Education, U.S.A.* (December 4, 1972), p. 80.

## INDIVIDUAL DIFFERENCES AND VARIED METHODOLOGIES

Another worry of the new teacher is how to deal with individual differences, which, as we know from an earlier chapter, are inevitable among human beings—differences in intellectual abilities, capacities for creativity, handicaps, and social attitudes.

Perhaps the best advice for the new teacher is that he continue to learn about individual differences among human beings and to explore the various methods he can use in his particular subject field or at the particular level—elementary, secondary, or college—at which he has chosen to work. Obviously the new teacher cannot provide for individual differences if his sole techniques are those he has too frequently been exposed to in his own learning experiences—lectures or question-and-answer recitations. The lecture is, by definition, aimed at the class group as a whole and usually is directed to the average student. Question-and-answer recitations provide for little more variation. Though a harder question may be asked of the more intellectually able student and an easier question may be asked of the less intellectual able, the teacher is aware that others are listening to the responses and that the recitation must be geared to the average or middle group. So if the teacher confines himself simply to such mass-education approaches as the lecture and the recitation, he will be unsuccessful in adapting his instruction to individual differences.

The new teacher might well focus on methods which have promise for differentiation. For instance, he might work with small groups within a class. In good modern schools, committees of students often carry on studies which illuminate problems or topics that are the concern of the whole class. In this case committees report to the group as a whole, working out a wide variety of presentations: a panel, a dramatic skit, a radio program, an interview, a mural, a chart, a map, or even a dance. Within such committees some students make a more significant contribution than others. Members are encouraged to go as far as they can and to contribute at the highest level they can reach.

Another teaching technique is the use of extensive individualization. Children and young people can be encouraged to work independently on topics or problems of greatest interest, geared to individual ability. Individual reports may be made to the class as a whole; the teacher may help the individual find materials and consult with him on his progress. Independent work can flourish in schools organized to provide both teachers and students with time for such activity. Schedules which provide for individual work in laboratories, art rooms, libraries and for face-to-face conferences with teachers are more challenging than the old classroom organization of set periods and inflexible scheduling.

Meeting individual differences may often be achieved through using media to which individuals particularly respond. Some learn a good deal from resources with visual and auditory appeal—films, television broadcasts, radio programs, recordings, and filmstrips. Some gain particularly from panels, symposiums, and debates; others learn better through field trips, social travel, and community participation.

Educational technology is also in the process of providing aids to individualization. Programmed instruction is geared to the individual learner who works at his own program and proceeds at his own pace. Computer-aided instruction provides an even more sophisticated approach to individualized learning.[15] Hicks and Hunka say:

> There exist today many CAI systems which, controlled by suitable computer programs, can be used for an astonishing variety of educational activities. The systems can give drill and practice exercises to dozens of students simultaneously. They can provide instruction in which the lesson-writer, through his CAI program and like a tutor, *guides the learner* step-by-step through the material. At another extreme, they can provide the opportunity for "investigation" in which the *student chooses the questions* he will answer and the educational resources he will use in finding the answers. Through CAI, many students can make experiments simultaneously on the same piece of laboratory apparatus, or the students can make a variety of experiments requiring no real laboratory apparatus but only clever CAI programming that "simulates" the apparatus.[16]

However, critics of computer-assisted instruction point to formidable cost factors, reluctance of teachers to accept CAI, and inadequate "software." They believe a major effort in research and development will be necessary before CAI is widely used; they regard the first round of development during the late 1960s and early 1970s as a failure.

Obviously such brief mention of possible techniques cannot substitute for the information on methods and materials which can be acquired in courses in general methods and courses in special methods of teaching. If the prospective teacher takes advantage of the opportunities which his future courses should provide him, he will learn the materials and methodologies that will markedly reduce his insecurity concerning ways of providing for individual differences.

Skill in using varied methods and materials should be accompanied by deep concern for motivating students. The new teacher must constantly provide stimulating experiences in which subject matter becomes a resource for new insights into human behavior, new pleasures in liv-

---

[15] Don D. Bushnell and Dwight W. Allen (Eds.), *The Computer in American Education* (New York: John Wiley & Sons, 1967); John I. Goodlad, John F. O'Toole, Jr. and Louise L. Tyler, *Computers and Information Systems in Education* (New York: Harcourt, Brace & World, 1966); Paul I. Jacobs, Milton H. Maier, and Lawrence M. Stolurow, *A Guide to Evaluating Self-Instructional Programs* (New York: Holt, Rinehart and Winston, 1966); B. L. Hicks and S. Hunka, *The Teacher and The Computer* (Philadelphia, Pa.: W. B. Saunders Company, 1972); H. A. Lekan, *Index to Computer Assisted Instruction* (New York: The Sterling Institute, 1970); A. E. Hickey (Ed.), *Computer-Assisted Instruction: A Survey of the Literature,* fourth ed., (Newburyport, Mass., ENTELEK, 1969).

[16] Hicks and Hunka, p. 22.

ing, and a means of developing new skills, whether intellectual, social or manipulative. When he finds students who do not respond to the curriculum, his responsibility is to attempt to find out why. Is the problem a matter of reading skill? Are physical factors, such as eyesight, involved? Is the student exhausted because of some environmental circumstance? Does the classwork seem irrelevant to the student?

Different responses are called for by different situations. If the problem is reading, then remedial reading is called for. If the problem is physical—such as eyesight—the cooperation of the nurse and the family is needed. If the problem is exhaustion, investigation of the family situation and cooperation with school or community social work agencies are required.

If the problem is curriculum relevance, close examination of one's own approaches as a teacher is called for. Is subject matter becoming an end in itself, with the growth of children and youth secondary? Can the content be adapted so as to contribute to the lives of students? Can more concrete illustrations be used? Can applications be stressed? Can a conception of possible future uses be built, especially uses for living a better life? Can more able students help others perceive greater relevance? Has the new teacher begun where the learners are? After all, there is nothing more useless to a student than an answer for which he doesn't have a question! Of what use is a solution for which a student does not have a problem?

General psychology and psychology of education courses for teachers in training can be particularly useful in helping the new teacher to become more competent in motivating students. The beginning of wisdom on motivation is to motivate oneself to learn more about motivation!

## CONFRONTATION

Until recently the worries identified so far would have constituted the major problems arising in the context of teacher-student relations. But by the 1970s, a technique of social action borrowed from college campus dissent and from black protest had appeared in American high schools, junior high schools, and even a few elementary schools—the technique of confrontation. Confrontation can be variously defined. For our purposes, it means confronting authorities with demands for changes accompanied by explicit or implicit threats of disruption if the demands are not met, usually within a specified time. Confrontation does not proceed through the normal processes of communication or the usual channels of action (or perhaps inaction); the usual processes may have been tried and found wanting or simply bypassed. Confrontation may or may not take the form of violence.

Protest is a wider term than confrontation. Protest may take place through the normal processes of communication and customary channels

The days of dictating policy to students seem to have passed.

*Howard Petrick, Nancy Palmer Photo Agency*

of action in a school. It may also take the form of confrontation. Before condemning all student protest and confrontation, one should take into account that the United States was established through a protest which eventually took the form of a confrontation — the American Revolution. Such rights as freedom of speech, freedom of the press, and the right of the people peaceably to petition their government are built into the Bill of Rights as legal channels for protest.

According to a survey of more than 1,000 public and private schools reported by the National Association of Secondary School Principals in 1969, the majority of secondary schools were then experiencing protest activities of some sort. Nor was protest confined to the senior high school. Fifty-nine percent of the senior high school principals reported protest activities and, contrary to expectations, almost as many junior high school principals (56 percent) reported protest activities. City schools and suburban schools were the major focus of protest with a rate of 67 percent. In rural areas, the rate dropped to 53 percent, yet even in rural America the majority of secondary schools were experiencing protests.

What were the students unhappy about? At the head of the list were dress and hair regulations. One-third of the principals reported objections to the dress code. One-quarter of the principals reported conflicts over hair lengths and styles. Other matters drawing protest included smoking rules, the conduct of the cafeteria, assembly programs, choices of speakers, censorship and regulation of school papers, the matter of underground papers or pamphlets, and scheduling of such events as sports and social occasions. Problems in the area of race relations were reported by only ten percent of principals. But when racial problems occurred they tended to be characterized by substantial anger, hostility, and sometimes violence. A major object of sharp dissatisfaction was the school program itself. Forty-five percent of the principals cited student protests related to teachers—quality of teaching, assignment of teachers, lack of freedom to choose teachers; to the content of the curriculum; to groupings in classrooms; and to schedules, homework, grades, and examinations.[17]

In the early 1970s student protest in secondary schools ebbed. Tides of protest in secondary schools apparently are influenced by the existence or nonexistence of activist protest in colleges and universities. When university protest decreased, largely through troop withdrawals from Vietnam and reductions of draft calls, high school protest also decreased. Another contributing factor may have been greater sensitivity by high school educators to the necessity for involving youth in policy and planning. High school principals gave serious attention to ways of decreasing conflict, as the titles of recent publications of the National Association of Secondary School Principals indicate. They include *The Reasonable Exercise of Authority*[18] by Robert L. Ackerly, chief counsel for the organization—a pamphlet which defines due process, suggests positions on ten issues, and cites landmark cases; *Disruption in Urban Public Secondary Schools*,[19] by Stephen K. Bailey, which surveys literature on school disruption and reports on the experiences of nineteen schools throughout the country; and *Protest in Black and White: Student Radicals in High Schools*,[20] by David A. Kukla.

Court decisions have also clarified issues by affirming and defining student rights. For instance, in a Supreme Court decision, *Tinker v. Des*

[17] "Survey Finds Dissent Moving Into Lower Grades," *Education, USA* (March 10, 1969), p. 151.
[18] Robert L. Ackerly, *The Reasonable Exercise of Authority,* (The National Association of Secondary School Principals, 1969).
[19] Stephen K. Bailey, *Disruption in Urban Public Secondary Schools,* (The National Association of Secondary School Principals, 1970).
[20] David A. Kukla, "Protest in Black and White: Student Radicals in High Schools," *National Association of Secondary School Principals Bulletin* (January 1972), pp. 72–86.

*Moines Community School District,* the court ruled, "students in school as well as out of school are 'persons' under our Constitution. They are possessed of fundamental rights which the State must respect just as they themselves must respect their obligations to the State."[21]

All teachers have the potential to reduce or eliminate the causes of student unrest through involving students in a genuinely democratic process, characterized by respect for each individual whether teacher or student; by more teacher-pupil planning in classes; more relevant curriculum; more emphasis upon varied ethnic studies in the curriculum; and more opportunities for students to express themselves.

The new teacher may be able to make a special contribution since he is usually closer in age to the junior and senior high school student than is the typical teacher. He has a strategic opportunity to serve as a middle-man or moderator or advisor in student dissent. For example, he is often acutely aware of problems arising from dress codes; he himself may have experienced the impact of such restrictions in schools or colleges he has attended. In 1972 when the Supreme Court refused to hear the case of a young man who did not conform with a school regulation on hair codes, Justice William O. Douglas dissented from that refusal as follows: "It seems incredible that under our federalism a state can deny a student education in its public school system unless his hair style comports with the standards of the school board.[22]

The new teacher might be a helpful participant in committees with student membership which have responsibility for drafting improved disciplinary regulations. He might be helpful in removing grievances, such as discrimination in selecting students for recognition in student government, in athletics and honor societies, and in determining membership in clubs organized to serve special needs.

As he works with students who are reaching out for greater involvement in the world of school and community life, the new teacher must be always aware of the changes that are necessary if institutions that deal with human values and human needs are to be remade and revitalized. In her contribution to *Student Unrest: Threat or Promise,* Maxine Greene counsels those who teach:

It is not really hard to understand the disenchantment of our students. It is not even hard to understand their objections to the traditional teacher-student arrangements, their resentment of the authority which seems to inhere in the very presence of a person standing in front of a classroom and addressing people who, in their very willingness to sit and listen, are accepting inferior roles. We need to be as imaginative as we can about the protest, as empathetic as we can. And we need continually to concern ourselves with creating the kinds of conditions and learning situations in

[21] "Justice Douglas on Hair Codes in Public Schools," *The Washington Post,* January 24, 1972, p. A16.
[22] *Ibid.*

which students feel that we welcome choosing and involvement and making sense in an open world. To do this, we have to think about restoring to the young a sense of potency even as we try to communicate the values of competence, the excitement of patterning, of mindfulness.[23]

## DIMINISHING YOUR WORRIES

These then are some of the things which the new teacher worries about—maintaining discipline, helping individual students who have problems that disturb the class and/or prevent them from learning, providing for individual differences through a wide range of resources and methods, and dealing with confrontation. There are no easy answers which will completely eliminate such worries. There are no panaceas that supply infallible prescriptions to solve such problems.

The new teacher must explore for answers, whether independently, through organized courses, or in interaction with experienced teachers and administrators. Fortunately, the more the new teacher learns and the more his abilities grow in coping with any one of his worries, the more his other worries should diminish. For instance, the more the new teacher can skillfully deal with individual differences, the more likely he is to have rapport with students and the less likely he is to have discipline problems. The problems considered in this chapter are interrelated, and the overcoming of one helps in the conquest of the others.

## DISCUSSION

1. What is your opinion of the major worries of individuals planning to enter teaching? What are some of your own major worries in this connection?
2. What is the meaning of discipline? Does it differ from "control"?
3. What is the case for "being one's self" in matters of discipline? What are the cases for the alternatives?
4. What are some of your personal experiences with school discipline? Interpret these experiences in light of what you now understand about teachers and teaching.
5. In what specific ways have teachers you have respected dealt with discipline problems in their classrooms?
6. What is the essence of the fully functioning self-actualizing personality?
7. What are the implications of the self-actualizing personality theory for the problem of discipline?
8. Is it ever legitimate in the classroom for teachers to be angry, irritated, or hostile? If so, why? If so, when? How about corporal punishment?

[23] Maxine Greene, "The Spectrum of Disenchantment," *Student Unrest: Threat or Promise* (Washington, D.C.: Association for Supervision and Curriculum Development, 1970), pp. 32–33.

9. How would you describe your view of discipline to a group of parents whose children were in your classroom?
10. Whom do you remember as being a particular problem to one of your teachers? What insights do you now have into what caused him to become a problem and into the teacher's method of handling the problem?
11. What are some possible approaches in dealing with the individual problem student? What resources does the teacher have to call upon?
12. What do you see as the role of a classroom teacher in dealing with an emotionally disturbed child?
13. What is the relationship between curriculum content and instructional methodology and the problem of discipline? Is it likely that planning with students will lead to better or poorer discipline?
14. What are some characteristics of methodologies which provide for individual differences? What techniques seem to you most promising? What new technology is developing?
15. What are some key factors in motivating students?
16. Why is readiness on the part of the pupil so significant for learning?
17. What is the meaning of confrontation? How does it differ from protest? How widespread is contemporary student protest and confrontation? What do you think are the implications of protest and confrontation?
18. What are the major grievances of dissenting students? From your experience, are some of these grievances valid? Can you visualize any contributions which you can make to dealing constructively with protest and confrontation as a new teacher?
19. How are the worries of teachers interrelated? In what ways does dealing with one problem aid the teacher in dealing with an allied problem?

## INVOLVEMENT

1. Conduct a survey among class members about their worries as they contemplate becoming a teacher. What proves to be the most usual worry?
2. Try role playing in a series of discipline situations. (One student plays the role of a teacher, another a student, another the principal, another a parent, another an administrator, etc. A discipline situation is described in general and the actors improvise their lines and responses.)
3. Visit a school and observe the interaction in a class. What ways does the teacher use to exercise control? Are they verbal or nonverbal? Are they threatening, punishing, praising? What appears to be the climate of the classroom—laissez-faire, dictatorial, or democratic? Why?
4. Try the role of a fully functioning self-actualizing person by earnestly and consciously attempting to follow this pattern for a period of time. Note whether you encounter any unusual responses from people who are not aware of the nature of your attempt.
5. Try various possible approaches to discipline with young people with whom you have some relationship through family, organizations, etc. Note what seems to succeed with them and speculate on why.
6. Attempt to develop a characteristic curricular experience in your field of specialization. Speculate on whether or not certain discipline problems might or might not occur under these circumstances.

7. Relate these concepts to discipline:
   security            recognition
   responsibility      belonging
8. Present a case study of a problem student observed by you in schools. Discuss possible approaches to such an individual.
9. Visit a classroom. Keep a time diary to determine the percentage of time you observe the teacher doing the talking. How much time is given to students' talking? To quiet study?
10. List some of the possible methodologies to provide for individual differences which you could use in a class you might teach. Share these with other students. Which techniques seem best? At which level or in which subject fields? Are there common denominators?
11. Practice making anecdotal notations about children as you observe them at work. Share these with another student and criticize one another's work.
12. Prepare a personal file of sources for instructional materials. (See audio-visual suggestions at the ends of each chapter.)
13. Visit a school and observe a class for an hour. What teaching methods are used? What materials are used? How are they used?
14. Observe situations in which educational technology is used to see whether individual differences are truly provided for and to assess the general atmosphere surrounding the work of students.
15. In your estimation, how will the use of instructional devices such as teaching machines and programmed books alter school objectives? Computer technology?
16. Conduct your own study of the incidence of confrontation in schools and the apparent causes.
17. Define some of the contributions you hope to make in dealing with confrontation and protest activities in schools in which you will be teaching. Analyze your own strengths and weaknesses as a mediator.

## FURTHER READING

Birmingham, John. *Our Time Is Now.* New York: Praeger, 1970.   Students speak out on topics which concern them, such as civil rights and student rights.

Erickson, Carlton W. H. and David H. Curl. *Fundamentals of Teaching with Audiovisual Technology.* Riverside, N.J.: Macmillan, 1972.   Audio-visual techniques and their use in both traditional and innovative teaching.

Hart, Richard L. and J. Galen Saylor (Eds.). *Student Unrest: Threat or Promise?* Washington, D.C.: Association for Supervision and Curriculum Development, NEA, 1970.   Papers contributed by theorists and practitioners at an ASCD conference on student unrest.

Hook, Sidney (Ed.). *In Defense of Academic Freedom.* New York: Pegasus, 1971. Essays in defense of the value of academic freedom by writers who see it as in great jeopardy. In general, the writers oppose techniques of violence and confrontation and question the assumption that the university must become an agency of specific social and political programs.

Jenkins, Herbert. *Keeping the Peace.* New York: Harper & Row, 1970.   A police chief looks at his job, including his relationships to militant black and white youth.

Libarle, Marc, and Tom Seligson (Eds.). *The High School Revolutionaries.* New York: Random House, 1970. High school radicals speak for themselves.

McGrath, Earl J. *Should Students Share the Power?* Philadelphia: Temple University Press, 1970. A useful study of the role of students in college and university governance including background, the pro and con of student participation, and techniques proposed and practiced for achieving student participation.

Mead, Margaret. *Culture and Commitment.* New York: Doubleday, 1970. By the distinguished anthropologist who holds that everyone born before World War II is an immigrant in time struggling against unfamiliar conditions of life in a new era and that today's young generation is akin to a first generation born into a new country. Like all of Mead's work, lively, provocative, discussion-rousing.

Postman, Neil and Charles Weingartner. *The Soft Revolution.* New York: Delacorte Press, 1971. A handbook written for students interested in "turning schools around." Also useful to teachers concerned about their relationships to students.

Silberman, Melvin L. (Ed.). *The Experience of Schooling.* New York: Holt, Rinehart, and Winston, 1971. A book of readings by educational writers concerned about what schooling does to children. Deals with "the hidden curriculum; teacher favoritism; crowded classrooms; the threat of evaluation; student powerlessness; peer group tensions; and students' views of schooling."

Tickton, Sidney G. (Ed.) and the Academy staff. *To Improve Learning: An Evaluation of Instructional Technology.* 2 Vols., New York: R. R. Bowker, 1970. A report to the President and the Congress of the United States by the Commission on Instructional Technology, including selected working papers.

Today's Education: NEA Journal. *Discipline in the Classroom.* Washington, D.C.: National Education Association, 1969. Selected articles on discipline which are of continuing value to elementary and secondary school teachers.

Tyson, James C. and Mary Ann Carroll. *Conceptual Tools for Teaching in Secondary Schools.* Boston: Houghton Mifflin, 1970. A new and important approach to teaching methods which focuses on two themes: theory and methods of teaching for concept attainment and theory and methods for the development of responsible behavior. The latter section is important to prospective teachers who are worried about discipline.

Wiener, Daniel N. *Classroom Management and Discipline.* Itasca, Ill.: F. E. Peacock, 1972. Maintaining an effective classroom climate for learning. Emphasis on methods for changing behavior and on specific classroom problems.

## SELECTED AUDIO-VISUAL MATERIALS

*Behavior Modification in the Classroom* (16 mm film, 24 min., color, University of California, 1970). Demonstrates the use of operant conditioning and modeling procedures in three different classroom situations. Discusses appropriate rewards and teacher training techniques.

*Controlling Classroom Misbehavior* (35 mm filmstrip, 74 frs/record, color, National Education Association, 1969). Presents some control techniques for misbehavior. Shows how motivation affects control and the effects of punishment and reward.

*Critical Moments in Teaching: A Child Who Cheats* (16 mm film, 10 min., color, Holt, Rinehart, and Winston, 1968). A girl who is "average" begins to make scattered high test scores. Most of these scores are the same as those of the child who sits next to the girl. The teacher is faced with a problem of what to do about this situation.

*Critical Moments in Teaching: I Walk Away in the Rain* (16 mm film, 11 min., color,

Holt, Rinehart, and Winston, 1968). A high school student does only what is necessary to get by, even though he is capable of doing quite well. The problem is to get this boy to work up to his potential.

*Critical Moments in Teaching: Image in a Mirror* (16 mm film, 9 min., color, Holt, Rinehart, and Winston, 1968). An elementary child is convinced she is going to fail. Even though she makes excellent grades she still lacks self-confidence. How may the teacher deal with this problem?

*Critical Moments in Teaching: Less Far Than the Arrow* (16 mm film, 8 min., color, Holt, Rinehart, and Winston, 1968). The teaching problem of motivating a class in a secondary school.

*Discipline in Education—A Series* (35 mm filmstrip, captions, color, Educational Film-strips, 1964). A discussion of the problems of discipline in the school and at home. The History of Discipline (42 frs.); The Need for Discipline (42 frs.); The Teaching of Discipline (40 frs.).

*Finding Out* (16 mm film, 30 min., b. & w., BBC-TV: Time-Life, Inc., 1967). Primary children are encouraged to handle objects, ask questions, and design experiments. Methods of teaching and learning in the primary school are discussed.

*Glasser on Discipline* (16 mm film, 28 min., color, Media Five, 1972). Presents a successful new approach to an old problem. Emphasizes that discipline is not punishment but rather following common sense rules of courtesy and mutual respect.

*Learning and Teaching—A Series* (35 mm filmstrip, color, Bel-Mort Films, 1960–69). A series of filmstrips on teaching methods and procedures. Titles include: Asking Questions; Determining Students' Grades; Explaining; Grouping Students for Effective Learning; Instructional Materials; The Logical Dimension in Teaching; The Measurement of Learning; Methods of Teaching; Pictures and Words; Planning a Unit; Teaching Science, Photosynthesis; Transfer of Learning.

*Looking at Teaching* (35 mm filmstrip, 73 frs/record, color, Colonial Films, 1967). Illustrates the relationship between the teacher and student, showing that the instructor must adjust to the learner's initial behavior and learning ability. Discusses the subjects of preplanning, motivation, involvement and testing as they relate to the teaching and learning process.

*Motivation in Teaching and Learning* (35 mm filmstrip, 72 frs/record, color, National Education Association, 1968). Summarizes the field of motivation for the classroom teacher: how to motivate students, the role of the teacher's personal characteristics, and the student's record of success or failure as a motivating factor.

# TWENTY

# What is the work of the new teacher?

Variety, which the poet William Cowper called "the very spice of life," is characteristic of teaching and education. The three million American teachers are individual persons. They work on a variety of levels—preschool, nursery school, kindergarten, elementary, junior high, senior high, college, university, and adult, each with its characteristic mode of operation. There is a considerable range in their salaries and their organizations are numerous. Most teach in the public school system while some work in independent private schools or religiously sponsored schools.

Consequently, generalizations concerning the work of the American teacher must be made with the recognition that a wide range of differences exists which is not indicated by deceptive averages. Forewarned, let us approach our generalizations about the work of the teacher with caution. In the school in which you will teach, things may be quite different. We will begin with facts about number and size of your classes, co-curricular activities, homework, and other characteristic duties. Then we will look at your tools—textbooks, the library, audiovisual and new instructional technology resources. Then we will consider your community relations, including parent-teacher meetings, parent conferences, and community participation.

## CLASSES AND RELATED RESPONSIBILITIES

### Number of Classes

The number of classes that you might teach varies according to the level in which you teach. In general, if you are a preschool, kindergarten, or elementary school teacher, you will work with a single class. If you teach

A Project Head Start preschool—group play for social development.

in junior or senior high school, college, or graduate school you will usually work with several classes. If you are in adult education you will sometimes teach a single class and sometimes teach several sections of the same course.

The typical preschool, kindergarten, or elementary school teacher stays with a single class from the beginning of the school day to its end. (However, a number of elementary schools use some degree of departmentalization; teachers meet several classes in their subject area daily, as is done in high school.) If you teach in a self-contained class on one of the childhood levels, you will find your free time limited. However, team teaching and open education may include time for joint planning with other teachers and usually does allow you some flexibility in time use. Sometimes a teacher has an aide. Otherwise, as a preschool, kindergarten, and elementary school teacher, you will depend for free time largely on recesses in which one or more teachers may be in charge of a large group or on the occasional conduct of a class by a special teacher of music, physical education, or art.

If your level is junior high school you will find that the typical junior

Elaine Keenan

Audio-visual materials aid in teaching and learning.

high school operates on either a six- or seven-period day. Eight out of ten junior high schools follow this pattern. A few schools have a program of fewer than six periods a day and schools with eight-period days are increasing as the curriculum of the junior high becomes crowded with more subjects.[1] In most cases a junior high period averages 50 minutes, exclusive of time for passing from one class to another. So as a typical junior high school teacher you will probably teach five or six classes and have one period free. ("Free" should not be taken too literally; during a so-called free period teachers often hold conferences, mark papers, prepare for classes, fill out forms, or catch up on what is happening about the school.)

The senior high school day is also conventionally divided into equal periods. The senior high school teacher too usually has one period free. However, as computerized scheduling develops and senior high school programs increasingly are fitted to the needs of the individual student, the faculty has a variety of teaching assignments and corresponding variety in unscheduled time.

Whether the contemporary American teacher teaches kindergarten or

[1] William Van Til, Gordon F. Vars, and John M. Lounsbury, *Modern Education for the Junior High School Years* (Indianapolis: Bobbs-Merrill Company, 1967), p. 63.

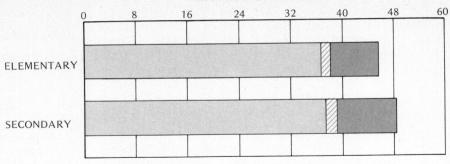

MEAN HOURS PER WEEK

|  | SEC. | ELEM. |
|---|---|---|
| Length of Required School Week | 36.8 | 36.3 |
| Other Compensated Duties | 1.9 | 1.6 |
| Noncompensated School Related Activities | 8.4 | 7.9 |
| All Teaching Duties | 48.1 | 45.8 |

FIGURE 20-1 The Teacher's Working Week

NEA, Research Division, *Status of the American Public School Teacher, 1970–71*, Research Report 1972–R3 (Washington, D.C.: The Association, 1972), pp. 32–34. Copyright © 1972 by the National Education Association. All rights reserved.

senior high school or any of the intervening levels, there is little difference in the length of the teacher's day. The range of in-school time is from seven hours to seven and a half hours (see Figure 20-1). The length of the school day for pupils, including lunch and recess, ranges between six and seven hours, with the exception of the kindergarten in which the length of the typical school day is from two and a half to three hours for the child.[2]

On the college level, the American Association of University Professors, the major organization of college and university teachers, recommends a maximum undergraduate teaching load of twelve hours per week. The AAUP indicates that no more than six course preparations during the academic year should be scheduled. The AAUP suggests as a preferable undergraduate pattern a teaching responsibility of about nine hours per week and fewer course preparations. Junior or community colleges usually follow the former pattern of twelve hours a week or indeed, sometimes more, and so do many private and public four-year colleges. Staffs of the four-year colleges which are actively working toward excellence sometimes achieve the preferable pattern of nine hours of undergraduate instruction. On the graduate level, the AAUP sanctions a teaching load of nine hours per week but regards six hours as preferable.[3]

[2] Educational Research Service, *The School Day for Teachers and Pupils, 1970–71,* Circular No. 4. (American Association of School Administrators and NEA, Research Division, 1971), pp. 2–3.
[3] Statement on Faculty Workload, *AAUP Bulletin* (Spring 1970), p. 31.

number of pupils per class was 26 in 1971.[5] Classes in independent private schools tend to be smaller and classes in typical parochial schools tend to be larger than classes in the typical public school at both elementary and secondary school levels.

In considering the average number of students in an elementary or secondary school class, one must take into account the growth of team teaching and nongraded classes. Situations are increasing in which three teachers work with perhaps seventy students in a team teaching, and/or nongraded organization especially in the primary, upper elementary, and junior high school.

On the college level, there is indeed wide variation. Classes range from small and comfortable seminars of perhaps a half dozen or a dozen students to giant introductory courses with enrollments in the hundreds. Faced with increases in college enrollments, some universities have adopted television instruction for hundreds of students, supplemented by occasional discussion groups of moderate size. So wide is the range that to cite averages might be misleading.

On the graduate school level, a wide range in size persists, though the range is somewhat narrower than on the undergraduate level. As a fifth year of study for teachers has become increasingly required for professional preparation, master's degree classes have increased in size. Though doctoral programs are on the increase in American universities, the universities have so far managed to keep class sizes down.

Teachers prefer fewer students in their classes. They point out that with relatively smaller numbers they can achieve greater individualization and are able to pay more attention to individual differences. They also say that better discipline can be maintained. "Working with too many students each day" was first on a list of critical problems described by teachers in a 1972 assessment of problems by the NEA. Yet research studies to date concerning the relationships of class size to effectiveness of instruction are ambiguous in their results. Evidence as to whether improvement is related to reduction of class size is conflicting and confusing. However, in the drive for better working conditions and higher quality in education, it is predictable that teachers will continue to seek public support for smaller classes. It is also likely that the public will continue to resist smaller classes because of additional costs.

**Co-curricular Activities**

Co-curricular activities are a part of the teacher's work, especially in secondary schools and occasionally in colleges. Though the co-curricular program in junior and senior high schools is no longer regarded as "extracurricular," for teachers the program involved is "extra" in that it is

---

[5] NEA, Research Division, *Status of the American Public-School Teacher, 1970–71,* Research Report 1972-R3 (Washington, D.C.: The Association, 1972), pp. 30–31.

not part of the regular class load. However, teachers often approach co-curricular activities with anticipation, since many such activities reflect their own interests and hobbies. Sensible school administrators schedule teachers for co-curricular activities related to individual hobbies and interests when this is possible. A new teacher interested in dramatics may find himself the director of the annual school play; a new teacher with an interest or background in debate may find himself coach of the debate team. When a co-curricular program is highly varied, new teachers may find that even unusual hobbies may be reflected in the program. Quite literally, the range may be from A to Z, from an archery club to a zoology group. Yet sometimes as a new teacher you may be saddled with a club that no other teacher wishes to sponsor.

The co-curricular program of the school is usually more informal than the regular class program. Consequently, one of the rewards for you as a new teacher is coming to know students who share your interests in a relaxed, informal, non-compulsory situation. Interpersonal relationships are advanced as students proceed at their own pace. A new teacher sometimes learns from co-curricular activities some techniques to make regular classroom instruction livelier and more informal. The rewards of co-curricular activities to the teacher are often financial as well. A 1970 NEA study reported that of 1,142 1969–70 salary schedules surveyed, 489 (or 42.8 percent), paid supplements for directing certain extracurricular activities. Although athletic activities dominate the supplementary salary picture, various nonathletic activities such as dramatic events, the school newspaper and yearbook, and vocal musical events are also well represented.[6] In general, the typical junior and senior high school teacher sponsors one major co-curricular activity each semester.

### Homework

Some teachers also have another out-of-class activity—the homework they assign which must be read, graded, etc. The extent of homework in American schools varies from level to level. Homework, in the sense of required activities and studies after the student has returned home from school, is not characteristic of preschool, nursery school, or kindergarten education and is frowned upon by most elementary school educators. Critics of homework point out that the success or failure of home study depends heavily upon the home environment and the interests and educational background of parents. Children generally perform homework adequately when the parents are inclined to supervise and guide the child. But children from home environments in which parents are uninterested in schooling often have trouble doing homework. Instead, many

---

[6] NEA, Research Division, *Salary Schedule Supplements for Extra Duties, 1969–70,* Research Report 1970-R4 (Washington, D.C.: The Association, 1970), p. 6.

or recess supervision, responsibilities in connection with study halls, supervision of corridors, and a variety of paper work. Teachers sometimes remark that they have little time to teach. In an effort to reduce the volume of such responsibilities, perceived by teachers as essentially routine and nonprofessional, a new group of workers has been employed by some schools. Educators are finding that the new staff increasingly goes beyond routine work and plays a useful personal role in the education process by working with individuals and small groups. Students are gaining from relationships with a variety of adults.

The most popular terms for the new personnel are teacher aides and paraprofessionals. The new workers free teachers for greater concentration on teaching activities and individual needs; they often enable the teacher to introduce more creativity into his work. Unfortunately, sometimes the new workers conflict or compete with the established teacher corps. Because of such situations, teacher unions and teacher associations have sometimes viewed the new workers with a degree of reserve and even opposition.

The numerous occasions on which teacher aides and paraprofessionals have proven to be helpful to the teacher have resulted in a steady decrease in opposition by teachers and their organizations to new patterns of staff utilization. In 1970 the American Federation of Teachers (AFT) in New York launched a campaign to organize paraprofessionals for higher pay and benefits. Particularly in schools in underprivileged areas, paraprofessionals and teacher aides recruited from the local community and often from minority groups have made significant contributions to effective education. In Pittsburgh for instance, neighborhood mothers worked in black areas. In New York City, the Public Education

**TABLE 20-1 Types of Assistance Given by Teacher Aides as Reported by Teachers***

| | |
|---|---|
| Secretarial assistance | 72.2% |
| Assistance with lunch duty | 45.8 |
| Assistance with grading papers with objective answers | 40.3 |
| Assistance with playground duty | 35.6 |
| Assistance with instruction of small groups | 26.9 |
| Preparation of instructional resources | 26.9 |
| Assistance with classroom environment | 26.4 |
| Assistance with instruction of individuals | 25.7 |
| Use of instructional resources | 20.4 |
| Assistance with bus duty | 15.5 |
| Assistance with grading essay-type papers | 5.6 |
| Other | 5.8 |

* Compiled from sample survey of public school teachers.
"Teacher Aides in the Public Schools," *NEA Research Bulletin* (March 1970), p. 12.

Association encouraged unpaid volunteers to foster remedial work. Such helpers frequently know neighborhoods intimately and students personally.

The utilization of teacher aides and paraprofessionals is on the increase; estimates of their number range from above 200,000 to near 300,000. A report by Associated Organizations for Teacher Education says:

The traditional concept of the teacher—one person with a set number of pupils within a self-contained classroom—is gradually being modified by the concept of a teaching team composed of persons of widely differing competencies, training, and life experiences. The team may include not only the teacher as diagnostician, leader, and participant, but also other professionals like curriculum specialists and paraprofessionals. The team might also have volunteers or older students in a youth-teaching-youth program.

In such a setting, the teacher, rather than substitute a management role for his central instructional one, adds management responsibilities to his instructional functions, mobilizing pertinent resources to meet the learning needs of children and youth.[9]

The school paraprofessional may be a teenager or a grandmother, an elementary school dropout or a Doctor of Philosophy, a suburban wife or a retired worker. Paraprofessionals may wear many labels—instruction aide, teacher aide, education aide, school aide, community aide, media aide, clerical aide, teacher assistant, educational associate, family assistant, family worker, parent/community aide, social worker aide, community liaison worker. Volunteers range from young children to mature adults.

In *A Learning Team: Teacher and Auxiliary*, the authors propose that the goals of a team made up of teachers and auxiliaries should be:

. . . first to establish rapport and mutual trust between school, home and child; then to create a learning environment in the school which is rich, varied and alive; next, to analyze each student's behavior within the environment so as to identify his needs, his interests, his anxieties, his goals—conscious and unconscious—his learning style, his modes of attacking a problem, and his apparent feelings toward self and others. The final step in the process is to restructure the environment, while providing the medley of supportive services that are needed, as the learner meshes his strivings to an educational task which is consonant with his goals, and at the same time replete with opportunity for his growth and development.[10]

[9] Wiggins, Sam (Ed.), *Educational Personnel For Urban Schools,* Prepared by Associated Organizations for Teacher Education (Washington, D.C.: The American Association of Colleges for Teacher Education, 1972), pp. 14–15.
[10] Gordon J. Klopf, Garda W. Bowman, and Adena Joy, *A Learning Team: Teacher and Auxiliary* (Bank Street College of Education, for the United States Office of Education, 1969), p. viii.

Your introduction into teaching would be still more significant if it could include experience comparable to those of an aide or paraprofessional, culminating in an internship. You would come to know and appreciate the team approach to the teaching-learning situation. You might check into any local possibilities of your participation in a team as part of your teacher preparation program.

## THE TOOLS OF THE TRADE

### Textbooks

The use of textbooks for the grade level or the courses which you will teach constitutes a crucial problem to you as a new teacher. It is not that textbooks for your use will be unavailable; in all but a small fraction of contemporary schools, textbooks will be readily available though they may not always be most appropriate or most up-to-date or even best suited to your class's reading level. Nor is it that the process of obtaining them is difficult; in the large majority of school situations (but not in all) textbooks will be ready and waiting for you. Yet despite the existence and easy availability of textbooks for your grade level or courses, the use of textbooks involves problems for you which are likely to test the high resolutions you have made as to the kind of teacher you will be. You have a choice as to whether your textbooks will dominate the content, methodology, and total approach of your teaching.

As you look over the textbooks supplied, there may be powerful forces at work urging you toward becoming the type of traditional teacher who rarely deviates from the text adopted. Your own natural nervousness in an unfamiliar situation will encourage you in this direction, as will your insecurity about your ability to translate into practice your own ideas about education which you formulated in college courses, student teaching, and discussions with friends. Another force takes the form of the attitudes of some experienced teachers who may advise you to take the easy way out by simply following any textbook provided. It may even occur to you that the administration of your school and system by the very act of supplying you with textbooks is implicitly advising you to teach the textbooks. And, frankly, a beginning teacher has little leeway in choosing texts or ordering alternatives.

While your situation is by no means as serious as that of Faust who sold his soul to the Devil, you may feel that there are some similarities! The easy way would be to forget your resolutions and what you may have learned and to allow your textbooks to completely dominate your teaching. You can find many arguments to support this position: the textbook was presumably written by an authority who knows the subject intimately; the activities suggested by the textbook writer may be better than any you could devise; with increasing investment in production, textbooks presumably grow better and better.

The harder way is to use your textbooks as tools, not as your sole instruments in the struggle to achieve your educational goals. If you take the harder but more challenging way, your textbooks will be one among several tools you use. To the extent that your textbooks are useful in developing the best possible education for each student, you will use them; to the extent that other media or approaches are appropriate, you will select them. The backgrounds of students should be taken into account in deciding on the appropriateness of the content of the textbooks; if textbooks do not fit the students, alternative materials should be used. More materials than the textbooks alone are usually available to the classroom teacher. Many modern school administrators would prefer that you use your textbooks selectively rather than slavishly; such principals and supervisors may help you devise multi-resource lessons. Perceptive teachers avoid using textbooks which are racist or sexist; they compensate for omissions as to the lives of Mexican-Americans, women, etc., through use of supplementary materials.

Concerned teachers approach decisions about the use of textbooks with care and deliberation. You might carefully appraise the teaching situation in which you find yourself, including student backgrounds, community expectations, school practices, administrative viewpoints, etc. You will discover that some textbooks fit well into your plans. You will find that other textbooks are useful as resources to supplement and extend your teaching. You might find still other textbooks which, in your situation, should be avoided or minimized, to the extent that you can avoid them or minimize their use. Frequent student-teacher evaluations might help you develop varied ways of using your available textbooks. Seek the aid of an experienced teacher or librarian to check on the existence of other media and materials.

Some may advise you that to follow a text doesn't make you a traitor to ambitions growing from preteaching experiences. They may regard the Faustian analogy as overly dramatic. They may suggest that you begin conservatively by using your textbooks and branch out only as you develop more confidence. On the other hand, how we begin sometimes determines where we end up. Robert Frost said it well in "The Road Not Taken":

> Two roads diverged in a wood, and I—
> I took the one less traveled by,
> And that has made all the difference.[11]

### Library, Audio-visual, and New Technology Resources

Many resources are housed in libraries, audio-visual centers, and technological collections. Very early in your acquaintance with a new school,

---

[11] From "The Road Not Taken," from *The Poetry of Robert Frost*, edited by Edward Connery Lathem (New York: Holt, Rinehart and Winston, 1969).

you might become familiar with both the school and the public library holdings related to your grade level or subject area. In most cases, librarians are on your side and are interested in the use of their facilities and eager to help you become familiar with their procedures. Certainly, you will realistically appraise the reading levels of your students, for little good can come from using library materials which are beyond the interest, or intellectual level of the students you teach. As you consider what your students should read, you might well use existing bibliographies rather than always start from scratch. Again, the librarian's professional help can be useful to you.

Some newly constructed school buildings contain materials centers which go far beyond libraries in their scope. Not only do they contain books; they have clustered together packages of materials dealing with a particular topic or problem. Such packages may include pamphlets and clippings in addition to books; cassettes and loops in addition to films and records; lists of community resources in addition to technological aids. The industrial revolution has certainly reached education and the new learning resources centers are packaging the latest products created in a technological era.

Today schools vary widely in availability of audio-visual materials. Some schools have a learning resources center which may be an integral part of the library; some have little or nothing at schools or even at district centers. But even such schools often have access to state or university depositories of films, filmstrips, film loops, and recordings. Of course, the use of such resources requires ordering weeks or even months in advance and thus the spontaneity that comes with easy availability is diminished. Yet, with advance planning, teachers in schools lacking learning resources centers can still make good use of audio-visual materials.

There are hurdles other than availability to overcome in using audio-visual materials. One obstacle may lie within yourself—the possible inclination to view the showing of a film or the playing of a record or tape as an opportunity to relax from the none too easy business of teaching. It takes some self-discipline to recognize that a film or a tape or a record should be previewed before it is used or, should this not prove possible, that careful descriptions of the content of the material should be studied in advance of screenings or listening sessions. It takes some self-discipline to recognize that one must be selective about audio-visual materials, using them when they are appropriate and for purposes which should be clear to the teacher, and which ought to be made clear to the learner.

Too, students who constantly encounter records, television, drive-in movies, etc., in their environment outside of school have often developed habits of only partially paying attention to audio-visual aids. It may take some effort to get students to listen attentively and to watch carefully if material is less exciting than skillful mass media productions. If the teacher suggests things to look for and questions or problems to have in mind before presenting the audio-visual program, and follows the presentation with discussion, the outcome may be better communication and consequently better learning.

The availability of new teaching technology in American schools also varies widely. In a growing number of schools, television of several types is accessible. In some schools, the only available television programs are those that happen to be broadcast by the major commercial networks. While some of these may well be germane to your purposes as a teacher, most of them, including the better documentaries, plays, and news programs, occur during evening hours. Given the wide access to television that American young people currently have, the teacher might well request or require listening to a selected program for follow-up consideration in class the next day.

In addition to commercial programs, some schools have access to and make use of television broadcasts from educational television stations. *Sesame Street* and *The Electric Company* are examples of educational television programs developed for the young child. Then, too, some school systems have their own closed circuit broadcasts directed to certain grade levels or subject areas; a few schools prepare their own television materials. Whatever the approach, the new teacher will soon learn of it because staff members, including audio-visual personnel, are usually interested in wide dissemination.

A minority of schools also employ programmed instruction in the form of so-called teaching machines, or, less frequently, may use computer-assisted instruction. Again, there is seldom a problem of learning about the existence of such resources; there is a greater problem of learning to use them well to meet the needs of students. Your own college may use machines for instruction; if so, observe their use or abuse. Sometimes machine instruction is planned for a class as a whole; sometimes machines supplement the learning requirements of individuals. In most cases, the school leaders find it necessary to supply inservice training for both experienced and new teachers with respect to available educational technology. You might get a head start by including audio-visual instruction in your total undergraduate program, experimenting with it during pre-service experiences. The industrial revolution in education is here to stay. The new teacher should learn to use the new machines constructively without allowing the curriculum to be dominated by too arbitrary and rigid use of programmed materials, ETV, and curriculum packages (some of which are advertised as "teacher proof").

### Equipment and Supplies

As a new teacher, you will soon discover the inevitable and potentially highly helpful "office." The secretaries and assistants who maintain school offices are your resources for information on a variety of equipment and supplies, whether they take the slight form of a pencil or the bulky shape of an overhead projector. These clerical workers follow procedures developed by the system or the individual school so any basic questions and certainly any complaints or proposed procedural revisions should be channeled to administrators, including department chairpersons or others. Learning the established routines for equipment and supply use early and heeding these procedures should put the new teacher in the good graces of those who preside over offices and make life easier for the teacher in quest of equipment and supplies. Nor should the importance to you of the custodian be forgotten; he is a good man to have on your side when the time comes for moving furniture, rearranging desks, or even when frantically hunting at the last moment for a piece of chalk.

## PARENT AND COMMUNITY RELATIONS

### Parent-teacher Meetings

One type of teacher-community relationship is through the meetings of parent-teacher organizations. Though attendance at parent-teacher meetings is seldom compulsory for teachers, most schools heartily encourage teachers to be present. Attendance at such meetings and participation in activities of the association can provide the new teacher with a rudimentary introduction to the community in which he works.

Some parent-teacher organizations are independent of national organizations and are autonomous bodies associated with a single school or single district. Other parent-teacher organizations are part of the National Congress of Parents and Teachers. The latter group is also organized along state lines. The national organization, popularly termed P.T.A., states its purposes as follows:

1. To promote the welfare of children and youth in home, school, church, and community.
2. To raise the standards of home life.
3. To secure adequate laws for the care and protection of children and youth.
4. To bring into closer relation the home and the school, that parents and teachers may cooperate intelligently in the education of children and youth.
5. To develop between educators and the general public such united efforts as will secure for all children and youth the highest advantages in physical, mental, social and spiritual education.[12]

By a margin of six votes, the P.T.A. in 1972 took a national stand in favor of busing to reduce racial isolation. At the group's national conven-

[12] *The P.T.A. Magazine* (September 1972), inside front cover.

tion, a resolution to ask the P.T.A. to develop "other viable alternative methods for providing quality education" was amended to include "solutions that could by rational means reduce racial isolation through transportation." But at the 1973 national convention the delegates voted two to one against court-ordered busing. However, approval by 31 state assemblies would be needed if the measure were to become an item for action. In 1972 the P.T.A. also dropped a long established policy that the P.T.A. "will not interfere with administration of the schools and shall not seek to control their policies." The new position indicates the P.T.A. "shall seek to participate in the decision-making process establishing school policy."[13] These activities seem to indicate a trend toward activism by the 8.5 million member National Congress of Parents and Teachers, which has usually stressed noncontroversial activities and emphasized its policy of noninterference in the conduct of the school. The 40,000 local P.T.A. units usually emphasize such activities as raising money for playground equipment, encouraging programs to prevent drug abuse, and urging that traffic signals be installed near schools.

The new teacher is not usually called upon to make any particular contribution to his first parent-teacher meetings. You will probably do little more than be recognized when introduced to the group as a new teacher. Therefore, you should have abundant opportunities to learn not only from the formal program of the meeting but also from its implications. A parent-teacher meeting affords you the opportunity to speculate, for example, on which parents attend and which do not. Are any groups of parents conspicuous by their absence? Or presence? Are the attendants at the meeting representative of the students in your class or classes? Is attendance skewed toward the more prosperous and economically influential parents? Is attendance representative of the distribution of your classes in terms of racial, nationality, and religious dimensions? Which parents set the tone for the meeting? Is the meeting the creation of the school administration or of the parents or of both groups jointly? Careful observation of such meetings can make some contribution, however elementary, to your understanding of the locus of power in your school and community.

The new teacher can also learn from the substantive content of the meeting. Does the meeting deal with the real problems of the children or youth whom you have come to know through your classes? Or does it deal with peripheral matters? Is the meeting concerned with shadow rather than substance through emphasis placed upon formalities and rituals? What else could the meeting focus upon? The parent-teacher meeting is often a reflection of the parents' and the community's conception of and commitment to education.

---

[13] "News Front," *Education, U.S.A.* (May 29, 1972), p. 219; "The P.T.A. Takes Stand Against Forced Busing," *New York Times,* May 24, 1973, p. 22.

The attitudes of his colleagues and administrators toward the meeting should also be of interest to the perceptive new teacher. Do teachers welcome the meeting or do they attend grudgingly, if at all? Do they see such meetings as significant and useful? Does the administration regard the occasion as an opportunity for genuine sharing? Or does it apparently fear such meetings? Does the administration manipulate the meeting to reinforce the present school programs by simply acquainting parents with the status quo rather than regard the meeting as an opportunity for parental suggestions and possible program improvements?

The first active role the new teacher is likely to play in a parent-teacher organization will come sometime during the school year when a meeting attended by parents takes the form of a program of visitation of individual classrooms accompanied by discussions with teachers. As a new teacher you may be fearful of such occasions, for you recognize that they might bring to light not only your successes but also your failures—and you will probably have both. However, a new teacher might use the occasion to describe his program and purposes and, when appropriate, to ask for the kind of cooperation from parents he most needs. He would be well advised to try to differentiate between that part of the visit with parents which deals with the experience of the class as a whole and those inevitable parent-requested conferences about the progress of individual students. To discuss individual students in the larger parent meeting is clearly a dubious practice, even when a parent urges or invites the new teacher to do so.

### Conferences with Parents

While parent-teacher meetings are obviously useful to the teacher, individual parent conferences often supply him the clues he needs to be more effective with young people. Whether a parent actively seeks a conference is often largely a function of the parent's social class. For instance, most upper middle class parents will not hesitate to request a conference with a teacher, particularly when disturbed about some aspect of the school program or the student's progress. The lower class parent may also be concerned about the program or the child but will usually not request a conference; such a parent often feels uncomfortable or out of place in a typical school atmosphere. But, whether a conference is parent- or teacher-initiated, the new teacher must demonstrate a reasonable amount of skill in human relations. Teacher sensitivity can convert the possible initial discomfort of the meeting into a constructive and cooperative relationship. College study of the behavioral sciences, as well as out-of-school activities in programs such as Head Start and youth work, can prepare the teacher to deal skillfully with parents and their concerns.

The problem of knowing how to act and what to say, however, is really secondary to the problem of obtaining parent conferences with those parents who never request them. Somehow the new teacher has to find a way of getting in touch with the parent who does not volunteer to come to school to meet him. Sometimes a request for the parent to confer at the school is in order. The new teacher, however, would be well advised to recognize that for many parents such an invitation is a summons and a potential threat. Some parents find that the invitation conflicts with their working hours or responsibilities to children not yet in school. If they come at all, they may have their defenses up.

The new teacher may find that the better way to communicate is, by careful prearrangement, to visit the parents at home. Sometimes this is easily arranged; at other times because of parental reluctance, embarrassment at poor home conditions, or occasionally because of the high crime rate in a neighborhood, arrangements may prove difficult. But, when made, such home visits are often rewarding; new insights come to a teacher when he visits the home which day after day has been contributing to a student's experiences, whether positively or negatively.

### Community Participation

One of the most realistic approaches to understanding the school's community is to work actively in that community as a participating citizen. The range of possibilities is as wide as your interests, concerns, and hobbies. Some recreation oriented teacher-citizens participate through the programs of Y's, whether YMCA, YWCA, YMHA, etc. Some manage Little League baseball teams or organize youth hostels. Some work in neighborhoods through their churches. Some socially conscious teacher-citizens work with community centers or settlement houses. Some become involved in community action campaigns, such as fair housing programs or community fund drives. Some participate in political action through working with political groups. In all such cases, the teacher-citizen becomes a contributor, sharing in at least a segment of the total community life.

In his community activities, the teacher has the responsibility to continuously make it clear that he is proceeding as a citizen rather than as a spokesman or a representative of the school as an institution. Two classifications of rights and responsibilities of the American teacher should be clearly differentiated. As a teacher of children and adolescents, a teacher has certain rights and responsibilities. His rights include freedom to teach so that young people may learn; his responsibilities include living by a professional code of ethics and the fostering of the use of intelligence by students. As a citizen of the United States, the individual who is a teacher also has certain rights and responsibilities. A teacher not only *may* participate in the common life as a citizen, but to be a truly democratic citizen he *must* participate. He must run the risk of reaching a conclusion on race relations or foreign policy or the economy or any other controversial issue which does not happen to be the majority position of that moment. Active citizenship always involves the possibility that one may espouse unpopular causes as well as majority beliefs.

The new teacher should not assume, however, that his claim to citizenship or to freedom to teach will go completely unchallenged. It is possible that frequent peer and/or community pressures will be felt to restrict teacher activities both within and without school. Evidence to support this is, unfortunately, all too readily available.

Jonathan Kozol, in *Death at an Early Age,* tells of his dismissal from the Boston schools for refusing to restrict his classroom reading and reference material to a list of approved publications. School authorities and certain community elements particularly objected to his use of the poem "Ballad of the Landlord" by Langston Hughes with his fourth grade class.[14]

Charles James, a teacher at Addison High School near Corning, New York, was dismissed because he wore a black armband in class in symbolic protest against the Vietnam war. In 1972 the United States Court of Appeals for the Second Circuit ruled that school officials had violated the teacher's constitutional rights. Judge Irving R. Kaufman's decision said:

> More than a decade of Supreme Court precedent leaves no doubt that we cannot countenance school authorities' arbitrarily censoring a teacher's speech merely because they do not agree with the teacher's political philosophies or leanings.
>
> This is particularly so when that speech does not interfere in any way with the teacher's obligations to teach, is not coercive and does not arbitrarily inculcate doctrinaire views in the minds of the students.[15]

Not all cases of teacher dismissals are related to broad national and international problems. Take, for instance, the carrot case. The contract of Mrs. Mildred Downs, a second grade teacher who had 25 years of teaching experience, was not renewed because of "(1) insubordination, (2) lack of cooperation with the administration, (3) teaching her second graders to protest." In connection with a unit she taught on nutrition, her students had written to the cafeteria supervisor and expressed their preference for raw rather than cooked carrots. On another occasion Mrs. Downs had written letters to fellow teachers asking whether they too objected to the fumes and debris from an open burning incinerator in the school yard, which she saw as a health and safety hazard. The U.S. District Court reinstated Mrs. Downs to her teaching position with back pay and said that when a school board punishes "a teacher who seeks to protect the health and safety of herself and her pupils, the resulting

[14] Jonathan Kozol, *Death at an Early Age* (Boston: Houghton Mifflin, 1967), pp. 225–232.
[15] "Teacher Is Upheld On His War Dissent," *New York Times,* May 25, 1972, pp. 1, 36.

intimidation can only cause a severe chilling, if not freezing, affect on the free discussion of more controversial subjects."[16]

In some southern states which have resisted desegregation, black educators often were overtly discriminated against when jobs were reassigned. Representative of this group was Fred McCoy, a principal of an all-black elementary school in Natalbany, Louisiana, who was reassigned to teach a fourth grade class in the mornings and do janitor chores in the afternoon.[17] Harvest Mitchell, a black coach in basketball, football, and track, was demoted to assistant coach after a desegregation order closed his school; the U.S. Court of Appeals for the Fifth Circuit ordered him reinstated as head coach in the desegregated Florence, Alabama, school system. The Appeals Court said: "If a school official, administrator, teacher, principal, or coach is demoted or dismissed as a result of a desegregation order, and if his objective qualifications for his former position did not diminish . . . then he must be given the opportunity to assume any new position equal to the one he lost, prior to the offering of the new position to any new applicants."[18] At an Atlanta conference in June 1973, education and civil rights organizations charged that 6,000 black teachers and principals had been dismissed and that thousands more had been demoted during desegregation and merging of dual school systems in southern and border states.

Teachers are not completely without protection in such cases as have been mentioned. Actions by school authorities, if arbitrary, can be contested in the courts.[19] To aid teachers in expensive and time consuming legal action, the NEA, for example, maintains the DuShane Emergency Fund to provide teachers with financial and legal assistance when their rights are challenged. Also, teachers have increasingly moved toward negotiated agreements with school boards which detail their professional rights and responsibilities. The struggle for teacher rights is a continuing battle.

In September 1972, the NEA publication, *Today's Education,* reported, "On June 29, an event of great consequence to teachers occurred. The U.S. Supreme Court affirmed that publicly employed teachers may not be denied a new contract because they have exercised the rights secured by the First Amendment to the U.S. Constitution."[20] The authentic American tradition is that the citizen has a right to hold his point of view and to

[16] NEA DuShane Emergency Fund, "Teacher in Arkansas' Carrot Case Wins Her Job Back," DuShane Fund Reports (Washington, D.C.: National Education Association, July 20, 1971), p. 2.

[17] "The Bad Side of Integration," *Time* (July 13, 1970), p. 32.

[18] NEA DuShane Emergency Fund, "Significant Victory for Black Educators: Demoted Headcoach Wins Job Back," DuShane Fund Reports (Washington, D.C.: National Education Association, May 25, 1972), pp. 4–5.

[19] David Rubin, *The Rights of Teachers: The Basic ACLU Guide to a Teacher's Constitutional Rights* (New York: Avon Books, 1972).

[20] NEA DuShane Emergency Fund, "U.S. Supreme Court Supports Teachers' Due Process Rights," *Today's Education* (September 1972), p. 37.

defend it through legal means. Once we accept any doctrine that educators as citizens do not have the same rights and privileges as do other American citizens, we open the way to the application of a variety of illegitimate pressures upon individual teachers.

## SOME PROBLEMS ENCOUNTERED BY THE NEW TEACHER

In your first year of teaching you may encounter formidable problems partially because of the practices of your school system. Or you may encounter substantial sympathetic help through better procedures. You may even encounter a strange mixture of both.

The operational practices of many school systems often contribute to the difficulties of the beginning teacher. Some school systems, particularly in the large metropolises, have established the tradition of assigning the newest and therefore least experienced teachers to the most difficult teaching situations, those in the slums and the ghettos which are rife with social and educational problems. It is usually neither malignancy nor stupidity which accounts for this type of assignment. Openings for teachers annually are usually more frequent in disadvantaged areas. Teacher transfers from such areas often take place when the teacher, after achieving tenure, may be offered the option of teaching elsewhere and chooses an area nearer home or in a less trouble-prone neighborhood. True, many teachers, given the choice, remain in the difficult or disadvantaged situation; they accept the challenge of contemporary education or they like the work. But a larger number of teachers move out of the ghetto or slum school when the opportunity occurs.

In the particular school in which the new teacher works, he sometimes is assigned a class or classes unwanted by experienced staff members. Again, while there are many teachers who enjoy the challenge of working with relatively low ability groups, most teachers, given a choice, choose the average or above average section. Thus the new teacher, despite inexperience, finds himself frequently facing the difficult task of working with low ability students who are often less motivated to school achievement.

There are even situations in which new teachers unfairly are assigned excessive after-hours duty, older textbooks, etc., though such situations are clearly indicative of discrimination by administrators who practice favoritism toward experienced teachers. Fortunately such practices are rare.

## SOME HELP FOR THE NEW TEACHER

Yet there exist systems which use procedures which provide substantial help to the new teacher. (Paradoxically, some systems both provide help to new teachers through positive procedures and contribute to the difficulty of new teachers through negative operational procedures!) Such help may be informal through friendship and earnest advice; it may be formalized through meetings for new teachers prior to the opening of school, regular meetings throughout the school year, conferences with principals and supervisors, readiness to help in emergencies, etc. There are schools in which the staff leans over backward to be helpful to the new teacher. His in-service education may be co-sponsored by the school system and a local university. He may be given a lighter load than experienced teachers. Though he will inevitably encounter problems, he has much within the existing system going for him. For some new teachers the transition to actual teaching may be eased by a teacher-education program that carefully inducts the new teacher into teaching not only through classroom instruction but through multiple opportunities for observation, participation, work as aides, helpful student teaching, periods of internship, etc.

Inevitably there are dropouts from teaching as from study. The majority of teachers work through the problems which a first year in any occupation or profession presents and come back for more of the combination of joyous achievement and painful frustration which teaching often involves. Good teaching can make a change in the lives of human beings, and a good teacher, whether experienced or inexperienced, knows it and persists.

## DISCUSSION

1. What are the advantages and disadvantages of working with a single class throughout the day, rather than different classes for shorter periods throughout the day?
2. Discuss the kinds of knowledge an elementary school teacher should possess in order to teach in a self-contained classroom.
3. List what you consider to be the advantages of organizing subject matter for elementary schools on some basis other than separate subjects.
4. What co-curricular activities do you feel you are qualified and prepared to sponsor? Why do you feel that these particular activities are important to students?
5. What types of activities do you think should be conducted by teachers with no extra compensation? with extra compensation?
6. What has been your own experience in respect to homework during your years of schooling? Do you believe it has made a significant contribution to your learning? What is the case for or against assigned homework?
7. Should different homework policies prevail at different levels of the educational ladder? Are some types of homework more beneficial than others? What types?
8. How would you like to see children and youth spend their after-school time? What role should homework play?
9. Defend the position that daily homework is a necessary part of a student's school experience.
10. What are some of the relatively routine responsibilities of teachers about which

educators complain? Which of these can be allocated to assistants and which are inevitable characteristics of the choice of education as a field of work?

11. What do you believe should be the position of the teaching profession in relation to the use of paraprofessionals? What is the role of aides in the teaching profession?

12. How does an assistant sometimes unwittingly handicap a new teacher? What are some of the ways in which a new assistant might attempt to help a new teacher?

13. Under what circumstances might a teacher adhere closely to a textbook? Under what circumstances might he deviate, even to the point of abandoning the textbook? What other tools of the trade are available to teachers?

14. How might a new teacher most readily become familiar with library, audio-visual, and technological resources? What are some benefits from using such resources with students? What are some cautions to be observed?

15. What are the most frequent uses of television in American schools? To what extent has educational technology other than television been adopted in American schools?

16. What are some of the ways in which the teacher might come to understand the community in which he or she works?

17. What are the functions of parent-teacher meetings? What kinds of parent-teacher meetings are most effective? Least effective? What can one learn from attendance at the parent-teacher meeting if one is a new teacher?

18. In your opinion, what should be the role of the National Congress of Parents and Teachers? What should be the role of the local P.T.A.? Do recent developments in the program of the P.T.A. seem promising or unpromising to you?

19. How can parent conferences be made useful for all involved, including students, teachers, and parents? What approaches to the conference might be most workable?

20. What alternatives does a teacher have when a parent is unwilling or unable to come to school? Do you see possible problems in visits to students' homes?

21. What is your own view on what teachers as a professional group and a teacher as an individual should do under circumstances of attempted restriction of rights? What protection do teachers have in such cases?

22. What is your opinion as to how a successful first year of teaching might be fostered by the school system and the new teacher?

## INVOLVEMENT

1. Check into research on the relationship between class size and the effectiveness of learning. Does the evidence seem conclusive to you?

2. Spend an afternoon with the extracurriculum of a typical junior or senior high school. Then attempt to generalize on the importance or lack of importance to the students and teachers involved. Do you observe any instances of gain to individuals?

3. Review your own experiences with homework as a student. How do these compare with the experiences of other students in your group?

4. Interview an intermediate elementary student, a junior high student, and a senior high student to determine the type and amount of homework they are expected to

complete in a week. What are their reactions as to the importance and helpfulness of these assignments?

5. Visualize a typical homework assignment which you might make in your subject field and at the level of instruction at which you will teach. How important is your proposed assignment? How creative? Could it have been done within supervised study time in class?

6. Interview a teacher on the amount of time he teaches and the amount of time which is given to activities he regards as routine. What suggestions does he have for reduction of routine work? What attitudes does he take toward aides or paraprofessionals? What is the length of his working day?

7. If paraprofessionals work in the schools which you visit, interview several about the nature of their work. Determine whether they have particular grievances. Ask them what aspects of their work give them most satisfaction.

8. Examine several textbooks you might use in your future teaching. Ask yourself how you might most effectively use such textbooks. Look particularly at proposed activities, which are usually found at the end of chapters.

9. Develop a plan for teaching for approximately a week which leans heavily on the best of the textbooks which you have examined. Develop a teaching plan for a week which almost completely avoids the use of a textbook. Note how much time preparation of each plan took. Ask yourself which plan seems most valuable for learning by students.

10. Examine a textbook on the adoption list in the state and in the subject or on the grade level on which you plan to teach. What are its strengths and weaknesses in light of what you expect to teach in that particular area?

11. Build a bibliography for future use in your teaching. Obtain the help of a librarian in doing so.

12. The next time you see a classroom film, ask yourself what questions you would have raised before showing the film and what discussion you would foster after student viewing.

13. If a school in your vicinity is notable for its use of technology, visit it and become acquainted with the resources and their uses.

14. Attend a parent-teacher meeting as an observer. Follow the suggestions contained in this chapter in observing what is said in the meeting and perhaps what is unsaid.

15. Obtain whatever catalog of films you are most likely to use in your own teaching in the community in which you tentatively plan to teach. Check off the films which you would most likely use in your particular field of instruction.

16. Check with parents of children and youth of school age who are among your acquaintances as to the extent of their relationship to the schools through parent-teacher meetings, conferences with teachers, etc. Ask them about the kinds of relationships they would like to have with the schools attended by their children.

17. Establish your own relationship with the community through some organizations or groups which fit your patterns of interest or conviction.

18. Follow closely cases of infringement of teacher rights or freedom to teach. When it seems appropriate, play a role as a citizen in such incidents.

19. Determine what the school or school system in which you hope to teach does to help teachers in their first year of teaching. Inquire too of assignment policies as they apply to first-year teachers.

## FURTHER READING

Cooper, James A. (Ed.). *Differentiated Staffing.* Philadelphia, Pennsylvania: W. B. Saunders, 1972. Concerning differentiated staffing through dividing the role of the teacher into different professional and paraprofessional subroles while making concurrent changes in scheduling, curriculum, decision-making power, and individualization of instruction.

Dreeben, Robert. *The Nature of Teaching.* Glenview, Illinois: Scott, Foresman, 1970. An analysis of schools and the work of teachers through a primarily sociological mode of inquiry. Emphasized are "the occupational characteristics of teaching; the teacher's work setting; the technology of teaching; setting for teacher training; occupational careers in teaching; and teaching, present and future."

Fischer, Louis and David Schimmel. *Civil Rights of Teachers.* New York: Harper & Row, 1973. The extent to which teachers are denied civil liberties accorded other members of society.

Hiemstra, Roger. *The Educative Community.* Lincoln, Nebraska: Professional Educators Publications, 1972. On the community, the community school, the modern family, and need for community coordination, cooperation, and change.

Hyman, Ronald T. *Ways of Teaching.* Philadelphia: J. B. Lippincott, 1970. Teaching methodology, especially the discussion method, role playing, questioning, with a reappraisal of the recitation and lecture methods.

Pickarts, Evelyn and Jean Fargo. *Parent Education.* New York: Appleton-Century-Crofts, 1971. A book to meet the need for parent education which stresses content and methodology in parent education and which describes ways of working with parents in advantaged circumstances and in low income communities.

Salk, Lee. *What Every Child Would Like His Parents to Know.* New York: McKay, 1972. Aid to parents by a pediatric psychologist concerned for psychic needs of children.

Samalonis, Bernice L. *Methods and Materials for Today's High Schools.* New York: Van Nostrand Reinhold, 1970. A comprehensive methodological guide to basic planning techniques, the craft of teaching, and broader professional responsibilities.

Warren, Earl. *A Republic, If You Can Keep It.* New York: Quadrangle, 1971. An essay on the relationship of the Constitution to the expansion and protection of freedom.

Watson, Paul G. *Using the Computer in Education.* Englewood Cliffs, N.J.: Educational Technology Publication, 1972. A review of current studies in the use of computers by an advocate who is also willing to recognize shortcomings.

## SELECTED AUDIO-VISUAL MATERIALS

*At the Center* (16 mm film, 29 min., color, American Library Association, 1970). Presents the role of the school library media specialist as a dynamic force in school media centers.

*Differentiated Teaching Staff* (16 mm film, 28 min., color, Stanford University, 1966). Dwight Allen discusses an approach to teaching which emphasizes a range of teacher competencies in a variety of staff positions.

*Educational Media* (35 mm filmstrip, 93 frs/record, color, National Education Association, 1969). Suggests principles and procedures that may be applied in the classroom in using educational media. Based upon scientifically validated findings and expert opinions.

*Let Them Learn* (16 mm film, 27 min., color, Encyclopedia Britannica Educational Corporation, 1967). Examines the characteristics of educational films which make them significant teaching materials.

*The Media Center in Action* (16 mm film, 14 min., color, Coronet, 1972). Presents today's modern media center working with schools to enrich the learning process and help students achieve their learning potential.

*Programming Is a Process—An Introduction to Instructional Technology* (16 mm film, 32 min., color, University of Illinois, 1967). Introduces viewers to the basic process of instructional technology—programming an instructional sequence for maximum student learning. The steps of the programming process, applicable to all media, are described as a means toward instruction.

*The Remarkable Schoolhouse* (16 mm film, 25 min., color, CBS-TV: McGraw-Hill, 1967). An innovative look at educational methods, revolutionary school designs, technological communication media, and the role of teachers in shaping the school of the future.

*Resource Center* (16 mm film, 28 min., color, Stanford University, 1966). Dwight Allen presents the functions and uses of resource centers for students in various academic areas, and discusses the staffing and administration of such centers.

*The Sound of a Stone* (16 mm film, 28 min., b. & w., Centron Educational Films, 196-). A high school teacher becomes suspect because a book he recommends is considered subversive. The waves of gossip and hate touch shores for which they were never intended. Community leaders and the parent who made the accusation try to undo the damage, but the reverberations continue in sinister and startling ways.

*Teaching the One and the Many* (16 mm film, 28 min., color, National Education Association, 1968). Illustrates how faculty and students utilize men, media, and machines. Stresses the development of "software" such as films, filmstrips, programmed materials, video tapes, and teaching kits.

*Television in your Classroom* (35 mm filmstrip, 44 frs/record, color, Great Plains Instructional TV Library, 1967). Outlines five basic elements of effective instructional television utilization—importance of study guides, the proper adjustment and placement of the classroom television set, the role of positive teacher attitude, the significance of effective follow-up activities, and the distinct usefulness of evaluation and feedback by the classroom teacher.

*Television Techniques for Teaching* (16 mm film, 23 min., color, San Diego Area Instructional Television Authority, 1968). Demonstrates some practical approaches to utilizing television in the classroom.

*Telling the P.T.A. Story* (35 mm filmstrip, 1 filmstrip/captioned, color, Universal Education and Visual Arts, 1967). Details the attainment of objectives of the P.T.A. to enable members to better understand and contribute to the P.T.A. program.

# TWENTY-ONE

# What about evaluation and guidance?

Since all teachers must both appraise and help students, the work of the new teacher calls for some acquaintance with two specialized fields which are important in teaching — evaluation and guidance. Ideally, the new teacher should study these fields in courses taught by specialists in the fields, for each involves important substantive content for the classroom teacher. Here, we will at least open up some issues and sketch some background for consideration by the new teacher concerning evaluation and guidance.

## EVALUATION AND MEASUREMENT

### The Process of Evaluation

Evaluation is a process of determining the value or worth of something through examining, judging, appraising, estimating, and measuring. Thoroughgoing evaluation in education includes (1) identifying the purposes of education, (2) gathering data and evidence to show whether the purposes are being achieved, (3) interpreting the evidence and data gathered, and (4) making the changes called for by the interpretation. As we have already seen from Chapter 16, the determination of purposes of education is no simple matter; it is marked by substantial conflict in viewpoints. Gathering and interpreting data and evidence presents technical problems and making changes based on evaluation is difficult. Yet it makes little sense to educate people without determining whether the education they have experienced produces effective results.

In attempting to evaluate, educators have developed a variety of formal and informal measurements. Measurement is only part of the total process of evaluation and tests are one way of measuring. In ancient China, examinations were used to select civil servants, and in European universities during the Middle Ages examinations for both professors and students were common. In the United States, Horace Mann campaigned for written rather than oral examinations in school districts in Massachusetts.

Late in the nineteenth century, Joseph M. Rice, a pediatrician and a muckraking journalistic crusader for better schools, called for reforms in education to be based on data gathered through objective tests. At the close of World War I, Edward Thorndike developed many techniques for objective testing and popularized this approach to testing. Ben D. Wood fostered cooperative test development and programs, encouraged state-wide surveys of achievement through tests, and pioneered in electrical equipment to score tests.[1]

In our own times, the attempt to evaluate the outcomes of educational programs is accompanied by a call for accountability. Educators are being asked to be accountable or responsible for the educational product. Sometimes educators are asked to agree in advance that they will be rewarded or penalized in accordance with evaluation findings as to the degree to which they attained specific results. Goals are established along with performance oriented objectives. The success of the educational program is then determined through evaluation. The results are shared with the community.

Proponents of accountability believe that this approach will make the schools more responsive to the communities which support them. They believe that, in turn, citizens will see the relationship between high quality education for all students and the resources which are invested by the public in the program. The hope of the advocates of accountability is to combine resources provided by communities and teaching efforts provided by educators in order to improve the quality of education. Critics of the accountability movement think it overemphasizes academic outcomes and disregards humanistic goals. They reject emphasis on accountability as too mechanistic an approach to education. They dislike reward-penalty motivations in teaching.

### Measuring Aptitudes and Interests

Today educators are concerned with aptitudes, interests, personality, and values, as well as with so-called objective and other tests of academic achievement. For instance, educators use aptitude tests in an attempt to learn more of the individual's potential to master a specific series of skills, such as skills in algebra or modern languages, in verbal reasoning

[1] Robert L. Ebel, "Measurement in Education," in American Educational Research Association, *Encyclopedia of Educational Research,* 4th ed. (New York: Macmillan, 1969), p. 778.

or quantitative analysis, or in clerical or mechanical abilities. Critics believe that aptitude tests are better at predicting potential failure than potential success. Such critics say that past performance is a better predictor of aptitude than a paper and pencil test.

Contemporary educators also use attitude inventories to attempt to identify specific personality problems or characteristics. Such inventories or check lists include the Minnesota Counseling Inventory, the California Personality Test, the Mooney Problem Check List, the Science Research Associates Youth Inventory, the Adjustment Inventory of Stanford University and the Minnesota Multiphasic Personality Inventory (used primarily with adults and college students).

Personality instruments sometimes come under fire. Some groups of parents, especially those representing strongly conservative views on school and society, criticize some personality inventories as an invasion of privacy which uses the prestige of science and the sanction of research to justify offensive probing into the personal and private affairs of young people and their families. Supporters of personality tests respond that skilled teachers and counselors will use the findings with discretion and for the personal development of the young person.

Some specialists in counseling point out that there is no real evidence that personality questionnaires can be used for personal development; they say that nontest devices, such as private conferences, personal history questionnaires, autobiographies and biographies, diaries and logs, supplemented by sociometric methods and staff reports, can be more useful in helping the young person with his personal perplexities. Also, tests can be faked. For instance, Merle M. Ohlsen says:

One does not have to be a tests and measurements expert to discover why most personality questionnaires used in the schools fail to identify children needing special help. If one takes his favorite personality questionnaire, reads the directions, and responds to the items, he will discover that he is able to present whatever picture of himself he wishes to present. This is true for pupils, too. What a pupil tells a staff member about himself through use of the questionnaire will depend on his awareness of his problems, his ability to see the similarity between his problems and those presented in the questionnaire, his ability to understand the statements made, and his willingness to report his problems to those who will see the test results. Whether pupils can, or are willing to, trust those who will see their responses, and whether they can face their problems, will also determine how they respond to the test.

All in all, other sources of information prove more helpful than personality questionnaires.[2]

Interest inventories are also used to determine the likes and preferences of students for vocational guidance purposes. For instance, two long established interest inventories are the Strong Vocational Interest

[2] Merle M. Ohlsen, *Guidance Services in the Modern School* (New York: Harcourt, Brace & World, 1964), p. 255.

Blank for Men and the Kuder Preference Record-Vocational. The argument for the use of such interest inventories with fifteen- or sixteen-year-olds is that they may be used to identify occupations from which clients may obtain job satisfaction. Critics of interest inventories claim that too early use of data and too specific application to occupations may tend to oversimplify the complex matter of occupational choice. However, as Ohlsen has pointed out, a counselor can note the problems critics cite and still find interest inventories useful in helping young people identify groups of activities of importance to them.[3]

Since the administration of intelligence and aptitude tests and attitude and interest inventories is usually conducted by means of a school-wide or system-wide testing program, the new teacher normally first encounters his problems of measurement and evaluation in connection with tests of achievement in his or her class.

### Tests of Achievement

Lively controversy surrounds the use of various tests of achievement at grade levels and in subject fields. For instance, there is considerable disagreement as to the desirability of using objective instead of essay tests.

Teacher supporters of objective tests defend true-false, multiple-choice, and similar tests because of their convenience and economy; they claim that they provide scores which are precise and objective. Defenders of essay tests claim that essays provide for a demonstration of a variety of reasoning and communication skills that objective tests cannot measure. In turn, the defenders of objective tests point to the difficulty of appraising essay tests as shown by the wide variety of judgments of essays by presumably qualified readers.

But sponsors of objective tests have their critics too. Banesh Hoffmann, for instance, is particularly critical of multiple-choice tests. He claims that the brighter students often see in the so-called "incorrect responses" some answers which are more creative and intelligent than the responses which the test maker considers correct. So Hoffman writes articles against objective testing with such titles as "Tyranny of Multiple-Choice Test"[4] and "Psychometric Scientism"[5] and a book titled *The Tyranny of Testing*.[6] Defenders of multiple-choice tests claim that Hoffmann's evidence is insufficient and that mis-keying or indeterminacy in responses is far less frequent than he claims. Nor do the supporters acknowledge that objective testing is a kind of guessing game, for they believe that a sufficiently long objective test avoids any impairment of the score that might be caused by guessing.

Standardized achievement tests are often used at the beginning of a

---

[3] *Ibid.*, p. 293.
[4] Banesh Hoffmann, "Tyranny of Multiple-Choice Test," *Harper's* (March 1961), pp. 37–44.
[5] Banesh Hoffmann, "Psychometric Scientism," *Phi Delta Kappan* (April 1967), pp. 381–386.
[6] Banesh Hoffmann, *The Tyranny of Testing* (New York: Crowell-Collier, 1962).

school year to determine where students stand in achievement as a new school year begins. The tests can then help the teacher plan to identify and meet the student's needs and learning problems. The results of standardized tests also provide answers to parents' questions about their children's standing. Parents are often supporters of standardized testing because it helps them know how their children are doing as compared to national norms.

Standardized achievement tests come under fire from critics who charge that teachers often teach simply what the tests attempt to measure. Teachers are said to concentrate on instruction intended to enable the student to pass such tests as the Regents examinations of the State of New York, a state-wide testing program that has been in existence more than a century. About 70 percent of the students in New York State take Regents examinations which are given in 21 subjects. In 1972, the State Board of Regents voted to continue the examinations for the present. However, three members of the twelve-man board voted against the action and charged that the Regents examinations system was obsolete and an obstacle to creative thinking. Particularly critical was board member Stephen K. Bailey of Syracuse University, who said that the present Regents examination system

. . . has helped to impose unimaginative, standardized curricula upon massively bored teenagers. It has helped to promote an invidious caste system within our schools. . . . It has arrogated to central educational direction both curricula and examination mandates which have undermined the local educational creativity. It has provided a "Linus blanket" for poor teachers and a prison for inspired teachers.[7]

A Commission on Tests of the College Entrance Examination Board concluded, after reviewing criticisms of current tests and their use, that the College Board should continue its testing functions. However, the Commission recommended that the present tests given by the Board, such as the Scholastic Aptitude Test (S.A.T.), were in need of considerable modification and improvement. Since the current examinations fail to recognize and appraise the wide variety of skills, mental attributes, and talents among students, the Commission recommended additional tests. Called for were tests measuring not only verbal and mathematical ability, but also such aspects of student competency as musical and artistic talent, sensitivity and commitment to social responsibility, political and social leadership, ability to adapt to new situations, etc. There are indications that the recasting of the role of the College Entrance Examination Board will take place throughout the 1970s.[8]

Yet despite such criticisms, standardized testing prospers and prolif-

---

[7] "Regents Decide to Retain Tests," *New York Times,* June 24, 1972, p. 16.
[8] Commission on Tests, *Report of the Commission on Tests: I. Righting the Balance* (New York: College Entrance Examination Board, 1970), p. 54.

erates. A major organization in the field is Educational Testing Service of Princeton, New Jersey. Educational Testing Service not only constructs, administers, scores, reports, and analyzes tests; it also carries on research concerning testing and other educational matters.

Yet many teachers use their own teacher-made tests in their classes in addition to or as a substitute for a variety of standardized tests. They argue that the teacher knows best what he is attempting to achieve and can best devise the particular test that tells him and the students whether results are being obtained. In other words, they feel that their own tests can be tailor-made to fit the needs of the pupils. Supporters of objective testing, however, doubt the individual teacher's competence in test making. They point out that some tests are homemade in the worst sense. But it is probable that most of the tests used in classrooms are made by the teachers themselves.

Meanwhile, some educators and, apparently, a growing group of students believe that tests of all types, whether standardized or teacher-invented, are overused in American classrooms. They see tests as handicaps to effective learning, and as sources of confusion, frustration, and hostility on the part of students. They point out that in a world in which nothing succeeds like success, nothing fails more dismally than failure—and it is the fate of the less academically able students to be constantly confronted with failure on tests. The sponsors of perceptual psychology are particularly critical of the destructive effects of an excessive use of tests on human personality.

In the middle 1960s, when a national assessment program was proposed, critics such as Harold Hand of the University of Illinois opposed national assessment. He feared that the result would be a rigid national testing program similar to that used by ministries of education in European, African, and Asian countries and foresaw damaging social consequences to education.[9] The Association for Supervision and Curriculum Development has also viewed national assessment as a step toward federal control of education and a uniform national curriculum. The sponsors of national assessment say that they are simply attempting to provide data through national assessment on the attainment of groups in different regions, residential environments, economic status, and age ranges. They compare the data they gather to the economic information needed to achieve a better economic order in the country.

In 1970 the National Assessment of Educational Progress reported on national results in science and citizenship, two of ten subject areas in the survey. Through tests, measurements, and interviews, about 100,000 people between the ages of 9 and 35 were sampled in these two areas. Among the findings of the federally supported survey was "that the

---

[9] Harold C. Hand, "National Assessment Viewed as the Camel's Nose," *Phi Delta Kappan* (September 1965), pp. 8–13.

knowledge and learning skills of students and young adults are greater when 'textbook' information is reinforced by practical experience.''[10] To minimize the accusation that national assessment could lead to curriculum uniformity, the National Assessment of Educational Progress reported results and encouraged readers to reach their individual conclusions; it avoided presenting highly specific recommendations for national curriculum changes.

In 1972, the National Assessment of Educational Progress reported on reading ability. Nearly 100,000 persons age 9, 13, 17, and from 26 to 35, took the reading tests and fared better than the test makers had anticipated. The respondents did best on practical reading exercises which asked them to understand word meanings and to gain facts. They did less well on critical and interpretive reading. For instance, whereas 95 percent of the 13-year-olds could read the labels on merchandise, only 24 percent answered questions correctly after reading a poem by Shakespeare.[11] In the debate on whether schools test too much or not enough, the public is split, though public opinion leans in the direction of support of more testing.

### Standards for Grading and Marking

Perhaps even more controversial than testing is the question of grades or marks, whether on assignments, examinations, or courses. (Sometimes in the following material we will use the words "grades" and "marks" interchangeably; however, in education the word "mark" often is applied to grades recorded for courses, rather than to "grades" on examinations and assignments.) In general, there are three viewpoints: (1) grading by comparison, (2) grading by achievement of individual potential, (3) abolition of grades.

Supporters of grading by comparison believe that pupils should be graded or ranked on assignments, examinations, or courses in comparison with other pupils. Implicit in this assumption is the belief that some kind of standard should be established and that those who achieve beyond this standard should receive marks above the average while those who achieve below the presumed standard should receive lower than average marks. Yet proponents of this view sometimes have difficulty in defining exactly what the chosen standard actually is.

Since the standard must be in relationship to the performance of some other group, the question arises as to which of several groups to use as a standard.

1. Should a national group of a given grade or age be used as a standard for grading performance? If a national standard were used in the United States, the vast majority of students in the slums would be

[10] "Learning + Experience = Knowledge, Survey Shows," *New York Times,* July 8, 1970, p. 1.
[11] "Reading Results In Study Hailed," *New York Times,* May 9, 1972, p. 9.

graded somewhere between failure and below average, whereas the majority of students in suburban areas would be graded somewhere between success and above average.

2. Should the mark be based on some smaller unit for comparison, such as community or the school itself? But schools differ as to social class and local factors within a community. If the grade level of a given school is the unit used, problems arise when there are several classes at the same grade level or in the same subject area. What should be done about groups which are sectioned in terms of ability? Should all "fast" sections have a heavy preponderance of high grades and all "slow" sections have a heavy preponderance of low grades and failure? What happens then to the motivation of less able students who are constantly deprived of opportunities for success as measured by grades? If an honors group must demonstrate extremely high accomplishment to receive a high grade, does this penalize such students and reduce their motivation to enroll in an honors group?

3. So a third proposal is to judge the comparative performance of the individual in his own class. The teacher assumes that he knows what a desirable standard or average for his class is and he grades accordingly. Some students receive high grades and some lower grades, depending on academic achievement alone. No consideration is given to the individual's effort or potential. Some criticize this approach as unfair and inhumane.

4. Another possibility in judging performance is to depend on the teacher's idea of what is, in general, typical for the age level or grade or subject. But estimations of what is typical in general vary widely from teacher to teacher. No clear reference group is involved because individual teacher's standards are vague and undefined.

An alternative to grading based on the comparison of the individual with some group, whether national, school-wide, class, or "typical" of children and youth everywhere, is grading the student on the basis of his own achievement of his potential. In this system of grading the student who proceeds at his maximum capacity receives the better marks. The student who is achieving less than he is capable of achieving receives lower than average marks. The student who is proceeding normally presumably receives an average mark.

The approach to grading on the achievement of potential is defended as opening up the possibility for success to each student. After all, the student is not being graded on someone else's ability—he is being graded on the basis of his own achievement in relationship to his potential. But opponents of this form of grading ask how is the teacher to know whether the student is living up to his potential? Can the teacher really assess this? Some point out that there is a danger that students will be marked high if they are docile, compliant, dutiful, and industrious, and marked low if they are unruly and skeptical, or perhaps creative and original! Still other critics point out that the world is essentially competitive and that grading on the basis of individual achievement might be socially misleading to pupils, and thus in the long run no help to them at all. The academically weak student who tries hard might discover that only the school, not the competitive world, regards him as "A." The brilliant student who does not live up to his potential might be cheated or handicapped by "C's" interpreted as evidence of low ability by college and graduate school admissions officers.

### Symbols in Grading and Marking

In both grading by comparison and grading by the achievement of one's potential, symbols are used to represent marks for the course. A mark is "(1) a single summary symbol, (2) covering achievement in some substantial segment of the educational enterprise, (3) given by an instructor, (4) for purposes of record and report." [12]

The most frequent symbol system used in marking in American schools is A, B, C, D, and F (for some reason, E is usually neglected), sometimes accompanied with modifiers in the form of plus or minus. This system is largely used on the junior and senior high school levels; numerical grading is its nearest competitor. On the elementary school level, marking according to "S" for satisfactory and "U" for unsatisfactory has gained some ground especially in the kindergarten and primary grades. School systems exist in which all three approaches may be used. For instance, the primary teachers may mark on the basis of "S" and "U," the upper elementary school teachers may use the alphabetical marking system, and the secondary school teachers may use the numerical approach.

### Criticisms of Grading and Marking

Fundamental challenges to grading and marking come from those who are critical of the symbol system in education. For instance, a vigorous analysis of the traditional system is *Wad-Ja-Get? The Grading Game in American Education,* a book written in the form of a novel about a school system which reassessed its grading policies. [13]

Some opponents of the symbol system say that marks are extremely inaccurate as a judgment of competence; that marks differ from teacher to teacher, from school to school, subject field to subject field, community to community. Marks, it is argued, focus the attention of both teacher and learner on tests and examinations; they cause both teacher and learner to ignore the major objectives of the educational program. Marks, argue the

---

[12] Robert L. Thorndike, "Marks and Marking Systems," in American Educational Research Association, *Encyclopedia of Educational Research,* 4th ed. (New York: Macmillan, 1969), p. 759. Copyright © 1969 by American Educational Research Association.
[13] Howard Kirschenbaum, Sidney B. Simon, and Rodney W. Napier, *Wad-Ja-Get? The Grading Game in American Education* (New York: Hart Publishing, 1971).

critics, are no way of communicating with parents about a child; to do so requires all of the letters of the alphabet arranged into words, phrases, sentences, and paragraphs! A single letter such as "B" alone tells the parent (and the child) very little about his work. The standard marking system is too cold and impersonal to build good relationships between school and home. The communication goes in one direction only, from the school to the home which presumably simply absorbs the information.

Marks, continue the more aggressive of the critics, threaten the welfare of some children by constantly reminding them of their failures. They support a "rugged individualism" and dog-eat-dog attitude on the part of the student. They distort what the school is actually attempting to do in the way of building humane values. Pressures for high marks on courses and good grades on assignments and examinations lead to cheating and lack of honesty.

### Alternatives to Grading and Marking

The critics of current marking systems call instead for what they conceive as better communication concerning a student's progress. They are frequently proponents of conferences between teachers and parents. In a conference, two-way communication exists and the teacher can learn from the interaction. Parents can learn ways of being helpful at home in the interest of better learning by the young person. Both the program and the potential of the individual student can be considered in a situation which is flexible and adaptable. Such conferences are especially valuable when students also take part.

Skeptics concerning dependence upon conferences point out the amount of time they require. Teachers have so many students, they say, that they simply do not have time for conferences. Nor are all teachers qualified to carry on an effective conference with parents. Nor will all parents wish to come to school for conferences year after year. On the

TABLE 21-1 **Methods Used by Elementary and Secondary Teachers to Report Pupil Progress to Parents***

| Method used | Elementary | Secondary |
|-------------|-----------|-----------|
| A report card with a classified scale of letters | 71.6% | 83.1% |
| A scheduled conference with the parents | 59.9 | 20.0 |
| A written description of the pupil's performance | 24.3 | 10.4 |
| A report card with a classified scale of numbers | 10.0 | 8.8 |
| A report card showing percentage grades | 2.4 | 10.0 |
| A report with either pass or fail | 8.2 | 2.6 |

* Compiled from a nation-wide sample survey.
"Reporting Pupil Progress," *NEA Research Bulletin* (October 1969), p. 75.

junior and senior high school levels, conferences with several teachers would be necessary. In addition, say the doubters, teachers do not really know their students well enough to hold a conference with parents, since many teachers are essentially subject oriented and have only vague impressions of the individual pupil's personality.

Another proposal by those who oppose the current marking system is the writing of letters by teachers to parents concerning the progress of the child. Such a letter usually describes both the general work of the class and the individual performance of the individual student. Teachers in schools using reporting through letters have set aside long weekends approximately twice a year for the writing of such communications to parents.

Again, the critics raise the factors of time and teacher abilities in communication. They also point out that a letter is not a two-way communication and that some of the flexibility claimed for the conference approach is lacking. After a while, say the critics, the teacher begins to write the same letter over and over with only minor revisions and thus individualization in communication is not achieved.

Confronted with such criticisms, the exponents of abolition of the marking system often either stand firm on advocacy of conferences and letters or settle for expansion of report cards. Expanded report forms provide an opportunity to say more about a student than can be conveyed through the brief symbol. For instance, categories as to achievement and attitudes may be spelled out and the teacher has an opportunity to check specific factors in several categories. The proponents feel that such an expanded report is much more useful than a few symbols. From such check lists the teacher may develop a profile of the young person which should be useful to the parents. Again, the critics cite the factor of time and point out that teachers often do not know students intimately and consequently react to them with generalized approval in all categories producing a positive "halo" effect or, on the other hand, with generalized disapproval in all categories.

In answer to the above criticisms, the opponents protest, oftentimes impatiently, that the criticisms are essentially expedient. If the problem is time, the proper solution is to provide the teacher with more time to make conferences, letters, and reports meaningful, rather than to insist upon the inanity of brief symbols. If the problem is money, the community had best provide it, rather than sanction a system of grading which is fundamentally harmful. If the problem is teachers knowing the students, then class size should be reduced and the emphasis should be placed upon individualization in instruction. The proponents of marks regard such proposals as Utopian.

Some advocates of changes in the traditional marking and grading system have proposed a possible middle position. For instance, the authors of *Wad-Ja-Get?* describe at the close of their book the recommendations of the committee on alternatives to the grading system in their fictionalized school. Among the recommendations were:

1. In September of the coming school year, Mapleton High will convert to a "Two Track Grading System." One track will be traditional grading (A, B, C, D, F); the other track, grading on a credit/no credit (CR/NC) basis.
2. As soon as possible this spring, teachers and students will indicate whether they would like to be part of the traditional grading or the CR/NC track. Students must have parental permission — signed and kept on record in the guidance office — to participate in the CR/NC grading. . . .
3. A teacher may elect to teach some of his courses in the traditional grading manner and others using the credit/no credit system. Thus, a teacher himself can experiment to see which he prefers.[14]

In 1972 a group of educators formed an alliance, the Center for Grading Alternatives, to help individual school systems improve their reporting systems and to work with college admissions offices on grading alternatives. Some school systems are reevaluating their grading policies in response to the criticisms of humanistic psychologists and the development of individualized instruction, open education, and alternative schools.[15]

### Social Significance of Grading and Marking

The new teacher will probably encounter continuing controversy concerning marking and grading as he works with fellow teachers, administrators, parents, students and community members. In some schools or systems, grading and marking has become a focus of community controversy. Practices as to grading and marking are deeply established in American schools and society. When the grading system is changed in an American school, other factors operating in the institution are also affected, such as ground rules for reward and punishment. Some community citizens perceive changes in or abolition of marking as a threat to the competitive social system which they support. Thus changes appear to some subversive and unAmerican. Consequently, to change a marking system involves considerable persuasion which often encounters vigorous opposition.

## GUIDANCE AND COUNSELING

### The Nature of Guidance and Counseling

In the school setting, guidance is the cooperative effort of the counselor and his colleagues to further a child's normal development and help him

[14] *Ibid.*, pp. 233–234.
[15] "Educators Drawing Together to Reform Grading," *Education U.S.A.* (Washington, D.C.: National School Public Relations Association, November 20, 1972), p. 67.

recognize his problems and improve his adjustment as he moves through school. Counseling is one of several guidance services provided by the best schools.

Merle M. Ohlsen describes several possible guidance services:

*Counseling services* are needed when a reasonably well-adjusted pupil encounters problems that he cannot solve either by himself or with the assistance of such important other people as parents or teachers. . . .

The *child study* service is needed: (1) to determine a pupil's readiness for a school experience or a next phase in the school program—e.g., to begin formal instruction in reading; (2) to help pupils and their teachers determine whether the pupils are making satisfactory progress in their school work; (3) to identify and to diagnose learning problems and to plan appropriate remedial programs for individuals; (4) to identify pupils for special programs involving exceptional children, including both the gifted and the talented as well as the various types of handicapped children; (5) to help individuals discover what they feel they need to know about themselves in order to make intelligent educational and vocational plans; (6) to help pupils to identify and to cope with those distracting and disturbing forces which are interfering with efficient learning and healthy living.

*Orientation* is designed to help pupils prepare for and adjust to new situations as they progress through the schools—e.g., from home to kindergarten, elementary to junior high school, and senior high school to college or to employment.

The *information service* is a cooperative effort of teachers, counselors, and librarians to obtain appropriate materials, to organize them for the pupils' most efficient use, and to help pupils understand the significance of the materials for them when they cannot do so by themselves. The need for educational and vocational information is obvious. Social information is needed, too. As children grow up, their questions suggest that they want and need a great variety of information.

*Educational and vocational planning* is especially important in the United States where we have a strong tradition that every man has the right to choose his life work. To choose well a pupil must understand his abilities, aptitudes, and interests, and be familiar with vocational opportunities available to him. He also must be able to relate this information to his perception of himself and to his other important life goals. Similar knowledge of himself and of the opportunities available to him is needed to make intelligent educational plans. For most students these are difficult decisions, and for many the assistance of well-qualified counselors is needed.

*Job placement* can help a student avoid drifting into a job, often obtained with the assistance of friends and relatives, that has little or no relationship to his most salable skills. For best vocational placement, most youngsters need assistance in identifying and in developing their salable skills, in identifying appropriate jobs for these skills, and in selling themselves to a prospective buyer.

A good *follow-up service* can provide a high school's students with helpful information on what they may expect when they leave school, and provide the staff with suggestions that they can use to improve the school's program. Both types of information are needed by every school.

A carefully planned program for *leadership and social development* provides for the identification and training of prospective leaders, encourages school activities which provide leadership experience, and assists in the development of meaningful

*Lida Moser, D.P.I.*

The teacher and the counselor work together for the benefit of students.

social and extra-class activities. It also enlists pupils' assistance in planning and developing meaningful social experiences.

Except for educational and vocational planning, job placement, and follow-up services, which are not essential for most pupils below grade seven, the basic services described above are needed by all youth.[16]

### The Teacher's Responsibility for Guidance

The teacher has a responsibility to further the student's normal development, to help the student recognize his problems, and to improve his adjustment. Again and again, teachers are called upon for informal guidance in both academic and social situations as problems of students arise and as students' perplexities become apparent to teachers.

The teacher's responsibility for more formal guidance, including counseling, varies in practice from level to level. Counseling is an accepting, trusting relationship between a counselor and one or more clients. Within this relationship clients learn to face, express, and cope with their problems, identify alternative solutions, develop the courage and self-confidence to act, and change their behaviors. Students and staff must perceive the counselor as a nonjudgmental, trustworthy confidant. Failure to provide such a safe environment in which youth can solve their problems and develop their relationship skills, as well as the

[16] Merle M. Ohlsen, *Guidance Services in the Modern School* (New York: Harcourt, Brace & World, 1964), pp. 18, 19, and 20.

schools' and colleges' failure to provide meaningful participation in solving real social problems, accounts for much of youth's hostile reactions today. They also are saying to teachers, "Merely tolerating us isn't good enough. We want our teachers to care, too, and to help us develop as persons as well as scholars."

Every teacher should exhibit genuine concern for every pupil and be concerned about his general development. But the teacher is not a counselor. Though he does not have the preparation to do counseling, he can and should encourage his pupils to talk to him privately, assess pupil growth, foster growth, and provide appropriate educational, personal, and social information.

At some educational levels the professional help of counselors is currently available; at others, the professional help of counselors hardly exists, though it is steadily growing. With respect to guidance, the preschool, nursery school or kindergarten teacher is still almost always on her own and without the aid of counselors; guidance help, if available, comes from community agencies or school psychologists. The elementary school teacher is also largely dependent upon her own resources, even though elementary school counseling is rapidly increasing. In 1971 there were 7,982 elementary counselors in public elementary schools in the 50 states plus the District of Columbia and the Virgin Islands. Seventy-eight percent of these counselors in public elementary schools were employed fulltime while twenty percent worked half-time or less and two percent less than half-time.[17]

Merle M. Ohlsen comments:

Most educators recognize the importance of the elementary school teacher's role in furthering children's normal social, emotional, and intellectual development; increasing their desire to learn; maximizing their independent learning; helping them learn to understand and accept themselves, including what they have a right to expect from themselves; helping them learn to accept and relate to classmates; and helping them discover and develop special interests, abilities, and aptitudes. These goals can best be accomplished with the consulting help of a competent elementary school counselor.

Sometimes a counselor can provide this help best by observing a child in the classroom in order to assess the others' impact upon the child and the child's impact upon others, including the teacher. For other teachers the best assistance is provided in individual sessions. For still others their needs can be best served in groups. For teachers who are helped by such consultation, certain common ingredients seem always to be present: the teacher perceives the relationship as a safe one in which he can participate in his own development; participation is voluntary; the counselor does not function as an evaluator; and the relationship is a mutual one—each giving and

[17] William H. Van Hoose and Jon Carlson, "Counselors in the Elementary School: 1970–71," *The Personnel and Guidance Journal* (April 1972), pp. 679–682.

Ford Foundation (Arthur Leipzig)

Counselor helps student fill out applications for part-time employment.

receiving aid. It is safe for a participant to admit his problems and his efforts to change are reinforced by the other person or group members.[18]

Specialized help from counselors on the high school level has been more frequently available to students. For instance, in 1971, about 42,000 people were engaged in counseling in American public secondary schools. Some of these were part-time workers.[19] During the middle 1960s it was estimated that the full-time equivalent of counselors was 31,000 people and that the number of counselors as compared to pupils was a ratio of 1 to 507. Yet, at the time, such educational statesmen as James Bryant Conant and such leaders in guidance and counseling

[18] Merle M. Ohlsen, "Elementary School Counseling," *Contemporary Education* (November Supplement 1969), p. 10.
[19] U.S. Department of Labor, Bureau of Labor Statistics, Bulletin 1700, *Occupational Outlook Handbook,* 1972–73 ed. (Washington, D.C.: U.S. Government Printing Office, 1972), p. 61.

as C. Gilbert Wrenn were recommending a 1 to 300 ratio in public secondary schools.[20]

So despite the growth of counseling, encouraged by increased support of the federal government, teachers still retained a substantial responsibility for guidance—the whole responsibility when counselors were lacking and a shared responsibility when counselors were present in schools.

When teachers share a responsibility for guidance with counselors, perplexing questions frequently arise. What is the responsibility of the teacher? What is the responsibility of the counselor? To some, the question is not an issue; they believe that guidance and education are one and the same and that all counselors are teachers and all teachers are counselors. This position is frequently taken by those who hold a broad concept of the functions of the teacher. On the other hand, some think that the special province of counselors is to help pupils to choose among the possible courses of action open to them. According to this point of view, the guidance function emphasizes decisions, goals, value judgments, and plans, whereas instruction is a matter of acquiring knowledge, skills, facts, concepts, etc. Obviously this is not a satisfactory description of instruction from the point of view of those who hold that instruction should meet the needs of the individual learner, or throw light on the social realities of the times, or develop value judgments, or all three.

A sensible resolution of the question of the responsibility of the teacher and the responsibility of the counselor is to recognize that, though school counselors are educators, they perform specialized services which require specialized knowledge and skills different from (but not better than) teachers. The counselor's role stresses helping relationships. A good counselor works with students on problems on which they want help. He helps students come to know themselves. He helps them locate and appraise information about opportunities available to them. He helps them to learn to make decisions. He consults teachers, administrators and parents as he works. In short, the effective counselor *counsels.*

In the present state of education the counselor needs all of the help from teachers he can obtain with respect to guidance and counseling. On the secondary school level, for instance, the counselor often finds himself busy helping students with their choices of college and their planning of high school programs. It is usually his responsibility to counsel low achievers and to counsel on subject matter difficulties. Project Talent found that "adjustment counseling was practiced regularly in a majority of the schools only insofar as it pertained to students' problems with

---

[20] Martin Katz, "Counseling—Secondary Schools," in American Educational Research Association, *Encyclopedia of Educational Research,* 4th ed. (New York: Macmillan, 1969), p. 248.

teachers (thus perhaps overlapping the academic area); counseling on personal and family problems, or on relations with classmates, took place regularly in only about a third of the schools."[21] Counselors, like teachers, find themselves engaged in a variety of activities such as clerical work, supervising study halls, scoring tests, etc., and are unable to give as much time as they would wish to their central activity, which they describe as "counseling students."

In order to protect school counselors from being assigned duties which damage their relationship with students and staff and to allow more time for essential professional duties, the American School Counselors Association (1967) published a carefully prepared job definition. These duties stress the counselor's helping relationships: counseling students concerning the problems with which they want assistance, helping students to get to know themselves, helping them locate and evaluate information concerning the opportunities available to them, helping them learn to make decisions and learning to act upon their decisions.

## THE NECESSITY OF GUIDANCE AND EVALUATION

The teacher is a guidance worker too. He tries to understand the behavior of students and identify their problems. In his own way, he tries to be helpful to them as to vocational planning, educational decisions, and personal problems. He tries both to create an accepting environment for growth through the schools and to help parents with the needs of their children. He tries to help a student develop values, appraise himself, develop a healthy self-concept, make choices, and achieve his potential. Guidance is an inescapable aspect of the teacher's work.

However, without the help of a qualified counselor the teacher is limited in what he can do. With the help of a qualified counselor, the quality of the teacher's services can be improved by the addition of the counselor's specialized services.

Equally inescapable is evaluation. Evaluation today is not limited to the field of academic achievement alone; it also embraces attitudes and interests. Contemporary controversies over testing include not only the continuing debate between advocates of objective tests and those who support such tests as essay examinations; today testing in American schools, whether standardized achievement or teacher-developed, is regarded by some critics as excessive. Grades and marks are also under fire; newer ways of reporting progress—check lists, conferences, and letters—are proposed. Proponents of grades and marks are forced to clarify which groups they propose to use when they make comparisons.

[21] *Ibid.*, p. 243.

Recognition grows that testing and grading programs are not simply matters for technicians but, instead, have significant social implications in American life.

## DISCUSSION

1. What are the several phases involved in evaluation? How is evaluation different from measurement? Are there ways of measuring other than testing?
2. What are the various methods that you as a teacher will use to evaluate the progress of your pupils? Which of these methods will be completely "objective"? Can *any* method be completely objective?
3. Why do schools use interest inventories? Attitude appraisals? Personality inventories? Are these matters any of the school's business?
4. What basically is the meaning of accountability? Does the movement termed accountability seem promising to you? Any dangers?
5. Why are personality instruments frequently considered invalid? What arguments support their use?
6. Should the same achievement or aptitude test series be used throughout all grade levels? Why or why not?
7. What are your arguments in favor of the use of teacher-made tests? In opposition?
8. What are the uses and abuses of tests and grades?
9. Do you believe performance should be graded in relation to national norms, group norms, or individual norms? Defend your position.
10. What grading procedure do you intend to use with your classes?
11. What is your own viewpoint on the use of symbols in grading as contrasted to more substantial reports? What alternatives to symbols do we usually have?
12. Why does a change in a marking system frequently prove controversial? Is there a relationship between grading and marking and an American social system characterized by competition?
13. What are the major guidance services of a good school? Which of these are you aware of from your own experience as a high school student?
14. What are the teacher's and counselor's guidance roles? How might their respective areas of responsibility best be defined?

## INVOLVEMENT

1. Compile a useful list of intelligence, achievement, and personality tests that you can use as a teacher. Be sure to include the title, authors, publishers (with addresses). Indicate opposite each test its principal use.
2. Explore with your class the various personality and interest inventories members may have experienced. Is there any evidence from accounts of these experiences of "faking" or "beating the tests"?
3. Using a familiar class level and subject matter for illustrative purposes, cite the major arguments supporting the contention that pupil evaluation is most successful when based on limited, well-defined educational objectives. Why do proponents of accountability insist on the importance of limited, well-defined objectives? Does this overly limit and narrow the educational framework?

4. Write several specific objectives in your area of specialization and have other class members criticize them.

5. According to class members, do tests of achievement constitute valid instruments for college admission, for decisions on whether one passes courses, etc.? Explore the implications of opinions by class members.

6. List outcomes in your teaching area that could not be measured by an (a) oral test (b) essay test (c) short-answer tests.

7. Consider your own college or university's grading policies. To what extent do they seem sound or unsound? If a consensus exists in your class, you might decide to communicate it to the administration of your school.

8. Discuss the matter of grades and marks with an experienced teacher. What are his reactions to the various points of view expressed in the chapter?

9. Visit a community agency which engages in counseling with school-age children and youth. What training do such counselors have? What relationships do they have to the schools?

10. Interview elementary and secondary school counselors. How do they see their role in relation to their student clients and the other school personnel?

11. Spend a day with a classroom teacher. In what ways does he or she use counseling skills in dealing with all the personal relationships in which he or she is involved?

12. Inteview the personnel director of a school system. What does he or she see as the role of the school counselor? How does he or she evaluate the relative success of the counselors in the system?

## FURTHER READING

Beggs, Donald L. and John W. Wick (Eds.). *Evaluation for Decision-Making in the Schools.* Boston: Houghton Mifflin, 1971. An attempt to bridge the gap between teachers and the researchers, statisticians, and test experts in education who are mathematically sophisticated. Deals with evaluation as a whole and includes achievement tests, homogeneous grouping, evaluation of teacher effectiveness, etc.

Grier, William H. and Price M. Cobbs. *Black Rage.* New York: Bantam, 1968. Two black psychiatrists look at the potential for violence in American blacks.

Grobman, Hulda. *Evaluation Activities of Curriculum Projects.* Chicago: Rand McNally, 1969. The context of curriculum evaluation, what to evaluate, whom to evaluate, how do we evaluate, and some reasonable expectations from evaluation of projects.

Johnson, Dorothy E. and Mary J. Vestermark. *Barriers and Hazards in Counseling.* Boston: Houghton Mifflin, 1970. Barriers and hazards encountered by the counselor and the counselee which get in the way of desirable interaction.

Linden, James D. and Kathryn W. Linden. *Tests on Trial.* Boston: Houghton Mifflin, 1968. For the test consumer in search of information about tests and testing. A resource which provides data on selected tests in common use.

Shane, June Grant, Harold G. Shane, Robert L. Gibson, and Paul F. Munger. *Guiding Human Development.* Worthington, Ohio: Charles A. Jones, 1971. Foundations and procedures of counseling and guidance for the counselor and teacher in the elementary school.

Shertzer, Bruce and Shelley C. Stone (Eds.). *Introduction To Guidance: Selected*

*Readings*. Boston: Houghton Mifflin, 1970. Selected readings for counselors beginning their preparation. Included are sections on today's adolescents, contemporary views of guidance, and issues and trends in guidance.

Van Hoose, William H. and John J. Pietrofesa (Eds.). *Counseling and Guidance in the Twentieth Century*. Boston: Houghton Mifflin, 1970. An unusual historical book containing an autobiography, an article, and a list of selected writings by 22 outstanding contemporary leaders in counseling and guidance.

Worthen, Blaine R. and James R. Sanders. Educational Evaluation: Theory and Practice. Worthington, Ohio: Charles A. Jones, 1973. Includes conceptual frameworks proposed for educational evaluations and practical considerations for conducting such evaluations.

## SELECTED AUDIO-VISUAL MATERIALS

*Afraid of School* (16 mm film, 30 min., b. & w., McGraw-Hill, 1965). When children are morbidly afraid of school, there is need to look to home and family relationships.

*As They Grow—Elementary Guidance—New Dimensions in Meeting Pupil Needs, Part I and II* (35 mm filmstrips, Pt. I-52 frs/record, Pt. II-62 frs/record, color, Guidance Associates, 1966). Examines the role of the guidance counselor and describes how he interprets tests, counsels students, refers students to outside resources, and maintains records.

*Challenge of Change: The Case for Counseling* (16 mm film, 29 min., color, NET: Indiana University, 1962). A view of the guidance process in schools and the individuals who should be involved.

*Counseling Discipline Cases* (16 mm film, 20 min., b. & w., Psychological-Cinema Register, 1963). A counselor explores reasons for school absences and works with a student who is frequently absent and has forged an excuse.

*The Family in the Purple House* (16 mm film, 13 min., color, King Screen Productions, 1970). Is a family without a father really different? Designed to promote understanding and appreciation of different life styles in families.

*Critical Moments in Teaching: Report Card,* (16 mm film, 12 min., color, Holt, Rinehart and Winston, 1967). An open-ended film which examines the problem of the basis on which students should be graded.

*Evaluation* (35 mm Filmstrip, 45 frs/audio tape, color, Venicet Associates, 1966). How the efficacy of instructional efforts is to be judged—preassessment, test design and data interpretation.

*Role of the Counselor in the Secondary School,* (35 mm filmstrip, 77 frs/record, color, Guidance Associates, 1965). Probes functions of the secondary school counselor, such as interaction with teachers and parents, assistance with career and course selection, record keeping and interpretation.

*Testing: Its Place in Education Today* (35 mm filmstrip, 2 filmstrips, color, Guidance Associates, 1966). Analyzes what educational tests can accomplish, how they have evolved over the years to meet the changing needs of education and the difference between standardized and teacher-made tests.

*What's the Good of a Test?* (16 mm film, 12 min., color, Journal Films, 1965). Describes how to use tests, what tests measure and how to prepare for and take a test. Explains and illustrates composition or essay questions, objective questions, and standardized tests.

TWENTY-TWO

# What will the schools of the year 2000 be like?

For many, the year 2000 may seem quite distant. But a person born in 1954 will be 46 years old in that year, and a person born in 1956 will be 44. While these may not be the most eagerly anticipated birthdays in a person's life, they do represent the middle, rather than the old age years. Neither the person born in 1954 nor the one born in 1956 will reach today's usual age of retirement, 65, until about the end of the second decade of the century. So, should you choose teaching as your career, the year 2000 will represent perhaps the most productive segment of your life. You should be near the top of your form, professionally speaking, in the year 2000. It is, in reality, that *near*, rather than that *distant*.

What might education and society be like in the year 2000? Some may regard this question as both foolish and fruitless, saying that the future is impossible to predict. To support their contention, they cite earlier efforts of intellectuals to define the future, including the Utopian dreams developed throughout the ages, from those of Plato to those of Edward Bellamy, and the Inferno-like predictions of Dante, H. G. Wells, Aldous Huxley, and George Orwell.

In the mid 1970s, in "the best of times" and "the worst of times," it is quite evident that neither the Utopian dream nor the predicted Inferno has materialized, and that neither Heaven nor Hell has yet prevailed. For reasons such as these, some scholars believe that speculating about the future is no more reputable than consulting the astrologer, and that it is about as reliable as the predictions contained in the farmers' almanac.

Yet speculating on (or attempting to identify probable characteristics of) the future today is conducted differently from the tradition of prophesying Utopias or Infernos. Scholars today have better tools for use in speculating on the future than their predecessors. Consequently many reputable scholars are today engaged in "futurism," and have developed some noteworthy analyses of "future states."

The American Academy of Arts and Sciences devoted an issue of *Daedalus* to a report by the Academy's Commission on the Year 2000. In this publication, outstanding scholars, primarily physical and behavioral scientists and some humanists, presented papers relating to various aspects of the future, and interacted with each other.[1] *The Year 2000,* by Herman Kahn and Anthony J. Wiener, provides a comprehensive fact base for making assumptions about the future.[2] A versatile social scientist, Donald N. Michael, specifies the dangers which lie ahead for "the unprepared society."[3]

Many educators are also playing a role in contemporary speculation on the future. In an earlier chapter of this book (Chapter 2), you were introduced to *The High School of the Future.*[4] Harold G. Shane has contributed several insightful articles in *Phi Delta Kappan,* such as "Future Shock and the Curriculum,"[5] and "Future-Planning and the Curriculum."[6] The author of this book has written *The Year 2000: Teacher Education*[7] upon which he will also draw in this chapter.

Especially helpful to educators are the publications that were prepared by a project in eight western states called *Designing Education for the Future.* Highly important to new teachers are three volumes in the series which deal with prospective changes in society, the educational implications of these changes, and emerging teacher education.[8]

In the early 1970s, reports Harold G. Shane, futures research was being carried on by large corporate entities such as Rand Corporation

[1] *Daedalus* (Summer 1967).

[2] Herman Kahn and Anthony J. Wiener, *The Year 2000: A Framework for Speculation on the Next Thirty-Three Years* (New York: Macmillan, 1967).

[3] Donald N. Michael, *The Unprepared Society: Planning for a Precarious Future,* 10th John Dewey Society Lecture (New York: Basic, 1968).

[4] William M. Alexander (Ed.), *The High School of the Future: A Memorial to Kimball Wiles* (Columbus, Ohio: Charles E. Merrill, 1969).

[5] Harold G. Shane, "Future Shock and the Curriculum," *Phi Delta Kappan* (October 1967), pp. 67–70.

[6] Harold G. Shane and June Grant Shane, "Future-Planning and the Curriculum," *Phi Delta Kappan* (March 1968), pp. 372–377.

[7] William Van Til, *The Year 2000: Teacher Education* (Terre Haute: Indiana State University, 1968).

[8] Edgar L. Morphet and Charles O. Ryan (Eds.), *Prospective Changes in Society by 1980,* Designing Education for the Future, Number 1 (New York: Citation Press, 1967); idem, *Implications for Education of Prospective Changes in Society,* Designing Education for the Future Number 2 (New York: Citation Press, 1967); Edgar L. Morphet and David L. Jesser (Eds.) *Preparing Educators to Meet Emerging Needs,* Designing Education for the Future, Number 7 (New York: Citation Press, 1969).

and large industrial complexes such as The Singer Corporation, by consultation groups such as the Institute for the Future, by educational policy research centers at Stanford and Syracuse Universities, by individual scholars at large universities, such as the University of Massachusetts and the University of Minnesota, and at small colleges such as Alice Lloyd College in Kentucky, by the Hudson Institute and the Academy for Educational Development. Reports of current research are often carried in *The Futurist,* a magazine published by the World Future Society, and in *Notes on the Future of Education,* published by the Educational Policy Research Center at Syracuse University.[9] The literature of futurism steadily increased during the 1970s.

Some of the more promising efforts relating to probable futures differ from the types of prophecies used to describe the Utopias and the Infernos in that they incorporate the concept that various kinds of futures are possible. Today's scholars are therefore concerned with describing *alternative futures,* rather than with describing a single predestined future.

Kenneth E. Boulding, a distinguished economist and student of society, provided a valuable insight concerning the idea of *alternative futures* with his concept of "system breaks."[10] System breaks refer to discontinuities, surprises, turning points, or sudden changes in the characteristics of a system—all of which are unpredictable or only partially predictable in advance.

If system breaks are distinct possibilities (and past history has repeatedly demonstrated that they do occur), then those who are concerned with forecasting probable futures cannot assume that present trends will continue and that the future will simply be an extension of the present. Such scholars must also include provision for the possible futures that may exist as a result of system breaks. On the basis of all pertinent information, the futurist sets forth or forecasts the future (or futures) most likely to emerge.

Since in contemporary futurism alternative futures are set forth and considered, speculation on the future can be an important aid in clarifying alternative courses of action in the present. In other words, futurism can help modern men, including educators, to confront their present problems squarely and to systematically plan for feasible solutions. Contemporary futurism is not a form of escapism. It is a procedure that tends to force man to face realities.


## POSSIBLE SYSTEM BREAKS AND THEIR CONSEQUENCES

Because of the nature of system breaks, it cannot be predicted when they

[9] Harold G. Shane, "U.S. Futures Research in Education: The Status of the Field in 1972," in *The Potential of Educational Futures,* Michael Marien and Warren Z. Zeigler (Eds.) (Worthington, Ohio: Charles A. Jones, 1972).
[10] Kenneth E. Boulding, "Expecting the Unexpected: The Uncertain Future of Knowledge and Technology," *Prospective . . . 1980,* p. 203.

will occur. Scholars can indicate, however, that they *may* occur at some point in time. This was true in the case of the discovery of ways of harnessing nuclear energy, and in the development of materials designed to increase agricultural production. System breaks of this nature have occurred in the past. System breaks, of the type listed in the sampling below, *may* occur in the future:

Developments in automation and cybernation may increase production to an unimaginable high, and at the same time make possible more leisure time than may now be thought possible.
Developments in communications may make possible virtually exponential increases in man's ability to communicate with fellow men throughout the world.
Developments in oceanography may make possible whole new sources of food.
Developments in energy sources may result in "clean," nonpolluting fuels.
Developments in medicine, geriatrics and biochemistry may result in discovery of techniques whereby the education of a person may be facilitated through drugs, chemicals, and transplants.

System breaks of the type described above are potentially beneficial. Other types of system breaks related to the development of nuclear weaponry, poisonous and nerve gasses, environmental pollutants, famine, overpopulation, and social imbalances are, of course, potentially harmful. But regardless of possible consequences, system breaks, if and when they occur, will cause the role of education to change dramatically. Consider the following implications for education of the five potential and beneficial system breaks described above:

If, in the year 2000, the average worker only had to devote 20 hours per week to his task, the educational system would have to place major emphasis upon *leisure-time* experiences, rather than upon *work-experience* activities.

If, in the year 2000, it is possible and feasible to converse, through both audio and video media, with people throughout the world, the educational system would have to place much emphasis upon "human-to-human" aspects of education.

If, in the year 2000, production of new sources of foodstuff from the oceans proves to be economical and feasible, the educational system will have to provide entire new curriculums devoted to "marine agriculture."

If, in the year 2000, nonpolluting energy sources are available at reasonable costs, industry will be able to produce, at an even greater rate than at present, goods for all people, and mass transportation facilities will be available to virtually everyone. The educational system will have to assume major responsibility for the development of people who are capable of using such goods and facilities in the most advantageous manner.

If, in the year 2000, it is possible to induce or facilitate learning through drugs, nerve stimulants, or transplants, the educational system would have to include not only persons trained in the educative process, but persons trained in medicine, biochemistry, and applied psychology as well.

It may well be that by the year 2000 none of the types of system breaks described here will have occurred. On the other hand, it is entirely possible that at least several will have taken place. An even more likely possibility exists that portions or segments of the developments described above will have occurred.

Obviously, all system breaks are not always pleasant to contemplate. Here are a sampling of horrible possibilities:

1. The potentiality exists of nuclear war which would create global devastation through reducing much of the world to rubble; such a war would exterminate many human beings.
2. The potentiality exists of world-wide famine accompanied by the poisoning of air, land, and water through a combination of an unchecked population explosion and an unstemmed pollution of the earth's natural resources and a critical shortage of sources of energy.
3. The possibility exists of a social revolution taking the form of anarchy in a society in which the establishment wages war but is unable to cope with domestic social problems and in which the poor, the alienated minorities, and the young destroy the social institutions.

If any of these system breaks prevailed, what would education be like in the year 2000?

If the year 2000 saw the United States participating in a global nuclear war, schools would be converted into hospitals and refugee centers. To the extent that education was maintained, the attempt would be to develop manpower for the war effort and ingenuity to insure national survival. As to values, the schools would probably teach unquestioning loyalty to our side.

If overpopulation and pollution prevailed, human beings would be so busy averting famine and environmental disasters that all available young people would be working for survival. The schools might be used simply as assignment centers for needed jobs.

If the year 2000 were a time of a revolution characterized by anarchy, the schools, as a representative of social authority, would be occupied by mobs, and destroyed by burning and vandalism. New versions of education would take place in nonschool settings.

You may well point out that such extreme scenarios are unlikely. You may be quite right that these are unlikely alternatives. We hope so. Yet possible system breaks, even as drastic as these, must be taken into account as we speculate on the future and must influence our own planning today toward desirable futures.

Rather than such extreme system breaks as those described above, the year 2000 may be a time when such tendencies are overcome or at least contained by the going system. For example, war may have been eliminated or may take the form of small-scale regional "brushfires," readily contained, or may be reduced to sporadic guerrilla warfare such as the murders of the Israeli athletes at the Olympic games in Munich in 1972 and the Israeli retaliations. Overpopulation, pollution, and energy lags may have been conquered or world-wide effective famine relief systems and emergency approaches to particular environmental problems may have been put into effect. The causes of anarchic revolution and social imbalance may have been overcome as ghettos and wars are eliminated and effective education and meaningful employment prevail or the social structure may prove resilient enough to contain a continuing degree of violence and social anger. Should any of these developments take place, there would be substantial changes in American society but not sharp system breaks.

## THE MOST LIKELY AMERICAN SOCIETY OF THE YEAR 2000

If we assume that substantial social changes—based on prevailing trends rather than on major system breaks—will take place in the United States between now and the year 2000, we can speculate on the American society most likely to exist at that time. Obviously, there is no inevitability in the trends described here; they are simply statements of the way things appear to be going. Note too that the next several pages present a *national* analysis, not a *global* projection; system breaks emanating from "the Third World" could sharply alter these trends.

So we will make the assumption that in the year 2000 the United States will still exist as a nation and as a major world power. By that time the states of the Union may number 52 instead of 50, should Puerto Rico and perhaps the Virgin Islands be admitted. Or even more if novelist Norman Mailer has his way; he ran for mayor on a platform of making New York *City* a separate state.

The United States of the year 2000 will be more heavily populated than is the United States of the mid 1970s; current estimates place the probable American population from 251 to 300 million at the turn of the century. This population will live primarily in urban areas. A report of the National Goals Research Staff, *Toward Balanced Growth: Quantity with Quality*, issued in 1970, predicted that by the year 2000, 70 percent of the population of the United States will live in twelve metropolitan areas.[11] By 2000, several metropolitan areas will have agglomerated into three megalopoli, in which will be found almost half of the American people, according to Kahn and Wiener, who call these urban complexes Boswash

[11] "Panel Finds Need to Inspire Debate on Nation's Goals," *New York Times*, July 19, 1970, pp. 1, 47.

FIGURE 22-1 Suggested U.S. Megalopoli of the Year 2000

Herman Kahn and Anthony J. Wiener, "The Next Thirty-Three Years: A Framework for Speculation," in Daniel Bell (Ed.), *Toward the Year 2000: Work in Progress* (Boston: Houghton Mifflin,
1968), pp. 73–100.

(the Boston to Washington complex), Chipitts (the Chicago along the
Great Lakes to Pittsburgh complex), and Sansan (the San Diego to Santa
Barbara—eventually San Francisco—complex).[12]

The futurists expect that the United States will have a substantially
higher gross national product (GNP) than the 976 billion of 1970 or the
1,050 billion of 1971.[13] (A severe energy shortage could negate this.)

The increase in the GNP is related to the predicted further increase
in scientific knowledge and technological development in the United
States. Productive power in the year 2000 will be increased by continued
growth in computer technology, and by further automated, cybernated,
and electronic expansion.

As the United States continues to develop, it (paradoxically) is expected to follow both centralizing and decentralizing tendencies. The
United States has developed as "a national society," depending heavily
upon centralization in government, in mass media, and in modern transportation.[14] Yet at the same time there may well be an expansion or extension of "creative federalism," with governmental power delegated to
states, regions, and localities. For instance, the $30 billion five-year

[12] Herman Kahn and Anthony J. Wiener, "The Next Thirty-Three Years: A Framework for
Speculation," *Daedalus* (Summer 1967), pp. 718–719. See also Kahn and Wiener, *The Year
2000*, pp. 61–62.
[13] U.S. Department of Commerce, "U.S. National Income and Product Accounts, 1968–71",
*Survey of Current Business* (Washington, D.C.: U.S. Government Printing Office, July 1972),
pp. 12–13.
[14] Daniel Bell, "The Year 2000—The Trajectory of An Idea," *Daedalus* (Summer 1967), p. 643.

revenue-sharing program of 1972 caused federal funds to flow toward statehouses and city halls. A leading political scientist has predicted that: (1) all governments will continue to grow; (2) sharing will increase; (3) the states will have to act with great vigor to maintain their traditional position in the governmental structures; and (4) localities will have to struggle for policy control—as distinct from administrative control—of new programs.[15]

The nature and role of work will be influenced by the possibility of plenty in the American society of the year 2000, with problems of production largely solved because of (1) the ability of Americans to combine industrial facilities with a good geographic location, (2) a substantial resource base, and (3) a constantly innovating technology. As a result there likely will be different work patterns among the population. Many, perhaps most, Americans will work about a 30- to 32-hour week.[16] Colm points out that typical hours of work by 1980 may become approximately 36 hours. "In addition it may become common to have a sabbatical for labor; that is, a period in which a worker, after several years of work, may need retraining or additional training, travel, or to pursue some other activity of his choice."[17] But while the employed worker is working his shorter work week, the unequipped or unemployable or unable population may not be working at all and may be supported at a subsistence level in a welfare oriented state. Meanwhile a leadership group, holding specialized key positions by virtue of their intellectual capabilities may be overworking themselves because of a combination of forces, factors, and drives. Key personnel will work hard for reasons of prestige, status, increased income, and a sheer desire to accomplish and lead. The leisure-time problems and needs of each of these groups—the employed workers, the unemployable population, and the specialized leaders—will obviously be very different each from the other.

Meanwhile, the knowledge explosion will continue its convulsive leaps, and full utilization of knowledge sources will become essential for anyone who aspires to leadership and social regard.

One of the most fascinating areas for speculation is the question of goals or directions for American society in the year 2000. It is difficult to extrapolate curves into the future as to norms and values. Yet if we do so, the likelihood is that America will move from the older established tradition of stressing hard work, thrift, and spare living and toward a more leisure-oriented, free-spending and hedonistic pattern of living. One can already see indications of this direction in books on contemporary youth such as *The Age of Aquarius*,[18] *The Greening of America*,[19] and *The Making*

[15] Daniel J. Elazar, "The American Partnership: The Next Half Generation," *Prospective . . . 1980*, pp. 111–115.
[16] Kahn and Wiener, *The Year 2000*, p. 175.
[17] Gerhard Colm, "Prospective Economic Developments," *Prospective . . . 1980*, p. 92.
[18] William Braden, *The Age of Aquarius: Technology and the Cultural Revolution* (Chicago: Quadrangle Books, 1970).
[19] Charles A. Reich, *The Greening of America* (New York: Random House, 1970).

*of a Counter Culture.*[20] One might even speculate that of the familiar trilogy of the Declaration of Independence, "life, liberty, and the pursuit of happiness," the latter may come into its own.

The rights to life and liberty will probably be taken for granted; these will be expected by the population as a matter of course, even though struggles relating to the latter may take place, primarily in resistance to invasions of privacy and impersonal bureaucratic controls. But it may well be that the pursuit of happiness will be of paramount concern to a pleasure-seeking America. In the society of the year 2000 there may be time available for members of that society to enjoy life—to engage in avocational activities, travel, cultural enrichment, and other self-renewing activities. Thinkers such as Kahn and Wiener see a basic long-term multifold trend toward "increasingly sensate (empirical, this worldly, secular, humanistic, pragmatic, utilitarian, contractual, epicurean, or hedonistic) cultures."[21]

Commentators on future American society tend to agree that it will not be a Utopia by the year 2000. Just as Americans of the 1970s have their problems relating to war and peace, integration and desegregation, energy and environment, urban ghettos and suburban enclaves, and alienated youth and conservative middle age, so also will the citizens in the year 2000 be faced with problems that are somewhat similar in nature, including obsolescent housing, organized crime, environmental pollution, and difficult intergovernmental relationships. A serious gap exists between our *professed values* (what we say we believe) and our *operative values* (what our actions demonstrate our real beliefs are). The degree to which society and education will be able to resolve or alleviate those social problems of 2000 will depend, in no small measure, on whether this gap in values can be narrowed.

In summary, many scholars are suggesting that the most predictable and probable forces and factors that will have shaped American society by the year 2000 will be these:

1. The continuance of the United States as a nation and as a world power
2. An expanded U.S. population estimated at 251 to 300 million
3. Increased urbanization
4. Increase in urban megalopolitan complexes containing almost one-half the people
5. A markedly higher gross national product
6. Continued expansion of scientific knowledge and technological development—especially in computerized, automated, cybernated, and electronic areas

[20] Theodore Roszak, *The Making of a Counter Culture: Reflections on the Technocratic Society and Its Youthful Opposition* (Garden City, N.Y.: Doubleday and Company, 1969).
[21] Kahn and Wiener, "The Next . . . Years," p. 706.

7. An increasingly national or centralized society concurrent with increasing sharing with states and localities
8. Less working time for the ordinary worker; unemployability for the untrained or unable; hard work by the leadership group
9. Expansion of the knowledge explosion
10. Expansion of the pursuit of happiness goal in American life as hedonism increasingly replaces puritanism
11. The continuance of social problems
12. A delay in the arrival of either Utopia or Inferno—but all bets are off if particular system breaks occur.

## THE MOST LIKELY AMERICAN EDUCATION IN THE YEAR 2000

In order to examine the probable educational system of the future, one must begin with population and its distribution. Which levels of the educational ladder will be characterized by sharp population increases and which will simply hold their own? The predictions given below are cautious, and are limited to the years until 1980.

The increase at the elementary school level should be the most manageable of all increases. In the United States, elementary education for all of the children of all of the people, with negligible exceptions, has already been achieved. At the secondary school level we have not yet achieved secondary education for all of the youth of all of the people. The dropout rate for the nation is still about one out of four students. A major problem facing secondary education, therefore, is to absorb as many as possible of those who now drop out, in addition to those who enter high school as a result of population growth.

The largest increase in terms of percentages should occur at the college and university levels. In 1971, the Carnegie Commission on Higher Education anticipated that college enrollments would double during the 1970s, 80s, and 90s and would reach a total of at least 16 million students by 2000.[22] (But some commentators in 1973 thought such 1971 estimates to be overly expansive and the Commission reduced some of its estimates.)

Community colleges should especially increase their enrollments. Open admission policies in city colleges and state universities should also account for much of the anticipated enrollment growth. Upper undergraduate years and graduate years should reflect increased enrollments too; however these increases should be less sharp than the prospective increases at the level of the first and second years of higher education. To accommodate the increase anticipated by the Carnegie

---

[22] Carnegie Commission on Higher Education, *New Students and New Places: Policies for the Future Growth and Development of American Higher Education* (New York: McGraw-Hill, 1971), pp. 136–137.

Habitat, Montreal. Experiment in urban housing.

Commission (1971) the country would need by 1980 between 175 and 235 new two-year community colleges and between 80 and 105 new four-year colleges, especially in large metropolitan areas.[23]

However, in the 1970s enrollment growth lagged in the nation's colleges and universities. In the 1972–73 school year only 2 percent more students enrolled in higher education institutions than in the previous year. In 1973 the Carnegie Commission advised caution as to expansion.

If the projected increase in the gross national product materializes, Americans can clearly afford to support education adequately out of that expanded gross national product. Whether Americans will choose to spend their money for education, however, is another matter. On the side of the probability of increased support is the increasing recognition that knowledge is power, and that education is the indispensable key to leadership and that education (as we indicated in Chapter 11 on "What About Money to Support Schools?") is of great value in the economic development of the nation.

On the other side of the ledger is the very real possibility that renewed revolutionary assaults on universities similar to those of the late

[23] *Ibid.*, pp. 107, 109.

1960s may result in social repression and increased budgetary slashes for higher education. Indeed, a minority of students may bring about a system break of anarchy by destroying the universities and other social institutions. A different system break is predicted by Michael Young in his fascinating *Rise of the Meritocracy, 1870–2033*.[24] Young foresees so much emphasis on the training of an intellectual elite at the social controls that the masses will revolt by the year 2000.

In a nation that can afford education and has established its value to society, the likelihood is that there will be continuing support for the various types of resources—human, technological and physical—that will be needed in the educational system.

Students in the year 2000 may have little contact with teachers who view their role as only that of imparting knowledge. Instead, students—learners—may be interacting meaningfully with teachers who perceive their role to be that of *facilitators* of learning, and who will be constantly guiding the student toward that end. Meaningful methods or techniques for motivating learning, utilizing ability and evaluation as guides, may be the cornerstone of the teaching-learning process.

If the above developments take place, students will view methods of accumulating relevant information in a meaningful context as being of far more significance than the "old-fashioned" concept of memorization of data, so characteristic of many twentieth century schools. They will rely heavily on information storage and retrieval banks, and will be concerned primarily with *how* to locate and utilize needed information.

Kahn and Wiener have surmised that "computers will also presumably be used as teaching aids, with one computer giving simultaneous individual instruction to hundreds of students each at his own console and topic, at any level from elementary to graduate school."[25] Richard L. Shetler has provided an even more dramatic portrayal:

> Just imagine the staggering possibilities of having all the world's great libraries, the accumulated knowledge of mankind, at your fingertips, of being able to select from them the information that is desired, and at the same time having a machine that can analyze, sift, integrate, and calculate for us.[26]

As to curriculum, the possibility is that curriculum making will increasingly be done by federations of professionals. Groups of educators, including liberal arts specialists in disciplines but also increasingly specialists in the foundations of education, in various media, and in curriculum, will then develop concepts and create materials to implement their ideas. Instead of a single curriculum design for a field, such as PSSC physics, it is likely that there will be multiple designs offered to schools

[24] Michael Young, *The Rise of the Meritocracy, 1870–2033* (Baltimore: Penguin Books, 1958).
[25] Kahn and Wiener, *The Year 2000*, p. 90.
[26] Richard L. Shetler, "Major Problems of Society in 1980," *Prospective . . . 1980*, p. 266.

through research and development laboratories. Yet the curriculum
change problem of obtaining sufficient teacher involvement and participation will probably persist as curriculum making moves more and more
into the hands of experts. A counter possibility exists that curriculum
making may move in a highly individualistic direction if open education, alternative schools, and the ideas of the compassionate critics prevail.

Though the National Education Association and the American Federation of Teachers may be effectively merged long before the year 2000,
the number of educational associations will probably grow larger with
the growth of specializations and the necessity for the representation and
the professional information which such associations can provide. Some
foresee the development of superorganizations similar to holding companies to relate specialized educational groups to larger concerns.

By the year 2000, the teacher in the self-contained classroom may
well be obsolete. Already, increased numbers of supporting personnel
are coming into education. The available technology is expanding. Spe-

Education of the future may include studying at home with a computer.

Arthur Schatz, Time-Life Picture Agency

cialization is increasing. By the year 2000, a coordinating teacher may take for granted the presence of a supporting staff including secretarial workers, teacher aides, instructors and assistant teachers. The help of technicians, evaluators, and researchers may be available to teachers. If so, the role of the coordinating teacher will increasingly be that of "the master of the mix," as O. K. Moore, the creator of the talking typewriter, has phrased it. "The mix" upon which the teacher would draw would include readily accessible libraries of books, television programs that could be replayed, films, sound tapes, computer consoles, etc. Such a teacher would also utilize field trips, independent study, guests and visitors for instructional purposes.

One might even speculate that the teacher of the future will divide his six-hour working day into approximate thirds. One third might be spent in the classroom (or community or laboratory) in supervising or facilitating learning of a particular discipline or interdiscipline. Another third might be spent working with the staff members as they coordinate and plan future learning experiences. The final third might find the teacher engaged in some particular specialty, such as individual therapy, conducting analysis groups for discussion of values, preparing television presentations or tapes, working with specialists in programming computers, developing evaluation techniques and tests, etc.

Management of the individual school may be correspondingly complex. In the future it might be shared by an administration specialist and a curriculum specialist. The latter might work on program while the former might be concentrating on community relationships and the coordination of the total enterprise through managerial and political skills.

Brickell visualizes the changing roles of teachers and administrators as follows:

The present role of teacher will gradually evolve into a cluster of roles encompassing such discrete functions as team leader, formulator of detailed objectives, instructional sequence planner, script writer, presenter of information, evaluator of pupil responses and designer of supplementary pupil experiences. The new administrative and supervisory specialties will include position titles such as Specialist in Outside Developments, Supervisor of Professional Training, Director of Equipment Acquisition and Maintenance, Chief of Materials Production, Program Assessor, Coordinator of Temporary Personnel Assignments, Professional Librarian, and Travel Officer. We can anticipate that an Assistant Superintendent for Development and Training will cap off the pyramid of such positions in the central office of the school system.[27]

Yet Brickell also says, quite possibly with tongue in cheek, "Very probably (I regret to assume) if one opens the door to a typical 1980 classroom

[27] Henry M. Brickell, "Local Organization and Administration of Education," *Implications for Education of Prospective Changes in Society,* Designing Education for the Future (New York: Citation, 1967), p. 227.

and walks inside, the teacher will be standing up front talking."[28] This could very well be true in the Year 2000 as well.

A fundamental change for the student as to schools may be that he will not need to go to school so often! For, in addition to schools, students will have opportunities for learning through home information centers. A home learning and information center might include "video communication for both telephone and television (possibly including retrieval of taped materials from libraries or other sources) and rapid transmission and reception of facsimiles (possibly including news, library materials, commercial announcements, instantaneous mail delivery, other print outs)."[29] While home learning and information centers may turn the student's steps homeward, the development of extended recreational facilities of schools may turn his steps schoolward. Just as college campuses have developed student unions, gymnasiums, natatoriums, and the like, elementary and secondary schools may develop expanded recreational facilities as part of master plans for the improvement of the environment surrounding youth.

Again we might sum up the *most likely* American pattern of education *if* the *most likely* American society of our earlier projection actually prevails. (All bets are off if major system breaks take place.) In such a society, the typical school would reflect the following influences and characteristics:

1. The elementary school population would increase to a minor degree; the secondary school population would increase but less rapidly than in recent decades; college and university enrollments would also increase.
2. The typical school would be an urban school.
3. About half of the nation's children and youth would go to schools in megalopolitan complexes such as Boswash, Chipitts, and Sansan.
4. A markedly higher gross national product would be potentially available for educational support and thus the school would have potentially sufficient funds to build needed facilities, to buy needed supplies and equipment, and to pay teachers a substantial wage.
5. The schools would make use of computer technology not only for purposes of scheduling but also for instruction through an elaborate electronic network.
6. Schools would depend heavily on a curriculum making process developed through national curriculum projects engaging a wide variety of experts. (Yet greater individualization may prevail instead.)
7. Educational organizations would proliferate.
8. A coordinating teacher would be a key person in an educational pro-

---

[28] *Ibid.*, p. 216.
[29] Kahn and Wiener, "The Next . . . Years," p. 714.

gram involving paraprofessionals, clerical workers, researchers, computer specialists, and audio-visual technicians.

9. A teacher would teach, coordinate staff members, and engage in an individual educational specialization.

10. Management of the individual school would be shared by an administration specialist and a curriculum specialist.

11. In addition to the school's extensive facilities for storage and retrieval through material centers, computer technology, and library materials, students would have access to home information centers containing substantial technology.

12. Recreational facilities in relationship to the schools and as part of the total environment would be markedly expanded on both the elementary and secondary levels.

What would be the crucial life decisions which students would be making in such schools? In the kind of society we have envisioned for the year 2000, in which neither Utopia nor Inferno prevails, students would be attempting to meet their needs through rich and diversified educational opportunities. They would also be dealing with the crucial human problems which pose difficulties as to survival of their society. They would be engaged in vigorous discussion of value choices, including decisions on the better ways of using leisure in a period providing many competing opportunities; they would also be considering the fundamental value question of how a man or woman should best live.

## DISCUSSION

1. How old will you be in the year 2000? Others in your family, among your associates, among the younger people you know? When presumably would you retire if the retirement age remains approximately 65? How near is the year 2000 to you?

2. What system breaks other than the ones mentioned by the author do you see as conceivable by the year 2000? Do you believe that anyone can possibly conceive all the potential ones? Why or why not?

3. Discuss with class members their estimate of the most likely system breaks. Consider the question of whether human beings can influence system breaks or whether system breaks are inevitable.

4. What have been some of the classic Utopian speculations? Infernos? How does today's "futurism" differ from such past speculation? What is the significance of the concepts of "alternative futures" and "system breaks?"

5. Read some of the Utopias and Infernos and check the authors' visions with your own value preferences. Do they jibe?

6. What are your opinions on the general directions of norms and values in American society? What evidence is there for and against the "pursuit of happiness" hypothesis?

7. What are the outstanding characteristics of the most likely American society of the year 2000? Why is the matter of population a key factor? Or the energy crisis?

8. How would you rephrase the probable characteristics of the "most likely American society of the year 2000"? What type of society would you prefer, if any, to the society envisioned here?

9. What can an individual human being do to influence the future?

10. What might education be like in the year 2000? What seems most likely to you? Can you relate your projection to social forces and trends?

11. Do you see any particular advantages or disadvantages in the education you have projected for the year 2000? How does your projection differ from that in this chapter? Can you differentiate what you expect education to be and what you would like education to be?

12. After your careful thinking during this course, what do you see as changes in the educational system, including teacher education, that could better prepare you to be a teacher in the year 2000?

13. What can you do to bring about the type of future education you support? You individually? You collectively with others?

## INVOLVEMENT

1. Examine news magazines and TV reports for predictions on the future. Do these predictions have any bearing on education in America?

2. Write out your own projection of the most likely future society and the most likely future education, using the year 2000 as a target year. Compare your projections with those of others in your group.

3. Carry on your own independent program of reading as to contemporary "futurism."

4. Initiate the formation of a group of people particularly interested in "futurism." Meet regularly outside of class to discuss alternative futures and how human beings might influence them for the better.

5. Involve two or three high school students (or friends or neighbors) in a discussion of what they believe good education should be like in the future. Do they consider education as a road to a "better life"?

6. Attempt to envision some of the technological media which may be characteristic of the year 2000. Compare what you envision with technological media with which you have become familiar through visits or through your own college or university.

7. Consider the possible specialization which you might follow in future years. What could be done now to move in the direction of such specialization? Should you attempt to do so? Compare your proposal with those of others.

8. What is your own preparation for teaching in the society and education contemplated for the year 2000? What could you do now or in the immediate future to improve your preparation? Or is any preparation for the future completely unthinkable? Take whatever action seems indicated by your answers.

## FURTHER READING

Eurich, Alvin C. (Ed.). *Campus 1980: The Shape of the Future in American Higher Education.* New York: Delacorte, 1968. To bring closer together the present plans for change in higher education and future probabilities on the campus and in the nation.

Eurich, Alvin C. (Ed.). *High School 1980: The Shape of the Future in American Secondary Education*. New York: Pitman, 1970. Projections by a group of specialists on the shape of things to come in the American high school. A series of explorations and projections.

Foshay, Arthur W. *Curriculum for the 70's: An Agenda for Invention*. Washington, D.C.: National Education Association, 1970. An examination of the teacher's viewpoint on education, teaching as it appears now, and the kinds of decisions needed during the immediate future. Advocates both self-fulfillment and meeting the needs of society.

Krug, Mark M. (Ed.). *What Will Be Taught—The Next Decade*. Itasca, Illinois: F. E. Peacock, 1972. Trends for the future in a variety of subjects and fields: English, visual education, science, foreign languages, mathematics, social studies, and teacher education.

Michael, Donald N. (Ed.). *The Future Society*. Chicago: Aldine Publishing Co., 1970. Articles on social changes, strains and conflicts within the American system which have appeared in the lively social science magazine *Trans*-Action.

Roszak, Theodore. *Where the Wasteland Ends: Politics and Transcendence in Post-Industrial Society*. Garden City, New York: Doubleday, 1972. A spokesman for the counter culture condemns man's confidence in science and finds hope in the romantic movement and in transcendent religious revival.

Theobold, Robert (Ed.). *Futures Conditional*. Indianapolis: Bobbs Merrill, 1972. A fascinating anthology of fiction, social science, and pictures which suggests various ways in which the future can be seen, presents materials being printed about the future, sets forth a number of ways in which a person can participate in affecting the future.

Toffler, Alvin. *Future Shock*. New York: Random House, 1970. Stresses the drastic adjustments and consequent shocks to people in today's world as the future becomes a reality.

Van Til, William (Ed.). *Curriculum: Quest for Relevance*. (Revised edition, 1974) Boston: Houghton Mifflin, 1971. An anthology on curriculum that stresses the present and the future through selections dealing with current criticisms of the curriculum, alternatives in curriculum, proposals for curriculum for the 1970s, and speculation on alternative futures for curriculum.

## SELECTED AUDIO-VISUAL MATERIALS

*Anatomy of Youth* (16 mm film, 21 min., color, ABC Media Concepts, 1970). The generation gap, an international phenomenon produced as an aftermath of World War II, created a post-war world radically different from any known to man. Anthropologist Margaret Mead suggests that parents should stop talking of things they don't know about and realize that drastic changes are inevitable.

*At Home, 2001* (16 mm film, 25 min., color, CBS-TV: McGraw-Hill, 1967). Increasing self-sufficiency and more spare time will allow man to conduct everyday affairs from his home, including the education of his offspring.

*California 2000 A.D.* (16 mm film, 40 min., b. & w., BBC-TV: Time-Life, Inc., 1970). An absorbing and sometimes chilling preview of a brave new world dominated by technology.

The Child of the Future (16 mm film, 59 min., b. & w., McGraw-Hill, 1965). Interviews Marshall McLuhan on educational technology. Pictures a variety of audio-visual devices and their role in the education of the child of the future.

*The Class of '01: The College of Tomorrow* (16 mm film, 25 min., color, CBS-TV: McGraw-Hill, 1967).   A glimpse of what universities of the future will be like. Explores the use of multi-media, television, computers, and the use of human resources.

*Communications: The Wired World* (16 mm film, 22 min., color, Document Associates, 1971).   Looks at some of the methods that will probably be used in the future to disseminate information and examines the nature of the world we are soon to live in.

*Education: No More Teachers, No More Books* (16 mm film, 22 min., color, Document Associates, 1971).   Explores the new role of the teacher in a technological society and the emerging directions that formal education may take.

*The Family: Lifestyles of the Future* (16 mm film, 22 min., color, Document Associates, 1971).   The family unit is undergoing change and transition from the old fashioned family group to an isolated unit of two adults and their children. How can the family unit adapt itself for survival?

*The Future and the Negro* (16 mm film, 75 min., b. & w., NET: Indiana University, 1965).   Depicts a panel discussion by noted commentators on the future of blacks, the economic position of the Negro, racism, and the relationship of the American Negroes to Africa. Features actor-writer Ossie Davis.

*Future Shock* (16 mm film, 42 min., color, McGraw-Hill, 1973).   Based on Alvin Toffler's important book with a narrative by Orson Welles.

*The Futurists* (16 mm film, 25 min., color, CBS-TV: McGraw-Hill, 1967).   Analyzes some of the physical, social and economic problems which face the world today and in the future. Ten leaders in world government, science, technology, and sociology give their views. Narrated by Walter Cronkite.

*Geopolitics: The Shape of Things to Come* (16 mm film, 22 min., color, Document Associates, 1971). Can we control our destiny or do we merely react to events? Discusses man's future as a creature of the world community and the forces that will shape the world of tomorrow.

*The Identity Society* (16 mm film, 28 min., color, Media Five, 1971).   Explains the major cultural shifts in society that affect our contemporary lives. Individual roles now precede societal goals as motivating forces.

*Technology: Catastrophe or Commitment* (16 mm film, 22 min., color, Document Associates, 1971).   Provides a perceptive analysis of both the advantages and disadvantages of technology in the future.

*The World of Future Shock: Crisis in the 800th Lifetime* (16 mm film, 22 min., color, Document Associates, 1971).   Examines the type of problems the individual and society will face as a result of never-ending change.

# TWENTY-THREE

# Is teaching for you?

Now is the time to review a basic decision. Is teaching for you?

Throughout the earlier chapters of this book we have urged you to make important subordinate decisions concerning teaching. For instance, why teach? At which educational level? Who else teaches in American schools? Are salary and status important to you? What educational organizations do you incline toward? We also asked you to consider advantages and disadvantages of teaching in public, independent, and parochial schools. We raised questions about who is in charge in American schools, what is expected of teachers, and where the money comes from. We sketched social, psychological, philosophical, and curricular foundations of education. We asked, what does the new teacher worry about? What is the work of the new teacher? How about evaluation and guidance? What will the schools of the year 2000 be like? Your thinking, however tentative, on all such matters should contribute to your basic decision—is teaching for you?

## TIME FOR A DECISION

We could supply you some check lists to guide your decision-making. But we won't, because we believe it is better for each one of you to make your own list. We will suggest a process for making your basic decision, tentative or firm, whether or not to become a teacher.

Build a list of factors you intend to take into account as you decide whether teaching is for you. For instance, you might ask yourself what you really want in your future work and, indeed, in your life. Be completely honest with yourself. Pull no punches. Show the list to no one. Or show the list only to the person (or persons) who shares your most important decisions with you. Then take your list and check each item on whether it leads you as an individual toward or away from teaching. You might use a five point scale: (1) heavily toward, (2) somewhat toward, (3) neutral, (4) somewhat away, (5) heavily away.

One category in decision-making will probably prove to be your own goals. Do you want to make a difference in the world? If you do, jot down this goal unashamedly. Say it your own way. If this goal is not important to you, skip it. Do you want to work with people? If so, list this in your own words. Do you want to communicate the excitement of some subject or some ideas that have set you on fire? If so, say it out. Do you want to help people cope with their problems? Or help them lead more meaningful lives? What are your other goals with respect to your work and your life? Now use your five point scale in making your own personal interpretation as to whether your goals lead you to or away from teaching.

Try the same approach as to your own life-style. Are you somewhat individualistic? Are you group-inclined? Do you generally go along with life as it is lived around you? Do you struggle against things as they are? Are you often a leader? Are you usually a follower? Are you a good student? Are you not particularly inclined to intellectual matters?

Try the same approach with respect to the economic aspects of the teaching profession, including money, tenure, security, vacations, etc. For instance—having a good deal of money is important to me. A moderate living standard satisfies me. I couldn't care less about money. Economic security is important in my thinking. I simply can't think in terms of security or tenure. I must admit the long summer vacation is important to me. Think of related statements and put them down. Then judge the relationship of these welfare-related factors to teaching.

Give yourself your own personal version of merit rating in the form of a self-appraisal. Who am I? What do I do well? How do I relate to people? What are my personality characteristics? How is my health? Am I relatively stable emotionally? Am I resourceful and adaptable? Cooperative? Translate the questions into positive descriptive statements about yourself. How does this self-appraisal (which should neither be overly generous nor overly condemnatory) relate to teaching? Do aspects of your self-appraisal lead you to or away from teaching?

We suggest nothing as simplistic as just totaling up your score. Instead we suggest that you take a long look at this total profile of yourself with respect to teaching.

Here are illustrative sets of factors jotted down by three hypothetical individuals. Read over these sets and ask yourself how you would check them on a five point scale if you happened to be Ann, Zelda, or Tony (who, indeed, might check them differently from you). Even more important, write down your own list and check it as to which items lead you toward and which move you away from teaching.

### Ann

I really like to work with people.
I genuinely like kids and I think they like me.
I intend to get married.
I think I am both an individualist and a person who likes to work with others in groups.
I like to vacation in new places, though I like my home community and hope I'll work here.
My major hobbies are tennis, theater, and movies.
A moderate standard of living is all I need; keeping up with the Joneses is not for me.
I couldn't care less about security or tenure.
People see me as patient and tolerant (perhaps I am not as much so as they think).
I would like to be a "self-actualizing" person, and at least I'm trying.
I think people like me and I generally like them except for certain freaks.
I think I'm resourceful when new problems come about.

### Zelda

In all honesty, I am mostly concerned about me, not other people.
When it's all over, I want to say that I have really lived.
Above all I want to travel widely and often.
I put a good deal of emphasis on clothes.
I want to live as an individualist in one of the colorful cities of the world.
Let's face it, I need money to enjoy life.
Security is for the birds.
I think I could do my job well, whatever it might be, but I would never let it become overly important to me.
Emotionally, I'm often up or down.

### Tony

There is a lot wrong with things as they are and I propose to help change them.
People do not pay attention to the humanities in this practical, science-oriented world.
I read a good deal and have been called a "culture-vulture."
However, I don't believe in the ivory tower; I think that human beings should also act.
I would like to write a book — some time I might.
I would like to help people to see potential in literature for the enjoyment of life.
At this stage I don't think I really care much about money.
Ditto security and tenure.

I get along all right with people, particularly people who have something important to say. I'm impatient with idiotic people.
I believe I am a hard worker.
I get angry too often, particularly at things as they are.
I'm more of an individualist than a collectivist.

With or without the suggested self-analysis inherent in such a check list, some of you have concluded or will conclude that you are not going to be a teacher. To you, we wish good luck in whatever your chosen work proves to be. Possibly a few ideas about education which you may have acquired in reading this book will be helpful to you. Possibly you will be a better parent for knowing more about education in your American schools. You might even be a better citizen through understanding one of mankind's central activities, the education of the young. Perhaps you will be a more constructive critic of education and a more vigorous supporter of good schools than you would have been without the experience of reading this book.

## TO THOSE WHO WILL TEACH

Some of you have already decided or will decide soon that teaching is for you. If so, we suggest that you be a *good* teacher. Be a good one because you owe it to yourself to be competent in whatever you do. Be a good one because only good teachers are needed in the mid 1970s and beyond. Be a good one because you owe it to children and youth. Be a good one because you are being entrusted with a tremendous responsibility by your fellow men. Take seriously and carefully your steps toward becoming a good teacher.

### Undergraduate Education

Step one toward becoming a teacher is an undergraduate education that combines sound general education with effective teacher education and which results in a bachelor's degree. In all likelihood you already know the particular combination used in your own college or university and can state the requirements involved. (If you don't know them, we suggest that you stop reading right now and turn to the college catalogue!) But to get the most out of whatever pattern is used at your school, take advantage of the formal and informal sources of information which exist concerning getting the best possible education at your institution.

Formal sources include your advisor—how long has it been since you talked with him? If by some chance you don't happen to have an advisor, a trip to the dean's office will soon remedy that deficiency. Formal sources also include your professors, past and present, and the courses in which you are enrolled.

Informal sources include the student grapevine, which often

suggests professors and courses which are indispensable as well as, sadly enough, professors and courses to be avoided if at all possible. Informal sources include the activities of the Student National Education Association which probably exists on campus; the program and the magazine *Impact* may offer you ideas and information on education not readily available in the standard education courses.

### Certification

Step two in becoming a teacher is to be sure that your program leads you to certification to teach. Certification for teaching, like certification for any other profession including law, medicine, nursing, etc., has a long history and is a subject of controversy. Ideas vary widely as to desirable certification practices. In education (as in other professions), opinions range from the view that any college graduate can teach anything regardless of patterns of preparation, over to advocacy of rigid prescriptions of unalterable requirements. Opponents of certification requirements often dramatically point to an eminent leader in some field of study and declare that in such-and-such a state in this nation he would not be allowed to teach in public schools without further courses—to which proponents of certification retort hotly that such a leader must know more than subject matter to teach children and youth effectively in contemporary public schools. The controversy is lively and worth your attention.[1]

For your immediate purposes, however, what you need most is clear and reliable knowledge of the requirements for certification in the subject field and/or at the level in the state or states in which you propose to teach. Look up the practices of your own state as to elementary school or high school minimum requirements.

But facts are fleeting and certification requirements change, so you should be aware that a booklet for teachers, counselors, librarians, and administrators exists, *Requirements for Certification for Elementary Schools, Secondary Schools, Junior Colleges.* It is published annually and is currently edited by Elizabeth H. Woellner.[2] You should know also that *A Manual on Certification Requirements for School Personnel in the United States,* is published every three years by the National Education Association.[3] Even so, you should write to your own State Department of Educa-

---

[1] Margaret Lindsey (Ed.), *New Horizons for the Teaching Profession* (Washington, D.C.: National Education Association, National Commission on Teacher Education and Professional Standards, 1961); James D. Koerner, *The Miseducation of American Teachers* (Boston: Houghton Mifflin, 1963); James Bryant Conant, *The Education of American Teachers* (New York: McGraw-Hill, 1963); Robert M. Weiss, *The Conant Controversy in Teacher Education* (New York: Random, 1969).
[2] Elizabeth H. Woellner, *Requirements for Certification for Elementary Schools, Secondary Schools, Junior Colleges,* 37th ed., 1972–73 (Chicago: The University of Chicago Press, 1972).
[3] *A Manual on Certification Requirements for School Personnel in the United States* (Washington, D.C.: NEA, 1970). Retitled edition scheduled for 1973–74 publication.

tion (or Public Instruction) for the latest certification data concerning your subject field and/or level. Most important, you should talk to your advisor and if your school has an office devoted to certification, use it for your purposes.

It makes good sense for you to be certain on certification matters if you intend to teach in the public schools. The era of "limited" certification—emergency or substandard or conditional permits to teach—is over; though one in seven teachers taught on such permits just after World War II, today very few teachers do so and they are under pressure for full certification. Though certification for teaching in parochial and independent schools is regulated only in a minority of states, the most probable direction that such schools will take is toward greater emphasis on certification.

### Study the Situation as to Supply and Demand

The ratio of graduates seeking teaching jobs to the number open to them was about 2 to 1 in 1972–73 (NEA, 1973). Not everybody who wants to teach may be able to find a position in education in the years immediately ahead, for the annual supply of potential beginning teachers exceeds the demand for additional teachers. Even certification will not guarantee your employment as a teacher. But through a careful review of your own situation, you can increase your chances of being employed in the particular type of post you most want.

For one thing, you should look carefully at the most up-to-date information you can obtain on the distribution of opportunities to teach at the present time. You will find that some fields are marked by higher supply and lower demand than others and, conversely, some are characterized by lower supply and higher demand.

For instance, for the 1972–73 school year, 46 State Departments of Education recorded either a *low* supply or an *extremely low* supply of qualified teacher applicants in the following assignments:

. . . special education, 30 states; trade, industrial, vocational, technical, 27 states; industrial arts, 24 states; special assignments in remedial reading, speech correction, etc., 23 states; special assignments directed to educationally disadvantaged children, 23 states; librarians, 15 states; and mathematics, 14 states. The most frequently listed assignment areas in which the 46 states expect that schools systems generally will have to employ persons with substandard qualifications are special education, 9 states; remedial reading, speech correction, etc., 5 states; industrial arts, 4 states; and trade, industrial, vocational, 3 states.

Assignments most frequently reported as having an *oversupply* of qualified applicants were:

. . . social studies, 39 states; English language arts, 34 states; men teachers of health and physical education, 33 states; elementary school teachers, 26 states; foreign languages, 18 states; women teachers of health and physical education, 16 states; home economics, 15 states; business education, 14 states; and art, 13 states.[4]

However, notice that the assignment areas in which a low supply of qualified applicants were reported involved relatively few of the total number of positions to be filled. In other words, the low supply assignments were also relatively low in student enrollment. On the other hand, assignment areas marked by an oversupply included such fields as English language arts and social studies and such a level as elementary education. Such fields and levels are the areas with the highest student enrollments. Consequently, relatively large numbers of English and social studies and elementary school teachers were employed, despite the fact that the supply was generally abundant for these positions. And, of course, all qualified people in the low supply fields were employed too, though numerically they were relatively few if one considered the teaching profession as a whole.

As to supply and demand you may point out plaintively that you can't completely shift your specialization at this stage of your career. This is certainly true for most of you, though it is not necessarily true for all. Some schools of education offer programs to help teachers modify their present patterns, such as summer workshop opportunities for teachers of regular elementary classes to become teachers of special education.

Yet what many potential beginning high school teachers can do, if they find themselves in currently crowded fields, is to increase the scope of the classes they are qualified to teach. This can be done by (1) minoring in a subject field which is in higher demand than one's major, and (2) broadening one's major field. For instance, a broad background in several fields of the social studies, certainly including history, would be preferable to an endorsement only in economics and sociology. (See Table 23-1 on suitable combinations.)

### Obtaining Your First Position in Education

So you find yourself well on the way to completion of your undergraduate education and to meeting some pattern of certification requirements. You try your hand at student teaching and you like the experience. The time for securing your first teaching position then draws nearer. How to proceed?

Obviously, you begin with your preferences plus qualifications. Level? Subject field or fields? Public, independent, parochial? Any preferences (social or antisocial) as to social class or ethnic group backgrounds? Rural, urban, or suburban? Region, state, community?

Have you taken into account that education is far more extensive

[4] NEA, Research Division, "Preliminary Report: Teacher Supply and Demand in Public Elementary and Secondary Schools, Fall 1972" (Washington, D.C.: September 1972), p. 4.

**TABLE 23-1 Suggested Subject Area Combinations to Increase Job Opportunity**

| Subjects | Suggested combinations |
|---|---|
| English<br>Speech<br>Journalism<br>French<br>German<br>Latin<br>Spanish | Other subject areas in this block tend to make good combinations.<br>Speech or journalism majors might consider a combination with English to expand job opportunity.<br>Foreign language majors might consider a combination with English or perhaps another foreign language.<br>English and library science often make a good combination. |
| Biology<br>Chemistry<br>Earth Science<br>General Science<br>Physics<br>Mathematics | Science majors with no minor should attempt to secure certification in two or more science areas in this block.<br>Science majors certified in only one or two areas might consider a combination with math.<br>Math majors do not need a minor area; however, increased opportunity may result for people certified to teach chemistry or physics. |
| Social Science<br>Economics<br>Geography<br>U.S. History<br>World History<br>Political Science<br>Sociology | Social science majors should attempt to secure certification in at least four areas in this block if they do not have another subject area.<br>Social science majors with less than four areas might consider a minor area in math, English, or any other subject area in greater demand. |
| Physical Education<br>Men's<br>Physical Education<br><br>Women's<br>Physical Education | Preparation in another teaching area may be critical to securing a teaching position for boy's physical education candidates. Math, industrial arts, and English appear to be good subject combinations.<br>A teaching area for girl's physical education majors is not as critical as for boy's physical education. Students are encouraged to secure an area major which would permit teaching at both the elementary and secondary level. |
| Business<br>Education | Shorthand appears to increase job opportunity in many areas. |
| Art<br>Industrial Arts<br>Special Education<br>Home Economics<br>Music<br>Library | No subject combinations appear to be necessary at this time.<br>Certain areas in this block make good combinations with subject areas in the above blocks. |

"Teacher Demand and Supply in the Great Lakes Region," The Great Lakes Association for School, College, and University Staffing (March 1972), p. 10.

A teaching intern with her first class.

than the field of teaching in American schools? Leo J. Shapiro has pointed out the growing need for people to train and retrain continuously in business and industry: "As information and knowledge expands, they will have to be communicated to people, whether in the schools or in business and industry. Because of this, teachers will have the opportunity to move in and out of the schools in performing their professional function."[5]

Obviously, some positions will require more experience and training than you now have, such as a superintendency, a principalship, supporting central office staff positions, etc. But how about working for

[5] Leo J. Shapiro, "Teacher Supply and Demand: A Perspective," *AACTE Bulletin*, American Association of Colleges for Teacher Education (June 1972), p. 6.

professional organizations or teacher unions? State departments of education and federal agencies? Educational publishers or educational technology or educational television? Agencies specializing in youth work, in recreation, etc.? Domestic programs like VISTA? And the world of international education — Peace Corps, American Dependent Schools Overseas, Agency for International Development? In education, it's a wide wide world.

Perhaps you have a head start. For instance, you may have done your student teaching or your internship in the school in which you would like to teach. You may even have graduated from the school in which you would like to teach!

But most new teachers have no head start; they use the services of the college or university placement bureau for which there is usually no charge. As you fill out the various blanks and forms provided by your placement bureau, try hard to communicate to the prospective reader who you uniquely are and what you uniquely can contribute. Most placement forms ask you to supply references; they are essential and are not to be minimized. If possible, provide references from people in varied walks of life but certainly include one or more professors who know you quite well. But experienced employers are apt to assume that your references will speak favorably of you (after all, that is why you suggested these endorsers), so they will look long at other phases of your papers. They will be interested in how well you worked in your student teaching assignment. They will study your responses to whatever opportunities the forms afford you to talk about yourself and your ideas; many placement forms supply you a blank candidate's page for you to fill out. As he reads your papers, a prospective employer often asks himself, "Is this candidate right for us? Do I want to learn more about him or her through more correspondence or through a personal interview?" Then, at some point, he places your credentials in a grouping which conveys to him "promising — follow-up" or "middling" or "reject" and turns to the next set of papers. By then you have had your opportunity to present yourself to him for initial acquaintance; the "promising" grouping will be followed up through interviews.

A good placement officer will do his best to bring your credentials to the attention of school administrators. The higher the demand for teachers and the lower the supply, the more the administrators consult the placement bureau. Conversely, in times of high supply, the administrator is less likely to encounter your particular papers. In either case — and especially in a situation of high supply and low demand — much of the initiative rests with you. You are the person who should be writing to the school system or school in which you would like to work, describing what you have to contribute and suggesting that the administration acquire your credentials from the placement bureau at the college or university. Shun misspellings and grammatical errors like the plague; the excuse of "too busy to proofread" is quite unpersuasive to your reader and

With the teacher's aid, a child grows and learns.

reproducing machines will impersonally duplicate and perpetuate your errors from now till eternity.

As to interviews, both naturalness and empathy are recommended. Be yourself, yet also put yourself into the interviewer's place; he genuinely wants to know you well and wants to make no mistake concerning you. What can you tell him that will help him make a sound decision? As the interview develops, you might even quietly ask yourself whether you would employ you if you were the interviewer!

In addition to the placement bureau, there are other avenues for placement which you might use. Some state departments of education and some teacher associations maintain placement agencies—your placement office will know if this is the case in your vicinity. Commercial placement bureaus also exist; of course such services usually make a charge for registration and collect a commission from your first year's salary. The United States Employment Service also maintains local and state offices.

Some of you will be appointed to posts you hoped to get. But the fact remains that others will not get the particular posts that they most wanted. Some may have to settle for alternatives. For instance, let us return to Ann, Zelda, and Tony. Perhaps Ann may not get the elementary school position in the community she grew up in, despite her hopes. (But the result might be a broadening of Ann's horizons as she finds a post in a preschool program in another state.) Perhaps Tony won't get the position teaching the humanities in the upper middle class suburb to which he applied. (But maybe Tony will prove to be a good teacher of humane values in an inner-city situation or in a rural area; the book he

*Richard Bellak*

VISTA volunteer finds satisfaction in teaching in poor rural area.

has promised to write some day may be improved by his broader framework of experiences.) Maybe Zelda won't get a post in a "glamour" city like San Francisco. (But possibly teaching is not Zelda's cup of tea anyway—so perhaps it's just as well.)

## ONLY THE BEGINNING

When the day comes for you to teach your first class, your advanced education will also begin. For true education is continuous and never-ending. Not only will you learn from experience; there will be many informal and formal opportunities for your further education.

Informal opportunities include your own reading and viewing. Whatever relates to the individual, to society, and to values—whatever relates to psychological, social, and philosophical foundations—should be grist for your mill, whether encountered through books or films or television. The printed word alone as to education is voluminous and embraces professional and trade books, popular and professional magazines, pamphlets and journalistic columns. Be sure to include new books about school and society which are the subject of lively discussion among informed people.

584

Formal opportunities include in-service education. A major enterprise of school systems is the improvement of the work of teachers. You will encounter in-service education first in the form of an orientation program for new teachers which customarily takes place prior to the opening of schools in the fall. The scope of such in-service sessions for orientation ranges from lectures on ideas by consultants to the homely details of setting up one's classroom in readiness for students. Many school systems often continue orientation sessions for teachers throughout the academic year. In the better of these programs, new teachers have opportunities to present their problems for discussion and interaction among themselves and for expert advice from experienced staff members. In addition, many school systems provide in-service sessions for all teachers. The focus may be upon acquaintance in broad terms with organizational innovations and curriculum content changes or the focus may be on a particular problem or approach upon which the school system is concentrating. For instance, a school system may concentrate in a given year on case studies of children, or meeting the problem of drug addiction, or revising the social studies program, etc.

Formal opportunities also include graduate work. As five years of higher education for teaching becomes increasingly taken for granted, teachers will either defer beginning to teach in favor of continuing into a fifth year of preparation or will continue their formal education during summers, late afternoons, and occasional evenings while being fully employed as teachers. In either case they will probably study for and obtain a master's degree. Most teachers who work toward the master's degree concentrate on the levels and/or subjects they are currently teaching. But the new teacher should also recognize that the master's degree program can also help him to move toward some specialization in education which now attracts him. True, doctoral level study is required increasingly for full opportunities in such specializations as school superintendency, the principalship, and the curriculum director's post. Yet many educators begin their preparation for such positions at the master's degree level and many other central office posts than these are open to people who specialize in such fields as supervision or audio-visual education on the master's degree level. Consequently new teachers often combine study for greater competence in their teaching field with at least a beginning on specialization in some administrative, curricular or supervisory responsibility.

So your education in the field of education is still in its initial stages. Through these pages, an attempt has been made to introduce you to education. But an introduction is only a beginning. For you as an educator there is much more to know, many more experiences to be had, much more living to do. May you learn much, experience widely, and live well in your years as an educator! For yours is a career field where the action is and where human beings *can* make a difference.

## DISCUSSION

1. As you have made important subordinate decisions concerning teaching while reading the earlier chapters, which ones of these decisions were especially important to you? Why?
2. What are some of the factors which you would advise individuals to take into account as they decide whether teaching is for them? Which of these factors seem most important to you?
3. What might be the value of a book like this one for an individual who decides not to teach? Dead loss? Some possible gain? Substantial gain?
4. What is the combination of general education and teacher education which characterizes the college or university in which you are now enrolled? What criticisms do you have of the combination? What suggestions do you have for improvement?
5. What is the argument for certification of professional people? Are there occasional excesses with respect to certification? What is your own view on certification?
6. How can a teacher who is looking for a first position in teaching or who contemplates a transfer from a present position best utilize placement offices, employment agencies, etc.?
7. What type of in-service program seems to you to be potentially most helpful to new teachers?
8. What is your own thinking concerning a fifth year of preparation? What are your own plans in this connection?
9. Why educate? Why teach?

## INVOLVEMENT

1. If you have not already done so, build the list of factors you intend to take into account as you decide whether teaching is for you. Check it and examine the resultant profile. What seem to be some possible implications for you?
2. Put yourself in the place of Ann, Zelda, and Tony and check their list as you think they should. Do any implications for their possible careers emerge?
3. Carry on a careful investigation of the certification requirements which affect you and the steps you should take to achieve certification. Share your findings with others to make sure that you have not overlooked any important matter.
4. Investigate carefully the current situation with respect to supply and demand, particularly as it affects you. In so doing, call on whatever sources of help you need, such as state department of education sources, teacher association and union sources, local university resources, etc.
5. Try your hand at a preliminary draft of your placement papers. Check this with friends and associates to get their reactions. Make changes and improve your first draft of your papers.
6. Widen your horizons on possible positions in education through reading up-to-date sources on current careers for those contemplating work in the broad field of education. Role-play an interview with an administrator who is supposedly considering you for a post in his school or system.
7. Gather information from universities in which you might study for a master's degree. Contrast and compare the various patterns of programs, requirements, etc.
8. Take a long look with other students at the many further ways you can acquire

competency in education following the conclusion of the course in which you are enrolled.

## FURTHER READING

Beck, Carlton E. (Ed.). *Perspectives on World Education.* Dubuque, Iowa: Wm. C. Brown, 1970. Original essays on education written especially for this volume by scholars from many nations and dealing with education in Europe, Asia, the Middle East, North America, Latin America, and Africa.

Biegeleisen, Jacob I. *Careers and Opportunities in Teaching.* New York: E. P. Dutton, 1969. Informal overview of teaching opportunities at levels ranging from very young children to college and university and including teaching careers abroad.

Bigelow, Donald N. (Ed.). *The Liberal Arts and Teacher Education: A Confrontation.* Lincoln: University of Nebraska Press, 1971. A book about the past and future of the liberal arts and teacher education intended to help merge liberal arts education with professional education.

Callahan, Sterling G. *Successful Teaching in Secondary Schools.* Glenview, Ill.: Scott, Foresman, 1971. A book to help in the development of instructional techniques. Emphasized are teaching principles, planning for teaching, specific teaching procedures, special teaching problems, and recent developments in teaching.

Coyne, John and Tom Hebert. *This Way Out: A Guide to Alternatives to Traditional College Education in the United States, Europe, and the Third World.* New York: Dutton, 1972. Useful for students seeking alternatives to traditional education and for faculty counselors and others who advise young people. Included are a guide to learning on one's own; descriptions of about 100 innovative U.S. programs; and information on studying in Australia, Western Europe, Latin America, Africa, and the Middle and Far East.

Henry, Marvin A. and W. Wayne Beasley. *Supervising Student Teachers: The Professional Way.* Terre Haute, Indiana: Sycamore Press, 1972. A useful guide for the cooperating teachers who will supervise your student teaching.

Lucio, William H. and John D. McNeil. *Supervision: A Synthesis of Thought and Action.* New York: McGraw-Hill, 1969. Theories of supervision in education, including the scientific management theory, the human relations theory and the authors' revisionist view.

Sergiovanni, Thomas J. and Robert J. Starratt. *Emerging Patterns of Supervision: Human Perspectives.* New York: McGraw-Hill, 1971. A book on supervision which deals with supervising the human school and the human curriculum. Emphasizes as a primary goal the humanizing of American education.

Unruh, Adolph and Harold E. Turner. *Supervision for Change and Innovation.* Boston: Houghton Mifflin, 1970. Highly helpful book which discusses supervision and demonstrates the theories presented. In-service education programs are fully described.

Zerfoss, Evelyn and Leo J. Shapiro. *The Supply and Demand of Teachers and Teaching.* Lincoln, Nebraska: The Nebraska Curriculum Development Center, 1973. The supply and demand for teaching, both in and out of schools, by the Committee on Information Systems of the Study Commission on Undergraduate Education and the Education of Teachers.

## SELECTED AUDIO-VISUAL MATERIALS

*Finding Your Job* (35 mm filmstrip, 6 filmstrips/records, color, Eye Gate House, 1972). How to find the right job for you. How to write a resumé. How to conduct yourself on an interview. When to look for another job.

*Professional Commitment* (35 mm filmstrip, 70 frs/cassette, color, Educational Filmstrips, 1967). Designed to heighten the sense of career commitment in new teachers and renew dedication in experienced educators.

*Student Teaching and Teacher Orientation* (35 mm filmstrip, 150 frs/records, color, Bailey Film Associates, 1968). Presents a beginning student teacher in various situations and in interaction with her college supervisor and her supervising teacher.

*Your Future in Elementary Education* (35 mm filmstrip, 79 frs/record, color, Guidance Associates, 1964). Discusses becoming a teacher and teaching in an elementary school. Explores student teaching, educational curriculum, requirements for certification, and children's learning processes.

*The University of the Future* (audio tape, 15 min., National Center for Audio Tapes, 1970). A proposal to reward faculty for effectiveness as teachers and scholars.

# Index